Adoption Parenting

Creating a Toolbox, Building Connections

More than 100 contributors create a practical, hands-on approach to parenting your adopted child.

Edited by Jean MacLeod and Sheena Macrae, PhD.
Foreword by Adam Pertman

EMK

EMK Press • Warren, New Jersey

EMK Press, a subsidiary of EMK Group, LLC
16 Mt. Bethel Road, #219
Warren, NJ 07059
www.emkpress.com

Photo credits:
Rick Connors 81-2, 309-2, 310-1; Carl David 334-1, 334-2, 334-3; Martin Landesvatter 253-2; Gerallt Llewelyn 114-2; AnnMarie Mannino 358-2; The Picture People Cover, 203-4; Portrait Corporation of America, Inc. (PCA) 309-1 Jeffrey Potts 1-4, 406-2; Ken Rada Photography 81-6; Hope Rogers 405-6 Dean G. Turk 127-2, 165-2, 166-3, 221-1, 221-3, 333-3, 432-3

Publisher's Cataloging-in-Publication Data

MacLeod, Jean.
   Adoption parenting : creating a toolbox, building connections / edited by Jean MacLeod and Sheena Macrae ; foreword by Adam Pertman.
   p. cm.
   Includes resources and index.
   ISBN 097262445-7
   ISBN 13 9780972624459

1. Adoption. 2. Parenting. 3. Adopted children–Psychology. 4. Adopted children–Family relationships. 5. Child rearing. I. Macrae, Sheena. II. Pertman, Adam. III. Title.

HV875.55 M33 2006
649.145–dc22   2006922063

Manufactured in the United States of America

06 07 08 09 00 01 02 03 04 05

For my mother, Christine, and her legacy of love.

J.E.M.

To each and every one of the global
community of writers in this book!
Your parent toolkits and perspective have
broadened our community's wisdom,
and inspired me to parent my children better.
May you go on to inspire our readers as you have me.

S.M.M.

Language 81-112

Food 113-126

Baggage 127-144

Learning 253-282

School 283-308

Race 309-332

Older Child Adoption 333-356

Challenges 357-404

Support 405-430

Therapy 431-450

Journey 451-485

Resources 487-492

Index 493

Tools and Connections
The Key to Adoption's Changing World
By Adam Pertman

For far too long, we adoptive parents lived in a world of make believe. To be fair, it wasn't a world of our own creation; that monumental task was accomplished by a culture that decided there was only one right road to family formation–and it wasn't the one we traveled to form our families. But we all lived in that world and we generally played by its rules: Don't talk about infertility or birthparents or any other 'personal' subject and, most of all, just proceed with your lives as though you'd become moms and dads the old-fashioned way.

Lots of wonderful families were formed during the decades in which we played out that fantasy, and many people–parents and their kids–felt (and were) blessed. We paid a high price for the benefits we received, however, and we pay it to this day. Some of us lied to our own sons and daughters about their pasts, and they are mightily ticked off as a result. We relegated untold thousands of birthmothers to the role of baby-making machines, and they are deeply wounded as a result. We barely whispered about the way we formed our families, and too many of us remain insecure about them as a result; and, because it's very hard to shape thoughtful attitudes or practices about secrets, all sorts of laws and policies in our society are antiquated, misinformed, and even detrimental as a result.

Fortunately for everyone concerned, our world is being transformed. In most ways, it is becoming more honest about and more respectful of everyone involved in the adoption process, and it is recognizing that many different paths can lead to the formation of a whole, loving, normal family. I'm also confident that the changes occurring all around us are becoming so entrenched that, as is so often the case with social progress, legislators and policy-makers will ultimately catch up with the altered reality on the ground.

Adoption Parenting: Creating a Toolbox, Building Connections probably would have languished on a dusty shelf in the old world; it simply tells too many stark truths. It is premised on the understanding that adoption isn't the revelatory 'win-win' solution we used to pretend it was. But that doesn't mean this book portrays adoption as a downer or

inferior or inherently problematic or anything of the sort. Quite the opposite; we can truly honor an institution that provides homes for kids who need them, gives adults the opportunity to revel in the joys of parenthood, and does those things in an honest, respectful way. Recognizing that there are unique challenges in 'nontraditional' families–whether led by single parents, step-parents, divorced parents, grandparents, gay parents, adoptive parents, or any other sort of parents– doesn't diminish those families. It just recognizes the differences within them, and that's a very good thing because parents generally do a better job when they understand their children's (and their own) realities and needs. And those realities and needs are especially important to address when the family has so many layers of complexity because it is multinational, multicultural, and/or multiracial and was formed through adoption.

In our new, improving world, *Adoption Parenting* deserves to be front and center. It deserves to be in the hands of parents, would-be parents, adoption practitioners and others (let's start with teachers, doctors, and mental-health professionals, shall we?) who profoundly affect our families. Its thoughtful, accessible approach is not about wallowing in problems and challenges, but about sharing knowledge, making connections, overcoming obstacles, and doing a better job for the sake of our kids. In our new, improving world, *Adoption Parenting* is indeed a useful toolbox, but it is far more. It is a celebration of how far we have come, and it is a roadmap toward an increasingly successful future.

Adam Pertman is the Executive Director of the Evan B. Donaldson Adoption Institute, the pre-eminent research, policy and education organization in its field. He also is the adoptive father of two (Zack and Emmy) and the author of Adoption Nation: How the Adoption Revolution is Transforming America, *which has been reviewed as "the most important book ever written on the subject." Pertman has received numerous awards for his work, lectures and writes internationally about adoption and children's issues, and has appeared on programs including "Oprah," the "Today" show and "Nightline'.*

With Thanks

A book of this sort doesn't just happen.

This book started it's journey over 3 years ago with the founding of a yahoogroup list serve, called aptly, Adoption Parenting. The people we have met and gotten to know have formed the foundation of the sharing and learning that is this book. The voices we have heard, internalized, and included in one form or another include adoptees, birthparents, and adoptive parents. Each of these individuals have given us pause for reflection and challenged the way we think. We hope they will do the same for each of you.

I'd first like to thank my co-editors: Jean MacLeod and Sheena Macrae. Their tireless efforts in making this book a reality I hope will be appreciated by all who read this book. It has truly been a labor of love. To our families: Molly, Lily, Hanna, Donald, Heather, Zoe, Rob, Annette, and Natalie, we thank you for allowing each of us the time to spend on this monumental undertaking and for the wisdom and understanding you have provided to each of us.

To the mentors we have developed and relied upon, Sherrie Eldridge, Beth O'Malley, Gail Steinberg, Adam Pertman, Hollee McGinnis, Analee Matthews, Indigo Williams Willing, Brian Boyd, Leceta Chisholm Guibault, Jill Lampman, Dick Fischer, Suzanne Chambers, Susan Caughman, Pat Johnson, Karen Gillet. To each and every parent who has risen to the challenge and become the expert they needed to be to parent the child who has come to them, we thank all of you for sharing your wisdom and helping others with your hard won understandings and truths. To each of you who read this book in it's various incarnations; your comments and insights have helped to shape this book, and we thank you.

To the voices in the adoption community that have moved adoptive parents along the path where sometimes we would rather not go, Jane Brown, Cheri Register, Sonja Sun Johnsen, Kim (Eun-Mi) Young, Tobias Hübinette, Chris Brownlee. We have listened and we hope that the material presented in this book will allow others to hear as well.

To Doris Landry for looking at this book with an eye of a professional, the perspective of one who has seen much, and the understanding of a parent.

To Chi-Ying Jan who tirelessly tracked permissions, read for common sense and understanding, and came away changed with a new understanding and perspective. To Barb Fraser for helping to find typos and inconsistencies. Any that still remain are the fault of an over-tired publisher hurrying through the final pieces of this book.

To every parent who has shared images of their children scattered throughout the pages; they are our reminder of why we wrote this book, for the children.

And to each of you who continued to ask "When will this book be done?" as we struggled with the sheer complexity of it and the enormity of task. We hope it was worth the wait.

Carrie Kitze
Publisher

Getting Started

Adoption Parenting 101
Why Do I Need This Book?
by Carrie Kitze, Publisher, EMK Press

As each of us takes the steps on the journey of adoption parenting, at some point, we come to realize that we need to reach outside ourselves to effectively parent the children who have come to us. For some of us it comes upon the return home with sleeping and feeding issues. For others, it may come later as our child discovers that to get the family they are with, they had to give up another. Wherever the challenges lie, it is so important to find a practical, accessible resource that understands the layers of adoption as they relate to parenting. We hope you will find this book to be such a resource.

   This book is the vision of EMK Press, but its has been made possible by the collaboration and shared wisdom of the parents, parents experts, and experts who have come together to share what they have learned in parenting their children. Skillfully assembled by co-editors Jean MacLeod and Sheena Macrae, who understand that it takes a village to raise a child, this book comes from a wonderful global village of parents and children, reaching out across the world. It is composed of 'tribal wisdom', passed from parent to parent, enriching our community, but allowing each of us simply to use those tools and thoughts that work for us, based on each of our unique parenting perspectives and the circumstances and issues faced by our children. We call this the Adoption Parenting Toolbox, and it is something no adoptive parent should ever be without. Adoptive mom Bonnie Shute said it well...

   "What makes more sense than thinking we have scaled the mountain is to understand that we need to take a toolkit on the climb. I may need different things in my toolkit than you do, but we all need the bag and strategies, re-regulating when things are all out of whack. This should be a goal for all our kids–those who have experienced early challenges may need a bigger bag, with more strategies than others. Some kids who have been in secure homes from the beginning have special needs in this regard, too. Our job is to make sure the bag isn't empty."

A Different Perspective

Imagine for a moment…

You have met the person you've dreamed about all your life. He has every quality that you desire in a spouse. You plan for the wedding, enjoying every free moment with your fiancée. You love his touch, his smell, the way he looks into your eyes. For the first time in your life, you understand what is meant by "soul mate," for this person understands you in a way that no one else does. Your heart beats in rhythm with his. Your emotions are intimately tied to his every joy, his every sorrow.

The wedding comes. It is a happy celebration, but the best part is that you are finally the wife of this wonderful man. You fall asleep that night, exhausted from the day's events, but relaxed and joyful in the knowledge that you are next to the person who loves you more than anyone in the world…the person who will be with you for the rest of your life.

*The next morning you wake up, nestled in your partner's arms. You open your eyes and immediately look for his face. But **it's not him!** You are in the arms of another man. You recoil in horror. Who is this man? Where is your beloved?*

You ask questions of the new man, but it quickly becomes apparent that he doesn't understand you. You search every room in the house, calling and calling for your husband. The new guy follows you around, trying to hug you, pat you on the back. . .even trying to stroke your arm, acting like everything is okay. But you know that nothing is okay. Your beloved is gone. Where is he? Will he return? When? What has happened to him?

Weeks pass. You cry and cry over the loss of your beloved. Sometimes you ache silently, in shock over what has happened. The new guy tries to comfort you. You appreciate his attempts, but he doesn't speak your language-either verbally or emotionally. He doesn't seem to realize the terrible thing that has happened…that your sweetheart is gone.

You find it difficult to sleep. The new guy tries to comfort you at bedtime with soft words and gentle touches, but you avoid him, preferring to sleep alone, away from him and any intimate words or contact. Months later, you still ache for your beloved, but gradually you are learning to trust this new guy. He's finally learned that you like your coffee black, not doctored up with cream and sugar. Although you still don't understand his bedtime songs, you like the lilt of his voice and take some comfort in it.

More time passes. One morning, you wake up to find a full suitcase sitting next to the front door. You try to ask him about it, but he just takes you by the hand and leads you to the car. You drive and drive and drive. Nothing is familiar. Where are you? Where is he taking you? You pull up to a large building. He leads you to an elevator and up to a room filled with people. Many are crying. Some are ecstatic with joy. You are confused. And worried.

The man leads you over to the corner. Another man opens his arms and sweeps you up in an embrace. He rubs your back and kisses your cheeks, obviously thrilled to see you. You are anything but thrilled to see him. Who in the world is he? Where is your beloved? You reach for the man who brought you, but he just smiles (although he seems to be tearing up, which concerns you), pats you on the back, and puts your hand in the hands of the new guy. The new guy picks up your suitcase and leads you to the door. The familiar face starts openly crying, waving and waving as the elevator doors close on you and the new guy.

The new guy drives you to an airport and you follow him, not knowing what else to do. Sometimes you cry, but then the new guy tries to make you smile, so you grin back, wanting to "get along." You board a plane. The flight is long. You sleep a lot, wanting to mentally escape from the situation.

Hours later, the plane touches down. The new guy is very excited and leads you into the airport where dozens of people are there to greet you. Light bulbs flash as your photo is taken again and again. The new guy takes you to another guy who hugs you. Who is this one? You smile at him. Then you are taken to another man who pats your back and kisses your cheek. Then yet another fellow gives you a big hug and messes your hair. Finally, someone (which guy is this?) pulls you into his arms with the biggest hug you've ever had. He kisses you all over your cheeks and croons to you in some language you've never heard before.

He leads you to a car and drives you to another location. Everything here looks different. The climate is not what you're used to. The smells are strange. Nothing tastes familiar, except for the black coffee. You wonder if someone told him that you like your coffee black. You find it nearly impossible to sleep. Sometimes you lie in bed for hours, staring into the blackness, furious with your husband for leaving you, yet aching from the loss. The new guy checks on you. He seems concerned and tries to comfort you with soft words and a mug of warm milk. You turn away, pretending to go to asleep.

People come to the house. You can feel the anxiety start to bubble over as you look into the faces of all the new people. You tightly grasp the new guy's hand. He pulls you closer. People smile and nudge one other, marveling at how quickly you've fallen in love. Strangers reach for you, wanting to be a part of the happiness. Each time a man hugs you, you wonder if he will be the one to take you away. Just in case, you keep your suitcase packed and ready. Although the man at this house is nice and you're hanging on for dear life, you've learned from experience that men come and go, so you just wait in expectation for the next one to come along.

Each morning, the new guy hands you a cup of coffee and looks at you expectantly. A couple of times the pain and anger for your husband is so great that you lash out, sending hot coffee across the room, causing the new guy to yelp in pain. He just looks at you, bewildered. But most of the time you calmly take the cup. You give him a smile. And wait. And wait. And wait.

How would each of us handle all these changes?
How would this impact us for the rest of our lives?

Written by Cynthia Hockman-Chupp, Cynthia is an adoptive parent like many of us. She was a longtime school teacher for a variety of grades who has learned from her children how to parent a child with attachment issues. Analogy courtesy of Dr. Kali Miller.

Each of the chapters in this book is a Toolkit, filled with advice and experience from which we adoptive parents can select the tools with which to address the issues that we–with our intercountry/transracially adopted children–face. The chapters, like the issues, aren't discrete. They flow into each other and will overlap in ways that are unique to each family. This is not a book to be read at one sitting–but instead to be digested over time as understanding and needs allow. You will discover that as you create a personal adoption parenting toolbox, you may find tools in any number of the chapters that are helpful and allow you to look at something with a different perspective. You may also discover over time that your tools will change.

Adopted children come to us with a variety of pasts. Each child will have had different experiences–and the temperament and abilities to handle what life has dealt them. Parenting an adopted child is different from parenting a biological child. There are many places where your toolbox will be the same as parenting biological children, but there are places where your toolbox should be different. And that is primarily what this book addresses.

Why should the toolbox be different? Because we are parenting from loss! Our adopted children have an extra layer we need to parent. When we leave to go off to the store, they know deep down that there is a possibility that we might not come back. It has happened before and can happen again. It is the most fundamental, foundation shaking loss. Sometimes our children come to terms with it early in their lives, others in the teen years, others as adults. But it is there. It adds another layer to the parenting we need to do.

Is parenting from loss hard to do? Well, just like our children, each of us comes to parenting with the baggage of how we were parented and how we want to assimilate the things we have learned from home....or not. What we need is an understanding of where our children come from and where we come from and how to fit that all together. And as we put a circle of connection around the adoption triad, we also need to think about the impact our children's first families have on us and our children–and we need this, whether we have an open adoption or not.

The Most Important Tool–Perspective

Perspective is an essential tool. It is interwoven with almost everything we do as a parents; it also spills into everyday life. It makes us walk a mile in the shoes of others to help us understand who they are and why they do what they do. This overlays all the adoption parenting work we do; it's a powerful and fundamental tool. It's a tool which allows us to know to help our children, and also to empathize with them on how being adopted feels.

The seemingly simple analogy in blue on the preceding and facing page helps us understand our children's initial feelings on being placed with us, coming to us from loss of family, community, and country. It puts into perspective how our joy at welcoming them may have sat uneasily with their fear of us as new and strange. Our children have to learn that we care, and have to learn also that we would hold true to our pledge to care for them. And we have to understand their loss, anger, and contain it. We become the safe haven for them, the place where they learn that families are where kids grow, safely. No matter what, we are there to help and to catch them

The most important thing that perspective teaches is empathy. Empathy for the feelings our children have that might not be what we would have thought. Empathy for where the behavior has come from, not just reacting to it. And empathy in knowing that we both need to understand where the feelings come from, and how to get them out to see the light of day so we can understand them, learn from them, and put them back inside changed. Sympathy, understanding, and care flow from empathy and it all flows back to connection.

The Hardest Tool to Use–Feelings

Another critically important tool interwoven throughout this book is learning how to recognize feelings, whether they are misplaced or on target. How our feelings make us act and react is one of the hardest tools for each of us to use, but one of the most essential ones we must learn how to access. Watching your child navigate big emotions can often trigger your own response to a similar emotion; resolved or unresolved. And we need to learn that creating calm out of chaos will only work for the short term if the big feeling underneath is unaddressed. Understanding feelings is so important; it's a process that is ongoing as we learn to help our children with their feelings and how we fit as a family. Understanding feelings and how to apply them is crucial to choosing tools in your adoption parenting toolboxes and having them truly work.

The following article *"The Parent/Child Connection: Shared Feelings, Strong Families"* by Jean MacLeod starting on page 7 details the ways we need to teach access to feelings to both ourselves and our children. It is the basic primer, the sharpening tool you need to understand and to really access the best of the other tools you may need in your tool box. In this book, we've utilized the research of Silverstein and Kaplan whose premise is that there are Seven Core Issues in adoption which are detailed on the following pages. These are basic and fundamental, and affect all parts of the triad (adoptee, adoptive parent, birthparent) because we all share loss and gain in the making or the loosing of our families.

The premise behind these is simple and Jean's article takes you step by step through each of the seven. This article can be re-read as we read the book, and re-read as we return at later stages of our parenting journey.

This book is not the final resource on any given topic, rather a jumping off point. Visit our website **www.emkpress.com** for the most up to date resources and links associated with this book. Also, this book is not a substitute for professional guidance. But it can help make you aware of when you need to reach out to people skilled in helping families like ours on the journey.

The Parent/Child Connection
Shared Feelings, Strong Families
By Jean MacLeod

Love, anger, loss, and grief. Most of us would prefer to not have to deal with adoption fall-out. It is emotional, messy, complicated stuff that most of us were not raised to handle. But somewhere between the ages of four and ten, our adopted children begin to realize that in gaining an adoptive family, they have suffered some very significant losses. Suddenly, they need help interpreting both their positive and negative emotions and they need acceptance for what they're feeling on all levels. They look to us for help, and if we can't, or if we come up short, they proceed on a long, lonely journey, all by themselves.

Adoption fall-out is an opportunity that parents should grab with both hands! It is a chance for you to stretch yourself as a mom or dad, and a chance to keep your child fully in your life. Typically, fall-out first begins in the car, on the schoolyard or at bedtime. It may start with a single question. It can enter your life with a child's amazing and bewildering breakdown, or creep in silently with a child's sullen look and angry silence. It is often attributed to 'ages & stages', and it may go underground…but it doesn't go away.

Once we parents realize what we're dealing with, how do we ever equip ourselves with the tools to help? How do we teach our internationally adopted children to cope with the sources of adoption fall-out, and how do we give them what they need to grow? How do we help our children, mostly pre-verbal when adopted, express the feelings of anger, sadness or confusion over the life choices that were made for them—emotions that they may carry but can't explain?

Teaching our children to understand their emotions and allowing them to express their feelings about the beginning of their lives is a powerful first step toward fall-out containment. Many of our internationally adopted children come to us with very little history, and a very big need to know the 'facts' of how and why they began with one set of parents and ended up with another. They crave a structure of knowledge that will help them navigate the enormously complex feelings that accompany abandonment. They need hands-on context to aid them in keeping their self-esteem while dealing with feelings of unworthiness, and the ultimate core question: why didn't my birthparents keep me?

The Seven Core Issues in Adoption
The seven core issues can provide parents with the insight and information needed to create a toolbox that will enable them understand the feelings of an adopted child. Deborah N. Silverstein, LCSW, and Sharon Kaplan Roszia, MS, have identified universal adoption issues that trigger emotions that are experienced, to some degree, by every single adoptee:
1) Loss
2) Rejection
3) Guilt and Shame
4) Grief
5) Mastery/Control
6) Identity
7) Intimacy
These seven issues are the basis for an adoptee's thoughts, feelings and reactions. They are

A Note to Parents

Adoption-parenting can be challenging, puzzling and frustrating. Our children are huge joys, but they come with to us with a history that we sometimes need to work to connect to. Attachment or adoption therapists are trained to understand the needs of internationally adopted children, the issues of loss, and the effects of post-institutionalization. For parent-recommended therapists, and therapists registered with the national organization ATTACh, go to the following websites: **www.attach-china.org** and **www.attach.org**

a parent's key to understanding a child's perceptions of herself and her view of her biological and adoptive families. The seven issues are inter-related and overlap, and they decisively affect most every aspect of an adopted child's life.

Rather than being viewed as a pile of negative emotional baggage, the seven core issues can be utilized by an adoptive parent to guide a child to self-awareness, strength and resiliency. Some of the seven issues have a panacea– 'prescriptions' that a parent can apply to help a child grow and heal, while others simply demand acceptance. One of the hardest things for any parent is to see a child in pain and not be able to make the pain go away, or fix what is wrong. Especially in adoption, a parent's role must sometimes be the 'facilitator', instead of the 'fixer' that we'd really like it to be. The facilitator role is an important one, however, and it is essential to an adopted child and her family circle.

Psychologist Doris Landry has created a set of four prescriptive tools for parents to use to help them steer their children through the seven issues, and to alleviate some of the alienation and confusion categorized by Silverstein and Kaplan Roszia. Children who are dealing with core issues may be helped with one or more of the following:

Education   Understanding
Ongoing Awareness   Acceptance

A parent's job entails guidance and support; it requires a mom or dad to allow and encourage a child to feel every emotion deeply, while using the education, understanding, awareness, and acceptance tools that give a child permission to move forward. For an adoptee stuck in a core issue, the world is a scary, insecure place. Mom or Dad might not be able to fix the world, or a child's losses, but according to therapist Dee Paddock, parents have an important role. A parent…

"…can model doggedness, mastery, moral courage, love and hope. Our adopted children can grow into adults who are optimists, who believe it is possible to transcend sorrow and fear, and that things do change."

1) Loss

Through abandonment and adoption, our internationally adopted children lost their birth-parents and biological siblings, and their extended family of aunts, uncles and grandparents. Our children lost their birth country, birth culture, racial identity, and language. Some of our daughters and sons lost orphanage caretakers that they cared about, others lost foster families that they had loved and lived with since birth.

Children who have lost their birthparents, foster parents or primary orphanage caretakers have had the rug whipped out from underneath them one too many times. They come to expect fear and loss as a normal consequence of loving and living; they know it can happen at any time and without warning, because it's happened to them before.

Internationally adopted children can suffer from intense separation anxiety, and have difficulty with transitions and separations of even the innocuous kind. Camp, sleepovers, moving, or attending a new school are small hiccups that can re-awaken conscious, or unconscious loss issues. A parent's death, divorce, or hospitalization, are severe trials that need to be recognized as major earthquakes for a child with a previous loss trauma.

Focusing on adoption loss does not equate with fixating on unhappiness.

Birthmother loss is especially poignant for an adoptee. [See **Loss & Grief** page 165] A birthmother's rejection cuts deeply, sharply and permanently. If a child was adopted as an infant, the birthmother is the person the child 'remembers' on an unconscious, primal level, and is symbolic of the 'loss soup' that contains the overwhelming longing an adoptee may feel for her previous life. As a parent you can give your child permission to love two mothers, one who gave her life and one who will take care of her, make good choices for her and love her forever. You can also give your child permission to feel anger at the choices a birthparent made for her. Abandonment may have been the birthmom's only choice, but even if a child understands this intellectually, it still hurts and the hurt needs to be expressed. Your child may even need permission to express feeling angry with you–for not being there when she was a baby and needed you, or for 'stealing' her away from her birthmother and country. Some children get caught in birthmother loss and need concrete ways of processing:

- Include the birthmother in normal conversation with your child.
- Celebrate adoption day, your child's birthday, or Mother's Day with a birthmother honoring ceremony the day before ('Mother's Day Eve'). Help your child make the day of her own symbolic design, using letter writing, picture drawing, cake-baking, candle-lighting or moon-wishing.

Reinforcing a place for two 'real' moms within one family is a unifying gesture, and one that affirms the reality of a child's love and loss, past and present. Focusing on adoption loss does not equate with fixating on unhappiness.

There is no tool to 'cure' loss, and there is no closure. A parent's understanding of a child's loss won't make the loss go away, but it will forge an empathic parent-child liaison based on honesty and trust. Acknowledging loss is an important first step in acceptance and in moving forward for our children. We have to stop ourselves from trying to amend their reality by painting an entirely rosy picture of their early lives—a rosy picture that may not entirely jibe with what they are feeling inside. Our children don't need us to make life pretty; to grow, they need to be taught to examine their feelings and be able to decide if loss is unfairly over-influencing an emotional reaction. Adoption loss can't be eradicated, but a child can learn to recognize it, own it, channel it and control it.

2) Rejection

A child's feelings of rejection are directly related to abandonment. Children without a way to express their confusion, fear, sadness, and anger over their perceived rejection by their birthmother, may act out with inappropriate tantrums or behaviors. Or they may act in, with depression, boredom, and withdrawal. A child may be extra controlling, or exhibit intense anxiety about loss or separation. Adopted children may feel shame ("I must be bad/unlovable for my birthmother to have given me away") and live with poor self-esteem. Adoption is a lifelong process; understanding the ongoing need for communication and learning the words to use may feel simplistic, but it is part of the prescription.

Does your child have words to identify and regularly express the four basic emotions that people are born pre-wired for?

Angry   Sad   Scared   Happy

Some children really have no idea why they are feeling the way they do inside–no one has helped them make the connection between their lives/losses in their birth country and their current feelings. They do not understand what is triggering their reactions, and over-reactions. They honestly do not know why they are feeling angry, why they are taking it out on their mom or dad, and why they carry so much inexpressible emotion. Once they become aware their relief is often immense, and they can begin to work on coping mechanisms.

Does your child have your permission and encouragement to express her feelings? "I wish I still had my birthmother" is hard for a child to say if she believes her mom would be sad or angry in hearing the truth about what she thinks or how she feels. If the mom takes it personally, it is far too risky for a kid to be honest ("my mom will leave me if I tell her this"). Our children's number one fear is of abandonment, and they will suffer in silence if that's what it takes to avoid causing the unthinkable to happen again.

3) Guilt and Shame

Guilt and shame are by-products of rejection. They are a child's paralyzing, toxic reaction to the belief that something must be intrinsically wrong with them, or that they must have done something really bad, to have caused their own abandonment. Shame is secret and silent. Adults understand that birthparents have grown-up reasons to relinquish a child, but children view the act personally as a reflection of themselves, and are deeply ashamed of not being 'good enough' for a mother to keep. The prescription for shame is to blast it out in the open and help children understand that their 'rejection' and abandonment was not about them.

Detect it, Expose it, Dump it!

Shame and guilt can only exist in dark, untouched secret places. Bringing the reasons for a child's self-incriminating feelings out into the light and exposing secrets to the truth will begin to eliminate shame, rejection, and guilt's internalized triple grip.

4) Grief

A pro-active parent can help their child explore the past, live fully in the present, and develop the resilience necessary for the future. Therapeutic parenting is a term that describes the extra level of pro-active parenting that is required to help a child discover and recover from their childhood trauma. Children exhibit expressions of grief according to their experience and their temperament, and they may present grief in very different ways. Some children display sadness by fighting, some are unable to play, and some children demonstrate little expression and no excitement about life in general. Others are excessively nervous or shy, and worry more than is normal. A therapeutic parent uses all four tools to help a child with grief:

Understanding   Awareness   Education   Acceptance

A parent can gain valuable insight into a child's feelings by introducing sensitive or painful topics, by really listening, and by being watchfully aware of a child's activities. The content of a child's imaginative play is a window into what they are feeling, and by observing without interfering, a parent may be able to decipher if a child is trapped in the grieving process. Without skills to become 'un-stuck', a child will repetitively play out his or her issues. A useful twist on 'misery loves company'; a therapeutic parent using the four tools can relieve a child's burden by sharing play and conversation, and by examining and validating the child's emotions. Part of the miracle of therapeutic practice is that simply talking about an inner issue like grief can take the issue outward, re-shape it, and change a child's perceptions about it.

5) Mastery/Control

Paradoxically, post-institutional (PI) adoptees suffer from a lack of control over the early-life decisions made for them, and also suffer from taking too much of the unnatural kind of control, too young. Ideally, a child learns autonomy in steps, and learns control over their world under the watchful eye of their mother. A healthy bio infant/toddler trusts that their world is a safe place to investigate and master (control). An abandoned PI child skips over the trust, to desperately trying to control their environment in order to survive. A child who is having difficulty dealing with the seven core issues is unable to let herself believe that 'parent knows best' and will engage in continual power struggles with her parents, and anyone else in authority. These children must control friends, play-dates, conversations and parental attention. Some children will feel pushed to hoard food, tell lies, or even steal, in order to demonstrate complete control over their own world. A child lives through an orphanage experience by taking care of herself; to later trust an adult to take care of her feels dangerously life-threatening.

Part of the control problem is solved when the parent and the child recognize what the underlying problem really is (an adoption issue), and what is fueling it (a child's base fear for survival). Working on changing control patterns takes dedicated, non-punitive action and lots of loving, but firm limit-setting. A parent needs to withdraw the unnatural control and decision-making from the adopted child and work at building a basis of trust and love. The adoptee has to learn to allow the adoptive parent to make good choices and decisions for her, while the parents continually demonstrate trustworthiness. Giving the child the gift of healthy, inner self-control is based in attachment-parenting plus parent control, enforced with kindness and affection. When an adoptee feels safe and in control of her inner self, some of the need to control the outward universe disappears. Although frustrating, the hard work a parent does with an adopted child on her post-institutional behaviors should be an affirming experience for both; shame is debilitating for a child and anger is self-defeating for the parent. [See **Discipline**, page 145]

6) Identity

"Adoption, for some, precludes a complete or integrated sense of self... Adoptees lacking medical, genetic, religious,or historical information are plagued by questions such as: Who are they? Why were they born? Were they in fact merely a mistake, not meant to have been born, an accident?" (Silverstein and Kaplan Roszia)

Helping a child develop an identity that includes the past, the present, and the future is integral for a child to feel whole. An adoptee's realization of the blank space in their family history exacerbates the hollow spot they carry inside, with a profoundly sad result.

Past Identity: Without a foundation to build upon, a structure crumbles. Creating an honest life narrative, or Lifebook,helps provide a sense of history, or life structure, for adopted children. [See **Narratives**, page 221] Our internationally adopted sons and daughters come to us encoded with information that we can backtrack, react to, and connect with. Everyone has a story, but the facts of an internationally adopted child's babyhood are not as important as how she feels about her early life, how she interprets pre-adoptive events, and how she views her place in the world. Resilience, a trait that allows a person to view and react to adversity as a challenge rather than as a trauma, plays a large part in how a child defines herself through 'past identity'. A child who suffered a harsh orphanage experience had a difficult start in life, but can be taught by a parent to be re-defined by her bravery and courageously strong survival skills. A 'powerless victim' internal working model can be changed; not by ignoring sad facts, but by embracing them.

Resilience may not be innate to some, but it can be learned. Parents play an integral role in modeling behavior and feelings, and by demonstrating their own resilient responses to life. Resilience researcher, Dr. Steve Wolin, believes that the give-and-take, the emotional insight, and the support that are components of a healthy reciprocal relationship, ultimately generate self-esteem and permanent, integrated strength in an individual building internal reserves.

Present Identity: A child's identity in the present is, to a large degree, familial. It is a huge comfort for a child to feel that she belongs in her adopted family, that she has full membership along with her parents and siblings, and that the membership can never be revoked. A child derives strength from kinship and claiming behaviors! Emphasize family by celebrating connections, and by dedicating time and importance to building family. Building awareness and mutual acceptance entails that parents and children:
- work and play together
- describe the special attributes of each family member

- describe family goals
- talk about family unity
- design simple family rituals
- draw or talk about what families do to stay close (See Page 67, Raising Family Awareness)

Some adopted teens and adults cite feeling alienated from their adoptive families; it makes sense that time, effort, and priority should be put toward underscoring the fundamental need to be together. A strong family provides a safe base to explore from for a child, and a secure safety net for a teen experimenting with independence.

Future Identity: Family claiming and connection, life narratives, and Lifebooks are tools to help a child learn to integrate her past, understand the present, and take charge of her future. Giving a child ownership of her life story and her thoughts and feelings builds a foundation for further construction. Kaplan Roszia and Silverstein warn that a: *"Lack of identity may lead adoptees, particularly in adolescent years, to seek out ways to belong in more extreme fashion than many of their non-adopted peers. Adolescent adoptees are over-represented among those who join sub-cultures, run away, become pregnant, or totally reject their families."*

Helping a child develop an identity that includes the past, the present, and the future is integral for a child to feel whole. An adoptee's realization of the blank space in their family history exacerbates the hollow spot they carry inside, with a profoundly sad result. Reinforcing your child's whole identity, co-creating and re-framing her story while facing the difficult truths together, and giving her the tools to develop pride in that identity, will strengthen your child's trust in herself and help give her the resilient fortitude to live with past, present, and future shadows. (For more information on racial identity, see page 311.)

7) Intimacy

For a young child, intimacy is measured in peer friendships and in a child's relationship with her parents. If a child is grappling with adoption issues, it can interfere with all of her interactions. Grief, shame, loss, and rejection may motivate a child to steer clear of any relationship with potential to bring more of the same.

"Adoptive parents report that their adopted children seem to hold back a part of themselves in the relationship. Adoptive mothers indicate, for example, that even as an infant, the adoptee was 'not cuddly.' Many adoptees as teens state that they have truly never felt close to anyone. Some youngsters declare a lifetime emptiness related to longing for the birthmother they may never have seen." (Kaplan & Silverstein)

Working on the intimacy issue requires a great deal of trust, communication, and vulnerability from children, and from adults. A parent must be willing to discuss topics that are uncomfortable (infertility, for example) and be willing to participate in painful conversations (a child wishing for her birthparents). It is up to the parent to introduce adoption subjects, and to be willing to accept a child's biological family as part of their own. A parent who is distressed or embarrassed talking about personal issues or who refuses to visit the loss-laden 'dark' side of adoption, will not be helpful to their child and will probably not get many shots at parent-child intimacy, either.

Holly van Gulden and Lisa M. Bartels-Rabb, authors of *Real Parents, Real Children*, suggest using the Pebbles Technique to open a conversation about a sensitive adoption

For Further Reading:

Lifelong Issues in Adoption By Deborah N. Silverstein, LCSW, and Sharon Kaplan Roszia, MS

Doris Landry, MS, **www.adoption parenting.net**

The Art of Resilience By Hara Estroff Marano Psychology Today.com

Orphans and Warriors, The Journey of the Adopted Heart By Dee Paddock, MA, MTS, NCC

The Resilient Self: How Survivors of Troubled Families Rise Above Adversity By Steven J. Wolin, MD and Sybil Wolin, PhD

Real Parents, Real Children By Holly van Gulden and Lisa M. Bartels-Rabb

topic. *"Pebbles are one-liners, not conversations, that raise an issue and then are allowed to ripple until a child is ready to pick up on it."* An example might be mentioning your child's beautiful, black hair and wondering out loud if she got her hair from her birthmother… essentially, throwing out a conversational pebble for the child to catch. If a child chooses not to respond to the pebble, the parent has still communicated a willingness and ability to talk about difficult subject matter. You can toss out another pebble at another time.

Because adopted children are fearful of hurting their adoptive parents, and are unwilling to risk rejection, parents must be the discussion initiators. Parents must model behavior and leadership, and pro-actively be part of a child's internal world. An un-addressed intimacy issue can quietly decimate an important relationship, leaving a child alienated and a parent sad and confused. How intimate we are with our young children now will have direct repercussions on their teen years:

"When an open, accepting environment in which the child can talk about and tackle adoption-related issues is established early on, the child will feel freer to turn to his parents to talk about problems as a teen. If parents deny their child's feelings or sweep them under the rug, then the family—parents and child alike—will have no system for addressing them when they intensify in adolescence." (van Gulden and Bartels-Rabb)

Adoption fall-out is a blessing in disguise. Our children's sadness, anger, confusion, and questions are all there for us parents to pick up and run with. Adoption issues will continue to re-appear at times of transition throughout our children's lives: entering school, moving, marriage, pregnancy and birth, divorce, medical interventions, deaths of friends and family, mid-life and old-age. How our children handle each challenge depends on their personality and on their preparation. The Seven Core Issues and parenting prescriptions give us tools to interpret our children's thoughts and emotions, and allow us the insight to guide them to self-awareness. We can't fix the fall-out, but we can help our children with their feelings, and with their healing. We can demonstrate our own resiliency and teach our sons and daughters that their journey of adoption is more than survivable; that it has shaped them in remarkable ways, and with our help, it can also make them strong.

~ By Jean MacLeod

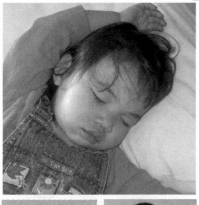

Sleep

Whatever Happened to "Sleeping Like a Baby"?

by Claire McDonald, Ph.D.

In the years before I actually had children, I imagined a nighttime ritual with illusions that only a non-parent could muster. It went something like this: bathe the baby, cuddle and read her a few books, give her a last bottle, and lay her in her crib for the night. After the baby's good night kiss, I imagined my husband and I would be free to work, pay the bills, exercise, and watch a movie. In other words, once the baby was asleep, our nighttime lives would look a lot like they did before we became parents. We were both teachers, and we knew (or thought we knew) all about raising children. It was just a matter of finding the right combination of love, humor, and structure. Parents whose children were problem sleepers had obviously failed to take the proper approach…

When we were finally united with our own precious child in China and our first evening together arrived, we followed our original plan. We cuddled our baby as we gave her a last bottle, and promptly at seven p.m., as advised by the orphanage doctor, we turned out the lights and laid her in her crib. She dutifully fell asleep…for exactly one hour. The orphanage doctor told us that our baby slept without waking from seven p.m. to six a.m.! (More likely, these are the hours when the lights are off in the baby room in the Suzhou Social Welfare Home.) At eight p.m. on our first night together, my husband and I were for the first time in our sheltered lives, witnesses to abject terror.

Hours later, we dispensed with the crib, laid our sweet, scared baby on my chest and eventually coaxed her back to sleep in our bed. Later that same night, I awoke to a sound, loud and rhythmic, that I could not immediately identify: our baby was wide awake, sucking her middle and ring fingers and watching us sleep. In those eyes, deep and black, I saw an ancient woman-child studying the two who had become her parents.

Well into her sixth year, our daughter, who is a healthy and happy little girl during the day, wakes up each and every night one to three hours after going to sleep. We have been through night terrors, nightmares and night-waking.

> *"People who say they sleep like a baby generally don't have one."*
>
> Leo J. Burke

Sometimes my husband and I have despaired of ever having more than thirty minutes of couple time. From our first night together, we embraced the Family Bed, and have since introduced the Big Girl Bed, trying any number of methods for helping our daughter to stay asleep.

For us, though, what has worked best has not been a strategy or even a tool; it was a change in our attitude. We have been led to the realization that this particular child cannot help the fact that she cannot yet fall asleep alone, or stay asleep throughout the night. It is not about power, and she is not a willful, out of control child. Her mind simply moves so fast that it will not give her any peace. Most nights, she can get to sleep and then later, back to sleep, fairly quickly; some nights she cannot. Learning to accept unpredictability has been one of the most challenging lessons in my education as a mother.

Our ancient woman-child has taught me a great deal: about sleep and its primal connection to trust, about patience, and about giving children what they need rather than demanding what we, as adults, want. My daughter frequently needs her mother at night. My job is to be there for her, and for now, this is my real work.

A Universal Issue

Over the years, I have discovered that my family is not the only one working on sleep issues. Perhaps the number one topic on adoption parenting e-lists is sleep. Parents just home with new members of the family are confronted with the whole gamut of sleep issues:

- Child screams when she sees the crib.
- Child wants to sleep with parents.
- Child wakes many times every night.
- Child has night terrors.
- Child has nightmares.

Why do children who seem to be doing reasonably well during the day struggle so at night? It is not all that surprising. If you are like many adults, you, too, have confronted sleep issues at various times during your life. How many of us can honestly say that we have never laid awake at night thinking about job-related problems, health concerns, or troubled relationships? At night, all the distractions of the day fade away, and we are left to consider the reality we may prefer not

Baby's cries really are a language, but early in the mother-child relationship they may seem more like a foreign language. The more you listen and respond, the better you will get at understanding what your baby is saying.

William Sears, M.D. & Martha Sears, R.N. Authors of numerous common sense parenting books including *The Attachment Parenting Book*

to think about. We should not be shocked when babies and toddlers, with far fewer emotional and intellectual resources than adults, may also find nighttime difficult.

For those who have adopted internationally, it may be useful to know that many of our children (especially those from China) were abandoned at night or in the very early morning. It is a crime in most countries to abandon a child, and many birthparents who feel they must take this course of action do so under the cover of darkness. While some of our kids escape that early imprint, many do not. Add to that what must be, at times, a lonely, terrifying night environment in an institution, and our children are set up for sleep trouble.

Crying it Out

So why not just follow the advice that we have all heard so often–let the child cry it out and eventually she will sleep on her own? You absolutely will hear this advice from almost every one you know–from your mother-in-law to your co-workers, from your sister to three other mothers at the playground.

Perhaps the best known advocates of allowing children to cry as a method for sleep training are Richard Ferber, who wrote *Solve Your Child's Sleep Problems*, and Gary Ezzo, author of *On Becoming Babywise*. Ferber, who is the director of the Center for Pediatric Sleep Disorders at Children's Hospital in Boston, generally recommends a strategy called controlled crying. Parents put their baby in her crib and allow her to cry. They then check on and comfort her over gradually lengthened periods of time.

Should Baby Cry it Out?

By William Sears, M.D, and Martha Sears, RN
Authors of numerous common sense parenting books including
The Attachment Parenting Book
Reprinted with permission.

Sometime during your parenting career, someone is going to suggest that the solution to your baby's crying is to let your baby cry it out. Don't do it, especially not in the early months of getting to know one another. Let your baby cry it out is a piece of advice that can do far more damage than good. Let's take this insensitive admonition apart so that you can see how unwise and unhelpful it is.

Let 'your' baby It's very presumptuous for a person with no connection to your baby to lecture you on how to respond to your baby's cries. Even if the advice comes from Grandma or another loving relative, realize that this person does not know your baby the way you do. She's not the one who is listening to what those cries sound like at 3 am. To people who give this kind of advice, probably out of concern for you, a cry is an annoyance. But really, a cry reflects a need.

'cry' What exactly is a baby's cry? To the cry-it-out crowd, a cry has no meaning. But in fact, a baby is trying to communicate. He is desperate to communicate his needs. How you respond to the cry is also a way of communicating. Not only is the cry a wonderful tool for babies, it is a useful signal for parents. Cries are designed to motivate parents to respond.

'It' What is the *it* in cry *it* out? Is it an annoying habit that must be broken? That's unlikely since a need cannot be called a habit. And babies don't enjoy crying. Also the belief that crying is good for a baby's lungs is just plain wrong. Excessive crying lowers baby's blood oxygen levels and raises levels of stress hormones. To an attached parent, a cry stands for a need. The it in cry it out won't go away until the need is filled.

'Out' What actually does a baby cry out when you let him cry, and where does it go? Does the infant cry out the ability to cry? Can he just get all that crying over with and be done with it? No! An infant can cry for hours and still retain the ability to cry. What the baby loses is the motivation to cry, and some other valuable things along with it. When no one responds to baby's cry, the baby has two choices: He can cry louder, harder, and produce a more disturbing signal, hoping desperately that someone will listen; or he can give up, become a 'good baby' (that is, a quiet baby) and not bother anyone. Think how you would feel if you had a need and tried your best to communicate that need, but no one listened. You would be angry. You would feel powerless and unimportant, and you would believe that no one cares about you, since your needs matter little to anyone. What goes out of a baby left to cry is trust: trust in his ability to communicate and trust in the responsiveness of his caregivers.

> *What goes out of a baby left to cry is trust: trust in his ability to communicate and trust in the responsiveness of his caregivers.*

Something goes out of parents as well when baby is left to cry it out. Parents lose sensitivity.

Advisers may tell you that you must harden your heart against your baby's cries and even may suggest that you should do this for the sake of your baby. This is wrong. You go against your own biology when you consciously desensitize yourself to your baby's signals and shut down your instinctive responses. Yes, it's true that eventually crying won't bother you, but this has serious implications for your parenting. You will lose your ability to understand baby's primitive language. This is what happens when parents view crying as a control issue rather than a way of communicating.

Sweet Dreams?

Many of our children were abandoned at night, in the 'illegal safety' of darkness.

Orphanage babies experience night/sleep as a time with fewer staff and, perhaps, with physical or emotional needs not being met as needed.

Many of our children have experienced extremely abrupt transitions of care, with no understanding or explanation of their multiple caregiver losses. For them, the world becomes an unpredictable, un-safe place, where being left alone (or waking to find a 'new' parent) is always a possibility in their mind.

Crying, especially in a pre-verbal or child with subtractive language loss, is a universal to show discomfit. Crying communicates. It is part of 'the dance of attunement' between mother and child, and sometimes the only means the child has to gain the mother's attention.

'Ferberizing' as a method of sleep training is extremely popular in the United States, and many families have found success using it. Most people, it appears, turn to the section with specifics on controlled crying and do not read the entire book. However, Dr. Ferber's book is well worth reading in its entirety because he clearly states in almost every chapter that his method is not necessarily appropriate for children with anxiety issues, or with a background of trauma. Bottom line: traditional Ferberizing is not an appropriate method of sleep training for many of our adopted children.

Like Ferberizing, the approach advocated in Babywise has garnered great popularity. Gary Ezzo's strategy, which begins in the first week of life, involves regimenting every aspect of the baby's world—feeding, playing, and sleeping. Parents are urged to get the baby on a fairly strict schedule as soon as possible and to resist the urge to create 'dependency' by fulfilling a baby's needs upon the baby's request

Many other experts also endorse the 'cry-it-out' approach. A typical example, taken from *What to Expect: The Toddler Years*, suggests for a two-year-old that: "If she cries when you leave, don't go back into her room immediately. Give her 15 or 20 minutes to comfort herself to sleep". Parents adopting internationally should understand that popular child-rearing literature is aimed squarely at healthy children whose childhoods are spent in their cultures of origin, with their birthparents. With my oldest daughter from China, I read book after book, but nothing truly addressed my daughter's needs, especially when it came to sleep.

The Reason Why

Adoptees (particularly those who have lived in institutions) come to us with far more emotional wounds than the typical child who lives out her childhood with her birthparents. Before we begin to worry about sleeping alone and sleeping through the night, we need to concern ourselves with attachment. In the years since my husband and I spent that first night with our daughter, we have learned that almost all of the issues around sleep (going to sleep, staying asleep, dreaming, and waking) are intimately connected with issues of trust and, ultimately, attachment.

Babies who are adopted have been through quite an

ordeal. The sense of well-being and trust that a baby is born with can be severely damaged when she is relinquished or abandoned—even if this event occurs immediately after birth. Research clearly indicates that newborns instinctively know their birthmothers and crave closeness with her. When a baby is abruptly separated from her birthmother, after nine months in the womb of this woman, the loss is often felt well into adult years.

The ability to form healthy attachments depends upon something called the cycle of need or the attachment cycle. Essentially, the cycle works as follows:

- Baby feels a need (hunger, wetness, gas, etc.).
- Baby expresses this need.
- Caregivers respond to the need.
- Child calms with parent help.

Over time and through thousands of repetitions of this cycle, the baby learns that crying is worthwhile: someone cares! He learns that he matters in the world, that the world is basically a good place, that someone will meet his needs, and that he can trust (and eventually love) his caregivers.

When institutional care follows abandonment/relinquishment, babies may not experience the cycle of trust that every child needs for healthy emotional development. In many orphanages there are far more children than caregivers can possibly handle and caregivers are often untrained in promoting attachment. Responding to every cry from every child is simply not a realistic option. The result? Many children who have spent much of their infancy in orphanages have learned that crying is not worthwhile, that no-one answers, and that the world is unfriendly and unsafe.

It is also important to understand that adoption itself, while such a happy event for us as parents, can be a terrifying, inexplicable event for a baby or toddler. Orphanage care may be abysmal, but it is what your child has become accustomed. The transition into a new home—especially if the adoption is international, transcultural, and/or transracial—can be yet a third disruption.

When our children come home, and they begin to allow us to move through the cycles of attachment that were broken by relinquishment and the adoption process, it is a miracle of sorts. Children who have been through a number of disruptions need us to complete the cycle of trust each and every

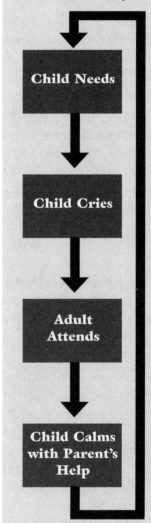

Cycle of NEED

To meet a child's emotional need, a parent must complete the circle, As a result, the child feels loved and secure, and trusts her parents with her safety.

Child Needs

Child Cries

Adult Attends

Child Calms with Parent's Help

You Made Me Feel Better
I Feel Good
You Are Good
The World is a Good Place
~Doris Landry, MS

time they express a need. And nighttime is perhaps the most vulnerable of times for children who have been adopted from institutions. Karleen Gribble states in *The post-institutionalized child*, published in The Benevolent Society, February 2004. *"Children may be able to consciously control their reaction to the stress of the new environment during their waking hours but in a more relaxed state during sleep their anxiety and or anger is exposed. Night is also a time when grief can more easily surface and the losses that a child has experienced are revealed."*

If your child has lived in an orphanage and/or has a diagnosis of Post Traumatic Stress Disorder (PTSD), you have even more reason to resist the 'easy way' to sleep train your child. Karleen Gribble adds *"Since sleep difficulties are a symptom of a deeper problem, sleep training techniques such as controlled crying/comforting are not suitable for children who have lived in an orphanage. Such techniques can cause further damage to an already hurt child as they learn that they cannot trust their parents to respond to their cries."*

Even for the seemingly well-adjusted international adoptee, controlled crying as an approach to sleep training simply should not be on the list of adoption parenting tools. So, are you destined to stay awake until your child goes to college? Should you just feel sorry for your child and allow her free reign at night in an effort to compensate for her early losses? Certainly not! There are many effective techniques for coping with sleep problems, and while some of us may struggle for a time, eventually almost everyone finds strategies that work for our children. Sleep is crucial—not only for the sanity of the entire family, but for the healthy development of the child himself. Lack of sleep contributes to everything from general fussiness to significant behavior issues.

The Basics: Getting Ready for a Good Night's Sleep

For most parents in the adoption process, there is a fairly long wait between the paper-chase and the actual adoption. This is a wonderful time to think about sleep! Now, when you still have the luxury of your own eight hours of uninterrupted slumber, do some reading. Decide what your goals are for your child:

- Are you comfortable with the Family Bed?
- Is there a solid reason (for example, parental health issues) for asking your child to sleep on her/his own from the beginning?
- Is there some middle ground you could aim for?

Regardless of your choices and preferences, there are things you can do right now to set the stage for good sleeping habits. Consider some of the following features inspired by Elizabeth Pantley, author of *The No Cry Solution: Gentle Ways to Help Your Baby Sleep Through the Night,* in the room where you expect your child will sleep:

Lighting. Be sure to include adequate lighting for day and nighttime activities but also consider choosing one fairly dim light (25 watts). When it is time for bed, you can use this soft light at reading time as a signal to the baby that the day is winding down. Also, think about installing a night light so that you can change the baby or feed her in the middle of the night without triggering her biological clock to wake up fully.

Color. Think carefully about using significant amounts of bright yellow or red in your

Sleep Patterns: The First Days

When we receive our children from their caregivers, we need to ask not just about sleeping routines but also about napping and feeding routines. These routines will have been mapped by the child onto the rhythm of the whole day (over twenty-four hours). The child's new world will seem more of a crazy disoriented place if we remove the routine of these 'sign-posts' straight away.

We need to find out when our children were fed. Many institutionalized infants are woken through the night to be given bottles. Fostered kids might be breastfed. A hungry child will come to anticipate nighttime feedings. Many adoptive parents faced with a screaming child in the dead of night have found with some relief that the child is not so much traumatized as looking for an expected bottle.

Keep in mind that feeding/sleeping information can be a little skewed in translation, or even just plain wrong! If the 'instructions' aren't working, be creative! Ask for advice from others who have adopted children from your child's orphanage, or email your adoption facilitator in your child's birth country for input.

We need to find out how and where our children slept. In a crib, in a bed? In the dark, with a light? Alone in a crib, or with another child? On the floor? With a caregiver/foster mother? All of these factors, if we can discover them, may help us settle our children in their first days with us. Some children are so affected by the fact of the adoption that this itself stops an easy transition to sleep. The child may not in fact be reacting adversely to new parents, but will be reacting to the hyper-stimulation of new places, new people, and new smells. Turn it to good effect! One adoptive father whose child would not sleep unless being walked out in the bustle of busy night streets in China, felt that he was introducing her 'to the world'. He made a win: win of her not sleeping by ensuring the time was spent bonding.

However, we still need to moderate how much 'excitement' the child should be exposed to; many therapists recommend very low-key levels activities by day for newly adopted children. This helps regulate their behavior, which in turn will positively affect their sleeping clocks. All these functions are linked by what scientists call 'circadian rhythms' (a daily rhythmic activity cycle, based on 24-hour intervals, that is exhibited by many organisms); de-synchronize these, and breakdown in adjustment becomes more likely.

Families who have adopted internationally also need to remember that their new child's diurnal clock, with its settings set for time-zones far apart from those of the new adoptive country, will initially prevent routine sleep. Re-setting the circadian rhythm may take time, and may take longer time than our jetlag.

~ Sheena Macrae

child's bedroom. Color theorists (and fast food restaurants!) have long known that red and yellow (warm colors) are color 'stimulants' while soft blues and purples (cool tones) tend to relax people.

Sound.   Consider investing in a sound machine for your child's room. Especially when children have lived in institutional settings, they may be used to a considerable amount of nighttime noise. Waking in the middle of the night to a silent house can be quite scary. Conversely, if your family lives in a city, the night noises outside your home (cars, sirens, etc.) can also be very disturbing. White noise helps remove the issue of sound from the sleeping mind. A small CD-player with lullabies can work the same wonders.

Safety.   Whatever option you choose, be sure to set up the child's bed (family bed or a crib) with great attention to safety. This is also a terrific time to do some problem-solving in advance. Think about how you would handle a child who:

- takes a long time to go to sleep
- cries a great deal
- wakes often in the night
- struggles with night terrors

If there are two of you, it may help to agree on an alternate-night plan or a weeknight versus weekend alternation schedule. Perhaps one parent consistently takes 'night duty,' but that parent also gets weekend naps. Remember, you will be a better parent if you can sleep once in a while! This is also the time to come to an agreement about your family's philosophy of sleep. The last thing you want is to be standing by a screaming child arguing about whether you should let her cry it out. If you are parenting as a single, line up some 'relief' workers now — perhaps a cousin or grandparent who would be willing to help you at night if things get rough.

And finally, prepare yourself emotionally for this new challenge. Get your sleep now. Have a few wonderful 'last dates'. Stay out late with your best friend. Finish up projects that are hanging over your head, or decide to shelve them for at least a year. In other words, clear your schedule as much as you can!

Many, many children will join their families and will not experience significant sleep issues. If, however, your baby does have trouble sleeping, understand that you are not alone, and most likely are not 'doing it wrong.'

Bringing Baby Home

Once your child is home, you can begin to establish good sleep patterns immediately. Accept that you may have some sleepless nights and make whatever arrangements you can to lighten your load. Good nighttime sleep patterns begin in the daytime. Some key elements of the baby's day include:

Food.   Babies need to eat enough during the day to meet the needs of growing bodies. For Post Institutionalized (PI) kids, initially getting enough to eat can be quite a task. It is not unusual for PI babies to put on a pound a week in the first weeks home. Babies who are constantly hungry have a difficult time falling and staying asleep.

Exercise and Fresh Air.   Be sure your little one is getting enough exercise. By all means, resist the urge to turn on the television during the day! Television, and especially evening viewing, has been linked with a wide variety of sleep problems.

Naptime. Babies need naps! Missing a nap does not necessarily mean that children will fall asleep faster at night. Too little daytime sleep will result in an over-stimulated, cranky baby who has a difficult time getting to sleep at night.

When nighttime comes, you may well have to try a number of strategies before you hit on one that will work for your baby. I would recommend that you experiment with having your baby go to sleep alone, only if he is willing to cooperate (some babies will!). Ideally, your baby will begin life in your family with sleep associations that allow him to go to sleep by himself and to sleep peacefully through the entire night. If you find that this is not the case, you have a choice to make. Which is more important to your child: immediately learning to sleep alone, or learning that mom and/or dad will always be there for him? If there is a choice to be made, you may elect to delay teaching him to sleep alone until after attachment is secure.

Emotional Age. It is important to understand, too, that when a child has been institutionalized, his emotional age and her physical age can be dramatically different. Noted psychologist, Doris Landry, who specializes in attachment and adoption, recommends treating your baby's emotional needs as though he were a newborn—even if he is ten months or a year old. In those first weeks and months, the primary goal should be promoting attachment and a sense of

~It Worked for Me!~
Sleep is Your Job...

I was frazzled beyond repair at our night ritual–my whole evening was taken with getting my three year old daughter to sleep. I sat her down one night and told her I could not continue with what we were doing. It was making me an unhappy, grumpy mommy. I told her that it was my responsibility to fix it. I told her from that night forward my job was to get her ready for bed, read her books, and tuck her in with her special songs. Her job started after we said goodnight. It was her job to stay in bed–but she didn't have to fall asleep. That would have been too much pressure for her to handle. She could sing, she could play with a flashlight, play with her doll, whatever. It didn't matter, she just had to stay there in bed.

My one exception to this rule was if she was frightened. I told her she could always call out to me if this happened, and she understood this. At first staying in bed was very hard for her and I compromised. I checked in later to say another goodnight to remind her exactly what her job was. Initially it took her a very long time to fall asleep, but about six months into our going-to-bed plan, I realized that most nights my daughter was asleep in under five minutes.

My daughter was proud that she had a job to do just like mommy, and she loved to hear how well she was doing at it.

~Debbie Carr-Taylor
adoptive mom

trust and security. Learning to go to sleep alone and to stay asleep without assistance may need to wait.

The Sleep Routine

Once night falls, then how do you proceed? Perhaps the best piece of advice, agreed upon by virtually all experts–from Ferber to Sears–is to set up a pre-sleep routine and follow it every night. Keeping your child's routine as consistent as possible in the first months home can pay incredible dividends.

Establishing the routine may be very difficult in the first week or two if your child has been adopted internationally, because both you and the child may be struggling with jetlag. Days and nights may be reversed for a while, and it may take several weeks for your child to fully re-adjust. Patience, and a sleep relief worker, can work wonders.

A sample sleep routine might look like this:
- Give the baby a warm bath.
- Turn off bright lights and use low watt lights and even a sound machine.
- Read her a story or two and snuggle.
- Give her a last bottle (rocking chairs are soothing!)
- Try to put her down drowsy rather than asleep, in her crib or your bed.

During this time, remain very calm and do not engage in play. Bedtime is not a good time for tickles or any games that might be stimulating. Try to be as boring as possible!

It is quite likely that she will cry. This is your chance to complete the attachment cycle discussed earlier:
- Have all physical needs been met?
- Is her diaper wet?
- Does she have gas? (New brands of formula, formula with iron, and unfamiliar foods can wreak havoc on a baby/toddler's intestinal system)
- Is she teething and in need of medication?

If you are certain that her physical needs have been met, try patting her and see if she calms herself without you picking her up. Keep it bland and boring. Do not talk to her other than to say 'Shh…Shh.' If she can not calm herself, go ahead and cuddle her, rock her, or walk the floor with her. Do what you feel she needs you to do. Trust your instincts as a parent. (And please, if the crying goes on too long or the child appears to be in severe pain, by all means call the pediatrician. She expects to hear from new parents—yes, even in the middle of the night.)

The Bottle, the Sippy, the Pacifier. Pediatricians and dentists advise against giving a toddler or preschooler a bottle of anything other than water to take to bed. But if watered down juice, milk or formula gets your child to sleep, you might want to go with the flow, so to speak, and just be extra-vigilant about teeth-brushing. If there is not a severe medical/dental contraindication, and comfort-sucking provides your child with a degree of relaxation, then ignore advice to take away your child's baby bottle, sippy cup or pacifier at nighttime (or at an arbitrary, pre-determined age). Wait until your son or daughter is ready to go to bed without these sleep aids before taking them away.

The Bed

Crib Fear. If you've chosen a crib as the place where your baby will sleep, it may be helpful to know that some PI children experience an extremely negative reaction to cribs. Our children, especially when they are newly home, do not understand what is obvious to us. They do not know that we are in the next room; they do not know that we will definitely be there when they wake up. Indeed, if a child was abandoned, experience teaches him that it does not pay to go to sleep alone. In his experience, parents do disappear in the night.

For children who have been in foster care abroad, cribs may seem entirely alien because they have been co-sleeping with their foster parents for months or even years. If sleeping alone in the crib appears to be the issue, consider some of the following alternatives that many adoptive (and non-adoptive) families have used with success:

> ## Swaddling?
>
> Some babies respond to being swaddled snugly with a light baby blanket around their legs and torso (leave arms free to move). Whether from wearing layers of clothing in a cold orphanage, or from sensory preference, swaddling seems to help some babies and toddlers relax enough to fall asleep.

The Family Bed. Allow your baby to sleep with you. Be sure, though, to follow all the recommended safety procedures: never sleep with a child after ingesting alcohol, use tight fitting sheets, dress the baby warmly enough so that he does not require sheets or a quilt, and use a properly installed bed rail to be sure that he does not fall out of the bed. I would be remiss if I failed to note here that the American Academy of Pediatrics recommends against co-sleeping due to the possibility that newborns may be smothered.

Early on, our family used the Family Bed and we occasionally revert to it. I stay with the children until they are asleep and then get up for the evening. Frankly, every member of our family appreciates the Family Bed, and I am convinced that my daughters are very close to one another because for years they woke up together each morning in such a loving environment. Many adoptive parents throughout the country indicate that the Family Bed often puts an end to many common nighttime problems.

Two Mattresses on the Floor of Parents' Room. Some parents, concerned about having a baby in the bed with them, put two mattresses (usually their regular mattress and a twin) on the floor of their bedroom. The baby is then close to his parents without actually sharing the same bed. If the baby has a difficult time going to sleep on his own, a parent stays on the twin mattress until the baby is asleep and then moves to her own mattress for the night.

Side-car or Co-sleeper. Place the baby in a specially-designed mini-crib which hooks on to your bed. This approach, endorsed by Dr. William Sears, the Attachment Parenting

Infant/Child Massage

A lotion massage after a bath can promote relaxation, and can be an attuning, quiet time for a parent and child. Use a gentle but firm pressure to avoid tickling, keep lighting low and play sleep-time music.

Here are some books to get you started:

Infant Massage: A Handbook for Loving Parents–Vimala Schneider McClure

Baby Massage for Dummies by Joanne Bagshaw and Ilene Fox

guru, has gained popularity in recent years. There is little danger of rolling over on the baby with this method; parents can keep an eye and ear on the baby; and parents are available to hold hands or pat a back as necessary.

While I strongly advocate some form of co-sleeping for children who are newly home, I also understand that families sometimes have very good reasons (parental health concerns, parental sleep disorders, a parent who snores loudly, a child who is a violent sleeper, etc.) for choosing a crib for their child. If you feel that co-sleeping will not work for your family, consider the following strategies:

Daytime Fun in the Crib. Elizabeth Pantley recommends that parents whose children are apprehensive about cribs use the Family Bed while re-orienting their baby to the crib during the day. This is especially helpful if you have tried the controlled crying method unsuccessfully and inadvertently created negative associations with the crib. Place the baby in the crib for very short intervals during the day and stay with the child. Play games like peek-a-boo through the slats. If you can create new and positive associations with the crib during the day, you may well succeed in moving him to the crib at night.

Mattress or Chair in Baby's Room. Using this method, one parent stays beside the crib on a chair or mattress in the baby's room, while the baby sleeps in the crib. Some parents hold the child's hand while she goes to sleep. Gradually the child gets used to her own bed, the hand-holding stops, and eventually, the parent no longer needs to stay with the baby. In another version of this method, the parent verbally reassures the child with the same 'cue' words—"good night" or "shh, shh"—but avoids picking the child up as an immediate response to distress.

Medical Possibilities

If you have tried many of these suggestions and you are not finding success, have your pediatrician check into the following physical possibilities, all of which are fairly common causes of sleep problems for international adoptees:

- Enlarged or infected adenoids or tonsils (can cause sleep apnea)
- Vitamin or mineral deficiencies
- Constipation (formula with iron can be difficult for some children to digest)
- Asthma/allergies (causing sinus headaches, coughing, wheezing)
- Scabies
- Eczema

- Lactose intolerance
- Teething
- Ear infections
- Intestinal parasites
- Acid Reflux
- Sensory Integration Disorder (DSI) can cause difficulties with texture, movement, space, body position sound, and smells.

You should also consider the possibility that your child is processing emotional issues that require professional help. Many PI children suffer from PTSD which can interfere with sleep. Indeed, noted adoption specialist Deborah Gray lists sleeping problems of all sorts–falling asleep, staying asleep, nightmares– especially when they are combined with other symptoms of being on 'high alert', as possible signs of PTSD. Look for a therapist who has significant experience dealing with international adoption. And yes, even a very young child can be helped by an experienced practitioner. You may find that once you start addressing these issues, sleep problems are either diminished or eliminated altogether.

Patience is the key to this early phase home with baby. Remember, however, that you need your sleep every bit as much as your baby does. If things get really rough, look for nighttime relief. If you have a partner, devise creative ways to be sure that you both have the sleep you need.

Transition into Toddlerhood/Preschool Years

Not all children are adopted as babies. What if you are bringing home a toddler? Many of the suggestions in the section above can be implemented with the preschool set. There are a few differences, however. Toddlers and preschoolers are much more mobile, and they are willful. Once they have an idea in mind, convincing them to move in a different direction can be harrowing. What follows are some ideas for handling children in this age range:

Daytime Routine. While older children may look like they can handle more flexibility in their schedule, the truth is they need routine every bit as much as they did when they were babies. Meals need to be served at the same time every day; early bedtimes should be enforced.

Exercise. Perhaps most important for promoting healthy toddler sleep is exercise. Young children need an extraordinary

The Handbook of International Adoption Medicine: *A Guide for Physicians, Parents, and Providers* by Laurie C. Miller, MD

This is the medical source book for parents and pediatricians who are looking for information targeted specifically at international adoptees. Dr. Miller provides preparatory advice about health risks of particular sending countries, and a post-adoption heads-up on medical conditions that are infrequently encountered in the western world. The basics are covered in detail: growth and development, parasites, immunizations, infectious diseases, neurocognitive and behavioral issues, and the child's emotional transition to his or her new family. Clinical, but readable, and an invaluable parent/ physician tool.

Sleep Deprivation

Exhaustion plays a role in undermining the capacity of parents to cope, develop a support network, and find time to sleep

Swap child-care in the night with a partner

Trade sleep/a shower with good friends who understand, and return the compliment

Use family who can be around as loved stand-ins while you grab an occasional whole night's sleep

Talk the whole thing through with a family doctor who understands your child's institutional background and attachment needs

Buy a baby monitor and use it. You will hear a lot that will help hone parenting skills

Nap when the kids nap OR when they are at school

Try therapy for a child with trauma that interferes with sleep

~ Sheena Macrae

amount of daily exercise—as those of us who have adopted late in life can attest! It will be difficult for them to sleep with excess energy.

Television: Turn it off. Toddlers, especially toddlers who are joining a new family, need stimulation from you, not from the television. Avoid television, particularly in the hours before bedtime, as evening viewing has been linked to many sleep disturbances. Researchers also strongly recommend that families do not allow children to have televisions in their rooms.

Bedtime Routine

The bedtime routine for a young child should look a lot like the routine you would follow for a baby. What if the child does not want to go to sleep on his own? While this problem can be difficult with an infant in a crib, it can be extraordinarily trying to keep a terrified and mobile toddler in a toddler bed. Again, the emphasis is on attachment; a young child who is newly home needs to know that you will be there for him 'no matter what'. Consider the strategies listed in The Bed section: the Family Bed, the side car arrangement, two mattresses on the floor of parents' room, a parent mattress on the floor of child's room. Many adoptive families have found that they work as well for young children as they do for babies. In addition, there are several other strategies that may be worth a try:

The Lovey. Help your child choose a lovey—a special blanket, a stuffed animal, or a doll that he will sleep with every night. Some parents use a t-shirt that belongs to (and smells like) Mom or Dad to cover the child's pillow. Even if your child can not yet go to sleep without assistance, virtually all sleep experts indicate that the lovey can help later as you make the transition to sleeping alone.

Sippy Cup. Give the child a sippy cup with water. The child can't suck on it all night in the same way that she could with a bottle, but it will short-circuit the famous "I need a drink of water" problem. Especially when my children have colds, having a drink of water handy will often cut short a coughing spell.

Naps. This is a tricky one. As children move out of infancy and into toddlerhood, their need for naps varies quite dramatically. One of my daughters, around the age of three, had a terrible time falling asleep at night. When I removed the nap, she suddenly nodded off at eight p.m. every night without a fuss. On the other hand, if a child is unready to give up a nap, being extra tired will only ruin the latter half of the day and make going to sleep at night even harder. Experiment a bit and consult with your pediatrician about sleep needs for different aged children.

Sleep Coach. If your child has a relative or adult friend that he particularly likes, have that person speak to your child about sleep. Have your child 'report in,' especially when she has a good night (sleeps through the night, goes to sleep alone). For some children, it helps to know that they have someone external to the immediate family rooting for him.

Personalized Book Get out that digital camera and take photos of the child going through the bedtime routine. If you can, snap a photo of the child sleeping. Together, write a little book about sleep. The easiest way to 'publish' it is to print it off of your computer, or just buy a small photo album and insert the photos with a little text. Your child is guaranteed to love this activity, and the book will probably become a favorite.

Professional Help. Again, if you have worked with many of these tools and you are still struggling with sleep, consider the possibility that you need outside help. By all means, have your pediatrician rule out physical cause. Think about consulting an attachment therapist, especially one with significant experience with international adoption. A qualified therapist can be invaluable in addressing a child's core issues and related sleep problems.

No Right Way

Had I believed that room sharing or the Family Bed was the only way to parent a newly adopted child, I can imagine my first daughter would have thought I was nuts. She had lived her entire life in a Romanian orphanage and hated any crib on sight, but once she found that toddler bed of her very own...in her very own pink room....with her very own toys and more...she couldn't have been happier to go to bed and slept twelve to thirteen hours a night with nary a whimper or peep.

When her sister came home from China I was very open-minded about sleep. Thank Goodness! My second daughter feared sleep like it meant death. The terror she exhibited was heart wrenching. When we first arrived home, we dismantled the crib and moved it right next to Mommy's bed. It took a very gradual process over the next four months for her to slowly relax and go to sleep first with Mommy right next to her crib, then with Mommy sitting on the bed, then in a chair in the room, then walking in and out of the room. For months she continued to wake up every few hours to make sure she was not alone.

I'm so glad I didn't assume that because my first daughter transitioned sleep wise into her own room so easily, that this was the right way! Every child is different and some are going to need different arrangements than we have originally planned. We really need to be open minded about many aspects of parenting until we really get to know the children who've joined our family.

~ Jill Lampman, adoptive mom

Making a Change

Regardless of how much you may love the Family Bed or enjoy cuddle time while your child falls asleep in your arms, no doubt you hope that the time will come when attachment is reasonably secured. The child then needs to learn to go to sleep without your assistance. Some children will decide on their own that it is time to sleep in the Big Kid Bed. I know of one young man who slept in a family bed until first grade, when he went to his first sleepover at a friend's house. He was scared, but he managed to spend the night away from home. After that, he told his parents he would prefer to sleep in his own room. Not all of us are so lucky.

If you find you need to do more work to accomplish a change, consider the following tools:

Understanding Sleep Associations: If you are considering a change to your child's sleeping arrangements, you must consider that child's sleep associations. Children and adults come to rely on these (the right size pillow, a ceiling fan, a certain weight quilt) in order to go to sleep. If you are a primary sleep aid or trigger for your child, she will find it difficult to go to sleep without you. Your goal is to set up a new set of sleep associations. Soft music can be a soothing sleep aid. If night waking is an issue consider a player that will repeat the music throughout the night. This avoids setting up a sleep association that won't be replicated if your baby rouses during the night. If she awakens and misses the music she associates with sleep, you will be notified! The lovey can also become a primary sleep aid, allowing you to gradually and patiently withdraw from the routine. Use the lovey (especially the t-shirt that smells like a parent) to reassure her that she always has a part of you.

Music Can Work Magic!

Heartbeat Music Therapy for Babies and Children Works for All Ages
Special arrangements of traditional nursery songs using the actual human heartbeat recorded from the chest as the rhythm.CDs and tapes-
www.babygotosleep.com
Chinese Lullabies by the Beijing Angelic Children's Choir
Ethereal and hypnotic: these lullabies from around the world create a feeling of tenderness and comfort. Find online at places like Amazon
Peaceful Go-to-Sleep Imagery for Children
Mindworks for Children CDs
www.sound-remedies.com
A great collection of gentle, sleep lullabies
www.serenitysupply.com

TIP: Play your children's nighttime CDs and tapes on repeat mode. Sometimes the sound of the music turning off can awaken a light sleeper.

Talk with your Child. As your child gets older and more verbal, it is well worth having several serious conversations about why he needs to acquire the skill of sleeping on his own. Get his concerns on the table if you can. One little girl I know recently confessed to her mother that the reason she was resisting learning this new skill was that she feared she would never be allowed back in the Family Bed. Her grief at this possibility of permanent rejection was overpowering her natural tendency to embrace new challenges. Her mother gently explained that knowing how to sleep on her own would not mean that she was banished from the Family Bed. Together, they came up with a schedule of times (father away on a trip, child ill, Friday nights) when the family would return to co-sleeping.

Taking the Gradual Approach. Much as you might love to announce that tonight will be the night when your child goes to sleep alone, sleeps through the night, or sleeps in the Big Kid Bed, your chances of success improve if you take it slowly. You may be tempted at this point to go the Ferberizing route and get it all done in just three days. Think carefully about this idea. Consider how hard you have worked to make this child feel safe. Don't undo all the hard work you did helping your child come to trust you! Instead, work on breaking the transition into small and reasonably painless steps. (Some examples of how to do this include moving from the Family Bed and the check-in method.) Work, too, on clearing your nighttime routine for several weeks so that you are entirely focused on making the change work.

Moving from Family Bed to the Crib. Try putting the crib right beside your bed. Hold hands as the baby falls asleep. Over a few nights, shorten the hand-holding period. Over a few weeks, gradually move the crib away from your bed and toward the door. Eventually, move the baby into the hall (if possible) and then into her room.

Moving to The Big Kid Bed. Have your child help pick the new bed out, or have her help choose the bedding. Set it up in her room, and let it stay there for a few days or weeks —unless of course she is fired up about trying it on the first night. (A stroke of genius led us to paint our bedroom and tell the kids that the fumes would be bad for them at night so they had to sleep in their own room. As it turned out, they loved it.) Create positive associations with the bed; read to her or play simple board games on it during the day. If you are moving her out of the Family Bed, lay down with her just as you did when you were all in the same bed. After a few days, move to sitting up in bed, work your way to the end of the bed, then try sitting in a chair near the bed every night for a couple of weeks, then try sitting in the doorway.

Some children are excited about the Big Kid Bed but then will not stay in it long enough to go to sleep. You may have to devote some nights to sitting quietly beside the bed and calmly and lovingly (but without conversation) putting your child back in bed over and over. Toddlers, especially, can be quite determined, and you will need all the patience you can summon to make this work. Do not get angry as this will only create negative associations with the Big Kid Bed! If you have a partner who does not normally do the bedtime routine, try having that person use this strategy. If your child melts down or gets hysterical, stop! Return to the crib or the Family Bed and try again in a few weeks or months. Have faith that your child will get there eventually.

Self Soothing

Adopted children often self-soothe by using sensory means. While thumbs and blankies are common, peaceful means to sleep, some adopted kids scratch or masturbate themselves at bedtime.

Is the child manifesting and replaying previous abuse? The child who inappropriately self-soothes may be trying to tell that he has had to devise a premature ability to cope with actual fears, frights, and bad dreams.

Parents need to work with children like this by day, and may need to seek help from a therapist in dealing with a child's underlying trauma. Ideally, a child needs to be able to trust his parents enough to allow mom or dad to soothe away his need for defense at night.

Co-Sleeping with Siblings. If you are making the transition out of the Family Bed, it may be easier to set up a double or queen size bed with a sibling who is willing to co-sleep. Sometimes, just having someone in the bed beside a child will be reassurance enough to allow the child to fall asleep and stay asleep. Be sure to add bed rails for safety's sake!

Using the Check-in Method. If your child is relatively verbal, this method may help to teach him to sleep on her own. After your normal routine, tuck the child in and give him a kiss. Tell him you will be back for another kiss in 2 minutes—whatever you think he can tolerate (we started with 10 seconds.) Then set your timer and by all means, don't blow it! On good nights, I use this method to cope with night waking with some success. Often, my daughter is asleep by the second or third check-in.

Nighttime Disruptions

Even for children who go to sleep relatively easily, there remains the issue of staying asleep through the night. There are three major categories of problems that occur during the night: night waking without distress, night terrors, and nightmares. To understand what is happening in each of those situations, a quick review of sleep theory may help. Children (like adults) go through sleep cycles of varying lengths at night. As sleepers pass from deep, restorative sleep into REM (rapid eye movement) sleep, they tend to arouse very briefly. Those brief arousals are the points when children and adults tend to experience problems–either fully arousing or getting 'trapped' in a partially awake/partially asleep state. Nightmares, on the other hand, occur during REM sleep.

Problem #1: Night Waking

Some babies and children routinely wake spontaneously at least once during the night. They do not appear to be in distress and they are clearly wide awake. Try to put your child back to sleep as soon as possible. We made the mistake of responding to night waking in one daughter's toddlerhood by allowing her to stay up with me—thus making a nighttime wakening emotionally rewarding and habitual. Though our situation was more complicated than a simple bad habit, I wish, in retrospect, that I had treated returning to bed as a higher priority.

Some possibilities for coping with this situation include:

Check for Immediate Physical Causes Is the room too hot or cold? Is the child over or underdressed? Is the baby eating too much close to bedtime and suffering with an upset stomach? See the possible physical or medical causes listed under The Sleep Routine section.

Eliminate Nighttime Feedings. If your child is still waking for nighttime feedings long after he is home and your pediatrician feels that he no longer needs nutrition during the night, consider the watering-down method advocated by Dr. Sears. This method is appropriate only if your child has attained an adequate body weight, which for many international adoptees may take many months. Over several nights, change the balance in the baby's nighttime bottle in favor of water. Eventually, give him a bottle with just water. Generally, if his body is only waking for nutrition and he is getting only water, the body will stop looking for a meal at that time, and he will cease the nocturnal awakenings.

Look at the Child's Sleep Associations. If you have determined that your child's room and clothing are reasonably comfortable, that she is not waking for food, and that there are no physical problems involved in the night waking, you will want to think about the way that your child has learned to fall asleep at night. If you are one of her sleep associations at the start of the night, she will have a very difficult time going back to sleep when she hits the normal brief arousal period between deep sleep and REM sleep. At that point, like all children and adults, she will become dimly conscious of her surroundings. If she associates sleep with a parent and the parent is not there, she will waken fully and start to cry or set off in search of you. If you are still in the period of promoting attachment over sleep training, however, you

Nap Terrors

We adopted our oldest when she was ten months old; she had lived in an orphanage in China since she was around three days old. She didn't sleep well from the first night we knew her. Naps were tricky too; about three times a week, she would fall asleep. But my husband and I grew to hate the naps. Our daughter woke up in a rage or terror, and I later started calling these episodes nap terrors because she really wasn't fully awake, and they were very similar to night terrors. She would scream and rage for up to thirty minutes upon waking up, or looking like she was waking up. For awhile, we just thought she woke up in a terrible mood. Yes, we were inexperienced parents. A baby doesn't know a nap from night time sleep. I learned later that both nap and night time terrors can stem from Post Traumatic Stress Disorder (PTSD). We think that our daughter's PTSD-based terrors are probably due to being abandoned while sleeping, as experts think is the case for many abandoned children.

We revisited the napping conundrum with our second child too. So both my kids existed on little sleep in the beginning. As they became more secure (and for my youngest we worked on sensory issues), sleep became easier. Both of them napped later. When everyone else I knew was complaining that their kids were giving up the naps, my kids were just starting to nap consistently! For both kids, this was around three years old.

~Tia Marsh, adoptive mom

may decide that you need to live with some night waking. If you feel that your child is ready to learn to sleep alone, look at the suggestions in the section on Making a Change and implement these gradually. Sleep researchers tell us quite conclusively that once children know how to go to sleep alone, night waking is usually eliminated.

Keep a Sleep Journal. Keep detailed notes as to your child's day and the specifics of the night-waking. You may find that particular activities (visitors to the house, television late in the day, changes in routine) trigger night waking.

Try Controlled Awakenings. Use your sleep journal to determine when your child is likely to awaken (e.g., ninety minutes after falling asleep). Just before the child would normally awaken, go to him and gently rouse him by patting his back. Some families have found that this strategy short-circuits the night-waking. After two weeks or so of this preventative waking approach, children will sometimes simply lose the habit of waking up.

Consult a Therapist If you have worked through the suggestions above and the night wakings continue, consider the possibility that your child may be dealing with larger issues than just a sleep training problem. The young lives of too many of our children have been fraught with emotional (not to mention physical) danger. Many of our children come home with PTSD and other emotional issues. Several trauma specialists, including Deborah Gray and William Steele, note that unprocessed trauma is often initially evidenced in sleep disorders. If you suspect that this is the real issues underlying your child's sleep problems, look for a qualified therapist in your area. If PTSD is the real issue, your child will not simply grow out of it. If your child's situation is serious enough, you may want to speak to the pediatrician about doing a sleep study.

Problem #2: Night Terrors

Richard Ferber describes night terrors, or sleep terrors as "incomplete awakening[s] from deep non-dreaming sleep." The spectrum of partial arousals ranges from talking in one's sleep (which is no cause for alarm), sleep walking, and full blown sleep terrors in which the sleeper screams and thrashes wildly. A child in the midst of a sleep terror may appear to be awake–eyes open and body in motion–but, in fact, the child is trapped between sleep and waking. Sleep terrors typically occur during the first half of the night, within four hours of bedtime. They can be extremely scary for parents and other family members who witness them, but they often disappear with time. When a night terror is in progress, the following steps may be helpful.

Stay Close but Do Not Awaken the Child. This is good advice, but it is extremely hard to do when your child is thrashing about and screaming in a panic. However, sleep researchers believe that intervening in a night terror will only prolong it and may terrify the child when she comes to full consciousness. Restrain the child only if you believe she is about to hurt herself.

Show the Child the House. Many parents in the adoptive community have reported that they have good results turning on all the lights and walking the child through the house. Speak calmly to your child as you give him a guided tour of her home. This strategy worked for us. When a child has lived in a number of vastly differing circumstances in a

Nighttime Parenting

Some kids need more parenting at night than others....this isn't an indication that they are spoiled or that you haven't set the right boundaries–just that they are more insecure and have other needs that should be met. If you're not finding the Family Bed will work for you (and the Family Bed is a very appropriate option), then a sleeping bag on the floor is also a good one. Check around your room for a spot that is the least likely impede to anyone's pathway and then show it to your child. Place a small, kid-sized sleeping bag under your bed, or near it, and let your child know that she is welcome to pull it out on her own and come sleep in your room when she's feeling scared. Also let her know that everyone needs to sleep so it's not time to visit in the middle of the night. This was a terrific solution for my daughter when she was six and seven years old, and unlike what some will tell you, it doesn't create a monster or set up habits that are impossible to change! It's just responding to the individual child's needs, and figuring out a way for everyone in the family to get a good, solid night's sleep (which is so important).

~ *Jill Lampman, adoptive mom*

short period of time, he may need to be grounded in the present when he gets stuck in partial arousal.

Do Not Mention the Night Terror. A child will have no memory of a night terror the next day and discussing it will only reinforce the sense that she is out of control. In the long run, you may feel that you need to do more than just live with night terrors as a regular feature of your family's life. When sleep terrors become a permanent element of the night, they are extremely disruptive to everyone in the family. If you get to that stage, here are some suggestions:

Look at the Child's Routine. Jodi Mindell has noted that both insufficient sleep and irregular bedtimes can be triggers for sleep terrors. According to her research, children who have too little sleep one night are prone to night terrors the next night.

Keep a Sleep Journal. Note what seems to set off the terrors. It is well known among families adopting from China that the first visit to a Chinese restaurant, especially if your baby receives a lot of attention, can trigger night terrors. It did for us. Medications can also be the culprit, so keep records.

Try Controlled Awakenings. This is described under Night Wakings

Consider Other Physical Causes. This is also described under Night Wakings

Consult a Therapist. Several sleep experts believe that night terrors are developmentally appropriate in babies and young children. According to Ferber, parents should begin to look for a psychological component to sleep terrors if they persist beyond the time when the child turns five or six. He advocates psychotherapy, noting that, "When she allows herself to express her feelings during the daytime, even inappropriately, she will have less need to guard against those feelings at night". For children who are adopted,

Resources

Sleeping through the Night: How Infants, Toddlers, and their Parents Can Get a Good Night's Sleep by Jodi A. Mindell This is a 'kinder, gentler' version of Ferber and a controlled crying approach is not appropriate for many adopted children. However, all of the other sections, from night terrors to calming yourself as a parent are excellent and well worth reading.

The No-Cry Sleep Solution: Gentle Ways to Help Your Baby Sleep through the Night by Elizabeth Pantley Contains excellent suggestions for gradually teaching your child to sleep through the night. It's slow and gentle approach is very appropriate for adoptive families.

The Attachment Parenting Book by William Sears, MD, Martha Sears, RN and *The Baby Sleep Book* by William Sears, MD, Robert Sears, MD, James Sears MD, and Martha Sears, RN These are part of the Sears Parenting Library and great resources for understanding the relationship between you and your child and how to teach your child to sleep.

Solve Your Child's Sleep Problems by Richard Ferber This book is wonderful—and terribly misunderstood. You will need to read the entire book and understand that some children have emotional issues that must be addressed before sleep training can begin.

particularly those from an institution, it is advisable to begin to look for psychological roots to sleep terrors well before the age of five. Indeed, the window for improving a child's emotional health is open long before that time. Don't wait and allow your child and your entire family to suffer!

Problem #3: Nightmares

Unlike night waking and night terrors, both of which occur in transition as the sleeper passes from deep sleep into REM sleep, nightmares occur during REM sleep. Nightmares tend to occur during the second half of the night when most people spend more time in REM sleep.

Immediately following a nightmare, parents should work to reassure the child.

Hold your Child. Comfort him. If he is verbal, get him to talk through what occurred in the dream. One of my children is most comforted by turning on all the lights, moving to a different room and processing the dream right away. The other prefers to give me the briefest of accounts ("Emily hit me"), get a quick hug, and return to sleep with as little fuss as possible. In any event, this is an ideal time to go through the attachment cycle and meet an emotional need. Help your child to feel as safe as possible.

Try Art. Hand the child paper and crayons or markers (or play dough, if that works better), as soon as she awakens from a nightmare. See what she creates. One child I know of drew her orphanage, a building with 20 or more windows and no doors, after each nightmare. She felt trapped, terrified and angry in the orphanage, and her sleeping mind was just beginning to give her access to those feelings. Art can be incredibly helpful in figuring out what underlies nightmares. If nightmares persist, you may need to look into the following factors:

Consider Immediate Physical Causes. A room that is too hot or too cold may inspire nightmares. Similarly, heavy foods (pizza, for example) or high dose vitamins just before bedtime may also be a factor.

Consider Immediate Emotional Causes. Did the child just start preschool, or meet a new caregiver? Is there a new member of the family (a sibling, a live-in grandparent, or a new partner for a parent)? Is there marital or partner discord in the family? Has there been a recent death or divorce? Are there problems at school or on the playground? Has a best friend moved away? If there are emotional stressors in your child's life, you will need to address them before the nightmares will end.

Look at the Child's Routine. As is true for both night waking and night terrors, change in routine or lack of sleep can be an important contributing factor in creating nightmares.

Keep a Sleep Journal. Note what seems to set off nightmares and make efforts to minimize those factors. Helping your child feel safe during the day and during the night may reduce nightmares.

Consider Physical Causes. Again, many of the physical issues listed in the section on Night Waking can contribute to nightmares.

Consult a Therapist. Nightmares are very common among children who are adopted, especially those coming from institutions. Whether our children have a diagnosis of PTSD or some other disorder, or no diagnosis at all, persistent nightmares should not be ignored. Whatever the child is trying to process during the night must be brought into the light of day and dealt with. Taking the step of consulting a professional may just be the best gift you can give your child. Preschool and older children can be given psychological tools to help them combat their fears.

This, Too, Shall Pass

For adoptive parents facing sleep issues, there is much good news. Research into sleep has evolved a great deal in recent years, and there are many, many strategies and tools for us as we teach our children to get the rest that they need. In my

Sleep Needs

Sleep needs are idiosyncratic. It's something adoptive parents need to keep in mind when worrying about a child who doesn't sleep. Perhaps your child just doesn't need a lot of sleep compared with her peers? Until you know your child's sleep patterns, and have eliminated any post-institutional issues, it's hard not to be concerned when a child won't sleep.

It's our job to gauge when we need to be firm about bedtime, and when being content in bed and awake is fine. Letting kids have toys, books, headphones (for the older ones) often is the best route, rather than insisting they sleep. Most children who don't need so much sleep like to know where we are. An open door policy often allows parents their own time downstairs while the children rest easy because they hear the sounds and know where their parents are!

experience, however, the most important tools of all are the hardest to teach and the most challenging to learn:

Your Attitude. In the end, your attitude can make all the difference. Some of our children come home with significant problems: post traumatic stress disorder, anxious attachment, sensory integration disorder, to name but a few. When you are tired, coping with these issues can be overwhelming. It is all too easy to let frustration, annoyance and even anger take over. For an excellent discussion of self-calming techniques for tired parents, read *Sleeping through the Night: How Infants, Toddlers, and their Parents Can Get a Good Night's Sleep* by Jodi Mindell.

A Commitment to the Gradual Approach.   If there is one lesson my darling oldest daughter has taught me about parenting, it is that the gradual approach is, in the long run, far easier and more successful than any seemingly quick solution. More than most, our children need to believe that they can trust us and that we will not attempt a quick fix just to serve our own needs.

Hang in There. The single hardest thing for me about each sleep challenge has been that I did not know when it would end. If someone could have told me for sure that my newborn would need just one feeding a night by the time she was eleven weeks old, it would have been so much easier to handle the nights when infotainment TV at two a.m. was my best friend. It appears, however, that parenting (adoption or otherwise) is not about reading time charts. It is about working hard at finding solutions for our children and having the patience to try many if necessary.

Adoption parenting is quite a journey, and if you are to make it in the long run, you will need to take care of yourself. Find ways to help your child sleep, and look for ways to get the sleep you need so that you can be the parent you want to be. Sleep deprivation may feel eternal, but hold onto the time-tested truism: absolutely, eventually, this too, shall pass!

Claire McDonald, PhD is an adoptive mom, freelance writer,
past Head of the Upper School at University Liggett School
in Grosse Pointe, Michigan. She holds a BA from the
College of William and Mary and an MA and PhD
from the University of Massachusetts-Amherst.
She regularly gets eight hours of sleep a night and
hopes to continue that pattern when her
third child comes home.

Claiming

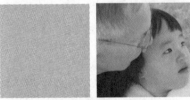

Circle of Love:
Attachment and the Adopted Child
By Susan Olding

There's a photo on my desk. It's an image of me with my husband, Mark, and our about-to-be-adopted daughter, taken just moments after her orphanage director brought her to us. Mark and I are looking into one another's eyes. The shot isn't a close-up, so you can't see the tears of joy glistening there, but you can feel them in the shape of our smiles. His arm curves around my shoulder; I lean slightly in his direction. After years of waiting and infertility, we're thrilled to be beginning the grand adventure of parenting together, and our happiness and deep attachment and attunement to one another are as bright and self-evident as a sunflower.

But what of our new daughter? My arms envelop her body; my hands hold her tight. Her plump cheek rests softly against my shoulder. She clings to me and explores the bare skin of my arms with gentle, curious fingers. But her legs hang limp against my hips. She stares, not at her new father and me, but blank-eyed into the distance, and on her face is an expression of such sadness, worry, and fear that I can hardly bear to look at it.

In that photo, I read the history of our daughter's struggles to attach to us. Her clinging arms, snuggled cheek and curious fingers show her intense desire and her need for love. But her averted, frightened eyes and her limp legs suggest the challenges we will confront in teaching her what love means and how to give and receive it.

Many of us who adopt post-institutionalized children will face similar challenges. All internationally adopted children are affected by their early experiences of neglect and loss, but some seem more profoundly affected than others. For reasons we don't fully understand, these children struggle harder to form secure attachments in their new families. Luckily, there is growing recognition of the importance of attachment among prospective parents, agencies, and professionals, and together we are learning what we can do to help build healthier relationships with our wounded children.

Definitions and Theory
As a new parent, the phrase 'Reactive Attachment Disorder' (RAD) struck fear into my heart. Our social worker hadn't even mentioned that attachment might be an issue for post-institutionalized children, but I'd heard several cries of warn-

ing from exhausted and frustrated parents on the big International Adoption e-boards, and I had read the angry and defensive responses ("Our kids don't have problems like that!"). While I carefully filed those posts about attachment on my computer's hard drive for future reference and read the relevant sections of Mary Hopkins-Best's *The Weaver's Craft*, secretly I prayed that once our daughter joined our family, I'd never need to think about the subject again.

I didn't understand then that attachment is not an all-or-nothing proposition, but instead occurs on a continuum: from the securely attached, to the insecurely attached, to the completely unattached. Several classificatory systems have been proposed to describe this arc, and you can also find a list of problematic symptoms, and warning signs of attachment impairment on page 55. Reading them, you may be tempted to ask, "Don't all kids do that sometimes?" Apart from the most extreme behaviors, such as fire setting and deliberate violence towards animals or people, all kids do show some of these symptoms some of the time. The difference is in the severity and persistence of the behavior and the reasons the child is engaging in it. The child with attachment issues is not just 'testing boundaries'. A part of her wants to hurt her caregiver or drive her caregiver away.

Attachment can be defined as the close, trusting tie between two people; or in particular, as the reciprocal relationship between an infant and her primary caregiver (usually her mother). Healthy attachment occurs when the infant experiences her caregiver as consistently providing emotional essentials such as touch, movement, eye contact and smiles, as well as the basic necessities such as food and shelter. In ideal circumstances, where the bonding cycle is proceeding as it should, the mother's consistent response helps to regulate the child's level of arousal; eventually, over many repetitions of the cycle, the child understands that it is safe to trust, and learns to modulate her responses to fit the situation. This capacity for modulation grows in part because throughout the cycle the mother is providing the infant with physiological experiences (rocking, swinging, sucking, touch) that are foundational for all future sensory, cognitive, and affectional development.

It's obvious, then, why children who suffer trauma, abuse, neglect, or multiple placements during their first few years of life are at special risk for attachment impairment. When an infant's basic needs are not consistently met she is suspended in a state of helpless arousal leading to anxiety and anger; put simply, she can't trust. Also, because she has been short-changed of experiences of touch and movement that help to build complex neural pathways, she has difficulty processing sensory messages from the environment in as efficient a manner as her more 'typical' peers.

Instead, as recent research on brain development and trauma by Bessel van der Kolk, Alan Schore, Bruce Perry, Daniel Siegel, and Daniel Amen confirms, she relies on more primitive areas of the brain and shows an exaggerated fight or flight response to stress. Even when conditions improve (when she joins a loving home, for example) she may remain developmentally 'stuck' in ways that aren't always obvious to the casual observer. It's not surprising, then, that post-traumatic stress disorder (PTSD) and Sensory Processing Disorder (SPD), as well as other disorders such as ADHD, Autism, Institutional Autism, Bi-polar Disorder, Oppositional Defiant Disorder, and Tourette's, often appear together with insecure attachment in our adopted children. Most of these could be classified under the very broad umbrella of 'regulatory disorders'. All have to do with the child's capacity to modulate emotional, behavioral, and sensory responses, and in internationally adopted children, all have their roots in the trauma and neglect of their first few months or years.

Parenting a child with attachment issues or regulatory problems is a challenge, and the degree of difficulty will depend on a combination of factors: her temperament and yours, the type and extent of trauma she suffered, the overall environment in which you are raising her, and her inborn sensitivities and gifts. Some of our children can be healed by attachment-oriented parenting alone. Some need a special kind of therapeutic parenting. Some need that, plus therapy for attachment issues and/or grief/loss and adoption issues. Some will need additional therapies or medication; my daughter, for instance, has received occupational therapy for her sensory integration difficulties. Some of our children may need all of these, and even then they may struggle with some degree of attachment insecurity.

And yet, there is so much room for hope. Children with attachment disorder can heal. And by helping to heal a child who hurts, you are giving her the gift of better relationships for life. A child who has struggled with insecure attachment and learned to love may become wise and empathic beyond her years. A child who has struggled with insecure attachment and learned how to love may love all the more deeply, when she does love, and may treasure her relationships more consciously than other children.

My own daughter, despite four years of parenting-for-attachment and several months of therapy, continues to show signs of anxious-ambivalent attachment. Yet I can't count the times that others have commented to me on our obviously strong bond. "It's wonderful seeing you two, as you always seem so happy together," said the mother of one of her pre-school friends. "You seem to have so much fun together," commented another acquaintance. "You two adore each other!" said a third. And we do. I can't imagine feeling closer to any child than I feel to M. For her part, she says that she loves me to 'infinity and beyond'. Could it be that we treasure our connection all the more for its being so hard won?

Problems and Issues

A child whose needs have not been met during her first year of life will learn, at a very basic level, that she cannot trust adults. Her sense that she cannot rely on anyone will engender high levels of anxiety, which may show itself in:

- Hyper-vigilance and seemingly preternatural recall
- Unusual fears or sleep issues
- A tendency to 'check out' or dissociate
- Hyperactivity, continual chatter and impulsiveness

As she gets older, she'll often try to dispel her anxiety through excessive bids for control in the form of extreme opposition and defiance, passive-aggressive behavior, or manipulation. She will also feel a great deal of shame and rage about her unmet needs. She may try to repress those feelings, presenting a mask of 'the perfect child' to the world. Or she may express those feelings through frequent or intense meltdowns, outbursts of violence towards others, or attempts to harm herself. Ordinary 'good parenting' practices seldom work; the child continues to engage in dangerous or troubling behaviors regardless of the methods parents use to put a stop to them. For loving parents, this can be deeply frustrating and confusing.

People outside the family may not recognize the complexity of the problem. Even professionals can miss the subtle signs of attachment impairment. They may attribute the child's behaviors to a developmental phase. Psycho-educational testing may identify cognitive or physical delays, or areas of giftedness, and the child's 'differences' or difficulties may be blamed on those. But her behavior may reflect her maturity level, her cognitive strengths or weaknesses, plus attachment strain (and PTSD or other related problems). A concrete example: Many pre-schoolers 'chatter' almost constantly. A child with a special facility for words and relative weakness in other cognitive areas will talk even more than her peers; she uses language to mediate her world. But a young, verbally gifted child with attachment strain will give the phrase 'non-stop talker' a whole new complexion. Normal children talk to communicate thoughts and feelings to another person, or at an early stage, to themselves. Children with attachment problems do that, sometimes. They also talk to make noise, to prove to themselves that they exist, and to control their world by forcing another to listen and to respond to seemingly endless questions and comments. They use language to manipulate rather than to connect.

> ### Building Relationships With Young Children:
>
> *Toddler Adoption: The Weaver's Craft*
> by Mary Hopkins-Best
>
> *First Steps in Parenting the Child Who Hurts*
> by Caroline Archer
>
> *Attaching in Adoption, Practical Tools for Today's Parents* by Deborah D. Gray
>
> *Parenting the Hurt Child: Helping Adoptive Families Heal and Grow*
> by Gregory Peck and Regina M. Kupecky

Parenting a child with attachment issues can be isolating and lonely. Many children with attachment issues present one face to the world and another at home, and parents frequently find themselves disbelieved when they try to talk about the difficulties they are experiencing. Children with attachment issues, like all children, change as they progress through developmental phases, and sometimes parents are fooled into thinking that the situation has improved when, in fact, the problems have simply gone temporarily underground. Even when parents acknowledge that the family has a problem it can be very difficult to find professionals who understand the issues and who are experienced in working with post-institutionalized children. Parents themselves fall prey to feelings of anxiety, guilt, shame, and rage when 'experts' suggest that they try techniques that they have already tried to no avail. It is painful when friends advise them that 'all kids do that' or imply that they should 'lighten up' or 'be stricter'. It is humiliating and uncomfortable when strangers stare disapprovingly, or offer comments about (overly friendly) 'delightful' children. It is very important that parents take good care of themselves, and seek understanding support in order to withstand the parental and societal stress they are under.

Nurture and structure must be properly balanced before a child will heal. Each child will respond best to different elements of nurture and to a different intensity of structure. Some feel most connected when their parent plays with them one-to-one; others feel loved when their parent cooks their favorite foods or expresses appreciation for a job well done. Some accept limits easily, and some need the stronger containment of a 'steel box with a velvet lining.' It may take some time to figure out what type of parenting best suits your child, and you may have to make some adjustments to your preferred or default style. Not only that, but you will need to learn new techniques and strategies as your child moves

Resources

Raising Your Spirited Child: A Guide for Parents Whose Child Is More Intense, Sensitive, Perceptive, Persistent, Energetic by Mary Sheedy-Kurcinka

The Difficult Child by Stanley Turecki

Parenting With Love and Logic: Teaching Children Responsibility by Foster Cline and Jim Fay

Love and Logic Magic for Early Childhood: Practical Parenting from Birth to Six Years by Jim Fay and Charles Fay, PhD

The Challenging Child by Stanley Greenspan

The Child With Special Needs: Encouraging Intellectual and Emotional Growth by Stanley Greenspan

Creating Schedules for your children: To create some great visual schedules for kids of all ages including free picture cards and daily organizers. **www.do2learn.com**

through various developmental stages and achieves new levels of healing. You may also discover that your philosophies of child rearing change as a result of parenting a child with attachment difficulties. Parents are on a growth curve, too!

The specific tools you use to secure your adopted child's attachment to you will be as unique as the two of you. But if I could offer one general piece of advice to new parents, or even to more experienced parents who find themselves feeling discouraged about their relationships with their children, it would be this:

Find at least one activity involving touch, movement and eye contact that you both enjoy, and do it every day. This is especially crucial in your first few weeks and months together. Your shared activity might be dancing with your baby in your arms; it might be swinging with your toddler at the park; it might be blowing bubbles, reading stories, singing songs, or feeding one another bits of delicious fruit. Whatever you choose, a few minutes a day of shared pleasure can help lay the foundation for a richer connection.

From Rejection to Connection

What happens if your baby or older child rejects you, refuses to look at you, and does not want to be near you? This is without question one of the most worrisome situations for a new parent. But try not to despair. By moving gently but persistently into your child's comfort zone, you will find a way closer to her heart. If you find yourself in this difficult position, reach out for professional help and parent-to-parent support. Seek others who will understand and make suggestions. Online support groups can be invaluable.

Tools that Build Connection: Nurture

1. Floor Time or 'Special Time'. This means 15 to 30 minutes of focused, one-on-one imaginative play with your child, during which you allow her to set and develop the theme. Rather than directing or evaluating your child's play, you facilitate, by describing what she is doing, interpreting her facial expressions, and mirroring and elaborating on her feelings. When you play this way regularly with your child you make her feel valued. You also foster trust, and you may make some interesting discoveries about her fears and preoccupations. It was during a floor time session that I learned about my three year old daughter's fear that if she were very naughty she might be sent back to the orphanage. It was during floor time that she asked some of her first questions about birth parents.

More information and a full description of floor time can be found in the work of Stanley Greenspan.

2. **Outdoor/Active Time**. Many of our children seem 'busier' than is typical. Many suffer subtle developmental delays or sensory processing disorder as a result of inadequate early stimulation. They need opportunities to move, both to curtail anxiety and to build important neural connections. Running, swinging, crashing, climbing, and jumping, either in a gym class or at the park, all help to develop the proprioceptive (body's sense of motion that detects the movement or position of the body or a limb) and vestibular (body's sense of equilibrium) systems. These systems are both constantly activated under normal infant circumstances, when a parent picks up/puts down and carries around a new baby (it's how a baby learns spatial skills!) Movement is great for parents, too. It helps us deal with the stress of parenting our often demanding kids. Spending time outdoors can also help anxious children to slow down. Walks in the woods or at the beach or in a local park can prime a child for closer connection at other times of the day. Days when our daughter spends significant time outdoors are typically easier days for everyone in our family. And besides, being active together is fun!

3. **Food.** Some attachment impaired children struggle with hoarding and gorging. More information about how to deal with this issue can be found in the **Food** chapter pages 61-74. When problems of this kind are not serious, food can be used to cement connection. Some new mothers choose to breast feed, and where it's feasible for both participants, this can be a wonderful opportunity to be close. Many children enjoy a 'bottle time' long past toddler-hood. Some therapists recommend offering sweets in limited amounts. Games involving Cheerios, bits of fruit, candies or small crackers promote eye contact. And as children grow older, cooking together can become a fun family project.

4. **Co-sleeping.** Many experienced parents and some attachment therapists recommend the 'family bed'. Co-sleeping can reduce children's anxiety. Note, however, that some children have to build up to this level of intimacy. Highly active children like my daughter may thrash and kick too much in their first months with the family. They may be over-stimulated and unable to sleep at all. Some families put children in the same room, on a pallet next to the parents' bed. Our daughter seemed most comfortable in her own room for her first year with our family. Gradually she began to come into our bed whenever she'd wake in the night. Now, for a

Adoptive Breastfeeding

Breastfeeding can help children and mothers connect with one another. It provides skin-to-skin contact, sweet food, comfort, and nurturing. While some children actively seek breastfeeding with their new mothers, many children need some time to develop the relationship with their mother before they can cope with the intimacy of breast-feeding. Mothers who have breastfed their adopted child state that it is a powerful tool for relationship development.

The Adoptive Breastfeeding Resource Website **www.fourfriends.com**

La Leche League **www.lalecheleague.org**

Mental health, attachment and breastfeeding **www.international breastfeedingjournal. com/content/1/1/5**

-*Karleen Gribble*

variety of reasons, we co-sleep for the whole night. In other words, we've moved towards more night-time contact rather than less, which is a pattern that is the reverse of what most families might expect. But I'm sure she will ask to sleep on her own when she is ready and for now, when she wakes, rather than crying out in fear, she simply touches us and goes back to sleep. We are all better rested as a result. Families should experiment to find what works for them [see **Sleep** chapter pages 1-26].

5. Smell and Skin-to-skin. Our olfactory sense taps into the most primitive parts of our brain. Sharing shampoo, lotions, and laundry detergent can be a powerful way to make a child feel that she 'belongs'. My daughter's favorite 'blanket' is really an old shirt of mine; she loves to sniff my hair and sweaters. Skin-to-skin contact is also important. Bathing together, showering together, and swimming together can be wonderful opportunities to build closeness.

6. Get Silly. Tickles, blowing raspberries, pat-a-cake, hide and seek, nursery rhymes and family jokes: all of these feed a sense of shared fun and pleasure. They also promote eye contact and the kind of touch that some children find less threatening than kisses and embraces.

7. Song and Story. Music is a powerful tool for connection. Think how songs stick in our memories and remind us of specific periods of our lives. Similarly, stories, in the form of literature, life books, trauma and claiming narratives, and anecdotes about 'when I was little' and 'when you were littler'. These all help create a sense of security and belonging. More information can be found in the **Narratives** chapter (pages 221-252) of this book. In our family, we used one of those children's tape recorders to good effect. I read stories and sang songs onto tapes for my daughter; and she listened to them nightly after tuck-in time. She calls these tapes (and now, CDs) 'Mama's Voices'. They were especially comforting to her when I had to be out in the evening or had to go away for a few days.

8. Regress the Child to Her Emotional Age for Nurture. Many internationally adopted children enjoy bottles, rocking, swaddling, nose-kisses, and 'peek' games far longer than one might expect. These children missed out on babying they needed and deserved; you are not indulging them by re-parenting them to meet these needs. Even if children resist cuddling, touch is important to their healing. Woo your child. Cuddle her and hug her daily.

Tools that Reduce Anxiety, Build Self-Esteem, and Teach Self-Control and Self-Regulation: Structure

1. Relaxation and Visualization Exercises. Children can begin to practice these even when they are pre-schoolers. Good examples of audio materials to help children relax are available from the Child Anxiety Network (www.childanxiety.net) and from MindWorks for Children (www.mindworksforchildren.com).

2. Yoga, Deep Breathing, Meditation. My daughter responds well to the request that she take three deep breaths when she is becoming over-excited or angry. It helps if I do this with her. 'Strong Sitting' is a technique promoted by Nancy Thomas. Parents direct the child to sit straight and quiet on a mat for a few minutes at a time. This helps the brain 'shift gears' and promotes the development of the limbic system and the neo-cortex. 'Strong sitting' is not meant to be used as a 'consequence' or 'punishment'; it is instead a meditative practice.

3. Provide Visual Sequences and Schedules. Children with insecure attachment often profit from visual charts or 'pictograms' that outline the day's or week's events. Knowing what will happen in advance frees them from worry. See www.do2learn.com for free picture cards and daily organizers.

4. Learn about Temperament and Teach your Child to Recognize and Value her Strengths. Is she stubborn or persistent? Impulsive or spontaneous? Viewing your child's characteristic responses through a positive lens doesn't mean that you'll find them any easier to live with. And whatever you attribute them to or call them, some qualities and habits, taken to extremes, will contribute to her problems in relating to others. But reminding ourselves about how temperament influences behavior can help us view our children's intensity in a slightly different light and offers a language to teach them self-respect and self-love.

Online support groups can be accessed through these websites:
Attach-China-International
www.attach-china.org
(not just for China adoptions)

Attachment Disorder Network
www.radzebra.org

Older Child Adoption
www.olderchildadoption.com

Attachment Disorder Site
www.attachmentdisorder.net

ATTACh
www.attach.org

Child Trauma Academy
www.childtrauma.org

Trauma Center
www.traumacenter.org

5. Provide Opportunities for Success. Fulfilling family responsibilities or succeeding in a sport or in their schoolwork gives attachment challenged children reasons to feel good about themselves and can reduce their inner sense of alienation. Notice your child's natural strengths and encourage her to pursue them. Get psycho-educational testing to find out about her preferred learning style and her cognitive abilities. Set high expectations and help your children meet them (see the **School** chapter pages 281-308 for more on sports.)

6. Teach children to recognize their bodies' signals and to monitor and maintain their own levels of arousal. A helpful guide is the Alert Program for Self-Regulation, How Does Your Engine Run? (www.AlertProgram.com) Designed by two occupational therapists, this manual promotes awareness of how we regulate our own arousal states and encourages the use of sensorimotor (senses and movement) strategies to manage our own levels of alertness.

7. Consider Occupational Therapy or Programs such as Brain Gym®. Movement tailored to the child's specific deficits will help develop neural pathways in the brain. Often participants are encouraged to 'cross the mid-line', meaning, use both the right and left side of your brain to think, feel, and respond. This bilateral stimulation seems to help modulate emotional responses and organize thought. Significantly, EMDR (Eye Movement Desensitization and Reprocessing), recommended as a treatment for trauma and useful for children with attachment difficulties, is also based on bi-lateral stimulation.

8. Help children identify and name feelings and provide safe outlets for strong feelings. Some insecurely attached children will try to deny all negative feelings, including anger. These are the 'too-good' children. They can be helped with feelings charts, narratives that allow them to experience feelings vicariously through the characters, and with

Why Grandma Can't Pick the Up the Baby

Newly adopted children often arrive into our families stressed by the transition and confused as to what family is and what's special about parents. It's a two-way thing–we also need time to learn our new children! We need also to have courage and knowledge to tell people in our circle of friends and family what we know to be best for this, our child. Here are some tried and tested bonding tips. If friends and family protest, print this sheet and give it to them.

- New experiences are hard to cope with during stressful times so minimize the stimulation your child receives in the early days post-placement.
  Save the welcome party for later!
- Control the contact your new child has with others until your child understands that family is special; this is especially important if your child is actively seeking to engage others as opposed to you. In the early days and months even Grandma may have to wait to cuddle!
- If you will use caregivers other than yourself from early on, bring them into your bonding circle, but try to ensure that the care givers defer to you on how to feed the child, how much excitement you think is appropriate, etc.
- Keep your child in close proximity to you–carry them if you can. Slings are useful even for older toddlers and pre-schoolers. Your child will begin to recognize your special feel and smell!
- Do not ignore your child's cries to avoid 'spoiling' them or to teach them 'to go to sleep'; this will be detrimental to their developing trust of you.
- Arrange for physical closeness so that you are within arms reach and line of sight of your child at night.
- Avoid hard baby carriers, baby seats, high chairs and strollers which put distance between you and your child. Slings and front-facing strollers allow eye-contact.
- Provide the experience of nurture through food via bottle feeding/feeding games. Hold your child on your lap at mealtimes.
- Provide lots of touch and skin-to-skin contact via massage, swimming together or co-bathing.
- Be persistent but not invasive when nurturing your child. Your child may take some months or more to become comfortable with your care-giving. Becoming familiar rather than strange takes time, but the bond forged will last a lifetime.

Some families use visual aids to help their children understand the 'circle of love'. Draw your child at the heart of concentric circles with those on the outside furthest from your close family relationship, where kisses and cuddles are permitted. Think up your version of this! Display it on the fridge – and live it for real. Show it to doubting friends and family. They – like your child – will get it!

Sheena Macrae and from Karleen Gribble BRurSc, PhD, Adjunct Research Fellow in the School of Nursing, Family and Community Health at the University of Western Sydney, NSW, Australia and adoptive mom of

parents who identify and share their own feelings. Other children will try to deny all 'soft' feelings, such as sadness, fear, and even happiness; these kids tend to act angry a lot of the time. Still others will show all their feelings, but in extremes. These children need experiences of 'containment' where they learn that they are loved unconditionally, regardless of how angry or frightened they might be inside. Some families have benefited from keeping a 'family feelings journal' or a mother-daughter journal. This can take the form of words or, more often, artwork. You might provide the angry child with a special jar; suggest that she can write down or draw pictures of her angry feelings and put them into the jar as an alternative to acting them out. Some kids will enjoy a special pillow that they can punch; others like to throw a substance like Gak Splat at a (parent-approved!) wall. Play and humor are also safe outlets for feelings. **Parents should seek professional guidance about whether and how to practice therapeutic holding.**

9. Respond to the Child's Emotional Age. If you feel tempted to shout "Act your age!" consider that your child may already be doing just that. She may be acting her emotional age, instead of her chronological age. When a baby pulls the cat's tail, we don't put her in time-out; instead we tell her to stop, then take her hand and show her how to touch gently.

When a three year-old throws a tantrum, we don't ground her for a week; instead we stay near her until she is calm (possibly holding her) or we offer her another safe place such as her room where she can regain her balance. Then we reassure her and help her process her feelings. That's not to say that you should ignore unacceptable behavior. On the contrary, most insecurely attached children need to know that their parents are in control, and maintaining firm boundaries is one way of conveying that. But be aware of your child's emotional state. Has she been triggered into a PTSD reaction from another time, place, and age? Before imposing consequences, you may need to help her reach equilibrium.

10. Recognize What your Child can Handle. Part of responding to your child's emotional age means recognizing how much in the way of stimulation, freedom, choices, and privileges she can handle. Many internationally adopted children need quiet environments when they first join their families. Some do poorly in crowd situations, particularly crowds of other children, for months or even years, post-adoption. Nancy Thomas advocates returning children to 'the basics', as in limiting stimulating activities to those we provide for babies and young toddlers until the child shows she is ready for more. The 'basics' for all children include stories, active play, building blocks or stacking toys, markers or crayons for drawing, and cuddles!

Once a child has shown that she can make good use of these playthings and can remain 'respectful, responsible and fun to be around,' then she can gradually earn more privileges and freedom. Especially for children who are impulsive and/or violent, a system like this can be very helpful.

11. Model the Calm Response. Children with attachment issues push their parents' buttons. Every parent of an attachment impaired child will 'blow it' once in a while, and probably far more often than she would like! But anger, while understandable, is usually counter-productive. Try to model the response you hope your child will emulate. Keep in mind psychologist Dan Hughes' PLACE attitude for parents: Playful, Loving, Accepting, Curious, Empathetic! (see page 57)

Use natural and logical consequences wherever possible, without showing irritation about your child's poor choices. Allow the consequences to do the teaching and refrain from lecturing. Some parents find the 'Love and Logic' approach very helpful.

12. Reward? Children with serious attachment issues generally won't respond well to behavior modification techniques such as rewards for desired behavior. It is because they find few, if any, things worth holding dear. We can only speculate that this is due to not 'owning' things during an impoverished life and not feeling special themselves.

But children whose issues are less serious can sometimes be helped by rewards in specific situations, or rewards of a particular kind. You may need to experiment. If rewards or incentives seem to motivate your child to tolerate greater closeness, to treat others with greater respect, or to use the calming strategies you've taught her more consistently, then by all means, reward her. The more fun to be around your child becomes, the more you will enjoy her; and the more you enjoy her, the stronger your attachment will grow.

13. Set and Maintain Limits: Rehearse, Replay, Rewind, Repair, Repay. Children with attachment impairment and/or cognitive processing problems often need opportunities to rehearse expected behaviors and desired social skills. Role play is a useful technique. For instance, if your child has a habit of grabbing or interrupting, in a calm moment you can stage a similar scene and then allow one character to choose a better alternative. You can 'play' the characters yourselves or you can use puppets. Model the responses you hope your child will internalize. You can also re-play situations that did not go well and play out more positive endings. 'Replay' can be a consequence. If your child has done something unintentionally rude or socially clumsy, you can ask her to practice the better response. This is empowering.

Offering children a chance to rewind and start over for minor infractions of rules or for unwanted behaviors can also be a way of maintaining limits and encouraging appropriate behavior without inducing shame. If my daughter uses an unpleasant tone of voice, for example, I can cue her to self-correct by saying "Would you like to rewind that?" This teaches that mistakes can be forgiven.

Children who hurt others or themselves, who break things, or who waste parents' time in constant opposition or control battles need to repair the damage and repay the person they have hurt. If they make a mess, they should clean it up. Repayment or restitution can take the form of chores or a fine, or time spent making something for the person they have harmed. Deborah Gray and Nancy Thomas offer other ideas.

14. Give Alternatives for 'Calm Down'. Deborah Gray, author of *Attaching in Adoption,* recommends giving children specific parent-generated alternatives to help them defuse. Children whose PTSD has been triggered or who explode in anger will often settle more quickly when given a choice: "You can calm down in my lap or you can calm down in your room."

15. Reconnect after Conflict. All children need to reconnect after the relationship has suffered a rupture. Insecurely attached children can experience even the mildest limit setting as threatening, yet they will push and push the boundaries. For them, reconnecting after conflicts becomes all the more important. After your child has fulfilled the consequence for misbehavior, make sure you hug her and let her know she's loved. If you lose your patience and shout at her, apologize. Children who rage or who make impulsive mistakes need help to process their difficult feelings. After the outburst or the incident, parents can ask children what happened, what they were feeling before it happened, how they handled their feelings, how their choice worked for them, and what they could do next time. These questions prompt children to take responsibility and to try different approaches. This approach is found in the works of Nancy Thomas.

Therapy

Therapy for attachment strain can be very helpful. Talk therapy, cognitive-behavioral therapy, play therapy, and art therapy, are potentially useful adjuncts (especially for the child who is only mildly affected or the one who is already well on the way to healing), but may not get to the primary problem: the child's impaired trust of her primary caregiver. Nor do they address the trauma and resulting neurological deficits that underlie her broken trust. Therapies that appear more useful include:

- Dyadic (a reciprocal parent-child relationship) Developmental Therapy. Variations of Daniel Hughes' DDP therapy model may, or may not, involve nurturing Holding Time, practiced either at home or in the therapist's office
- Family Narrative Therapy
- EMDR
- Theraplay (therapist-led play)
- Neurofeedback

(See **Therapy** chapter for resources and a discussion on how to choose a therapist pg 431.)

Useful additions to these for many children are Occupational Therapy (OT) for sensory work, along with other forms of Physical Therapy, including Massage and Cranio-Sacral Therapy. Doris Landry, an attachment oriented family therapist, believes that for a child who has been 'unmothered', attachment work must go hand-in-hand with OT for either therapy to be completely effective. Some families have also experimented with nutritional supplements such as Omega-3 fish oils or diets. Whatever the form of therapy chosen, the right therapist will:

- understand that the parents are not to blame for the child's difficulties
- will not allow the child to triangulate (a child who sides with the therapist against the parents is an example of triangulation).
- will work together with the parents, coaching them and supporting them in practices that will move the child further along a path of trust and healing.

Attachment therapy in general, and therapeutic holding in particular, remain controversial in some circles. Much of this is due to some confusion of terminology and a horrifying episode several years ago resulting in the death of a child during a 'rebirthing' session. Reputable attachment therapists do not practice 'rebirthing', and the type of holding they support is completely different from the type involved in the incident that made headlines. But parents should ensure that therapists are experienced and that they do not subscribe to abusive practices. In the USA parents may consult a national organization called ATTACh (www.attach.org) for recommendations and therapeutic guidelines. Parents may also find therapist recommendations through their local support associations for adoptive families, or in some cases, through their adoption agencies or social workers.

Taking Care of You

Parenting a child with attachment issues will demand all your energy, and then some. Many parents become clinically depressed or suffer vicarious trauma. Take time for yourself every day to replenish body and spirit. Find or create a support system (in person or online–preferably both). And if necessary, seek therapy for yourself. Your child's trauma may trigger trauma or unresolved issues from your own childhood. You will parent more effectively if you're able to recognize your 'hot spots' and look after your own emotional needs.

Full Circle

Recently my daughter and I were getting ready for her bedtime stories when she asked me to pause for a minute while she looked around her room for one of her stuffed animals. "Wait," she said, snuggling back into the crook of my arm. "Kitty wants to be inside the love circle."

Kitty is a stand-in for my daughter. These days, she is a full and eager participant in family hugs. Does that mean our struggles are over? Far from it. Every day remains a challenge. But it's been years since I saw the worried face of our early family photos. Sometimes she leaps forward quickly, sometimes she spirals backwards, sometimes she slides sideways, but day by day, step by step, hug by hug, my daughter is learning it is safe to love.

~ Susan Olding is step-mother to three (now adult) children and an adoptive mother of a daughter from China. A former secondary school teacher, she holds a BA in Philosophy and a B.Ed. with additional qualifications in Special Education.

Bubbles of Happiness

My mommy goal is to create 'bubbles of happiness' each day. As many as I can! I check in with my children often, and ask them regularly, "What's the best thing about today/this month/this week?" Then I ask them what they remember most in the same time frame. When both things match, I count that as a success.

What they will take with them into their adults lives are the small joys, celebrations, and successes-- moments of fun and laughter. Creating these bubbles each day, both in thought, mind, and experience, and shaping the meaning my children are making from their lives is something that I have lots of fun with. This brings things down to a very achievable goal that is more often successful than not. Success encourages me to keep working; the more positive interactions I have with my children, the stronger our relationship becomes.

Since I chose to adopt children with significant mental, emotional, and cognitive challenges, to me it feels like I'm in a race. My race is to build the strongest possible parent/child bonds before we begin to negotiate the rapids and whirlpools of the teen years.

We each shape how our children make their own meaning and weave their own tapestry. How we frame things, how we teach values, how we weave our perception of their personal tapestry might be something that we haven't truly been conscious of before. How do we do that? What skills do we have? What resources do we have? How might we improve what we're doing now? Not in the 'I have to be perfect' thinking, but in the spirit of continued self assessment and forward growth.

~ By Deborah Anderson, birthmom, bio mom, and adoptive mom

The Attachment Spectrum
Attachment is a Long-term Process
Edited by Doris Landry, MS, LLP

Attachment Theory indicates that children do not break former attachments but rather, add more attachment figures, suggesting that parents of adopted children need to understand how their child has been emotionally affected by a history that may have included multiple caregivers, loss, malnutrition, illness, abuse, and neglect. Helping our children move from the insecurity of less-than-adequate treatment to seek closeness as a means to a healthy and secure attachment is of primary importance. A child's secure attachment to his parents will benefit every aspect of his life, and contribute immeasurably to our own joy in parenting. The following are styles of attachment:

Secure
Secure babies freely explore and even engage strangers while with their mothers. They will be visibly upset when separated from mom and greet her with pleasure and excitement when reunited. They mold to the shape of their mother's body when consoled, hang on to their mother when scared, and enjoy playful facial games and eye contact. Secure children develop trust, self-regulation and learn self-reliance. The development of meaningful relationships and an ability to cope with stress and frustration allows for the attainment of their full intellectual potential.

Anxious/Ambivalent
Traits of an Insecure/Avoidant child:
- Anxious of exploration and of strangers in the presence of mother
- Inconsolable and in distress when mother departs
- Reunions with mother are resentful, yet needs closeness ("hold me close/let go of me!")
- Resistant when mother initiates attention

Older children may:
- Make parent work hard to find ways to satisfy child's needs; controlling
- Exhibit extreme anxiety which may be exhibited by constant movement or chatter
- Ask for hug, and then cry out "it hurts"
- Ask for help, then make the parent feel inadequate

The deprived infant/child, the one not held, fed, cuddled and 'claimed', needs to be given the opportunity to experience missed sensations. This is most often accomplished through occupational therapy but the missing component is usually the parent... treatment needs to be experienced within the context of a meaningful relationship.

Further, it is suggested that the treatment be through the parent. This means the occupational therapist must work with the parent to teach them to do the interventions.

Doris Landry, MS

More Than Love

Many adopted children carry with them scars of their history that unconditional love alone cannot fix, heal or remove. I've learned as a parent that some-times love is simply not the answer to helping my child. I could not love the anxiety out my daughter, I could not love the fear out of her, I could not love the trauma out of her. Sometimes loving our children will mean dif-ficult choices and painful decisions.

There will be issues that arise where the love we have for our children will force us to parent in ways that we never thought we could or would. Loving them the way they need to be loved may mean finding someone to help us understand why they are the way they are, and why they think the way they think.

Our love must be more than unconditional... it has to be proactive, and endurable. Parenting is about a lot more than just love.

~ Jill Lampman
adoptive mom

Insecure/Avoidant

Traits of an Insecure/Avoidant child:
- Avoids and ignores the mother
- Does limited exploration even with mother present
- Strangers not treated much differently than mother
- Expresses little emotional range, less able to pretend play
- Passively resists efforts to be soothed

Older children may:
- Find ways to care for self, not needing others
- Show little interest in parents; exhibits no fear of strangers
- Exhibit stilted play; won't ask for help

Insecure/Disorganized

Traits of an Insecure/Disorganized child:
- Lacks a coherent style or pattern of interacting due to erratic care
- Perceives that caregivers are frightened (and are frighten-ing)
- Acts alarmed, freezing in place under stress
- Acts rejected or abandoned
- Often behaves in ways indicative of abuse

Older children may:
- Exhibit hurtful behaviors to animals or other people
- Exhibit behaviors of former abuse with little or no remorse

Reactive Attachment Disorder (RAD)

Children age five or younger can be diagnosed with Reactive Attachment Disorder if one of the following is present 1) their behavior is reactive to care that had a persistent disre-gard for their basic emotional and physical needs, or 2) they had repeated changes of primary caregivers (i.e., no one to attach to prior to adoption). After the age of five, Reactive Attachment Disorder can manifest in children as Oppositional Defiant Disorder, progressing to more severe problems such as Conduct Disorder. These children may have little conscience or fear of consequence, will hurt, lie and steal without remorse, and will not respond normally to nurturing or discipline. A baby or young child with Reactive Attachment Disorder is an extremely traumatized child, and requires intensive treatment and specialized parenting, as does an older child exhibiting opposition to authority, defiance, or general disturbed conduct behaviors.

Creating PLACE
Parenting to Create a Sense of Safety
By Daniel Hughes, PhD

A child can best be understood by focusing not so much on the behavior that you can observe, but rather on the nature of the child's intentions which underlie the behavior. The child's intentions include the thoughts, feelings, perceptions, and motives that are associated with the resultant behavior. Often these features of the child's inner life are associated with previous events that were traumatic and/or shameful, so the meaning of the behavior is often closely tied to the meaning of those past events in the child's mind.

To ignore the child's inner life, we will have only the most superficial understanding of him. To encourage the development and expression of his inner life we need to first make him feel safe. If he knows that he will be judged negatively for his intentions, they will remain hidden. To provide the experience of safety, a parent might well consider PLACE. Representing the five parent-attitude qualities of Playfulness, Love, Acceptance, Curiosity, and Empathy, PLACE creates a sense of safety that facilitates self-discovery and communication. PLACE also describes the nature of a home which serves both as a secure base for exploring the world, and a safe haven where one can return when the world becomes too stressful.

Playfulness. Playfulness characterizes the frequent parent-infant reciprocal interactions when the infant is in the quiet-alert state of consciousness. Both parent and infant are clearly enjoying being with each other while being engaged in the delightful experience of getting to know each other. Both are feeling safe and relaxed. Neither feels judged nor criticized. These experiences of playfulness—combined with comfort when he is distressed—serve as the infant's original experience of parental love.

During frequent moments of playfulness, both parent and child become aware of how much they like each other. Playful moments reassure both that their conflicts and separations are temporary and will never harm the strength of their attachment. Playfulness also provides opportunities to convey affection when more direct expressions may be resisted. The child is likely to respond with less anger and defensiveness when the parent is able to convey a touch of playfulness in her discipline. While such a response would not be appropriate at the time of major misbehavior, when applied to minor behaviors playfulness keeps the behavior in perspective. The behavior is a threat to neither the relationship nor the worth of the child.

Love. When it is the central motive for the parents' interactions with their child, love enables the child to have confidence that what underlies the parents' behaviors involves the intention to do what is in the best interests of the child. Love, when it is expressed most fully, conveys both enjoyment and commitment. The child needs to know that basically his parent 'likes' him, enjoys being his parent, and looks forward to having fun together. While at times enjoyment may not be obvious, for the child to feel loved, he needs to be confident that commitment is always present even when moments of reciprocal enjoyment are not. During these moments there remains an assumption that this basic 'liking' will return.

Fundamental to the sense of being loved is the child's conviction that his parents will do what is in his best interests. The parent will do whatever it takes to keep him safe and

Strategies for Building Attachment

with Your Newly Adopted Child

Prepare

• Learn what you can about the sort of experiences your child might have had pre-adoption, what this might mean for their emotional development, and what sort of caring strategies might be helpful.

• Educate family and friends about how you might need to care for your child post-adoption and how and why this early attachment work is important.

• Talk with family and friends about how they can support you post-placement.

• Plan your move from the self-focused mental attitude of the adoption process, to the child-focused attitude that you'll need post-placement in caring for your child.

Recognize

• Acknowledge the loss and hurt in your child's past, and that the placement in your family was a stressful (or even traumatic) event for them.

• Evaluate that how you were parented will impact your parenting; be prepared to change your beliefs and parenting style if necessary.

• Accept that your child has special needs as a result of their past and that these special needs may be anything from minor and short-term, to major and long term.

• Admit that while it is quite normal to be rejected by your child initially, it is also very difficult!

• Affirm that as the parent you are the expert on your child.

• Believe that 'gut feelings' you have about your child are significant, and should be treated seriously.

• Be aware that others may not understand what you must do to meet your adopted child's needs; you may have to act contrary to the advice of family, friends or health / child care professionals whose opinion you value.

• Realize that your child's emotional age may be much younger than their chronological age, and that it is appropriate to provide nurture that is in line with their emotional needs.

• Value the hard work that may be involved in meeting your child's needs early on in the relationship, because it will bear fruit in the long-term.

Nurture

• Because new experiences are hard to cope with during stressful times, minimize the stimulation your child receives in the early days post-placement.

• Keep your child close by frequently carrying them (children up to five or six years of age can be carried with the assistance of a sling).

• Control the contact your new child has with others until your child understands the specialness of family; this is especially important if your child is actively seeking to engage others.

• Provide physical closeness during the night via co-sleeping, or other sleep arrangements that keep you within arm's reach and line of sight of your child at night.

• Avoid using devices that place physical distance between yourself and your child, including hard baby carriers, baby seats, high chairs, and strollers.

• Breastfed, or otherwise provide the experience of nurture through food via bottle feeding.

• Provide lots of touch and skin-to-skin contact via massage, swimming together, or co-bathing.

• Respect that your child may initially not want to be close to you, or receive nurture from you, and that it may take some gentle persistence and patience before they are able to tolerate the intimacy involved in nurturing.

• Be responsive in your caregiving; in making decisions about caregiving choose options that encourage closeness rather than distance between your child and yourself.

• Do not ignore your child's cries to avoid 'spoiling' them or to teach them 'good sleep hygiene'; this will be detrimental to their developing trust of you.

Refuel

• Don't be too proud to ask for help if you need it, or too polite to reject offers of help that interfere with parent-child attachment.

• Seek contact via online or face-to-face support groups, with others whose children have similar histories and experiences.

• Prioritize, so your time and resources are spent on what is important.

• Don't expect life to be 'back to normal' soon after placement.

~ By Karleen Gribble

to ensure that his basic needs will be met and his rights will be respected. 'Hard times' will pass without abuse, neglect, or abandonment because the child's welfare is at the core of the parents' daily motives, decisions, and behaviors with regard to their child. Children who have lost their first parents for whatever reason need ongoing signs that their relationship with their adoptive parents is permanent—that they will never be 'given away' regardless of the crises or conflicts that lie ahead.

Acceptance. Unconditional acceptance is at the core of the child's sense of safety, value, and relaxed sharing with his parent. Within acceptance the child becomes convinced that his core sense of self is worthwhile and valued by his parents. His behavior may be criticized and limited, but not his 'self'. He becomes confident that conflict and discipline involves his behavior, not his relationship with his parents or his self-worth. While the behavior of the child may be evaluated and limited, the thoughts, feelings, perceptions, and motives of the child never are. The child's inner life simply 'is'; it is not 'right' or 'wrong'. Am I suggesting that if a child says to his parents that he does not like his brother and wishes that he lived somewhere else, such expressions are 'OK'? Yes—and the fact that your child disclosed his inner life to you may well reflect his trust that you will not dislike him because he has such thoughts and wishes.

If he is criticized for his inner life, he will most likely begin to conceal it as well as feel ashamed of that aspect of himself. When he is safe to communicate his inner life, his parents will be able to understand how he is struggling with his brother, the reasons for the struggles, and possible ways to reduce them. When he is not safe, the parent will be left with simply disciplining inappropriate behavior toward his brother, without addressing the underlying causes. When the

Books by Daniel Hughes, PhD

Building the Bonds of Attachment, Awakening Love in Deeply Troubled Children
The tragedy of the unattached child and the possibility of transformative intervention:

Facilitating Developmental Attachment, The Road to Emotional and Behavioral Change in Foster and Adopted Children
How to work successfully with emotional and behavioral problems rooted in deficient early attachments.

child knows that his parents understand his dislike and his wishes to have his brother 'go away', often his experience of his brother begins to change on its own, the behavior problems reduce on their own, and there is no need for the parent to 'fix' the problem. When the inner life is not expressed and accepted, the parent is often constantly managing conflicts between their children.

Accepting the child's intentions does not imply accepting his behavior. The parent may be very firm in limiting behavior while at the same time accepting the motives for the behavior. In fact, this combination of making a clear difference between unconditional acceptance of intentions and presenting expectations regarding behaviors is probably the most effective way for your child to experience less shame toward self and more guilt toward others when he engages in inappropriate behavior.

Inner-directed guilt, in the absence of pervasive shame, is probably the most effective circumstance for facilitating socially appropriate behaviors.

Curiosity. Curiosity without judgment is crucial if the child is to become aware of his inner life and then communicate it to his parents. Curiosity does not mean adopting an annoyed, lecturing, tone and demanding, "Why did you do that?" Curiosity involves a quiet, accepting tone that conveys a simple desire to understand your child: "What do you think was going on? What do you think that was about?" The child most often knows that his behavior was not appropriate. He often does not know why he did it or he is reluctant to tell his parent why. With curiosity the parents are conveying their intention to simply understand 'why' and to assist the child in such understanding. The parents' intentions are to assist the child, not lecture him nor convince him that his inner life is 'bad' or 'wrong'.

With curiosity, the parents convey a confidence that by understanding the underlying intentions behind the behavior, they will discover qualities in the child that are not shameful. As the understanding deepens, the parent and child will discover that the behavior does not reflect something 'bad' within the child, but rather a thought, feeling, perception, or motive that was stressful, frightening, and/or confusing and seemingly could only be expressed in behavior. As the understanding deepens, the child becomes aware that he can communicate his inner distress to his parents. There is no need for the inappropriate behavior. The behavior does not reflect his being 'bad'. He is much less likely to engage in that behavior again, since there is no need for it. He is also more able to step back from the behavior, be less defensive about it, and experience guilt about it.

For curiosity to be experienced as helpful it cannot be communicated with any annoyance about the behavior. Nor is it presented as a lecture that provides an excuse to 'process' a behavior in what amounts to rational blaming. Curiosity is a 'not-knowing' stance involving a genuine desire to understand and nothing more. When it leads to the child developing a deeper understanding of himself and a deeper sense that his parents understand and accept him, it will, when combined with empathy, naturally lead to a reduction in the inappropriate behavior much more effectively than will focusing on behavioral consequences.

Empathy. Empathy enables the child to feel his parent's compassion for him, just as curiosity enables the child to know that his parents understand him. With empathy the parent is journeying with the child into the distress that he is experiencing and then feeling it with him. The parent is demonstrating that she knows how difficult an experience is for her child. She is communicating that her child will not have to deal with the distress alone. She will stay with him emotionally, comfort and support him, and not abandon him when he needs her the most. The parent is also communicating her strength and commitment. The pain that the child is experiencing is not too much for her. She is also communicating her confidence that with her sharing his distress, it will not be too much for him. Together they will get through it.

Empathy enables a child to develop his affective resources so that he can resolve and integrate many difficult emotional experiences. He will be able to manage such experiences without being overwhelmed by anxiety, rage, shame, or despair. Curiosity enables a child to develop his reflective resources that will enable him to understand himself more deeply including his intentions underlying his actions. With both empathy and curiosity the parent lends herself to her child for the purpose of his developing the affective/reflective skills necessary for him to be able to act in ways that are in the best interests of both self and other. Researchers are increasingly clear that it is deficiencies in these affective and reflective skills that are often at the core of behavioral problems.

In essence, PLACE focuses on the whole child, not simply his behavior. PLACE facilitates attachment security and the closely related affective and reflective skills that are so necessary for maintaining a successful and satisfying life. The child discovers that he is doing the best that he can, he is not 'bad' or 'lazy' or 'selfish'. Through PLACE and the associated attachment security, he is discovering that he can now do better. He can learn to rely on his parents and they will facilitate the development of his inner life and behavioral choices in a manner that he could never do on his own. Then as he experiences PLACE first hand, time and again, these same qualities will become part of his stance toward others—now toward parents and friends, and later also toward his partner and children. He will clearly know that both intentions and behavior matter. He will also know that both 'self' and 'other' matter.

When we angrily lecture and scold our child about his behavior and our assumptions about his equally unacceptable thoughts, feelings, perceptions, and motives, our child is not feeling safe. He is likely to become shameful, isolated, and defensive, all of which will reduce the likelihood that he will change his behaviors. If instead, we relate with PLACE, he will be likely to feel safe even when his behavior is being limited. He too will strive to understand his inner life and associated behaviors. Feeling safe that the 'self' is not being attacked and that his attachments with his parents are still secure, he is likely to become motivated to change his behavior. When his inner life is respected, valued, felt, and understood, first by his parents, and then by himself, his difficult behaviors are likely to lose much of their reason for being.

~ By Daniel Hughes, PhD, a clinician specializing in the treatment of children and youth with severe emotional and behavioral problems

Attachment Problems
Subtle and Not-So-Subtle Signs
By Arthur Becker-Weidman, PhD

Attachment is fundamental to healthy development, normal personality, and the capacity to form healthy and authentic emotional relationships. How can you determine whether your child has attachment issues that require attention? What is normal behavior, and what are the signs of attachment issues? If you've adopted an infant, will you see attachment problems develop? These and other related questions are often at the forefront of adoptive parents' minds.

Attachment is the base of emotional health, social relationships, and one's worldview. The ability to trust and form reciprocal relationships affected the emotional health, security, and safety of the child, as well as the child's development and future inter-personal relationships. The ability to regulate emotions, have a conscience, and experience empathy all require secure attachment. Healthy brain development is built on a secure attachment relationship.

Children who are adopted after the age of six months are at risk for attachment problems. Normal attachment develops during the child's first two to three years of life. Problems with the mother-child relationship during that time, an orphanage experience, or breaks in the consistent caregiver-child relationship, all interfere with the normal development of a healthy and secure attachment. There are wide ranges of attachment difficulties that result in varying degrees of emotional disturbance in the child. One thing is certain; if an infant's needs are not met consistently in a loving, nurturing way, attachment will not occur normally and this underlying problem will manifest itself in a variety of symptoms.

When the first-year-of-life attachment-cycle is undermined and the child's needs are not met, and normal socializing shame is not resolved, mistrust begins to define the perspective of the child and attachment problems result. The cycle can become broken for many reasons:
- Multiple disruptions in care giving
- Post-partum depression causing an emotionally unavailable mother
- Hospitalization of the child causing separation from the parent and/or unrelieved pain. For example, stays in a NICU or repeated hospitalizations during infancy.
- Parents who are attachment disordered, leading to neglect, abuse (physical/sexual/verbal), or inappropriate parental responses not leading to a secure/predictable relationship
- Genetic factors.
- Pervasive developmental disorders
- Caregivers whose own needs are not met, leading to lack of awareness of infants needs

The child may develop mistrust, impeding effective attachment behavior. The developmental stages following these first three years continue to be distorted and/or retarded, and common symptoms emerge. Although I am listing several common symptoms it is very important to realize that when you are trying to parent a child with attachment difficulties you must focus on the cause of the behaviors and not on the symptoms or surface behaviors. It is the cause or motivation for the behaviors that must be your focus...otherwise you are like a doctor who treats a cough without figuring out whether the cough is caused by TB, an allergy, the flu, or lung cancer.

Not-So-Subtle Signs of Attachment Problems:
• Superficially engaging and charming behavior, phoniness
• Avoidance of eye contact
• Indiscriminate affection with strangers
• Lack of affection on parental terms
• Destructiveness to self, others, and material things
• Cruelty to animals
• Crazy lying (lying in the face of the obvious)
• Poor impulse control
• Learning lags
• Lack of cause/effect thinking
• Lack of conscience
• Abnormal eating patterns
• Poor peer relationships
• Preoccupation with fire and/or gore
• Persistent nonsense questions and chatter indicating a need to control
• Inappropriate clinginess and demanding behavior
• Abnormal speech patterns
• Inappropriate sexuality

The Underlying Causes of These Various Symptoms
The cause is some break in the early attachment relationship that results in difficulties trusting others. The child experiences a fear of close authentic emotional relationships because early maltreatment or other difficulties has 'taught' the child that adults are not trustworthy, and that the child is unloved and unlovable. Fundamentally, the cause is a developmental delay. The child may be chronologically six, ten, or fifteen, but developmentally these children are much younger. It is often useful to consider, 'at what age would this behavior be normal?' Frequently you will find that the child's behavior would be normal for a toddler. Chronic maltreatment (abuse or neglect) or other disruptions to the normal attachment relationship cause:
1. Fear of intimacy
2. Overwhelming feelings of shame. (Not guilt...shame causes you to want to hide and not be seen. So, for example, some children's chronic lying can be seen as a manifestation of this pervasive sense of shame. What is a lie, but another way to hide?)
3. Chronic feelings of being unloved
4. Chronic feelings of being unlovable
5. A distorted view of self, other, and relationships based on past maltreatment
6. Lack of trust
7. Feeling that nothing the child does can make a difference; which translates to low motivation and poor academic performance

8. A core sense of being bad
9. Difficulty asking for help
10. Difficulty relying on others in a cooperative and collaborative manner

So how does one distinguish the difference between a child who 'looks' attached and a child who really is making a healthy, secure attachment?
This question becomes important for adoptive families because some adopted children will form an almost immediate dependency bond to their adoptive parents. To mistake this as secure and healthy attachment can lead to many problems down the road. Just because a child calls someone 'Mom' or 'Dad', snuggles, cuddles, and says, "I love you", does not mean that the child is attached or even attaching. Saying, "I love you", and knowing what that really feels like, can be two different things. Attachment is a process. It takes time. The key to its formation is trust, and trust becomes secure only after repeated testing. Generally attachment develops during the first two to three years of life. The child learns that he or she is loved and can love in return. The parents give love and learn that the child loves them. The child learns to trust that his needs will be met in a consistent and nurturing manner. The child learns that he 'belongs' to his family and they to him. It is through these elements that a child learns how to love, and how to accept love.

Older adopted children need time to make adjustments to their new surroundings. They need to become familiar with their caregivers, friends, relatives, neighbors, teachers, and others with whom they will have repeated contact. They need to learn the ins and outs of new household routines and adapt to living in a new physical environment. Some children have cultural or language hurdles to overcome. Until most of these tasks have been accomplished, they may not be able to relax enough to allow the work of attachment to begin. In the meantime, behavioral problems related to insecurity and lack of attachment, as well as to other events in the child's past, may start to surface. Some start to get labels, like "manipulative," "superficial," or "sneaky". On the inside, this child is filled with anxiety, fear, grief, loss, and often a profound sense of being bad, defective, and unlovable. The child has not developed the self-esteem that comes with feeling like a valued, contributing, member of a family. The child cares little about pleasing others since his relationships with them are quite superficial.

When are problems first apparent?
Children who have experienced physical or sexual abuse, physical or psychological neglect, or orphanage life, will begin to show difficulties as young as six-months of age. For example, the signs of difficulties for an infant include the following:
• Weak crying response or rageful and/or constant whining; inability to be comforted
• Tactile defensiveness
• Poor clinging and extreme resistance to cuddling: seems stiff as a board
• Poor sucking response
• Poor eye contact, lack of tracking
• No reciprocal smile response
• Indifference to others
• Failure to respond with recognition to parents.

- Delayed physical motor skill development milestones (creeping, crawling, sitting, etc.)
- Flaccid muscle tone

What are the Subtle Signs of attachment problems?

Gail tells her seven-year-old daughter, Sally, to pick up the napkin Sally has dropped. As Sally crosses her arms a sad and angry pout darkens her face. Gail says, "Sally, I told you to pick up the napkin and throw it away." Sally stomps over to the napkin, picks it up, and throws it away. Crying and whining, Sally stands with her back to Gail. Sally, angry and unhappy, is exhibiting one of the subtle signs of attachment sensitivity that nearly all children adopted after six-months demonstrate.

Attachment is an interpersonal, interactive process that results in a child feeling safe, secure, and able to develop healthy, emotionally meaningful relationships. The process requires a sensitive, responsive parent who is capable of emotional engagement and participation in contingent collaborative communication (responsive communication) at nonverbal and verbal levels. The parent's ability to respond to the child's emotional state is what will prevent attachment sensitivities from becoming problems of a more severe nature.

Subtle signs of attachment issues:

- Sensitivity to rejection and to disruptions in the normally attuned connection between mother and child
- Avoiding comfort when the child's feelings are hurt, although the child will turn to the parent for comfort when physically hurt
- Difficulty discussing angry feelings or hurt feelings
- Over-valuing looks, appearances, and clothes
- Sleep disturbances. Not wanting to sleep alone
- Precocious independence
  (a level of independence that is more frequently seen in slightly older children)
- Reticence and anxiety about changes
- Picking at scabs and sores
- Secretiveness
- Difficulty tolerating correction or criticism

Internationally adopted children experience at least two significant changes during the first few months of life that can have a profound impact on later development and security: *Birth mother to orphanage or foster care, and then orphanage to adoptive home.*

We know from extensive research that prenatal, post-natal, and subsequent experiences create lasting impressions on a child. During the first few minutes, days, and weeks of life, the infant clearly recognizes the birth mother's voice, smell, and taste. Changes in caregivers are disruptive. The new caregivers look different, smell different, sound different, taste different. In the orphanage there are often many care givers but no one special caregiver. Adoption brings with it a whole new, strange, and initially frightening world. These moves and disruptions have profound effects on a child's emotional, interpersonal, cognitive, and behavioral development. The longer a child is in alternate care, the more these subtle signs become pervasive.

There are effective ways for a parent to help his or her child. Parents and the right parenting are vital to preventing subtle signs from becoming anything more than sensitivities.

Parenting consistently with clear and firm limits is essential. Discipline should be enforced with an attitude of sensitive and responsive empathy, acceptance, curiosity, love, and playfulness ("PLACE"). This provides the most healing and protective way to correct a child.

As Sally walks away to pout, Gail comes up behind her, scoops her up, and begins rocking her gently while crooning in Sally's ear. Gail sings songs and tells Sally she loves her and understands Sally is angry at being told what to do. Gail expresses sadness that Sally is so unhappy. At first Sally resists a bit, but she soon calms down and listens as Gail tells her how much she loves Sally. Sally is sensitive to feelings of rejection and abandonment that are evoked by her mother's displeasure, so Gail brings Sally closer to reassure Sally non-verbally. It is by experience that the subtle signs are addressed and managed. Nonverbal experience is much more powerful than verbal experience since most of the subtle signs have their origin in nonverbal experience and nonverbal memory.

Finally, Sally eventually did what she was asked to do and was praised for doing what was expected. In this manner, Sally experiences acceptance of who she is while becoming socialized. These types of behaviors or interactions do not constitute a mental illness or Reactive Attachment Disorder. They are subtle signs of attachment sensitivities. So, what can you do?

Maintain Attunement. The most important thing you can do is maintain an attuned emotionally close and positive relationship with your child even when your child is being nasty or pushing your buttons…it is at those times that the child most needs to feel loved and loveable, even if the behavior is unacceptable. Create a connection with your child and then discipline.

Physical Closeness. Bringing the child in close is better than allowing the child to be alone or isolate him or her self.

Verbalize. Talk for the child. Put words to what the child is feeling. This allows the child to feel understood by you, maintains a connection, and helps assuage the fear of rejection and abandonment. It also helps the child become self-aware, models verbal behavior, and facilitates a sense of emotional attunement between parent and child.

Provide Ready Food. Don't make food a battle. A child who steals food or hoards food usually has sound emotional reasons for this. Providing the child with food so that your child experiences you as provider is often the solution. Put a bowl of fruit in the child's room (be sure to keep it filled!) In some instances, I've recommended that the parents provide the child with a fanny pack and keep it stocked with snacks. This usually quickly ends hoarding and stealing of food.

Encourage Dependence. For the child who is overly independent, doing for the child and not encouraging precocious independence is helpful. So, making a game of brushing your six-year old's teeth, dressing your seven-year-old, or playing at feeding a nine-year-old, are all ways to demonstrate that you will care for the child. Keeping it playful and light, allows the child to experience what the child needs and helps eliminate hurtful battles.

Time-In Rather Than Time-out. When your child is becoming dysregulated, they need you to regulate their emotions. You do that by reflecting the child's emotions back to the child; putting into words what you think the child may be feeling. In this manner you demonstrate that you can accept what the child is feeling, that feelings can be tolerated and discussed; even if the behavior will be disciplined at a later time. Remember; first connect with your child, then discipline.

Reduce shame. Avoid shaming parenting methods and interactions that might be harsh or punitive. If the child is already experiencing too much shame, increasing that will only be destructive to the child and your relationship with your child. You set the emotional tone for the relationship, so keeping things positive is important. An example: your seven year old has just screamed "I hate you," because you said it's time to go to bed. I'd start by reflecting the child's feelings back to the child as you walk the child to bed with your arm around the child, *"Boy, you are really mad that you have to go to bed now." "You sure don't want to go to bed now." "I wonder what you think is making me send you to bed now?" "Maybe you think I'm being mean?"* Through this sort of dialogue you are demonstrating your acceptance of the child's feelings and your interest in the child's thinking and feeling…you are showing the child how to reflect on one's inner life.

These subtle signs are important reminders that our children have ongoing sensitivities that as parents we must address. Responsive and sensitive communication is essential. Attachment is a function of reciprocal communication; attachment does not reside in the child alone. It is very important for the parent to manage and facilitate this attuned connection within a framework of clear limits and boundaries, natural consequences, and firm, loving discipline.

Dr. Becker-Weidman is Director of The Center For Family Development www.Center4FamilyDevelop.com and co-editor of Creating Capacity for Attachment, Dr. Becker-Weidman was adopted. He has three children, one of whom was adopted.

Raising Family Awareness ~
Valuing Each Other

- Call a family meeting and include everyone in your household.

- Describe the special attributes of each family member.

- Describe family goals.

- Talk about family unity and draw or talk about what families do to stay close.

- Ask each member to list three things that make it difficult to stay close, then problem-solve the difficulties as a family.

- 'All for One and One for All'– attend each child's school/ sports/extra-curricular events as a family and celebrate each child's accomplishments. Make regular participation in an adoption support group, or visit to Culture Camp, a family outing; make it clear to all that it is an important part of your family life.

- Design simple family rituals to reinforce love and belonging, adoption and birth. Invite your children to share their thoughts and incorporate their ideas.

- Shine a daily 'ritual' spotlight: at dinnertime, ask each family member to describe the high-point and the low-point of their day–no interruptions from others, allowed!

~ By Doris Landry, MS, LLP

and Jean MacLeod

Mishaps and Milestones
Developmental Milestones May be Moving Targets

Parents tend to see children's developmental milestones as set in stone. Bottle feeding is 'set to cease' at 12 months plus, potty training 'needs' to be achieved by age two. Some children–particularly internationally adopted children where early deprivation may result in developmental delays–simply don't meet targets easily. Too often, as well, it is parents who hasten a child to a target because meeting the target helps the household run more smoothly! So a potty-trained child will be accepted in nursery school more readily than a child still diapered, and so on.

Post-institutionalized kids have had very little control over their lives. They didn't choose to lose their birthparents, be adopted, or be adopted overseas. All toddlers use their bodies for protest–hence The Terrible Twos, with screaming fits, temper tantrums, and little persons throwing their protests into whole-body language. Just so, older adopted kids, who've seemingly met developmental milestones–potty training and weaning–often simply regress to the ultimate in body language when under stress. Potty training may fly out the window, or they demand to be bottle fed once more.

Kids who regress under stress to 'body language' are signaling two things. The first is ultimate control – parents can't force a child to eat or go to the bathroom on demand. The second is their need at that time to be a baby once more.

Adopted children need our permission and understanding when they regress. They want us to confirm that we will look after them no matter what, and that we will meet their resurfaced baby needs. Adopted kids may regress at transitional stages in their lives – a new school, the arrival of a new sibling, a death or divorce, and significantly may regress as their understanding of their adopted selves progresses. So a child may soil and wet (whether deliberately or not) when he confronts the fact that adoptions are 'made'. The child recognizes that things that are made can be broken–and suddenly, all the losses he experienced flood back, and he needs to control once more as a baby does, by body language. It's the ultimate control and at the same time the ultimate display of weakness and need for care.

What do we adoptive parents need to do? First we need to eliminate any physical reason for regression. Second, we need to eliminate external pressures – playground aggression or even bullying. Third, having done all that we need to show our child we understand the need for regression. Gentle questioning will often reveal a child's fears. It's then up to us to administer the remedy. Often the child is simply seeking reassurance that we understand and we will be supportive. A child who fears the impermanence of adoption may need a reclaiming ceremony, or to see his adoption papers, or to sit with his parents and work through his lifebook.

Mishaps with milestones don't go away overnight – but they dissipate when our children understand that we know what their body language means....

~By Sheena Macrae

Learning to Play
Attachment's Magic Key

Child's play may be simple, but playing for a child's love, playing for keeps, is both imperative and purposeful. Nothing should be as satisfying to your young son or daughter as your touch, your eyes, and your smile. Therapeutic play between a parent and child recognizes the importance of a parent's position as nurturer, and places Mom or Dad in the starring role as 'The Best Toy in The World'.

Therapeutic play stresses the normal, healthy pattern of playful attachment that occurs naturally between a mother and her biological baby or toddler, and it re-teaches an adopted child the magical give-and-take of a reciprocal relationship. Reciprocal play reproduces and formalizes the healthy biological pattern, and is directed by the parent with a conscious goal of shared experience and playful intimacy.

Therapeutic play is focused interaction and eye contact and fun. Physical and emotional closeness can be frightening to a child with attachment issues, or even rage-inducing to a child with Reactive Attachment Disorder. Play can teach basic trust with disarming silliness, and promote re-parenting of the young child through a loving 'babyhood' he or she may never have had.

Play is one key to unlock an insecurely attached child's heart. It doesn't take the place of attachment therapy for children with difficult issues, but therapeutic play is a wonderful, additional tool for parents to practice regularly at home. To equip families for purposeful fun, therapist Doris Landry, MS, has put together a Bonding Box of supplies to keep on hand: Parent and child can take turns face-painting each other with cotton-balls or paint brushes. They can doctor imaginary boo-boos with body lotion and band-aids, play barber shop or hair salon, measure each others arms and legs, and look into each others eyes with a magnifying glass. A parent can read stories to their child by sitting knee to knee, and holding the book next to their face to receive their child's eye contact. Snacks can be fed to each other, face to face, and guessing games played with foods, materials and textures. Caring for baby can be acted out, with parent and child switching to play both roles.

Outdoors, tea-parties with mud-pies embellished with leaves and pebbles can be 'fed' to each other after a 'drive' to the party via swing (stand in front of the swing to push). Swimming together can also be a magical catalyst to imaginary

Bonding Box Items
for therapeutic play at home:

Silly String or Foam
Baby Powder
Hand/Body Lotion
Cotton Balls
List of Baby Songs to Sing
Mirror
Baby Blanket
Loving Story/Picture Books
Soft Baby Hairbrush
Band Aids
Favorite Snack Food
Tape Measure
Baby Bottle
Sippy Cup for Juice or Milk
Nail Clippers
First Aid Ointment
Magnifying Glass
Variety of Tactile, Sensitive Materials or Swatches
Paint Brushes– Small and Soft
Baby Spoon
Small Flashlight
Velcro Hair Curlers

play. The skin-to-skin proximity and the necessity of holding on to mom or dad, promotes physical and emotional closeness, dependency and trust. Sheena Macrae explains: "I have done most of our therapeutic play in the pool. 'Beauty Salon' is fun because you really can wet Mom's hair with the watering cans. The sinkers and hoops are the scissors, and the float-boards and noodles become seats and tables. Face 'makeup' is easy because it's water, and the amount of mutual bubble-blowing and toe-kicking is great. 'Hospital' is also a favorite drama. My car (a float) crashes, and the ambulance (my youngest on a floatable frog) must reach me. My oldest daughter can pull and push me in the water now, so she saves me. I am then doctored with the water toys turning into medical instruments. We end every pool session with a 'twirl' where I swing both of them together, horizontal on the water. The swinging, and the feel of the water, is bliss for them! We hop out to towels, shampoo and body lotion sessions, then on to hair gel and hair drying. *It is wonderful.*"

Parents can be creative with the backyard, the pool, and the contents of their Bonding Box, remembering that the point of play is to draw the child into a reciprocal, nurturing experience. The play may be child-led, but it is designed and engineered by mom or dad. Therapeutic play is interactive play with a purpose, and it can help to create the moments of intimacy that reinforce a healthy parent-child relationship.

~ By Jean MacLeod & Sheena Macrae

How We Fit

I have cared for many children through the years and though I have never given birth, I do not think that the fact of giving birth necessarily means that you love the child more. I have seen some absolutely horribly self absorbed and neglectful birth mothers, who have no feeling for their children once their fantasy of parenthood has been abandoned.

They say that it means more if you see your own physical characteristics, or those of the child's father, reflected in your child. But my adopted child reflects not my physical being but my way of walking, talking, thinking; just being in the world. When we spent time with my extended family (second cousin and her granddaughter) last summer, the similarity between the two girls' way of talking, responding and expressing themselves was uncanny. The family tradition of strong willed, plain speaking, no nonsense pioneer women is alive and strong in the personage of my little babe from China. And in many ways we seem to look alike; the way she walks and stands had folks at work in stitches. "It's not hard to tell who her mother is" was the universal comment. And I hear my own phrases and turns of speech repeated back to me in an most annoying fashion. She even answers the phone the way I do. The point is, for me that there is a lot more than the accident of biology that binds our children to us and us to them. And children I have loved and cared for years and years ago have looked me up and said "You were my first real mother". As they were my first real children.

Lynn Sherwood, adoptive mom

Day Care and Adoption:
Staying Attached
By Sheena Macrae

Nothing divides adoptive parents like a good, volatile conversation about day care! Most parents agree that ideally, adopted children flourish emotionally with as much time spent with mom or dad as possible. Post-institutional children often have deficits to fill up, and may need concentrated attachment-parenting in order to build a strong parent-child bond. Day care has been hung with the damning accusation that it is merely another orphanage stand-in, and that parents who use day care are oblivious to the needs of their children.

These provocative arguments are moot points for good parents who love their children and who must work outside the home. Day care is often a necessity, and there are ways of minimizing any ill-effects of time away from home, while maximizing the time a parent does have with her or his children. Attachment-parenting techniques (consciously parenting to promote child-bonding) can be helpful when applied over the day care experience, and focusing on a child's needs can cultivate a regular, non-traumatic separation.

How to Choose Care
How do you choose childcare? With care and sensitivity and an ear trained to the ground for good reports of the placement you think might work! Word of mouth brings news of where works and where doesn't. But gleaning 'insider info' can be hard for first time adoptive parents, especially those with no bio-born children. How do you tap the grapevine, the parent/mother network, when your children arrived without nine months of pregnant mom-to-mom networking?

Pre-Adoption Sleuth-work. If your agency or local friends can help, listen to their recommendations for day care centers, or home-based care. Look at local childbirth groups' notice-boards and you might see where every one wants to place their kids. Chance a visit, reserve a place for your child. Is there a local community care website? Check it out! Is there a day care facility available at your place of work?

Family Finance Planning, Fiscal and Emotional. Can you afford not to work? If the answer is no, how much of your income can you divert to childcare? What you can afford in terms of care will decide where you place your child. Like diapers and other essentials, it usually costs far more than you think. Can you and your partner agree to occasional 'respite' care? Will s/he give you time out or will you have to hire a babysitter to be sure of it? Can you use family or friends for care? What's the pay back? Are you comfortable with using grandma? What if you disagree with a good friend who is being paid to care for your child?

Post-Adoption Considerations. When your child is home, visit the places you have found and ask if you may stay a day to observe. Think before-hand what issues matter to you, and what issues you want the staff to be pro-active on. Questions you may want to ask:
• Will you be allowed to ease your daughter into day care over time? Can you stay with her during the transition?
• How does the staff support diversity? What are the rules against discrimination, teasing, bullying. What is the ethnic mix?

- How many staff understand and have been trained in child trauma? (senior staff should have some knowledge of this)
- Can you direct how your child is treated when your child's needs run contrary to the norm? (regarding food or toileting, for example)
- Can you give directives about child's contact and cuddling with staff? (important if you have an affection-indiscriminate child and are trying to limit number of caregivers)
- Do they provide daily reports on how your child is coping? Do you want to be called if she continues to cry after twenty minutes, an hour, two hours?
- How are leaving and re-uniting handled?
- How are naps are handled? (does your child have sleep issues?)
- How will they handle it if your child has oral-sensory issues or is unused to a western diet?
- What are their toileting and potty-training practices?
- What discipline style do they use? (isolation, 'shaming', or any form of corporal punishment is inappropriate for post-institutionalized children)

What Type of Day care Will You Choose?

Family Care. It is great to build bonds with grandma/grandpa, but care parameters need to be explained in advance. Can you 'direct' your mother/father? Some relatives refuse to 'see' attachment difficulties, and some continue to use racial slurs around trans-racially adopted children. And if you don't hire care, you can't fire it! Family care absolutely depends on individual families, but if it works, it is ideal. Family care can be a truly wonderful experience for everyone.

Home-based Childcare Providers. These professionals (make sure you see the official accreditation) who care for a group of children in their home, can be excellent or awful. It's vital to ask to spend some time with them, because you must see how they deal with anger, anxiety, and control issues with their charges. What works with the kid down the street might not be appropriate for a child adopted from Russia.

Nannies.   They make have very specialized qualifications (top-end) or they may be au pairs, workers or students from abroad who attend classes and look after your kids. Check accreditation and references. With top-end nannies, breathe deeply and get a top job yourself to pay for them! Will you mind that your child comes to love them? Will you feel replaced, or can you work as a team? Will your children cope when Nanny 'moves on' and they are bereft of a loved person from home? How will you deal with this? Will you breathe a happy sigh because if your child is well-cared for at home, then that's one less stressor when you're not there to care?

Day Care Centers.   Most are designed to optimize their hours to suit working families; center hours may start at six am and go through till seven pm. Staff are likely to be trained, but not necessarily in the issues adoptive families deal with. Again, spending time before committing your child is vital, as is checking accreditation and listening to testimonials. If you are a working mother, and opt for full-day care, you might need to consider whether or not your child is assigned a designated caregiver, and whether or not you like her. Can you cope if your child begins to bond with her? This is part of the deal; you should be amenable to accepting this, but will you? Bonding with a day care giver does not mean that she is supplanting you, just that you have to consciously establish what your being mom means.

A Toolbox for Coping

Work is a necessity for many of us, but adoptive parents with children in day care do need to consider what being absent for part of the day means to a child adopted from institutional or foster care. Initially, our children may not trust the difference in day care, to the regimes they had in their birth country. We parents may end up looking like a 'senior caregiver' popping in and around their daily routine. We need to ask:

• How do we make ourselves special over our chosen caregivers, but still allow the caregivers to become significant others in our children's lives?

• How do we tell our kids that we will always be there, but caregivers may move on? (There is no easy answer, apart from the simple fact that time, and the cycle of caregivers coming and going, proves our staying is permanent).

Settling into Day Care. The ritual of the drop off, with a kiss and a hug and a special remembrance of mom /dad become important. And the ritual of the return, when we go right into the care facility and pick our kids up, when there is time for a hug, a quiet sit-together, some (shared) food. We also need to acknowledge that our kids will need to make bonds with their caregivers because we need to allow our kids to settle and feel secure. It's a question of balancing how attached our children become at day care, to the detriment of attaching to us. It's important to be able to talk this over with staff, and have them problem-solve with you, if necessary. It's also important for the children to see, and the staff to emphasize, that parents drop their kids off, and parents return. In fact, learning by watching that the other children have mothers and fathers and are always collected, may enhance our children's notion of belonging to a family. To maintain this trust, it's important to ensure not being late to pick up a child. If another adult is picking your child up, make sure you talk about it with your child in advance. Be clear that no matter who picks up, you will return!

Making it Work. Parent and child may need time to settle together into the facility, with a planned withdrawal of Mom or Dad. This requires the support of the staff. Some facilities may require the settling to be concluded over a day, over a week, or even over months. Be sure you know, and understand what your child can handle! Settling also requires that we parents continue to assess both what the staff reports to us about our child and how we find her at the end of the day. A child whose behavior regresses to baby stuff or escalates to violence after a 'honeymoon period' at day care, may not be suited either to that particular facility, or to day care, or both.

Deciding on placement in care is a matter of judgment, but it is useful to take along a friend who is versed in how adopted children fare in day care with you to help observe. It's also at this critical stage that having chosen a facility with staff able to comprehend a child's difficulties comes into its own: staff should be able to advise us if our child displays readiness; this is part of what we pay for.

Integrating a child into day care, and day care into your family, takes time, nurturing and patience. Every family needs to find what works for their specific circumstances, but there are keys to making day care run smoothly and keys to staying connected to your children after being separated during the day. Devising day care 'sacred ground rules' for your family (and sticking to them) will help you stay aware of what you can do to make your child feel loved, while you are together or apart.

~by Sheena Macrae

A Day Care Family

Pre-adoption, I always thought I'd be a stay at home mom. But then was another sort of family. Now, I think we've constructed a good life together even though I work full time. I believe it is possible for some families to build a strong, supportive, family in this way. I also believe that there are children (adopted and not) who are too damaged or fragile to handle this lifestyle.

Day care children need to be able to develop the ability to understand and trust that you're going to come back. My kids attend a day-care where they feel cherished, safe and are supported in ways that leave them free to learn how to be comfortable and happy in the world. I take them to this good place each morning. Thus, they trust that I, too, keep them safe. We are free to keep growing deeper as mother and daughters.

~ Becky Miklos

My Sacred Ground Rules
Making Day Care Work for Us
By Becky Micklos

- I eliminate all separating from my children except for the time they spend in day-care. We sleep together. I don't ever leave my two year old with anyone, not even her grandparents. If my five year old chooses to, she can go to her grandparents for a few hours on the weekend. No evening separations on school days, ever.

- I do lots of attachment parenting stuff, everyday. Giggles and stories in the mornings. Rock-a-bye baby with kisses and eye contact at night. Wrestling, tickling, giggling. A bottle for the baby at morning and night, and for my big girl on request. Hair fixing, lotion rubbing, shoe-lace tying are all opportunities for eye contact and attunement. Videos are watched with a kid in my lap.

- I never speak of day care as being optional or non-compulsory. This is how our family operates. Period. Some days I don't like to go to work, and you don't like to go to school. It happens, but we go.

- I never speak of going to day care in terms of punishment. It's neutral. A fact. Sure, we'd all rather be together all day everyday. But this is how our family works.

- I try to keep our mornings routine and low stress. Find and set out everything the night before. The kids eat breakfast in the car. We have to be out the door by seven am; there's major potential for yelling and disconnect if things go awry and I'm concerned about being late for work. Nobody needs that anxiety.

- I remain neutral when dropping off. Pleasant and matter of fact. Goodbye honey (hug), I love you (kiss), have fun, I'll see you later. If you're too upbeat, too much on the sell, kids sense ambush.

- I always pick up the little one myself. On the occasion I've taken the little one for a doctor's appointment, I'll let grandparents pick up the older one and bring her straight home, but only by pre-plan.

- I avoid all activities (even running errands) after day care. They've had enough stimulation for the day. I run the errands either on my lunchtime, or squeeze them in just before I pick up the kids. We don't meet family or friends for dinner or fun on school nights. It's way too disruptive and tiring for all of us. When kids are tired, they're more apt to feel anxious and unsafe; we have to maintain optimal emotional health by staying rested and grounded. There will be years in the future for entertainment, stimulation, going out into the world. At this point our family is still connecting and it is best done at home.

- I always have a comfort object in the car for each child when picked up from day care. The big one gets her blankie, the little one her bottle. This is an immediate easer of tension and anxiety. It's a simple way to reconnect by giving them something good that comes directly from me. Never, ever forget it; they trust that you will have it there for them.

- I keep to the same routine every evening. We get home at six pm and I feed them as quickly and simply as possible. Everybody's crabby when they're hungry, and since we only have two hours before bedtime, I really try to keep it friendly, pleasant and loving. I don't waste our brief time together prepping meals or doing chores. When they're older and can help (without trying my patience too much) we'll do these things together. For now, I have a healthy snack before I leave the office because I can't eat macaroni and cheese or ramen noodles every night!

- I know their teachers. I'd advise this of everyone using day care. Be respectful of the teachers in front of the child. Be pleasant and demonstrate your friendship with the teachers to the child. Laugh and talk a bit about the child's accomplishments. Show the children that you trust this person, you like them, and you are a team in caring for the child. Be relaxed. If you have serious issues to discuss, do it by phone, out of the child's earshot. You need the teacher. A good teacher will be able to tell you a lot about your child. They are neutral tools for getting information about how your child lives in the world away from you. They have experience with tons of kids and can have a good sense about when children have serious issues.

- I keep in contact with the teachers. At the start of every school year I write the teachers a note about my children, their life before me, our family situation, and any current concerns I might have about their behavior or development. It might be a shameless prod for special treatment, but I don't care! My kids are little and I need this to work. I need the teachers to be sympathetic, empathetic, aware, and otherwise on our side. If I do a bit of education about the differences of post-institutional kids, they are usually very receptive, interested and observant. My older daughter receives daily Occupational Therapy from one of her teachers for her Sensory Integration issues, though the teachers were shocked when I first suggested that there could be a problem and that I was having her evaluated. Now they see how much she loves it, and that it makes her calmer and a bit more attentive. My daughter sees the OT as something special her teachers do for her. It makes her feel safe.

~ Becky Miklos is a single mom to two daughters from China. She also volunteers for Altrusa, administering donation sponsorships for children in foster care in JiangXi Province

"Why Do You Ask?"
Questions from Total Strangers and Strategies to Handle Them
By Cheryl Leppert

"Where are your kids from?" It happens at least once a week. Total strangers approach me in the grocery store, at the park, in the library. Most days I'm happy to answer, but sometimes I admit I just want to shout, "It's none of your business!" Locally–for example in our church–everyone knows who we are: We're the family with the two girls from India. They may not always remember our names, but our faces are indelibly etched into their consciousness. That's not necessarily a bad thing. The response has been overwhelmingly positive. One family from our church even chose to adopt after seeing the joy our children have brought to our family. But that feeling of being on display never goes away. So how do we handle invasion of our privacy?

I have learned some strategies to help me evaluate which questions are OK, and which invade the privacy of our family and ask for information private to my children. I also am teaching my children how to evaluate situations - essentially, teaching my children how to speak for themselves. This is really important. One day soon, if it's not happening already, your daughter or son will start moving around in this world without you. It may begin at preschool, dance class, scouts, or elementary school. But when that day arrives, your kids are going to need to be prepared with some idea of how to handle the questions when you are not there to help answer them. Here firstly are my tools for teaching my kids how to evaluate situations

- Model good responses.
- Ask their opinions. "How could we have handled that differently?" "Were you comfortable with me answering that question?" "Is it OK for me to share that information?" See W.I.S.E Up in **School** chapter page 284
- Role play with them. Ask what situations they've encountered and work together to come up with responses that might work.
- Let them know it's OK to ask for help. If a child at school is too persistent in their questions, who can your child turn to for help in deflecting the problem?
- Let them know it's OK to not give an answer, and demonstrate this when out in public. It's parents' jobs to defend their children, it establishes boundaries and it teaches how to establish them

Five great strategies for formulating a response

Strategy 1: Give a brief, but honest answer, when appropriate. More often than not, this will end the conversation quickly. "Where is she from?" "She was born in India."

Strategy 2: Answer their question with a question. "Why do you ask?" This puts the ball back in their court. If they're being inquisitive, they'll probably feel uncomfortable saying so and will let it drop. If they have a good reason for asking, you can decide where to go from there.

Strategy 3: Show them how invasive the question is. "Do your children get their looks from their father?" A quip is in order sometimes: "I don't know. I never met him." And a snappy response to "Are they really sisters?" is to reply with, "Yes, they are now. Thanks for asking! And do all your children have the same father?" The point here is not to cast doubt upon the questioner's virtue, but to help her see a comparably personal question.

Strategy 4: Defer to your children. Depending on their age, you can make a point of asking them if it's OK for you answer the question, or, if they're a bit older, you can invite them to do the answering. It's good for the children to see that you respect their ownership of the information, and it can be a good chance for them to practice how they want to answer when strangers ask.

Strategy 5: Invoke the cloak of privacy. Privacy is different from secrecy. Secrecy connotes that there may be something to be ashamed of. Privacy is the barrier that allows you to keep personal information to yourself. Would a total stranger walk up to a woman with a newborn and ask how many stitches she received after childbirth? No. Some things are personal and private and it's OK to say, in as tactful a way as fits the occasion, that it's none of their business.

One thing I have discovered is that my primary obligation is to my children, not to the person who has asked the questions. Using that premise to set boundaries and to model responses for my children has been the key to handling intrusive questions for my family.

~ Cheryl Leppert is a freelance writer and adoptive parent of two children, both from India

Using your Body to Communicate

Turn. Allow your body language to indicate the question is out of order with a look or by physically turning. Your children will come to learn from you that boundaries are important for matters that are personal and private.

Silence. Sometimes the sound of silence is most expressive. When someone asks a question which in your view is outrageous and simply violates family privacy, it isn't necessary to answer.

Look. You can also add a slow gaze slipping over the person questioning you as you disengage. That tells the person your view more directly than words.

Loving Hands
Caring for Your Child's Hair is an Act of Love…

Hair care is of great significance among the African American (AA) community. Hair care is not just about keeping a neat appearance, it is about bonding with family and friends, and it gives other parents an idea of how much value you place on your child. Children with unkempt hair are considered to be uncared-for, or neglected by their mothers. Adoptive parents who simply 'don't know how to do hair' really do need to learn!

It's hard for children to sit still, and it can hurt a little for an AA child to have her hair properly worked on. I have several AA friends who prefer to take their daughters to a salon to get their hair done because they aren't as good at styling (or don't have the time). There is no stigma to taking your child to a salon; it really is acceptable and I think you would be nicely surprised by how kind those at the salon would be to your family.

A salon can be a friendly place to make AA connections for your child. People will see that you, the parent, are taking the time and effort to do your child's hair correctly and giving her a resource to learn how to care for it herself. This clearly demonstrates that you do understand the importance of hair among AA people.

If your daughter is really tender-headed, it may take a couple of trial visits to the salon to get all of her hair done during one visit. I don't know if you have ever seen a small AA child with half a head of hair 'done' and the other half 'just brushed out'? It is relatively common to see AA children like that (usually when they are quite young) because they are tender-headed and cannot sit still during the time it takes to braid their hair (it can take up to three to four hours to do one child's head, depending on the condition of their hair, and how intricate the hair style is).

Adoptive parents with an older child might sit down with her and talk about the fact that you know she is tender-headed, but that doing her hair correctly will only entail some discomfort on her part until she gets used to it (and she will quickly become accustomed to it). You can also talk to her about how her hair will grow more healthily, be more lustrous and will really become 'her crowning glory'. If she is old enough, a little natural self-esteem/vanity may get her to be more willing to have her hair done. And there are also the pretty beads, clips, and barrettes!

When you go to the AA salon, ask them to show you how to oil your daughter's head between visits (there is a bit of a trick to it, being careful to not use too much or too little). This helps to keep her hair conditioned and her scalp healthy. It can also be a really wonderful bonding time with your daughter: you get to talk about how much you like taking care of her, and how beautiful you find her hair to be. You can start building the type of 'belonging' and bonding that many AA parents create with their children through hair care. In addition, the oil and conditioners smell great, which is a nice, pampering, girly thing for the two of you to enjoy.

~Sasha Brooks

Connecting through Ceremony
Rituals Add to Family Glue
By Carrie Kitze

On days when our children might be thinking more about how they joined our family and where they fit into it all, (birthdays, anniversary days, life milestones, Mother's and Father's Days) we can try to talk a bit more on how they joined–and we can make a special ceremony. Children are very ritualistic; being claimed as well as claiming by rite matters to them. And a ceremony doesn't need to be complicated to be effective. Ceremonies are living pictures–short action narratives that help children grasp complex meaning. Here are some easy ideas which help make new rituals and ceremonies for adoptive families:

Plant a Tree. A fitting and visual reminder....plant a tree for each of the moms or dads your child has. Make them different kinds, or the same. It's your choice. You could plant fruit or other ornamental flowering trees or one that is beautiful at a certain time of year: pretty colored leaves in the fall, cool bark if the birthday is in winter, unusual leaves if in the summer, flowering for spring. Plant one for each of your children, adopted or not.

Write a Letter. Letter writing is powerful as children get older and can articulate their thoughts and wishes better. You can burn the letter and send the wishes up in smoke, attach it to a balloon (although that isn't too great for the environment), or save it in a file for later (or both if you are quick!) If you have birthparent contact, this is a nice time to send this letter and let them know what the child is doing/thinking. These snapshots of feeling make great additions to a co-created lifebook.

Create an Honoring Ceremony. Kids love ceremonies–especially the ones that they get to participate in and that make them be at center stage. My littlest one loves to blow out candles. So for us, a ceremony with candles is a great choice. Here's what we have done. Each of us has one candle for our parents (all of them) and one for our selves. We also have one main candle, which is the family candle. Help your little ones to light their parent candles and the candles representing themselves from the family candle. Talk about how each person (moms and dads, too) joined the family. Mom and dad through marriage, bio children through birth on their birthdays, adopted children, on their adoption days. You can add some detail each time you have the ceremony like the day of the week they were born, what the weather was like. You can also drop a thought about the gifts each of them have and how those are genetic or learned. Have them blow out the candle with thoughts or wishes. This can be repeated as many times as you need until all the thoughts and wishes are out on the table. This is one to follow the lead of your children. There are no right or wrong answers.

Share Thoughts With the Moon. Another powerful symbol of connection is the moon. Regardless of where we call home in the world, we all look at the same moon and this can be a wonderful way to allow your child to create a personal and private tool for connection. We sometimes sit on our back porch and gaze at the moon and send wishes to people we aren't with at the moment. Do it for grandparents, cousins, or aunts and uncles who don't live close and also for birth family.

It's important to be able to voice and accept the feelings that come from memories and ceremonies and rituals will help your family do just that.

A Root and a Rock
Making Sense of Two Mothers
By Sheena Macrae

Somewhere between a root and a rock is my child–and she envisages herself as growing from and on two mothers.

We use the run up to Mother's Day and Mother's Day Eve as a special time to let our kids talk about their birthmothers and families I find it a helpful tool for me–talking and letting adopted kids open up about birthfamily is quite tough for adoptive parents as well as our children! This is a time which helps forge connections between our mutual families, connections celebrated on Mother's Day. So whether or not my kids do a lot of talking and thinking, having this time to think, maybe 'send a letter' or even let go some balloons in honor of their birthmums is good. It's freeing, and it tells them I am open to them loving two sets of parents. Kids do need permission to love birthparents, even if they have never met their birthparents. They need it–despite what the circumstances of their abandonment may have been.

For some years now my older girl has 'planted' a daffodil she's cut from the garden in honor of her birthmother–because, as she says, that's a bit how her relationship with her birthmother is. Cut off. This year she took her thinking a little further and a little more bitter-sweetly. She said her birthmum is the root, she's the flower, and birthmum went snip, snippety snip and cut her off. Then, her orphanage put her in a vase of water where she wilted, and might have died and then 'she was stuck onto us to grow'. She looked at me hard, paused, looked again then said 'Thing is, Mum, it's hard growing on you and Dad, because we're not the same plant'.

I had to phone a friend–in fact it was a transatlantic call! I needed help! And we discussed how I might talk about grafts, and how plants that are grafted on to others often grow more strongly thereafter. And so I did. But my daughter swept ahead of me, as children do. Their thinking is often simpler and truer than ours. She decided that since she is Heather (her birthcountry name also means purple flower), she will be a heather, that I am her rock, and she is rooting on me. She remembered that heathers keep on growing roots in water when uprooted, and so she is nestling in close to my rock to put down new roots. Putting down new roots, of her own, which are also born of the roots that her birthmother gave her.

I love this–she is changing the ending of her own story! It takes the power of narratives to new places (see **Narratives** chapter pgs 221-252). It's powerful when kids get a grasp of their own stories and decide to overcome! It's even more wondrous when our children prove that experts are talking sense after all. Heathers are feisty plants and I am overcome yet again by this child and her elastic band of living–she is resilient in a way that I have never had to be. I am privileged to be this child's mother.

And I am glad she is growing on a root and a rock.

Language

Building Love

from Language Losses and Communication Gains
by Sheena Macrae, PhD

Medical experts with a special interest in intercountry adoption (ICA) tell us that in terms of our children's development, around one month's loss is experienced by our children for every three they are institutionalized or placed in non-optimal 1:1 care. And so when we receive our children, we should expect that at least initially, in terms of language development, they will be 'behind' children who have never been institutionalized and who remain in the language environment of their birth and pre-birth. Experts call this developmental language delay. All other developmental skills, from the physical to the social, may also lag.

It's our job to ensure that we have our children assessed for language delays as soon as we can and, more seriously for language disorders. Experts advise speech and hearing 'tests' should form part of the battery of tests run to evaluate the health of our children on arrival to our country and our home. It is only by learning how we may mitigate language losses that we can be fully empowered to create communicative gains.

In looking at our children's language skills (and which of these require assistance), we need also to look at their communicative needs and skills. Children who have been institutionalized, perhaps with less than optimal nutrition, physical care and attention, may be affected both in terms of cognitive and social development. A child raised with poor nutrition, quite literally, doesn't have the energy or material to age-appropriately develop the neurology of communication and speech because the brain has not developed as it should. A child raised with no special caregiver attending to physical and social needs gives up trying to be heard. A child raised with the trauma of separation from birthmother locked within, lacks the capacity to communicate because fear is the key to this child's existence, not communication.

In assessing our children's needs we have to face their history:

1. Environmental factors (e.g. factory emissions, lead levels) in the sending country also affect physical and cognitive development and have a possible effect on speech and

cognitive capacity. Standard of care can affect health; a child doesn't thrive with environmentally-linked illnesses such as gut and respiratory problems, and a child who doesn't thrive physically most likely doesn't thrive across the whole spectrum of development.

2. An orphanage is a place where learning either to speak age appropriately or to communicate (social interactive skills) is not likely. Noise levels in the corridors may be loud, and paradoxically staff may speak rarely to the children, more amongst themselves. The children are 'in a world of their own'. Their speech and communicative skills are not comparable with children in their birth country who are living outside orphanages.

Doctors and researchers specializing in ICA and speech/communicative development are beginning to see that communication skills–gestures, knowing how to play–are a significant predictor of catch-up in speech for our ICA children, and also predict how quickly our children will learn our language after whatever start they had in the language environment of their birth and care pre-adoption.

It seems critical that as responsible parents we address both the speech and communicative environment of our children. We need to talk and sing and read to them, yes, but we also need to ensure that we are communicating with all the senses of touch, hearing, taste, smell, and sight. These underpin social communication and are the basis of rich communicative gains. For most children, development in the broader domain of communication skills, activity, movement and social roles has gains in language skills predicated upon it. And for those children for whom language skills can never be assisted back to a 'normal' age appropriate expectation, the teaching of the communicative skills helps them navigate our social world.

Stanley Greenspan, in his book *Building Healthy Minds*, reminds us that parents don't pay enough attention to the skills that teach children how to relate, communicate and think. These include acceptance of sensory sensation, an ability to fall in love with parents, being a two way communicator, and being an interactive problem solver and creator of ideas, with the ability to connect between ideas and relationships. Greenspan holds that "These are the essential building blocks of higher-level skill".

"Remember, if a child has had normal language development in a first language, the second language should come relatively easily. If it does not, this could be a sign of a more basic language learning problem, which probably also affected the first language. Seek help with therapists who understand your child's circumstances."

~Mark Sebba

Part 1: Understanding Language Losses
The Nuts, Bolts, and Cracks in Language

Understanding what language losses our children may have–beyond developmental language delay–takes away the fear of the unknown, and assists in knowing when to ask for help. Specialized help should always be sought if a parent has a gut feeling that something is wrong. We parents need to learn to listen very carefully to other experts our children may encounter, as teachers and day-care workers may pick up on problems as fast as we do.

Speech, Language, and Auditory Disorders

There are many speech, language and auditory disorders that have roots in genetics, trauma and environment. If our children have functional difficulties in making sounds, with voice tone and in sequencing language structures, we may need to consider the possibility of speech, language or auditory disorders–or a combination of all three.

Speech Disorders are where the speaker has difficulty producing sounds or has problems with voice quality. Problems include stuttering, difficulty in articulating sounds or with pitch and voice quality. Sufferers often suffer from a bundle of problems. Those listening to a speaker with a speech disorder may find it hard to understand what is being said.

Language Disorders are where there is breakdown in capacity to understand and use words in context. Typically speakers use words inappropriately; sometimes the capacity to form grammatical sentences is lost, and vocabulary is limited. Sufferers sometimes find it hard following directions. Sometimes language disorders are found in speakers who also have language learning problems and/or developmental language delay.

From The National Institute for Deafness and other Communication Disorders (NIDCD) is a brief definition of auditory processing disorder:

Auditory Processing Disorder(s) Auditory processing is a term used to describe what happens when your brain recognizes and interprets the sounds around you. Humans hear when energy that we recognize as sound travels through the ear and is changed into electrical information that can be interpreted by the brain. The 'disorder' part of auditory processing disorder means that something is adversely affecting the processing or interpretation of the information.

Home & School Listening Therapies for Audio Processing Disorder and Learning:

Fast ForWord **www.scientificlearning.com**

Earobics Step 1 and 2 **www.earobics.com**

Lindamood-Bell Learning Processes (including LiPS and V/V) **www.lblp.com**

The Listening Program™ **www.rmlearning.com**

NCAPD (National Coalition for Auditory Processing) **www.ncapd.org**

ASHA (American Speech-Language-Hearing Assoc.) **www.asha.org**

American Academy of Audiology **www.audiology.org**

We are not sure what causes APD (also referred to as Central Auditory Processing Disorder, or CAPD). Human communication relies on taking in complicated perceptual information from the outside world through the senses, such as hearing, and interpreting that information in a meaningful way. Human communication also requires certain mental abilities, such as attention and memory. Scientists still do not understand exactly how all of these processes work and interact or how they malfunction in cases of communication disorders. Even though your child seems to 'hear normally', he or she may have difficulty using those sounds for speech and language.

While the cause of APD is often unknown, auditory processing difficulty in children may be associated with conditions such as dyslexia, attention deficit disorder, autism, autism spectrum disorder, specific language impairment, pervasive developmental disorder, or developmental delay. Sometimes this term has been misapplied to children who have no hearing or language disorder but have challenges in learning.

Undiagnosed and untreated, children with auditory processing disorders find it difficult to follow the 'social rules' of school and making friends. They can not sequence and hear (the bones of social interaction), and they may act out in frustration. We need therapeutic help with such children, both in ensuring vestibular (inner ear) stability and in ensuring they learn the rules of 'how to hear' in complex auditory environments (such as in a classroom). Many children with ADD and ADHD are possibly misdiagnosed; they simply may be too stressed to hear.

Cognitive Loss

Cognitive loss is a highly emotional subject for parents of adopted children whose development has been arrested by poor conditions prior to adoption. Under-stimulation and lack of a supportive, creative daily environment can cause a child's communicative brain to atrophy, out of lack of interest, and out of lack of care.

Children placed into adoptive homes with rich communicative environments may be able make up losses. There are experts who assert that a child's brain is 'plastic' (it can take on board new experiences and use them to develop previous developmental gaps). So, although a child's development has points where the brain hardwires available experience, the brain permits 're-tries' with new experiences at later dates. For us this means hope within the richer communicative environment of the adoptive family.

Adoptive parent Nancy Hemenway is hopeful that with the right treatment, therapy, attention and environment, cognitive loss can be overcome. She states *"A child's brain has been found to have a great deal of plasticity. Plasticity is the ability of the brain to rearrange the connections between its neurons. It is the foundation of the memory formation and learning processes, and can also be important in compensating for brain damage by allowing the brain to create new networks of neurons. These local changes to brain structure depend on the environment—and represent an adaptation to it.*

"One can not separate early deprivation and brain function, or a diagnosis like Reactive Attachment Disorder or (Post Traumatic Stress Disorder with brain function, because the 'emotional' is tangled with the chemistry of the brain. Many issues once considered genetic are now known to be plastic.

"A single traumatic experience can actually alter an adult's brain chemistry and also its structural design. Researchers have now found that abuse and early neglect have severe effects

on the brains of children. How plastic the brain remains gives hope in the ability to reorganize and restructure the damage.

"For example, trauma begins with being afraid, so let's look chemically at what happens, how fear induces a reaction. Once afraid, adrenaline rushes, the heart pounds, blood pressure rises and the body is readied for its physical expression of Fight, Flight, or Freeze. A chemical in the brain called cortisol (a hormone secreted by the adrenal glands in high amounts during stress) is released. This chemical helps the body respond to danger.

"There is mounting evidence suggesting that children neglected in orphanages have a short circuit in this system of response, which manifests in unbalanced cortisol levels in the children. Megan Gunnar, PhD, a professor at the Institute of Child Development, University of Minnesota, has found that developmental delays and cognition problems correlate directly with irregular cortisol levels.

"Dr. Gunnar and other professionals believe too much cortisol leads to damage in the brain's hippocampus. This damage leads to memory lapses and anxiety.

"Cortisol can also affect and alter areas in the brain which determine attention. Hyper-vigilance is common in children who look around as if their environment is a dangerous place to be. They may even incorrectly interpret the 'innocent' action of a peer or teacher to be life-threatening. According to trauma specialist Bruce D. Perry, MD, PhD: "Children who are aroused [from fear] can't take in cognitive information. They're too busy watching the teacher for threatening gestures, and not listening to what she's saying." These children see their world as a constant threat, and one they have to cope with in order to be safe. Anxiety and hyper-vigilance is displayed even in sleep. All of this takes its toll on the development of language and problem-solving skills.

"Experts until recently were unsure of when the door of plasticity closes. The thinking among professionals is that there is still a great deal of plasticity even through the teen years, and even adult brains now have more plasticity then once was thought."

However, not all loss can be made up or restored by loving care. Some families have children whose poor environmental pre-adoption care, compounded with a predisposition for language learning disorders, mean that the child is left, for example, unable to process differences in color, size, or hot versus cold. These children need specialist help, and some families report that their children will need help in understanding 'daily living' all their lives. Families in these circumstances suggest that their children were severely neglected, spending days in cribs without interaction or communication.

Boris Gindis, PhD a licensed psychologist and a certified bilingual school psychologist also reports on a different type of cognitive loss which can occur as our children transit from being primary speakers of their birth language to primary speakers of English, and move from the language skills required at home to the language skills required in the classroom. This aspect of cognitive loss is related to subtractive bilingualism. Gindis notes that language is used both for communication, but also at school and work for reasoning.

Dr. Gindis calls this difference 'communicative language' (also known as BICS, Basic Interpersonal Communicative Skills) and 'cognitive language' (or CALP, Cognitive Academic Language Proficiency). Gindis suggests that children adopted between the ages of four and eight are most vulnerable in not being able to make the leap from home to school, from communicative to cognitive language.

The reason? Children adopted under the age of four have a longer time at home before they go to school, and that time allows English to take root as the foundation for both communication and reasoning. Children adopted after age eight have their birth language in place, may be able to read and write, and may well be able to reason. While these older children may have developmental delays, or other learning difficulties and speech/language disorders, Gindis asserts that these are more easily recognized in the older child and more evident for treatment.

The four to eight year-olds fall between the cracks. Their primary language was lost before their new primary of English was learned, so the foundation for English is shaky. Families who have reported with pleasure how 'quickly' their children learned (communicative) English are shocked to find that when their children are in school, end of school reports note the children's difficulty in using language for reasoning, which of course affects academic study across the whole curriculum.

Subtractive Bilingualism

Subtractive bilingualism needs to be considered as part of an international adoptee's developmental language delay. Receptive language (being able to understand speech) typically precedes communicative language. So a child will act on an instruction long before there is any verbal response. For those of us who have adopted children old enough to have developed receptive language skills in their first language, we need to consider what it means for them to be removed from their first linguistic environment and be transplanted to ours. We need to remember that receptive language acquisition may well begin in the womb, as the child listens to its birthmother talking as she goes about her everyday life. Our children, even at only months old, will have begun to internalize and understand their spoken birth language.

Coming from the environment of their first language to us, our children are lost on a sea of unanchored sounds and unfamiliar structures. Even gestures, which children use to augment their understanding, may well change from one culture to another.

Boris Gindis notes that our adopted children have linguistic challenges quite unlike children who come as immigrants and who also must learn English in order to communicate. The difference is that our children's home language, upon adoption, also becomes English. We don't support the continuation of their first language, because we can't. We are not native speakers. Our child effectively is deemed to have English as his or her primary language from the minute s/he enters the adoptive home.

What does this mean for the adopted child? It means that the child can not use a primary language (the language of home) in order to scaffold learning English. There is no use for the child's first language, and the focus of the family is probably to have the child learn English.

Compare this with the immigrant child. A rich interaction in the primary language is available in the home, and the child can use the primary language's underlying structures to test and compare with the underlying rules of English.

Learning a language when a primary language remains 'live' is termed additive bilingualism. Subtractive bilingualism is where the new language replaces the old–before the child has full grasp of the first. When this happens, there is limited potential for the child 'to check' the underlying systems that support his new language.

English as a Second Language (ESL) or English for Speakers of Other Languages (ESOL) programs, which are in place in schools to assist new learners of English become fluent, are built on the assumption of additive bilingualism, and may not meet the learning challenges of our adopted children.

Children need a particularly rich linguistic and communicative environment in their new homes if we are to truly assist them take English as their primary (but second) language. We can help them:

Taking things beyond simply looking at the development of language into the realms of the development of communication means that we look at language along with all the senses and systems of body management, in interaction with the world.

1. Turn off the TV. Learning a language takes the live interaction of two people, and TV is a passive partner. Start talking/telling stories/making up stories together.
2. Sing: anything from silly songs to nursery rhymes.Rhyming helps a child learn the sound pattern of a language.
3. Swim (with lots of shouting and splashing). Feel the water, hold your child, blow bubbles!
4. Swing in the backyard or park. Talk about how it feels!
5. Sand play in the garden or on the beach. Talk about the things you are making!

Part 2: Creating Communication Gains
The Language of Love

Speech is human. It's perhaps the pinnacle of the processes that support human communication and connection. It is accompanied by and builds on the systems of gesture, touch, movement, hearing, and smell; which make it possible for us to 'know our loved ones' and connect. All are vital for the nurture and sustenance of babies. But perhaps voice, the precursor of speech, is critical to the mother/child bond. A newborn turns to the voice of the birthmother–because that voice has become known from the time within the womb. And the baby knows that this is his mother, and so expects to be held and kept secure. Babies are secure simply in knowing their mothers. Destroy that intimate knowing and a baby is lost. Without mother, there is no communication and no love.

Communication

We are story-tellers and historians. Our cultures the world over reflect events re-told in song, in drawings, in books, papers, diaries, and in everyday speech. Why is this narrative history so important to us? The success of humankind probably rests on developed ability to 'share the load', learn and teach again how best to protect ourselves and our children. We don't have to re-invent the wheel. The immense success of the internet is just the latest tool we've developed to support our basic need to communicate.

Do we communicate because we are basically a vulnerable species? Looked at in terms of physiological strength, we are weak. Looked at in terms of how we can communicate, we are powerful. Our communication skills are crucial in bringing up our children. Of all creatures, we humans have the most vulnerable babies. Experts note that our children are, in fact, born 'too soon', physically immature but with a head large enough to contain the brainworks that makes us the best communicators in the world. Our vulnerable children need help to find themselves in space and in loving arms. This primes our brains for everything else. Walking, talking, math, and reading–all derive from the first senses of being held, attentively, by mom. Senses underlie understanding of them–which is all that math and reading are, an extension via thinking of walking and talking! And because our children are so physically vulnerable, our human bonds of love for our children depend heavily on the senses that underpin communication. Voice, touch, and playful movement all conspire to make a child and his mother a pair.

So, speech (and the development of the language process) requires to be securely based on all other forms of communication in order for use as a social tool. Some experts suggest that speech delays–and perhaps even cognitive disorders–may be linked to a child's not having access to a fully enriched communicative environment at critical points in his or her development. Research also predicts that a child who 'gets' social cues develops language skills more easily. Speech is far more than the naming of parts. It's about claiming a place in a discussion–and that's how it is from the first gaze of a mother and baby to the last handclasp of a grownup child and a dying mother.

I share my mother's taste in most things, art and literature in particular. My mother was an artist, a painter. But while I am not without creative talent completely I do not have her gift in my hands. This talent does not predominate in the genes that I inherited. A short time before my mother died in 1997 we had our last visit together. I sat, as I always did, on her bed before retiring and we talked. We held hands. With both of our hands clasped together. Hers old, lined and fragile and mine middle aged with the beginnings marks of lines. I belonged in this place, with this mother of mine. Our hands tied together not by bonds of heredity but by the bonds of kinship and family.

~Mary Hart

Separation: Voices Lost

For our adopted children, what does being separate mean? Separated from mother, placed in care, with multiple caregivers and multiple placements? How does this affect speech and language development? How does it affect social development, and communication skills? How does it affect capacity to love and accept love?

Children who've become separated from their mother in the first six to nine months of life have not just lost their mother; they have lost part of themselves. We noted that the human child is born immature, and has no 'self' other than the mother. It's only when the child finds 'self' reflected in the communicative gestures that are the foundation of normal mother/child relationships that allow healthy baby separation. The game, the dance, the sweet eye-contact and the kisses-with-baby-words tell the baby that someone else (and she is an important else) thinks 'this baby' is a wonderful partner. It's an invitation to dance,

The New Language of Toys, Teaching Communication Skills to Children With Special Needs, a Guide for Parents and Teachers,
By Sue Schwartz, PhD and Joan E. Heller Miller, EdM

This book talks about language by developmental ages, possible causes of language delay, recognizing early speech and language problems, and playing and learning. Filled with easy parent-child activities that involve very basic toys. It explains each activity in detail and gives examples of dialogue to use with the child. For post-institutionalized children, start with the birth to 12 months section regardless of your child's age. Post-institutionalized children missed the interactive, developmental play that is key to language development, and would benefit by building on the earlier activities in the book.

and psychologists Dan Hughes and Dan Siegal endorse this. We learn our worth and how to navigate the world from the reciprocal bow, and the act of 'dancing' with our mothers.

What does it do to a baby to find that voice gone? Quite simply, experts believe it is the end of the world as that baby thought the world was. And more, what does it do to a baby to find her mother 'there' but angry and depressed? If the mother is 'there' but unable to meet the child's needs (food and eye contact, nutrition of the body and the soul), the child will inevitably become depressed (because she is still part of the mother), and communication between them regarding the baby's needs will fail.

This is essentially the basis of 'failure to thrive' in children where communication systems fail, and the child cannot get needs met, neither emotionally nor physically. Without eye-contact, without interactive play, without food, smell from the expected mother, the child's interest in developing communication wanes.

How many of us 'know' our adoptive children in this description? We adoptive parents often parent children who have lost or never known the joy of communication. How do we repair this gap? Can we? We do it by 'learning' our children as we would have if we were their birthparents. Our difference? We learn our kids, we learn their loss and we parent the combination. We reach out with all the senses that underpin communication and ask our children into our arms. We ask them if they'll let us help them belong. Claiming the right to parent a child with profound loss (which all adoptive children have), doesn't mean we are there to remove their loss or right to grieve it. We are there to help our children bear it, which they can do through the security of knowing us, being held by us, and communicating with us. And we can give them back a sense of understanding of their past, by talking and sharing our thoughts on their loss, and listening to their thoughts right back.

Creating a Communication Environment

Many of us have wonderful adoption video and pictures. When we re-watch them later how many of us are forced to rethink what is happening there, and how our child is feeling and reacting to us?

For many children, the handover or first meeting is fearful. The child meets us. He peeps from behind known caregivers (perhaps the care isn't good, but it's the familiar, and the norm for our child). We are happy, we smile, and we outstretch our arms. Yet, the child's gaze may avert from us, or lock gaze with the caregiver. Our kids are using their whole body to say no, I am not yours. *And that's where we must start our work as parents.*

Whether our child becomes ours as a baby, a small child or a school-age child, it's a new start. We are, parent and child, born to each other that day. It's our job as responsible adoptive parents, to begin again the Dance of Attunement that might have/should have begun at birth, with mother and child together. Except we are dancing our child to a broken tune, and it's our job to take that on and make our dance positively swing. It's only through this new dance, say psychologists Dan Hughes and Dan Siegal, that adoptive parents can link to their child. It's only by learning how our child feels that we can gently reconnect the damaged connections our child brings to us from abandonment, loss of first family, and first mother.

Playing together, reading together, talking together is powerful. It allows us precious time and space in which to play and come to know each other. Later on it allows us to open the dialogue more comfortably about the tough topics of adoption, race, and feelings. We need to learn how and when our child likes to talk, play, learn, and communicate. Different children have different styles, and so do parents.

> There is no use in addressing any one of our children's issues; we need an umbrella approach, covering and supporting all. Communication is more than 'just' speech or language. It is fundamental interaction with our environment and the people in it. And communication ability which moves outward from the mother/child interaction and the secure bond that forms there–is the gateway to the world.
> ~ *Sheena Macrae*

This learning curve is the basis of attunement to the child's communicative needs. It's our job to appreciate how our child needs parenting, and to get out of our comfort zone and accommodate them.

- Buy them great art materials, and sit with them as they draw–even if we can't draw.
- Listen to tapes while walking together, or simply talk when walking if you are a bookworm and your child loves to move!
- Sit with your child if they are a couch potato and love TV: don't condemn it all of the time, instead discuss it. Buy books associated with programs, buy music, do drawings.
- Practice being the animals in films which is great fun for budding actors! When your child grows up, make films together. Or sit and watch theirs!
- Make journals; bind your children's drawings and stories. Work on it together.
- Work on your child's Lifebook together.
- Create a family history and include your child's 'notable deeds'. Funny words, funny stories, and achievements become the fabric of your family.

When Communication is Difficult...

What of the child who resists contact? Who won't allow touch, who doesn't 'hear' voice and who certainly doesn't permit eye contact? A sector within attachment theory and therapy is predicated in the fact that certain children who have suffered loss and trauma may often use standard modes of communication as barriers against being cared for by a new person. They may defy, avert from eye-contact, may not hear, and every attempt at touch is resisted as if we are abusing them. They may have sensory problems as well as attach-

Baby Signs

We used a small set of 25 signs with all three of our daughters. I am a definite believer in the power of communication –to which signing is an amazing tool. We still use some of our basic signs to 'remind' our daughters when necessary (e.g. thank you, please, eat, more, toilet...)

Here's a list of the signs we found most useful, with those that were particularly helpful when our youngest daughter came home from China at the top of the list. Most of our signs surround eating/food. This is the time that we found was most urgent for all three girls to be able to communicate with us. Best way to go about it was to introduce only one or two signs each week. This way we were able to learn and remember the signs too!

More–this is by far the best sign we taught!

Eat

Please

Water

Milk

Tired/Sleep

All done

Full

I Love You

Thank You

Book

Apple

Bottle

Cookie

Strawberry

Sing/Song

Diaper

Father

Mother

Toilet

French Fry

Friend

A good book on baby signs is:

Baby Signs: How to Talk with Your Child Before Your Child Can Talk By Linda Acredolo, Susan Goodwyn, Douglas Abrams

~ *Karen Freed, adoptive mom*

ment problems. These children may have been neglected children and they have resisted being social because they trust only themselves. How do we give them the essential help to become social? *We work to understand what caused their withdrawal from sociability and work to engage via all communications channels–from a handclap to a hug and onto words...until our child responds.*

And what of the traumatized, inward turning child? The child for whom the transition to our family triggers fear based in the changes and loss in their short lives before us? How do we help these children communicate with us? What of the child whose language is delayed beyond the developmental delay expected in post-institutionalized children? Or a child whose history includes multiple caregivers? And what of the child who hugs too hard, or falls up the stairs or hates to swing or swim? *We work to understand what may underpin these delays, and work to engage the child in 'just' the appropriate but ever-changing load of sensory input from the external world. We–as responsible parents–need to discover how our child is able to process this. It's what we do with the finding that makes the difference!*

New and exciting research suggests that trauma impacts on a child across all the senses, not just the emotional plane of feeling. A hurt child, quite literally, withdraws inside himself and is unable to communicate or make her body work in space. To restore the child to a level closer to age-appropriate capacity for communication and movement, it's thought the child must be re-stepped through all the stages of motor (physical) and emotional development that were halted with the onset of trauma. A child trapped in a trauma bond at under a year old may sometimes behave and move as a baby, even at age five or six or seven or eight. *It is our job as parents to help our child know the world via their senses–otherwise they cannot know it with their minds.*

So, what do we do to help, reach and comfort a traumatized child, the child with attachment bonds that are broken? Research suggests that a child (pre-birth and post-birth for up to nine months) is regulated totally by its mother. Sensory experiences are modulated by her. The bond that is formed post birth between them through the senses (touch, voice, smell, balance, and gaze) is also modulated hormonally, via the hormone oxytocin, the hormone of 'love'. The bond is based on trust. Take that essential contact and bonding away, and a child cannot move from the neurologically primed response which freezes a child in the face of fear. They have no capacity to do anything other than feel the fear. They have no fear reflex, which alerts, and gives capacity to move, seek and check the fearful stimulus. How many of us see our children stuck, unable to do other than feel the fear when they first come home?

Can we adoptive parents remedy this? Can our being available and close, work for our hurt kids? Yes, because we don't aim to replace people, but simply become the loving hands that will hold our child safely, the loving voice that will help our children rest. We are not usurping a place, but simply filling a void with feeling, words, and touch.

Communication: Building Love

The way forward is to recreate for the child the comfort and closeness of the mother and child that was their birthright as children born into this world. That's love, basically. We can attempt to re-modulate these hurt children by recreating the bonding movements. Some of us may use various forms of therapy, some of us may not, but we all need to get close to our children to 'reach them'. To achieve this balanced mix of love we'll use: eye contact, voice contact, touch, smell, and movement. Find these in rocking, cradling, lifting, swinging, gazing, talking, singing, touching, and listening to our children. Therapists may suggest very specific techniques to achieve this (even for older children) by using slings, ball ponds, womb-like spaces and more to create closeness between mother and child. We can learn interventions that re-create a close and rich sensory bond for our children.

For little kids, peek-a-boo games introduce eye contact, the fact that mom is still there and the notion of permanence. Mom holding a kid trying to walk/ride a bike is another: mother is the model for the child who is not quite built for a task yet! Board games are communication tools and involve turn taking, a prerequisite of social dialogue. Ball games are a dance of partners. Team sport is an extension of board games; kids learn that dependency is a worthy tool and makes us humans stronger. Camp fire songs draw together soul-mates. We can do all of these interventions in some way or other from babyhood to teens. We become the mothers and parents of our children, parenting the child and all the losses they bring with them.

Using these tools, we balance the child and permit real and psychological movement out from mother, as our child checks back with us for regulation and approval, that's communication. And when we smile and they smile back...that is love.

~ Sheena Macrae, PhD has loved how words work since she can remember. Her first degree covered language and literature, her PhD took her to the nuts and bolts of language, language acquisition, and change. Her adopted children have taught her the power of communication—and how international adoption can affect language development.

How to Find a Speech-Language Pathologist or Audiologist

American Speech-Language Hearing Association
www.asha.org

American Academy of Audiology
www.audiology.org

Canadian Association of Speech-Language Pathologists and Audiologists
www.caslpa.ca

(UK) Association of Speech and Language Therapists in Independent Practice
www.helpwithtalking.com

Speech Pathology Australia
www.speechpathologyaustralia.org.au

~ *Karen E. Pollock, PhD, CCC-SLP*

Language
When Our Kids Come Home
By Mark Sebba, DPhil

A Sea of Babble?

Imagine you have spoken one language all your life. Suddenly, without warning, you find yourself in a new environment, where your language is not spoken and only barely understood. What is more, you are expected to understand and use the language of this new place. People keep speaking to you in it, and expecting you to respond. How would you feel? Uncomfortable? Bewildered? Panicky?

This scenario is what actually happens to many children who are adopted internationally. So is this what a child experiences, when abruptly placed in a new language environment where his or her first language is not used at all? Bewilderment and panic?

Not necessarily. There is one big difference between the adult and the child. The child is developmentally designed to learn language, and has a special sensitivity to all aspects of human language: the intonation, the sounds that make it up, the grammatical structure, the words. Although there is some disagreement about whether there is a critical age at which this language-learning ability is lost, it is very clear that a two year-old is good at learning language in a way that a 32 year-old is not.

To a child who is 18 months or three years-old, encountering a new language is not a problem. If they are exposed to it sufficiently and have a reason to want to learn it, they will learn it. What is unusual and almost unique to the situation of international adoption, is that just as the new language arrives on the scene, support for the first language abruptly stops. In other words, instead of learning a new language at the same time as being able to use and continue developing the first, the child is immersed in a new language but can't use the old language to communicate. *These children are not just trans-nationally adopted; they are 'trans-linguistically' adopted.*

Change Equals Problems?

Will the sudden change of language cause communicative and development problems for an internationally adopted child? When I adopted my daughter in China at age 14 months, I was prepared for her to be behind other children who had been learning English from birth, at least for the first year or so–perhaps longer.

My daughter started to use English words within a few weeks of arriving. She romped ahead; by age two she was making simple sentences and had a vocabulary at least as broad as other two year olds; at two and a half she began to attract remarks from parents and daycare staff to the effect that her language was very good for her age. Now at five, she has excellent verbal skills–no longer so outstanding among other five year olds, but still impressive.

What Research Says

From research and from my own daughter I learned that it is a mistake to assume that there will be a problem.

For many children the switch from birth language to second primary language won't be a long-term problem. Professor Karen Pollock, in some fairly large-scale studies of children adopted from China into North American homes, has shown that by and large, the children do not have more speech development problems than the general population. In fact as a group, they tend to do better than average–in one study of 55 preschool age adoptees, 27% were classed as 'high scoring' and the great majority performed at or above average. Rather than accounting for poor performance, the researchers have been driven to explain why so many of the children did so well in their tests.

Research on children adopted from Eastern Europe gives a somewhat different picture. Early reports of international adoptions from this region indicated a high incidence of speech and language development problems–up to 60% in one study. Sharon Glennen, a specialist in language development, who is herself the mother of two children adopted from Russia, reports that in her recent study of 28 newly adopted children from Eastern Europe, 'most of the children did well, with average English language standard scores within normal limits'; nevertheless about a third of this group of children had problems and were recommended for speech and language early intervention. Another recent study by Glennen of 46 children, ages six to nine adopted from Eastern Europe as babies, showed that about 11% were regarded as having speech or language impairment, even several years after adoption.

Sharon Glennen relates developmental delays directly to the conditions in the institutions where the children live. When adopting her own daughter, she was able to spend eight days observing life in a Russian orphanage. Although the conditions there were good in many respects, with the physical needs of the children well catered for, there were few opportunities provided for interaction with their caregivers or older children. Caregivers worked shifts and changed frequently; older toddlers ate independently at small tables; younger children were given help with feeding but caregivers

rarely talked to them. When children were talked to, it was typically in the form of simple commands such as "come here", "sit down", and "don't do that". Under such conditions, it is not surprising that children would experience delays in language development.

Outcomes

It is important to keep this in perspective, however. 'Delay' may just mean a 'late start'; it does not necessarily mean an ongoing deficit. My own daughter was 'late' learning to walk; on the day of her adoption, at 14 months, she could only walk with assistance. Two days later, when we visited the children's home, we quickly realized why: though the building was light and airy, it was quite cramped, and the children were confined to their own rooms or a short corridor. There was simply no where to walk! Six weeks later, in her new home and with lots of opportunities to practice, she took her first independent steps. Likewise, if children have lacked linguistic stimulation, they can and often do catch up. After adoption, as the majority of children receive the kind of interaction they need in order to develop language normally, most have no ongoing language problems. In some cases, early problems do not resolve themselves and a proportion of children continue to experience problems after starting school. Two big questions come out of this for the adoptive parent:
1. What can I do to give my child the best chance of normal language development?
2. How do I know if something is wrong and my child needs to be assessed by a therapist?

What Can I Do to Help My Child's Language Learning?

If our children lacked (among other things) linguistic stimulation for the first year or two of life, let's create a stimulating language environment for them.
- Talk to them.
- Interact verbally as much as we can.
- Provide them with lots of interesting play activities, using lots of talk.
- Build on their existing communication skills, which are not dependent on any particular language.

Attaining Bilingualism

If you are able to keep your child in touch with his or her original first language, it is more likely to help than to harm. Being able to communicate through the original language might give him some extra confidence in the early stages and the child is unlikely to be confused learning two languages.

It is not possible to say exactly how much exposure to each language a child needs to become fluent in two languages, but unfortunately, it is clear that the limited time many parents can provide in the first language are not enough. This is not to say that there would be no benefits, but do not be surprised or disappointed if your child seems to make very little progress in their original first language.

If support for the original first language continues at a high level, your child may eventually become a true bilingual. There is evidence that bilingualism has benefits–educational, social, and possibly cognitive. At least in theory, some of these benefits may result even if your child has only a limited knowledge of his or her original first language.

When to Seek Help

The finding that most children make an easy and fairly quick transition to their new language is good news, but it's of great importance for another reason. It means that where children are having difficulties or appear to be adapting very slowly to the new language, we should not assume that this is due to the change of language. Where a child has had normal language development in a first language, the second language should come relatively easily. If it does not, this may be a sign of a more basic language learning problem, which has probably affected the first language as well.

When a child is transplanted from one language environment to another, some degree of delay in learning the new language is inevitable. No one could learn dozens or hundreds of new words overnight, let alone a new set of grammar rules. So how long should we wait before deciding that the child is having difficulties that would warrant checking out with a speech and language therapist?

As a very rough rule of thumb, children adopted at 18 months or less might need six months to a year to catch up, and children adopted at over 18 months might need one to two years. Where speech is concerned, by three years of age, most children adopted trans-linguistically as infants or toddlers are at more or less the same level as their monolingual peers.

If you suspect a problem, consult a speech and language therapist who is knowledge-able about internationally adopted children, and provide them with as much background information as you can obtain. To decide whether or not a child has a language delay, a speech and language therapist has to carry out an assessment. The only valid assessment for a child who has just arrived in an English-speaking country from China or Russia, for example, is one based on other children who have only just begun to learn English as a new language. An 18 month old recent adoptee cannot perform in English the same as an 18 month old who has been exposed to English all his or her life, and Early Intervention workers who assess new arrivals may not always be aware of this. Assessment should be done in the first language if at all possible.

Remember, if a child has had normal language development in a first language, the second language should come relatively easily. If it does not, this could be a sign of a more basic language learning problem, which probably also affected the first language. Seek help with therapists who understand your child's circumstances.

~ Mark Sebba, DPhil.
is Reader in Sociolinguistics and Language Contact at Lancaster University, England.
He has a doctorate in Linguistics from the University of York.
His interest in the language development of transnationally adopted children
stems from the fact that he is father to two Chinese adopted children.

Saying Very Little~My Experiences with Language

We brought Joanna home from Shenzhen, PRC at age 27 months. Before we brought her home in May 1997, I heard one of the top international adoption doctors, Dr Jeri Ann Jenista, give a talk on development delays. Dr. Jenista said that for every year a child was in institutional care, it took about four months to get caught up; some children never catch up. So, we had Joanna tested for language and physical capacity when she was 29 months old and the results showed her receptive language was at the level 'of an 18 month-old' with expressive language at the level 'of a 15 month-old' child. She walked like a 15 month-old and only weighed 19.5 lbs. We received speech and physical therapy administered by the county school system. The special services we received were top notch. I could not have been more pleased–and it was all free!

Joanna said very little and the words came slowly. How did we help her? We used lots of expressive body language in our conversations and she responded accordingly; she is my little actress! Her speech therapist came once a week and played games with puzzles, play-dough, shapes, and colors. She knew her colors before the kids across the street and they were not adopted.

One day I was putting laundry away. I can't remember exactly how old she was, but she was able to string two words together and had just started to put three words together. I asked her to carry her clean shirt to her room (I had a full basket). She threw it down and said 'Dirty'. I handed it to her and said, "It is clean. Let's put it in your drawer." She threw it down, "Dirty". After three times of this I said "OK, I'm putting these things away. You can help me if you want to come." She didn't come for a minute or two. Then she appeared behind me with the shirt and said (in the same tone of voice her older brother often used with me), *"OK, OK, OK! You dribum (are driving) me nuts*!" I almost fell over! Where would she have heard that? The words were starting to come–and we still say "you dribum me nuts!"

Joanna's speech therapy ended after first grade. She didn't need it. However I was concerned that her reading skills were not what they should be. As she learned to read, she often made up her own words. I don't mean that she just said the wrong words; I mean she made up words for the ones she didn't know. We called them 'Joanna words' and she thought that was really funny. My son had a lot of funny words as a toddler, but Joanna had a book full. She liked reading and didn't want to slow down. She didn't slow down to 'chunk' the words–as the teachers call sounding out the syllables–just racing over them. It dawned on me somewhere along the way that she was learning to read just like she learned to talk, using words as she thought they were, right or wrong. Now age 10, a pupil mentor in an English as a Second Language Class, and two straight As on her report card–I realize she has caught up as Dr Jennista suggested. But I miss her funny words!

~ By Jane Mulliken, adoptive mom

Top Ten Tips
For Speech and Language Acquisition in Internationally Adopted Children
By Karen E. Pollock, PhD, CCC-SLP

Parents of internationally adopted children often have questions or concerns about their children's speech and language development. Our children have a unique experience with language learning–with an abrupt loss of exposure to their birth language and simultaneous onset of exposure to their new language. They are unlike other groups of language learners–they are clearly not monolingual, but they are also not bilingual because they are not acquiring or maintaining two languages at the same time. They are also not like most ESL (English as a Second Language) learners, because they often do not yet have a solid developmental base in their birth language, due to their young age and/or delays resulting from insufficient language stimulation in orphanage care. In fact, their language learning situation is so unique that researchers on the topic have coined a new term, '**second first language acquisition**.'

So, what should parents of second first language learners expect in terms of speech and language development? When should we be concerned, and how do we go about getting professional help? Here are my Top Ten Tips for ensuring your child's speech and language needs are met:

1. Don't Panic.
The odds are in your favor. Several recent independent studies of children adopted from China and Eastern Europe have found that although there is considerable variability during the early months post-adoption, after one or two years in their permanent homes the vast majority of children adopted as infants or toddlers are performing at or above age level on tests of English language proficiency. This good news suggests that given sufficient exposure to English in a stimulating, language-rich environment, most internationally adopted children will become competent speakers of English in a remarkably short period of time.

2. Be Proactive.
Even though there is a good likelihood that your child will eventually achieve normal English speech-language abilities, most parents are not content to sit back and wait to see what happens. Many of us waited a long time to become parents, and are eager to give our children all of the support we can to help them compensate for any early deficiencies. We also know that it is better to identify and address problems early than to waste precious time that could/should have been spent providing critical early intervention. You can do a lot by making your home a language-rich environment. For example, talk to your child about what you are doing and where you are going. Repeat and expand upon what your child says, and read to your child (at a level appropriate to their interest and attention span). Many parents have found baby signs (simple gestures used to represent words and ideas) useful as a way of reinforcing early communication skills and acting as a bridge to spoken words.

Parent training programs for enhancing children's language are also available in many communities. In addition, some families take advantage of opportunities for more structured early intervention programs. In most areas, our children qualify for early intervention because they are 'at-risk' for speech-language and other developmental delays. Most early intervention is family-focused, and will also provide you with techniques for facilitating and supporting speech-language development at home.

3. Get a Hearing Test.

All internationally adopted children should have their hearing tested as soon as possible after returning home. Consider it comparable to the newborn hearing screenings that are routinely done before children are sent home from the hospital. Good hearing is essential to speech and language development, and you want to know that your child is beginning this task with all of the necessary tools. In addition, the first step in any evaluation of speech-language concerns is a hearing test to rule out poor hearing.

   Speech-language pathologists can 'screen' for normal hearing through a variety of conditioned behavioral response methods (such as turning towards a sound source, or dropping a block in a bucket in response to hearing a tone). But if your child does not respond to such methods, or if they do not pass the screening, follow up with more in-depth testing by a qualified audiologist. In the early months home, some children may not respond to behavioral testing methods, due to stranger anxiety or a lack of understanding of what is being asked. Audiologists have other objective ways of ruling out hearing loss that do not require a behavioral response.

4. Trust Your Instincts.

If you have concerns about your child's communication abilities, act on them. Don't be overly influenced by other parent's experiences, or put off by well-meaning physicians or family members who tell you to just give it more time. Parents are known to be very reliable reporters of their children's speech-language difficulties. After all, you know your child better than anyone else. If you have difficulty understanding their communication attempts, or think that their abilities are not up to par, seek professional help.

5. See a Qualified Speech-Language Pathologist for an Evaluation.

Although you may want to first discuss your concerns with your child's doctor, recognize that not all pediatricians and medical personnel are familiar with or have experience in assessing speech-language development. If you have concerns, seek an evaluation from a qualified speech-language pathologist (SLP), more commonly referred to as a speech-language therapist (SLT) in the UK. You do not need a physician's referral to see an SLP although you may need to go through your local health care system unless you are paying with private funds. Ask for recommendations through your local school district or health authority, or use one of the searchable databases on the websites for national organizations of speech-language pathologists and audiologists (see page 40).

   The type of evaluation the SLP conducts should vary according to both the age of your child and the length of his/her exposure to English. For example, assessments during the first month or two home should focus on universal (and not English-specific) aspects of communication:

* Does a newly arrived 10-month-old vocalize to get the attention of an adult?
* Does s/he babble repetitive strings of syllables such as ba-ba or da-da-da-da?

- Does a newly arrived 16-month-old imitate simple gestures, such as clapping hands, or push away unwanted objects?

These types of communication skills, which are not specific to the language being learned, are most predictive of newly arrived children's language development status. Over the next year, as the child has more and more exposure to English, it may be possible to estimate the number of different words the child understands or says and compare them to preliminary norms for children adopted at similar ages from Eastern Europe and China. Keeping a record of these vocabulary estimates over time will also give an idea of the rate of change, which may also be predictive. By two years (or perhaps even after one year) post-adoption, commonly-used speech and language tests developed for and 'normed' on monolingual English speaking children can be used, although they should still be interpreted with caution.

6. Be Prepared to 'Inform' The Professionals.

Do not be surprised if you know more about speech and language development in internationally adopted children than your speech-language pathologist (SLP). This statement is not meant to insult my professional colleagues. Research on this population is still in its infancy, and most SLPs have not received any formal training in how to assess or treat 'second first language' learners. Results of early studies are beginning to appear in our professional journals, but best practice guidelines for assessment and intervention with our children are not yet widely available. Internationally adoptive parents are highly educated and dedicated parents who seek information from a variety of sources, and have an extensive network for sharing that information. So you may have access to new information before they do. If your SLP does not have extensive experience with assessing internationally adopted children (and remember, they are different from bilingual and ESL children), share with them copies of articles on the topic, or refer them to the relevant websites. Armed with these additional resources, they will be able to work with you to properly interpret assessment results and make appropriate recommendations.

7. Learn as Much as You Can About Your Child's Communication Development.

One critical piece of information that is often missing when our children are brought to an SLP for an evaluation is what their communication abilities were like in their birth language. Not knowing how their development was progressing in the birth language makes it more difficult for SLPs to determine whether a child is likely to catch up on their own, or require speech-language therapy. If at all possible, try to get as much information as you can by interviewing their caretakers or sending a translated list of questions to their orphanage. Recognize that not all attempts to obtain such information will be successful, however, due to time constraints and/or level of cooperation of orphanage staff.

Another alternative might be to have an assessment conducted in the birth language after arrival. The feasibility of this option depends on the availability of a native speaker (in the child's local dialect) and the extent to which the newly arrived child is comfortable interacting with strangers. In addition, because attrition is rapid, in order to get an accurate picture of the child's abilities any assessment in the birth language should be conducted within the first few weeks home.

8. Don't Assume that all Problems are Adoption-Related.

No doubt many of our children are at risk for speech and language disorders due to less-than-ideal stimulation in orphanages or other related developmental delays or medical issues. But it is a mistake to assume that all of our children's difficulties with English are due to the fact that they were adopted. For example, I've been asked more than once if a child's difficulty with the /r/ sound is due to them not hearing /r/ during first year of life, because /r/ was not present in their birth language. I point out that difficulties with /r/ are also quite common in monolingual English-speaking children, and many do not master it until eight or nine years of age. In fact, most of the speech sound errors that internationally adopted children make are common developmental errors.

Internationally adopted children are difficult to assess because of their late onset of English exposure, but if all else is developing normally they should make the switch to English with relatively little difficulty. However, somewhere between two and eight percent of all children have developmental speech and language disorders, regardless of whether or not they were adopted or switched languages midstream. If your child is not progressing steadily, consider the possibility that there may be a problem and seek help.

9. Be Prepared to Advocate for Needed Services.

Our internationally adopted children are often caught in the cracks of eligibility for speech-language services. For example, I know of school-aged children who were denied speech-language services because they were viewed by the school system as ESL learners. Because a pre-adoption assessment in the birth language was not conducted, there was no proof that they had a more basic, underlying language deficit that would qualify them for speech-language services. Another common example are preschoolers who are too old for early intervention services, but whose problem is not severe enough to make them eligible for other special programs prior to entering the school system. Parents should be prepared to advocate for services, if necessary with the assistance of a private practitioner.

10. Take Time to Enjoy Your Child's Development.

It's easy to get caught up in the day-to-day concerns about whether or not your child is progressing adequately, or if they are getting enough of the right kind of help. Too often we forget to sit back and watch the miracle of a young child discovering the joy of communication and its power. Jot down those cute little mispronunciations, made-up words, and ungrammatical attempts at sentences, and marvel at the adaptability and resiliency of our children, who really do 'say the darndest things!'

Karen E. Pollock is a Professor and Chair of the Department of Speech Pathology and Audiology at the University of Alberta in Edmonton, Canada. She is also a single parent to a 7-yr-old daughter adopted from China and a 12-yr old biological son. For the past five years, she has been actively involved in the conduct of research on speech and language development in children adopted from China. Recently, she has expanded her work to include children adopted from other non-English-speaking countries, such as Haiti. Karen has presented the results of her work at both professional conferences and parent support group meetings, and published in academic journals as well as adoption support group newsletters.

Your Child's Language Development:
Evaluating Pre- and Newly- Adopted Babies and Toddlers
What's Normal? What's Delayed?
By Sharon Glennen, PhD, CCC-SLP

Verbal and Non-Verbal Behavior

Between the age of 12 to 24 months, children begin to say their first words. By age 24 months, normally developing children are expected to produce a minimum of 50 words and to put two or more words together in simple phrases. Children raised in orphanages rarely meet these developmental milestones. Parents should not be surprised to learn that their 18 to 20 month old child hasn't begun to talk. Nonverbal social interactions, unlike spoken language abilities, appear to be less affected by the orphanage environment. Parents of children under 24 months of age should focus closely on nonverbal social interaction skills. As children reach age 30 months, some words should begin to emerge. A child who is not talking at all by two and a half years of age may have additional factors suppressing language development that need to be considered.

If videotapes of the child are available in the orphanage, or if parents are able to meet the child, then questions should be supplemented with observations. Children at this age typically do not interact well with strangers or in new situations. (My own two adopted toddlers followed this scenario. During our first interactions, one sat stone-still in my lap like a passive lump, the other screamed every time we came near). Children this age should be videotaped interacting with an adult caregiver whom they know well, in a room they know best.

Parents meeting children for the first time should later ask to watch the child interacting with well-known adult caregivers, also in a room that is familiar to the child. Luckily for my children, we had previously seen videotapes of them interacting with familiar adult caregivers and knew their reactions to us were based on the fact that we were total strangers. In addition to being with familiar caregivers in a familiar room, children tend to talk more when playing with toys or objects that are familiar. Children should be observed or videotaped playing with toys or objects that they know; when children this age are introduced to new toys they tend to spend most of their time exploring what the toy will do, and spend less time interacting with others. Questions for adoptive parents to ask, or skills to observe:

Children 12 to 18 Months

Eye-gaze and Facial Expressions

- Does the child make frequent eye contact with adults during interactions?
- Does the child show signs of enjoying interactions with a familiar adult, especially when eye contact is made?
- When another person begins to talk, does the child turn towards the new voice?
- Does the child make 3-point gaze shifts by looking at a toy in hand, then at an adult, then back to the toy?
- If more people are in the room, does the child make 4-point gaze shifts by looking from a toy in hand to one person, then the other, then back to the toy?

Reaching and Gestures

- Does the child show objects in hand to an adult (without actually giving them)?
- Does the child push away unwanted items?
- Does the child engage in give and take games when holding objects?

- Does the child imitate simple gestures such as clapping hands or waving bye-bye?
- Will the child hand an object to an adult to ask for help with it?
- For children closer to 18 months, does the child shake his or her head "no"?

Play with Objects

- Does the child attempt to actively explore toys? Does the child push or spin parts of toys, turn toys over, roll them back and forth?
- Does the child repeat interesting actions with toys? If the child makes a toy produce an unusual noise, does he attempt to make the noise again?
- Can the child imitate simple play activities? If an adult bangs two blocks together, will the child try to imitate?
- Does the child know what to do with objects used on a daily basis? When given a spoon or cup does the child attempt to feed himself? When putting on clothes does the child begin to lift his arms in anticipation of a shirt going on?

Language Comprehension

- Does the child turn when his or her name is called? (This skill is often delayed in children raised in groups because it takes longer for children to sort out which name is theirs.)
- Does the child momentarily stop what he is doing if an adult says "no" in a firm voice?
- Does the child follow simple commands such as "sit down" or "come here" without adding gestures to the commands?
- Can the child identify two-three common everyday objects or body parts when asked "Where is _____?" (Make sure the child has frequently seen the items on a daily basis, for example: 'shoes, cup, spoon'. Don't use items such as a 'ball' if the child has rarely played with one).

Spoken Language Production

Of all areas of language development, this will most likely be delayed in children raised in orphanages. Children raised in orphanages will probably not be using words by this age.

- Does the child vocalize communicatively to get attention, to ask for help, to ask for a toy or food?
- Does the child vocalize in response to an adult's talking?
- Does the child stop vocalizing when an adult is talking?
- Does the child try to imitate adult words or vocalizations?
- Are several different consonant sounds heard during vocalizations?
- For children who are using gestures, does the child pair vocalizations with gesture attempts?
- Does the child look at an adult when vocalizing to communicate?

Oral Motor and Feeding Abilities

- Does the child eat from a spoon? When eating, does the child's lips close around the spoon to clear the food?
- Does the child eat and enjoy foods with soft textures that don't require chewing? (oatmeal, yogurt, mashed potatoes)
- Does the child eat and enjoy foods that require a little chewing such as soft cookies, overcooked pasta, rice, or bananas?
- For children closer to 18 months, does the child try foods that require more chewing such as bread, cheese, or soft meats such as sausage?
- When sitting at rest, does the child keep his mouth closed or is the mouth frequently open? If the child has a cold or allergies, the mouth needs to be open to allow the child to breathe and the child will drool more than normal. If the child doesn't have allergies or a cold, the mouth should be closed most of the time.

Children 18-24 Months

Children this age should do most of the items listed above plus the following:

Eye-gaze and Facial Expressions
- If an adult points to an item across the room and says "look" does the child follow the adult's point to see what is being pointed to?

Reaching and Gestures
- Does the child point with a finger to communicate?
- Does the child use a variety of gestures to communicate?
- Does the child consistently vocalize when producing gestures?
- Does the child wave "hello" or "bye-bye"?
- Does the child take an adult by the hand and lead them to things?

Play with Objects
- Does the child attempt simple pretend play actions such as stirring spoons in cups, pretending to eat, or pretending to clean up?

Language Comprehension
- Does the child appear to understand 50 or more words?
- Can the child point to body parts when asked "Where is your eyes, nose, mouth?"
- As the child nears 24 months, can the child follow a 2-object command such as "Give me the block and spoon?"

Spoken Language Production
- Is the child attempting to say any words?
- Does the child attempt to imitate words such as "bye-bye"?

Oral Motor and Feeding Abilities
- Does the child feed him or herself?
- Does the child readily eat and enjoy foods that require some chewing such as bread, sausage, or cheese?

Children 24-30 Months

Children this age should do most of the items listed above plus the following:

Reaching and Gestures
- Does the child shake his head to indicate yes and no?

Play with Objects
- Does the child attempt two and three part sequences of pretend play? Can the child stir a spoon in a teapot, pour tea into a cup, then pretend to drink the tea?

Language Comprehension
- Does the child appear to understand most simple sentences and commands?
- Can the child identify a variety of objects in the room and body parts?
- Can the child follow a command that requires getting objects out of sight? For example if asked to "go get your shoes" can the child go to another room and bring them back?

Spoken Language Production
- Can the child say 10 or more words?
- Is the child beginning to put two or more words together into phrases?
- Ask for examples of the child's three longest sentences. Write them down with translations.
- If the child is putting three to four words together into sentences, is the child adding any grammatical markers like verb tense, plurals, or articles?

Oral Motor and Feeding Abilities
- Can the child self-feed from a regular cup without difficulty?

Sharon Glennen, PhD, CCC-SLP is the Department Chair of Audiology, Speech Language Pathology & Deaf Studies at Towson University. Dr. Glennen is the parent of three children, the two youngest adopted as toddlers from Russia.

Listed skills are based on several sources including Rosetti (1990), Wetherby and Prizant (2002), and Glennen and Masters (2002).

Language and the Older Adopted Child
Understanding Second Language Learning
by Sharon Glennen, PhD, CCC-SLP

Older internationally adopted children undergo the same changes in language and culture as younger adopted infants and toddlers. The key difference is that younger children have several years to develop English before beginning school. In contrast, most older adopted children have to begin school soon after arriving home. They are presented with the complex task of learning academic skills in a language they don't initially speak or understand.

One issue that clouds the language learning process for older children is the notion of bilingualism. Internationally adopted children are often considered to be bilingual when in reality they are not. Bilingual language learners are learning to speak two languages. Some children are exposed to both languages from birth, others learn one language at home and are later exposed to a second language when they reach school-age. In both cases, proficiency in the first language is used as a scaffold to help learn the second language.

In contrast, internationally adopted children are not bilingual. Prior to adoption they learn a first language, the birth language, which is prematurely stopped when the child is adopted because most adoptive parents do not speak the language. The child then begins learning a new adopted first language (or second first language). The process of prematurely halting language development in the birth language before it fully develops is known as 'arrested language development'. Loss of the birth language occurs quickly after adoption even in older children. Dr. Boris Gindis noted that Russian children adopted at ages four to eight lost expressive use of their language within three to six months of adoption and all functional use of the language within a year. In summary, internationally adopted children are only bilingual for a very short window of time after adoption.

The loss of the first language before the new adopted language develops leaves the internationally adopted child in a linguistic and educational limbo. Unlike the bilingual child who has a strong first language to fall back on, the internationally adopted child has no language until English develops. This lack of a functional language is not an issue for younger children who have several years to develop English before starting school. It is a significant issue for older adopted children who need to begin school right away. Because the children are not proficient in English, cognitive and linguistic development is often negatively affected.

Consider these facts: the typical six year-old understands over 20,000 English words. A five year-old child adopted from another country would need to learn an average of 54 new words every day in order to fully catch up in language comprehension abilities by age six. If the catch up timeframe is stretched out to two years, the adopted five year-old would still need to learn an average of 27 new words every day to fully catch up by age seven. However, while the adopted child has been playing catch-up, his six year-old friends have also added an average of 5,000 words to their vocabulary. By age seven, the typical child understands 25,000 words. In order to fully catch up within a two year window, the adopted five year old needs to learn an average of 34 words per day. In summary, expecting older adopted children to develop proficient English language skills within one or two years of adoption is unrealistic.

Learning a new language to proficiency takes years. Although internationally adopted children are not bilingual, information about second language learning in bilingual children provides some insights into what to expect. Cummins studied second language learning in a large number of bilingual children. He determined that proficiency in the first language was the single best predictor of learning a second language to proficiency. It is important for parents to determine if the child had difficulty understanding or speaking the birth language. Children who spoke the birth language well should easily pick up English. In contrast, children who had difficulty speaking or understanding the birth language will likely need extra help to learn English. Cummins divided the development of language proficiency into two levels.

The first level is known as **Basic Interpersonal Communication Skills (BICS).** BICS proficiency is attained when bilingual children are fluent in a second language for day-to-day social interactions or interactions that have lots of contextual cues. This level of fluency is achieved quickly, typically within one to three years of exposure to a second language. BICS fluency often masks the fact that the child hasn't mastered full comprehension of the language.

The second level of proficiency is known as **Cognitive Academic Language Proficiency (CALPS).** This level indicates the child has acquired all vocabulary and grammar concepts necessary to have full language proficiency in the academic setting, especially academic situations with reduced contextual cues. This level of proficiency takes anywhere from five to nine years to achieve.

The concept of swiss cheese is a good analogy for understanding the language abilities of a child who has BICS fluency without CALPS mastery. Although the overall size and structure of the cheese is there, it is riddled with holes placed in unpredictable places. The holes occur when:

• The child doesn't know certain vocabulary words.
• The child knows the words but hasn't learned all of their subtle shadings in meaning.
• The child knows the words but lacks the correct context for understanding them.

One example is the older adopted boy who decided to make a picture of a dugout for his learning project on Native Americans. When he finished, he proudly showed his mother a picture that looked like a baseball stadium. Another child wanted to know why there was no 'fast hand' on a clock. When told that some clocks don't come with second hands, he replied: "No, it has a second hand, it's missing the third hand." The reality is that most children adopted at older ages will lack full proficiency in English for many years and may require extra tutoring or speech and language services to keep up academically. Because proficiency in spoken language is the basis for developing skills in written language, older internationally adopted children who have not achieved CALPS levels of language proficiency are at significant risk for having academic difficulty.

Speech and Language Services for Older Adopted Children

The older internationally adopted child is not truly bilingual and will not have proficiency in the new adopted language for several years. This creates a dilemma for the child who is having educational or language difficulties in school. The American educational system is set up to:

1. Provide special education services for children with delayed language development or language learning disorders, through the federally mandated Individuals with Disabilities Education Act Part-B (IDEA).
2. Provide bilingual education services for second language learners through ESL programs developed at the level of the local school district.

The school-age internationally adopted child who hasn't developed full English language proficiency is like a square peg trying to fit into round program holes. Neither type of program fits exactly. Increasing the problem is the difficulty of validly assessing academic or language abilities in a child who is not proficient in any language.

When children adopted at older ages enter school, the typical first response of the school program is to offer bilingual education services. Parents need to realize that bilingual education programs are not mandated by the federal government. The extent and scope of services is left up to the local school district. The only exception is when state law, such as California's Proposition 227, mandates bilingual education policy across all districts within a state. Therefore bilingual education programs vary widely from state to state, and school district to school district. Common bilingual education models include the following:

English Classrooms with Support
- All instruction is provided in English in regular classrooms
- Individual tutoring provided as needed
- English as a Second Language Pull-Out services
- Minimal teacher modification of instruction
- Teaching is focused on academics

Bilingual Classrooms
- Teaching occurs in English and the birth language
- Teaching is focused first on academics and second on English language mastery
- Transitional Bilingual Classrooms–shift from the first language to English quickly
- Maintenance Bilingual Classrooms–shift from the first language to English gradually

Sheltered Immersion Programs
- Teaching is in English with substantial modifications designed to increase student comprehension of the material (i.e., added pictures, shortened directions, simplified vocabulary, etc.)
- Teaching is focused on academics and English language mastery

Most schools offer classroom support services for bilingual children. Schools with high numbers of culturally diverse children offer bilingual classroom programs, however the instructional language is usually Spanish. Sheltered immersion programs are offered by school districts that have many children speaking a number of different first languages. Children from various cultures are merged together into the same sheltered immersion classroom.

Although **English as a Second Language (ESL)** Programs are better than nothing, they do not fit the internationally adopted child because the child is not truly bilingual. As stated before, bilingual children have a first language that can be used for instruction if a concept isn't understood in English. In contrast, when internationally adopted children do not understand concepts in English, there is no other language to fall back on.

A better classification for newly adopted school-age children is to consider them as having **Limited English Proficiency (LEP)**. The classification of LEP indicates that a child is not proficient in English to a level needed for academic achievement and the classification of LEP can be made regardless of the child's proficiency in the first language.

Children who need more than bilingual education services need to qualify for speech and language or other services under the federal IDEA-Part B act. The federal government wisely states in its regulations that all children needing services under IDEA should be assessed in their first language. These mandates were created so children who didn't speak English proficiently weren't unnecessarily pushed into the special education system. The problem for many internationally adopted children is that by the time someone identifies that special services might be needed, the child has lost the first language and is not yet proficient in English. The 'Catch 22' is that the child now has no language to use for valid testing, yet needs to have language skills tested in order to qualify for speech and language services.

Parents need to advocate for their children and remind professionals that the internationally adopted child's first language, and only language, is now English. If the child is not proficient in English, the child is not proficient in any language and therefore at significant academic risk.

One way to resolve these issues is to provide better documentation of the child's language abilities prior to adoption. Parents adopting older children should try to obtain information on the child's language development in the native country. Ask the orphanage or school staff to put their language or academic concerns in a brief note that can be translated at a later date. If the child is known to have language delays prior to adoption, the documentation can be used to help qualify the child for immediate speech and language services upon entering school.

If orphanage or school staff feel the child is delayed, parents are urged to have the child's skills evaluated in the birth language within the first two to three months home. If the assessment takes place after three months home, the child's birth language will already have begun to disappear which will lower test scores. The assessment should focus on the child's language, cognitive, and academic abilities. These skills should preferably be evaluated by a speech language pathologist or psychologist who speaks the birth language. If a professional who speaks the language is unavailable, then a translator can assist. The American Speech Language Hearing Association (ASHA) maintains a registry of speech language pathologists who are proficient in other languages. ASHA can be contacted for referral information via their website, www.ASHA.org.

Speech and language issues are an important concern for the older internationally adopted child. Parents and professionals who are actively dealing with language learning following adoption are urged to learn more about bilingual language learning, and educational law regarding bilingual language services and IDEA.

~By Sharon Glennen, PhD, CCC-SLP, the Department Chair of Audiology, Speech Language Pathology & Deaf Studies at Towson University. Dr. Glennen is the parent of three children, the two youngest adopted as toddlers from Russia

Portions of this document were first published in Glennen, S. (in press). Language development following international adoption. In Families for Russian and Ukrainian Adoption (FRUA), Medical Issues Facing Our Children (2d Ed.). Merrifield, VA: FRUA Press.

Birth Language Learning: *Two Reasons Why Some Children Need to Wait*

Parents involving their adopted children in birth-language learning need to be aware that language can be a powerful trigger for the 'psycho-social' trauma that some children may exhibit over some unexamined parts of their early life. *(based on the work of Boris Gindis, PhD).*

Speech and language are also powerful connectors. If they become mildly or severely delayed or scrambled, stabilizing the child in your family should be your first priority. Language 'work' should be done in the parent's language while they work to strengthen the adoptive parent-adoptee attachment process. *(based on the work of Doris Landry, MS).*

Taking the time to listen to the cues from our children can make learning their birth language a much more positive and productive experience.

Developing a Birth Language Learning Playgroup

By Catherine Bickley

We developed a playgroup for our children–adopted from China–to help them learn their birth language called the Riverdale Mandarin Playgroup. But the outline can work for others too! It's fun; we meet two out of three Saturday afternoons, and we have kids of all ages. To a casual observer it might seem unstructured and chaotic. However, each session is anchored by a carefully thought-out lesson plan with clear learning objectives that underlie the seemingly free-flowing and informal class. Our teacher is pivotal; she is a native (Chinese) speaker who immigrated to Canada as a teenager. We have a maximum of six children per class. The class is very interactive and we feel that with any more than six per class the children wouldn't have enough opportunity to be actively engaged. The classes are divided by age. We ask parents to stay with their kids in class.

Playgroup Learning Structure

When our group began, we focused on vocabulary that our then 2.5 year-olds already knew well in English: animals, colors, numbers, body parts, and food. These children's vocabulary has increased in breadth and complexity over time, and that's reflected in their work with us–but we still start incoming little ones from that entry point. Each class has the same basic structure:

• Greetings (including a check on feelings and their words)
• Songs (which the children choose from picture cards)
• Tone practice
• Story and/or games or craft
• Snack
• Goodbyes

We devise our curriculum to meet demand. Since three of the six families in the older class were planning trips to China, the teacher dedicated two or three classes to useful vocabulary for the trip. The students learned how to answer questions about their names, ages, and where they lived. They even role-played 'how to bargain' in a Chinese marketplace. From the beginning the teacher, my co-coordinator, and I have met once or twice a term and talked about what is working well and what could be improved. A current issue is how to adapt the class to keep the attention of the older kids.

~Elements of Success~

The Teacher
To run a successful, long-term language-learning playgroup, a committed, qualified teacher–with a gifted way with children–is necessary.

The Parents
Parental involvement is important; we require parents to stay for their children's classes. We often use parents as 'props'–an intended side effect is that parents pick up vocabulary and are able to reinforce the language with their children at home, and motivates the parents to begin their own studies.

Classroom Facility
We meet in a very bland room in a church. We find that this makes the teacher the most interesting thing in the room!

Teacher's Salary
We pay the teacher a set fee per Saturday, collected from parents at the beginning of each term. The participant fees operate as cost recovery only, on a non-profit basis.

Registration
Registration is via email and phone. We have a simple one-page form with room for name, contact info, food allergies, past exposure to Mandarin.

Playgroup Administration
We need a committed co-coordinator, with the group held at a size that can be managed by a minimum of volunteers.

Community Building is Key
We've always seen the classes as part of community-building in the China adoption world. Our threads of connection are playgroups, adoption support groups, parental connections–and more!

Resources
See BrainGym **www.braingym.org** for more suggestions of how learning is enhanced through movement.

Here's How Our Playgroup Works:

Greetings. Our teacher greets each child and parent with a cheerful "Ni hao!" (Hi!) as they enter the class. Then our teacher asks each person how they are feeling that day. Using picture cards with faces portraying different emotions as a cue, the children respond that they are happy, sad or tired. Interestingly, the parents almost always report being tired!

Songs. We use the same songs over and over again, gradually expanding the number of songs as the children and parents learn them. In many ways, songs are easier to learn than spoken vocabulary as the music and rhythm carry people along and seem to imprint more strongly on the brain. The classes involve a lot of physical movement–pre-schoolers seem to learn much better when not anchored in place, and they are allowed to move freely. To take advantage of our use of songs and our feeling that 'learning through movement' works with little kids, we arrange it so that many of the songs are accompanied by activities.

- The Hello/Ni Hao song is sung while everyone holds hands and moves in a circle. As the children's vocabulary develops, our teacher will ask, in Mandarin, if they want to sing fast or slow.
- Rain, Rain, Go Away has the teacher uses a spray bottle of water and starts off by spraying children. Or parents!
- Twinkle, Twinkle Little Star in Mandarin uses cut-out cardboard stars in different sizes and colors that the children hold up while singing. The process of selecting which star each child wants involves talking about size; it also involves the words for colors.

Tone Practice. We make practicing the four Chinese language tones a very physical activity. Everyone stands up and physically reproduces (with swinging arms) the shape and direction of the tone markings that are used in pinyin to indicate the sounds. It's easier to demonstrate than to describe!

Crafts. The craft segment is tied to seasonal activities, for instance: Halloween, Chinese New Year, Hanukkah, Christmas, and the Autumn Moon Festival.

Snacks. The snack part of the class is always popular. It seems a bit Pavlovian at times, but it works! The children progress from simply saying the name of the food that they would like, to more complex sentences.

Goodbyes. We end the classes with a very simple goodbye song, which again gives the children an opportunity to use their vocabulary to make choices (fast, slow, loud, quiet, me first, my turn).

Follow-Up. The teacher emails the new vocabulary to each family after each class. Many of the songs we use in the class are on a CD that accompanies a book, and families listen to it at home to practice between classes.

~ Catherine Bickley , co-founder of the Riverdale Mandarin Playgroup that introduces young Canadian children adopted from China to their birth-language and culture. Catherine lives in Toronto, Canada, with her spouse and two daughters.

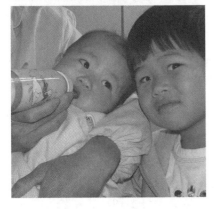

Food

Food
Feeding the Child Who Has Never Had Enough
By Leann King, BSN, RN

Best Laid Plans...

In the days after completing my home study, I immersed myself in the typical reading of expectant parents. I found myself thinking about the kind of parent I wanted to be, and I regarded my idealism as 'gospel'. I was fortunate to read about attachment disorders online and consequently had a pretty good arsenal of attachment activities under my belt when I boarded the plane to China. I believed my daughter would attach to me because I knew what to do to promote attachment. In retrospect, I was so idealistic that I set myself up for some significant failures.

In my musings on parenthood, one thing I became very clear about was not passing on my own food issues to my child. I grew up in the 'clean your plate' generation, as many of us did, and this along with other feeding taboos (rewarding, bribing, withholding food as discipline), have resulted in ongoing issues with food for many adults. No way was my child going to have this kind of relationship with food! I believed that it was my responsibility to provide three healthy meals a day, and snacks if needed, but it was my child's responsibility to decide what and how much she ate. I would not reward, bribe, or withhold food for any reason and, of course, I would have a wonderful, appreciative, self-regulating eater.

The Reality of a Malnourished Child

I was poorly prepared for the child who became mine. She came to me at almost 11 months-old, malnourished and obsessed with food. I had read that a baby will turn her head and give very clear cues when she is full. This is not the case in a baby who is starving or who has never had enough. As a new parent, I had no idea how much she should eat. So I let her eat and eat and eat, feeding her as long as she opened her mouth. Of course, it didn't take very long for vomiting and diarrhea to start. And everything I had come to believe about feeding a child was quickly rejected.

Initially, I was very worried that there was something wrong with my daughter. My nursing background had me contemplating every possible gastrointestinal disorder while trying to understand her food 'intolerances'. *Time and hind-sight have allowed me to see the issue for what it really was–a child who couldn't be filled up.* After about one month of this cycle of gorging and vomiting and diarrhea, I had to essentially start over, as one would feed a much younger baby. We went back to only the basics–formula, rice cereal and a few fruits and vegetables. I made a conscious effort to have food always available to her. I had a bottle of formula, a plain rice cake, a few cheerios, and some small pieces of banana set on the coffee table in the room where we spent most of our time. Interestingly enough, this alone hugely eliminated her need to overeat. Even in such a young child, the need for control of her food was clearly evident.

> *"Time and hindsight have allowed me to see the issue for what it really was–a child who couldn't be filled up."*
>
> Leann King

Feeding

My daughter was not able to initially feed herself because of fine and gross motor delays, so this made it difficult to allow her to control her intake. Also, as she had significant attachment issues, I wanted food to come from me. I wanted her to understand that I would always feed and look after her, and that this was a mother's job. When she eventually developed pincer grasp, she was able to help herself between meals. I still fed her at meal times and held and rocked her for bottles. Very quickly, the food that sat on our coffee table went untouched. Having it there allowed her some control and subsequently, she was able to relax and trust that food would always be available to her. As her attachment grew, and she trusted me more, she was able to relax around food.

Now at five years-old, she is a great eater in comparison to many of her friends and she is an awesome self-regulator. She has a sweet tooth, but can put down chocolate to eat an apple. She is much pickier now and has clear favorites which unfortunately, do fall into the category of normal kid fare: pizza, hot dogs, macaroni and cheese, and chicken fingers. This is contrary to her initial gorging of anything and everything! Thankfully, she also has some very healthy favorites and enjoys tomato and feta salad, potstickers, salmon, and broccoli.

She has her own cupboard in the kitchen, stocked with crackers, cereal, dried fruit, fruit cups, and cookies, and she has easy access to the fruit bowl. She is free to help herself at anytime, even just before dinner. I will remind her as she helps herself that dinner will be ready in five minutes, and sometimes she will return her snack to the cupboard. It is her decision to eat mandarin oranges before dinner and I do not comment on it, even when it 'spoils' her appetite. I think this is necessary in order for my daughter to self-regulate her food intake.

A basket holds all of her treats which she is free to have at anytime. I recently threw out some Christmas chocolate that was getting stale and her Easter chocolate will, no doubt, have the same fate. When she was smaller, I used to put her treats in a high cupboard and she would ask for them constantly. Now that she has control over them, she rarely indulges in more than a small portion.

Finding Hunger, Finding Thirst

We have faced my daughter's inability to recognize her own hunger. Some of this is developmental, as toddlers are often poor advocates of their own physical needs, but in my daughter's case this went on much longer than usual. Although her early obsession with food might indicate a hyper-vigilance with regards to hunger, in reality, the exact opposite occurred. Her survival instincts had taught her to eat whatever and whenever she could. *Her actual cues for hunger were buried by repeatedly not having her hunger needs met.*

It has been our most longstanding challenge and five years later, my daughter is just now articulating her own hunger and thirst. I have tried modeling my own physical cues, describing the sensations, and anticipating her hunger and thirst (especially if her mood or behavior is deteriorating). When she is in the throes of a hypoglycemic meltdown, she cannot see her own hunger. However, she is finally becoming aware of the role this plays in her behavior.

Although our children may have significant food issues, they may not be able to identify hunger per se. When hunger is an unmet need, the natural correlation between hunger, food, and fullness is disrupted. I think that it is important that we try to teach recognition of hunger, and this may be very challenging in a child who wants to eat all the time as an issue of control. Their opportunities for feeling hungry will be significantly diminished in the beginning. As the need to control their food lessens, they will allow themselves to get hungry, trusting that food will be there when they need it.

The most difficult lesson for me was understanding that birth children normally come to us self-regulating their intake as they are filled up with enough food and a mother's love. Post-institutionalized children may have had neither. Those who have never had enough food struggle with the eat-to-survive instinct they developed early in their lives. Parents struggle with the sad reality that our children have been chronically hungry for much of their early lives.

I recognize that these eating/feeding issues are not as easy to address in an older child who has habits of survival more deeply ingrained. I do believe, from my connections to others parenting post-institutionalized children with significant food issues, that allowing as much control as possible is paramount to the child developing a healthy relationship with food. My daughter still takes a sippy cup of milk to bed with her, because knowing she has something if she wakes up hungry is very important to her.

If the child is allowed choice, then we should eventually see a reduction in dysfunctional eating practices. If we do not want these issues to become full blown eating disorders (obesity included), then we must bow gracefully out of the picture as our child re-learns self regulation. And, although initially, an unhealthy cycle of gorging, vomiting, or obesity may be distressing, we need to trust that our children need us to provide the right environment for them to learn to meet their own nutritional needs in a healthy way. If we understand Maslow's hierarchy of needs, we know that emotional needs cannot be met when there are unmet physical needs. By providing our children with enough food and shelter, we open the door to love. Food is part of the cycle of attachment that creates a secure individual, and can play a big role in the relationship between mother and child.

~ By Leann King, RN (ICU), BScN, single parent, co-moderator of attach-china, a yahoo
group for parents with an adopted child with attachment or trauma issues

~Making Eating Easier When You First Come Home~

- Post-institutional children may have been malnourished in the orphanage, or at least not fed optimally. Research shows that learning and behavioral issues (e.g. ADHD and possibly attachment issues) can be related to poor diet. What we feed our children, once at home, matters!

- Know what is good nutrition for a child; get further help from your pediatrician if your child is malnourished, has parasites (see page 125) or a chronic digestive illness. Learn modern nutritional thinking on the balance between the various food groups.

- Don't get upset if your child doesn't want a particular food. Know the food groups, and substitute until you find something in the group that they like.

- Remember that your child will be used to food at different temperatures, textures, and types to those you use at home. On receiving your child, try to find out their diet and feeding schedule.

- If your child seems averse to eating, use the opportunity to baby him. Don't be afraid to grind or blend food, or even to rely on baby cereals and formula (if your child is under two).

- Children's blood sugar peaks and dips as they use up food eaten in energetic play. They have small tummies too! We need to feed our children smaller, more frequent, healthy snacks to keep energy levels high.

- Children are more likely to act up if hungry than if full. If a child has a period in the day when tantrums most often happen, look to see if the child is simply low on fuel.

- Bring a nutritious small snack when you pick your child up from school or day care. The 'gift' reminds the child you have been thinking of their needs, assuages hunger pangs, and helps in avoiding crankiness.

- Play games with food to help bond with your child–have races to push marshmallows round a plate by blowing with a straw, or share a popsicle!

- Before using over-the-counter food supplements, check first with your pediatrician and find out if it's safe for your child to have them.

~Sheena Macrae

A Taste of Home

What are our toddlers and older children used to eating prior to adoption?
It depends on their age, the region of the country they are living in, and also
whether they have been in an orphanage, group home or foster-care.
For some children, easing into a new culture with tastes from their old home
makes the transition a little easier.

Colombia

Hot chocolate, cheese, bread, cereal, eggs, soup, chicken, salad, rice, juice with sugar, guineo (green bananas)

Guatemala

Tortillas, maize (corn), rice, beans, eggs, fish, bananas, papaya

India

Government milk (a cow/water buffalo mix), boiled and mashed plantains, rice with yogurt, rice or rice-cake with dal (a thick cereal similar to cous-cous, with tumeric, onions, and vegetables), orange or sweet lime juice

Korea

Yogurt, juice, sugar water, seaweed soup with soft cooked rice, miso soup with rice and small tofu chunks, soybean soup, sweet potatoes (baked or steamed until soft), fried eggs, kimchi (spicy cabbage), pork

China

Noodles, rice, steamed eggs, cooked green vegetables, chicken, soup, rice congee (rice porridge), dumplings (mostly pork), steamed bread, watermelon

Russia

Infants in Russian orphanages are fed foods like kasha (cereal made of buckwheat or other grains), rice, cabbage or other vegetable puree, fruit puree, formula, kefir (a yogurt like drink), and weak tea or milk and tea. Toddlers get kasha, broths and soups with rice or pasta, brown bread, cheese, boiled eggs, pureed vegetables, pureed fruits, mashed potatoes, cucumbers, beets and milky tea. Older children report eating soup, soup, and soup! In addition to the foods mentioned, older children also have foods like sausage, dried fish or meat, broth, soups, and stews. They also drink tea with meals. Depending on the orphanage, children of all ages might get juice, bananas, and other fresh fruits as special treats.

Finding the Formula
Your new baby is in your arms, and it's time to eat.

What do you give him? What if he won't drink the formula you packed and carried halfway around the world? How do you know what baby or toddler formula to choose?

- Ask the orphanage caregivers or foster parents, via your adoption facilitator, for a feeding schedule with times and types of formula or food. Some parents have found that seemingly sleepless kids were simply hungry, because they had been fed through the night.

- Ask about the bottle temperature the baby is used to, and whether anything is normally added to the formula (the only way one parent could get her new daughter to drink her bottle in China was to add a couple of sugar packets to it).

- Some orphanages enlarge the hole in the bottle nipple to get the child to drink more quickly. Some babies may refuse to suck on the bottle nipples until the nipple is altered to flow faster. It may be helpful to duplicate the type of nipple used in the orphanage (which usually can be purchased locally). Avent bottle nipples are sold with different sized openings, if your baby needs a faster flow.

- Try to buy a supply of the formula the baby has been used to in the orphanage and use it to wean the baby gradually onto your formula of choice.

- Ask if your child was being weaned onto other foods. Meat 'soup' is often given to babies; think stew, ground and watered!

- Some children in foster care are weaned to regular solid food at a very young age. Watch your baby's hunger cues and his interest at the table while you are eating.

- Ask specifically for the type of milk formula provided in the orphanage, social welfare institute, baby home or hogar. Some Chinese orphanages, for example, use rice milk and wean onto rice congee. Think laterally and buy local equivalents in China, or carry some with you (dry rice pudding flakes re-constitute a close equivalent to rice milk).

- If you are travelling to adopt, leave the iron-fortified formula at home to be introduced gradually. Iron is very constipating and can disrupt a baby's digestive system.

- Be aware of the local foods your child may have been exposed to in their birth country, and what they might enjoy once home. Ask what all of the children are commonly fed in your child's culture.

- Some Asian born children are lactose intolerant, which means dairy milk-based formulas may cause colic or won't be properly absorbed. Lactose-free or soy formula are options; check with your pediatrician.

- Don't make an issue of food. A newly adopted baby or toddler may be in shock and won't eat. Concern yourself that they are drinking water initially.

- Children generally thrive on a wide variety of foods. Once home, experiment with formula and food, but do so in conjunction with a pediatrician if you are concerned about your child's eating habits, development, or weight.

- Remember, an initial upset tummy may be less about food and more about parasites. Check dirty diapers and run parasite testing to be sure.

Feeding Your Toddler

Experienced feeding tips from a mother of three grown children,
one daughter from China, and 35 foster children.

I feed toddlers when they are hungry. Dinner at 5 pm may not be convenient for the adults, but kids often need to eat at that time. If the parents dine later, the toddlers can join in again, for snacks and social hour. I have learned to offer food several times a day. When my daughter first came home she had four meals a day, plus snacks. Do not get into the habit of cooking separate meals for toddlers; keep offering them whatever the rest of the family is eating.

Although toddlers want to be independent they do not always have the stamina or patience to eat their whole meal alone. So some feeding by the parent and some by the child is a great way to keep toddlers eating and occupied. Keep a few special items near the feeding chair to bring out when interest in the food is flagging. It can be simply a container of pegs, while you spoon in a few more mouthfuls. I never force a toddler to eat.

Separate high chairs do not allow toddlers to eat as part of the family. Get one that puts the child at the table. You can remove the tray on some to do this; otherwise use a booster seat. Feed a newly adopted child on your lap and from your plate (great for facilitating attachment).

Toddlers who drink more than three cups or two bottles of milk a day are not going to be hungry. Drinking lots of juice also spoils the appetite. With adopted kids, I do not believe in taking away bottles too soon, so substituting water for the milk will reduce the milk consumption. Another trick is to switch to smaller bottles. Insisting the bottle is only drunk while in a parent's lap is another good tactic. This is great for teaching the child to depend on the parent to meet their needs, and helps build the parent-child relationship.

With a picky eater it is essential that everything eaten is healthy. So snacks should not be high in fat or sugar, or low in nutrition: no candy, cookies, or fizzy drinks. Fruit will satisfy a sweet tooth. A sweet potato will sweeten a vegetable soup, as will sweet corn. Offer fish and lots of high protein foods like eggs and meat. Some children will really like flavorful food, some prefer it bland. Here are some suggested nutritious foods that are easy to serve to toddlers, and are foods that they all generally enjoy:

- any kind of melon
- soft fruits like bananas
- strawberries
- peaches, plums and oranges chopped into pieces (freeze them for a summer treat)
- yogurt for fruit-dipping
- slices of avocado
- cooked carrot and other cooked vegetables
- strips of cooked chicken can be used to dip into yummy dips like hummus, or served on their own
- pasta with meat sauce, or shredded vegetables hidden in tomato sauce

Pancakes with small pieces of meat or fish with finely chopped veggies added (grated potato or carrots, for example) are also fun, and you can cook a stack and freeze some for later. Shred some vegetables and mix with egg and rice and form into patties (don't forget to add a dash of flavoring such as soy sauce or oyster sauce), and cook in the frying pan.

Some toddlers are very suspicious of new foods and may take awhile to accept them. Even if a new food is initially rejected, keep offering it and one day the toddler may surprise you and eat it. Try not to overwhelm a toddler with a plate piled high with food. Instead, offer small portions and refill the plate. Toddlers love it when you give them food from your plate, so put extra on yours to allow for this.

I find toddlers love eating off of brightly colored dinnerware, with their own child-sized cutlery. Cut food into pieces that are easily held or bite-sized. Allow a lot of messy finger feeding. Some parents choose to initially feed all food by hand (from their fingers to the child's mouth), encouraging eye contact as they offer food. Toddlers do strive for independence though, and in time will insist on feeding themselves.

Teething toddlers may find metal spoons cold and hard on tender gums. Use chopsticks to feed them, or soft plastic baby spoons. Toddlers like to help with meal preparation or table setting. So get them involved in any way they can. No one likes mush! Small proportions of individual foods served in an attractive way are better than a plate of mashed veggies or white pasta in a white sauce.

Expect messy eating from a toddler and allow for it. Large bibs and a mat under the toddlers chair to catch dropped food are essential (owning a dog helps, too!). Expect food in the hair and a bath after after dinner! Kids always eat better at other people's houses, especially when there are other kids around. So invite friends over and let the kids eat together. Do not expect much in the way of manners till around three. Meal time should be enjoyable! Picnics are great fun and can be as simple as a lunch in a local park or in the backyard garden. Toddlers love eating outdoors, and with friends along it is even better. Eating is very social.

My most important advice about feeding a toddler? Don't worry, and never let the child know you are concerned about their eating. Food issues can quickly become control issues. If your child has no known food allergies or intolerances, no parasites, and is growing, then she will not starve.

~ By Jeanette Carrison
Single mom to four, foster mom to 35, a teacher of young
children in migrant communities among other things!

'Regular Food'

When a child turns up her nose at foods from other cultures, and declares she only wants 'regular food', it becomes a teachable moment. At my house, I tell my children that Chinese food *is* regular food in China. We talk about how Lo Mein is like spaghetti and Mushu is just a type of pancake. We talk about how cultures develop and swap food ideas. The pancakes and Lo Mein are among the Chinese foods my kids enjoy, because we have cooked these at home and discussed the food connections. They also eat mooncakes because we make our own, and they help (we don't put an egg yolk inside, though. I guess that's cultural fusion!)

~ Kathleen Klavey
adoptive mom to two
children from China

Food Aversions and Obsessions
Some Tools for Parents

Many of our post-institutionalized children come home developmentally delayed simply because of life in an institution. Babies, toddlers, even pre-schoolers and beyond may not have had the opportunity to try foods of many different textures, tastes and types. When we try to offer them food, they may gag. They may not know what to do with lumpy texture, or meats. Strange looking food may turn them off. Some children who have suffered from lack of sustained emotional care may also have control issues over food–they may want to gorge or may refuse to eat what we offer. Food is a mother's weak spot! Our love somehow gets cooked into the meals we create, and a child who rejects our food 'rejects us'. We have to get creative with our culinary and emotional tools and find a way to ensure our child learns that food is a pleasure, and that in our home, it's not a battle ground.

Food Aversions
For children with sensory issues in chewing and swallowing food, we have tools:
• Never force a child to eat.

• If you suspect that your child hasn't experienced food textures, his mouth won't be ready for textures and hard foods; don't be afraid to make the dishes blander and smoother.

• Take some tips from occupational therapists and other experts and gently brush teeth and gums (let the child do it too). It helps harden the palate.

• Make a game of eating. Zooming 'airplane' spoons of food may not work, but kids love trying to get food off their top lips!

• Blowing bubbles, drinking from sippy cups and straws all encourage mouth and tongue activity.

• Introduce new foods gradually. And remember, children often take time to really decide they love a food (don't bulk buy).

• Let a toddler help make a simple meal (put grapes on plates, or carrot sticks and cheese dip). If they create it, they may well eat it!

• Teach older kids table manners, and take them out to try different cuisines (as well as that of their own ethnicity).

• Don't ban a food (even candies and chocolate); most kids once home a while will self-regulate their food choices.

• Make meals social and sit with your child while they eat.

• Make sure your child is sitting upright. Digestion will not be optimal if the child is slumped and can't handle getting food from utensil to mouth.

- If your child won't eat, don't end the meal in an adult storm.

- If your child doesn't eat and fails to thrive, consult your pediatrician.

~Sheena Macrae

Food Obsession

Post-institutional children who are obsessed with food may be reacting to early starvation, or to under-feeding due to poverty or lack of orphanage personnel. Malnourished children may also have been sick, carrying parasites, or allergic to the formula used in the institution. Healthy children who continue to be obsessed with food post-adoption, might need your physical reassurance or professional help:

- Allow your child to carry a healthy snack in a ziplock bag (cold noodles, green beans, fruit) at all times, especially when you are in the car or away from home.

- Try re-training your child to equate love and attention with you, instead of with food. Don't deny food or take food away, but try re-directing your child from wanting food to bonding activities that require your child to participate (pat-a-cake, pretend face painting, and dancing together, for example).

- If you're dealing with post-institutional eating behaviors (bingeing, hoarding, stealing food, severe sensory difficulties with texture or swallowing) check with a doctor, a psychologist specializing in adoption, or a hospital that has a specialty clinic for children with eating/feeding problems.

~Jean MacLeod

Food is LOVE: Vietnam and Cambodia

My daughter Thao was adopted in Vietnam aged four months. She'd been breastfed on demand and given a thin porridge substance. Her birthmother gave us ingredients and instructions to make the porridge. Thao had a tough 24 hours as she went from demand breastfeeding to bottles. I had given her birthmother bottles and formula so Thao would be familiar with them, but she chose not to use them. She was concerned about the contaminated water supply and that the formula might upset Thao's stomach. One mild shock for me was that when I adopted Thao she was really quite plump. Not at all what you expect from intercountry adoption.

My daughter Srey Leah was adopted at 12 months, having spent all but a couple of days in the orphanage in Cambodia. She was eating rice, fruit, vegetables, meat, and fish. We were advised by the American pediatrician that saw her that she was malnourished, probably due to a lack of protein. There was money to pay for food at the orphanage, but I think Cambodians find it difficult to come to terms with how much protein a child needs as it's generally in such short supply. For Srey Leah, food was an enormously bonding experience. Even at nearly three years old, if you cuddle her like a baby and let her feed herself from a bottle, her eyes roll back and she reaches an almost transcendent state.

~ By Jane Reeves, attorney, adoptive mom to children from Cambodia and Vietnam

Cooking Lessons
The Importance of Feeding a Hungry Heart

I picked up Yan Kit's Classic Chinese Cook Book in the time between my referral and traveling to China. I felt that my new daughter, Mai Qiang, who was three and a half years-old at referral time, might crave the taste of food she knew, especially when everything else would be so unfamiliar.

A week after returning from China, I gingerly picked up the cookbook for the first time. A well-seasoned cook, I still didn't recognize most of the vegetables and other food-stuffs that I saw in the outdoor markets in China and in Chinatowns I'd visited—or the ingredients in Yan Kit's book. I knew I had a lot to learn and I wanted to be able to whip up Chinese dishes for my daughter so she would feel at home, at least in this small way.

I was soon to find out that one doesn't produce a Chinese dish or meal quickly It's an ancient cuisine prepared with time-intensive techniques that worked before the days of instant everything and techno gadgets. It was my daughter who taught me the most about Chinese cooking and life. I'm a single mom so she had to occupy herself playing while I cooked. She exhibited very little pleasure in the food I prepared, and in fact, her attitude was defiantly silent. She didn't appreciate my Chinese-food love-offerings.

When she had enough English to express herself, she looked at me one night and said, *"You no make the food. I want you. Too long."* I immediately got the message. She would rather have a microwaved mac and cheese and my attention than any time-sucking, Chinese meal I could produce. It was among the first of many lessons she has taught me.

~ By Susan Hipsley
This article is excerpted from one originally published in the FCC-MetroDetroit Threads

A Menu for Physical and Emotional Connection

- Make the food connection through bottles and sippy cups held by mom when the child is quiet and receptive. Continue this as long as the child wants it. Re-start it when your child is emotionally needy or feeling stressed.
- Provide three healthy meals a day with extra helpings readily available.
- Provide the child with her own always-accessible cupboard or drawer stocked with healthy snacks.
- Provide a basket or bowl with treats for the child.
- Provide a supportive environment for the child to re-learn self-regulation (refrain from commenting negatively on overeating, poor food choices, or hoarding).
- Provide the child with snacks to take when on the go.
- Know your child's energy dips and lows. Carry snacks!
- Instill in your child that she can be responsible for her own nutrition. Model it.
- Be sensitive to the unique needs of each child and make adaptations as necessary (follow the child's lead).

~ Leann King

The Uninvited Guests
Dealing with Common Parasites

Many of the places internationally adopted children come from are areas that might have few resources to maintain a clean water supply or have adequate food preparation facilities. The outcome can be unintentional visitors who piggyback inside our children for the ride home. Often, symptoms can be difficult to pinpoint in conjunction with other issues facing a newly adopted child.

Tapeworms are flat and ribbon-like, and are normally passed in small segments (although can be many, many feet long inside the body). There are three human tapeworms, and they are contracted by eating raw or undercooked pork, beef or fish.

Roundworms, or their eggs, are found in the soil contaminated with human feces and can be picked up on the hands and transferred to the mouth (or enter through the skin). Two of the most 'popular' types of roundworms with international adoptive families are Ascaris (Ascaris lumbricoides) and Pinworms (Enterobus Vermicularis).

Ascaris is a type of roundworm that looks a lot like an earthworm; it ends up living in the intestinal tract, can multiply profusely, grow to be about a foot long and can cause plenty of related problems.

Pinworms (Enterobius vermicularis) are easily passed from person to person and can run rampant among groups of children. The worms hang out in the anal area to lay their eggs, and cause intense itching; children scratch, then pass the eggs on to others with unwashed hands. If a child is diagnosed with pinworms, all members of the family must be treated with medication to eradicate the infection.

"The most common procedure for collecting the pinworm eggs is a rather simple one involving swabbing the anal area with the sticky side of a piece of transparent Scotch tape, and transferring the tape to a slide for examination." (National Institutes of Health)

Tapeworms and roundworms can make a very dramatic entrance, either into your baby's diaper, or into the toilet bowl. Don't flush! Retrieve the worm, put it in a container, and take it to your pediatrician. It will make diagnosis much simpler and you will be able to immediately start your child on an effective medication. Some children will vomit up their 'uninvited guests', making retrieval a little easier, but no less dramatic!

Giardia (Giardia lamblia) is the parasite causing giardiasis. It is passed from person-to-person, and is caused by contact with infected feces (either directly or through contaminated water). Symptoms are nasty, but resemble many other gastro-intestinal problems which makes it tough to identify: *"foul-smelling diarrhea; excessive gas; abdominal pain; bloating; nausea; tiredness; and loss of appetite. Upper gastrointestinal symptoms such as vomiting may predominate" (from the National Institutes of Health)*. Stool samples need to be

The American Academy of Pediatrics "Red Book"

(also available as an e-book from www.aap.org)
The Red Book includes information on active and passive immunization, care of children in special circumstances (internationally adopted children), and management of about 200 specific conditions and childhood infectious diseases including parasites.

www.aapredbook.
aappublications.org/
about/

collected over a period of three days (and sometimes for as long as four or five weeks).

- An older child can use the toilet after you place a large plastic container right into the toilet bowl. Avoid getting toilet water into your sample; use a container with a large opening and tall sides.

How to obtain a 'clean' stool sample from a child out of diapers:

- Lift the toilet seat up and place a sheet of clear plastic wrap from one side of the toilet to the other. Make a little trough in the middle of the plastic wrap, so that urine trickles into the toilet bowl and the feces is caught.
- Be sure to wear surgical gloves and wash your hands thoroughly when working with stool samples, or when changing the diaper of a baby that is in the process of being tested for parasites.

How to obtain a 'clean' urine sample:

- A baby in diapers can have a plastic bag taped to his or her bottom (use the type of surgical tape that doesn't hurt to be pulled off). Immediately feed baby a bottle and wait for quick results. Empty bag into clean container.

Getting a positive identification on a parasite can be a long, frustrating experience. Physicians in the USA are not always familiar with many of the parasites and infections commonly found in our children's sending countries. Parasites can cause serious digestive problems, cause sleep disturbances, and exacerbate asthma and reflux. If there is a parasitical-type problem with the child, but inconclusive test results, parents may wish to consult a doctor who specializes in international adoption medicine. International medical clinics (commonly associated with large hospitals or universities) can be easily found by searching online.

~Jean MacLeod

Baggage

Adult Attachment:
Becoming the Parent I Need to Be
By Kathy Reilly, PhD

For all of us, our ways of interacting with others have some constancy and consistency across relationships. And, whatever our style of interacting, it is always expressed when we interact with our children! Further, how we interact with our children impacts how they learn to interact with others... So how do we learn enough to change how we relate to others if our style of relating impacts on our children? How I 'am' and how I relate to my daughter was brought home a while back at a play date where my daughter, Rachel, and I met with my friend Michelle and her daughter Sara.

Both children were adopted from China. Rachel has been diagnosed as anxiously attached by a therapist specializing in adoption, and has trouble feeling completely safe unless I am nearby. I have worked hard to understand my daughter's needs. Sara shows many of the same signs of anxious attachment as Rachel, but her mother takes a different approach. Michelle has done no reading or consulting around attachment issues and feels that many people make too big a deal out of these issues. She feels that if she and her husband provide regular, good parenting, her daughter will be fine. Michelle is a very different kind of mother than I am, and is generally not over-worried about how her daughter is feeling. Feelings are not her focus–but she is a good mother and cares for her daughter very well. As the play date progressed I saw how my anxiety impacted on my daughter–and I believe that my friend's lack of empathy for her daughter's also impacted on that child

As our daughters are playing I am very aware of my daughter, where she is playing and how she seems to be feeling. At one point she seems to be preoccupied or unsettled. I go over and ask her if she is all right. She says she is fine and goes on playing. She does not like me to ask how she is feeling, but I feel a need to be sure that she is okay. When Michelle goes to get food she leaves the play area without telling her daughter. Sara misses her mom while she is gone, and I explain to her where her mommy is. Sara stares for a while in the direction of her mommy, then eventually resumes playing. Michelle returns and Sara comes running to her. Michelle says, "Oh honey, you are all right," and proceeds to get the food ready. At times Sara wants to cuddle with her mom while eating. Michelle cuddles a bit, but then encourages Sara to sit in her own seat and play with Rachel.

Clearly, Michelle and I are very different kinds of mothers. How do our relating skills with our children affect how they behave?

- I am an anxious, worried mother. I am never quite sure that my daughter is okay, and I am always checking on her.
- Michelle is a more minimizing mother. She minimizes her daughter's feelings, and will tell her daughter that she is okay, regardless of what her daughter may be feeling.
- I smother my daughter in an attempt to make her feel safe.
- Michelle ignores her daughter's own feelings in an attempt to smooth a situation.

We both have good intentions, but for both of us, our mothering styles don't necessarily translate into accurately hearing what our children need from us.

Michelle and I have different styles of interacting, different ways of relating with adults and children. How did we get to where we are? There is research available which strongly indicates that how we relate to others in adulthood depends on how our parents related to us as children. That is how attachment styles form–it's all in how we relate to and are comforted by our parents.

The pioneer in observing and identifying childhood attachment styles was Mary Ainsworth. The three childhood styles (each related to a particular way of being parented) as identified by Ainsworth are:

Secure Attachment. Children with this kind of attachment style tend to have had consistent, predictable, and nurturing caretaking. Their caretaking has not necessarily been perfect, but at the same time, there have been few, if any major let downs or traumas. For these children, the world has treated them well, and they expect it to continue to do so.

Anxious/Ambivalent Attachment. Children with this kind of attachment style have had inconsistent and unpredictable nurturing. They have had some nurturing and they are attached to a caregiver, but the caregiver has been notably inconsistent. These children are not sure that they can count on the world to meet their needs. They generally do not feel safe, and they vacillate between being clingy and angry.

Insecure or Avoidant Attachment. Children with this attachment style have had mothers or caregivers that have tended to not be available for nurturing. These children have not received much emotional support from their caregivers, and they have learned not to expect much. (For more on attachment, see **Claiming** pages 42-80.)

Parenting Style Dictates our Children's Attachment Style

Ainsworth's observations show us that our parenting style impacts the degree to which our children will be able to trust and interact in the world. The more consistently and predictably we can nurture our children, the more trust and ability to attach they will have. In the 1980's Mary Main, a developmental psychologist, developed a method assessing adult attachment. It was found that unless there were significant intervening variables such as therapy or further trauma, childhood attachment styles are carried into adulthood. Main found that children usually develop the same attachment style of their primary caregiver. If a mother is dismissive, a child will have to learn to be dismissive. If a mother is anxious, a child will learn to be anxious, and will not be certain the world is a safe place. If a mother is secure, responsive, but not smothering, a child will learn to feel safe in the world and know that there is a reliable home base to which they can always return.

Of course this makes sense, but it was a stunner for me. As mentioned before, my

A Different Dance

Biology is powerful. It choreographs an invisible, important, tightly-stepped mother-baby dance. There is an extra 'base-level' of connection inherent in a biological mother-infant relationship, a connection knit by nature, and that connection is perfect trust.

Adoption is different. Not in what we feel for our children, but in parenting around loss, both our children's and our own. A securely attached biological child who hasn't been abandoned by a birth parent, would never believe that his mother would ever permanently leave him, for any reason. And primal loss will always be a deep, dark possibility for our internationally adopted children, because the unthinkable did happen to them. It happened to them, it severed their connection, and it spun them halfway across the world...

Understanding the importance of the connection forged by healthy biological parenting, helps adoptive parents to proactively fill in some of our children's missing pieces. We can adoption-parent to build feelings of trust, safety and love in our adopted children. We can work to replicate the natural dance of attunement a bio-child has with his mother, while acknowledging a different adoptive mother-child dance. The music is there; we just need to teach our children to trust our lead, to hold on tight and to follow our steps. Adoption is not lesser than biology, but we can apply the biological two-step to our adopted children to help keep our families in-tune, and attuned.

~ Jean MacLeod

daughter is anxiously attached. My husband and I are spending a great deal of time, energy, and money on therapy and other activities to increase my daughter's ability to feel safe in relationships. And, the one thing that will have the greatest impact on her attachment style is me and my attachment style. I realized that no matter what else I do, if I do not address my own attachment style, my daughter will have the same attachment level and fears that I do. My own attachment level will limit her.

Getting Beyond the Limits...

That my own attachment level could limit my daughter was a tough realization for me. I would like to think that I could parent my child perfectly, out of my good intentions or out of all the love that I have for her. After exploring the adult attachment issues, it became clear to me that no matter what else I do for my daughter, if I do not understand my own fears and issues in relationships, my daughter will not surpass my level of trust with others. This would be also be true if my daughter were my birth child, but since my daughter has her own adoption-related attachment issues and we are working so hard to help her in this area, this insight seemed even more important to me. The lifesaver is that along with the above finding, Mary Main also found another, very encouraging finding. She discovered that adults who started with less than secure attachment styles, could, with work, reach secure attachment status. Main called these adults "earned secure," and she found that these adults could raise securely attached children, just as other securely attached adults do.

In her research, Main measured adult attachment by asking adults to talk about their childhood memories, and to place them in a coherent life narrative. Main found there to be four categories of adult attachment, three of which corresponded with Ainsworth's findings for children, and a fourth category that Main added based upon her research. Main categorizes adult attachment as:

Secure. These adults were able to describe their childhood in a way that made sense in terms of all the characters or people, and included the strengths and weaknesses of each.

Preoccupied. These adults, when talking about childhood memories, could not help but still have some anger, frustration, or some part of their histories that did not really make sense to them.

Dismissive. Main labeled as dismissive those adults that often spoke of their parents in very positive terms, but had trouble giving examples to demonstrate the qualities of which they spoke. Generally, these people are cut off from the emotions that they and others feel.

Disorganized. These adults have experienced physical, sexual, or emotional abuse, or the loss of a parent in childhood. These kinds of events are so overwhelming and confusing that people who have experienced these events often have unusual, confused behavior that was different than any other category.

How Do We Assess All This?

The most encouraging aspect of Main's research was the finding that adults who started with anxious, avoidant, or even disorganized attachment styles, could reach secure attachment status and raise children with a secure attachment style. The lifesaving finding is that an adult can move to being earned secure. This is possible by working on understanding their own style of forming relationships, and understanding how past events impacted them. How do those of us with insecure childhoods move toward an earned secure attachment status? We find earned secure:

- in our willingness to emotionally work through and understand the feelings from difficult experiences in our childhood.
- with therapy, where we learn to understand or 'hear' the difficult emotions that we experienced as children. In leaving denial, we gain peace over our childhood experiences.
- by gaining perspective, tying in our feelings, and providing a coherent story or narrative about our past. Gaining insight about our childhood and how we were parented allows us to be understanding, while still acknowledging our feelings and emotional reactions.

Earned secure status occurs when both anger and denial from past events have been mastered so that a person is fully present in the moment, and able to make present-moment choices based on current events, not on past feelings. It is the unprocessed or 'unheard' feelings of the past that make it difficult for us to tell what is really happening in the present. Once we have heard and understood the feelings from the past, we are able to see the present more clearly, and are able to be available to our children so that we can provide them the consistency and nurturing they need. Children need us fully engaged with them, so we need to start a parallel process of meeting our own needs as we attempt to meet those of our children. It might help if we keep a stage or two ahead!

Doing the Best We Can (and Our Parents May Have Said That, Too)

In attempting to understand feelings from childhood, people are uneasy about blaming their parents. It's thought to be to easy an excuse and that it is disloyal. I would agree that our parents probably did do the best they could; we are all human and we have our strengths and our weaknesses. But what we need to understand is that our parents perhaps did the best job they could, but at the same time, their 'best' may not have been ideal for us. Our feelings and reactions to what may not have been ideal for us are important as well, and need to be validated. The trick is to be able to hold in one part of our mind how it was for our parents; at the same time, in another part of our mind, realize how it was for us…and be compassionate with both. Discovering how our life experience has impacted us is important. So is understanding that our parents did the best they could with the tools, experiences, and information they had at the time.

And What of Me–As an Adoptive Mother?

I've sought therapy since the play date I described, and I am proud and grateful to say that I am not the same mother I was then. I still have tendencies and inclinations to be an anxious mother. But, I am increasingly able to try to judge what my daughter needs, versus what I fear. My relationships with friends and my husband have also benefited, and I am having more fun, with less anxiety.

I believe understanding these issues with an adopted child can be even more important than doing so with a birth child. An adopted child's attachment issues may interact / clash with the adoptive mother's issues in ways that are not as likely to happen with birth child and birthmother pairs. With birth children, to a large degree, attachment style is derived from and runs parallel with the birthmother's style. In adoption, there are two different processes occurring:

• Adoptive mother and child may have different attachment styles, making it difficult to connect

• Adoptive mother and child have the same insecure style, doubling the anxiety or anger or dismissiveness between the two! In this case it may be hard to identify the attachment issues, as both the parent and the child may be most comfortable at a distance.

Each attachment style combination is unique and presents its own special challenges. But, because there are so many more variations, and because they can impact and spiral off of one another, I believe it is even more important in adoptive families to have some understanding of how these issues interact. If I had not been an adoptive parent, I would not have been forced to explore my own attachment issues nearly so deeply. My child's life would have been much more limited by my own attachment issues than I ever would have known. As it is now, my daughter is thriving due to the attachment work we have done, and I am thriving, too. I now take risks and become involved in things I would not have in the past. I can tell in subtle ways that my friendships are deeper, nicer and more satisfying, and my marriage feels richer, as well. Attachment work is not easy, but I feel good about what my daughter and I have accomplished together. I wouldn't have life any other way, for my daughter or for me.

Tools for Getting Help

Once we realize that our adult attachment style will impact and limit the attachment style of our children, our first task is to begin to assess what our adult attachment style might be.

Assessment. The best method for identifying adult attachment style is assessment by a professional familiar with Main's Adult Attachment Interview system. Therapists trained in infant mental health, child attachment, foster care, or adoption, will be familiar with the interview, as they are more accustomed to assessing attachment issues.

Books. If a formal evaluation is not readily available or possible, reading can also be of great help. Books can be extremely helpful for exploring and examining adult attachment issues.

Self-reflection. Thinking about the following questions can also be a tool in evaluating attachment issues:

- How did you interact with your parents in your early childhood?
- Did you feel safe with your mother and father?
- What is your earliest memory with your mother?
- What is your earliest memory with your father?
- What did you 'not get enough of' in childhood?
- What do you fear in relationships?
- What do you fear for your child in relationships?
- What do you think was difficult for your parents to do in childhood? Why?
- Did anyone die in your early childhood?
- Were there other adults that were significantly involved in your caretaking when you were young?
- Were there other adults that you could rely upon as you were growing up?

The Use of Therapy

I believe that therapy is by far the most effective way to become 'earned secure', or to 'hear' those parts of us that have not yet been heard.

The most important factor in finding a good therapist is to find someone that you are comfortable with, someone you can talk to with complete honestly. It is perfectly legitimate to shop around for a therapist to make sure you find someone you like and respect. It can be a good idea to talk to several different therapists, either on the phone, or in person, to see who feels right for you. As a good friend of mine says, "We don't expect the first pair of shoes we try on to fit, so why would we expect the first therapist to fit?" Some therapists will be willing to meet without a fee for the first session to facilitate finding a good working relationship; this is worth asking about.

The therapist should also be well trained and familiar with attachment or developmental theory. Good therapists can include social workers, psychologists, or psychiatrists. Ask how long they have worked as a therapist, and if they've helped

---

How to Become a Terrific Parent Even If You Didn't Have One...

Parenting from the Inside Out, How a Deeper Self-Understanding Can Help You Raise Children Who Thrive by Daniel J. Siegel, MD & Mary Hartzell, MEd

The Whole Parent, How to Become a Terrific Parent Even If You Didn't Have One by Debra Wesselmann

Mothering Without a Map: The Search for the Good Mother Within by Kathryn Black

Growing Up Again - Second Edition: Parenting Ourselves, Parenting Our Children by Connie Dawson, and Jean Illsley Clarke

others do adult attachment work. When deciding who is right for you and how you feel about them, trust your gut instinct.

Finally, there are many kinds of therapies that can be helpful in working on adult attachment. Among those available are: Psychodynamic, Interpersonal, Cognitive, Humanistic, Imago, and Infant Mental Health work with adults or families. EMDR (Eye Movement Desensitization Reprocessing) is a somewhat new technique for processing past trauma, which can be incredibly helpful within a short amount of time. For all these types of therapies, find a professional who specializes in the technique, talk to them about how applicable it might be for you and what you hope to accomplish.

~Kathy Miller Reilly has a PhD in Clinical Psychology from the University of Detroit, and a Master's Degree in Social Work and a Master's Degree in Personality Theory from the University of Michigan. She is married and is an adoptive mom.

In My Own Words–*It takes more than love...*

One very real, but often overlooked, symptom of emotional pathologies like attachment disorder is an unhealthy family dynamic. To paraphrase Nancy Thomas (author of *When Love is Not Enough*), emotional pathology is contagious. My current attachment therapist told me she can practically diagnose an attachment disordered child by simply talking to the mother! Is the mother depressed, angry, frustrated, or stressed out way beyond the point of a regular parent? Is her relationship with her husband or partner strained? Are the other children in the house acting prematurely responsible and covering for the attachment disordered child to keep peace?

I am sad to admit that I was thrown in a deep depression from living with a child who rejected me, was not compliant, was destructive, and who caused chaos constantly. Not only was I unable to find love for her in my heart, I became anxious and super-charged with adrenaline whenever I was near her! Needless to say, I was not the ideal parent. To make matters worse, I had an immense sense of guilt and failure that was heightened by the well-meaning words of those around me, who told me to just 'love my child more' and to 'change my expectations'.

In order for me to help my family heal, I had to first get myself to a better place. One major turning point was finding a therapist who validated and recognized my feelings as 'normal and completely expected' for a parent of a child with Reactive Attachment Disorder. I was freed by the notion that I could be a good parent without feeling much love or attraction for my child. All that was required was a *desire* to love her and a *desire* to help her. Of course, this is not easy. We are tired, over scheduled, and financially strained (therapy is not cheap or fast!) Every moment of every day is a living practical exam on how much I want to love her and how much I want to help her.

Every whine, every blood-curdling scream, every repetitive chant, every stiff hug, every averted look, every lie, every deliberately spilled or broken item is an opportunity for me to do the right thing. If I miss it, it is not long before I am given another chance! My daughter's gift to me is to give me endless chances for me to redeem myself and become the mother I want to be: the one that loves her children and is strong enough and wise enough to heal her family.

~ By Lisa Kastner, adoptive mom

Post Adoption Depression Syndrome
What It Is and One Mother's Experience
By Sheena Macrae

The birth-Baby 'Blues' are pretty much understood within our society and empathetic help is offered to new mothers by family, friends and physicians. While depression after childbirth is thought to be hormonal, the outcome in how mothers behave often fits doctors' diagnostics for a true depression. Normally, bio Baby Blues are short-lived, and new mothers return to 'normal' as hormone levels balance.

> "I thought I was the failure: that I couldn't mother well. In fact, neither I nor my child was the problem. Each of us was coping with the transition to family as best we could, given the raw circumstances of international adoption."

When we adopted our daughter, it was clear to me in China that she was an angry child: she bit me, hard! I was a medical case! I was afraid that she'd do it again; and she did. I became afraid of her …and this was a child of only eighteen months old. My husband felt it was only natural that she be angry, and went through the litany of all the disruption we had caused to 'her world', no matter how limited that had been. I felt that her anger went deeper.

But what if an adoptive mom feels depressed post-adoption? Is this like birth- Baby Blues? Post Adoption Depression Syndrome (PADS) is a term coined by June Bond in 1995 in an article for Roots and Wings magazine. Bond's suggestion that the Baby Blues can affect adoptive families took the adoption community by storm.

When we came home, my husband returned to work within a week. I was left to cope with a traumatized toddler (I am quick on the mark enough to have judged this was the case except for the first few days in China when I hoped it was teething). She could be a bonny, attractive, and smiling child, and indeed she was to others, including my husband. Friends commented on how easy she was, how social. But what I got was a child who swung from lengthy anger outbursts to complete autistic-like shutdown. At night she had sleep terrors.

June Bond's article on PADS, coupled with a survey conducted by Harriet McCarthy with families who adopted from Eastern European countries, alerted other adoption workers to the possibility that post-adoptive families "are not always the happy families we all think they should be".

It was a hard first year. But the anchoring thoughts of other mums already parenting post-institutionalized children let me understand about attachment disorders, and how these are prevalent in institutionalized children. I also began to understand how differing children respond to events, why some suffer the effects of trauma and loss and others emerge truly unscathed. I realized that my child was a 'sensitive' child, with sensory issues; every knock and noise on the physical and emotional level set her jangling. I understood that she zoned out because she was overwhelmed at all the changes that had overcome her.

I called medical advisers for help, but, but they saw only the social child, and suggested I deal with the 'Terrible Two's' by putting the child in the hall and walking away. I had enough raw sense to realize that this would be counter-productive. I knew that my daughter wouldn't dare let herself trust, and was trying as hard as she could to push me away. So I didn't do the 'time-outs', and I lost confidence in my pediatrician. But I learned I needed to build her trust in me.

Post adoption depression can be a product of environment: of emotional highs and lows and of a feeling of inability to cope with a new child whose issues may be far from the 'facts' presented on the referral sheet. It also tends to strike those who have already had a history of being depressed, or emotionally fragile themselves. All families, but perhaps especially those for whom there is a history of depression, should be on the alert to deal with the stressor that adoption can be. No matter that society says it should be the happiest of events.

I got so angry with the effect her anger and her zoning-out had on me that I spent a lot of time diffusing my frustrations on our gravel driveway; there is a lot of sensory relief crunch-jumping on the path! I was also extremely upset that I was not better able to sort my own emotions. How on earth could I sort hers if I couldn't sort my own? A neighbor watching me push my daughter in her stroller commented afterwards that she had felt so badly for us both that first year—my child hardly ever raised her head from her chest, and I pushed sometimes as if all the vitality had gone from me.

Advice to agencies, social workers and families post adoption needs to center on getting help to affected families, and not to make it a shameful matter that help is sought. It is critical to understand that children from institutional or foster care may well enter the adoptive home with specific and demanding needs of their own. For them to 'come home' to parents whose own needs swamp the child's is a double whammy. There is a great deal of research available to show that children of depressed parents do not thrive easily or heal emotionally until the parents are whole once more. We parents have a great responsibility to our children to look after ourselves.

I thought I was the failure: that I couldn't mother well. In fact, I understand that neither I nor my child was the problem. Each of us was coping with the transition to family as best we could, given the raw circumstances of international adoption. I felt was alone and isolated in a situation where I would now recommend to others to get help as fast as possible. My husband couldn't see the problem, friends couldn't see the problem, and I was deflated. I struggled pretty much on my own, losing friends along the line when they couldn't see what I saw in my child, and feeling pretty isolated in my marriage, too.

Some Resources:

The Post-Adoption Blues: Overcoming the Unforeseen Challenges of Adoption by Karen J. Foli, PhD and John R. Thompson, MD

Attaching in Adoption: Practical Tools for Today's Parents by Deborah D. Gray

Babyshock! by Jean MacLeod. *EMK Press Parent Resource,* **www.emkpress.com**

Attach-China/International **www.attach-china.org**

A 4everFamily **www.a4everfamily.org**

Adoptive Parents need to ensure a backup system and support network prior to bringing home baby and enlist the help of social workers, adoption therapists and doctors in the assessing realistically the emotional and physical needs of a post-institutionalized child.

What definitely saved me was learning to trust in my judgement as the parent of my child. I knew her anger and her shutdowns were similar to the Terrible Twos (and Threes and Fours)

but they went further. I would urge any parent with a child who has inappropriately intense emotions or intense lack of emotion (zoning out) to consider that this small child might have disregulated emotions.

Parents can:
- Enlist the help of the adoption therapists or social workers to help parents cope. Inform your family and friends what you may be trying to accomplish with your child (attachment work with an avoidant child can be tough work). Let them know how they can help you!
- Make realistic preparations for time off work (if your child is not ready for you to return to work when your leave of absence is up, do you have a back-up plan?)
- Make realistic plans for keeping self and home together while dealing with baby and self…prioritize, and let go of what is not important!
- Decide who you need to allow into the care-plan for the child, and use grandma or an understanding friend for short respites.
- Plan partner time (a glass of wine together while the child sleeps–or doesn't–is good partner fuel). Realize that parenting, especially parenting a traumatized child, can be a bumpy transition. Be supportive of one another and communicate.
- Plan fun time with your new child, or at least get out with the child in the fresh air, or sing some songs in the park. Making good times happen with PADS is easier if an outing is planned.

Adoption Professionals and Health Care Professionals need to be aware that adoption, like many life milestones, may bring with it a sense of intense fatigue or burnout instead of the anticipated sense of achievement. They also can:

PADs Checklist

Don't allow depression to make you unavailable to your baby, or ruin what should be an exciting time in your life. If you are experiencing the post-adoption baby blues and it shows no sign of lifting, ask family or friends to help you make an appointment with a therapist or physician. A consultation with an attachment therapist or a therapist specializing in adoption issues could be very beneficial, as they usually have experience with international adoption and understand the parallel family issues. PAD can creep up on you slowly; the following are some questions that may help you identify whether you're just having a bad day, or whether your depression is larger and should be treated. If you answer 'yes' to a number of these questions it is highly recommended that you discuss your feelings with qualified personnel. If you answer 'yes' to the last question, you **must** seek help immediately:

- Loss of interest in being around other people?
- Always on the verge of tears?
- Difficulty concentrating--unable to make decisions?
- General fatigue or loss of energy?
- Difficulty sleeping or an increased need for sleep?
- Significant weight gain or loss?
- Excessive or inappropriate guilt?
- Feelings of worthlessness?
- Feelings of powerlessness?
- Feelings of hopelessness?
- Loss of enjoyment in things you like?
- Irritability?
- Recurring thoughts about death or suicide?

Information provided by the American Psychiatric Association

Expect the Unexpected

Realize that parenting a baby or child that is coming to you from an orphanage or foster care will present you with issues that you aren't going to find covered in Dr. Spock or in What *to Expect the First Twelve Months*. If your parenting style is not effective on your post-institutional child, then you need to adapt it to what works! Most of us were not taught, pre-adoption, about our post-institutional child's deep need for 'control', or clingy, anxious attachment, or what to do about lingering orphanage behaviors. Parenting a new child with adoption issues can be exhausting, overwhelming and bewildering. It is extremely depressing to feel like you are a failure at parenthood, but you are not! You may simply be working off the parenting role model you were raised with, and it doesn't necessarily work with our post-institutional kids.

~Jean MacLeod
Babyshock!

- Be aware that adoptive families may have bonded in the hearts with a fictional child. Reality (a child with real and perhaps overwhelming emotional or physical special needs) brings grief for the 'might-have-been' dream. This grief in turn may re-trigger other, older losses, such as infertility or divorce, or even an adoptive parent's own childhood trauma.
- Be proactive in offering families local help, national help and the opportunity to plug into the global community of the adoption internet. The adoption community can help support moms and dads, and teach them the skills of adoption-parenting.

Fast forward four years from our first daughter's adoption. Her new sister is home, and health advisors have come to our home to check her over. My daughter acts out mercilessly, then zones out. The nurse watches it aghast, then shakes me by the hand and tells me she never did believe me before. She does now that she has seen it all.

- Be ready to offer pre-adoption discussion and facts as a total matter-of-fact-course. Families should first hear of the possibility of PADS through social workers and agency pre-adopt seminars.
- Families who adopt and have a parent with a depressive history need particular help from primary health care providers. If a parent is depressed, they cannot be the parent that their new child needs them to be. Seek counseling, anti-depressant medication, help from a spouse or extended family, and parenting support groups. Asking for help is in fact being a responsible parent

And fast forward with us all to the present, eight years from that first bite. I have a loving, intense first daughter, still prone to drama, but attached most solidly to our family. With knowledge, emotional work and adoption-parenting skills, we have come through her early trauma, my PADS reaction, and the addition of a sibling, to become a whole family. .I still use the gravel path on occasion. But I'm often joined by my daughters--crunching can be fun!

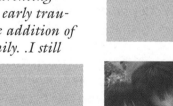

~Sheena Macrae

The Resilient Parent
Healing Yourself, Mothering your Child
By Debbie Carr-Taylor

My daughter lived in my psyche for two decades before I met her, but my thoughts didn't carry melodies of the mother-daughter dance. I had no memories of tender moments between a mother and her child. Mostly they were of the horror I felt at risking a repeat of the physical and emotional abuse my mentally ill mother rained on me, during my childhood and young adulthood.

During those decades, as a solution to ending the cycle of abuse, I vacillated between swearing I would never have children and a cautious and growing optimism that the hard emotional work I was doing would allow me to become a parent.

On the day I met my daughter I promised her I would strive to be the mother she deserved. I felt the responsibility of being the best parent I could be so that I wouldn't become yet another stumbling block from her difficult, early life circumstances.

I am a social scientist by profession and a researcher at heart so I spent my time waiting for my daughter reading about what might be expected of me as the parent of a post-institutionalized child. In addition to reading about general adoption issues, I focused on attachment issues. I felt it was so important to be able to recognize signs of attachment difficulty (or hopefully, signs that my baby was open to attaching), learning attachment-promoting activities, and preparing to welcome my daughter.

Happily, my seven-month-old daughter gave indications that she had her attachment abilities still alive within her. She made strong eye contact, quickly came to prefer me over others, and was happy to let me fully care for her. The first bottle I prepared for her was so telling. Her tiny hands came up to hold it, but as soon as she felt me continuing to hold it she released the bottle and never touched it again in all her months of bottle-feeding. I could feel her relax into my body that first time as her eyes searched my face. It is an understatement to say she was simply open to my mothering. In retrospect, I think it was she who started to draw me to her.

As my days of motherhood unfolded, I found that there were times when I felt overwhelmed by my daughter's physical and emotional demands and I would simply 'space out'. I would suddenly realize she'd been crying in her crib and I hadn't 'heard' her, or she would be sitting in my lap and a poke or baby sound from her would pull me back to attention. She definitely noticed when I was not fully present with her and did not like it. I had to force myself into a constant 'mental checking in' to keep me from tuning-out when I was tired or overwhelmed. While this served my daughter well, it was exhausting for me. There was little room in my life for other things and I knew this was not a sustainable pattern.

Over time, I was drawn again to the attachment literature I had read in preparation for parenthood. As I re-read old resources and found new books on the subject I came to see myself in them! I could see myself as the 'avoidantly-attached' child who had grown into a dismissively-attached adult! This was such a revelation to me; I gained a deeper understanding of some of my characteristics and behaviors.

Of particular help to me were the books that included adult attachment styles, not just children's, and information about how adult attachment affected parenting. I saw a way of healing myself and of becoming a better parent to my daughter. I found these books tremendously empowering and I was excited and impatient to make the necessary changes in my internal geography!

I spent a year of focused emotional work including therapy, an intense sort of "holding session", lots of reading, reflecting, writing, and sharing with trusted friends. In this process I learned that how I was parented affected how I mothered my daughter, and why I needed to heal hurts that were deeply buried beneath my surface. I started this emotional work out of my profound commitment to my child.

Resilient Parent–Resilient Child

I no longer need the constant vigilance to keep myself tuned in to my daughter. It happens naturally now, even when I'm tired or overwhelmed. I have more confidence in my relationships and I'm not nearly as afraid to state my true feelings or needs. I've been able to re-envision my life being connected to people, rather than being on the outside, looking in at people in satisfying relationships.

During therapy, I considered why I have been able to bounce back from some tough childhood experiences and move toward an 'earned secure' attachment style in my adulthood. I also began to wonder why some international adoptees have been able to manage the effects of their very difficult beginnings and why others seem totally overwhelmed by what they've experienced. I was introduced to the concept of resiliency during this time and I recognized it as an invaluable life skill or trait, and one I wanted to pass on to my own daughter. In scientific terms, resilience is "a universal capacity which allows a person, group or community to prevent, minimize or overcome the damaging effects of adversity" (Grotberg, 1995). Or, as the popular quotation says, "the ability to get knocked down ten times and get up eleven". Some people are born with resiliency skills, but many have to work to build and internalize them. The traits of a resilient child or adult (*from the International Resiliency Project*):

I HAVE:
- People around me I trust and who love me, no matter what
- People who set limits for me so I know when to stop before there is danger or trouble
- People who show me how to do things right by their actions
- People who want me to learn to do things on my own
- People who help me when I am sick, in danger or need to learn

I AM:
- A person people can like and love
- Glad to do nice things for others and show my concern
- Respectful of myself and others
- Willing to be responsible for what I do
- Sure things will be all right

I CAN:
- Talk to others about things that frighten me or bother me
- Find ways to solve problems that I face

- Stop when I feel like doing something not right
- Figure out when it is a good time to talk or take action
- Find someone to help me when I need it

The previous points are from Edith H.Grotberg, PhD, Senior Scientist, Citivan International Research Center, University of Alabama, Birmingham, who conducted the International Resiliency Project www.resilnet.uiuc.edu/library/grotb97a.html.

A resilient person has a cluster of these characteristics. These may be innate for some people, but all can be learned, modeled, and/or taught–which is the true value of resiliency! You can learn to bounce back or help your children learn to bounce back, even if you're not a natural 'bouncer'.

Bouncing Forward. Teaching or learning resiliency is adding new ways of responding to situations. It is learning new dance steps for old tunes and even writing whole new songs to dance to. These are invaluable skills for all of us, but particularly so for parents of adoptees and our children whose early lessons on how life works may not be serving them well.

There are many books written on learning resiliency in personal and professional life. To start with, it is helpful to get a sense of how resilient you are. A quick and interesting resiliency test can be found at www.resiliencycenter.com. After you get a sense of how resilient you are, you may want to pursue different resources for beefing up your resiliency.

What I've Learned... Don't give up on yourself or your child! It is very often possible to heal from difficult childhood circumstances. Each step toward healing is empowering and allows bigger challenges to be successfully taken on. Emotional well-being is a process, not a destination. There are different issues to address at different points along the way. For me at least, there was a point where the process changed from a survival mode (I have to do this emotional work or I just cannot function) to a journey of increasing richness, and satisfaction with the results. Resiliency is perhaps the most important skill in life. It helps you pick yourself up when you trip. It will keep a person forging ahead, seeking happier, healthier options. It allows a person to truly be in the moment, rather than bogged down in past difficulties. It provides a level of creativity and innovation in thinking and actions that can add richness to any life. It provides a foundation for strong personhood. It dramatically enhances parenting ability.

Resiliency is what keeps a mother dancing to lovely tunes with her child, rather than being trapped alone on the sidelines with an ugly noise from the past replaying in her head.

~ Debbie Carr-Taylor is an adoptive mom
She was a research sociologist for the federal government before becoming a mother.

Resources

The Resilience Factor: 7 Essential Skills for Overcoming Life's Inevitable Obstacles by Andrew Shatte and Karen Reivich

The Resilient Self: How Survivors of Troubled Families Rise Above Adversity by Steven J. Wolin, MD, and Sybil Wolin, Ph.D

The Power of Resilience by Robert Brooks and Sam Goldstein

Becoming Attached: First Relationships and How They Shape Our Capacity to Love by Robert Karen, PhD

Loss of a Dream, Gain of a Child
Adoption and Infertility

Resource
Adopting After Infertility by Patricia Irwin Johnston
Not a how to adopt book but one that allows you to understand the emotions and feelings of both ways to build a family.

People adopt for many reasons. Some parents are first time elective adoptive parents, some elect to adopt after the birth of birth children, and sometimes election to adopt doesn't arise from infertility. Many families come to adoption after unsuccessful attempts to conceive, carry, and give birth to 'bio babies'. Adoption preparation courses often deliver on 'loss in adoption', but how often do they ask parents coming to adoption after infertility to use their own losses to find empathy, a common place, with their adoptive child? While it's not the same loss, it is loss of the familiar; the child, and the parents who were each 'expected' by those same children and parents.

Adoptive parents can use their own insight and experience of the profound loss of the possibility of birth children to illuminate how their adopted children may feel. As the children grow, it can be hugely enriching to discuss the 'what-ifs', and how both adoptive parents and their children grow to encompass the loss each has and grow to meet the loss in the joy of being together! In families where children and parents have each suffered loss, empathy often allows a parent to attune faster to a child's loss. Working to heal a child's losses often takes parents on a parallel journey, where, as the child heals, we also gain insight into our own hurts. That's the plus side. There is however the darker side of the moon that we need to be aware of, and which good pre-adoption preparation should highlight. Our child's journey–both emotional and simply how they look– may raise ghosts: the 'might-have-beens' of the parent who has lost the dream of a biological child.

It's about life and its milestones. As our adopted child peers in the mirror to find whose nose is reflected in her pretty nose, and whose feet gave her those long toes, we may be peering silently round the edges of the mirror wondering what a bio child of ours might have looked like. As our adopted child excels at sport, fails at reading, and is the most wonderful mimic ever, we may wonder how much of that is nurture and not nature. We may ask what of our adopted child we did make–and wonder if that would have been less, more or just the same had we had bio children. And if our adopted child flunks rather than succeeds where it's important to us to succeed, how far must we move away from ascribing that 'failure' to genes? We absolutely must. We need to step away from the losses of what if to the gains of what is.

Older adoptive parents report also that when adopted kids leave home (perhaps to rejoin communities representing their birth culture), marry, make sexual choices, and have kids, it's tough. Becoming a grandparent is another time that the past losses can be triggered. It's tough realizing that the feelings may still surface–as you look at a child that is not biologically related to you as well. But–growing up never stops, nor does the giving that makes a parent 'real'. Never mind velveteen rabbits and loved, worn noses– we have to know our losses, recognize their triggers, and never stop seeking to understand if we want to stay real parents.

~By Sheena Macrae

10 Tips
from a Do-Over Dad
By Richard Fischer

I have often referred to myself as a 'second chance dad'. In what seems like a lifetime of perpetual parenting, I seized the exceptional second chance to parent a duet of infant daughters, united with me through the miracle of adoption. Thirty years had passed since my first round of two a.m. feedings, sterilizing bottles, and the unending procession of cloth diaper washing, but the memory of those experiences was still fresh in my mind. The experience wasn't entirely positive and still lingering was the uneasy memory of what I neglected in my juggle between family and career. I was about to become a do-over dad, but I vowed this time would be different. I prepared for a higher level of fathering skills, anticipating that my Chinese-born daughters, already separated from their first families, would need the special touch that only an understanding and better disciplined dad could provide.

From the beginning, I understood that Jing Ying's world was about to be turned upside down. In one brief exchange of loving arms, all that she came to recognize and experience in her few short months of life would vanish into a too-soon faded memory. Sights, sounds, smells, and the culture of her birth, along with the familiarity of her caregiver's touch, would now be replaced with her new dad. To transition her life experiences and to help her learn to trust and love her new 'baba', I would need to call upon both old and new dad to communicate the love I ached to share. I wanted more from this parenting connection than the 'hurry and grow-up' routine that was my initial version of fathering.

For the new and soon-to-be dads, I will share with you a China dad's dim sum of thoughts and experiences that have made fatherhood akin to heaven on earth for me:

1) Take your time, and savor every moment of those first months and years of being a dad. Your child has but a short time to be a kid without the pressures that accumulate with the teen years and the metamorphosis to adulthood. Allow them the freedom to live the "kid experience" and enjoy this magical time at their own pace. This may be your last chance to be a kid again, too!

2) Communicate at their level, both figuratively and philosophically. Get down on the floor, connect eye to eye and share a simple dialogue sparked with excitement and imagination. Teach your child to dream, explore the world around them and learn to "just imagine" by finding animals in the clouds, building bedspread forts in the living room or floating Popsicle stick ships down the gutter after a spring rain. A simple touch can be magic too. My daughter Jing Ying loved to touch and be touched, often falling asleep while lying on my chest, listening to my whispers and feeling the beating of my heart next to hers.

3) Make yourself available to spend quality time with your child, and be spontaneous. Unscheduled outings with dad can be adventurous or a great time to share an ice cream, with a few giggly butterfly kisses added for good measure. When you are with your child, give her your undivided attention. I put my personal hobbies on hold for a few years and learned to fish with only my daughter's fishing pole in order to give her my undivided attention. Now at age ten, she still loves to fish with dad and often makes dates with me to share a picnic lunch (and passes along her tips for catching the most fish!).

4) Remember you are building a family, not just adding a child. If there are older siblings, set aside private time to build and strengthen those relationships. Let them know you value their input and encourage them to claim ownership in the decision to adopt. Striking a comfortable balance between work and home is an important issue to address. Plan on spending as much time as possible with your family, especially in the first days and weeks of a new arrival.

5) Give yourself an emotional green light to talk to your children about their feelings, fears and emotions. Validate their concerns and practice being a good listener. Don't be afraid to show your emotions and try to refrain from telling your teary-eyed three-year-old that "big boys and girls don't cry". It sends the message that expressing the pain of minor injuries or lamenting emotional losses in life isn't allowed.

6) Avoid the 'Superdad Complex'. It's not dad's job to fix every problem, be the ultimate sports authority or provide all of the gifts to your children. Parenting is not about meeting your expectations of being the greatest dad; it's about being the best and most consistent dad you can be.

7) You can't relive your life vicariously through your child's activities. It's their turn to be the star athlete, studious scholar or heralded artist as they choose. It's your job as dad to be the counselor and cheerleader, and it doesn't hurt to keep your chauffeuring skills intact.

8) Praise, praise, praise at every opportunity the efforts and accomplishments of your children. Encouraging the 'can do' attitude early on will make a big difference in how they perceive and adjust to

difficult situations in the years ahead. I often tell my daughters, "I'm proud to wear your name; thank you for being my daughter."

9) Connect. Share meals together to start the day and reconnect after work, school or play. Turn off the television and talk; make plans together or share a laugh as a family. Experience connectedness in sharing the simple pleasures of being together.

10) Adopting a child of a race different than yours brings the responsibility to educate and prepare your child for life in a color conscious society. Learn to be sensitive to the issues your child may face and provide a cultural connection that will promote a positive identity and healthy self-esteem. I suggest participating in one of the cultural camp programs that offer workshops and activities for both children and their parents. The children get to interact with other adoptees that share their cultural connection, and parents get access to the adoption professionals and experienced adoptive parents who will become the nucleus of a life-long support network.

~ Richard Fischer is the publisher of Adoption TODAY and Fostering Families TODAY magazines, a Congressional Angel in Adoption Award recipient, and an adoptive dad.

Discipline

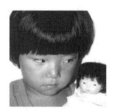

Anger and Control Issues
Using Empathy to Reduce Anger
Helps Parent and Child
By Christopher J. Alexander, PhD

Children who are adopted certainly don't have a monopoly on anger as an emotion. It is quite common, though, for this group of children to manifest anger in ways that can appear excessive, confusing, and threatening. While most children will protest if they are bothered or angered by something they don't like, it sometimes seems as if the anger expressed by adopted children is in excess of what we believe is called for at the time. This can include having an explosive outburst to seemingly minor things, such as not getting one's way, a parent arriving late, a casual remark, or an innocent touch.

Adoption specialists point out that adoptees often feel anger in response to being given away by birth parents, feeling like second class citizens, and feeling unworthy of having anything good happen to them. We must also stay mindful of the fact that many adoptees come from backgrounds where there is a family history of poor impulse control, psychiatric disorders, substance abuse, or other factors that can contribute to a poor modulation of emotions. Thus, when the child is angry, he may have little recognition or control over how intense his response is. Also, children who grew up in violent or chaotic environments had aggression and rage modeled for them and they quickly learn that it is an effective way of getting attention and perhaps even getting one's needs met.

As parents, we must always strike a balance between understanding possible causes of our children's rage, while taking care not to enter into power struggles or do things to harm or shame the child. This is incredibly difficult, as children are highly skilled at being able to identify and push our buttons! It is inevitable that children will make us angry.

Particularly if you are adopting an older child, he or she may come from a background where there weren't adequate limits set. The child feels entitled to doing or getting what he wants and resents it when the adoptive parents try to bring order and an alternative reality to the situation. Issues of trust are paramount with adopted children and many of these kids will resist trusting the adults who adopt them. While we recognize that our efforts to bring boundaries, safety, supervision, and guidance to children are in their best interest, they may perceive it as a threat to the foundation of their being.

Many parents are surprised to find themselves in huge power struggles with very young children over basic requests such as telling a child to get ready for bed or to wash hands before dinner.

For many people, anger is expressed when they feel out of control. What I find with a lot of adoptees, though, is that they use anger to feel in control. This is why the child may react with anger or rage after a period of calm or when he has shared intimacy with a parent. This may trigger feelings of vulnerability in him, which he defends against by getting mad and physically or psychologically pushing you away. The anger is used to help him feel safe. When parents respond with anger, it confirms to the child that people can't be trusted and that the world is a threatening place.

But what if we respond to the child in the opposite way? When you're angry with a friend or partner, do you want them to battle back with you? Probably not. That just leaves you feeling discouraged and wondering why he or she doesn't understand you. What if, on the other hand, the person we were angry with said something like, "I can see how mad that makes you," or "You're really mad at me," or "That really hurt you?" Even if we are being irrational with our words and behaviors, there is a quality to that level of response that helps to diffuse the situation. Maybe a more balanced discussion of the issues can be had at a different time. But when someone responds to our anger with compassion, we feel less defensive and we pull back from our attack.

In every presentation I do on raising adopted children, I emphasize the role that empathy has for these kids. All of us—children and adults—want to feel that someone understands our needs, confusion, and hurt. Given the isolation and alienation that so many adoptees feel inside, the importance of receiving empathic responses takes on heightened importance. Empathy communicates "I can see how you feel". It doesn't offer answers or solutions for painful feelings or events, but it communicates to the child that we can see into their hearts and minds and recognize the impact that things have on them. When parents offer empathy for a child's anger, he often feels closer to them, as the parents convey that the relationship is strong enough to withstand his rage. Parents also communicate that the relationship they share with the child is more important than any conflict that is going on.

It is a good bet that your child knows what makes you angry, how to get you even more fired up, and in what ways you are likely to react. For a young being who feels so little control in life, imagine how powerful that must make him or her feel, knowing they can bring you to the boiling point without much effort on their part. Next, be aware of what your typical response to being angry is: are you the kind of person who says or does things to make other people feel bad when you're angry? Are you likely to throw or kick things? Do you feel the need to discuss the event in minute detail at the time you and the other person are angry? Do you need to be alone, away from others when you are angry?

What is important about becoming aware of your own response to anger (in yourself or others) is your knowledge of what you are modeling or communicating to your child. If you want others to hurt inside when you are mad, what will the effect be on your child if you make comments that cause him to feel bad about himself? If you need to be alone when you are mad, how will you handle this need if you are raising a young child and it is just the two of you?

Other strategies that I find helpful in dealing with anger and power struggles include:

Try lowering your voice instead of raising it. Imagine the impact on the child of hearing the parent gently say, "If the trash is not taken out in the next five minutes, I will put the video games in storage for a week." If a parent yells this, it sounds threatening. If, on the other hand, it is said in a matter-of-fact tone, the child receives the message, "Do as you will. I'm not going to battle with you. I trust you know the consequence for not complying."

Recognize when you are most vulnerable. If you are likely to be rushed, tired, or on edge on certain days or at certain times, this increases the chance you will get angry and reactive at those moments. What can you do to add a buffer during these times? How can reduce the stress? Will it help to wake up earlier, avoid cooking on certain nights, or tell your partner you need more of their help? Will you need to set limits in advance with your child, such as saying, 'No TV' or 'No friends at the house' during those times?

Don't forget to breathe. When I'm angry, I hate hearing that one. But it really does work. Taking one second to breathe deeply or counting to five shifts the brain from 'fight or flight', to 'focus' (thinking of more rational responses). Remind yourself to breathe, focus attention, and to carefully think through what your reaction to stress/conflict will be.

Anticipate your child's triggers. Oftentimes, it is possible to predict when your child will get angry. This might be on Monday morning when they have to shift away from weekend mode, on anniversaries or holidays due to the memories they raise, at bedtime, at mealtime, or when they have to do homework. When you can anticipate these events, you are in a better position to think of how to defuse conflict before it arises. This might include giving the child advanced notice, such as, "I know tomorrow is your brother's birthday and it seems like that is always a rough day for you. What can we do in advance, to help make it a better day for all of us?"

Follow through afterward. Whether the conflict, power struggle, or rage episode with your child was major or minor, and whether it was expected (He always fights with me at bedtime) or unexpected, it is important to talk with your child about what happened. But do it after the tension has settled. For example, while bathing your child, tucking her in, or folding clothes together you can say, "You were really mad at me earlier when I said you couldn't have ice cream." Permit your child to share their thoughts or feelings, but try to educate him or her about the impact their words or actions have on others: "When you throw things like you did, it scares the dog and that's why he doesn't want to sleep in your bed." "It hurt my feelings when you called me that name. Clearly, you wanted me to feel bad and you succeeded." "That ice cream was your father's and he had been waiting all night to have it. It's important that we share in this family. Tomorrow, we'll go out and buy treats that we can all have." "I'm sorry I called you a brat. I don't think badly of you. Your behavior makes me crazy at times, but I still think you're the best kid in the world."

~Christopher J. Alexander, PhD is a child psychologist, specializing in the treatment of foster and adopted children and the author of Welcome Home: A Guide for Adoptive, Foster, and Treatment Foster Parents

Discipline
With an Adoption Twist
By Deborah Moore,
based on the work of Doris Landry, MS with permission.

How many times have you been in the check out line at your local grocer, calmly flipping through your favorite magazine, when the shrieking wail of a tantruming four-year-old echoes through the aisles? "I want candy NOW," he bellows, his face purple with rage, lying flat out on the floor, kicking and banging his legs into the linoleum. His mother, bending down on her knees, pleads with him to get up and 'be a good boy'. Near tears, she fights her own rage at her son's behavior, and feels humiliated and embarrassed. Finally, out of desperation and with gritted teeth, she tells him to get his candy fast, so they can get out of the store.

Before I had children, I self-righteously vowed that no child of mine would ever act that way, especially in public. I would never have children who were so demanding or who acted so inappropriately, and I would never give candy to my children just to get them to stop screaming. My children would be sweet, kind, and quiet, and would immediately obey every word from my mouth. It's amazing what a few years and two children later will do to change a person's perspective!

Now when I witness a child melting down in the candy aisle at the grocery store, I look with tremendous sympathy to the poor mother. I want to go up to her, put my arm around her shoulder, and tell her I know exactly how she feels. I want to offer her candy from the stash I keep in my purse for my own kids at all times!

Raising children is more difficult than it looks. Like it or not, our kids need boundaries, and it's our job to set them, and our job to enforce them. For me, the area of discipline has proven to be one of the most challenging areas of adoption-parenting.

While waiting for our first referral, I read all the latest parenting books and thoroughly researched the most popular disciplinary techniques. I felt well prepared and ready to parent, and assumed I would know exactly what to do with my oldest daughter when she came home from China at fifteen months old. I would know how to feed her when she was hungry, change her when she was wet, rock her to sleep when she was tired, and comfort her when she was hurt or sad. And for the most part, that

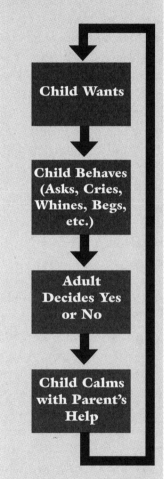

Cycle of Want
Assuming emotional needs continue to be met, an older child learns to calm and self-regulate through a parent's yes or no response to their 'want'. The circle must be completed for positive learning to take place.

Child Wants

Child Behaves (Asks, Cries, Whines, Begs, etc.)

Adult Decides Yes or No

Child Calms with Parent's Help

Parent says yes or no based on what is best for their child. Calming is what completes the cycle, not saying 'yes' for peace and quiet. You teach self control and belief in parent.
~Doris Landry, MS

was true. What I didn't expect, and didn't know how to deal with, was her intense need to be in control at all times. My baby wanted to be the boss!

How could such a tiny, beautiful, child cause such havoc with her demands? Out came all the parenting books, and as our daughter grew older, we tried all of the discipline techniques we had read about: time-out, taking away toys and privileges, scolding, and even spanking.

But our daughter didn't respond to the discipline methods at all like the 'experts' said she would. When we placed her in time-outs, she became terrified and clung to me as if I were her life line; when we scolded her, her eyes became empty and she hung her head in heart wrenching shame. Our loving disciplinary methods were not producing the results we had been 'promised' in all the books! Our methods only seemed to exacerbate our daughter's feelings of shame and loss, without correcting any of the bad behaviors that had prompted the correction in the first place. It was then that we realized that our daughter, like many adopted, post-institutionalized children, had some unique needs when it came to discipline.

Doris A. Landry, MS, LLP, a child psychologist who specializes in adoption issues in internationally adopted children, recognized the ineffectiveness of mainstream parenting books on post-institutionalized children. Doris created a new modality for adoptive parents, and called it Discipline with an Adoption Twist. There are many different types of disciplinary techniques, but all methods can be tweaked or 'twisted' to be most helpful for the adopted child.

Landry believes that the word discipline often brings to mind punishment for some offense or misbehavior. But what discipline is really about is socialization and behavior regulation. Correct discipline, lovingly applied will build a life-long alliance between the parent and the child. Parents sometimes mistakenly view spanking or isolation of the child as appropriate discipline techniques, yet these methods fuel a child's feeling of anger toward the parents, and leaves the adopted child feeling tremendous shame.

Shame is not feeling that what I did was bad, but rather, that I am bad. Shame is a significant issue with adopted children. Shame/guilt is recognized as one of the seven core (lifelong) issues of adoption for all members of the triad: the adoptee, the birthmother and the adoptive parent. For the adopted child, shame is the sense that they deserve rejection, because there must be something wrong with them or what they did, for the loss of birth parents to occur. Deborah N. Silverstein and Sharon Kaplan Roszia, state in their article *Lifelong Issues in Adoption* that, "Adoptees suggest that something about their very being caused the adoption". (See page 7 for more information.)

A child's sense of shame can inhibit attunement (the feeling of being 'at one') with his adoptive parents. If a child feels as though there is something intrinsically wrong with him–the 'real' reason why his birth parents left him–then why would his adoptive parents feel or do any differently?

Daniel A. Hughes PhD, author of the acclaimed book, *Building the Bonds of Attachment, Awakening Love in Deeply Troubled Children* states, "When infants have experienced a lack of attunement and pervasive shame through neglect…they cannot be reassured that they have worth. For these poorly attached children, discipline is experienced as rejection and contempt."

One evening the behavior of my youngest daughter (adopted from China at ten months of age) prompted me to give her a 'time-out' on my bed, while I was folding laundry. At age five, she was fully aware of why she was being disciplined, yet she was wailing loudly and letting me know that she did not like being confined or corrected. After five minutes, I stopped folding laundry, sat on the bed and took her into my arms. Before I could utter a word, she laid her head on my shoulder, and cried "Mom, I must have done something really bad for her to leave me."

Where did that come from? We hadn't been talking about her birth parents, her adoption, or anything even closely related. But there it was, from her heart and thoughts, into words, shame coloring her countenance. We sat for long time that evening, discussing her birth parents and the feelings she has about them and the reasons why they left her. Had I spanked her or isolated her in her bedroom for a time-out, I can only imagine what thoughts her sense of shame would have heaped on her small shoulders. Instead, because I was close by and stayed in tune with her during her 'time-out', I was privileged to be allowed inside her pain and confusion so I could help her understand the feeling for what it was. Being totally accepting of her and the feelings that she holds, binds us together in attunement where our feelings, thoughts and behaviors are in harmony. That evening, I know my daughter felt total acceptance from me, and felt intrinsically that she was loved.

Doris Landry states that appropriate adoption-discipline tools allow parents to:

- state behavior expectations
- stop a child's bad behavior
- correct a child without shame
- re-attune with a child

Our children are acutely aware of our non-verbal cues when we are disciplining them. They not only hear our words, they experience our facial expressions, the tone of our voice, and the hand gestures that we use. We mustn't forget that our children are more tuned into what we do and how we present ourselves, than by what we say. They need to sense our total commitment and empathy towards them during each episode of discipline, in order to obtain attunement.

There are times that our children need us to match their emotional experience. They need to see us involved with

Different Kids, Different Tools

I need different toolboxes for each of my children. Both of them spent an extensive part of their first year in an orphanage and that's about where the similarities of their needs end. A non-adoptive parent said to me a few months ago that she re-parents every single day. She has a 13 year-old and said what worked yesterday doesn't mean it will work today. A very simple statement, but one very comforting to me.

Keeping up with my ever-changing six year-old has put more than a few gray hairs on this head. It seems as if I am constantly refilling my toolbox with new and different things to meet her needs. My second child is officially special needs (hearing impaired) but I don't need nearly so many techniques with her as with my first child. No one thing works for us every single time.

~ Mary, mom of two from Eastern Europe

The Empathy Tool: Healing and Hugging

I've found that my kids react in a more positive way when I am seriously understanding of how really bad or ashamed they feel, deep down, when they do something wrong. My daughters more often have tears and need comforting when I go right to their feelings: "Oh, look at what happened; you must be feeling pretty bad about this."

I might continue to help my daughters understand the seriousness of whatever happened in a non-judgmental way, while addressing the sad/mad/scared inside feelings the child has over what they did. I do calmly/sadly/seriously express my own feelings if something of mine has been involved, or if they have hurt someone's feelings. When I use empathy, they feel worse about stuff on their own, than I would ever want to make them feel! They also like that I maintain control (it feels safe), and that I can help give them both emotional and concrete ways to go forward and self-regulate. They are then open to healing and hugging.

~ Jean MacLeod

their feelings and the pain, anger or disappointment that they are feeling. One way we can do this, is to match the intensity of their expressions. One day, when my daughter was screaming and out of control, I raised my voice, took on her feeling of frustration and yelled, *"I know you are so angry with mom right now. I feel your anger!"*

The pitch of my voice and the intensity I was exhibiting took her totally by surprise. She stopped screaming, and started talking with me instead. My sense was that she felt understood by me; that I felt the extent of her anger. This, of course, is not going to be appropriate every time you discipline your child. But it is helpful to keep this in your 'toolbox' of discipline techniques.

The Extra Layer

On top of whatever method of discipline you choose, Landry suggests adding these three basic tools to dramatically increase its effectiveness. Successfully disciplining an adopted child takes the extra layer of adoption into consideration:

Understand. It is important for us parents to help our children understand the meaning of their actions. For instance, children who were hit, slapped, kicked or restrained in their orphanage may replicate those behaviors under duress, without understanding why. When a child misbehaves, and you can recognize where the behavior comes from, it can be helpful to explain the relationship between his actions and his past.

Express empathy. With your empathy you can help a child see that while his behavior is bad, he is not bad. When you take him into your arms and engage in meaningful dialog about the 'why' of what happened, you are not condoning his misbehavior, but rather helping him understand the origin and the meaning of his behavior.

Re-attune. The child's understanding and the parent's empathy together lead to a re-attunement between parent and child, allowing for the child to express sorrow for hurting the other person. He is then able to learn and change and to openly accept your guidance and correction.

Our children will try our patience and push us to our limits. They need to be corrected and disciplined like all other children. But because they were adopted, our children have needs and issues unique to them. The added layer of adoption, along with perhaps the added layer of being a post-institutionalized adoptee, adds some complexity to our discipline models. Before my daughters came home, I had planned to discipline straight from the book, with a one-size-fits-all approach. But once my kids arrived, I quickly realized that that was not going to work. Their need for correction and discipline was the same as every other child's, but the way I handled it needed to be different.

Their past experiences necessitated that I consider different models. Some of the best advice I ever received about disciplining my children, was to have a 'toolbox' of techniques. Landry, in her "Discipline with an Adoption Twist" workshop, outlines seven different discipline 'tools'. These are all basic, well-known methods, but with an explanatory adoption 'twist' for our children's extra layers.

The Toolbox...

1-2-3 Magic. This book, written by Thomas W. Phelan, PhD, asserts that parents often treat children as little adults, and often spend way too much time trying to persuade our children that we are right. Parents talk too much and with too much emotion, which actually provokes the child. This can lead to yelling and even eventually to hitting. The 1-2-3 Magic philosophy:

1) A parent gives one explanation only.
2) A parent's authority is not negotiable.

After giving the one explanation, the parent then begins to count. If the misbehavior doesn't stop as a result of the explanation, the parent warns, "That's one". If the misbehavior continues, the parent says "That's two." If the child is still misbehaving the parent says, "That's three" and gives the child a time-out. The parent is not to argue with the child, or lecture the child. After the time-out, the child re-joins the family.

> **The Adoption Twist:** Parents should not send the child off to another room as suggested in 1-2-3. Rather, by keeping them close and modeling calm, controlled behavior you help the child regulate by not allowing him to escalate. This method takes the emotion out of the discipline, which will help the child re-attune with the parent.

How to Talk So Kids Will Listen & Listen So Kids Will Talk. This popular book written by Adele Faber and Elaine Mazlish give parents four techniques for suc-

---

Mommy or Daddy Time Outs

If your child's behavior has pushed every angry hot button you own, save your sanity and stop yourself from doing something you might regret. Give yourself a mommy (or daddy) time out and remove yourself from interaction with your child for a few important moments. Words to use: "I love you but I am very angry with your behavior. I need to go to my room and calm down for 10 minutes. After that, we will talk!"

cessful listening (a key piece of communication and attunement):

Listen with full attention. When you only half listen, children just give up even trying to talk with their parents. But when you give them your full attention, they feel special and want to talk with you even more.

Show a caring attitude. Children don't always want you to fix their problems. They may just need to know that you care about them and what they're feeling. You can often communicate your caring with just a word, such as "Oh" or "I see", or "Mmmm..." The child will know he was heard.

Deal with feelings, both the parents' and child's. How often do we as parents try to deny what our children are feeling? Our child will try to express emotion, and we quickly jump in telling him not to feel that way. Instead we need to help them deal with their feelings by naming those feelings. Statements such as "you are sad", "what a shock that was for you", or "you really cared about your friend" will help your child feel that you understand him.

You don't need to fix it. Don't try to solve the problem. Parents often try to explain things with adult reasoning. Telling a 2-year-old that you don't have any Toastie Crunchies in the house doesn't mean anything to him. All he knows is that he wants them now! Instead, give into the child's wishes and fantasy. How much easier it is for a child to go along with you when you fantasize right along with him about how wonderful a box of Toastie Crunchies would be. When mom wants it as much as he does, how can he argue?

Faber and Mazlish also offer help in gaining cooperation from our children. Parents can talk to their kids in such a way that the kids will naturally listen.

Describe the problem. Simply stating the problem as you see it is much better than blaming, yelling, or coercing. The point is made without blame and without emotion. It does not put the child on the defensive. Instead of *"You haven't taken the dog out all day. You don't deserve to have a pet.",* try *"I see Rover pacing up and down near the door."*

Use one word. Instead of yelling at your child again for walking out without her lunch, simply say 'lunch'. Again, you don't express blame or accusation toward your child.

Talk about your feelings. Instead of yelling at your child for pulling on your sleeve, tell him calmly, "I don't like having my sleeve pulled". It is more difficult for a child to argue with how his behavior makes you feel.

The Adoption Twist: The goal of the Faber/Mazlish method is to help children change unacceptable behavior without making them feel threatened, attacked or rejected, and also to help parents learn to listen so our children feel genuinely heard. This is particularly important for the adopted child, who may have a heightened sensitivity to not being heard or understood. The parents need to be mindful of not falling into the adoptive parent discipline trap, and should avoid:
- Giving in to the child's demands out of fear that the child won't love them.
- Being overly dismissive of the feelings that an adoptive child is trying to express (not really listening).

Behavior Modification. This relies on rewarding positive behavior in order to increase the frequency of such behavior. Any behavior will increase if followed by something pleasant. The reward can be either material, verbal or time spent together. Parents need to be careful when using this approach, and consider whether not reaching a reward will wrongly affect their child's self-esteem, and if the system is reinforcing the correct behavior.

One way to use the behavior modification technique is with the use of a reward chart. Once the problem behavior has been identified and agreed upon by the parents, it then needs to be discussed and agreed upon by the child. Allowing your children to help select the rewards and help in designing the chart is usually greeted with great enthusiasm. It's important to set a start date, and commit to a consistent time of filling out the chart. For some kids, behavior modification doesn't work. If, after implementing this technique, you see that it is not working for your child, then you need to question why. Perhaps it is because your child has significant control issues, or doesn't truly trust his parents to know what's best for him, both of which are not uncommon in adopted children. Parents may need to seek professional help.

The Adoption Twist: An important thing to remember about this discipline technique is that the rewards should be only positive, such as more time spent together, or choosing dessert for that night, or playing a favorite game together. Behavior Modification is really just a helpful indicator to measure if your child can be amenable to change…or if the problems run deeper. If a simple additional story at bedtime is motivation for a reward you are well on your way to a healthy relationship. If nothing motivates the child, then there is cause for concern; children normally are motivated by positive incentives.

Time-Out. Time-out is a common discipline technique that often needs modification in order to be appropriate for a child who:
- has been recently adopted
- has not fully attached to his parents
- struggles with anxiety related to separation from his parents

Time-out involves separation of the child and parent by sending the child to a designated room away from the family. But a child who has attachment issues, or who is just learning to trust his new family, should never be forced away from the parents. Using time-out, but with the adoption "twist", the parent still disciplines the child, but places them in a location close by.

Another adaptation of Time-Out takes place with the child sitting in the parent's lap to calm down and "think". A tantruming child can be kept safe in a parent's arms and lap while mom or dad is sitting on the floor. An out of control child may scream to get away, but desperately needs the calm, safe physical security of his parent.

For my daughter, a time-out, away from me, was torture. She would become overwhelmed with shame, and often would be unable to give me any eye contact. I could tell, by her body language and facial expressions, that she was not feeling healthy guilt, but rather a degrading shame, which rendered her unable to accept my love and forgiveness. I saw a huge difference when I began doing close-quarter time-outs with my daughter. I place her on a chair just outside the room I am in, but close enough that she can always see me. I explain once why she is being sent to time-out, that I will be very close by, and that she will not be alone. I set the timer, and go about my work. I don't speak to her or answer her call, but she can always see me. When the buzzer rings I go immediately to her side, gain eye contact and express my love for her, while still explaining that the bad behavior will not be tolerated. I noticed right away that this type of time-out helped alleviate her tendency to go immediately into shame. We are able to quickly re-attune and she was better able to understand why she was being disciplined, and apologize, because emotionally she was intact.

The Adoption Twist: Time out minimizes the shame response that adopted children are so easily prone to. This type of time-out is a positive example of disciplining a bad behavior, while always helping the child feel emotionally and physically secure.

Time-In. Time-in is a variation of the time-out technique mentioned above. According to Landry, the goal of time-in is for a chronically misbehaving child to experience a

Dealing With Control

Living with a child-sized control freak can be frustrating. Battling a child's tenacious will over endless inconsequential interactions is wearying work. Giving the child many choices over his or her daily life doesn't seem to end the ongoing problem, either. How can a parent help a child deal with a need for control that has invaded home, school, and the child's friendships?

Remove Yourself. It's not about the parent finding a way to eradicate the problem, it's about the child. A child's continued need for control is indicative of his feeling intrinsically out-of-control, and has nothing to do with what you might have attempted to do to help your child change.

Ask Your Child. Create a dialog with your child to really find out what is fueling the undesirable control-behavior. How does the child feel inside when he has the need to take control? What is going on within the child that needs to be addressed? A child who is helped to recognize the fear or anger his need for control is masking, can take steps toward awareness and consciously work at letting go the need for control. A securely attached child cares about what his parents think and feel, and wants to please them. Parents who understand the true issue of control can deal with the issue at its core, and not waste time and effort on the resulting symptoms. Needing control is a tough behavior to break, but a child who knows that his present negative behavior is based on feelings and experiences in his past, will be able to work on a new pattern with the guidance of his family.

~ Doris Landry, MS, LLP

successful day. When a child repeatedly misbehaves and does not respond to other disciplinary methods, a time-in may be appropriate. The parent explains to the child that she is going to help him have a good day by keeping him near by, and helping him make good decisions throughout their time together. The child is kept physically close to the parent, usually within arms length, for as long as the parent thinks necessary. As the parent goes about her day with her child beside her, they are able to talk together about his misbehavior and the feelings that caused it. The parent is also able to correct any subsequent misbehavior or bad attitude, because she can address the issues immediately, as they surface. The key to the success of this technique is for the parent to be very loving and empathetic toward the child, as the parent helps the child make good choices.

The Adoption Twist: The physical closeness of the parent and the time spent together give the parent and child an opportunity to process the child's feelings and surfacing behaviors. The parent must present a time-in as a help to the child, not as a punishment. The idea is to promote a "we are going to do this together" team feeling. Time-In is a wonderful opportunity to practice and strengthen attunement between parent and child.

Love and Logic.   Love and logic parenting, created by Foster Cline and Jim Fay, is an approach to raising children that puts parents in control and teaches responsibility to children. This is accomplished by parents setting firm limits in a loving way, and making sure the child knows in advance exactly what is expected of him. The child then experiences natural consequences for his actions, both good and bad, and is held accountable for his actions and for solving his own problems. The parent expresses empathy toward the child for making a bad choice, but does not bail the child out of the problem or try to solve it for him. The Love and Logic approach is normally a very positive technique, yet for the post-institutionalized child, or the child that has been neglected, abused, or shuffled from family to family, the "natural consequence" may not be known to him. Time is needed for the parent to teach and train the child, and to establish a basis of trust. If trust has not been established, then natural consequences can be shaming rather than instructive.

The Adoption Twist: Coaching the child may be a necessary adjunct to implementing Love and Logic, as some of life's lessons may have been missed (especially if the child was adopted from an orphanage or from foster care). Coaching focuses on teaching the child appropriate behavior. Instead of just telling a child to stop a behavior, the parent teaches the child societal expectations, and what appropriate behavior looks like. This builds an alliance between the child and his parent.

60-Second Scolding.   A 60-second scolding is another highly effective discipline technique. When the child misbehaves, the parent comes close to the child and makes eye contact, even gently holding his face if necessary. The parent tells the child, firmly but

Re-attunement

It's the emotional reconnection with your child after you've disciplined. This is really important in our family because our daughter can easily get mixed up between bad behavior and bad girl. She needs me to pull her close emotionally and remind her that she's never a bad girl, that I'll always love her no matter what she's done.

Re-attunement is not an optional thing; it must happen at the end of the discipline cycle. It helps keep kids from spiraling into shame and emotional disconnect.

~Debbie Carr-Taylor,
adoptive mom

without shouting, how the child's actions affected the parent. The parent then softens her voice, hugs the child and tells him how much he is loved and assures him it is the parent's job to take care of the child, and together they will work through the problem.

The Adoption Twist: The 60-second scolding is intense and honest, provides immediate intervention and ends on a nurturing note, affirming the parents love and commitment toward the child. Most parents scold, walk away and proceed with life as though nothing has happened. The adopted child is profoundly affected by disciplinary action, so the re-attunement "twist" is vital. This technique is powerful in its simplicity and works well for the adopted child, as it fosters a quick re-attunement between parent and child.

A wonderful word to remember, because we often forget to do this, is praise! We must never forget to praise our children. Sometimes a well-timed word of praise and encouragement can head off bad behavior before it even begins. Our kids covet our praise for hard-earned accomplishments, for behavior that is pleasing and appropriate, and for behavior that was not as bad as it could have been. No matter which tool we use from our adoption-parenting toolbox, our children who were adopted need our loving discipline. We must convey that nothing the child does will ever push us away, and that we love them enough to correct their behavior when it is wrong, with no strings attached. And even if they fail, they need to know our love stands strong.

~ By Deborah Moore, adoptive mom of two daughters from China. Based on the work of Doris Landry, MS, LLP

Guilt, Shame, and the Adopted Child
One is a healthy reaction to wrongdoing, one is toxic.
By Jean MacLeod

Shame is similar to guilt, except guilt is externalized ("I did something bad") and shame is internalized ("I am bad"). Shame in adopted kids can be traced in part to our children being abandoned or relinquished, and their resulting feeling of worthlessness:

- I must have been a very bad baby to make my mother give me away.
- I am so bad inside, that my own mother didn't love me.
- Everyone will know I am bad inside when they find out I am adopted.
- What do I say when kids ask "Why didn't your real mother keep you?".
- I was a bad baby so I'm a bad kid and I am powerless to become good.
- My adoptive parents don't understand how bad, how worthless, I really am.

Kids get stuck in shame because it becomes a vicious cycle: the child feels she is a bad person at her inner core, so why attempt goodness (or repair a mistake) when there is no hope to 'be' good? Shame feeds shame, and keeps the child frozen in place, unable to break the cycle. Shame needs to be addressed as an adoption issue, as a by-product of losing birthparents, abandonment and institutionalization. Kids need reinforcement and coping skills when learning to deal with feeling shame, and a parent's 'attuning' disciplinary choices are a key element of the learning process.

Coping Skills
Separate the behavior from the child. Help a child see the difference between "making a bad choice" and "I am bad so my choices are bad" by talking about the two. Everyone makes mistakes! A child who needs to be 'perfect' may be thinking that being less-than-perfect equals being worthless. Reassure the individual, while reprimanding the behavior:
"You are a smart kid, but that was not a good choice."
"I love you, but I can't talk to you about the cat when I am on the phone."
"You are always so generous; can you think of a better way to share with your sister?"
A reprimand that feeds shame: *You little brat! How many times have I told you not to hit your brother! Why are you so nasty?! When will you learn?*
A reprimand ending in re-attunement: *I am really mad at your behavior. Hitting is never appropriate! You must have been very angry at your brother but you need to apologize and I will come with you* (gently and firmly take child by hand to make an apology; follow with a big hug and "I'm proud of you" after the child apologizes).

Some adopted children need help in understanding the steps of reparation when they have made another person feel bad, or have accidentally hurt them. The child may have deep remorse for his words or action, but may be so frozen in shame that he is unable to see past his own self-focused feelings. Guilt is a healthy reaction; it urges people to make amends. Parents expecting a 'normal' guilt reaction from their child are puzzled by the child's apparent inability to care about the injured party—they don't understand that the offending child feels worse than they could ever imagine.

The parent needs to teach the child the social steps out of shame: a sincere apology for a misbehavior makes the hurt individual feel better and forgive, and makes the apologizing child who is feeling shame, forgive himself.

A Different Approach
Parenting a child with special behaviors requires special skill...

Those of us whose adopted children have attachment issues, sensory issues, Attention Deficit Hyperactivity Disorder (ADHD), Post Traumatic Stress Disorder (PTSD), high anxiety, autism, or other special needs, often face considerable public censure for our supposed contributions to our children's annoying behaviors. We may doubt ourselves and our abilities as parents. "You need to be more flexible," some experts might counsel, while others will insist that we ought to be more firm. Over time and with trial and error, we may in fact learn that we have to adopt a different parenting approach than the one that comes most naturally to us. But while we can definitely improve our children's chances by paying attention to the approaches that work best for them, our parenting is not fundamentally to blame.

Like all parents, we can (and do!) model appropriate forms of reacting and behaving, but our children's brain chemistry is out of kilter, and all the modeling in the world won't make an impact for our kids in the absence of more explicit teaching, repeated experiences of 'containment,' and sometimes other measures as well, such as dietary changes or medications.

To offer containment through a more structured environment to a child who needs it is not 'coercive' or disrespectful, any more than it would be 'coercive' or disrespectful to pull a toddler's hand away from a flame. But it is hard work to create that structure. And it is especially hard work to do it while maintaining a sense of humor and showing the child that she is always valued for who she is.

Ultimately, in terms of discipline, neither 'permissiveness' nor 'authoritarianism' cause our children's problems with self-regulation. People who are not parenting kids like ours might like to congratulate themselves that they are doing a better job, but frankly, they don't understand that we are parenting children who are 'different', and who need a completely different approach.

~ By Susan Olding

Being with Your Child in Public Places

Change Your Perspective on Tantrums and Change Your Child's Behavior
By Patty Wipfler, founder of Parents Leadership Institute (PLI)

We live in a society that has a demanding and judgmental attitude toward parents and young children. Often, the attitude toward children in public is that they should be seen and not heard, that the parent should be 'in control' of the child's behavior, and that children who are having feelings in public are a nuisance. In short, children are not really welcome. Their freshness, curiosity, and frank expressions of feelings are not seen as a gift.

In addition, the child rearing tradition that has been handed down to most of us sets us against our children when their behavior isn't convenient for adults. In the eyes of others, we are expected to criticize, grow cold, use harsh words and gestures, punish, isolate, shame, threaten, or physically attack a child who is 'misbehaving'. No parent really wants to act like an adversary to the child they love. We treat our beloved children in these ways when we can't think of anything else to do, or when we fear the disapproval of others.

There are certain situations in which young children often become emotionally charged. These situations include:

- Being with several people–with the whole family at dinner, at a family gathering, a meeting, a birthday party, the grocery store, church, or temple.
- Moving from one activity to another–leaving home for day care, leaving day care for home, stopping play for dinner, going to bed.
- Being with a parent who is under stress–you can supply your own examples!
- At the end of any especially close or fun-filled time–after a trip to the park, after a good friend leaves, after wrestling and chasing and laughing with Mom or Dad.

When children become emotionally charged, they can't think.

They simply can't function normally. They become rigid and unreasonable in what they want, and are unsatisfied with your attempts to give them what they want. They can't listen, and the slightest thing brings them to tears or tantrums. Their minds are full of upset, and they can't get out of that state without help from you.

The help your child needs at this time is to have you set kind, sensible limits, and then for you to listen while he bursts out with the intense feelings he has. This spilling of feelings, together with your kind attention and patience, is the most effective way to speed your child's return to his sensible, loving self. A good, vigorous tantrum, or a hearty, deeply felt cry will clear your child's mind of the emotion that was driving him 'off track' and will enable him to relax again and make the best of the situation he is in.

How are we parents supposed to listen to a screaming, flailing child in the middle of the supermarket? Several adjustments of our expectations are necessary before we can allow ourselves to be on our children's side as they do what they need to do in a public place.

Help Your Child Ward Off a Mad Attack

Things for Parents to Say

- "Stop and think. Make a good choice."
- "Remember to breathe when your tummy gets tight. Breathe. Let's breathe together."
- "Use your words, not your fists. People are not for hurting."
- "You can do it. I know you can get your mads under control."
- "I understand, right now you are feeling mad. Still, you can't hurt people, things or yourself."
- "You are the kind of kid who can take care of his own bad feelings."
- "Go to a safe place and draw out your mads."
- "You have a choice: Talk out your feelings or go to time out and get your mads under control."
- "Well, I'm feeling mad right now myself. I'm going to go cool off, then we'll talk."
- "I know how you feel. Sometimes I get mad myself. Then I tell myself, that it is OK to be mad if you are nice about it."
- "Thanks for sharing your angry feelings. Good choice in using your words!"
- "We are learning to be a 'Speak your feelings' kind of family. No more 'Mad Family' for us."
- "I believe in you. Sometimes it's tough, isn't it?"
- "You are one terrific kid!"

~ Excerpted from The Mad Family Gets Their Mads Out by Lynne Namka, EdD. Used with Permission **www.angriesout.com**

Every good child falls apart, often in public places. This is, for some reason, the way children are built!

Our society has trained people to disapprove of children doing what is healthy and natural. People disapprove of horseplay, of noise, of exuberance, of too much laughter, of tantrums, of crying, of children asking for the attention they need.

As parents, it's our job to treat our child well. When other adults criticize him, it makes sense to do what we can to be on our child's side.

Being parents means that we will have to advocate for our children in many settings. We need to advocate when we are with doctors and nurses, with teachers, with relatives, and with strangers.

Acknowledge that children legitimately need far more attention than it is comfortable to give. Adults who gave less attention to their own children, or who got little attention themselves as children, will be upset when they see you giving undivided attention to your child. We can expect these upsets, but we don't have to be ruled by them.

What do I do when my child falls apart in the supermarket aisle, or at the grandparents' house?

Spend one-on-one time with your child before you take him to a public place. Ensure that you and he are connected with each other before heading into a challenging situation. Then, stay connected. Use eye contact, touch, your voice, and short touches of your attention to stay with your child. This contact is deeply reassuring, and can sometimes defuse situations that your child often finds difficult.

When you see an upset beginning, immediately make real contact. See if you can find a way to play, so that your child can laugh. Laughter relieves children's tensions, and allows them to feel more and more connected. If, when you make contact, your child begins to cry or tantrum, do what you can to allow him to continue. His upset will heal if the feelings are allowed to drain.

Slow down the action, and listen. If getting into the car seat has triggered tears, then stay there, seat belt not yet done, and let the tears flow. Listen until he is done. Because of this cry, your whole day, and his, will improve.

If necessary, move to a more socially acceptable place. Go to the back bedroom, or move your grocery cart out the exit to the sidewalk. Do this as calmly as you can. Your child isn't doing anything wrong. It's sort of like a car alarm going off accidentally–loud, but not harmful to anyone. These things happen!

Plan what you will say to people who express their opinions or concern. It's hard to come up with a comment that says, "We're OK–don't worry!" in the middle of wild things happening, so think ahead. You can adopt some phrase like, "We seem to be having technical difficulties," or, "My daughter really knows how to rip!" or, "It's that kind of a day!" or, "After he's finished, it's my turn!" or simply, "We're OK. I don't think this will last all day." A comment like this reassures others, and gives the message that you are in charge.

As one parent I know put it, "I've finally figured out that it's my job to set a limit when he's going 'nuts', and it's his job to get the bad feelings out. As I listen to him, people might not be able to tell that I'm doing my job and he's doing his, but at least I know that's what's going on."

~ By Patty Wipfler, founder of Parents Leadership Institute (PLI) and Parenting by Connection. Parenting by Connection is the PLI approach to fostering close, responsive relationships between parents and children (www.parentleaders.org)

A Playful Solution to Anger and Aggression

"Feelings" Faces. Make paper plate faces attached to popsicle sticks. Have each child make faces for every feeling you can think of. Make sure the project is done with lots of laughs and exaggerated faces. Keep the faces handy and use them all day, every day. The minute someone acts up (don't forget to include yourself!) grab a plate face. Ask the children to pick a plate face to show how they feel. Some might be scared, mad, shy, or bug-eyed. Why? Because we all react in our own way to the same situation. Then ask everyone to pick another face to help make everyone feel better, especially the child who started the situation. *Do this everyday.*

~ Jane K.

Out of Control Parents
And How to Help Yourself get Back into Control

I figured out when my daughter was a toddler that I was fully responsible for most of her breakdowns! Not directly, but because I wasn't listening to her toddler cues. I was usually hell-bent on doing something I wanted to do and had dragged her along past nap-time. Or I hadn't properly prepared us to get somewhere on time, and I was irritable and trying to rush her. It all came back to mom. Making choices that were good for her was also a good plan for me. I learned to be a step ahead, to understand my daughter's dynamics, and to respect my hot-buttons.

It's okay to get mad. You get to model the 'dark side' to your kids, too, and teaching them how to safely cycle through anger might be the most important element in demonstrating the healthy rhythm of home and self-regulation.

I have worked really hard on my patience over the years. My family has not perfected tranquility by any means; I think what we have learned to do better is cycle our anger down non-destructively:

- I force myself to calmly verbalize my irritation to my kids a few steps before I lose it (and give them opportunities to quickly find a solution, or to rectify a bad situation if they are to blame). Verbal de-escalation is one of the big steps in my self-regulation, and I force myself to 'talk' before I need to yell.

- I use a 'special phrase' before needing to go to anger; this warns my kids that they have pushed me to my limit ("I have a really bad headache moving in" is my red flag!)

- We talk about our feelings a lot; I have found that using empathy on an angry child is a major de-fuser and a huge parent tool.

- If one of my kids has a melt-down, we analyze what went wrong afterwards and come up with better solutions to express mad without being out of control (sometimes we even role-play). This is a good follow-up to a child's tantrum, along with required hugs. If I have a tantrum, I apologize, and hug them even more!

Hearing your own 'monster mom' words screaming from your children's mouths, is never a proud moment. But at least you know they're listening! Use those as an example of how not to handle anger, and explain how you will work to make your 'mad' constructive.

Addressing the issues that interfere with the rhythm of the home doesn't mean brushing conflict under the rug. A parent keeps the family whole and in sync by catching negative escalation, dealing with it in a non-shaming manner, developing a behavioral structure for each child, and by modeling the behavior you want your child to internalize. Awareness is half the battle to taking back control of the home, and a calm, happy environment is easier to attain if family members are in harmony.

~By Jean MacLeod

Loss & Grief

Adoption Circle Gains and Losses
Each Part of the Triad Experiences Them.
By Vicki DuFour

As an adoptive parent you may have thought about what your child gained when she joined your family but you may not have considered what she lost. Or what you and your child's birth parents lost. Loss is a part of the adoption experience for everyone in the adoption circle. Each member will experience loss in different ways and at different times in their lives.

Adoptive parents gain in many ways; the opportunity to parent a child; to give love, wisdom and a family legacy. But they lose too. They lose a genetic connection with the child; the opportunity to give birth, and perhaps even the first years with the child. They lose the privacy and control involved in building a family without outside intervention. And if their child is from a different racial or ethnic group, they lose anonymity. On every public outing they become a 'conspicuous family'.

Adoptive parents often find it difficult to identify the losses that adopted children experience. They are so pleased at what they have been able to give the child that they do not want to think that the child may have lost something. But adopted children do experience losses. They may gain a loving, nurturing family, committed to their care forever, but they lose a biological connection and relationships with their birth parents, siblings, and extended family. For children from foster care, they may also lose the relationships with previous caregivers.

Many adoptive parents also find it difficult to imagine that there can be gains as well as losses for birth parents. Adoption is usually portrayed as a win for the child and the adoptive parents, and a loss for the birth parents. The losses are obvious–giving up the role of parent and the opportunity to nurture a child throughout her life. But there are gains for birth parents. They gain the freedom from the responsibility of parenting a child when not ready or able to do so; an opportunity to pursue different life goals, and particularly in open adoption, the security of knowing the child is in the home of a loving, caring family.

Adoption involves a series of tradeoffs for all members of the adoption circle. As an adoptive parent you may have already accepted the losses that you experienced when you adopted your child. Your child also needs to grieve her losses. If you are aware of her losses, you will be more able to help her accept and work through them.

"The biggest losses I feel as an adopted person are to do with lack of knowledge. Not knowing my medical history. Not knowing if I have siblings or not. The lack of racial identity. I feel an emptiness around what I don't know. I have so many unanswered questions, and a general sense of uncertainty about whether they will ever be answered."

"There's no doubt about it, my nuclear family is my number one gain. Being a member of my family is a huge part of my identity. When I got married I was adamant about keeping my maiden name. It is part of who I am. I have the best, most supportive family you can imagine. Even now, when I'm grown with a family of my own, my parents send me email telling me how important I am to them and how our family wouldn't be the same without me."

Possible Gains and Losses
Take some time to reflect on the unique circumstances of your own adoption experience and add to this list.

Gains for Adoptive Parents
* Opportunity to raise a child
* Fulfillment of having a family
* Siblings for other children
* Become a multi-cultural family
* Getting on with life after infertility
* Feeling prepared to parent

Losses for Adoptive Parents
* Genetic connection
* Experiencing birth
* Nurturing your child in his first few hours, days, months or years
* Privacy
* Control

"There were definitely gains from the adoption. I know I have had far better opportunities in life than if I had stayed in an orphanage. If I had grown up in Korea, I'd have no chance of a decent life. For orphans, no bloodlines, no status. And I wouldn't give up my family for anything. My parents, even if they irk me, have made a lot of effort. They are good people with the best of intentions. Living transracially in the United States has given me an understanding of diversity and a perspective on the world that most people don't have."

"When I visited Korea I was in my twenties and that's when I began to realize that it wasn't just a family and a birth mother that I lost, but also a culture. I realized that I could never see the country as a native, only as a tourist. I know that I am a true American at heart, which is nice, but also depressing. I'll never know what it is like to live as a Korean lives. I don't have those family traditions. I don't have the language. I tried to learn the language so I could communicate with other Korean people. All the time I was in Korea, I had this sense that my family was out there but that I would never know it. There's so much in that loss, I can't express it all."

Adoption Stories from *"Finding the Missing Pieces: Helping Adopted Children Cope with Grief and Loss"*

Gains for Adopted Child
- Permanence
- A loving, stable home and family
- Opportunity
- Security
- A sense of belonging

Losses for Adopted Child
- Growing up in his birth family
- Control
- Connections
  - to birth country and culture or neighborhood
  - to previous caregivers
  - to siblings

Gains for Birth Parents
- Peace of mind
- Opportunity to pursue goals
- Choice and a role in child's life (if open adoption)

Losses for Birth Parents
- Child
- Control
- Connections
- Self-esteem
- Choice and a role in child's life (if closed adoption)

Loss and the Adopted Child

Adoption loss is different than other types of losses such as death or separation from a loved one. Adoption seldom involves a single, identifiable moment of loss, and therefore is less likely to result in clearly identifiable stages of grief. It may not be permanent. The birth parents may be absent, but often they are still alive. There is the possibility of reconnection, especially in the case of a closed adoption that is opened, and in some kinship or foster care adoptions.

Adoption loss is also often realized after-the-fact. The adopted child may become aware of the losses related to adoption long after the adoption itself is finalized. This awareness grows and changes over time, so that at each developmental stage the adopted child reconsiders what has been lost.

Finally, adoption loss is unrecognized. Society often does not acknowledge that there is a relationship between an adopted child and a birth parent, so there is a limited understanding of the child's need to grieve the loss of that relationship.

Parents need to be aware of the various factors that affect a child's response to adoption loss when considering how their child is coping. First, and most importantly,

1) Consider the child's stage of development because this affects his ability to understand the loss. As the child grows older, his ability to understand the nature and cause of loss changes.

2) Next consider the age of the child at the time the loss occurred and the nature of the

> *"It was just in the past few years that I began thinking about adoption in terms of loss. My friend remarked that, as adopted people, our lives began with a loss. That one idea explained the anger and the feelings that I'd been unable to place. It made me realize how angry I felt toward my birth mother. I was angry that I would never be able to tell her that I was angry. And that led to another loss; I had to let go of the idea that she'd be in my life one day. I haven't really let that idea go through. I don't know if I'll ever really be able to let it go, until I know that she's dead."*

loss. A child adopted at birth with no conscious memory of his birth parents will grieve differently from a child who enters placement with memories of his birth family.

3) Consider the degree of attachment your child may have had with previous caregivers and the numbers of separations and losses that he experienced. Children who have experienced many previous losses may show few signs of obvious distress when moved to a new home. They have learned to cope with repeated losses by not allowing themselves to feel sadness.

4) Your child's temperament is another important factor in how he responds to loss and the most important indicator of how you will respond to his grief. You may already have some ideas of how he deals with difficult and challenging situations, and how you respond.

Your best strategy for helping your child deal with adoption losses is to be sensitive to the cues he is sending, and intervene when you feel it is appropriate.

Loss and Grief as the Child Grows Up

Children may grieve the losses surrounding their adoption many times throughout their lives and they will grieve differently as they grow older. Young children cannot express their grief with words; instead they show their feelings in their behavior. Older children may also display nonverbal indicators of grief. At each stage of development, the child's behavior and understanding of adoption will require a different response from the parent.

Infants and Toddlers. Even very young children can feel grief for the loss of a birth parent or a caregiver if they have grown attached to that person. Parents who adopt children at this stage should be sensitive to indicators of grief, including *changes in previous eating and sleeping patterns, lethargy, unexplainable crying, and separation anxiety. They may also regress, and begin acting younger than they are, ceasing behaviors that they have already mastered.*

The best strategies for coping with a young child's grief are patience, understanding and closeness, both physical and emotional. Let her cry, sleep longer, spend more time with you, eat foods that are comforting, and talk in baby talk, if that allows her to work through her grief. Provide consistent schedules and routines and keep major changes to a minimum.

Preschoolers. Preschoolers tend to be very literal and self-absorbed. They are interested to hear their adoption story, but often fail to understand what the words mean. They are also very sensitive to differences, and transracially adopted children may begin to ask questions about why their parents are a different color. *While they may not*

"Although I've known my birth mom for as long as I can remember, there was a time when I was a kid, maybe ten or twelve, when I thought about adoption all the time. What if I hadn't been adopted? What if I had stayed with my birth mother? When I thought about it logically, I realized that I would be in a totally different place than I am now, and it wouldn't be a better place. I just wouldn't have had the opportunities that I have now. I love my birth mother, but it's probably better that we live apart. We're so alike that if we lived together we'd probably have a really hard time!"

"There's always going to be grief in adoption. Whenever there is a biological history and a family history that have to be reconciled, there will be some grief. But it is not about having the grief that is the problem; it's what you do with it. Because what you need is openness, and honesty, and to be comfortable with it. If you can express your grief to someone who will understand and be empathetic, then you'll be ok. At least that's been my experience."

understand the losses surrounding adoption, they are capable of feeling them and may express these feelings in their behavior. They may engage in searching or pining behavior, asking strangers if they are their birth parents. Opposite reactions are also possible. They may be fearful that a stranger will come and take them away from their parents.

The more a child knows about adoption, the better equipped they are to handle the issues that arise. Begin by telling the adoption story early, increasing the level of detail as your child's comprehension increases. As you discuss painful information, reaffirm your closeness to your child by holding or touching her, but don't force her to make eye contact until she is ready.

Help your child model appropriate ways of expressing feelings. Reading books about adoption and about emotions is one way to open a discussion. Another is to play games with dolls, allowing characters to say things that she might not be ready to say for herself.

School Age. It is during the school years that children adopted at birth or at a young age move from knowing the words of the adoption story to grasping its implications. They now understand the concept of 'same' and 'different' and understand that adoption is a 'different' way to form a family. This may cause emotional conflicts and feelings of divided loyalties. They may begin to wonder about birth parents but may refrain from sharing those thoughts for fear of hurting their adoptive parents, or feel the loss of relationships with birth siblings or previous caregivers. Children, especially those adopted at an older age who remember their birth parents, may worry about their birth parents welfare. School assignments and questions of classmates may heighten their sense of difference and underscore feelings of loss. *Grief may be demonstrated in different ways. Daydreaming allows children to engage in fantasies about what the birth parents are like, possible reunions, and how life would have been different. This may result in withdrawal or obsessive questioning about facts. Anger, in particular for those who are placed at a later age or who have troubled pasts, may be a symptom of grief. A child, who in a moment of anger says, "You're not my real mom!" is expressing her anger, not rejecting her adoptive parent.*

The best thing parents can do for their grieving children is to give them permission to talk about what they are feeling. Children need to know that what they are feeling is not wrong, but that there are more and less acceptable ways to express these feelings. Let them know that it is okay to talk about birth parents. For example, if your child does particularly well at an activity, say "You're good at that. I wonder if you get that from one of your birth parents." Or "Tomorrow's your birthday. I bet your birth parents are thinking about you tonight." Use a Lifebook or Grief Box to focus on specific aspects of the child's loss history (see section Helping Children Cope page 172.).

Adolescents. Adolescence brings numerous changes to all children, but may be even more complicated for children who are adopted. Adolescents begin to wonder, "Who am

I?" and "What will I be like as an adult?" For adopted children, there may be additional questions like, "Who am I like, my birth parents or my adoptive parents?" It can add additional conflict as they search for self-identity. As they think about leaving home, it may revive feelings of loss and abandonment by the birth family. *Some teens may provoke parents by flouting parental rules. Older teens may become sexually active as a way of asserting their kinship to birth parents if the birth parents were teenagers when their child was conceived. Other teens might be prone to sullenness and depression. Parents should watch for signs of extreme depression, which may occur around events of loss, such as the breakup of a relationship or of separation, like high school graduation. If a teen shows signs of serious depression, like self-destructive behavior, thoughts of suicide, alcohol or drug abuse, or attempts to run away, seek professional help from a doctor or mental health provider.*

> *Adolescents do not outgrow the issues of adoption when they grow up and move away from home. Adjustment to adoption is a lifelong process for both parents and children.*

Help your teen cope with grief by letting her find ways to express herself in nondestructive ways. Encourage her to write feelings in a journal or in letters to her birth parents. The most important thing is to keep the channels of communication open, so that your child knows she can talk to you. Acknowledge her sadness, curiosity or concern as normal and understandable reactions.

Adults. Adolescents do not outgrow the issues of adoption when they grow up and move away from home. If there has been no contact with birth parents growing up, they may begin searching. The reunion process brings up many conflicting feelings such as curiosity, anger, resentment, guilt, fear, and of course, grief. Many adopted adults find feelings of loss also resurface when they have their own children. The biological connection to their child reminds them of the relationship they never had with their birth family.

Your job as a parent doesn't end when your child becomes an adult. If your child decides to search for birth parents, let him know that you support this effort. Share any information you have about the adoption, the agency and the birth parents. Adjustment to adoption is a lifelong process for both parents and children. At every stage children integrate their family relationships into their sense of self-identity. With each change comes greater awareness of what adoption means, and the gains and losses associated with it.

Triggers for Adoption Grief

Some parents assume that adoption is only an issue if their children bring it up. Other parents may assume that everything is adoption related. In reality, there are times when a child may feel adopted with a small 'a' and other times with a capital 'A'. Often a word or event will trigger a feeling and this may trigger a grief reaction:

Anniversaries. Often a birthday or Mother's Day will remind them of the person who gave birth to them, and will start a chain of speculation. *"Where is she now?" "Is she thinking of me?"* These thoughts often go unexpressed, but the child may continue to brood over them long after the event.

Transitions. Birthdays and holidays are not the only triggers–and may not be triggers at all for some children. Transitions or changes in family circumstances, like a new child in the family, moving to a new home, or the divorce of the adoptive parents may trigger fears

> *"At sometimes in my life I feel adopted with a Capital 'A'. It is the most important thing about me. But other times it's not so important. It's adoption with a small "a", one of lots of factors that describe who I am." Promoting Successful Adoptions: Practice With Troubled Families* by Jeanne Howard and Susan Livingston Smith

of loss or abandonment. Even small changes, like the end of the school year may remind children of the ongoing nature of loss.

School. School assignments that involve baby pictures or the construction of a family tree can be powerful triggers. A lack of complete information combined with the desire to fit in with classmates may result in various types of grieving behavior, such as anger, sadness or withdrawal.

Media. The media's portrayal of adoption and the relationships between parents and children can be very troubling. Stories about children who lose parents may disturb young children. Older children may find the use of the term 'adoption' in programs like 'Adopt an animal' or 'Adopt a roadside' offensive.

Think about your child and the various circumstances that might trigger an adoption-related response. Remember, just because he hasn't had a response yet does not mean that he never will. While it is impossible to know when someone might say or do something that will trigger your child's grief, you can be prepared to talk about it.

Sometimes children are adopted with a capital 'A' and sometimes they are adopted with a small 'a'. You won't always know which one your child is feeling, but you can be sensitive to how they respond to the changes and stress they experience as they grow up.

Helping Children Cope

Helping your child understand and express her feelings about adoption is critical. But children are not always comfortable talking about emotions, particularly difficult or painful ones. There are a variety of strategies you can use to encourage your child to explore her feelings, both positive and negative.

Talking and Listening. Talking about adoption should not be a one-time conversation; it should be part of your day-to-day family life. Indicate a willingness to talk about adoption so that she will feel free to talk about it when she is ready. Keep the information you say age appropriate and add details as she grows up. When your child asks questions about adoption, the words she uses do not always express what she wants to know. Try to understand what your child is thinking and feeling before you answer.

Adoptive Family Groups. Look for an adoptive family group in your area, or even online. They offer a place where children can meet others like themselves and understand that they are not alone in their feelings.

Reading Books about Adoption. There are many good books about adoption. Use picture books or storybooks for young children and novels, magazines and newspapers for older children. Read the books yourself first. Be careful to avoid books that ignore the child's life before adoption–these can reinforce the idea that the child either has no past or that it doesn't matter.

Lifebooks. A Lifebook tells your child's story from the beginning, includes information about her life before and after adoption and is a powerful tool, particularly for children who are adopted when they are old enough to have memories of their earlier life. The important thing to remember when using a Lifebook is that it belongs to your child. It is your child's story and she should be able to decide when and how to share that story.

Grief Box. A Grief Box can help a child identify the issues that make him feel sad and provides a technique for helping him work through his feelings. A therapist or parent should work with the child to create the Grief Box. Help your child list the things that make him feel sad and have him find items or pictures that represent those things and put them in a box that symbolizes his life. Have him talk about each item and explain how it makes him feel. Reassure your child and help him think about what he might learn from each item. Keep the box where he can add to it and examine the contents.

Rituals. Traditions and rituals provide opportunities for celebrating special occasions. 'Family Day or Adoption Day' celebrates the day on which the child joined the family. Another ritual is a candle-lighting ceremony for the birth and adoptive parents as well as for the social worker or anyone else involved in the adoption. Sharing the Lifebook on the child's birthday or on other days can also be a meaningful tradition.

Writing. Many parents encourage their children to write letters to their birth parents or birth siblings as a way to share feelings. Another strategy is to suggest that your child write herself a letter, taking on the role of the birth parent. Journaling can offer the same kind of outlet for children who prefer a less formal approach to the issue. Make sure your child understands that her writing is private and that you will not read it unless asked to do so.

> *"I remember participating in support groups of other adopted kids when I was in middle school. It was a great experience. There was no need to explain or give any background information because they'd had the same experience. It was very validating. People would talk and light bulbs would go on in your head. I find that it is still true, that my other adopted friends are great sources of support whenever I am struggling with my own issues."*

Grief and Growing

Learning to cope with grief and loss is not something that a child or family does once. Even it has been grieved over, a loss does not disappear. It may be revisited over and over throughout adolescence and into adulthood. By understanding and accepting the losses that are an inevitable component of adoption and employing strategies to deal with them, you, your child and your family will be stronger.

~ By Vicki DuFour, Executive Director of Adoption Learning Partners (www.adoptionlearningpartners.org), an online learning website serving the adoption community.

This article was adapted from Finding the Missing Pieces: Helping Adopted Children Cope with Grief and Loss available through Adoption Learning Partners (www.adoptionlearning-partners.org). Un-attributed quotations excerpted from Adoption Stories from the same work. Adoption Learning Partners offers education and training to the adoption community via the Internet through a series of e-learning courses of a variety of adoption topics.

The Right to Grieve
If it's unmentionable, it's unmanageable ~ Maria Trozzi

Children adopted internationally suffer loss of birthfamily, culture and country. It can be harder for them to resolve or 'find closure' for that grief because they have no absolutes to pack away. Will they ever find their families again? Is their birthfamily still alive? How would they feel if they were reunited?

We parents need tools to understand a child who might be feeling grief and loss. We need to help our child move to form fresh attachments, and help to place their grief and loss in perspective. Sometimes children need guidance in order to understand the story of their grief, and may need to be given 'different endings" and different ways of viewing what happened to them.

We need to understand our children's grief. To do that, we need to listen to what they tell us. We then can help them re-process it by offering different ways of looking at the loss, basically offering a new perspective. Life books can be very helpful in making the past available to the child – the book is literally in the child's hands. So also are 'lifelines'. Therapists at CASE believe that grieving children need to be taught coping skills, which help work through patches in their life when grief is strong. 'Lifelines' can be people, sports, thoughts or simply permission to call a friend and talk…

Grief is normal after loss. Parents need to children know that painful feelings are appropriate for hurts, and that with time and understanding, the feelings will diminish to manageable size

Children need to have the right for respect of their history. Adoptive parents can help children find pride in what has been lost. We can respect birthparents, and ensure our child has access to whatever personal property or information he brought to our family with him. We can celebrate the connection between the child, his birthfamily, and our family.

Children need to find a way to integrate their loss and move forward. If we work with our children to honor their loss, it can be incorporated, and the child can function as a whole again. Then grief and loss are still part of the child, but no longer the dominant part.

~ *Sheena Macrae*

Talking with Children about Loss By Maria Trozzi
Healing Loss in the Traumatized Child
By Marilyn Schoettle, M.A. and Ellen Singer, LCSW-C
Free download from The Center for Adoption and Support
Education, Inc. (C.A.S.E.) www.adoptionsupport.org

Authentic Beginnings, Real Bonds:

Honest Talk About Adoption

By Marcy Axness, PhD

The road to adoption is invariably a painful one for parents, marked by many losses: the child they might have had, but for infertility; the child or children they lost through miscarriage, stillbirth, or death. Sometimes even pieces of themselves feel chipped away—their sense of competence, wholeness, worthiness, and so many other essential, but clearly not immutable, components of self.

By the time their long-awaited adopted child is placed in their arms, parents usually—and understandably—just want to put all the heartache behind them and move on into the joyful realms of mothering and fathering. But their very real feelings of loss need to have a place in the story of their new family, or they can cast ever-lengthening shadows on the relationship between parents and child.

Adopted kids often grow up with the mantra "Being adopted is just another way to become a family." This is a dismissive characterization of a profound experience which has involved not only the parents' deep losses, but the child's loss of the parents who couldn't keep him. With the best of intentions, adoptive parents often convey half-truths about the implications of adoption to shield their child from the pain of loss which is inherent in the experience.

"Adoptive parents are really trying to do the right thing, and it feels like avoiding pain is the right thing, but it truly is not," says therapist Wendy McCord. "They need to look at their good intentions and re-frame them, because hiding from the feelings doesn't help their child."

"Other mommies and daddies had to take what they got, but we got to choose you," is another well-intentioned but ultimately destructive lie told to many adopted children. While it clearly wouldn't be appropriate to share with them what is often the actual truth—that they tried everything possible to have their own child before deciding to adopt—it is crucial for parents to share the essence of the truth with their adopted children, the feelings which hover beneath the facts.

Social worker Annette Baran, a nationally-recognized adoption expert, says, "Adoptive parents must weep with their child—We're sorry, too, that you didn't grow in mommy's tummy. I think parents don't realize they're allowed to show these feelings. They think they have to present an unflagging cheerfulness about adoption in order that the children will feel positive too, which is a misconception." Parents who demonstrate emotional openness send a healthy message to their child that he or she is allowed to express a full range of feelings, not just the 'nice' ones.

"Parents whose children express sadness usually feel that they need to reassure them, rather than feel the sadness along with them. But having lost an original set of parents is something to feel sad about, and the best any parent can do for a child is to allow them to share those feelings of loss with them," explains Baran.

Dr. McCord acknowledges that supporting a child in this empathic manner can be emotionally challenging for adoptive parents. "It forces them to feel their own loss about not having their own biological child, and it also will trigger any issues of what they may

Phone Home

My three year old got a new toy cell phone today. She was desperate to phone her Chinese Birthmother. So she rang her Chinese Mummy straightaway on the way home from the shops. Lots of chatting. Big Sister and I waited till teatime to ask what they'd said to each other. Here it is:

Chinese Mummy was crying and missing her (oh, Baby, what empathy!), so my little one promised Chinese Mummy that she'd send lots of toys to put in her bed so she won't feel lonely. My daughter's bed is packed with toys; she can't bear feeling lonely. .

Chinese mummy said she was missing my little one. So Babe told her that now she is a big girl she will come and visit her, but she will bring her English mummy, because without me, Babe will get lost. She also promised to make lots of visits, but she won't stay.

I was astonished at the surety with which she was negotiating her thoughts about her birthmother, and her birthmother's loss. She was dealing with that as well as her own fears about getting lost again, and the stability that English mummy brings. Watching the firm closed mouth she made when she announced she would visit but not stay made me realise also how much she is learning from Big Sister about belonging to two families but growing up in one.

And I was astonished at the sudden desperate need to phone now. It was desperate, we couldn't ignore it, and I am glad she has had her chat. Whether there will be more chats….I don't know. But as my Big Girl said, "Well Mummy, she's done better than you could. She found the number!"

That's right. She found the number.
~ By Sheena Macrae

have lost in their relationships with their own parents."

While it may seem easier—especially in the beginning—to avoid these uncomfortable feelings, glossing over them with cheerful slogans isn't the loving choice, for it ultimately deprives both parents and child of genuine intimacy. Children who grow up with that kind of pretense and denial often report that they have superficial, 'walking on eggshells' relationships with their parents.

By contrast, parents who allow a child to explore all of the complex feelings—and questions—that are a natural part of the adoptive experience, lay a solid foundation of trust and honesty for a deep, authentic connection with their child.

As any attuned parent knows, children are creatures of intuition—they respond to the truth behind our words rather than the words themselves. And if the truth we're telling them isn't the whole truth, they perceive in this discrepancy that there is something intangibly wrong about themselves. In my own experience, it took me until age 38 to unlearn that early, stunting lesson. To learn that there wasn't something unspeakably wrong about me, but rather, something that my parents couldn't face, and share—the difficult realities that surrounded my adoption.

When we deny adoption's losses, we also deny ourselves its fullest blessings.

~ Marcy Axness, PhD, is an early development specialist, adjunct professor at Santa Barbara Graduate Institute, and parent counselor. Using as a narrative foundation her experience as an adoptee and a mother, she writes and speaks internationally on adoption, attachment, and parenting, and is a leading expert on prenatal and perinatal development.

Your First Mother Will Never Forget You
One birthmother's hopes and fears.
by Piedad Yamille Agudelo Correa

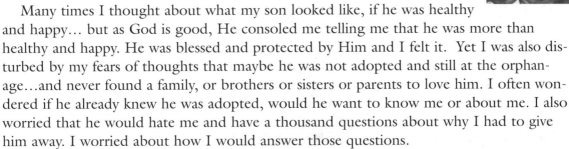

Before I received the first letter with news of my child I asked myself many times what would be the life of my child. My maternal instinct told me that he was well; but the conscience accuses you and betrays you, causing you to think the worse. I thought of him and I cried for him during the two long years until I received the first letter from his parents, and to learn he did not suffer.

Many times I thought about what my son looked like, if he was healthy and happy… but as God is good, He consoled me telling me that he was more than healthy and happy. He was blessed and protected by Him and I felt it. Yet I was also disturbed by my fears of thoughts that maybe he was not adopted and still at the orphanage…and never found a family, or brothers or sisters or parents to love him. I often wondered if he already knew he was adopted, would he want to know me or about me. I also worried that he would hate me and have a thousand questions about why I had to give him away. I worried about how I would answer those questions.

I think of my child often. I think of him at night, in the morning, and in the day. I will think of him during my tomorrows. In my prayers he is always with me and still more, when my other children cry or they laugh or they are happy. I think of what he might be doing at these moments and especially when his brother Andres Felipe does something good or bad; I wonder if Tristan carries himself the same way. Andres Felipe bears a striking resemblance to Tristan, for me they resemble each other a lot physically and in some things in their behavior.

Only once did I think of reclaiming my child. I would have reclaimed him if he were to stay in the orphanage. I went back to the orphanage. I was told that he was adopted and taken far away. Would I want to reclaim him today? To take him back, away from his family? No. I would never want to hurt my child nor his family.

What pains me in my soul is the pain of giving one child in adoption yet parenting other children. I feel sometimes that I do not have valid justification. I know a pain combined with a sense of peace and tranquility because it is so special a family that my son has, because they love him and give him a better life.

I often suffer guilt and remorse. I am alone to think that he is growing up and he understands the situation. My hope is that my child understands. I did not receive any understanding or support from my family and I did not count on them when making the decision. I was alone and I know that my mom and siblings did not want a heavier load as more children for such a poor family and home. They questioned me a lot and they caused me a lot of suffering when I was pregnant again. I felt so much alone and my life changed a lot since the moment I decided to relinquish my child for adoption. I was no longer the happy girl and I cried my grief in silence and I still do.

After relinquishment I prayed so to hear the voice of God answering me that my child was well. My pregnancy and relinquishment was not a secret. My family was embarrassed. They often spoke badly of me yet they also told me not to bring another child home to them. They asked me what I was to do with the child then did not support me.

I suffered so much! My mother, family and the father made me suffer and I felt they wanted to punish me. This was before I had contact and reunion with my child. Today we are all happy.

I worried a lot about my child. I think all birthmother's do. I worried about the difficulties he might face. I worried that someone would make him suffer and maybe touch him inappropriately or violate him the way some bad people do. I also worried that he would be killed and someone would steal his vital organs like it happens in many parts of the world. This practice can be found in the big cities and it is often mentioned on the news. This was one of my many worries. I did not want my child to suffer.

Sometimes people try to make me feel badly about my decision then I wonder if my child will love me or hate me. When I think of this and feel badly I wish I could speak my child's language, to be able to speak directly to him, look him in his eyes and really understand his feelings towards me. I want to understand his love or disaffection towards me. In my heart I know that I deserve the good and the bad. I am a realist.

The most difficult parts of the whole birthmother experience was if to be pregnant at my house and to endure the fights with my mom then the decision to give my child in adoption. The hardest by far was the third day after birth to have my child feed from my breast then sign the paperwork and to leave him there. I thought I would die. I so wanted to have him with me and my opponents impeded me.

More than 11 years after the adoption of my child my feelings are like that of any good mother, and I consider myself a good mother. I am full of love and have the best wishes and prayers for my son and my blessing and prayers are directed all to God, asking his protection and the guidance for the best road and my son obtains everything that he desires in life. My hopes were that in that time my child would be adopted by a good family that would give him a good education, to understand when he did a mischief, and did not mistreat him. I hoped they would give him medicine when was sick and a lot of love.

Today I feel very well, since I know that my son is with people that have truly accepted my child as their own and they give all the love that parents can give their children. I think that they are excellent people and of assurance my son will always be in good hands and he will be the same as born to them. For birthmothers who were young or single and can not have their children with them they can consider adoption. Adoption is a good option. Adoption is a better choice than abandonment or abortion. I want my boy to know that I love him and always wanted what was best for him and that is why I chose adoption and not to kill him in my womb or to throw him away. To me this is the decision of a good mother. I am here if and when he needs me.
Your first mother will never forget you.

~Piedad Yamille Agudelo Correa is a Birthmother from
Carolina del Principe, Antioquia, Colombia who has been reunited.

In My Words – My Children's Mothers

I think one of the most important things we do as adoptive Moms is give our children permission to explore the full range of feelings they may have at times, concerning the path their life has taken and the decisions that other people made for them. We are not and never will be the only mother in our children's lives. They have a birthmother, and how they think of her and feel about her is really their business. My children need to have the freedom to decide for themselves what they think about the circumstances that led to their adoption, and protecting my feelings should never been an issue for them as they work through that.

Their feelings will probably change as they mature and work through different issues, and we might not always agree with them...

~ they may 'hate' their birthmother, while we recognize that she was in a horrible position and did the best she could....

~ they may 'love' a birthmother they've never met...

~ they may 'love' the birthmother who abused and neglected them, and who they were legally taken away from...

They really need to know that whatever their feelings are, they are okay with us, because we **are** the mothers who are here now.

When I adopted my first daughter, I got to spend several hours with her birthmother spread across several days. One of the most incredible things she did was give me permission to love and parent my (our) child, passing the mantle of Mother along. That is something we now share –being this child's 'Mother'. I will never forget the moment when she turned to the translator and told him to tell me "I give this child to you with all my heart, and all I want for her is to have a wonderful life in America". It was overwhelming to me that she had the presence of mind in that heartbreaking moment to make me feel entitled to parent Elena, and to make sure I knew that she was certain her decision was the right one for her. My point is, even my youngest from China benefits from knowing about this one example of a birthmother's viewpoint...and it helps her feel a connection and love to her own birthmother, who she has not and probably never will get to meet.

~ By Jill Lampman
Adoptive mom to two daughters

Wanting to Know

When I look for courage, it is for the courage to support my child who does not have contact with birthparents half a continent away. This situation is much more difficult; it is painful for me, and it has caused my daughter more pain than any pain her brother's open international adoption has ever caused him.

My daughter cries over not knowing.

My son never cries about knowing.

~ Leceta Guibault
mom to two
internationally
adopted children

Our Mutual Son
Building an international relationship with a birthmother

An open adoption relationship should be built on respect and an understanding of the complex feelings of all involved. As adoptive parents, I think that we need to do a lot of work ourselves, coming to grip with the realities. Our children, as much as we adore them, were not born to us. They have a first family. Our kids know this too. They too must understand the truths of adoption. The birthfamily must also deal with their grief, sorrow, regrets, loss and most times guilt. As parents we must be comfortable in our role as parents and work on our fears of our children's biological families.

There is a lot of fear! A lot of 'what if's'. My son's birthmother, Piedad, wrote recently that as she prepares for our trip to Colombia, she is working on coming to terms with the fact that Tristan is from her, part of her, but not 'hers'. She is also working on the fact that as much as she can not wait to see him and touch him, she will have to once again let him go. That is so honest....

From my very first letter to Piedad, I was clear and truthful. I wrote from my heart, and I didn't ask questions. I told her why I thought opening the adoption, and contact, would be beneficial to all of us and especially to our mutual son. I told her that it was not my intention to cause her further pain but that I wanted her to know that Tristan was loved, happy, healthy, and alive.

My first letter was short, but I did understand the importance of photos. I provided Piedad with our full names and home mailing address. I already knew so much about her and her family from the written social history report, and I wanted her to know us...to trust us. Piedad wrote back immediately, saying that she welcomed the contact and that I caused her no pain:

"On the contrary...you have given me peace. A peace I never thought possible."

In the first letter she told me a little about her family and life. It was reassuring as it matched perfectly the social workers report. No lies! In my second letter I asked Piedad if she had any questions. She wrote back telling me that the photos said it all, and her only request was a photo of Tristan's daddy and me holding him. Piedad taught me that it was very important to her to see Tristan in our loving arms...not just alone.

Piedad and I nurtured our relationship. Our trust grew. I am glad that we did not jump on the first plane to Colombia after making contact! It would have been awkward. There would have been too many questions to be answered on both sides and it would have been rushed. Over time I've learned more and more about this remarkable woman. I now know her heart, her hopes and dreams and her everyday struggles. I now know "why adoption".

Piedad, remarkable woman that she is, helped me grieve my mother's death. This was an unexpected support! She was 'there' for me! Who would have thought this? I also helped her come to terms with the birth of a new baby six years almost to the day after Tristan was born and relinquished. She was overcome with grief and guilt over Tristan, felt unworthy of contact, and feared he would hate her. I told her that we celebrated the birth of a new soul into our extended family and that Tristan was very happy with the news.

He wanted to know more! What was her name? Could they send photos? I tried to help Piedad understand that the grief over losing one child was normal with the birth of a new baby. Many, many birthmothers had told me this and Piedad was no different.

I think that Piedad and I both took steps, from the very beginning to make this a positive relationship. We moved slowly, and did not rush each other. We both wanted this to be a long term relationship, one that brought both of our families together because of one child, yet also for the benefit of all touched by him. It has benefited my son, his sister by adoption, his siblings by birth, his birthparents and their extended families, and my husband and I and our extended families. As the years pass the significance has become clearer. This is right for our family...not just my child.

~ Leceta Chisholm Guibault is the adoptive mother of two children adopted from Latin America as infants. She is a Board Member of the Adoption Council of Canada, and a Board Member of the Federation of Quebec Adoptive Parents. Leceta was awarded a NACAC Adoption Activist Award for her work towards openness in international adoption.

In Front of the Mirror

The next time your young child asks you what his birthparents look like, show him pictures of people in your family who bear a distinct family resemblance to you (do you or your husband look a lot like one of your parents, siblings or cousins?). Have a discussion about inherited traits, then stand your child in front of a mirror and say that the next time he wants to see his birthparents, he can look in the mirror, because he has pieces of both of them in his own face, hair, eye-color, and body build.

- Cheryl Leppert adoptive mom of two daughters from India

The Facts of Life
and wishing we knew more

My little girl isn't so little any more! She is growing up. During her ninth year our conversations have shifted to topics of maturing, of becoming a young lady, and to be frank, of getting her period. I have always been open with Emily about my monthly menstrual cycle, the subtle annoyances of it all, the supplies, and the purpose. We've talked over the years whenever she's asked about "where do babies come from?" We've talked even earlier, when she wished that she had grown in my tummy but knew she hadn't. As our pets went through their various biological changes, she was eager to know 'how and why' and I had calmly and openly explained it all. What struck me about the whole process was this:

- When we were growing up we had our mothers and grandmothers to know approximately 'at what age' we would start our periods, and likely an idea of what our periods would be like.

- We have a sense of our own personal development based on generations before us, with diet and nutrition, and exercise and sports being the other key elements. Our daughters can look to us for information, but not for the important passing on of what it will be like for them physically. Their attitudes will come from us, but their biology on this aspect of their lives is predetermined.

- Our daughter's bodies will change at a pace unpredictable to most of us. What we do know is that they are maturing, and that it's our role to help them through this process and to make it as painless as possible for them.

Our daughters will likely feel some sense of loss, of not knowing about their birthmothers or sisters at this stage of their lives. It will not be about us adopting them or about being adopted. It will be the not knowing about their biological selves, not knowing what their birthparents gave them genetically. Their "what will my body be like?" questions will not be answered.

We, as international adoptive moms, need to be reading about the trends in the birth countries of our daughters, and the health statistics for immigrants from those countries. What are their statistics for incidence of cancer (cervical, breast, uterine), and for health factors such as high blood pressure, and heart disease? While we know that growing up in America will increase international adoptees life-expectancy dramatically, we don't know what roadblocks are ahead of them health-wise. It's something we need to learn about so our daughters, who will be dealing with an unknown health history all of their lives, will have some ideas of what to look for in their future.

~ By Jane Liedtke, PhD, Founder and CEO of Our Chinese Daughter's Foundation
and mom to a daughter who isn't so little anymore

Transitions

Transitions
How our Children Move Through
and Adjust to Change
~By Leith Harding

While all children experience transitions in their early years, adoptees with the challenges of loss, multiple placements, and the formation of attachments, may experience more frequent and more intense transitions. These transitions may be stressful for adults who are called upon by their child to provide security and safety with commitment and strength, at times when they themselves have been thrown off balance.

The ideal transition process is one which is carefully planned and well prepared in advance. Unfortunately, the transition experiences of many families do not meet this ideal. Some adopted children can be really 'thrown for a loop' during transition times, while other adopted children roll though transition with little or no problem. However, this may be a false sense of coping as they may completely fall apart at another, lesser transition. Similarly an event or transition might appear straightforward to us, but may be earth-shattering to an adopted child. Five of the biggest transitions for young adoptees are:

1) Adoption
2) Moving
3) Starting School
4) Understanding Adoption
5) Adolescence

So how do you know if a transition is going to be difficult or easy, whether it stirs up adoption issues, and how you can best help your children? You can't always know, but you can learn to recognize how your own child reacts to change, and what he or she needs from you in order to learn to cope.

1) Adoption: the Arrival of the Adopted Child

Adoptive parents have come to adoption as the result of a desire and longing for a child, preparation, and completing agency and government requirements. Even before the child arrives, parents have a sense of the child through photos, information and day dreams.

The child is in a different state of readiness for adoption placement. Children of all ages experience shock, fear, and uncertainty, including those who have had some preparation for the event. This time is traumatic for the child. Everything changes when they are placed in the arms of their adoptive family: smells, sounds, tastes, and styles of touch, holding, carrying, and sleeping. Some infants and young children have severe stress reaction with vomiting, diarrhea, sleep problems, and displays of grief. Older children may react with challenging behavior, acting out their grief at the loss of all they knew, their displeasure at the changes, and their need to control the situation. Infants may become fussy as they respond to different styles of parenting.

Tools: Pre-Adoption

Educate Yourself. Arm yourself with as much information as possible about the age and background of your child especially his/her care environment.

Discuss Expectations. Talk to siblings and extended family about the new child, and include both your positive and negative expectations. This helps your family develop a balanced perspective and begin to consider how to handle possible problems, attitudes and reactions. It is important to be aware that the child will have experienced loss, fear, shock, and disorientation. Discuss this with family and friends so they can help you and the child through the first weeks and months, when developing a bond between parent and child is so important.

Send Photos. If your waiting child is not an infant, send a snapshot album over with simple photos of mum, dad, sisters, brothers, pets, car, house, and bedroom. It is amazing how important it can be for waiting children to 'see' what they are waiting for.

Come Home to a Child-Ready House. Before you leave, child-proof your house. Fill the freezer, and tell friends who want to help to bring dinner over when you return.

Get Fit. Be rested, healthy and fit when you meet your child so you are in the best mental and physical state to become a parent. When traveling overseas, go a couple of days early if you can. Get a good night's sleep, and orient yourselves with the area, taking in the smells, sights and sounds.

Tools: Post-Adoption

Go Slow. While you will be so very excited to meet and hold your child, remember that you are a stranger to the child so take your time to watch her/him, introducing yourselves gently and making this special time 'sweet' for all of you. Do not try to do too much too soon, but keep your child near and learn all about him/her.

Limit Change. Keep further changes, outings, visitors to a minimum for a while and be sensitive to your child's need for time to process every new experience. Everyone will want to hold a baby or touch an older child but this may be scary and confusing for her/him and building trust and attachment with you is the highest priority.

Enlist friends and family. Extended family and friends can be really helpful during this time, assisting with household chores, helping with other children in the family, or shopping, so that you can focus on the needs of your new child.

2) Moving

The place your child calls their first real home is a very hard place to leave. For some adopted children moving may stir up feelings of abandonment, or fear of being left behind with the house. Moving to a new house is high on the life stress list. Adults find the process stressful, and children cannot be expected to take it in their stride. It is scary for them to leave the place where they feel comfortable, secure, and familiar.

Tools: Moving

Make an Album. Take inside and outside photos of the old house, old school, old friends. Include photos of the new house, neighborhood and school so they can become familiar with their new environment.

House-hunt Together. House hunting with kids can be difficult. It pays off to have them give their opinions and get used to the idea of moving.

Say Good-bye. Do farewells to the house (even rooms in the house), and say good-by to neighbors and neighborhood animals. It helps children understand the importance of farewells and can help them process other leave-taking events in their life.

3) Starting School

One of the events that mark a significant transition for both parent and child is the beginning of school. For many children this may be the first major venture into the world on their own, and it is both exciting and frightening. Boys and girls will form new relationships with other significant adults and further develop their own social skills through interacting with other children. For parents, there is the excitement of watching their child grow, mixed with apprehension at no longer being able to 'shield' him or her.

The transition to school can be a big step, especially for children who have been at home with mom, or in a home-based or small group care. For some children, the stress of negotiating a larger group of children and managing the teacher can raise issues of abandonment and fear of rejection. The reduction of daily attention may result in attention-seeking behavior, either at home or school, or both. Some children work hard to fit in and be good at school, and then fall apart at home; for others without an emotional connection to the teacher, it is the opposite.

Sometimes, for children who have lived in large group care before adoption, school can appear to be a re-visitation of that time. Jay (adopted at age 4) called school 'day-school'; when his teacher asked him why he called it day school he said "in Thailand we went to all-the-time-school", referring to the orphanage.

On the flip side, many children adopted at an older age struggle with their transition into the nuclear family and long for the group environment where they can be anonymous and interact with children rather than adults. School provides this environment, and some older adoptees even beg to go to attend. School can provide a brief time-out from the family, but the avoidance of family intimacy strains the attachment formation with the parents. In their confusion, an adopted child may begin to form a stronger attachment to a teacher rather than parent.

Regardless of the child's early experiences either overseas or here, the transition to school stretches the relationships and requires the child to manage their parent-child attachment in a goal-centered manner. This requires the child to control their parent proximity-seeking behavior and to rely on trust and delayed gratification.

Tools: School

Think it Through. Arrange for an orientation program for your child with mum or dad present the whole time. Cover what a typical school day is like. Prepare your child by visiting the classroom and rehearsing the separation. Think through and rehearse all possible reactions from your child (such as ambivalence, distress, pleading, quiet resignation, silent tears) and yourself (such as tears, guilt, distress, quiet joy, hurt, and anger).

Prepare for Success. Young children need to be adequately prepared for their transition to out-of-home environments such as day care or preschool programs. Children adopted from overseas, particularly, need to be informed and assisted in demonstrating the behaviors and skills expected of them in these learning environments. This includes pre-learning the rules, self-management related to activities such as eating and taking care of personal needs, and communicating effectively with adults and other children.

Reassure. Stay with your child for several visits and do not pre-empt their coping ability. You may need to attend class for a few days leaving later and arriving earlier than other parents. Also, arranging a seat outside where your child can see you when you arrive. This can remove the fear that you may not come when school ends and kids go in all directions.

Send Security. Allow your child to take a familiar item or a small gift that will help them remember that you are with them in this new adventure. Perhaps a little picture card, or soft toy that lives in your child's school bag. Inform the teacher of this security item.

Recognize the Event. Give a card or note to your child before or after the first day of school, and take pictures to recognize this special time.

4) Understanding 'Adoption Moments'

Adoption loss realizations can come at momentous occasions or just slip in during story time, the middle of a movie, or over breakfast. Children process their environment, and what they experience, hear and see, at different times according to their emotional and cognitive development. While a child may not be old enough to understand the concept of adoption, they may feel the sense of loss and seek to understand this feeling. Other children may not realize the connection between adoption and their loss of birth connection until much older.

Beau was adopted as an infant and was aware of his adoption from a young age. His parents had been open and felt he understood it well but at 11, he became quite sad and spend hours in his room just looking at the ceiling. He said he was feeling sad for his birth mother, and sad that he did not see her. Life events are commonly times of transitions. This means that at different times some seemingly insignificant event, like a movie, a surprise, birthdays, Mother's Day or Father's Day, or abandonment or adoption anniversaries may cause our adopted children distress or concern.

Tools: Understanding Adoption

Be Aware. Be aware that as a child's cognition develops, so does his knowledge and understanding of adoption. This may run on a different time line than what we might expect.

Be Ready. Be ready before it happens, rehearse with yourself, partner or a friend, how you may react when questions or adoption moments occur. How we respond to our children influences how they feel about themselves and their adoption.

Empathize. Do not minimize nor dramatize your child's 'adoption moments', but accept them, empathize and support your child as they explore their feelings.

The Care Will

Children who have been adopted worry about their adoptive parents' death and about being left alone. Many families have found that writing a 'Care Will' with their child has helped immensely. Sit down with your son or daughter and talk about what would likely happen if you got sick, went to the hospital, or died. Give them a chance to share their feelings and fears about it and then write down the optimal plan should anything unforeseen happen. Then together put it in a secret place. We added emergency phone numbers to our Care Will, and an action plan, as one of my children was the only person around when her birthmother got very sick. ~ Leith Harding

Typically, parents do not discuss the plans they have made for the family in case of their own death. But for children with loss issues and heightened fear or anxiety about losing another mom or dad, talking openly about the 'what ifs' that surround death, hospitalization or separation can be very therapeutic. There are good emotional reasons for discussing your legal documents and your plans with adopted children:

Finalizing protective legal paperwork for adopted children is an important wrap-up for parents who love their sons and daughters.

Children need to know that they won't be left alone in the world. Paperwork provides the concrete proof that a guardian has been chosen with care, that the child will have a good place to live, and that a child's financial needs will be met. The actual adoption documents work as 'proof' that a child's adoptive parents are legally 'forever', and that no one can take them away. The parent's Care Will and Care Plan paperwork reinforces an adoptee's security.

For some children, having a personal copy of some of these forms and phone numbers in a notebook will add to their feelings of security. Gauge your child's reactions during your conversation, and decide how much detail about life and death events is needed and appropriate. Your child needs to know that care has been taken so that he or she needn't live in fear of the results of being orphaned. For some kids the seeing of the paperwork doesn't offer much comfort. Telling them who will take care of them in our absence may be the most important part. The biggest issue for parents (adoptive or not) is actually to take care of the paperwork, and to keep reviewing it as time goes on. There are so many parents who don't do either.

Suggested paperwork for discussion:
- Child's Certificate of Citizenship
- Life Insurance (with an amount that covers college)
- Guardian
- Trust Fund
- Will (specifically stating that an adopted child is treated as biological)
- Patient Advocate Form/Durable Power of Attorney for Health Care
- Contact list with emergency phone numbers

Provide Information. Provide your child with age appropriate information as they seek to learn about their adoption.

Establish Rituals. If you are aware that special times like birthdays cause your child distress or concern, give your child time to process the upcoming event. Establish rituals to help your child manage their feelings, and celebrate or remember days or times of significance.

Equip Yourself. Arm yourself with knowledge to understand the issues of adoption, emotional development, and grieving so you are better equipped to know when adoption moments may arise.

5) Adolescence

Puberty is a time of confusion, overpowering emotions, control issues, and changing attitudes toward self and others. Adoption may complicate a child's transition from childhood to adolescence. With the ability to think more laterally and abstractly children are able to process the feelings of others, and begin to question how their birth parents might have felt about them. This raises a number of emotions and can begin a cycle of anger, resentment, and projection. These feelings are commonly directed at adoptive parents because they are the parents that are available.

Unfortunately, it is difficult to generalize how an adopted child will negotiate the mix of adoption realizations and realities with the emotional, social and physical changes that the teen years bring. An outgoing, open daughter can become a moody, withdrawn drama-teen or your delightful, self-contained, studious son can become the stormy, non-communicative, rap-loving upstairs resident.

Adoptive parents need to remain secure in the knowledge that their child loves them but is struggling with the 'big' feelings of growing up and with being adopted. As young people move through this integration process they seek greater control over themselves and others, which can generate friction at home.

Peers and role models (TV stars, musicians, teachers, older teens) become more important in your child's life. This is a normal part of growing up, but can mean that your adopted child is more vulnerable to racist remarks, the need to be accepted and the pressure to do things they would normally not do in order to fit. Being there, being aware of what they are doing and feeling is the role of all parents at this time. Adoptive parents are generally more protective because we know what out children have already experienced. Our assistance may help them through these times but also may create rebellion. Some parents who need to remember the good times when their child was a delightful toddler or a companionable eight year old, sneak into their teens' room and just watch them sleep to regain their perspective on their dearly loved child!

Cultural contacts that teens have as young children may become more difficult as they get older because they do not share the same culture as deeply as children raised within it. Mahesh had been welcomed into the Indian community soon after his adoption, joined the drumming team, attending cultural events and cricket matches. However, when he reached his teens he felt outside the group of Indian teens he had played with in his childhood. He commented that "they left him out and even spoke Hindi around him and laughed". He would not be an Indian adult, and needed to find where he fit.

Similarly society will view a trans-racially adopted child differently as they move away from the security of the family and close community. They are seen less as an adopted child and more as a racially different young adult in a predominantly white society. Adopted children need to be armed before they reach adolescence with some tools to help them through the confusion and turmoil of puberty.

Tools: Adolescence

Find Role-Models. Through the adoption community, look for significant adults with whom your children can identify.

Support Groups. An adoption peer group can be cultivated when children are younger Adoption heritage camps are ideal for teens to feel more 'normal' and to discuss issues that are common to all international adoptees. Also, group and individual counseling can benefit children who are experiencing difficulties, and who may derive support from the structure that therapy provides.

Make Contact. Establish strong communication and even set up activities (like walking the dog, or a movie night) that you will be able to continue to do together as your child gets older. Set up some 'thinking of you' or 'love you' rituals like hair brushing, shoulder massages, emailed notes or text phone messages, as these can be points of contact if things get rough.

Allow Independence. Consistently allow your child control over small things so they can learn to handle control as they get older. Be careful not to smother your child because of your concern; they need to find their own place in society.

Talk About Racism. Arm your child of color with the knowledge that others will view them differently as they move into the wider community without you by their side. Establish your own reactions to racism bearing in mind that you will be teaching your child how to react. The best advice I received was from a Sri Lankan mother who told me to teach my children to 'not react' to certain situations, as reacting will create more problems for them.

My anger, disgust and outspokenness will only teach my children to react with anger and this will only hurt them. Teaching them to ignore and walk away was the greatest lesson I could give them. There are many other transitions as an adopted child grows older: moving away from home, adult relationships, marriage, the birth of an adopted child's biological children, birth family reunions, and the death of close family members, including birth and adoptive parents. Helping an adoptee understand why transition and change may feel threatening, and teaching him or her about coping tools, will allow for greater self-understanding and for smoother life transitions.

~Leith Harding is mother to 7 children, 4 adopted internationally, adoption advocate, counselor, educator, and a researcher with a focus on adoption transitions.

Transition Tools for Anxious Children
Feel the Fear and Move Beyond It
By Jean MacLeod

A child's easy transition to new circumstances is based on an infancy and childhood of complete trust. While transitioning seems like a natural skill, it is really an outgrowth of temperament, a child's belief in a safe, secure world, and an unshakable faith in invincible parents. An adopted child has experienced loss and understands vulnerability at a primal level. For some adopted children change isn't necessarily a positive event, bringing fears that it could mean losing parents, friends and home. It has happened before. Change brings anxieties to the surface. There's no magic pill to help an anxious child learn to deal with change. There's just hard, steady progress based on:
- A parent and child's emotional work together on adoption and attachment issues.
- The child's firm grasp of truth.
- The child's trust in parental commitment (feeling 'safe').

Without a foundation of knowledge and awareness, and a parent who is willing to delve beneath the surface issues, the tools that enable a child to transition won't help. We have to 'do the work' with our children, before we move to do the fixing. Helping them understand the true cause of their anxiety about changes and giving them determination to overcome this is a responsible job for a parent, and only is possible if the child trusts us. Without this, we can't effectively develop a plan of action to deal with transitions. Knowledge and awareness come from an understanding of the Seven Core Issues of adoption, and the Four Feelings. Modulating an understanding of this with your child is key to preparing a toolkit for successful transitions.

Preparation is the key What makes your child comfortable in a new environment? Think about your child's pattern of behavior under stress, and what she or he intuitively does to feel better in a public situation. Ask your child to think-tank with you, so the two of you can come up with a list of personal transition-tools. Every situation has a 'hook' your child can use to ease into, step by step. To generate personal transition tools for your child, ask him or her:
- What do you need to feel comfortable? (example: a friend)
- What's the 'hook'? (example: pick one nice-looking kid and be friendly first)
- How do you do it? (example: your child role-plays with you prior to the event)

Putting the Plan-In-Motion
- Remain calm and confident for your child
- Acknowledge your child's fear–look at the core issue (see pages 7-14)
- Review the transition tools (above) together
- Tell your child it is OK to pretend confidence
- Reward trying and partial success
- Debrief the day–and be prepared to make tool changes!

It may not be easy, or always go smoothly, but empowering a child to own her fears and to fight them is a huge confidence-builder. Watching a child struggle to own and direct her behavior makes a parent understand that the real magic is not always in a transition's success, but in the heart and life-spirit of these children who work to be whole.

Facing Your Adoptive Parent's Decision to Divorce
When Love Doesn't Follow a Set Path
By Indigo Williams Willing

I was adopted from Vietnam and joined my adoptive parents and their two biological sons in the West in 1972. We spent many years together sharing our dreams, hopes, and love for each other. Then one day, as I was enjoying my twenties, living away from home, and studying at university, my mum told me she was separating from my father. She explained that they had a lovely marriage and that raising my brothers and I was the best thing in their lives, but how in the past few years they had come to grow apart.

When parents divorce, despite this being common, it is often painful for the children at any age. As a young adult with some maturity behind me to see reason, I tried to accept their decision in as rational a way as possible. I considered their perspectives and their needs. If they no longer were happy together, it was wasteful and hurtful for them to remain unified in marriage. However, there is no doubt that their decision lead to deep self-reflection and personal considerations, too.

My sense of security in the concept of the family (the idea it gives us the ultimate sense of belonging) and the concept of family home (the idea it represents our sense of historical self) became fragmented and set in doubt. What new ways would I have to re-orientate my sense of belonging, and sense of where I come from? This of course, has always been an issue due to my skin color indicating difference from my white family.

The new definition of how I had to see my adoptive family had to expand to my parents being in separate locations, and then with their new partners in new homes. I had brief thoughts of a promise being broken. My first concern was not the promise of marriage between my parents but the contract of me being adopted into an environment where they came as a stable package. This promise is only a sentimental illusion and was unrealistic–for my adoptive parents would always be mum and dad. Just separated.

The second concern was: how are my new stepparents going to treat me? As a strange foreigner juxtaposed in their western lives? Was there any xenophobia that might lurk beneath their pleasant-enough exterior? Or would they unconditionally accept me as 'one of them' in the warm, sincere way that my parents had done? All children meeting stepparents must go through issues of trust. I feel I experienced many doubts children have when their parents go through a divorce and settle in with someone new, only there was a fear of how they constructed race included as well. I felt particularly sensitive to having that feeling replicated within the safety of the sphere of family interactions.

Ultimately, what I had to fight was my deep fear of losing some parents all over again, after coming to terms that I'd lost my biological parents first time around. The terrible fear of being alone in the world. The fear of being rejected by stepparents also reverberated that maybe I was rejected by my birth parents.Of course, the power of dealing with parental divorce is to put things into a rational perspective and to reduce self-doubt and self-reflection to an awareness of what other people's needs and experiences are. My parents needed to be separated, they needed to be loved and accepted by new people, and they had the same fear of being alone and fear of rejection as everyone has in one way or another. I then felt more balanced, and ready to accept that love cannot always follow tradition. Which is what adoption is about too.

Adoption and Divorce
Use a Difficult Situation to Teach your Children Well

Divorce isn't the ending that any parent envisions when they begin the journey to adopt. In addition to the normal stress of a dissolved relationship, a parent may feel extra guilt over inflicting an additional trauma on a child with a history of loss. How you handle yourself during the process of divorce can mitigate some of the guilt: recognize that when a parent chooses to demonstrate a 'good' ending to a bad situation, it can set an incredibly important example. Whether a couple's divorce is amicable or acrimonious, a child needs to be guided through his own pain and confusion. When a parent is able to display emotional leadership, and implement a family emotional-behavioral plan to weather the upheaval of divorce, it teaches an adoptee that there is life-after-loss. Ask yourself:

1) What is your behavior modeling for your children? How are you 'teaching' them to handle adversity/sadness/anger?
2) Are you expressing your feelings in healthy ways?

3) Are you age-appropriately honest with your kids about your divorce? Do you answer (or bring up) questions in a straightforward manner, without getting overly upset?

4) Do your children truly understand that they had nothing to do with your divorce?

5) Are you allowing your children to mourn the loss of 'how life was' with two parents (even if the ex-spouse was less-than-perfect)?

6) Do you give spoken/unspoken permission to your children to love their other parent, and do you reinforce that relationship?

7) Do you validate your children's emotions?

8) Are you showing them how, in spite of divorce-loss, to be happy?

9) Are you allowing guilt over divorcing one of your child's parents to immobilize your good parenting (are you able to confidently set boundaries, and enforce house rules)?

10) Can you put your adopted children's emotional needs as your high priority over everything else for the first year after divorce?

   Marriage Role Models. You and your spouse are the marriage role models that your children internalize and replicate. Divorce is a sad solution, but worse, is staying in a bad/sad/mad marriage and allowing your children to understand your negative relationship with your spouse as 'normal'. Your marital relationship could become their family structure as adults. You cannot be the parent you need to be for your kids if you are chronically unhappy or in a dysfunctional relationship. It is important to get help or to leave the marriage if that is the case.
   Choices Parents Make. Avoid building a loving, fantasy parent out of an absent-by-choice ex-spouse. You don't want your child to be hurt by a parent who shows little inter-

est in visitation or who 'abandons' your son or daughter, but it is better to place an honest, non-denigrating explanation where it belongs (on the absent parent's personal problems, or sad choices, for example), and to help your child deal with this loss upfront. Covering for an ex-spouse in order to protect your kids' feelings will eventually backlash at you.

Therapy is Normal. Normalize therapy for your kids: Therapists are Feelings Doctors and we all could use a tune-up. If you are seeing a marriage counselor or individual therapist, tell your kids in a serious, but matter-of-fact manner. Talk about why smart people seek help. Your normalizing therapy as a healthy choice will go a long way in helping your child see a counselor, if it is indicated.

Divorce as a Trigger. Divorce will trigger an adopted child's loss issues. It is an opportunity to identify and talk about the core issue of loss, validate feelings, offer empathy, and help build your child's resilience with coping skills. An adopted child's awareness of his feeling that divorce = abandonment, and why he feels the way he does, is a huge step toward him being able to successfully deal with the stress of this major life change.

~By Jean MacLeod

When Does the Wind Change?

Attachment therapists tell us that we adoptive parents need to be attuned to what our children need, and that very often how a child behaves tells us a great deal about how they are feeling.

I'd been working hard on going where my child was taking me, but juggling empathy, attunement, and work is hard. My conscience had caved in as my work escalated and the children had been watching (too much) TV. They love the film Mary Poppins and they'd watched it two or three times in a row. Mary Poppins promises to stay with her charges till the wind changes–and her magic helps the family she has taken under her wing to grow strong. Mary is no longer needed; the wind changes and she leaves. Upstairs, my square-eyed duo were drinking this in.

At tea-time, a little face popped round the door, and a scared voice asked Mum, when does the wind change? Quick as flash I realized my troubled one was asking if I was going to be a permanent tool, always part of her armory against loss and hurt. Right then, through voicing her fright about loss, she helped me understand that attunement is not just about going where our children take us. It's about us needing to lead the kids, show them the way and model how they can regulate their loss.

It was easy this time. I simply picked her up for a cuddle and let her know that I wasn't Mary Poppins but her very own real mummy, there for keeps. She melted straight into me with total relief. The wind can change and change here, but I won't. I'm not going anywhere.

~ By Sheena Macrae

Disruption and Dissolution
Unspoken Losses
By Sheena Macrae

Introduction
Adoption is a way of forming a family, chosen by families who are sure that they can provide a loving home to a child who needs a 'forever family' But sometimes, a child comes home with needs that overwhelm the new family. These may be needs that the parents may not have been made aware of prior to the adoption. Families struggle; they haven't known the extent of the child's needs prior to placement. Counseling for parents through the adoption process and then post-adoption help, seen as vital in retrospect, is often thin.

   Sometimes difficulties arise in adoptive families. They arise because of the clash of cultures that occurs when children 'arrive' from economically disadvantaged countries where poverty and lack of public education leave a child ill equipped to succeed in the west. Sometimes there are unrealistic expectations on the part of adoptive families, where a family 'needs' a child to 'be grateful' for being rescued. Sometimes abuse, neglect and institutionalization leave a child with no experience in being part of a family, and the fit never happens. Sometimes, simply and catastrophically, parents and child are 'out-of-sync' temperamentally, which is something not confined to adoptive families. Or it can be any combination of these factors. Sometimes, because of all this, families want out. Dissolution occurs when an adoption is reversed legally in court after finalization, disruption when the process of adoption is halted before finalization. The term most often used for both is 'disruption'......

What Makes an Adoption Fail?
Adoption advocate Nancy Spoolstra, Director of the Attachment Disorder Network, insists that getting a family fit is one of the most critical factors in making an adoption work. She notes that adoptive parents–quite reasonably in her view–desire reciprocal relationships with their adoptive children. There is an anticipation that the children will give as well as receive, become interactive in developing an existing family ethos, and that parents will be enriched by their adoptive children as much as they enrich their children.

   However, adopted children often arrive with burdens of loss and an inability to understand sociability. Spoolstra forcibly remarks that some damaged children cannot recover enough ever to offer reciprocity. Many adoptions founder on this critical misunderstanding, that the children have no capacity to give what their parents had hoped they could give. Psychologist Doris Landry speaks powerfully on this too, stating that there are few prospective parents who could envisage the reality of some of the problems a hurt child brings to an adoptive relationship. She insists parenting any special needs child is a special and huge undertaking; it may challenge a family for life. She holds also the issues are parallel for birth-families and adoptive families... the element of surprise at issues can in stun in both.

   Agency Responsibility. It's a fact that around 10-25% of all US domestic adoptions fail prior to finalization. There is also increasing evidence being gathered from ICA placements, especially from research in placement into the USA from the former Soviet bloc countries, that disruption and dissolution is a growing problem in this specific adoption area. Why are these disruptions happening when people have gone halfway round the world to adopt, and at great cost?

Agency statistics point to the fact that the growing number of failing international placements may be related to the inability of parents to cope with the needs of children from institutions abroad, whether or not their agencies have made all the facts available. However, agencies are coming under fire for not fully disclosing children's histories, and for not preparing families for adopting children from countries where conditions can be very poor. Some people believe agencies should be more adept at helping client families formulate realistic aspirations for these children, given the disadvantaged start many of them have experienced.

Agencies are challenged for continuing to seek to place children from overseas without developing and devoting resources designed to maintain those placements. Why do they continue to place children without this? Is it not best practice for agencies to work with adoption counselors to ensure the adoptions they have facilitated succeed? There are those that surmise that agencies are more concerned with profit than assuming the mantle of responsibility for families post adoptive needs

Parent Expectations. Nancy Spoolstra suggests that blaming agencies is not wholly useful. She holds that in her experience parents cannot be prepared for what they don't or can't understand, or for what is beyond the general frame of reference of a pre-adoptive family. Adopted children quite often have needs that cannot be fathomed–until they are in your family. Nancy's website www.radzebra.org puns on similarities and difference. Zebras look like horses, but have a vital difference that most overlook despite the stripes…they are not domesticated, they startle at the merest whisper and they are they last to settle after being startled. Just so, many difficult adopted children may look very much 'any other child'–but underlying have very different issues to process which can throw the unprepared adoptive parent totally off a parenting course. These children are not used to the normalcy of family life.

The Impact of Dissolution and Disruption

The Impact on Parents. For the parents disruption can seem an admission of failure. The disruption can be total and catastrophic, where all personal resources are used and gone, and where the new child has totally undermined the safety of the entire family, emotionally and physically. It can mean financial difficulty, especially in the case of international placement where families can spend many thousands of dollars on the adoption, leaving little left to help the children post-adoption, or during and after a disruption. It can also mean quite legitimate feelings of anger that the child wasn't what the placing agency represented them to be.

The Impact on Children. There are few reports detailing how the children of disruption and dissolution cope. Children who disrupt an adoption are special needs children indeed. Some are deeply hurt. The wounds may stem from deprivations (environmental, social, and nutritional), from birthparent abuse leading to physical and emotional deficits in the children, from abuses in previous care (adoptive, foster, institutional) and sometimes deprivation because nobody cared enough to heal the wounds. For some of these children the responses they developed as coping mechanisms became pathological, resulting in behaviors too crude to be accepted in society.

Dealing with Disruption:
Stages of Grief and Loss

Stage # 1: Shock, Denial and Isolation. Shock, denial and the need to be alone are normal, biological, systemic reactions to trauma and pain. None of us who have experienced disrupting an adoption can say we have not been shocked by its trauma. Denial becomes a buffer, a breathing space, to accept the alteration to our personal reality that the disruption creates for us. Our need for isolation may take many forms: staying in our rooms, avoiding discussing our feelings, staying very busy, refusing to answer the phone or talk.

Stage #2: Anger. Anger is a feeling. Feelings are not good or bad, they just 'are'. It is how we choose to act or react that creates a positive or negative energy (and consequences) for ourselves, and for others around us. When we leave a relationship, as we do in disruption, we may find ourselves experiencing all of the feelings we have hidden away or repressed while our child was in our home It can be really crucial to find resources such as counseling and support groups, where it is safe to share our feelings.

Stage #3: Bargaining. During this stage we try to bargain with whatever we envision as our higher power to change events. With regard to disruption, we may try to bargain our way back into continuing to parent this child, at the expense of other relationships; we may find hope in small changes, where there really was no change; we may think if only we 'can do it right' that the child can continue in our family, and that we can continue to parent this child.

Stage # 4: Depression. Our feelings are numbed, minimized, and diminished. We avoid being social and may try to numb ourselves–too much to drink, to eat. Our feelings are pushed down, made very small, possibly because we are carrying so much pain that we cannot believe we will ever get through it, or that it will ever hurt less. Our child is a heavy burden on our day.

Stage # 5: Acceptance. This means coming to terms with the need to disrupt and the associated feelings, accepting the changes that have occurred, and moving on with our lives. This does not mean that we stop caring about the child, but accept that the best choice for this child is to find a family with different resources and strengths, which can help this child heal and grow.

Stage #6: Hope. This means moving past the acceptance of the loss to find some meaning or reason that ties together our past, present and future. It usually means taking time to look after ourselves, heal, and continue or begin counseling for our own fall-out from the trauma we have experienced.

~ Sheena Macrae

Elisabeth Kubler Ross's 5 Stages of Grief have been widely used to help outline how many people move through grief and loss to acceptance of it. Her book 'On Death and Dying' and additional information can be found at www.elisabethkublerross.com. Here, the 5 Stages are used with an adoption twist to outline how disruption may affect a family.

Disruption means **another loss** to these children, even if they 'designed' their behavior to avoid the sociability of family. Some children's deprivations are so deep that family care is almost impossible for them to accept; they have traveled too far from being able to trust outside a very specialized type of caring family. But nonetheless these children are entitled to leave the adoptive relationship with dignity and mementos (lifebooks, treasured goods); additionally, they are entitled to the best placement suited to their needs beyond the disrupting family.

The Impact on Family. The family will never be the same again. Other children in the family will have been affected by the arrival and then departure of a sibling. Just quite how this impacts on these sibs if they themselves have serious issues is a huge question. But families have to face this, and may need to provide therapy and counseling to address the damage caused by the disruption. Watching a sibling leave the home has a huge impact on the remaining child, who may rightfully fear another abandonment herself. Her relationship with her adoptive parents may deteriorate unless these issues are addressed; that she is safe though a sib has gone.

The parents in disrupting families have to be immensely strong in their feeling that disruption is in the best interests of the entire family; for the parents, the children who remain and the child who is leaving. Parenting is about making tough decisions. This is maybe the toughest decision an adoptive family may ever have to face. Yet the adoptive parents have to take a strong position because often what lies behind the disruption is a family in crisis.

The Effect on Sanity. Experts agree that any disruption is a trauma to all involved. Recovery is slow, and like all loss, recovery passes through stages. For parents, it is of paramount importance to acknowledge that if all possible routes were followed to avoid disruption, and it was eventually sought for the safety of the family, there is no questioning their parenting ability. Disrupting parents need to acknowledge that fact. Strong tough parents with good self-esteem can do this. Parents who disrupt may not initially feel good or strong or tough. If they are supported in their decision, they can regain their stability. Support comes from being in safe, supportive counseling and groups where parents can address their feelings.

Adoption advocate Nancy Spoolstra suggests the following protective advice for families who are considering or experiencing disruption:

Get Support. Begin by looking over the on-line resources accessible through the Attachment Disorder Network (ADN) www.radzebra.org. Online support offers a community of care and vital contacts through those who have 'been there, done that'. Connect with a list-serv that provides support and helps parents become strong enough emotionally to either become more effective therapeutic parents or end the placement. Local live support and online resources allow adoptive parents time to think through what is going to be best for everyone involved

Take Action. Analyze the factors leading to disruption in order to make clear decisions. Move to protect all family members in a safe environment. This requires action, especially if damage to other family members is involved; respite care for the child (removing them temporarily from the family) may be considered. *If sibling safety is involved, get pro-active immediately!*

Obtain Counseling. Validation of adoptive parents' feelings (acknowledgment of their loss, pain and guilt, their efforts at saving the placement, their sense of frustration) is needed to move the family forward in a healthy manner.

Protect Yourself. Work toward a protected disruption: use therapy to obviate hurt, documentation to validate your efforts (home video, detailed notes, letters/files from psychologists), and the police to corroborate (file police reports over every incident, as necessary).

Re-placement. Parent acceptance that they must take responsibility for placing their child outside the family–looking beyond the disruption to a re-placement within another family, group home or residential treatment center. *Families should be prepared for the 'Mack Truck Syndrome': the emotional pain and loss that hits unexpectedly after the child has left the home and the family begins to regroup.*

Avoiding Disruption
Pre and Post adoption Education
Adoption agencies need to be on board, both pre and post adoption. Adoption advocate Nancy Spoolstra suggests that in order to minimize disruptions agencies should consider:
- Parents' motives to adopt;
  how closely their expectations will match their potential reality
- Adult attachment profiling
  (family history of parenting, current parenting skills)
- Fit between adoptee and family
  (fit is critical)
- teaching attachment-parenting techniques to parents

Problematic Placements
Red Flags for Parents and Agencies.
- Parents who are planning an artificial twinning (new child matches age of existing child in family).
- Parents who are pregnant yet adopting.
- Parents who wish to adopt out of birth order.

These are criteria that shouldn't rule out a placement, but should place an individual family under tough agency scrutiny. It's important also to tell parents the why of these criteria. Many pre-adoptive families have never had a rationale given as to why artificial twinning is a red flag (parents find they cannot cope with a duo of special needs) or why adopting out of birth order is too (it affects sibling dynamics). Responsible discussion and responsible pre-adoption education should be concerned with these issues.

Building Connections. Parents have a responsibility to build a personal network of adoption-parenting advice and support, both pre-adoption and post-adoption. They need to actively seek out adoption education via workshops and reading materials. Agencies need to provide educational resources, provide parent training, and thorough post-adoption wrap-around services. Seeking professional help at the earliest sign of trouble, or inappropriate family fit, is vital as preventative support.

Letting the Child Go. A family who openly broach the subject of disruption with agencies and social workers most often has traveled the pre-disruption route and used all of the tools above. Adoption expert Nancy Spoolstra notes that when a family is 'talking disruption', it generally means that family intends to move all the way along the line to removing the child from family.

Parents have differing responses to dealing with the fact they had a child placed in the family, and then had this fact erased by law. Some, maybe tougher skinned, refer to the child of the disruption as just that– the child.   Others, more distraught, refer to the lost child as 'my son/daughter'. The child had a place in that family, and cutting legal ties is not the same as cutting emotional ties. Some families will be regretful, some grateful to have the placement ended. All should have reached the right decision for their family.

Children can and do go on to thrive in another placement beyond the disrupted placement. Letting go may be tough, but it may also give the family and the child a potential to heal, and be healed, without each other. Doris Landry holds that the words 'family fit' don't encompass what is needed when it comes to a new and healing family for a child from a disruption. Rather, she holds that success best comes when the new parents get into parenting with eyes wide open, knowing precisely that therapeutic care will be needed. Only by having the resources to reduce the risks of failure ready, will success follow.

Saying Goodbye. Goodbyes to the child should be as positive as can be achieved, with a wish (and thus permission) that the child be happy with the new placement. Sorrow that the placement did not work out is also necessary, and if this is tied to the positive hope for the future, the child may leave with the understanding that events did not work out, not that s/he will always be a failure.

Should an attempt be made to keep contact with the child post-disruption? Some families speak to the value of this; others suggest a clean break is necessary. Certainly, when the disrupting child has been abusing others in the family, contact should probably be terminated. Nancy Spoolstra believes that in some situations, it is in the best interests of the child and the disrupting family to maintain an 'open adoption'. Certainly, she recommends that the re-placement parents be open to contact with the disrupting family, allowing the child to retain a connection with the previous family. Many families make peace with this process by seeing themselves as the 'bridge' between a child's first life and their new (and hopefully successful) life. Clear boundaries should be agreed upon before placement in the new home to avoid contentions and more stress later. Written agreements, signed by all parties can ease the transitions, mitigate fears, and lead to a more successful transition.

The Child's New Future. It's important that the child be allowed to hold on to the fact that there had been a placement which failed, and that part of his/her history is always a part of her/him. Lifebooks should be updated to chronicle the disrupted placement, and in the new family, the child should be permitted to talk of their time in their previous home. Helping the child come to terms with the disruption is critical for a secure onward placement. Helping the child with the behaviors that caused the disruption is also imperative, and the post-disruption family should be prepared to use therapy (as recommended) for their new child.

Therapeutic Care for the Disrupting Family. Families must cope with explaining disruption to vulnerable children who remain in their family. This is hard when many parents have settled their adopted children by emphasis that this family is the forever family.

Many families have simply faced facts, and explained that it is parents' job to keep their family and children safe. Children understand and desire protection and safety. They can be helped to understand that for the displaced sibling, being made safe was not possible in their family, but that safety and care is being offered elsewhere.

Many adopted children will need therapeutic help if it's clear that the disruption is opening their own issues of safety, permanence and loss. Experts feel that therapy for all in the family is a vital part of the disruption process.

The Process of Disruption and Dissolution

The following is NOT meant to take the place of legal advice from a qualified and experienced adoption attorney, and personal research into parents' legal or other responsibilities

The process of disruption and dissolution can, in the USA, be achieved by public and private means. Where an adoption is finalized, severance of parental rights will have to be sought through a court order, but moving towards this can be achieved either through agency assistance, state assistance, or through private negotiation (if a new home has been found for the child) through a Family Law Attorney.

Writers in the sphere of disruption and dissolution are outspoken that to use agency or state placement teams in a disruption can be fraught with hidden emotional and legal dangers. Leaving the child to agency care or state care without a decision about the child's future, can be (and very often is) construed as criminal abandonment. Families remain responsible for their children's financial stability without a re-placement order. Private placements allow the disrupting families to ensure secure placements for their children without the deep hurt of being called inadequate by state or agency teams. However, some experts advise that that unless state considerations are met in full, the child and the disrupting family are both at risk.

Families should at all times follow legal practices governing moving children out of a family, in particular the Inter-State Compact on the movement of children (a guardianship measure). Nancy Spoolstra recommends that private re-placements work best if a facilitator is used, particularly one that knows the new family willing to take the child. She also notes that private placement can be 'buyer-beware' unless the facilitator has experience and integrity.

In ICA it is not a solution to return the child to the mother-country unless agency or sending government have a further placement for the child, and this has been negotiated.

It should also be noted that in a post-finalized adoption, unless and until legal dissolution is achieved, parental rights severed, and the child found a new adoptive home, the adoptive parents remain responsible for the financial welfare of the child until that child reaches adulthood.

Re-placement. There is a lot of information available online about placing kids beyond the family that disrupts. It perhaps should be written in bold, large print that disruptions should not be considered a cheap way to pick up kids (generally Caucasian) from international or domestic placements. Children from disrupted adoptions need specialized parenting. They need parents with knowledge of what the child has been through and who possesses parenting skills from hands-on experience with other kids.

Re-placement can be done through agency work and state placement. Experts say this is expensive, may not work out well and may remove any decision-making power of the child's onward placement from the disrupting parents. The cost of hiring an adoption lawyer and a placing agency can be overwhelming to a family who have already used up funds in making the adoption or paying for treatment.

It's advised by some workers in the field that personal or 'private' placements are better. The disrupting families get to 'interview' prospective adopters. This works in the USA as long as:

- All local regulations are adhered to.
- The Interstate Compact on the Placement of Children from home to home is adhered to.
- Guardianship arrangements are set up and adhered to.
- Financial arrangements made for the care of the child.

In the case of an adoption that has not been finalized, the process of disrupting is simpler, because placing agencies retain involvement in the adoption until legalization. But families can feel very bereft when the agencies simply remove the child. In ICA cases, where disruption occurs prior to leaving the sending country, negotiations will take place with the local authorities. Again, families will be left empty-handed, and the child returned to the sending country carers. The parents cannot expect any voice in how the child may or not be re-placed, although some families have managed to hear through the grape-vine how their disrupted child has fared in a re-placement.

Adoption after Disruption? In the framework of disruption, parents wonder if they will be able to adopt again. Will a disruption leave a stain on their potential to ask for another placement? In ICA, where a serious problem in the health of the child is discovered, and was not made material in the referral papers, it is very likely that the sending country will allow another referral, although not necessarily immediately. In most other cases, it will depend on the individual circumstances of the disruption. Many families do go on to adopt again.

What must be addressed is development of post-adoption services from agencies and other adoption workers to encompass the growing diverse needs of post-adoptive families, particularly those who have adopted internationally. It's important that families know that seeking therapy to preserve a family is strength, not weakness. It's also important that all adoptive families are encouraged to talk and think about disruption and dissolution. Only by talking, making resources available and easily accessible, will the adoptive community be able to deal with what are for now the 'unspoken losses' of disruption and dissolution.

~ By Sheena Macrae

Siblings

Siblings
Remembering Fair isn't Equal
By Becky Miklos

"Look, mama! Here's my baby Eva!"

Fumbling with the video camera and stumbling to wedge my big feet into baby room slippers, my three year old is way ahead of me, chirping excitedly about her discovery: her soon-to-be baby sister. In five days I will adopt this baby and realize my dream of mothering two daughters. For now, I am awed at the good fortune of our being able to visit her in the orphanage room where she has waited for a year, ever since her first week of life.

It is obvious from first glance that she is content and centered, a settled child. She grins and gurgles, reaching out delightedly without fear or hesitation, to touch the face of the three year old who is dancing and spinning inches away. Ah, yes, I think as the months of tension drain from my body: this child is perfect for us. Everything is going to be fine. Risking all, I have been gifted this pacific, generous, glorious baby girl...

Talking Two. Today I'm the single mom of two daughters adopted from China as small infants. My girls are wonderful siblings, due to a combination of luck, work, and personalities. The busy personality and high energy of my first child determined that she would have a sibling. OK, it wasn't that simple, but I had always dreamed of having a two-kid family; it was how I grew up. But adopting my first was hard, and for a time I didn't know if she could heal enough from the trauma and anxiety of her adoption, of losing her beloved foster family, to be able to also tolerate a sibling. Eventually, through attachment parenting and therapy, she did heal and moved on to exploring our home (including precariously scaling kitchen cabinets, appliances, bookshelves, and closets). She was into everything and keeping her safe was exhausting. I thought a sibling would distract her from her explorations and focus some of her energy along more constructive paths. She also remained an extremely controlling child who wouldn't tolerate being read to and who couldn't sit still long enough for me to teach her anything. Her diet consisted of macaroni and cheese and ramen noodles. I felt that a sibling would help this child to relax and to expand her world.

Preparing for a Second Child. My first was 20 months old and had been home for 10 months when I began paperchasing for child number two. By the time the referral came, she was three and old enough to be excited at the prospect of a sibling.

I never had any doubt that my first would travel with me to get her sister. We share a family bed and I'd left her for only one night during our time together. I couldn't see any benefit in leaving her for two to three weeks while I traveled to China, coming home with the insult of a 12 month old baby who would need lots of my time and attention! I felt that from the very beginning, my first child needed to have an investment in the well-being of the second and that she needed to be invested in our success as a family of three. I was lucky that my mom came along on the trip and that my first was comfortable enough to go with Grandma when I needed to focus on the new addition. During the trip, I expected a lot from my first daughter and she proved to be a wonderful traveler; enduring squat potties, orphanage, and foster care visits, and long rides along the bumpy, dusty, rural roads of JiangXi Province.

Setting Boundaries. Life in China with two was easy; my first was so excited that she was happy to be helpful, Grandma was there to help, and the new baby was happy, content, and easily amused. We also enjoyed room service, helpful guides, and clean fresh towels for the asking.

Realty hit when we got home, suffering from jetlag, and fighting a month long battle with bronchitis and sinusitis that all three of us contracted. I dropped my older daughter at daycare every morning so that I could focus on the new baby for the remaining six weeks I had off from work. For most of that time, we were recovering from illness; napping together on and off all day, until it was time to get my older daughter. She would fall asleep during dinner, and wake early every morning, demanding all the attention I could muster before the baby woke up. I remember her tears and anger at my fatigue and illness; I remember trying to placate her with yet another video, and commiserating that "yes, it's really not fair that the little bit of energy I have seems to go to the baby".

I felt terribly guilty about all of this until I remembered the title of a book I'd read in preparation for parenting two kids: *Loving Each One Best: A Caring and Practical Approach to Raising Siblings* (by Nancy Samalin).

Though I couldn't actually locate the book in the mess that had become my home, just focusing on the title freed me to survive the tough, early days. No, it wasn't fair. It wasn't ideal but it was enough. I was enough and we all had enough for now. I already knew how to love my older child and give her what she needed. I agreed with her that babies are yucky and not much fun and that took the edge off of her anger,

Making it Real:
Preparing Your Children for an International Adoption

Hang a large world map on the wall and pinpoint the country where the new sister or brother is waiting.

Cook dinners together with food originating from the new sibling's birth country.

Read books and watch videos together about the new sibling's birth country, and discuss what you've read or watched. Check your library, or browse these sources for family-friendly materials to purchase:

Culture for Kids
www.cultureforkids.com

Asia for Kids
www.asiaforkids.com

Celebrate the Child
www.celebratethechild.com

Tapestry Books
www.tapestrybooks.com

Chinasprout
www.chinasprout.com

Pack a Backpack

Will your son or daughter be traveling with you to adopt internationally? Pack a backpack with these possibilities:

- Camera (disposable, for younger children)

- Travel journal with pens and markers

- Blank drawing pad

- Deck of cards

- Books

- Mini music or CD player

- Small electronic games

- Snacks (non-melting, non-staining)

- A clean t-shirt (for inflight spills)

- Toothbrush and comb

- 52 Fun Things to Do on a Plane by Lynn Gordon (it's a deck of cards filled with interesting things to do in small spaces).

aligning her with me and providing a bit of forgiveness and generosity for her sister.

I tried to remember that **fair isn't equal**. My little one expected nothing, but my big girl had developed the expectation that I would meet her needs, and she deserved my best attention for the few waking hours we were together each day. Not that I neglected the baby; she had me all to herself while her sister was at daycare and I worked hard on attachment parenting with her. But when her sister came home my focus shifted. I praised my big girl. I "caught her being good" and she quickly became good. I remembered to ask my big girl to help by fetching a wipe or a toy, and I told her how special she was to be a big girl who could help mama, instead of a baby who couldn't do anything.

My one year-old wasn't terribly helpless, and was catching up fast. I felt the early weeks together were rare and precious, and I used them in setting up my girls to care for each other for a lifetime. My focus was on making them friends and playmates…and miraculously, it worked.

Now, three years later, they play well together, most of the time. No doubt it's a big help that my younger daughter is not bossy or controlling; most of the time she's content to follow along and be taught by my older daughter. She has an impish, quirky sense of humor that often escapes the intensity of my more straight-forward thinking, earnest older child. I am lucky that they are a terrific match, but I also believe that I've been able to build on this lucky match, and that I am helping them to be sisters. We have developmentally turbulent times ahead, but I hope and pray that I can continue guiding them to be friendly and supportive of each other, well into the future.

~ Becky Miklos is a single mom to two daughters from China. She works full-time as an accountant in South Florida. She dreams of someday turning her passions: adoption, parenting and attachment issues, into her bill-paying day job. She also volunteers for Altrusa, administering donation sponsorships for children in foster care in JiangXi Province: www.altrusa.ws

Preparing a Preschooler
for Adopting a Sibling

1) **Talk very honestly and *specifically* about what might change with a new baby in the house** (for example- "if we are reading a book and the baby cries we will need to finish our book later"), so that your child is prepared and won't feel so betrayed when/if a shift in your attention occurs. A three year old still won't be happy about sharing your time, but at least he or she will come to it with some understanding of the plan of action.

2) **Talk about what all babies need and deserve** (food, sleep, dry diapers, and lots of loving attention). Tell your child that's how you took care of him or her when he/she became your baby, and that's how you will take care of the new sister or brother.

3) **Prepare your child for the attention from others that the new sibling will bring.** Inform your son or daughter that all babies tend to bring this kind of attention; it's just how people react to little ones (it's how people reacted to him/her, too), and it's just a normal baby thing! Praise him or her specifically for handling all of the new baby-attention like a 'big kid'.

4) **Talk about the positive changes that will occur from being a Big Sister or Brother.** A new big kid bike? A weekly park date with just mom or dad? Talk about how she or he will be able to teach the baby sister or brother lots of important skills. Encourage your child to designate some of his or her 'younger' toys for the baby, and together choose a safe storage for treasures that your older child doesn't wish to share.

5) **Encourage regression.** Offer your child a baby bottle of chocolate milk and a chance to be held like a baby in your lap on a regular basis. Let him or her pretend babyhood. Offer tastes of baby food. Facilitate a bubble bath with your son or daughter and the new baby. If your child is new to potty training, expect regression.

6) **If your child likes baby dolls, buy one to give him or her while waiting for the sibling**. Demonstrate what babies need and how they like to be held; reinforce and reward careful handling!

7) **Give your child two special jobs to do that are all his or hers:** one that helps you out (for instance, place baby bottles on the lower shelf in fridge so he or she can run and get one for you as needed), and one that he or she designs to make the baby happy.

8) **Expect to do attachment work** (infant massage, parent-child bonding activities) on your preschooler for a period of time, in addition to meeting the new baby's needs.

9) **Use a hands-free baby carrier or sling so you can physically interact with your preschooler.** Holding hands anchors your connection to your oldest, while also carrying your youngest. Three hand squeezes = I Love You!

10) **Tell your child that he or she will always be your baby.**

~ Jean MacLeod

Parenting Siblings:
Biological and Adopted

I have worked hard on the sibling front. I mostly try to remove all elements of competition between the two girls. It is not always successful but often I make real headway. Two of my 'bibles' are the Adele Faber books, *Siblings Without Rivalry* and *How to Talk so Kids will Listen and Listen so Kids Will Talk*. They are not specifically targeted to adoption issues at all but I find the techniques definitely cross over. One of the most effective has been that each child is unique and therefore the absolute 'best' and most fabulous at being herself (there's nobody better in that department than you!), and we as parents cherish each child in their uniqueness.

The other concept I talk about often is that love is not a 'zero sum game'. A new child does not take a portion of love away from the existing children in the family, in my belief. And so I tell my kids this, and show it by how I act. I also look for every opportunity to reinforce and support the moments when they really enjoy each other and have definitely set an expectation that 'sisters take care of each other'. We work to make sure our son is not left out because so much time is consumed with his sisters' tantrums. And we make sure that he knows that they both adore him even though they can make him crazy.

The main area that I still grapple with is how to keep the adoptive nature of our family in balance. It is a defining attribute but not the only defining attribute and I don't want our two bio kids to end up feeling discounted in any way, or to grow up feeling that they had to take a back seat to the larger drama of our youngest child's adoption story. Of course, I also want our youngest to be totally secure as a full-fledged member of the family and also at ease (as much as possible) with her journey to it.

I remember reading once about 'normal' siblings of special needs kids and how difficult it was for them sometimes because of all the family energy that the special needs kids consumed, leaving significantly less for them. Also, I am the oldest of five so my concerns in this area are definitely related to my growing up experiences as well. I also worry about reading too many adoption books–will my biological daughter and son think I really only care about their adopted sister? So I am aware of my reading aware of the balance I require to have in my attitude to being mother to siblings. When we returned from China our bio daughter announced that she wanted to learn Chinese. I wondered if she thought that I only liked Chinese girls (why else did we travel halfway around the world?) So I asked her about it point blank while reiterating that nothing could touch my love for her.

She is eight now and in her fourth year at the Chinese language school (three hours every Saturday plus a tutor during the week). She says that when we go back to China she wants to be in charge (as our family translator and therefore the only one who knows the language). She is totally leading the charge on this front and we are incredibly proud of her. Our youngest will start language classes in the fall. It is a great boon that the language school, and the community around it, are already woven into our lives. In retrospect, her desire to study is a reflection I think of how out of control she felt when we were in China the first time. However, she has transformed that into a gift for all of us. Being part of the Chinese school community has introduced us to new friends, and provided a real bridge to the local Asian-American community that I am very grateful for.

~ Maureen Donely, adoptive mom

The 'Team Family' Approach
Helping Siblings Build Family Attachment
By Jean MacLeod

Adopting a baby, toddler or child is a joyous event. Older siblings are usually excited to be involved, and anxious to meet, greet and play with their new sister or brother. What happens when post-institutional reality counters their vision of a dream sib, with a toddler who needs vast amounts of parental time and special attention?

What happens is disappointment and resentment, unless big brothers and sisters are prepared to help the new sibling become "one of the family". Older siblings can be incredibly understanding of an adoptee's issues if they are given information in advance, if they are encouraged to ask questions, and if they are helped to role-play potential interactions.

Children who are adopted from an institution may have no concept of family, of what parents are supposed to do, or what exactly siblings are for. Children adopted from a foster home may enter a new family while grieving their foster family terribly, and rejecting everyone else in sight. Helping older siblings view your family (and themselves) *from the position of the transplanted adoptee* will give them a base for patience and compassion when dealing with their new sister or brother.

If your older children were also adopted, watching a parent teach the new child to love and trust may create a better understanding of their own babyhood. Be prepared to talk about what all babies need and why adoption happens. Listen to what isn't being said when your older child asks you questions, and be sure to address underlying feelings. Teaching your older children that helping the new baby or toddler to fall in love with you is your parent-job, and that they can promote this happening with helper-jobs of their own, is one way to pull them into the new child's bonding process.

Doing attachment work and activities with a newly adopted child can be emotionally draining if you are also worried about slighting the needs of your older children. Enlist

In My Words~ *Growing Siblings*

My adopted daughter is often the recipient of extravagant compliments while my biological son stands by. Had I known this would happen prior to the adoption, it would have broken my heart. But my son appears to enjoy the attention my daughter receives. He was previously a very shy child; painfully shy with strangers and acquaintances. He is transformed. Maybe this would have happened anyway, as age seven is an astonishing watershed. I suspect, however, that my daughter, largely because of the way she became part of the family, has contributed in a big way. My son came with us to adopt her. He was part of the process of the adoption himself. He took the photos on adoption day and wrote a diary. When we were in China, we compared notes with him on her progress. She helped enormously by smiling at him first, saying his name first, allowing only him to spoon feed her, giggling, flopping about, making a lot of rude noises, and generally acting in the sort of a way that all little boys must wish their sisters would act.
~Amanda Brookes

your kids, and have them work for you rather than against you! It's always better to take the time to train an ally, rather than ignore a problem and create an 'enemy'.

- If your baby or toddler has a breakdown or needs intense time with mom or dad, have a strategy in place with your older kids so they can help you handle it. Example of a pre-arranged plan of action: older children leave the room, dim the lights, turn music on low, bring a bottle, answer the phone if it rings, and have a special treat while they give you uninterrupted time to help your new child.

- If your big kid has a breakdown (a sudden, genuine need for attention), have a seat on the floor, put the baby down next to you, and pull the big kid in for a hug. Both can end up on your lap together!

- Create structured time for fun, loving activities with each child, but also plan on being flexible for triaging needs. Schedule times out of the house with each older sib where it is one-on-one, just like the time the new sibling gets. Tell them often what an amazing job they are doing as a big sister or brother, and how much you appreciate their hard work and help.

- Ask grandparents and extended family to spend some extra time with the older kids if the new child needs lots of your attention. Grandparents benefit from the same information and preparation about adding a sib that you gave your sons and daughters. They likely don't know about the extra issues you are dealing with if it's their first adoption, too. If your parents or in-laws are pros with adoption-grandparenting, let them know exactly how they can help when the baby arrives, and express your appreciation for their understanding!

- Older kids can be a conduit to you, and reinforce your emotional work with the new child. It is very easy (especially when a parent is tired!) to allow a baby or toddler to attach sideways to a sibling before he or she is fully, securely attached to a parent. It is great to see siblings interact, but if the new child is at all avoidant towards you then you initially need to be the only one filling her up with love. Give an older sibling the task of reporting to you when the new sib needs attention. If a toddler falls down and gets hurt, instead of your older child picking the toddler up and comforting him or her, your oldest can say "Let me get mom or dad for you–they can help!" and then you step in to be the one to meet the toddler's emotional/physical/safety needs. This also works for diaper changes or potty, dressing, and wanting to be picked up–for all of the basic, nurturing parental duties. Explain that this process is not going to take forever and eventually your older child can lavish all the caring attention she or he desires on the new sister or brother. This makes it a tough solo job for the parent. Older siblings make for a nice respite from the demands of a baby or toddler, but wait until your new child wants you over anyone, before letting her depend on anyone else.

Take care of yourself while you are filling the needs of a busy, growing household. You can't fill anyone else up if you are on empty! If the stress of juggling the needs of your new adoptee and the change in your family dynamics is wearing you down, call a family meeting and involve everyone in finding solutions:

• Everyone gets a turn to express their feelings, to bring up needs, and to ask the family for creative problem-solving. Sometimes just respectfully listening to a family member express their difficulties is helpful. A shift in the family structure, no matter how positive, can still be stressful.

• Delegate or re-assign chores. If your older kids are teenagers, then they can help pick up the slack and rotate laundry and dinner. Change expectations by talking about the changes in advance, and noticing your children's efforts.

• Get outside help for anything you can afford to have done, so you can concentrate on your kids without total burnout. If this is impossible, give yourself permission to let anything not of primary importance, to slide. Look upon facilitating the new addition to the family, and the family transition to multiple children, as a full-time job with a temporary 'intense' career assignment!

The Team Family approach can work very well; it is extraordinary what big sisters and brothers can do to help once they are informed about the issues, understand what you are trying to accomplish, and are given an action blueprint. Expect some bumps while siblings work out their new roles. The end goal is a happy, cohesive family, which contributions from all family members have helped to build.

~ By Jean MacLeod

Recommended Reading
for Adults:

Siblings Without Rivalry: How to Help Your Children Live Together So You Can Live Too
By Adele Faber and Elaine Mazlish

How to Talk So Kids Will Listen & Listen So Kids Will Talk
By Adele Faber and Elaine Mazlish

Loving Each One Best: A Caring, and Practical Approach to Raising Siblings
By Nancy Samalin

Beyond Sibling Rivalry: How to Help Your Children Become Cooperative, Caring and Compassionate, By Peter Goldenthal, PhD

For Young Siblings:

Henry's First-Moon
By Lenore Look

Sophie and the New Baby
By Laurence Anholt

Julius, the Baby of the World
By Kevin Henkes

Sheila Rae the Brave
By Kevin Henkes

A Pocketful of Kisses
By Audrey Penn

On Mother's Lap
By Ann Herbert Scott

Smile, Lily!
By Candace Fleming

For Special Needs Siblings:

Views from Our Shoes: Growing Up With a Brother or Sister With Special Needs
By Donald J. Meyer (ages 9-12)

Living With a Brother or Sister With Special Needs: A Book for Sibs, By Donald J. Meyer and Patricia Vadasy (for 13+)

The Sibling Slam Book: What It's Really Like To Have A Brother Or Sister With Special Needs
By Donald Meyer (ages 12 +)

The Reality of a Sister

My oldest turned three the day before I returned home with her little sister, who was 9 months old at the time. Despite months of preparation, reality hit with a vengeance. I'm convinced that age three is a really hard time to introduce a sibling, in part, because that's when kids are just starting to understand the concept of 'other'–and experiencing all the fears that go along with realizing the world doesn't revolve around them. I do know some three year olds who adjusted right away, but I know a lot who had a really challenging time, including my own! I needed some tools to cope! I did these:

1) Gave up on playing up the 'big girl' thing for my three year old. She had zero desire to be a big girl. She wanted to be my baby again. Instead, I worked on channeling the baby urges. We talked about when it was okay to 'play baby' and what she should do to let me know she was feeling a need to be babied.

2) Gave up on potty training for awhile for my oldest. It had been going pretty well, but she decided diapers were worth the extra attention from Mom, and there was no way I was going to 'win.'

3) Role-played what to do when the baby had something she wanted. And read and talked about the book *I Used to Be the Baby* by Robin Ballard, which is a great book.

4) Established two rules: No hurting the baby, and no waking the baby. That was it. My daughter didn't have to love the baby or like the baby, but she had to follow the rules. I never told her how to feel about the baby–although I often told them both how much I loved them.

5) Talked on the baby's behalf. When she smiled at her big sister or when she responded to something her big sister gave her I said, "Look! She saw you come in the room and smiled the biggest smile ever! I think she really likes you!"

6) Empathized with the angry feelings. We talked about other big sisters we knew - adults, like me and Nana. We talked about how sometimes little sisters are a big pain, and sometimes they are really cute , and even fun when they get old enough to talk and play better. We talked about how to deal with the angries–and read *Sometimes I'm Bombaloo* by Rachel Vail/Humi Yeo–a lot! That's another great book.

7) Followed the advice of a very wise adoptive mom, who said she gave her oldest a sense of control in the first two or three weeks home by removing the baby from her 'space' whenever the oldest felt her space had been invaded. No questions. No lectures.

It was several months before my oldest felt real affection for her sister. I had started to think she wasn't capable of it. But now they are five and three they have a relationship that's all their own and is incredibly sweet. The rivalry is there–the disagreements and misunderstandings and shouting matches–but it's also obvious they adore each other. And now I feel like I can help build the relationship by encouraging them to ask each other for help and work together on things. That was impossible before.

~ Gayle Kiser, adoptive mom

The Family of 'Others Like Me'
Keeping our Children's Connections

Connections for our children come in many forms, and the power of a connection can be amazing. We've had two important connections come to our family, one by circumstance, one by design; and both have been so helpful for our children.

Our first connection happened in China. One of the components of the China adoption program that appealed to us as potential parents was the trip over there: two weeks of getting to know each other as a family without outside intrusions, and two weeks of getting to know the country of our children's birth. We shared this very personal experience with twenty complete strangers. We were all giddy with the prospect of parenthood, and stupid with all the pieces we didn't know and hadn't prepared for! One rainy day in March, all of us shared one amazing, common bond: we were suddenly parents. Our children were thrust into the hands of complete and utter strangers, and the only thing that was familiar to them was each other.

We were fortunate that our agency placed all the families together in a block of rooms in each of the hotels we stayed at, and moms and dads got to know each other as we looped around the hallways with crying children at three in the morning. We all had an 'open door' policy and created a great support network; we held playgroups in the hallways, shared snacks and gradually got to know each other. And we watched our children play with the comfort of something familiar: each other.

Our guides also informed us that we wouldn't just be adding names to our holiday card lists, but that we would probably know each other for a lifetime. Our travel group, from all over the USA, decided to try to get together yearly, but none of us understood what these nine other families would mean in our lives and I am not sure that any of us envisioned that it would last more than a few years.

Fast forward to our first reunion. To see the children run into each other's arms and hug each other after seconds of their re-meeting was nothing short of amazing. These children weren't walking in China and now, a year later, were running at breakneck speed through a quaint B&B in Tennessee. It was like they had never been apart, and that hasn't changed in the six reunions we have had so far.

A Gift Only An Adoptee Can Give

We are a gift to one another! As adoption experts David Brodzinsky and Marshall Schechter put it, for adoptees, these connections *"are like food to a starving man."*

Many adoptees are starving for a sense of belonging akin to the bond shared in close-knit birth families. Fortunately, because all adoptees share a crucial piece of personal history—the loss of or separation from our birth families—much of our hunger to belong can be satisfied through each other.

~Sherri Eldridge author, adoptee and adoptive grandmother

Find her article on this subject at www.emkpress.com

Our group has made a commitment to meeting up with each other annually, and the connections continue with our group. I wouldn't be surprised if some of these girls head to the same colleges and are roommates. This primal connection to a fundamental piece of their past lives has been so powerful for them and we, as parents, feel that we need to do what we can to continue to foster these relationships. While the relationships between the

girls have changed as they grow, the connection for these 'orphanage siblings' is nothing short of amazing.

A second set of connections came more from my family's making than from circumstance. As members of 'Families with Children from China' (FCC) for a number of years, we watched our daughters age-out of event activities designed for new babies and toddlers. It was hard for kids to get to really know each other well within a large group.

Our solution was to start some small groups that are based on age/school grade, and it doesn't matter where the kids hail from. What we have discovered is that the kids relish the time they have to spend together. They are in groups where they look like one another, their family situation is not up for discussion since they all have many of the same circumstances in common, and we emphasize low-key activities that highlight friendly interaction. We also require the parents to stay.

It's a big kids' playgroup but it gives us parents the opportunity to get to know each other and to talk over issues we might be facing, as well. We organize events that don't require too much planning; there is usually a meal (everyone contributes), some kind of activity involved (usually minimal like a small craft), and plenty of opportunity for talk, play, and connections. These friendships continue to grow as we run into each other on the soccer field, at the grocery store, and other places around town.

While I stumbled on these connections, and intellectually understood their benefit, it wasn't until I read an article by Sherri Eldridge called *A Gift Only an Adoptee can Give* (you can find this article at www.emkpress.com, in the parent resources section as a free download) that I truly understood what a gift to our children spending time with other adoptees can be. Giving our children the chance to belong to a group where they seamlessly 'fit' without explanation has been priceless. It does take time and commitment from parents to make the connections happen, but in doing so, we help our children make their way in the world and help them to build foundations in the strength of the familiar...each other.

~ Carrie Kitze
adoptive mom, author, and publisher of adoption books and parent guides

Finding an Unexpected Sibling

By Susan Rittenhouse

Shortly after New Years, 2004, I was browsing our computer and noticed that one of the families, who had adopted a little girl from the same Social Welfare Institute (SWI) that our daughter was from, had updated their family website. My husband, Jim, and I usually don't follow the cyber-links that are posted on listserv groups, but this one was different. This other little girl shared the same first name as our little girl and they had been at the same SWI at the same time. We were curious, since the name we chose for our daughter (Meredith) is not a common one.

Jim emailed the other family, and said, "I saw your Meredith's photo on the internet. It looks amazingly like our Meredith" and provided a URL to our own family web site with photos of our daughter. The other mom sent back an email in agreement. I couldn't get over the likeness between the girls. It nagged at me until I finally sent the URL for the other Meredith to some friends and family, who all replied back to tell me that they also saw an amazing resemblance.

I began to think that maybe Meredith and Meredith might be related, and I hesitantly composed an email to the other mom. Knowing how crazy it sounded, I wrote the following: *"I can't seem to stop thinking about how much our girls look like each other. The older they get, the more they seem to resemble each other. I was looking at some of your Meredith's photos and even the tilt of her head is like our Meredith. Do you think that it is possible that they are biological sisters?"*

I also included a birthdate, a finding location, a brief description of our Meredith's likes, her current height and weight statistics and more links to photos on our family web site. Many emails and conversations later, our two families sent away for a DNA test kit. Weeks later, we received DNA results that confirmed our belief that the two girls were biologically related.

DNA Testing.   I wish I knew then what I know now about DNA testing. Even though I have Bachelors Degree in biology and took at least one course in genetics, I assumed that DNA results would be conclusive. They're not. Our test results indicated that the girls are at least half siblings. Siblingship DNA testing consists of comparing approximately 16 genetic markers. Known full biological siblings may share all markers (identical twins) or no markers. The calculated results are simply the *probability* that two children are related, and it may be a high probability or a low probability. The only way to get more conclusive results is to include at least one biological parent in the testing.

There is, however, more to establishing a biological connection than DNA. DNA tells only part (though a big part) of the story. Not all siblings look or act alike, but in the case where you have very little information, a similar look can be an important piece of the puzzle. Everyone that I know of who has identified siblings (I know of at least 80 families with more than 45 confirmed or suspected sets), all so far have happened on to a photo that looked amazingly like their child. They all had the same nagging suspicion, and each hesitantly contacted the other sibling's family.

Initial Contact.   When making the initial contact with the 'other family', email may be a convenient and non-threatening method to make the first contact. When you compose your letter (or prepare for your phone call), try to maintain a 'curious' tone. Remember that your enthusiasm could seem intrusive, threatening or pushy to the other family. They have not yet seen the connection that you see and may feel blindsided. Provide some information on your child's history:

- Province
- Orphanage
- Birthdates
- Abandonment stories
- Behavioral characteristics
- Possibly genetic medical conditions *(cleft issues, Thalassemia, etc.)*

Photos are invaluable at this stage. A picture is worth a thousand words.

Sharing Photos. Share lots of photos! You never know which photo will be the 'one' that is the clincher for you.Snapshots, not studio portraits, are best. Compare photos that are focused clearly. Costumes, hats, and sunglasses are cute, but can be a barrier to seeing facial features. Include poses that are 'typical' of your child, and include photos that are not 'typical' of your child. Include photos of your child at different ages. When comparing photos of two children, whole body photos can show similar body types. My daughter and her sister have a distinctive 'head tilt' in many photos, and that was useful for us. Once you've exchanged photos and are convinced that you see a similarity, ask friends and family members to take a look. Ask a trusted teacher or daycare provider for their opinion. Give them unlabeled photos and ask them who the children are.

Deciding to Test. If, after sharing photos and other information, you still think that your children may be siblings, you can proceed to DNA testing. When choosing a DNA laboratory, there is some basic information that you need to know. There are two tests that are commonly available: twin zygotic testing and siblingship testing Unless you are absolutely sure that you have twins, you should choose the siblingship test. The twin zygotic test will only tell you if a set of twins is fraternal or identical. Don't be tempted to take this test because it's cheaper and faster; it's worthless to only discern whether children who are not known twins really are twins. The siblingship test is more comprehensive.

It is important to choose a laboratory that has an appropriate (racial) database. In a siblingship test, most labs test 16 genetic markers. The lab looks at how often the genetic markers at a particular location match with the suspected sibling, and compares them to how often each marker/loci is found in people with the same racial background. Then the lab will do a calculation called a 'siblingship index'. The higher the score is on the siblingship index, the greater the possibility that the children are biological siblings.

Often, a personal meeting (before DNA testing) between the families is very informative. The interaction between the children can be very telling. It's also a way to make a connection with the 'other' family. In many ways, the connection between the families is very similar to that of 'in-laws'. In our case, we are very blessed that our families get along well.

Adoption and Biology. As adoptive parents, we are aware that it's not blood ties that make a family, and Jim and I tell our daughter that families are made in lots of different ways. It's not a competition between adoptive relationships and biological relationships. My daughter is an only child, but Sissy has a younger (also adopted) sister. This situation is new territory for adoptive families and I think that how the 'other' children are affected depends on how inclusive both families are. The connection between the biological sisters and the adopted sisters is different, but real. Often, the newly reunited siblings "adopt" their siblings' siblings as well. One way of demonstrating an inclusive relationship is to display photographs of all the children in both families; another is to include the "other" children when giving gifts and attention.

The biological connection is important, too. The sisters have a very strong connection that isn't explainable by anything other than genetics. The fact that my daughter has a biological sister is a part of her personal history. Sissy is a connection to my daughter's biological family…with Sissy, she can commiserate on what it's like to have a mosquito bite swell to the size of a golf ball, or share the same size dress-up clothes. My daughter once said about her sister and her 'in-laws': *"They are a part of my family and I am a part of theirs"*.

A Parent's Decision? Some adoptive parents, and even some adoptive professionals, feel that we do not have the right to look into our child's past, or to do DNA testing to determine siblings. It is my belief that when a situation like unexpected siblings is dropped in our laps, that it is our responsibility to gather as much information as we can in order to make an informed decision to declare two children siblings. We make potentially life-changing decisions for our daughter all the time: what schools to send her to, where to live, what extra-curricular activities to allow her to do, or whether or not to give her a sibling. As parents, we don't know which major or minor decisions of ours will trigger a child's intense reaction. I know that I would not want to face my daughter, tell her that I had information about a possible sibling, and that I had done nothing to find the truth.

A Parent's Responsibility. The connection between my daughter and her sister is inspiring. But it's an awesome responsibility to help our five year-old maintain a long distance relationship that is so important to her. The in-laws and 'Sissy' are in our thoughts and conversations daily. The tools that we use to maintain the relationship are the telephone, email, care packages in the mail, and weekend vacations.

It can get expensive depending on the distance between the two household. For younger children, it's the parents who take the lead in maintaining the relationship. We dial the phone, we mail packages, we email updates and information, and we make the vacation plans necessary for that very important personal contact.

Our girls understand that they were abandoned and split up, and they were/are angry about it. Finding a sibling makes it so much more real, because there is a living, breathing reminder. We've had anger and tantrums from the girls about missing each other terribly, and about living apart. We've also seen joy and love when they are together.

Our two families have learned to connect in many different ways: physically, mentally, emotionally, and spiritually. It's important to all of us and it's enhanced our lives. Through finding an unexpected sibling and the science of DNA, we've not only found in-laws… we've found friends.

~ Susan Rittenhouse is an adoptive mom to a daughter from China who found a biological sister who had been adopted into another family. Her family appeared with their sister family in the June, 2005 issue of Good Housekeeping.

DNA Testing for Siblings in Simple Terms

DNA testing compares Genetic Markers (or alleles) from saliva or blood. All DNA is distinct and different like a fingerprint, except for Identical Twins who have identically matching DNA. Without Parental DNA, other siblings may only show a percentage of probability of relatedness. The higher these percentages are, the more likely two individuals may be fraternal twins or full siblings. When enough markers match but produce a lower number, it usually indicates that they are somehow related (half siblings, cousins, etc.) but not full siblings.

The procedure itself is very simple.
- A Q-Tip-like swab is rubbed inside of the child/adult cheek to collect saliva and the swabs are then put into protective envelopes.

- The laboratory scientists break down the DNA from the saliva and separate out 16 specific markers (or Alleles) to be tested. There are 15 significant determining markers that are used by most laboratories to test against another individual's DNA markers. The 16th marker is used to determine the sex of the recipient.

- The laboratory analyzes each specific marker and they are then compared side-by-side, marker by marker with another individual's DNA markers.

- The more markers that match from person A to the markers of person B, the greater the chance that a biological relationship exists between them.

- The scientists then run the numbers through their calculated programs and databases to determine whether or not these two individuals are full siblings, half siblings, may possibly be related or are not related at all.

- Because of the distribution of DNA from both parents, occasionally true siblings test results will come out negative showing that they are not related.

When DNA samples are entered into a DNA database, each new DNA profile that is entered is run against every other DNA profile in the system. If there is a match, those two DNA profiles are flagged and the families are notified by Kinsearch and not the Laboratory, as their identities are coded for complete and strict privacy.

Barbara Rappaport, Executive Director Kinsearch Registry, adoptive mom.

Making a Pact for Proceeding;
What to do if the DNA tests come back as 'Don't Know'
By Elizabeth Catzel

My family and another family, both with children from the same orphanage in China, felt overwhelmingly from photographs and then from meeting in real space that our children looked so similar that chances were they were sisters. It was the early days of DNA testing, but we agreed to proceed with this although some laboratories warned that without parental DNA, results could not be conclusive. Proceeding was difficult but exciting. My son (also adopted) felt threatened by the thought of 'losing' his sister to a biological sibling. The net result? The laboratory that did the tests offered the result 'inconclusive'. Only one (European) lab consulted with the results, said a match was impossible given the DNA samples.

The result meant that the children, brought close together over the possibility, took different routes to coping with the end of their dream of a new sister. Now both families had to help our children deal with this loss of a potential sib. I believe that we owe our children any possible connections with their past, and we must help them fill the gaps in their history. We also must try to follow all avenues. It is important also, that we as parents proceed with caution and thought for our children's well being.

Given this, what have I learned from the experience of helping my child discover whether (or not) she had a biological sister? Here is the gist of what I learned, and I think the families considering DNA testing need to discuss these or similar issues with the other family. Agreement beforehand is a bit like a prenuptial contract: it sets out parameters for behavior and routes for advance and retreat.

Parental Obligations for your family
- Be prepared to put the brakes on early enthusiasm; a cool head is needed before a decision to involve the children in meeting, talking, and testing is made.
- Consider whether your child is emotionally healthy enough to take the strain of meeting and testing–given that inconclusive results can be devastating.
- If you decide to test the possibility that your child is biologically related to the other child (and they have met), ask yourself what needs are being met in testing. Would the children be happy enough to remain as 'orphanage siblings'?
- Work on keeping all your children appraised of the depth and commitment you have to them, which they also have developed for their adoptive sib.

Exchanges with the other family
- Work out with the other family in advance of testing or perhaps even meeting what you are likely to do if circumstances lead one way–or another.
- Work out with the other family how the initial meeting can be made so that you can withdraw without feeling pressure to proceed.
- Both families should take time to discuss why they think the children could be biologically related. It's worth asking other people who know them both, if possible.
- Ask help from people of the same ethnicity as your children. As transracial adoptive families, we may see similarities in 'type' far more easily than difference.

- Look at the cultural connections of your family and the family with whom you hope to forge a bond. Do you share a common understanding of what family is?
- Work out how you will maintain a bio sibling relationship when you both will also be maintaining adoptive family relationship. Let the other family know this.
- Can you afford the travel to keep connections going? Can you afford time to travel, make phone-calls? What if your lifestyles are different, and so is income? How would you determine that? Discuss this.

Preparing the children before, supporting them afterward
- If the tests are inconclusive but the children now have a bond, how will you maintain that bond? You must discuss this, and remember that children grow apart without regular contact.
- There may be emotional fallout from the test results. Can you sit down before hand and discuss how you will handle the different options of the results? Positive, negative, and inconclusive. All different. How will you broker responses?
- How will you handle the fact that a biological link might bring a need for closer legal ties? Would you consider becoming guardians for each others children if you should die? Would that include all the children in each family? You need to work this out.
- Work with your child on how to relate to the possibility of biological family as a matter of adoption course.
- Tell your children why you want to help them follow any leads that might take them to their biological family. It's part of your family ethos. Tell them you are doing this because of your strength as an adoptive family and that the legal ties of adoption are binding as much as the blood ties of biology.
- Watch how your child responds to your drive to help her connect with bio family. Ask how the other family thinks their child reacts to seeking connections.
- Listen to your child's reaction to the possibility of finding a biological sib who is adopted and living with another family. Find out about the other family's answers to these questions.
- Work out how to answer questions if your child asks if you will all go to live together. Share them with the other family!
- When you proceed with the other family, proceed as a family. Your child and her adoptive sibs are in this together. Consider all their needs. The other family must do the same.
- If the tests are negative, look after your child in the way she needs. Let the other family know that this is your priority.
- Comfort your child if she wishes that the test had been positive, and discuss how she can stay in touch with the other child. Have the possibilities worked out with the other family.
- Respect her if she decides that inconclusive is better read as no, and help her move on but respectful of the relationship that might have been. This should be part of the original 'compact' with the other family.
- Seek counseling for your child if the results affect her so deeply as to affect health.

Elizabeth Catzel is the adoptive mom to two children,
a daughter from China and a son from Vietnam.

Narratives

"When do you tell a child he was adopted?"
And Other Secrets We Shouldn't Keep
By Adam Pertman

It's one of the most common questions I hear. Most often, I like to answer with a true story. A friend of mine who is a social worker was placing an infant into the arms of her adoptive parents. The new mother leaned over to the social worker and whispered, "When do we tell her she's adopted?" My friend leaned over and whispered back: "On the way home."

It was the right answer; I think we should be honest from the start. Young children obviously won't understand what the words mean, but they'll always know their parents were comfortable with them and proud of how they came into their families. The details can be filled in over time, in an age-appropriate way. But I like to tell the story about my social worker friend for another reason: Why was the adoptive mom whispering? We keep secrets about things we are embarrassed about or ashamed of. ... and family formation should not be one of those things. We should be proud of who we are and truthful with our kids about their past and who they are. People who get whispered about can feel shame or think something is wrong with them. Our children deserve better.

Sometimes the truth can be hard, of course, especially for us (too often insecure) adoptive parents. Sometimes we don't want to face the truth or perhaps we don't know it. Maybe we are concerned that it will be complicated, or that our children won't understand tough material at certain ages. Can telling the truth be complicated? Sure. But not telling the truth can cause even bigger complications, especially when suppressed truths are later discovered–as they usually are. The reality of our family structure 'is' natural and normal for our kids. It is the reality they are living. Children figure out where they fit in situations of divorce, step families, single parent families, families with same sex parents, families in which grandparents are raising them. Why do we think they can't they figure out adoption? Of course they can, and they should always know that we're there to help them do it.

We often carry our own insecurities and worries about our children, then transfer them to the kids and assume they feel the same way. As parents, we are the guardians and the filters for the information we know about our children. We decide what we think is appropriate to know, and when. But we have to remember that our children are capable of assimilating more than we might think, and even harsh explanations can become good opportunities to tell the truth–in age-appropriate ways and with discretion, to be sure, but a lack of information rarely yields the best outcomes.

Adoption has come a long way from the closed practice of taking children home and revealing their history to them at teen-hood, or perhaps never. In the past forty years we have moved far from the 'just raise them as if you gave birth to them' model. A secretive past can be hard to overcome, and it's hard to learn much about secrets–so it's no wonder we've got a ways to go. But the good news is that we've moved out of the darkness and into the light; it's a far brighter, better place to be–and a much easier place for everyone involved to get educated and, consequently, to make even more progress.

Unfortunately, even the words we use relating to adoption still aren't either precise or well-accepted–which is no surprise, since it's hard to develop a good vocabulary about secrets. So we don't even have a ready way to describe people and make them understand their relationships are fine and normal. One example: My son and daughter are siblings, right? Well, they each also have biological siblings who are growing up in their respective birth mothers' families. Are my daughter's brother's sibs related to her? Are they related to my wife and me? We feel they are, but there are no words like 'in-law' to describe those relationships, so we don't have a way yet–as a culture and as individuals–of conveying the message that this extended family is fine and normal. I'm confident we'll get there, but adoption's covert past has made the job harder than it might otherwise have been. The way I see it, we've gotten to the point where we can discuss subjects like divorce, breast cancer, and Viagra in honest ways that have led to better outcomes; we can and will certainly do the same for adoption -- a topic that affects tens of millions of people in the most intimate, personal and important ways.

As an adoptive parent and an adoption educator, I want my children to fit into society without apologies or explanations. I want them to play and go to school without the stigmatizing, uninformed questions from strangers or acquaintances ("Why did your real mother give you away?"). I want them to grow up in a world in which 'you're adopted' is no longer used or perceived as an insult, in which the people who created them are not denigrated or relegated to secrecy, and in which neither money nor coercion are ever factors in how a family is formed.

I know how sappy and idealistic this may sound, but I want my kids–and all the people like them -– to be able to live their lives without the burden of wondering if their families are natural or real or authentic. I want to level the playing field so that every child, regardless of how he or she came to their family, knows that 'different' isn't better or worse–it's just different.

~ Adam Pertman is Executive Director of the Evan B. Donaldson Adoption Institute, and the author of Adoption Nation: How the Adoption Revolution is Transforming America. *He is most importantly the adoptive dad of two great kids.*

Opening the Dialogue
Why? How? and When?
by Sheena Macrae

When is it right to start talking adoption, and how do we start the ball rolling? We are told it's up to us to open the dialogue, talk to our children about why they needed adoption, came to us, and what they lost as well as gained on the journey. Many of us are scared, tongue-twisted and maybe even in denial that we need to do this! We have journeyed emotionally a long way and may have gone round the world to parent our adopted children. Why can't we simply relax and be their parents now they are home?

Why Do I Need To? The reason is that because we are their adoptive parents, we hold their losses in our hands, and it's up to us to show, by talking and holding them close, that there is nothing shameful and secret for us or for them about their adoption. Adam Pertman in his article on the previous pages, states that we need to start talking adoption from day one. If we start from then, perhaps before our kids even understand our words, we will have learned to say the words that come hard. We need to be able to say 'birthmother', 'loss', 'rejection', 'abandonment', and be able to talk about the love our kids may feel for their first families. Starting 'the talk' from day one is as much for our sakes as for our children.

We can read books and tell stories to our pre-verbal children about tough stuff. These begin to tell their story. That way we tell their story while communicating with them, rocking them, singing to them, all the while with them held safely on our laps. We are telling them that we are here now to help them face that past. We become the loving arms and the voice that holds them. We attune ourselves to them and their need, getting beyond our own.See **Parenting with Narratives** on page 228 for ways to use all kinds of stories to talk with your children.

How do we address our fears as we begin this dance of attunement, this very special need that adopted children have to know their history? What loss and insecurities have we brought into adoption? Do we fear that talking to our kids will trigger them? We need to top our tank to full in being able to cope with tough stuff. If we have tough stuff of our own to deal with, we need to deal with it before we will be able to be the parent our adopted children need. Psychologists say that when we parents are able to deal positively with our own 'story' (no matter how awful that story may have been), we become more powerfully able to parent.

We need a sense of delight in our children, that they have a history, and in talking about adoption, we signal that we are able to contain their needs, and be their effective adoptive parents. We cannot fill the gap our children have in the loss of first family; it's up to us to keep our kids safe despite loss. And this in itself creates ties that bind.

How Do I Do This? Every Adoptive parent I know has wondered how to read and talk about adoption, how to 'factor in' talks; questioning whether talks should be reactive to events. Is a toddler first noting different racial characteristics between adoptive mum and himself the real start of a more personal two-way talk? Is a young child who has been hurt by a playmate's taunt and comes seeking consolation a good chance to open the dialogue? Children often take us by surprise in what they have understood about adoption and difference. While using openings is great, we should be proactive and not keep silent if the child makes no comment. Children always hear what their parents say, even if they're not listening!

Your child needs to know you are his 'real mom' before someone asks if you are, and he needs to know that it's ok also to have a real birthfamily that he doesn't live with anymore. We need to be talking before our child asks. Because this lets our children know that talking about this subject is okay and that we can help them understand. This is done by commenting on how other people act, reading books, and creating books/stories where the child can see and talk about adoption, race, connections, and difference.

When Should I Start? Many experts suggest that that children's understanding of adoption alters as their intellectual capacity to understand develops. Often, when children reach the age of four and beyond they realize that adoption equals loss, and it's not just a fun way to be in a family. Their needs in 'talking adoption' changes, and it changes again most significantly during the teen years, where the crisis of identity may be doubled for an adopted child. Adopted teens may ask 'Who am I—and who made me who I am?'

Parents need therefore not to choose an age at which it's appropriate to talk adoption, but rather choose age appropriate ways of talking it from the start, from babyhood and tot through to teen and adult. Talking adoption never stops, and many adult adoptees affirm that how they perceive their adoption and their pre-adoptive history changes throughout the stages of their adult life. Many adoptees find how they perceive their adoption is spot-lit when they become parents themselves.

What if This Upsets my Child? Some families worry that their children don't want to hear their adoption story. They say that the kids are too settled to want (or need) to hear it. Some families want to know if their child could be unsettled by hearing the story—particularly if we parents are custodians of facts that suggest our children's history before our family was not pleasant.

All our children have suffered with the trauma of loss. Experts believe that rebuilding a coherent sense of self comes through rebuilding the whole narrative of their life. This is thought best done by 'filling in the gaps' through talking adoption and through offering the child their history through tools like lifebooks. In this way, the children develop a new narrative which binds them to their adoptive family as well as to the past. And beyond lifebooks come narratives of the family we have become with our child—don't forget these. The history of our family matters too, with all its anecdotes and funny photos and where our children fit in the picture.

What of the children whose behavior suggests that they were ill-treated or damaged by institutional care? Should that information even be shared as the dialogue of adoption is opened? Won't it cause further damage? Experts suggest that children whose early life was subject to other traumas and burdens beyond and as well as loss and abandonment or whose reaction to this is severe may need professional help to open the adoption dialogue safely. Therapists working with narrative therapy and therapeutic story-telling note that this work often offers the child a 'different ending' to the story that may have the child

Parent Resource

Twenty Things Adopted Kids Wish Their Adoptive Parents Knew by Sherrie Eldridge

This book gives a voice to adopted children's unspoken concerns and is an invaluable guide to the complex emotions surrounding adoption.

Tough Questions

They always seemed to catch me by surprise...

...in the car as I am merging onto a 4 lane expressway on rain slicked roads, or at 3am as we are lying side by side in the dark. They come at times that are 'safe', with little chance of eye contact.

I remember the first question coming when my oldest was not quite three. "Is my other daddy dead?" It was three am, she had experienced a difficult night of sleep up to that point and I was at my mental peak. Not!

My first thought was "I am not supposed to have to deal with this until she is six." But she didn't know that. She just knew what was in her heart. And what was there wasn't making sense to her. My next action was a deep breath and one of those age appropriate conversations. My next? A mad dash to get myself up to her speed.

~By Carrie Kitze
adoptive mom of 2

thinking they were bad and have caused these things to be done to them. Therapists support parents in carrying the work done in therapy to the home.

Do I Sit Them Down for 'The Talk'? Should a special time be set aside, or should a parent wait for a quiet walk or at bedtime so that the chat can be supported by a special cuddle? There are no special times or places. However, most parents and experts suggest that talk and connection often come best at intimate moments. But intimacy can sometimes mean away from the routine. Many parents admit that thunderbolt questions can often come at inconvenient-to-adult times, such as in the car in a storm on the busiest highway possible. So parents need to have rehearsed their thoughts to have an answer ready–or at least ready to be developed. Experts call these teachable moments, when a child stumbles upon a question that is a fundamental to their understanding of themselves and their past and present. The jury is out on who is taught by whom....

It helps to be close to a child when talking (and hearing from the child) tough stuff. Remember, our children have lived the tough stuff. The questions therefore live within them. It is our job as parents to make talking adoption safe. So eye-contact, reading while cuddling, swimming together when talking, building sandcastles when broaching birthparent concerns re-places our children's lost attunement to birthfamily. But note–talking is only one part of communication. For a child to engage, all the senses must be engaged making the child feel safe.

Adoptive parents of kids adopted at an older age ask how to talk to their children about adoption. Do they need different tools than the families with younger kids?

The basics remain the same. Be as open as possible as soon as possible and let the child own the past. With teens, communication probably plays the largest part, and some families have found that as opposed to the younger years, teens talk best and most openly if not required to make eye-contact. Experienced moms make themselves available while doing routine things like cooking, watching TV, reading a magazine. Asking a teen his views on something in a magazine often gets a better response then hoping for direct communication. Going to a movie together (or watching it on DVD) promotes exchange; just dive in and start the dialog.

Sheena Macrae is the mom of two who spends time with her children talking, writing, drawing, and dancing. Sometimes it is about adoption and sometimes it is just about life.

Opening the Dialogue "Only if they ask..."

Can we assume that if children do not ask, then they have no important questions about adoption? I have learned the hard way that, for my older daughter, it just wasn't possible, or true. Thoughts about birthfamily, the 'what if's, 'why me's', 'what's wrong with me that my parents didn't want me' and more were swirling around in her mind. I know this in hindsight! Such powerful, scary thoughts, and she had them locked away. Until one day I mentioned that she might be thinking about things that she didn't feel comfortable sharing. Reading some adoption literature clued me into the fact that my child was probably thinking adoption even if she wasn't asking.

It was the trigger.....
My then second grade daughter poured her heart out. How can I do justice to the fact of the weight of the movement? It started so slow, only a little at a time, but like a dam of water breaching the walls, once the breach happened, the flooded pain of her personality was irresistibly and irretrievably there. Nothing could stem that breach. She told how she didn't feel 'real', she felt like she was living someone else's life, like she didn't really belong here. She admitted that she thought about her birthmother every day. She was obsessed with returning to her birthcountry and once she admitted that truth, she began to beg to go back on a visit.

It was clear her self-esteem was so fragile, as if she couldn't hear enough how much we loved her, wanted her, cared about her. Her first rejection had so impacted her and given her a core belief that she was undeserving of our love. Don't think this was a disturbed, emotionally damaged child, don't think this! From the moment she came home she was happy, with a sunny and delightful personality. And yet, at the age of seven/eight we found ourselves seeking out counseling for her when it became clear she was having a breakdown with all of these issues overwhelming her mind.

I learned that I had to lead the way in opening up these conversations. I began to talk about "If I were adopted and knew XYZ then I might feel this way....what do you think?" We joined a parent/child discussion group where she had the chance to interact with other mid-elementary kids her age and make her own lifebook, talk about adoption, and listen to other kids talk about their feelings and experiences. She gained so much from this. We did take her back to her birthcountry and she got to meet her birthfamily and see her orphanage. This did so much to help her begin to resolve some of these issues, questions, and hurts in her life.

Today she's going into Tenth Grade and I couldn't wish for a more emotionally healthy, lovely daughter.....and yet I have no doubt that she wouldn't be who she is today if I had continued to wait for her to ask those hard questions and share what she was thinking.

By Jill Lampman, adoptive mom
For a list of questions that might be waiting to come out, see page 244,

Parenting with Narratives:
the A, B, C's of Adoption Stories
By Jean MacLeod

> *Stories need to have a central place in the ongoing development of the adoptive family.*
>
> Daniel A. Hughes, PhD

Once Upon a Time is a magical phrase that conjures up a faraway world from long, long ago. For our internationally adopted children, it is also a phrase that bridges the huge chasm between their early lives and who they are now. When life feels like a fairytale of good and evil, love and loss, reality and fantasy, it sometimes takes a story to create sense and meaning. How will your child see her or his adoption? What 'story' will they read into their own lives as they gain awareness of what happened to them as young children? Parenting narratives (stories with purpose) help the child to see a complex tale from different perspectives, and can give a child the opportunity to examine serious thoughts and emotions in a familiar format. They also allow the parent to present the truth in several age-appropriate ways and provide point-of-views that are personally empowering to the adoptee.

Parenting narratives can take shape through a parent's use of:
- Children's literature
- The oral tradition of storytelling (a favorite at bedtime)
- A co-created Lifebook or Life Narrative
- An adoption videos or photographs

Realizing that there are gentle and creative ways to approach the issues of adoption and the intense feelings of adoptees, and that children's books and story-telling can help provide the tools, is a relief for all of us adoptive parents who have taken on this monumental job without much tech support.

A child's attunement to his or her adoptive parents, and co-creating a Life Narrative with an adopted child, are both part of an overlapping, circular process. The parent-child narratives that are advocated within are NOT meant as therapeutic tools. Several forms of narratives are used by professionals to help children who have been traumatized or who are seeking help for specific social or developmental difficulties. An excellent source for further information can be found in the book and workbook from the Family Attachment and Counseling Center , or in the work of attachment therapist Daniel Hughes.

Adoption issues are normal. Some require a therapist's attention, but the issues that most often get expressed by adoptees are usually addressed at home by mom or dad. We want our children to express all of their feelings surrounding adoption because it allows us to do our job: we are the responsible parent and we need to encourage, support, listen to, and walk with our adopted children through their personal stories and beliefs.

The A, B, C's of Adoption Stories

Attunement and Attachment. Stories can help teach a post-institutional child the meaning of family, and help him or her to learn to love, trust and feel secure.

Building Identity. Children need a foundation for 'self'; they need the truth and they need to feel empowered by their story. Kids can't go forward without a past!
Communication and Connection. Children need to be able to talk about adoption's tough stuff, and they need to be able to count on their parent being next to them when they do

A = Attunement and Attachment:

Our internationally adopted children come to us missing the first steps of the Dance of Attunement. Attunement happens between a newborn and a mom as they learn to pick up and respond to each other's verbal and non-verbal cues. Voice, eye contact, facial expression and touch, all play into this amazingly essential give-and-take; a baby learns she has control over this all-important mom (equating to control over her own world), and she learns she can trust mom to understand and respond to her needs.

This natural dance between mom and baby is the foundation of attachment. It takes place in hundreds of moments every day, and is so hard-wired into healthy moms and bio-babies that it is not even noticed. When a child and a parent are attuned to each other the child is able to self-regulate. This doesn't mean that she is tantrum-free, but that she is able to draw upon the inner structures she has in place (from her mom) to calm down and make sense of her moods and feelings. A child who is securely attached is not ordinarily out-of-control angry or fearful; she is attuned to her mother's unspoken words and expectations. She knows the steps! What the mom offers, teaches and imparts to the child is reciprocated back to her in a solid relationship– it is the dance, tightly and lovingly choreographed. As a child pays attention to the mom's requests, and the mom pays attention to the child's needs, trust grows and invisible boundaries are laid and respected....

A post-institutional kid has missed the early formative groundwork that moms and infants do with each other, and must be taught to attune/attach. It is much harder to do with an older baby, toddler or child who has had their trust bruised, but it is crucial in having the kind of bond (and behavior) that brings joy to the entire family. In order for us to have the relationships that we dreamed of having with our children, we need to work a little more at connecting to them—and we need to teach them to connect to us. Attunement is a graceful dance between two people who know the steps, who can both lead and follow, and who can anticipate the change in music...

How do we foster this dance, this connection, in our toddlers and older children? Most of us are not experienced attachment therapists or adoption social workers, yet we parents can do what moms and dads have always intuitively done to connect: we can create shared emotional experiences with our children. We can involve our children's "perceptions, thoughts, intentions, memories, ideas, beliefs and attitudes" (Dan Siegel, MD). We can use our facial expressions, voice, and body movement to match and/or re-direct our children's affect and response. We can verbally help our children understand what they are feeling by communicating our own feelings.

We can tell stories. Stories are universal and personal. They can be utilized as shared emotional experiences, and we can use dramatic voices and active body language to help our children become involved. We can share our own emotions, and help a child reflect back on their own. When we are aware of our children's body signals and emotional cues, we can tailor our storytelling to feed our children's needs.

We can connect on the cognitive level, and from our hearts. Adopted children may need to re-learn to love, trust and feel safe. They may need to learn about families and relationships—children who have lived some or most of their young lives in an institution cannot be expected to understand the unseen structure of a family, or the role of a mom or dad. Stories and books don't make attachment happen, and they don't heal a traumatized child or cure attachment disorder. But used with a parent's awareness of attunement, they can provide a 'warm fuzzy' on the long chain of warm fuzzies that are necessary to build a loving relationship.

Children's Books can provide the tools to facilitate stories that promote parent-child attunement. Tools are not always easy to use…reading a story to a child is fun; reading a story that evokes emotion, shared conversation and empathy, is a little harder. The beauty of using narratives to adoption-parent is that it is already part of what most of us normally do with our children. It is just done consciously with an extra level of awareness, and with an end result in mind.

Storybooks can assist children who are navigating a new environment. They can be used to begin a conversation or open a topic, and can be personalized to a child's circumstances. Books are user-friendly and non-threatening, and can help a parent find the words that unlock shared feelings.

Almost any book with any kind of happy or sad 'feeling' can be used to leverage attunement. Older children can be similarly reached with a good tale and an exploration of its theme. I read the dog classic *Lassie Come Home* (the big, beautiful, illustrated version of the original, by Susan Jeffers/ Rosemary Wells) to my nine year old, who had been adopted from China as a baby. We were both teary-eyed by the end of the story, and I took advantage of the opportunity. I asked, "How do you think Lassie felt when she was lost and all alone?"

We talked about poor Lassie, who had been abandoned and who was searching for her birthparents—oops! I mean human family. Well, you get the idea… adoption, and the feelings a child has about her/his adoption, can be discussed via a story without an older child shutting down. The attunement came after we discussed Lassie's sad, dire circumstances: I told my daughter "If Lassie had been my dog, I never would have let her go! I would have searched every inch of England and Scotland, and I never would have stopped looking until I found her!"

I didn't change the sad stuff the poor dog had to experience, but there is always more than one take we can make on every finish. I like to acknowledge what the main character has or hasn't done with what has happened. What would my daughter do? What would I do? What are the choices? We ended up in a hug after sharing our sadness (and relief over Lassie making it home!), sitting close together, both of us enjoying the moment and each other.

When using stories to do 'the dance' with your child:
• Infuse your stories with drama and feeling
• Take verbal and non-verbal cues from your child (listen and watch!)
• Reciprocate with the next-step verbal/physical cue (show them!)
• Give actual words to shared emotion
• Encourage physical closeness

When reading stories, keep in mind:
Books that might appear 'too young' for a child's chronological age, may be very appropriate for that child's emotional age. Do not hesitate to use younger-level picture books that have stories that touch all ages on a deeper level. The books do not have to be about adoption to be useful.

Reading a book with your child in your lap is cozy and comforting. Alternate with having your child sit directly in front of you, knee-to-knee, while holding the book up and open. The child will see the illustrations, and also be able to read your face. "The most powerful of our non-verbal communication instruments is the face. A child's face, and yours, is a barometer expressing interest, investment, curiosity, joy, fear, anger, confusion, or doubt." (Dr. Bruce Perry, Senior Fellow of the ChildTrauma Academy.)

Some children are wigglers, and have a difficult time sitting still to listen. Author and adoptive mom Susan Olding suggests a solution that worked for her family: "A few disastrous experiences showed me that if I ever hoped to get my daughter to accept me as I am (somebody who loves to snuggle up with a book or twenty), I'd also have to show her that I accept her as she is (somebody who needs to move, to think!) So from the time she was about eighteen months on, I built in time before, between, and after stories to shake the sillies out. In our house this even included the special privilege of jumping on the bed. At that stage, I also read a lot of 'action' books to her (Eric Carle's Head to Toe comes to mind) and we'd both act out the pictures. I also allowed her to turn pages (until and unless she sabotaged that, in which case I would just put the books away.)"

Use a lot of expression! Be passionate! Use gestures! Some children have difficulty in 'getting' non-verbal cues, and are helped with story interpretation through exaggerated, dramatic interaction. Change the tone and volume of your voice (whisper to get a child's attention). Stories with repetition and catchy say-aloud lines are fun to read together.

Be aware of your child's physical and verbal cues. If a story makes him or her uncomfortable, stop and talk about it. Trust and emotional safety are key to attachment, and it is up to the parent to listen to the child, acknowledge the child's discomfort, and take the lead in either continuing the story, deciding to offer another story, or by suggesting a different joint activity.

Story-time can be an example of "reciprocal communication of thoughts and feelings, and shared activities" (Dan Hughes, Ph.D). Dr. Hughes' PLACE philosophy–Playful, Loving, Accepting, Curious, and Empathic interactions–reinforces attunement, and according to Dr. Hughes, facilitates the capacity for fun and love. Ask your child specific questions about what they think and feel about the story. Share your own opinion/feelings. 'Spin' the story and explore alternate endings. Have fun together! (see page 244)

There is no perfect, pre-determined set of children's books that work for every child. Therapists that work with narratives believe that the parent understands the child better than anyone else, and will have a better feeling for stories that will touch the child on some emotional level.

Narratives are a process. There is no 'right' way to tell a story; if you mess up, there's always another chance to re-tell it!

You will need to deal with Disney®. Disney movies are a particularly vivid form of cultural 'storytelling' that children (and parents) either love and cherish, or hate and fear! We can use these films, if our children are open to them. Elaine Hannah wrote: "Disney

What If's...

Talking 'what if' can be an immensely bonding family game, because it allows both our children and us to embrace possibilities that might have been, but were lost. Talking 'what if' is also necessary if our kids came from less than healthy previous families, care-settings, and institutions. It's our job to help our children look at that. And talking 'what-ifs' also is family glue–our children can speculate about what might have been, safe and empowered to do so by being in our families. It joins family histories and helps project for a future together. How we frame a perspective on possibility is hugely important for our children. In some instances our adult eyes, able to look at the politics of adoption, will affect how our children understand their past.

It's a very human thing to make sense of the present by making sense of the past. If we graft a 'story' of the past onto the present, it makes our identity more secure and our ability to cope more secure too. Moreover, if we parents are to maintain a close connection to our children as they mature into teens and adults, we need to expect that there might be a difference between their narratives of the past–and ours. As adoptive parents, we invested in a particular narrative on adoption–that 'story' which says our adoptive family would work. And we have worked as parents to make that story come true. It probably has. For our children, though, it's a different story. Most of them were drawn onto our storyboard without requesting it. We owe them a secure step from the past into our family. 'What ifs' allow us all to talk about what's good now–and what might have been.

~By Sheena Macrae

movies can be a wonderful starting point for discussing bigger life issues. When my daughter has expressed fear of the necessary mean character, be it witch, queen, or stepmother, I explain that without evil there can be no happy ending. Without a nasty character how would we measure the character of the good one? In life good things happen and bad things, there are good people and bad. There can't be one without the other. I try to boil the story down to the bone. There is challenge and evil, but courage and pureness of heart triumph and everyone lives happily ever after. Sometimes on a daily basis."

A Disney movie, like a dark fairy-tale, is an opportunity for talk, and for a release of emotion. It is an opportunity for a parent to attune with a child and help them emotionally 're-write' the ending. We can use Disney to declare what we, as parents, would do to help our children no matter what happened. And what our brave, creative, strong children could do to help themselves!

Claiming Narratives take parent-child stories a step closer and deeper, and offer a warm and caring 're-write' to a missing early chapter of the relationship. Typically, a claiming narrative is told in first person using storytelling's oral tradition, and is used to build or repair an emotional bond.

Claiming and Re-parenting
Mom or dad tells the story of how they would have taken care of the adopted child, if he or she had been born to them. The tale can begin in imaginary-utero and progress to the detailed, daily maintenance of a well-loved infant. Most children, even older children, like to be occasionally babied, and a claiming narrative allows a parent to physically act out caring for a 'baby' while simultaneously telling the

story. The emotional connection of re-enacting a happy, play-ful infancy is further reinforced by expressing the poignant, underlying wishes of both parent and child: Mom: *"I wish you had grown inside of me"*; or, *"I wish you had been my baby from the very first moment of your life"*; or, *"I wish I could have taken care of you the way you should have been taken care of"* Child: *"I wish you had been my birthmother"*; or, *"I wish my birthmother could have taken care of me"*

A child that expresses a wish to be with his or her birth-mother is generally not taking a personal shot at the adoptive parent. A child feeling 'safe' enough to express this kind of honesty is usually speaking to the loss that has rocked his or her world, and is not trying to be actively hurtful. It is actually a remarkable opportunity to attune: an adoptive parent that meets this sort of sad, wistful statement with empathy, and words of understanding, will help the child desire to turn to mom or dad for comfort. Dan Hughes said that a parent that helps their child "co-construct an interpersonal reality gives a child the tools that she needs to make sense of the internal and external worlds in which we live."

We parents give meaning to our children's experience, and we help them learn to analyze how they feel and what they think. Our children borrow our strengths, and our filters, and by sharing ourselves (our thoughts and emotions) we help them grow. Ultimately, an attuned dialogue on a sensitive topic like birthparents could prove to be an affirmation of the strength of the adoptive parent-child relationship. Children's books can provide an introduction into this kind of sensitive parent/child dialog:

> *I may never know you*
> *but I wonder*
> *who you are,*
> *and what you look like.*
> *Do you wonder too?*

> *The full moon glows*
> *heavy in the night sky.*
> *a beacon of*
> *beauty and truth.*
> *Why did you leave me?*

(excerpted from *We See the Moon* by Carrie Kitze)

Claiming and Family Membership
Claiming narratives have traditionally been used to pass on a family's history and rituals. Older adoptees can benefit from

---

Life Narrative Books for Children

Twice-Upon-a-Time: Born and Adopted
Eleanora Patterson

Tell Me Again About the Night I Was Born
Jamie Lee Curtis

Over the Moon: An Adoption Tale
Karen Katz

We See the Moon
Carrie Kitze

At Home in This World, a China adoption story
Jean MacLeod

When You Were Born in China Sara Dorow

When You Were Born in Korea Brian Boyd

When You Were Born in Vietnam Therese Bartlett

Through Moon and Stars and Night Skies
Ann Turner

When I Met You
Adrienne Ehlert Bashista

Before I Met You: A Therapeutic Pre-Adoption Narrative
Doris Landry, MS

Books that Claim and Celebrate the Parent Child Bond

I Don't Have Your Eyes
Carrie A. Kitze

Baby-Steps
Peter McCarty

I Love You Like Crazy Cakes
Rose A. Lewis

No Matter What
Debi Gliori

Even If I Did Something Awful
B. Shook Hazen

I Promise I'll Find You
Heather P. Ward

Little Miss Spider
David Kirk

Mama, Do You Love Me?
Barbara M. Joasse

The Runaway Bunny
Margaret Wise Brown

I Love You As Much...
L. Krauss Melmed

Hush Little Baby
Sylvia Long

The Little Green Goose
Adele Sansone

Hazel's Amazing Mother
Rosemary Wells

Owl Babies
Martin Waddell

Love You Forever
Robert Munsch

'family stories' that introduce their new family members (Great-Grandma Millie and Crazy Uncle Ed), and that include the adoptee in the group experience. It is a huge comfort for a child to feel that she belongs in her adopted family, that she has full membership along with her parents and siblings, and that the membership can never be revoked. A parent can emphasize family kinship by telling stories that celebrate connections.

Susan Olding made audio-tapes for her young daughter that recounted stories from Susan's own childhood, and used the connecting power of a mother's voice: "The stories on my daughter's most recent tape are indeed 'family stories.' Tales about me when I was a little girl, and a first version, story-book-style telling of her own baby story. The Family Narrative has been so important for my daughter. She adores those stories of my own childhood naughtiness or silliness. She likes to hear how her grandma (my mother) responded. This morning she asked me if Grandma was young when she adopted me. I gently reminded her that I was born to Grandma, not adopted by her. For a second I thought this might upset her. But instead, she said, "Hey! I know a birthmother!"

B = Building Identity

Helping a child develop an identity that includes the past, the present and the future is integral for a child to feel whole. For adopted children five to ten years old, identity may be the consuming core issue. Their realization of the blank space in their early family history coincides with the hollow feeling they may carry inside, with a profoundly sad result: they don't know who they are.

How do we help our adopted children develop a sense of identity? Particularly, how do we help international adoptees feel pride about where they were born, and help them be comfortable in the world they live in? **We can tell stories.**

*I still wonder about my life in China.
I love my parents very much and I
wouldn't want any other family, but
I think I will always miss knowing the
parents that weren't mine to keep.
My mom says that I am a brave kid
and that my life has been an amazing
adventure—that I have experienced
enormous changes, and I have survived
them all. I like to think about it that way;*

it helps me bring both my sides together.
I was born in China and now I'm from
here, and my before and after is all part
of who I am: one girl from two places
who is growing up to be at home in this
big, wide world.

(excerpted from *At Home in This World* by Jean MacLeod)

As parents, we also tell stories to change a child's view of themselves. For instance, the protagonist in *At Home in This World* has had sad things happen to her, but she is not a victim. She is coming to terms with her story and it's enigma, and she is empowered by her (and her parent's) particular view of her life.

How do we negotiate and interpret these important stories about identity in a way that allows our children to really integrate what we are saying about them? A narrative can help to change a child's reality (or 'internal working model', as trauma-specialist Dr. Bruce Perry calls it). Dr. Dan Siegel has been researching the kind of narratives that have the power to effect positive change in our adopted children. What he has found is that certain interactions can model and facilitate brain-integration of the thinking and feeling—the key is in using verbal and non-verbal signals at the same time to help integration of the story take place (language plus emotion, for example).

Dr Siegel uses the word collaboration for attunement, and he stresses that it can be taught to parents to use with their children. This includes engaging a child by sharing "eye contact, facial expression, tone of voice, gestures and timing and intensity of response." This also means sharing reflective dialogues about inner "thoughts, feelings, perceptions, memories, sensations, attitudes, beliefs and intentions."

Both Dr. Siegel and Dr. Hughes have researched and clinically validated the importance of marrying thought and feeling when working on attunement/collaboration and attachment. It is impossible to really help a child deal with their adoption stories or adoption issues, without having or fostering parent-child attunement. It is the basis for telling stories, and on a much deeper level, for building a child's identity. Healthy growth isn't possible without a firm foundation.

Attunement with our children helps them to create their own positive self-image. Therapist Denise Lacher said, "If you change the story, you can change self-understanding." I just call it 'spin', but they both work the same way. When you talk with your son or daughter about their birth story and abandonment, you have the power in your words to make your children feel like Heroes or like Victims. We are all multi-storied people, and we have choices we can make about our life-narratives.

Narrative Therapy uses a correlating concept called 'Narrative Spaces', that is helpful to apply to our kids. The media, for example, frequently tells our international adoptees

Using Narratives With Your Children

Connecting with Kids Through Stories: Using Narratives to Facilitate Attachment in Adopted Children
By Denise Lacher, MA, Todd Nichols, MA, MPAff, and Joanne May, PhD

Parenting with Stories: Creating a Foundation of Attachment for Parenting Your Child (Workbook) By Melissa Nichols, MA, Denise Lacher, MA, and Joanne May, PhD

The Right Stuff Narrative

Mom gave the facts of my pitiable birth story new light when she said that it only showed my determination to live. That baby was the determined child she saw before her now. There was no obstacle the future could hold that I could not overcome if I used that determination begun in me then.

She believed in my strength when all I felt was lacking! Lacking pictures, neat family history, and lacking her surname!

It is awesome to think that out of long ago moments of unwelcome conception, untimely birth, and unexpected survival; faith in self was built. Mom was never sure she would get it 'right'.

I guess you could say she gave me the 'Right Stuff Narrative'.
She was somethin'!

Barbara Jones, adult adoptee, mom to 8

(and the rest of society), pathetic or even horrifying stories about our children's early lives. An adoptee is used to getting his or her story told by the big, powerful storytellers (the media, looking for sensation), and has not had much choice but to internalize a demoralizing reality: "unwanted, abandoned, unloved, left on a street corner."

But the spaces 'in between' the media stories are equally powerful. A parent can utilize these spaces to bring a different, alternative meaning to what the media storytellers have proclaimed. For example, a space-in-between: a child who was left on a street corner as a baby and later adopted is not a pathetic, perennially wounded victim. He/she was a brave, strong baby with an iron will to survive, who overcame the odds… and who is imbued with traits to conquer the world!

By helping our children to see the spaces in their story and in the world around them, we can give them a tool that is truthful and life-changing. Words have the power to change lives; it is a force majeure to hand that power to our children, so they know that the rest of their story, their ending, is within their control.

A Lifebook, the chronicle of your child's life before they were adopted, can help define a narrative space, and an adopted child can better learn to acknowledge the empty places in her history when they are re-framed and normalized by the principal adult in her life. It's all about empowerment; a parent-child co-created Lifebook (shared words and emotion!) gives a child ownership of her life story, and all of her thoughts and feelings. Working closely together on a Lifebook gives a parent the opportunity to ask and to listen, and gives the child a chance to safely explore, express and react. The act of co-creating a Lifebook with a child is greater than the end product; the process is a joint venture of trust and love, of tackling narrative spaces and of facing the unspoken together. (See **Writing a Pre-Adoptive Life Narrative**, page 244)

C = Communication and Connection

Stories communicate our thoughts and emotions. They create a connection between people, and between the past, present and future. Life Narratives are an identity tool that can present an opportunity to use stories and mixed media as part of an attuning activity. Creating a Lifebook, watching and discussing an adoption video, and looking at pre and post adoption photographs together can combine the most basic attuning elements of Dr. Hughes' and Dr. Siegel's theories and research.

Adoption Videos and Photographs can be used as a jump-off point to conversations about a child's early life, and can give clues to a child's pre-adoption history. Looking at these tools analytically, a parent and child can discern the emotions of all involved and sometimes deduce relationships, level of pre-adoptive care, and a physical and developmental history.

In looking at your child's adoption day video or photos and the first months or year at home, it's important to talk about the emotions that the baby in the images might have been feeling, and the emotions your child has today watching herself on tape. It's okay to talk about the fact that she might have been scared, or grieving a caregiver or foster family during the adoption, and you might point out how your own happy expression does/doesn't match hers in the video. Ask her if she can see the difference, and can she guess why?

"Where did I come from? What did my birthparents look like... what will I look like? What was my life like before I met you? Why was I abandoned?" are questions my daughter has asked me, and she and I have looked for clues together. We might never find definitive answers, but we piece together what we can and find comfort in the process. How can adoptive parents make sense out of the sometimes trivial, sometimes confusing, sometimes emotionally overwhelming information we have for our children?

We can tell stories. My daughter and I watch her adoption video and discuss the feelings she had when she met us, that are evident by viewing her reactions on tape at ten months old. We talk about how happy I look, and how wary she looks. We watch her private interaction with her caretaker and understand more about her life in the orphanage. We watch, and talk about the area she is from, what the local people look like, and why she might have been placed where she was found. Without a lot of concrete answers to give our children, a lot of small clues can be surmised by viewing video footage or early photos of the adoption, and of the first months at home:

Photos and video helped to familiarize my daughter with her beginnings, and the visuals helped me to talk with her about the bittersweet side of adoption. Our video is part of my daughter's life story; it is part of my 'mothering' story. It is a precious piece, because it captures loss and love, and the first tentative moments of family connection.

Pictures do tell a story... but it's equally important to communicate how you and your child feel about what is gleaned from these visual puzzle pieces. An empathic, attuned parent-child relationship will remember the 'dance' steps through the questions of childhood, the angst of pre-adolescence, and the teen identity crisis. Ultimately, we want our children to be comfortable with all of their pieces and with who they are, and giving a child ownership over their history is part of a Parenting Narrative. Attunement, Building Identity, Communication and Connection:

The A, B, C's of adoption stories provide us with some of the fundamental tools of family. We can't be untruthful about a child's life story... but we can help our children connect a narrative that hangs together from the fragments that are known, and re-story the whole with our own love and strength.

~ By Jean MacLeod

The Sad Rabbit

A therapeutic story presenting the idea that children can express their grief through one or more actions or activities that represent their loss.

"Shaggy, the brown and white bunny sat...and sat...and sat. He didn't do anything. He didn't eat. He didn't play. He didn't think. He didn't cry. He just sat. Shaggy's grandmother had died last week.

Friends came by Shaggy's house. They asked him to come out and play. He said "no." They asked if he wanted to go for a walk. He said "no."

After several weeks of feeling a big hole inside him, he decided he needed to talk to someone. Someone who would help him feel better.

One person told him to be active, to play, to get outside, to stay busy. So, he spent a week running, and hopping, and playing, and running, and hopping, and playing. He still felt the same...like he had a big hole inside him.

Another person told to not think about it, not to be sad. So he spent weeks pushing the memories and thoughts of his grandma out of his mind. Every time he started to think of something nice or funny his grandma had done or said, he squashed that thought away. But, it didn't help. He still felt like he had a big hole inside him.

Another person told him to wait and the sad, bad feelings would go away. He thought to himself. I've been waiting. My grandma died weeks ago, and I still feel like I have a big hole inside me.

One morning he woke up and said, "I know who will help! I need to talk to Mrs. Owl." He hopped out of bed, hopped out the door, hopped down the path, hopped along the river, hopped through the woods, and came to Mrs. Owl's house. She was SO glad to see him!

Just as he had guessed, Mrs. Owl knew

exactly what Shaggy needed. First, she told him that that big hole inside him was normal. That everyone who has someone die, or move away, or who has a person go away from their life feels that big hole. Some people can't eat. Some people cry a lot. Some people feel lonely. Some people can't sit still. Some people are grumpy. She explained that everybody's sad is different. And, that's ok. "There are three things you need to do," she told him, "to feel better inside."

She sent him off to visit Mr. Turtle. Mr. Turtle was very pleased to see him. Mr. Turtle sat down with Shaggy and explained that one thing he needed to do was to tell his grandma that he was mad that she had died. "How can I do that?!" Shaggy yelled. She's gone! She's dead!" Mr. Turtle said, "Yes, that's true. But still, you need to say that you're mad."

All of a sudden, Shaggy's eyes got big, his chest puffed out, and he yelled, "WHY DID YOU DIE, GRANDMA?! WHY DID YOU LEAVE ME?! I'M SO MAD AT YOU! I MISS YOU!!" As soon as the words were out of his mouth, he began to cry. Softly at first, then loudly, he cried big tears, and more tears, and even more tears. Mr. Turtle just sat quietly and patted his head. After a long time, Shaggy looked up and said, "I think I... Maybe I feel... Why do I feel... a little bit better?" Mr. Turtle said, "Sharing your inside feelings help you feel better. And, crying helps you feel better, too."

Then, Mr. Turtle sent Shaggy off to visit Miss Robin.

Miss Robin was very pleased to see Shaggy. Miss Robin sat down with Shaggy and explained that one thing he needed to do was to tell his grandma what he missed about her. "How can I do that? She's gone. She's dead." Miss Robin said, "Yes, that's true. But still, you need to share all the things that you miss about her.

Shaggy curled into a little ball. His eyes almost closed. He whispered, "Grandma, I miss your cookies. You made the best cookies in the world. And, Grandma, I miss your voice. Your funny voice when you read silly stories to me. And, Grandma, I miss being in your garden with you. You had such pretty flowers and you used to tell me all the flower names…" After he stopped talking, he got very quiet. Then he began to cry. Softly at first then loudly, he cried big tears, and more tears, and even more tears. Miss Robin just sat quietly and patted his head. After a long time, Shaggy looked up and said, "I think I… Maybe I feel… Why do I feel… a little bit better?" Miss Robin said, "Sharing your inside feelings help you feel better. Remembering why the one you love was special helps. And, crying helps you feel better, too."

Then, Miss Robin sent Shaggy to visit Mr. Bear. Mr. Bear was very pleased to see Shaggy. Mr. Bear sat down with Shaggy and explained that one thing he needed to do was to build or draw or make or plant something that would help him remember his grandma for a long time. "But what can I do," said Shaggy, "I'm just a little rabbit?" Mr. Bear said, "Well, let's think about it…What could you do so that every time you look at it, you will think of your grandma, and smile…?

Shaggy thought and thought. I could draw a picture or I could make something with clay or I could write a poem… I know! I'll plant some flowers! The kind Grandma liked! I can plant them, and

water them, and look at them, and smell them…and it will make me smile because I will think of my grandma!" He got a big smile on his face, then the smile faded, then he looked sad, then he cried. Mr. Bear just sat quietly and patted his head. After a long time, Shaggy looked up and said, "I think I… Maybe I feel… Why do I feel… a little bit better?" Mr. Bear said, "Sharing your inside feelings help you feel better. Thinking of ways to remember people who aren't in our lives any more helps. And, crying helps you feel better."

Slowly Shaggy got up. He stretched. He said, "I feel soooo tired… and maybe I feel a little tiny bit better.

As Shaggy walked home, he thought about the three things he had done. He had told his grandma he was mad at her for dying. And he had cried. He had shared what he had missed about her. And he had cried. He had thought of a way to remember his grandma in a nice, long-time way. And he had cried.

He did feel a little tiny bit better.

When he got home and told his mom and dad about his idea for making a garden to help remember his grandma, they agreed that it was a wonderful idea! Over the next few weeks, Shaggy picked out seeds and planted them. He watered them. He pulled out weeds. And, soon, he had a beautiful garden. It wasn't exactly like his grandma's garden, but every time he looked at it, or pulled out weeds, or cut pretty flowers to put into a vase, he thought of his grandma, and he smiled. The nice memories of his grandma were with him every day. He still missed his grandma, but he felt a tiny bit better inside.

~ By Susan Ward

Lifebook Resources

Lifebooks, Creating a Treasure for the Adopted Child
Beth O'Malley, MEd

Adoption Lifebook, a Bridge to Your Child's Beginnings
Cindy Probst, MEd, MSW, LCSW

EMK Press Lifebook resources:
• Sample Lifebook for a 6 year old
• Sample Baby Lifebook
• *Adoption LifeBooks: Do's and Don'ts* by Beth O'Malley
• *My Experiences with Lifebooks* By Carrie Kitze

www.emkpress.com/parentresources

My Daughter's Most Important Story
How co-creating a lifebook created an understanding and a connection
By Carrie Kitze

I knew how important creating a lifebook would be for my children, but it always seemed to take a back seat to life. I had a plastic tub I affectionately called the 'Lifebox' chock full of things I was saving for when I had the time and guts to take the plunge. Writing a lifebook isn't easy. It forces us as parents to look hard at how we are presenting information to our kids that really isn't ours. We are just the caretakers of their story, the ones providing information in an age appropriate fashion. I was never left on a street corner, alone, scared, and crying loudly so that someone would hear me. But my daughter was. Somewhere inside she remembers that feeling of being alone and every now and again, she goes back there. The lifebook has allowed her to realize that the feelings she has have a root, a reality. And that reality is hers.

When I first started working on her lifebook, I had procrastinated until she was almost six. The time never seemed right, and something else had been difficult for me; I sensed it was wrong to approach writing it as frozen in time. I have friends who have created spectacular books with die cutting and fancy type. They are beautiful. I wanted to make such a book. I bought the supplies, and then tried to figure out the words that would take my child from toddlerhood to adulthood. I couldn't make it work. Words that were appropriate for a toddler were not the realities that my grade-schooler had discovered. As she approached six, she began processing her feelings in a big way and I knew that her story was a necessary part of that journey. I knew I had to make something that could evolve as my child understood more and more of her story.

I didn't have a year to get a beautiful book done either, so one day I sat down at my computer. I dragged out all the stuff I had and organized it into a simple narrative. I laid out the bones of the story complete with all the details we had from the paperwork and information that had been discovered through my orphanage specific e-group. I included all the photos we had from the earlier times, a scan of an ID card she had worn, details about the clothing she came in and some clues we had discovered about her journey before she came to us. I detailed the weather on the birthday she was given and details about the area of the country where she is from. For her, the interesting details were sensory in nature…what it felt like, or smelled like, or tasted like. They have helped her to construct a powerful image of what it was like.

Then I talked about what she looks like, and the skills and gifts she has. I added questions about where those gifts came from and what physical attributes may have come from whom. I know she has had difficulty with the one child policy. She has wished to be a boy because maybe then her birthfamily could have kept her. So we devoted some space in her lifebook to specifically talk about those questions. That was our first version.

 This was all done in a simple page layout program. Then, to make it hers, I added some questions to get her thinking about the information that she was reading in the book and how it made her feel. I left big blank spaces for writing and drawing. Then I hit print. My part of the book was done, but the benefit was yet to come.

Baby Lifebook

It's a lifebook with training wheels. Take copies of all the photos you have of your child's early life (caregivers, baby home, abandonment site, foster family, daily life) and put them in a simple photo book without captions.
Look at the photos with your child and talk about what you see. Your child will get used to the images while you are getting used to the words.

In the reading and conversations we have had subsequently about her life story, we have grown closer and more connected. We have laughed at the funny things that were her as a baby and cried together at the sad things no baby should have to endure. I have learned to listen to her heart and help her learn it is okay to listen to her heart too. I am so glad that I procrastinated in getting her book done, as this is the book that was right for her.

And it is just the beginning. It's her story, and she owns it. We have done several revisions since the first one and are about due to look again. Because the book resides in a file on a computer in addition to a hard copy, she can update her changing thoughts on her story, and save them as separate files. This allows her to watch her thoughts and understandings develop. We also can add new information on her past as it becomes available. The power of the electronic book means that no story is ever 'stuck' in a defined version.

I have now begun working on little sister's book. The story is different to her older sister's and her needs for understanding are as well. So her book will be unique and hers alone. But I am already thinking of the smells of China (they were burning off the rice and there was smoke everywhere), the sweet taste of the watermelon which is still her favorite food, and the things she struggles with most. And as we create her story, we will laugh and cry and connect as well.

~ Carrie Kitze, mom of two daughters from China, has always enjoyed telling stories.
The lifebooks co-created with her daughters have been the most
important stories she has ever worked on.

Lifebook Tips From Beth O'Malley

1) A lifebook can be the ultimate gift of communication for you and your child.

2) Don't think of a lifebook as a book. Instead—consider it a basic attachment tool. Attachment tools help to improve the quality of your child's life.

3) Worried about your artistic ability? Relax. Think about getting started and finished!

4) The best way to make a lifebook is with your child. Take a trip to a scrapbook store and let them choose papers, stickers and album.

5) Don't forget—the lifebook is your child's story. This means it includes their birth, birth parents, and reason(s) 'why' they were placed for adoption.

6) The lifebook is not your adoption journal. That's another album or journal.

7) Missing a few pieces of his or her story? Believe it or not there are more ways to deal with the unknown then you might think. If you get stuck or need to get re-energized, come to my website and sign up for my email lessons (no charge) which are part of my monthly lifebook newsletter:
www. adoptionlifebooks.comsignup.htm

8) Perhaps you're feeling anxious just thinking about this project. One parent bene-fit to wrestling with the words-to-use, is that you become grounded when it comes to adoption talk.

9) Think of the lifebook process as therapeutic. Only it doesn't cost anything and you can do it from home. *Smile*.

10) Love your child more than anything? Consider your time and angst over creating a lifebook another parent sacrifice. Certainly your children are worth it.

~ Beth O'Malley, MEd, an adoptive mom, adoptee, nationally recognized speaker and author of Lifebooks: Creating a Treasure for the Adopted Child. She has made countless lifebooks while preparing foster children for adoption.

Waiting Parents and Lifebooks

Waiting to adopt is such a stressful experience.
Time simply slows down, with a few 'hurry up and waits' in between.
Occasionally parents who hear about lifebooks make the mistake of thinking
"Oh, I'll get to that later." Big mistake! Get educated.
Find out what really goes into a lifebook. You might be surprised…

As you read about 'lifebooks' something magical happens. You start thinking differently about information, and about what's important.

There are once-in-a lifetime opportunities available when you travel and adopt. By knowing the right questions to ask, and including the answers in your child's lifebook, your child doesn't lose out on valuable pieces of information.

Journal, Journal, Journal. Not a writer? Write notes on scraps of paper. Keep old calendars, print out emails, buy a tape recorder and talk into it each night when you travel.

Don't lose your little scraps of paper. Have one safe place for the important stuff.

Prepare a list of photos you want to take. Otherwise you might end up with all pictures of just your child. Someday your child will want to know more.

Bring back a rock, packet of earth, or press a flower in between the pages of a book. Something tangible from your child's birth country that he or she can hold.

Get a copy of the local paper on the day you meet your child.

Record quotes from people on your journey. It makes for a more interesting read in the lifebook. Include your own thoughts and reactions.

Don't forget to include all your senses. What smells stood out? Noises? How did your child feel with that first hug?

Bring back anything that has the original smell on it. Don't wash the outfit they come in. Unless of course something yucky happened to it. Bring a plastic bag for it. Take a picture of it for the lifebook.

~By Beth O'Malley, MEd,
author of LifeBooks: Creating a Treasure for the Adopted Child

What Happened Before I Came to You?
Questions for Developing a Pre-Adoptive Life Narrative
Developed by Mary Ellyn Lambert (FRUA-Michigan) and
Doris A. Landry, MS, for Target: Lifebook—The Workshop

As you begin to think and jot down things about your child's pre-adoption history, you will be surprised by all the information you will be able to share. You can add depth and intimacy, even with little written documentation, and your efforts will come alive with feeling. Some questions that follow have been written as if your child were asking. This may help you step into their shoes and help you to answer some hard questions with compassion, empathy and a renewed respect for the plight of others. Many parents have found that Pre-Adoptive Narratives can reduce fears of abandonment, reduce shame, and strengthen their child's identity while increasing family intimacy.

In the Beginning...
Birthparents
Do you know them? What are their names? Why don't you know their names?
What do I call my birthmother? Birthfather?
Can you describe them physically? Like were they tall? Short?
What are their ethnic backgrounds? Were they married?
How did they make me? How old were they when they had me?
Do you have photos? Do you have pictures of their house or can you describe it ?
Did they work? What language did they speak?
Where are they today? Do you have their address?
Can I draw a picture of what I think they looked like then? Now?
Can I draw what I think their house looked like, or the hospital where I was born?
Can I write them a letter? Visit?
Birth Family
Do I have grandparents? Did you meet them? Do you know their names?
Do you know anything about them? Did they visit me? Can I meet them?
Do I have brothers and sisters? Do you know their names, where they are?
Do you know if they live with my birthparents? Why not me if they do?
What language do they speak?
Were they adopted like me? By whom? Are they still my brother(s), sister(s)?
Do I have other aunts, uncles and cousins? Can I meet them?

And then I Grew...
What happened during the nine months I was growing inside my birthmother?
Did I learn about what she sounded like? Did I smell the things she smelled?
Did I enjoy the foods she ate?
Did I hear the beat of her heart and feel the rhythm of her walk?
Could I tell when she slept and when she worked?

When she worried could I feel this too?
During the first three months, what did I look like and do?
What did I do the second three months?
During the last three months what happened?

And, I was Born...

What was my birth name?
How do you spell it? How do you pronounce it?
Why did you change my name?
What is my birth date? Do you know for sure or is it a guess?
How do they guess?
Who named me at birth?
Does it have a meaning like a family name or a flower?
What day of the week was I born on?
What was the weather like that day?
What was the first language I heard?
Do you have my birth certificate?
Was I big or little (reference appropriate standards)?
Do you think I had any hair? What color were my eyes?
Was I healthy? Why not? Was I born in a hospital? At home?
Why don't you know? Was I breast-fed?

Then there was Living...With Whom? Where?
Birthparents
Did I live with my birthparents for any time? What was it like?
Do you have any documents that tell a story?
Foster Parents
What did I call my foster mother? Foster father? Foster grandparents?
Did I have more than one foster family? Why? What are their names?
Can you tell me about them? Do you have photos?
Do you have any photos of their house? What language did they speak?
Where are they today? Do you have their address? Can I talk to my foster parents?
Foster Siblings
Do I have foster brothers and sisters? What are their names?
Where are they? Are they adopted too? Can I see them?
Caretakers
Did I have a special caretaker? What was her name? Where does she live now?
Can I talk to her? Was she important to me? How?
Other Children Who Were Like Siblings
What do I call them? Brothers, sisters? What are their names? Where do they live now?
Can I talk to them? Were they adopted too? Can we find them? Visit them?

Older Child Tip

Working with an older child? Parenting an older child? Don't have pictures? They hate to draw?

Try making a collage from pictures cut out from magazines.

Any type of art project seems to help kids relax.

Open up.

And the healing is the talk between the cutting and pasting.

~Beth O'Malley

Immediate Surroundings

What did the world around me look like?

Did I live in a family house? An apartment? An orphanage? Where was it located?

Was it a city, town, or village? Do you have pictures you can show me?

What was it like? Did I have toys? How did it smell and feel to you?

Were the people taking care of me happy? Were they nice? Were people smiling?

Were babies crying?

How many children lived there and how old were they?

Heritage

What can you tell me about my country of origin? Are there interesting things about it?

Does it have a long history? What kinds of cultural things would I find interesting?

How do they educate the kids? What kinds of religions do they practice?

Is this different than ours? Are there special foods? Special anything?

What are some social customs I might find interesting? Tell me about political issues.

Tell me about cultural issues. Why was I available for adoption?

Why couldn't I live with my birthparents? Why did they make me?

What does 'parental rights terminated' mean? What is 'abandonment'?

Did my birthparents just walk out of the hospital without me?

How can a mother or father just leave a baby?

Wouldn't someone bad take the baby if they were just left? What is an adoption plan?

How do the police just take a kid from their home?

Did my birthparents die?

Do parents leave babies if they are too much work? Who took care of me when they left?

What was my life like when they left me?

Were there financial issues? Tell me about it.

Why didn't family members, like grandparents, help my birthparents keep me?

Why didn't they take care of me? What is alcoholism? Drug abuse?

What is poverty? What is neglect? What is abuse? How can parents go to jail?

How can someone live on a street?

Once I know my story I might ask "How can someone leave a kid alone, sometimes for days, and without food?"

Finally... Why Did you Adopt me?

Not every question will fit your child's particular story. Understanding the questions your child might have inside will help you as parents work with your child to navigate her life story and understand a bit more of where she started, and who she is.

The Emotional Impact of Lifebooks
Lifebooks don't cause trauma, but they may expose it...

We are very lucky in that we met and are in contact with our daughter's birthmother. We have photos of our daughter at birth, and with her birthmother and fostermother the following day when she was taken to foster care, and all through her foster care with various members of her foster family. We have later photos of her birthmother, birthfather, siblings, grandmother, and the house they live in.

Because our daughter has language and developmental delays, I felt it very important to give her something tangible to use to understand her adoption. I created a lifebook for her. The book I wrote for her is about thirty pages long, with big photos or illustrations on each page, and with simple text. My daughter was just under five years-old when she first saw it. I don't think anybody anticipated the intensity of our daughter's reaction.

At first she was simply delighted. We gave it to her in the end of April and she wanted us to read it with her most days right through the summer. At first she focused on herself, then our family. Then she began to learn all the words of the text and all the names of her birth family and foster family. Then she focused on how, in foster care, she missed us and was waiting for us–always played out in a happy reunion sort of way. Once she said, "I want to see them" about her birth family. This is something we plan to do when she's a little older, and I told her that probably we will, but not soon. This seemed to be what she needed to hear.

In late May, the school dog died, which my daughter took hard. Then in early June, school ended. For the first time, I think she really understood the parting. She began to be clingy, anxious and weepy for the first time in her life. This continued through the summer. She was terribly anxious about any separation from my husband and me, and would weep and call out sometimes ieven if I just walked to the other side of the room. She could not be babysat by anyone but a grandmother. I couldn't go to the bathroom without her on many days. For six or seven weeks she needed both parents to lie down with her to sleep, or else she would weep in terror and be inconsolable. Going back to school was hard. We worked with the staff, and stayed at school with her at first. Now she is separating outside the classroom and not sad at all. She has a shared aide in school, and they draw pictures of her family and use social stories to help her cope, and it's working marvelously. But phew! What a hurdle!

What do I think? Well, I think the lifebook book worked. She got it. And, it triggered a great deal of grief and anxiety about separation which spread throughout her school, social life, and our family's life. It exposed anxiety over attachment figures. It was probably a healthy thing, and I am sure it's not over, just integrated on a certain level for now.

~Teresa M. Kohlenberg, MD
is a developmental pediatrician, child psychiatrist, and biological and adoptive mom.

Emily's Questions
The importance of learning to listen

When I was 11 years old I started having lots more thoughts and questions about my adoption. This made me feel uncomfortable. I just couldn't figure out what was wrong with me! I was adopted at birth and my parents have always been 'my' parents. They told me about my adoption from day one and they talked about it openly, for as long as I can remember. We have books and workbooks and more books. I think they felt that I was doing just fine–which made me even more afraid of going to them with my questions.

I have lots of friends and am a successful volleyball player and member of the student council. I do well in school and everyone says that I am smart and self-confident. I like hearing this and it is how I feel most of the time. But then the nagging questions about my adoption just kept coming and wouldn't seem to leave me alone.

I started to get moody, my mom said, and angry at little things. It seemed like I couldn't concentrate at school and my grades began to show it! No one knew what was wrong, not even me. I was very confused. My parents were getting worried because I wouldn't talk to them. Actually I would just often yell at them and secretly feel guilty. They seemed to be just as confused as me so they said we were all going to see a counselor who knew about kids who had been adopted.

I thought I was going to hate talking and not like any adoption counselor! What would she know anyway! But, for some reason it felt like she knew what I was thinking. It was kind-of-freaky, but not all that bad. She didn't 'make' me talk and seemed to understand what my parents told her. As I listened to her I was surprised to find out that I was not the only one who wondered about my birthparents and who felt like a traitor for doing so.

I didn't hate going to see the counselor as much as I thought I might. I didn't have to talk, and at first it helped just to listen. Since I was pretty quiet she asked me if I liked to write? Yes, I love to! She asked if I would write down some of the questions in my mind and bring them to our next meeting. I found myself writing about my adoption. No, not really 'about' the adoption, as my parents told me that part of the story over and over again, but about everything else. I found myself writing in a notebook here and there for days. After a week I had pages of questions. I didn't even know I had that many questions inside of me. They filled four pages! I looked at them a lot, thinking, "No wonder I can't think about anything else and get my homework done." I just couldn't believe it and I couldn't figure out how I even stored them up.

At our next counseling meeting I brought my notebook. I wasn't sure what we were going to do but somehow we just got to talking. I read some of the questions to my parents. I started to read and it seemed to go on forever. It was an amazing feeling to throw them all out into the air. I kept checking the looks on my parents' faces to see how they were feeling. I had twinges of guilt, twinges of happy, twinges of relief, twinges of scared, twinges of just about every feeling.

When I got to the last question I almost couldn't ask, it was the big question.... Why? ***"Why did they give me away?"*** I felt like none of the other questions mattered. I felt like I had wanted to ask that question all my life. I felt like it had built in my heart for 11 years and no one knew it was there. I was afraid to ask it, afraid for lots of reasons. My feelings of loss at that moment were so strong I thought I would never stop feeling so sad.

Now that the big question had been asked. I was afraid on one-hand that my parents didn't have the answer and, on the other-hand I was afraid that they did have the answer and that it might be something about me!

No, my parents didn't have the answer but I sure felt better asking. And, I sure felt better knowing that my parents really understood, they really, really understood! They knew how I wanted this answered and they understood how sad it made me not to know. I think we were all feeling the same thing. I think they would have loved to have made-up some answer for me but they didn't, they were just sad with me. It was nice not to feel alone.

Oh, and my parents seemed to be on my side. They didn't think I was a traitor for having questions, even four pages full! As I am writing this story I'm happy to report that my grades are better. And, I don't seem to be so angry with my parents. I don't think writing the questions were so very important. What I think is that they just needed to get out so I didn't feel so scared and worried.

My name is Emily and I was adopted.

This is based on a true story and excerpted from Underground Feelings *by Doris A. Landry, MS, LLP with Julie Kimball-Kubiak, MA, SW*

Abandonment
at the heart of the story

My adoptive parents tried very hard to suppress the truth, and did tell me my birthparents loved me (which didn't really make me feel any better). It didn't fill the hole of the feeling that somehow they left me behind. Why would you insist that abandonment = love? And why can't people accept the fact that unless you talked to someone who actually was involved in the situation you can't be sure about the facts in the documents. Documents can be easily forged and it's better, in my opinion, to bring that out in the open and speak honestly.

Through my adoption story, I can tell my daughter how people lied to me (intentionally or unintentionally), and about my forged documents, and 'fake' birth-date. I had to insist on the truth and wrangle it out of my adoptive parents. They kept making up stories and it backfired. It made me extremely angry at them and guess what– they lost my trust. I remember telling my husband that at some point in my life everyone just seemed to lie to me.

I don't think they really wanted to spare me the pain; more like they wanted to accept their version of the story. It's best to be honest; it's okay to say "I don't know" but that we hope our kids will find out the truth.

~by Riam Sangdoung Kidd, is a Thai adoptee who adopted her daughter from China

Using the 'A' Word
Why Should I Tell My Child that She was Abandoned?
By Doris Landry, MS, LLP

Abandonment is part of your child's identity and having a strong identity is one of the keys to a successful life. The word 'abandoned' is not only the truth but also the word that your child will hear in the coming years. If you begin to use this word it will not only become common/normal/usual in your family but will also increase the chances that your child will come from a place of strength when asked, "did your real mother leave you?" ("… abandon you?") Your child has already begun her journey of truth seeking, even if it has not yet been verbalized. This is true for all adopted children.

Early school years often begin the adopted child's journey of truth. The truth is already out there: lack of baby pictures for school projects, parents who look different, and no birth family name. The questions begin, such as, how did I get my name, or, how do you know my birth date? Your child can only be comfortable with the truth if you are comfortable with it. Young children seem to know that 'good' things are talked about and 'bad' things are not. In the years of concrete thinking, your child could assume that adoption, and the many things about it, are 'bad' if you don't talk about them..

Knowledge is power. The more you know about the possible reasons for abandonment, the easier it will be to explain. Research and understand the history and implementation within your child's birth country. Examine your own beliefs and opinions.

How Might My Child Feel About all the Information? It is important to first become comfortable with the idea that your child may be sad as you open the door to her truth. In order to gain something, loss needs to occur. Talking about coming together as a family, from loss (at times both the parent's and the child's) will allow a special connection between the two of you. This can bring about empathic feeling of 'sameness.' In using adoption terms at home, such as 'birthmother,' a child learns how to talk with others. However, parents must be comfortable using adoption terms. Test your feelings. *Remember, it is difficult for a child to gain comfort from a parent who needs comforting.* Your child's thoughts about her birth country and her birth family should create feelings of sadness, which may bring about tears. It is normal. Some children feel angry before or after they experience sadness. This, too, is normal. Anger is one of the steps often present during the grieving process.

What Should I Do and How Can I Help? Encourage your child to ask questions. "Some kids wonder if…" …you can love two moms? or…you can look for your birth family when you are older? or…all of the feelings you have about what happened to you are okay? Encourage her to draw to express her feelings and thoughts. Create and tell stories that end with coping skills that will empower your child. Expect delayed reactions from this story as some children need time to think and wonder. Be prepared; children's questions often come at the least opportune time! Explore the idea that there are many reasons why a child is available for adoption, just as there are many reasons why a family is created through adoption. Determine how your child best attends to talking about abandonment and adoption. Try talking in the first person, and, if not successful, use the third person. (Some children like to use dolls or stuffed animals to project their thoughts and ideas onto.)

An Adoption Collage: Putting the Pieces Together

A way to manage, memorialize, and make visual poetry of the past
By *Mary Anne Cohen*

Of all modes of art, adoption most resembles the collage: a collection of mixed materials, already pre-existing, brought together to make something new, interesting, and sometimes beautiful. The whole becomes greater than the parts. This is true at the beginning, especially in open adoption, but it is there in a less tangible way in closed or international adoptions as well; the inhabitants of the 'Ghost Kingdom', as author Betty Jean Lifton calls it, cluster around the everyday reality of birthparents, adoptive parents, and adoptees.

Collage Works Well. One big advantage of using the collage in art therapy is that it truly is something anyone can do, and those who are intimidated by the thought of having to draw or paint may be more comfortable with scissors, glue, and a pile of old magazines or found objects. Anyone can put stuff together, and often a surprising amount of emotion comes out in the process, the selection and combination of images, and in the finished product. Any adoptee or birth/adoptive family-member can privately make her or his own collage, or it can be done as a group activity at a meeting, at a conference or at a workshop It can be big or small, simple or elaborate, flat or three dimensional. It can be done as fine art (even Picasso did some collages), or as a strictly therapeutic tool with little thought to its artistic merit. It should be fun to do, although sometimes the emotions evoked by art done this way are strong and painful. There should be time to talk about those emotions, and about the finished product and the process, as well as time to do the actual work. The group leader should be available after the workshop for anyone who is distressed and needs further care because of the depths of emotions evoked. Sometimes we need help coming back to the world from that other place where dreams and art are made.

Advance Preparation Pays Off. I find that it works well to prepare in advance to do the collage, although it can be done on the spur of the moment with just a diverse pile of magazines to cut up, clean construction paper on which to assemble the images, scissors, and glue sticks. If you plan a collage meeting, instruct your group members to look through their adoption memorabilia, documents and photographs:

- birth certificates
- surrender papers
- decree of adoption
- search notebook
- baby pictures, family photos, reunion pictures

Internationally adopted children may also possess a certificate of abandonment, medical records, finding ad, police report, original passport and a certificate of citizenship.

Make copies of anything that might be interesting or meaningful to use. Some may want to make color copies which can get expensive. I like the look of black and white copies of photos, and prefer them for collage work. Depending on how elaborate you wish to get, people can also use small objects, cloth, ribbon, buttons, and junk jewelry. Craft stores are a good source of all kinds of little things (even tiny dolls) that can be used in many ways in collages. Junk drawers at home often have great and weird things, too. If you are making a three dimensional work, a glue gun is a good idea to have. They are very

Everyone's Collage will be Unique:

Some people will have just a few images, and lots of blank space, where others will have filled every inch, and have items overlapping. Some will have mostly text, a mix of text and images, or all pictures and no text. Some will tell a story, while others will be more abstract and just create a mood.

cheap and can also be found in craft stores. If you are working in a group, bring several, along with enough glue sticks.

Once you have gathered your materials, you can gather your group. You may want to play a tape of some calm and unobtrusive music in the background. Start with getting everyone to relax and quietly think about their adoption experience, while looking through the material they have brought with them and the magazines and other objects that are available to share. You can reassure the group that nobody will be graded or judged, and that what is important is to express inner feelings, and to have a good time working with a variety of images. Once things get rolling people should feel free to talk and compare, and ask for what they want if they are not finding it, as in "did anyone see a picture of a cat?" or "I need a red rose".

Conversation is as Important as the Art. When everyone is done, leave enough time for participants to show their work, talk about the images, and talk about what feelings came up in the process. There is something reassuring about the concreteness of the finished work, and the use of images that already exist gives a bit of emotional distance not present when one must draw or paint one's own images from scratch.

There is no limit to how photos, documents, words, pictures, and objects can be manipulated and combined in an adoption collage. It is a project that can be done again and again, always with new results. It can be a way to chart the progress and the shifting configurations of family and connectedness for the adoptee. It can be a way to manage, memorialize, and make visual poetry of the past. It can be a way to envision the future, to create fantasy, and to come terms with reality.

No Special Skills Required. Unlike written poetry, or most visual arts, it requires no special skill to create something that is eloquent, inventive, and often a source of continued insight into the mind and heart. It is often chaotic and messy, like real life, but there is still an element of choice and control over the situation that is helpful to adoptees, who had so little actual control over adoption, in most cases. It is a means, once removed, to explore the landscape of dreams and the subconscious, and to connect to archetypal and personal imagery that has deep meaning for the individual. What is unique about the collage is that those images can be collected and frozen in place, to be looked at again and again for deeper meaning.

Mary Anne Cohen is a birthmother who has been active in adoption reform since the mid '70s. She is the editor of Origins Newsletter, an essayist and poet with a degree in art, and has presented at many adoption reform conferences. Mary Anne is married and has three adult sons whom she raised; s he has also reunited with her surrendered son

Beneath the Mask, Understanding Adopted Teens, by Debbie Riley, MS, with John Meeks, MD also has some great resources for using art and crafts to process feelings.

Learning

Post-Institutionalized Children and Learning Issues
Children Gain when Parents Become Educators
By Susan G. Forbes, LICSW

I work as a therapist, specializing in adoption issues, particularly the issues of families with children struggling with the effects of post-institutional (PI) care. I do see several children adopted domestically from the U.S. with multiple problems due to being born to drug and/or alcohol addicted birth moms and/or a history of abuse, neglect, and trauma. The problems I see in the U.S children are very similar to those faced by children adopted from overseas countries who have been in institutional care.

My husband and I have two daughters, ages eight and a half and five. Both were adopted as healthy children from the People's Republic of China. When we adopted our first daughter, we did not receive any information about the potential problems post-institutionalized children might experience. Upon return, we had a battery of recommended blood work completed, and we saw a pediatric neurologist to assess any potential problems related to developmental delays, but he seemed to know very little about post-institutionalized children. He minimized most of the concerns I had regarding our older daughter's gross motor delays and he said our daughter was fine and would progress on her own with the opportunities for growth and development we were providing under our loving care.

Understanding the Challenges
As it turned out, both of our daughters have thrived under our care, but they also have challenges related to sensory integration dysfunction (DSI). My unfamiliarity with sensory integration dysfunction prevented me from seeking services for our older daughter. Our younger daughter also experienced a speech delay. Her sensory issues were the polar opposite of our older daughter. She was sensory seeking, hyperactive, and fearless. Our younger daughter was barely eligible to receive services through Early Intervention, but because of my insistence, we were accepted into the program. I did have to fight for Speech and Occupational Therapy services and waited way too long for each of them. My youngest entered the program at eighteen months, which only gave her eighteen more months of services (EI ends at age three). She did 'graduate' to the public schools service system, however once

again it was a fight to get services for her. She was not eligible for an Individualized Educational Plan (IEP), although was given a 'service plan'. In other words, we didn't have much leverage within the system and were 'lucky' to get what we got.

Currently, neither of our daughters is receiving formal treatment for their sensory, speech, or learning issues. Our younger daughter is often hyper-active, impulsive, and has difficulty regulating herself when she's angry, frustrated, excited, or anxious. She still needs speech for articulation and mechanical issues. Our older daughter has been experiencing some reading and math challenges that I believe may be related to tracking and visual processing. She continues to struggle with her gravitational insecurities and has hand-eye and foot-eye coordination difficulties. They make it hard for her to catch a ball, kick a ball, ride a bike, jump rope, roller skate, and go down stairs.

Why the orphanage/institutional care affects some children more than others will always be a puzzle for those of us who have adopted internationally, and who are without birth parent information. It's impossible to know, of all of the challenges our children face, which are the effects of institutional care and which are of a genetic base. So, many of us who have children with issues, become determined to help our children to the greatest extent that we can, without knowing the origins of their problems. For some, the hope is that if the problems stem from post-institutionalization than perhaps with proper interventions there is remediation. And if the problems are genetic, at the very least, we are doing all we can to provide our children with the best possible care so that they can function at a level as high as possible with their challenges

Families that receive services through Early Intervention can find it more difficult to obtain services once their child transitions into the public schools sector. If your child is obviously impaired, (autism, Aspberger Syndrome, ADHD, non-verbal learning disorder), receiving services might not be difficult to obtain. But for families whose children are functioning fairly well (although not necessarily up to their potential) they may find it more challenging to get the services their child needs in the schools. Additionally, school providers typically are not well versed in post-institutional issues, in particular sensory issues, attachment issues, emotional dysregulation issues, and the learning issues that often 'morph out' of sensory issues. If your child is bright in addition to having issues, it will prove to be that much more challenging to get services for them from the school setting. Insurance companies typically don't pay for issues that are 'developmental', indicating a lack of understanding and sensitivity to challenges that face adoptive families, particularly those without birthparent information.

Self Esteem

Self-esteem is an area of concern that I see with children who have learning issues. When children are younger and learning issues are not apparent, children play, learn, and interact on a level playing field. Once academic performance matters (which in some school settings can show up as early as kindergarten) children who are struggling are very aware that they are somehow different than their cohorts. Couple learning challenge differences with being adopted (transracially or not), and a scenario starts to develop where the child is feeling 'different'; they may become angry and depressed, and self-esteem can start to plummet. Behavioral issues can begin to surface or can escalate as the child is academically challenged and is not performing (cognitively, socially, emotionally, or behaviorally) in line with classroom expectations. Post-institutionalized children's issues are puzzling to educators. These children seem very academically strong in some areas and then very challenged in others, in ways that don't fit with how educators' understand learning disabilities.

The Long Reach of Malnutrition and Trauma

In Janina Galler's groundbreaking longitudinal study of infants in the United States, it was reported that *"60% of the children who experienced only one severe incidence of malnutrition, exhibited attention deficits, poor memory, distractibility, and poor school performance on follow-up testing at age 9-10 years old"*. Galler has also followed two groups of children in Barbados for more than thirty years. This study found that the children who experienced a moderate to serious episode of malnutrition during the first year of life, scored lower on IQ testing (10 to 12.5 points) than the healthy group and there was a remarkable difference between the two groups in the prevalence of attention deficit disorder. Nearly 60 percent of the children who experienced malnutrition showed symptoms of ADD – poor memory, short attention span, restlessness, and a tendency to be easily distracted.

Dr. Bruce Perry's work on the impact of trauma on brain development indicates similar findings: trauma, neglect, and maltreatment in early childhood can affect physical development, cause emotional/behavioral difficulties, and adversely impact attachment within the family and future interpersonal relationships. It appears that there are 'holes' or gaps in the brain development of children who have experienced early deprivation, neglect, malnutrition, trauma, etc. These 'holes' or gaps can create a non-typical appearance to learning disabilities and behavioral issues. As I have read and learned more about brain development and the short and long term effects of malnutrition, deprivation, neglect, and trauma, I have come to strongly suspect there is a correlation between sensory integration dysfunction/disorder and later educational, behavioral, emotional, and social issues.

Early Treatment

Educators hesitate to jump into identifying a child too soon as having a learning disability. I don't know if that's a fiscally driven decision or truly in the best interests of the child. But there is research that indicates that there are early indicators of dyslexia, and the earlier you treat the child, the better. If the learning disability is more in the form of ADD or ADHD, where the child's behavior is so difficult to manage that the classroom becomes disrupted by the child, the school may then decide an IEP is necessary. Sensory integration issues in the form of sensory seeking may look like ADHD/Hyperactive Type. Sensory integration issues in the form of sensory defensive can look like ADHD/Disorganized Inattentive Type. Some educators I have talked with, claim that if the child has a true learning disability, holding off with services until fourth grade won't hurt the child. I don't agree with that point of view, given that by that time, a child's self-esteem could have really taken a nose dive due to frustration, feelings of failure, and possible alienation from peers due to academic struggles.

Decisions about how to help their child are challenging for parents. As parents, our job is to be advocates for what we feel our children need. What if what we believe to be learning challenges in our children, are minimized by the school? What if we sense that the educators don't really understand the scope of our child's learning issues? Do we start to doubt ourselves, seeing that we're not professionals in this field, or think perhaps we're not seeing clearly because it's our child? How aware and accepting are educators to articles about brain development, trauma, attachment, learning challenges in PI children, sensory integration dysfunction/disorder and its impact on auditory and visual processing, hyper-arousal/anxiety/hyperactivity? How much do we push? How much do we step back and let the educators do their job?

Sharon Cermak, Professor at Boston University found similar learning problems in children adopted from Romania. Many of these children face multiple issues such as attachment, posttraumatic stress, sensory integration, language, cognitive, behavioral, and attentional concerns. Cermak states, *"Intervention for a post-institutionalized child should begin even prior to his or her adoption. Adoption agencies must be aware of the numerous issues these children face and share this knowledge with families so that they can make informed decision, understand their child's behavior, provide appropriate supports, and serve as advocates for their child. It is also important to provide these families with resources and professionals who are experienced in working with these children."*
These are tough questions and complex issues. My recommendation is for families to:
- Form support groups where they educate themselves, find good research articles about learning disabilities, post-institutionalized children and its long-term effects, and brain development, and then review and discuss the articles together.
- Learn how to navigate the special education service system offered in their area and become experts in advocacy and what services their child is entitled to receive.
- Be willing to explore non-traditional activities, therapies, and interventions; such as Yoga, Brain Gym, the Alert Program, Neurofeedback, Chiropractic, Nutritional supplements/Dietary needs, Vision Therapy, Listening Therapy, Equine Assisted Therapy, and Massage. Integrating these less traditional interventions into a therapeutic parenting model has the potential to stimulate the brain in ways that enhance regulation, behavior, learning, and sensory integration.
- Attend conferences and workshops on these topics so they're up to date on the research and can then present the most recent findings to their school district. We are and will always be the best advocates for our children.

As strange as it seems, we need to become educators ourselves, in much the same way many of us became Occupational Therapists and Speech Therapists for our children when they were younger. We need to be a strong force insisting on services that truly match our children's needs.

~ Susan Forbes is a Licensed Independent Clinical Social Worker in private practice in North Quincy, Massachusetts, specializing in post-adoption issues. She has worked in the field of mental health with children, adolescents, and adults for the past 18 years, and in the field of adoption for the past 8 years. She is also the proud parent of two daughters adopted from China. Susan has a particular interest in the area of sensory integration dysfunction (in post-institutionalized children) and brain development, and how sensory issues can impact children in the educational setting as they grow.

The Internationally Adopted Child at School
Becoming a Parent Advocate
By Julie Beem

'Wait and See'

As adoptive parents of internationally born children, we have become extremely adept at learning 'systems': the home-study system, the dossier system, the 'how to obtain citizenship' system. Once we are home with our beloved child and settled, we realize we are not finished with the systems we must learn to maneuver.

Most of us schedule an immediate appointment with a physician upon returning home with our new child. Many of us research doctors carefully, looking for one that has experience with internationally adopted (IA) children and the various diseases and disorders that may be associated with our child's particular country of origin. But few rush to have the child educationally evaluated. Parents adopting internationally are often highly motivated to learn all there is to know about international adoption, and read everything we can get our hands on about adoption, our child's culture, and parenting. We're eager, and we're anxious; we've waited a long time, and we want to do it right. Yet when a well-meaning 'professional' tells us to 'wait and see' or 'give her time to adjust', we begin to question any well-educated concerns we have.

The doctor smiled wearily. "Mrs. Beem," he said, "you have a beautiful daughter who seems to be developing very normally, given her circumstances. The tantrums you report are age appropriate and her language delay is normal considering she has only been home a year. I think you're just a little too worried about all this." I wanted to take this at face value and stop worrying about my child's behaviors and lag in language. After all, he was the head of the international adoption clinic (a clinic that I later learned had just opened that year). So I waited, and another six months passed with speech therapy provided twice a week through Early Intervention, and still no progress with her worsening tantrums.

The 'wait and see' approach makes so much sense on the surface. Our children have been yanked from the world they knew – their culture and their language. They have been taken from a sensory deprived environment and plunked into the sensory rich (and often overwhelming) lives we lead. Giving the child a period of adjustment sounds like a great idea, and professionals with little experience with IA children will almost always advise a very cautious, slow approach to assessments and interventions. If they do suggest interventions, they are always traditional in nature, like those we received through the Early Intervention program in our state (traditional speech therapy). They are rarely based on research about language acquisition in internationally adopted kids, emotional development of children who have been neglected or abused, or the effects of the lack of sensory stimulation on development.

After a few months of speech therapy, the Early Intervention staff transitioned our 'case' to the local school district, who immediately suggested full-time special needs preschool. Like any good mother, I wanted to do what was best academically for my budding three-year-old, so I agreed. After all, they were the professionals. So off she went out of our home for several hours a day into a classroom. The teachers were conscientious and caring, but the class was incredibly diverse. The children had a full range of disabilities (physical, mental, and emotional), making it a very complex environment.

Oh how I wish I'd known then what I know now! Here was my little one, home less than a year, whisked off to the exact wrong place for her to be. In all my reading and research, and appointments with 'professionals' no one ever told me what numerous parents have told me since:

- The first year home needs to be focused on attachment and bonding, regardless of the child's age.
- Getting the right assessments up-front, and repeatedly evaluating progress is the key to making sound academic decisions.
- School professionals don't necessarily have experience with dealing with children who have experienced multi-faceted grief, loss and trauma–so we parents really are the 'professionals' in assessing our children's needs.

The First Year Home

I was stunned and crushed at the news that my daughter was being kicked out of the church preschool. But I was not surprised. Her behaviors had been escalating over the last few weeks, and despite the gentle teacher's best efforts, she still hid under tables, interrupted others, and attempted to hit the teacher when corrected. It was incredibly humiliating for the mother of three other children, all honor students, to come to grips with this. Where had we failed her?

Most internationally adopted children do not arrive home ready for an academic school setting. Because of their resilient nature, high intellect, and some amount of sheer luck, some children land in school or preschool settings where they adapt with relative ease. But many more do not.

Knowledge is power!

Understanding what our kids need early and intervening proactively with services, may save them from a downward spiral at school. The *'wait and see'* method of evaluating our adopted children for speech and language (and other developmental delays), which is routinely used by pediatricians and Early Intervention, is not appropriate for post-institutional children. If you sense your child needs assistance, arm yourself with info and be prepared to advocate. A very helpful website:

www.wrightslaw.com

A healthy attachment to a primary caregiver is critical for a child's emotional and social development. But it is also a crucial building block for learning. Cause and effect thinking is specifically developed through the infant bonding cycle of a baby crying and having her needs met by a loving caregiver. The sensory stimulation that comes along with reciprocal play between infants and mothers is vital for the development of the child's sensory processing centers.

Armed with information about the importance of attachment to our children's brain development and capacity to learn, adoptive parents who are deeply concerned about our children's academic success must shift gears and realize that school achievement isn't the primary goal in our children's lives, regardless of their chronological age. We may have to make the decision to postpone schooling or to curtail our academic expectations, and instead focus on attachment activities and the re-parenting activities our children may need to make up for the developmental steps they have missed while not in our care.

Nancy Ng, an adoptive parent and editor for FAIR, captured it well in "What, Me Turn Down Services?" from *Adoption and the Schools* when she said, *"All activities are secondary to the essential task of building a firm attachment between parent and child....Efforts to prepare the child for a wider world of school and socialization must be provided in ways which allow healing, a healing that takes place in the loving, consistent crucible of the family."*

For the first year, parents of IA children should proceed cautiously with educational placements, remembering that the first and foremost activity is establishing a loving bond within your family, upon which a healthy emotional, social and academic life can be built. Many Early Intervention programs and services available through schools systems can be offered in the home setting or with parents present, if parents will be proactive in explaining to the educators why this is necessary for creating a healthy attachment and a safe environment for the child.

Getting the Right Assessments

Dr. Boris Gindis, psychologist and head of the Center for Cognitive-Developmental Assessments and Remediation, recommends full psycho-educational assessments of IA children as soon as they arrive home. He recommends conducting the assessments in the child's native language as quickly after adoption as possible, before the child has an opportunity to lose his native language ability. One reason for his insistence on the early evaluations (within weeks of arrival) is to immediately identify areas of remediation that are independent of the acquisition of new language. This is counterintuitive to the 'wait and see' approach schools prefer when dealing with a child acquiring a new language. This proactive approach is especially critical in the case of school-aged children, where quickly identifying possible deficits and learning disabilities enables the parents and the school not to waste any precious time in getting the services needed. Dr. Gindis' website (www.bgcenter.com) is filled with information and training opportunities for both parents and school personnel to learn more about conducting the right assessments for IA children.

Most international adoption clinics and many agencies advise parents of infants and toddlers to seek Early Intervention services, because it is an accepted fact that our children's early childhood deprivations usually lead to development delays. This is sound advice, and the services offered through these programs are readily available and generally provided at no cost or low cost. However, it is important to remember, that Early Intervention professionals are not usually experienced with children who have backgrounds of deprivation and neglect; parents may need to seek further consultation from private therapists, doctors and adoption professionals. Early Intervention programs in each state can be located through the National Early Childhood Center's website at www.netac.org/contact/ptccoord.asp.

Behavioral Differences

Many parents of IA children notice marked behavioral differences between their children and their non-adopted peers. In the best of pre-adoption scenarios, we are educated about the potential effects of early childhood deprivation on our children's emotional development. We gain a basic understanding of the effects of trauma, neglect, poor nutrition and even abuse on our child's developing brain. But educators do not have this perspective. Their experience with children from deprived backgrounds is usually very limited; in fact, ours may be the first internationally adopted child they have ever taught. They may pressure to fit our children into available pigeon holes.

Internationally adopted children do sometimes have ADHD. In fact some studies suggest that ADHD occurs at higher rates in adopted children than the general population. But often, behaviors that look a great deal like ADHD can be attributed to the child's inability to regulate their emotions and control their impulses due to their early childhood deprivation, and specifically to being traumatized. Parents often report schools pressuring them to identify ADHD as a possible issue and medications as a possible solution, because it is an issue with which the school is familiar. But for IA children, hyper-vigilance and inability to regulate their emotions can often be the real issues at hand. Next to their placement into our homes, going to school can represent the biggest change in our children's lives, triggering a variety of emotional responses and subsequent behaviors.

Often the behaviors our children exhibit in the classroom, whether they appear as withdrawal and shyness or impulsivity and hyperactivity, are anxiety-based. Because most educators have little to no training in the effects of childhood trauma, they may not recognize this or even see the triggers of the behaviors until incidents occur. Many teachers report that a totally compliant, easy-going IA child one day just 'exploded' or 'melted down' for no apparent reason. This is a good indication that something happened to trigger the child's anxiety. And many parents report that their children are often able to hold it together in the classroom all day, only to melt down upon returning home or to suffer stomachaches, headaches, or other anxiety-related issues.

Sometimes the child who appears overly active and aggressive may be repeatedly triggered with the classrooms behavior modification program. ("One more outburst Joey and you're going to be on the red light.") Children with PTSD and early childhood trauma hear this reminder (teachers sometimes call them 'cues') as a threat and their anxiety is triggered, so they act out more. Deborah Gray, author of Attaching in Adoption explains it this way, *"When children flood with anxiety, their ability to tell about what is happening inside of them is diminished. Sometimes they become aggressive, responding to all of the flight and fight energy that anxiety brings. They are the children who need the most structure given in the most nurturing manner. Instead, they often get the least nurture, with school systems using a tough, harsh approach. Traumatized children need a calm, consistent and nurturing approach in order to learn best. They do much better with a teacher who knows them well and can see when they start to get anxious. The teacher can often intervene with support before the child becomes aggressive."*

Sharing Information with the School

Parents are often reluctant to share a child's complete adoption story with the teacher, as they don't want their child labeled as 'bad' or 'different', or to be pitied in any way. These are valid concerns, but for behavioral issues in the classroom, it is important that teachers understand how the anxiety, fear, grief, and anger from IA children's early lives can impact their school experience. It is important that the educators, like the parents, recognize the anxiety in the child and the seemingly innocuous ways that these emotions are triggered. Many parents report that their child is immediately more successful when the teachers and parents collaborate on some easy interventions to increase the child's feeling of structure and safety. These simple tools can often help these children when their anxiety is heightened:

- Give the child a picture of mom to carry in their wallet.
- Encourage the child to go to a quiet corner to regain their composure.
- Teach the child to do deep breathing exercises.

Be Proactive: Communicate to Protect Yourself

The other major issue related to the child's behavior is his level of attachment to his parents. Children with unhealthy attachment or Reactive Attachment Disorder (RAD) will often exhibit overt behavioral problems that disrupt the classroom, or subtle, covert behaviors that may not get noticed by the teachers. Sometimes, the teachers will find the parents and their therapeutic parenting techniques to be strange and perhaps excessively hostile or harsh. The child may go to school and tell the teacher that the parent is doing something the teacher perceives as punitive or abusive. Or the child may relate some previous abuse they've received in their past lives to the teacher, who attributes it to the current parent. These are all reasons that parents should work closely with teachers to keep lines of communication open. One of the best tools for this is email. Families in this situation have also found it beneficial to enlist the help of their child's therapist, if appropriate, to meet with the teacher and discuss the child's disorder and the basis for the parenting techniques and interventions being used.

Language Development

Many internationally adopted children arrive with some degree of fluency in their native language. Parents often agonize over what to do to make the language transition go smoothly, and whether or not to help the child retain their native tongue. It is important to note that our children are not bilingual in the same way that children of immigrants are bilingual. Our children are immersed into the language of our homes and often do not come to us with 'healthy' language development in their native language. Studies have shown that many IA children acquire their new language more in a 'substitution' manner instead of adding the language to a primary one (like immigrant children). [See **Language** chapter pages 81-112]

This difference in language acquisition has a huge potential impact at school. Many school systems place newly adopted international children in ESL (English as Second Language) classes along side other non-English speakers. IA children simply don't have the same language scaffolding, and may fall behind in learning and act out because they simply don't understand.

Language is one of the major media used to learn in a school setting. Children who do not have a good grasp on context-based language (which for our children may lag behind becoming conversationally fluent) will struggle in the classroom. Additionally, many IA children have auditory processing difficulties and other speech or language impairments. Parents or teachers who believe that the child is still acquiring our language, and has the tools to progress normally once the language is acquired, might fail to identify that these learning difficulties exist. Traditional speech therapy and speech evaluations focus on vocabulary acquisition, fluency and articulation. Since IA children often come from both sensory and emotionally deprived situations, many of our children's language issues reflect true processing disorders and language impairments more than traditional bilingual issues.

Parents also report that **(Central) Auditory Processing Disorder [(C)APD]**, which is

Tell the Teacher!

As adoptive parents, we are our children's advocate and must help them broker adoption issues with other trusted carers, such as teachers. In particular, teachers need a steer from us on classroom issues that look familiar to them–but in adopted children may signify something else.

Experts are now beginning to understand the underpinnings of behavioral problems. In class, children who act out are getting a better understanding now that research shows that some kids simply (via genetics or background) are more vulnerable to learning difficulties and behavioral problems. Our adopted children may fall into this vulnerable class. Research is now starting to illuminate how orphanage life can seriously affect our children–and that may show in classroom life.

Early malnutrition can so severely deprive a child's brain that ordinary capacity to learn is hampered. Trauma can affect a child's capacity to store information, and may cause the child to act loudly in a way suggesting that s/he can control the environment. Birth language loss and the switch to the language of the adopted country may result in delays–when it comes to reading to learn.

What do we do?

Many experts and adoptive parents, who are also teachers, suggest that we appraise the school, and keep an open loop with class teachers. This isn't about presentations about adoption or birth culture or even diversity to school or class. It's about a factual summary of where current research on adoption, its issues and the classroom ability and activity of our child intersect.

Doing this means that before our school system logs our kid as ADHD, or with other learning difficulties that simply pigeon hole, we ask them to consider what other drivers there may be to our kid's acting out in class. It means that a kid who is lagging is given benefit of the thought that orphanage life may have caused some of the problems–and the child is given appropriate, funded, school district help.

We need to be aware of the issues if we are to tell the teachers. Advocacy for our kids means that we ourselves must always be proactive and learning.

~ By Sheena Macrae

Identifying Learning Problems in Adopted Children
www.schwablearning.org/articles.asp?r=689

often linked to sensory integration disorder and lack of stimulation and early deprivation, has been diagnosed as part of a child's speech delay, often years after the adoption.

Adoption and Cultural Issues

A discussion of international adoptees in school would not be complete if it did not address how transcultural and adoption issues are handled in the classroom. As adoptive parents, we often forget that teachers may not be 'adoption competent' and may not realize assignments that seem innocuous to them, like the ubiquitous family tree assignment, are causes of major anxiety and discomfort for adopted children. Mother's and Father's Day assignments, requests for baby pictures and birth data, and the inevitable genetics and sex education for older children are all laden with extra emotion for the adopted child. There's also the misusage of adoption language, illustrated by the class that participates in an 'adopt-a-highway' program or that 'adopts' a hamster as the classroom pet.

Knowing that these assignments and situations may be problematic, the proactive parent can offer teachers suggestions and resources for replacement ideas that are more appropriate. *Adoption and the Schools: Resources for Parents and Teachers* by Nancy Ng and Lansing Woods is a book with numerous suggestions for family tree assignments and for solutions to other adoption-sensitive issues in the classroom.

Cultural and racial issues can be a bit more subtle and sometimes much more difficult to deal with. Being prepared for the basic "Why don't you look like your mom?" is just the tip of the iceberg.

Imagine my shock and confusion when the teacher said she was giving my child 'credit' for 'Black English'—my Haitian-born daughter, adopted at 2 from a French-speaking land! I was uncertain about how to respond to their obvious ignorance about my daughter's speech, language and cultural issues.

Parents can be proactive in positive ways by volunteering to present culture and traditions to the classroom. But parents should be equally proactive when it is necessary to confront individuals' biases with regard to race, culture, and adoption—whether the individual is a student, a teacher, or district staff, or even if the bias exists within systems and procedures. Some parents and school administrators have a tendency to downplay any individual act of bias or prejudice instead of confronting it directly. This can be detrimental because silence sends a message of acceptance. Discussing your child's racial differences and the differences between your family and those not formed through adoption is important at each stage of your child's development. Addressing these issues before and as they occur, not only teaches your child how to handle biases he will inevitably face, but also shows your child the deep respect you have for him and his culture.

Age Appropriate Placement – A Good Idea?

Especially for families adopting older children, determining what grade level to place the child in can be a major decision. Conflicting opinions abound, and schools often have no-retention policies in place that force children into classes with children their same chronological age. While in many cases there are social and emotional benefits to being with children of the same chronological age, parents of IA children who are behind in their emotional development often find that initially placing a child in a class of younger children, with the appropriate academic supports, may be the answer. Younger children (those in early elementary) often respond well to being placed in a classroom where the children are on the same emotional level. Parents report that children who are placed in multi-age classrooms often fare even better, because they have a variety of ages to use as models for their socialization.

Convincing school systems to do things differently for your IA child is perhaps the most difficult part of dealing with the schools. Educators don't necessarily have the experience or answers for your child's unique issues. They also don't have the established systems and programs in place for dealing with the child's lagging emotional development, trauma, and behavioral issues, and language acquisition differences. But, some of our children will qualify for and benefit from special education services.

The Special Education Maze

(Note: all information about special education applies generically to special education within the public school system in the United States. Each state has variations on how the law is applied, so please research your state and local school system's programs. The information below does not apply to private schools or to those outside of the US)

All American children, regardless of their origin, are eligible, through the public school system for 'a free, appropriate, public education' (FAPE). This means that children with identifiable disabilities can receive special services and individualized educational programs tailored to their needs. The law is clear on what is generally referred to as 'special education'. How to access these services is not always as clear.

In July 2005 the updated **Individuals with Disabilities Education Act (IDEA 2004)** went into effect, replacing IDEA 97. This is the law governing most of the special education services in the USA. In addition to the IDEA 2004, **Section 504** of the Rehabilitation Act of 1973 and the **Americans with Disabilities Act (ADA)** of 1990 also apply to special education services. Through IDEA, federal financial assistance is provided to states, and ultimately to local school systems, for providing special education and related services to eligible children with disabilities. Section C of IDEA also provides for children younger than school age to receive services as preschoolers with disabilities. Infants and toddlers with developmental delays in cognitive development, physical development, communication, social and emotional development or other adaptive behaviors are eligible for services under the IDEA as well. These services are generally provided through programs called **Early Intervention** in most states. Local school systems usually take over the responsibilities of providing services for children ages three to twenty-one.

IDEA 2004 includes two concepts that impact our children. The first is FAPE; a student is entitled to receive 'free, appropriate, public education'. *"In a nutshell, FAPE is an individualized educational program that is designed to meet the child's unique needs and from which the child receives educational benefit." (Wrightslaw)*

The second is that each child's education must be provided in the **least restrictive environment (LRE)**. *"LRE means that, to the maximum extent appropriate, school districts must educate students with disabilities in the regular classroom with appropriate aids and supports, referred to as 'supplementary aids and services,' along with their nondisabled peers in the school they would attend if not disabled, unless a student's individualized education program (IEP) requires some other arrangement." (Wrightslaw)*

School Helps with Regulation and Control

I think school adds structure and routine, which many of our adopted children require to feel grounded and in control.

My kids are home with me, out of school, for a long summer. We are busy–keeping up with where school led! School at home, but with lots of time for play together and pretending which they enjoy.

However, I have already realized it that they miss the structure that the school day brings to their lives. They both enjoy their school. My oldest especially thrives in that environment. At home, they are a little out of whack. Of course, we could make a home environment more structured and I am sure they would get used to whatever it is. But for them the structure helps with self-regulation. They keep it together at school. It is routine. It is consistent and they like it.

Without school, we experience issues with self-regulation. My youngest, with has sensory issues, backslides into totally disorganized sensory behaviour. Areas I thought were over the hump have resurfaced again with a vengeance. Now I know that many kids get bored and are ready to go back to school well before summer is over. I see that, but for my kids it's deeper. Their inability to hold it is more about routine and structure. They need school because it makes them feel in control.

~ Tia Marsh, adoptive mom

Entering the Maze

Step 1. Identification. To enter the special education maze, a child needs to be identified as needing services. Many young IA children are referred to the Early Intervention program within their state, through which they are qualified as developmentally delayed and eligible to receive services such as speech therapy, occupational therapy and physical therapy. Depending on the child's progress, by age three they may be referred directly into the special education preschool services administered by the local school system and then on to the special education programs for school-aged children, being evaluated along each step of the way.

Children coming to this country at an older age or those who are not eligible through the Early Intervention program can be referred for evaluation by the parents, teachers or anyone else involved with the child. Schools are not required by law to evaluate a child based on a parent's request. However, most will and if the parent's request is not honored, the parent will be notified in writing as to why the child was not referred for evaluation. If a child is denied evaluation, the system provides for a way for the parents to formally disagree with this. Parents are encouraged to ask their school system for a copy of parent and student rights to understand the specific procedures and systems in their state and local district.

When a child is referred for evaluation the first step is referred to as identification. Most schools convene what is referred to as an SST (student study team). The team includes the child's teacher, principal or administrator, school psychologist or counselor, a special educator and you, the parent(s). There may also be others involved, depending on the areas of concern, such as speech and language professionals or occupational therapists. The SST will review the child's performance and reasons for concern, and will look to the parent to provide background information on the child's early development. Many parents are reluctant to share information about the child's early childhood and adoption, but need to realize that school evaluators must have the pertinent information about the child's history and the parents' concerns to understand the situation. Teachers will bring their observations and any interventions they have attempted in the classroom as well. The SST will decide if it's appropriate to try new academic or behavioral modification for a period of time in the general education classroom before further evaluation. After a period of time the SST will reconvene and determine if the child should be evaluated for special education services.

Step 2. *Evaluation.* Internationally adopted children referred for evaluation should receive a full assessment, which includes testing by the psychologist, special education teacher, speech-language professional, and others. You are an active part of the evaluation team and must sign off on any evaluations to be conducted; so advocating for a full assessment, since our children's issues are complex, is always a good idea. You will be asked both about your child's history and your observations about your child. Share any independent evaluations or observations by doctors or therapists that you think are valid assessments of your child's areas of concern.

The law is clear that the evaluations must be administered in a child's native language and must not discriminate based on race or culture. While this law protects immigrants and other non-English speakers, it often clouds the issues with IA children. Parents need to understand as much as possible about how their child is acquiring the English language and assist the school evaluation team in determining what may actually be a disability vs. a cultural or language difference or lag. Parents should question the types of evaluations given to their children and discuss the appropriate tools with the testing professionals. If evaluators employed within the school system are not qualified to perform the types of specific tests a child needs, independent evaluators outside of the school system must be employed at the school's expense. Parents of IA children have often been successful in having the school bring in experts in international adoption to conduct neuropsychological testing and specialized language testing to determine the child's educational issues.

The evaluation results are then used to determine the child's eligibility for special education and related services.

Step 3. *Eligibility.* To qualify, children must be identified as falling into one of thirteen categories. These categories are: autism, deafness, deaf-blindness, hearing impairments, mental retardation, multiple disabilities, orthopedic impairments, other health impairments, serious emotional disturbances, specific learning disabilities, speech or language impairments, traumatic brain injury, and visual impairments. The evaluations must have shown a discrepancy between the child's ability and their actual performance for the child to be eligible. It is extremely difficult to determine whether many of our children's issues are related to their limited opportunities to learn, or their acquisition of a new language, or if they are actual disabilities. Sensory deprivation concerns also further cloud the issue.

It's in the eligibility step that 'labeling' of the child occurs. Parents are often dismayed by the process of labeling our children and quite frankly, many IA children do not fit neatly into any of the special education exceptionality categories. However, to receive services, parents must understand that an exceptionality must be assigned. Since parents are active participants in this process, educating yourself on the exceptionality categories will allow you to assist in deciding which category best reflects your child's current functioning.

Step 4. Developing an IEP. An Individualized Educational Plan (IEP) is developed and updated annually for every child receiving special education services across the country. If your child is determined to be eligible for special education, an IEP meeting will be scheduled and you, the parents, will be notified. It is critical that you attend all IEP meetings and reviews. During this meeting (which will always involve at least your child's classroom teacher; a special education teacher or general education teacher if the classroom teacher is spec ed; an administrator; and you), the child's present level of performance will be summarized, specific educational and behavior goals will be defined, placement will be determined, and the types and amount of services the child will be receiving will be documented. From the IEP meeting the plan will be written that will define the goals for the child and the responsibilities of the various providers for carrying out the IEP. The IEP also defines how the progress is measured. Parents must give consent by signing the IEP and have the right to disagree with any portion of the IEP.

Step 5. Progress Reports, IEP Reviews, and Re-evaluations. Each school district handles reports differently. Parents should inquire about how they will be informed of the child's progress on IEP goals. These reporting schedules and methods are often established at the IEP meeting. At least once a year (or more often if parents or the school request it) the IEP is reviewed and revised. By law, your child will be re-evaluated every three years to determine if he continues to be a 'child with a disability' as defined by the IDEA and what the educational needs of your child are.

Section 504 Plans

When a child doesn't qualify for special education services under the IDEA, she may qualify under Section 504 of the Rehabilitation Act. Section 504 allows for a broader definition of disability than the one offered under the special education umbrella, but it does not enjoy the same federal funding as the IDEA. Therefore, schools may draw up a 504 plan for a child who is viewed to have temporary issues or who has more atypical or borderline issues. *"To be eligible for protections under Section 504, the child must have a physical or mental impairment. This impairment must substantially limit at least one major life activity. Major life activities include walking, seeing, hearing, speaking, breathing, learning, reading, writing, performing math calculations, working, caring for oneself, and performing manual tasks. The key is whether the child has an 'impairment' that 'substantially limits . . . one or more . . . major life activities.'" (Wrightslaw)*

The 504 plan usually provides for specific accommodations within a general classroom setting to address the child's particular areas of concern. 504 Plans are less regulated by federal law; instead the local school systems develop and enforce their own policies and procedures. Consequently, the use of 504 plans varies from state to state and school district to school district.

Many parents report that 504 plans have been 'just right' in giving their developmentally delayed child the classroom accommodations she needed to be successful, without the special education label or bureaucracy of establishing and maintaining an IEP. However, 504 plans do not give a child the same legal protection that they would have under IDEA 2004 (which also encompasses and surpasses what 504 plans have to offer). Define and research what your child needs in a classroom to be successful, and know which program will best ensure that success.

The Special Education Dance: Negotiation and Compromise

The IDEA 2004 establishes a multitude of regulations for the protection of children needing special services to receive an appropriate education. There are whole processes and frameworks for handling the various steps when parents disagree with the educators. It is important to know the rules and procedures. But it is equally important to understand the nuances and the way these rules are applied and sometimes misapplied.

As the parent, you have the right to disagree with evaluations, with denial of services, with proposed goals, proposed

The No Child Left Behind Act

This gives parents another resource for choice and 'quality control' over their child's public school education. Signed into effect in 2002 the NCLB Act requires and encourages educational reform and parent participation. Partial list of NCLB facts:

Accountability: NCLB holds schools and school districts accountable for results. Schools are responsible for making sure your child is learning.

School District Report Cards: NCLB gives parents report cards so they can see which schools in their district are succeeding and why. With this information, NCLB gives parents, community leaders, teachers, principals, and elected leaders the information they need to improve schools.

Public School Choice: NCLB may let you transfer your child to another public school if the state says that your child's school is 'in need of improvement.' Your school district may pay for transportation for your child. Contact your child's school district to find out if your child has this opportunity.

Extra Help with Learning: NCLB may also provide free tutoring and extra help with schoolwork if the state says your child's school has been 'in need of improvement' for at least 2 years. This extra help is often referred to as Supplemental Educational Services. Contact your child's school district to find out if your child qualifies.

Parental Involvement: NCLB requires schools to develop ways to get parents more involved in their child's education and in improving the school. Contact your child's school to find out how you can get involved.

~US Department of Education, www.ed.gov

Mama Bear Wisdom

"What's the one thing you wish you'd known as a parent advocate dealing with the schools, that you know now?"

1. **I am the professional when it comes to my child.** "I finally realized that no teacher, principal, counselor or other educational professional knew or understood my child's issues better than me. I am the expert on my child and I need to bring my expertise to the table every time I communicate with the school."

2. **Efforts to work together instead of fighting will almost always accomplish more**. "I went to the school prepared to fight and demand what we needed. I wish I had known that instead of going in prepared for battle, my most important function would be to research and study so that I could provide the school staff with the information they needed. Don't assume that they don't want to help your child."

3. **Document everything.** "If your child has special needs, sit down with the staff before the child starts school to identify the needs and make a plan (in writing). I wish I had been more proactive from the start."

4. **Polite, but firm, always works better.** "Advocate for your child, but do so in a cooperative manner. You will get a reputation as a 'squeaky wheel,' and that is not a bad thing."

5. **Don't assume that the teacher and others who interact with your child know about your child's issues.** "The teacher said she had no idea my daughter was adopted, much less had a history of trauma. There was really no way the teacher could have predicted my daughter's reaction without that information. This next school year I'll start by communicating closely with all the necessary staff about my child's needs."

6. **Know the regulations and don't assume the teacher does.** "I wish I had known how little the special ed departments know about special ed." Especially in smaller school districts or those with low numbers of children requiring special services, the teachers may not fully understand the procedures or regulations and how they apply. Knowing them yourself is always a good idea.

~ contributions from Julie Beem's Parent Advocate Group

placements and many other details. You have the right to seek independent evaluations, mediation and due process hearings if compromises cannot be reached. You may also file complaints directly with the state education agency. All of this is spelled out in the parents' rights information that the school provides.

But, as my grandmother was fond of saying, "You catch more flies with honey than with vinegar." And this is definitely as true in the special education dance as it is with international adoption. In the heat of the disagreement, you may want to reflect on the overall goal – to get your child the most appropriate education possible so that she can flourish. It is easy to get defensive and hostile when a school doesn't seem to understand your children's unique needs. Or it may be tempting to give up on the system entirely, because the bureaucracy of it all seems so overwhelming. Many parents turn to private schools or homeschooling out of frustration with the public school system. This is a viable option for some, but private schools are not mandated to provide the same types of special education services that are required from the public school systems, so many do not have the same resources as the public systems.

One of the nuances that must be recognized is that special education costs money. You don't have to sit through very many IEP meetings before you realize that some of the suggestions being made are made because they are less costly to the school system than other decisions. Administrators are under incredible financial pressures to keep costs down and minimize specialized personnel. In some areas, qualified teachers and specialists are in short supply. But that doesn't lessen the school's obligation to providing our children with a free, appropriate education. So, actively advocating for your child's specific individual needs, despite these factors, is necessary. But getting angry when they mention the financial aspect or declare "that's not the way we do it" usually serves no purpose. Just firmly and politely insisting that your child's individual plan meet her needs usually accomplishes much more.

Make the Teacher a Part of the Team

When reduced to the basic level, education is about a teacher reaching a student. And when you find the teacher (in whatever type of system) who is able to reach your child, you have hit the jackpot. So, it is important to know the system and the rules, but it is more important to open the lines of communication and establish relationships with the teachers working with your child:

- Talk to them and listen to them
- Attempt to understand and appreciate their perspective on your child
- Share what works at home and what you've learned
- Ask their opinions
- Send adoption-related materials to the classroom, if the teacher is open to the idea
- Work together on behalf of your child, and share in both the trials and the successes

There are many truly dedicated teachers out there. And many are often amazed and very pleased with parents who show interest, understanding, and appreciation of their situation. You will know that you're doing the special education dance correctly when teachers, specialists and parents encircle your child to encourage progress and to provide the best learning atmosphere possible.

What Parents Should Know about IEPs and IEP Meetings:

- Parents (and other participants) must be notified in writing at least 10 days prior to the IEP meeting that the meeting is scheduled.

- Parents are allowed to bring other people to the IEP meeting. Check with your state to see if advanced notification is required. Parents often find it useful to bring a parent advocate along with them. Parent advocates (paid or volunteer) are available in each state and are generally parents of children who have received special education and have become advocates because they understand the procedures, jargon, and regulations. Parents can locate advocates through their state's Parent Training Institute (PTI). Sometimes parents bring therapists or other professionals who have been working with their child as well.

- Taking notes or tape recording the meeting is a great idea. Someone on the IEP team will be taking official notes during the meeting, but it's always a good idea to take notes yourself. Often couples will attend the IEP meeting together and one will take notes.

- Don't be afraid to ask questions. The world of special education has more jargon and acronyms than the world of international adoption. If the rest of the team is talking about something you don't understand, ask for it to be explained. Keep asking until it is explained to your satisfaction.

- You should receive a copy of Students and Parents' Rights. If a written copy of your rights and all the appeal procedures has not been given to you prior to the IEP meeting, one should be provided during the meeting. If not, ask for it–it contains information you need to know.

- Exceptionality does not drive Placement. Determining which category a child falls into in order to receive special education services does not determine where a child will be placed (such as general education or special education classroom). There are numerous placement options that are considered during the IEP meeting and the overriding goal is to place the child in the least restrictive environment (LRE) where he will be successful. Parents should be active decision-makers in determining the right placement for their child, and should understand that even if a particular school doesn't have the type of placement your child needs, the school district is still obligated to provide it at no cost.

- For the IEP to be implemented, parents must sign their consent. For a school system to enact or change an IEP without the parent's signature requires a great deal of administrative and legal effort on their part. Therefore, the bottom line is that getting parents to agree to what is in the IEP is the easiest way for the IEP meeting to conclude. Knowing that you, the parent, have the right to say "no" to goals, placement or other details is empowering. As the parent member of the team, you are more than an active participant because your signature of approval is needed. But this places a special responsibility on you to understand the IEP process and to work with the team to reach solutions and resolve any differences of opinion.

- You should receive a copy of the IEP. If you don't get one–ask for it! It's important to file this and all other correspondence regarding your child's education in an accessible place. Some parents use large 3-ring binders divided by school year to house all related paperwork.

- Parents also have the right to review their child's official file, which contains copies of evaluations, notes from meetings and from observers, as well as past and present IEPs. Check with your local district for procedures on accessing this file. Parents have the right to obtain copies of anything within that file, but must be prepared to pay for the copies if asked.

~Julie Beem

Advocating for our Children: Becoming a Mama Bear

Somewhere in the experience of finding the right school situation for our children, we wake up and realize that we have become a true advocate: protective, proactive and tenacious. We have become a Mama Bear (even if we're not female!) It was not an instantaneous transformation, or even an intentional one, but one that happened over time, as the situations presented themselves and we rose to the challenges.

I treasure a Barbie® doll given to me by another Mama Bear, a doll that symbolizes who we've really become. We have named this doll 'Advocate Barbie' and she's best described as such: *"This Barbie sports tall boots for wading through all the bureaucracy and paperwork. Her accessories include a PDA full of specialists' names and numbers; a notebook full of medical reports, psychological evaluations and IEPs; a secret stash of chocolate bars ; and a cell phone with her child's teacher, the therapist, and other advocate moms. Her mini-van has a worn driver's seat from all the trips to school, therapies, and doctor appointments!"*

Hopefully, you're not alone in your transformation to an Advocate Parent. It is vital for your own well being that you find a community of support. The patience and tenacity we acquired as parents-in-waiting for our international bundles of joy are the same skills that can transform us into Advocate Parents for our IA children's educational needs.

~ Julie Beem is a 'mom three ways' (step, bio, and adoptive mom). She holds a B.S. in Secondary Education and an MBA in Marketing Communications. Julie is Director of Marketing & Fundraising for the Attachment Disorder Network, a national support group for adoptive and foster families raising traumatized children www.radzebra.org

Survey of Children Adopted from Eastern Europe
The Need for Special School Services
By Harriet McCarthy

For over fourteen years, children adopted from eastern European orphanages have been arriving in steadily increasing numbers to the West. As their numbers increase, so do their needs for special educational services.

- How likely is it that the child you have adopted or are going to adopt will need considerable help getting an appropriate education?
- Are adoption agencies and social workers adequately preparing families for what may lie ahead during school years, and are they supporting their families with post-adoption information and continuing education?
- Do school systems understand the cognitive and emotional dynamics of children who have previously lived in orphanages?

The Eastern European Adoption Coalition (EEAC) survey (to see the complete survey details, visit www.eeadopt.org and click on 'survey results') confirms what the experts have been saying for many years. These children are at high risk for difficulties in school. It's up to us as their parents to see that their educational needs are recognized early and that they receive the support services they need. In what follows below, we have been able to extrapolate from first findings from our Survey of Children Adopted from Eastern Europe to suggest areas that need highlighting.

Focus on Needed Educational Services

The specific focus of this first report from our Survey is on emotional and developmental issues. How do they relate to a post-institutionalized child's need for educational support services? When post-institutionalized children enter a classroom, teachers see them as members of culturally enriched families, whose parents are well-educated, predominantly middle-class, Caucasians. This is not the usual presentation of students needing special education services. Most of the time, teachers do not anticipate problems, and many students slip through the cracks of our educational system for too long during their early elementary years. Frustrated parents who recognize their children's challenges may have to fight for school resources and support. This creates tremendous stress for everyone in the family.

Developmental Delays, Language, and Learning Disabilities

Dr. Dana Johnson from the University of Minnesota is engaged in the largest longitudinal study of post-institutional children in the United States. He advises that all orphanage children will have developmental delays and are therefore at high risk. Sadly, there is an almost universal lack of understanding among adopting parents about what developmental delays really are, how profound they can be for the entire family, and how often they occur with other neurological impairment. Many educators and adopting parents think that most developmentally delayed children coming from institutions will just 'catch up' if given enough time and a nurturing environment. They miss the fact that developmental delays are a very strong indication of the need for future educational support.

The term 'developmental delay' is misleadingly innocuous, but daunting in its actual implications. It indicates delayed physical, emotional, and cognitive development - not simply a very small child who is immature and underweight. The physicians who evaluate video and medical referrals and/or examine a great many children coming from orphanages estimate that one month of cognitive and physical growth is lost for every three months spent in an orphanage (Aronson; Albers, 1997, Johnson, 2000). These delays are caused by missed critical milestones in development - foundational 'holes', so to speak. Because these deficits are foundational, and since all higher learning is supported by a child's developmental foundation, it is impossible to ignore missed milestones hoping they won't be critical later on. Missing information needs to be identified, appropriate therapies need to be implemented, and consistent support needs to be given to both the child and the parent. A developing child's progress is directly proportional to

1) health, nutrition and prenatal care of birth mother
2) length of term and birth weight
3) availability of dependable primary caretaker and nurture
4) level of physical stimulation, emotional interaction, and language exposure
    during the first critical and formative years of life.

For orphanage children, age at placement, and duration of time spent in an institution are also critical factors. If all the environmental variables are positive, and if a child spends a minimum amount of time in an orphanage environment and has strong survival skills, that child will have a decent chance of closing any developmental gaps. Regrettably, that seldom happens. Birth weights of orphaned children are frequently low due to prematurity, maternal illness, drug addiction or alcohol abuse, malnutrition or smoking. Primary caretakers don't exist in orphanages. Appropriate levels of sensory stimulation are missing. Language delays and language processing problems affect large numbers of children in institutions (Groza, Ileana, Irwin). Many children live inside an orphanage for years before they are adopted. If developmental delays are present at the time of the adoption, and if early intervention isn't implemented immediately, precious time will be lost that may never be recovered.

How do such children cope at school? Every day at school comes another large serving of instruction. Normally developing children can keep pace with the new material pouring in because they draw upon their early learning, vocabulary, and culture. Post-institutionalized children who come with delays have a terrible time assimilating this rapid flow (Glennen, 2002). They have incomplete early learning, weak language skills, and lack of cultural exposure. These children don't possess fundamental tools for academic success. During the early school years, their symptoms may include fine and gross motor problems, trouble with learning their alphabet, inability to grasp basic math facts, or difficulty remembering or retelling a simple story. They may have general memory problems or appear inattentive, hyperactive, sensory seeking or sensory defensive. They may start to exhibit a lack of phonemic awareness or have problems with sound/symbol associations. These are all clues that intervention is required immediately. This is the time for parents to start advocating for their children and asking for special services in the form of IEP's (Individualized Education Plans).

Some children may be functioning well enough that an hour in the Resource Room will suffice (this is called an Inclusion Plan). Some will need more help and may be placed in a special self-contained classroom for learning or emotionally disabled children. Still others may need a full-time aide and/or assistive technology to help them through the school day. Many children will need tutoring in addition to special services while in school (Barth, Gibbs, Siebenaler, Health and Human Services).

Dr. Boris Gindis suggests that there is an additional negative component to language delays in Post-Institutionalized children. He has labeled it "cumulative cognitive deficit", and says that it "refers to a downward trend in the measured intelligence or scholastic achievement of culturally/socially disadvantaged children relative to age appropriate societal norms and expectations." It leads to low self-esteem, lack of interest with and frustration with most of the work schools concentrate lesson plans upon. What is the cumulative deficit founded upon? Lack of care and lack of caregivers. Babies learn very quickly that if they cry, no one will come (Groza, Ileana, Irwin). Older children lack the opportunity to talk to adults. The end result is an eerie silence inside these institutions. It's a symptom of dramatic and damaging changes that have occurred inside the brains of traumatized and neglected children–changes that lead to disruptions in normal sensory processing (Perry). Lack of exposure to meaningful language, lack of nurture and individual attention compounded with the stress of being totally powerless over their surroundings causes neurological changes which may have negative effects on a child's life in his new adoptive family and at school.

Language professionals who work with post-institutionalized children have recommended that older adoptees be tested in their primary language as soon as they arrive. Clear articulation does not guarantee successful language development and, in fact, may mask a significant problem. The appropriate therapy if a child is language delayed takes place with a Speech/Language Pathologist. America's state run Early Intervention Programs may help if a child is young enough to qualify, but it's likely that complete success may need the assistance of a private Speech/language professional. Parents should bear in mind that this kind of language therapy will be of significant duration and expense. Language delays have the greatest detrimental impact on future learning potential because learning requires reading and "reading relies on the brain circuits already in place for language" (Shaywitz, 2003). See **Language** Chapter pages 81-112 (articles by Glennen, Pollock and Sebba). Researchers believe that when children in orphanages displayed clear deficits in social and cognitive functioning compared to same age children attending kindergarten, then these children would have learning difficulties in the future. " (Groza, Ileana, Irwin)

The Effects of Prolonged Stress

Alcohol-Related Neurological Disorder.   There is another important issue to bear in mind when considering causes for learning disabilities over and above inherited traits or the effects of early deprivation, and that is Alcohol-Related Neurological or Neurodevelopmental Disabilities (ARND). ARND as a diagnosis is difficult to nail down without documented maternal history or alcohol abuse, but a significant number of participants answered that their children had been diagnosed with ARND, and more said they suspected ARNDs. Please see **Challenges** Chapter and FASD Articles.

Post Traumatic Stress. Boris Gindis says that cumulative cognitive deficit may occur concurrently with or as one of the consequences of Post-Traumatic Stress Disorder (PTSD) and Attachment Disorder (Gindis). This is the most frequently found psychiatric diagnoses in our Survey. Post traumatic stress within our community of families has also been described as 'adoption stress', a term which can be applied to all parties in an adoption. "The reality is, when we look closely at adoption, we realize that traumatic stress is pervasive–often impacting several, if not all, of the parties involved. Unfortunately, this traumatic stress, 'adoption stress', is generally not recognized and its impact is misunderstood." (www.adoptiondoctors.com). Misunderstanding of the effects of post-traumatic stress is perhaps deepest at the school level. Children's responses to stressful situations differ from that of adults. What may appear to be hyperactivity, inattention, oppositional behaviors, cognitive difficulties, memory issues, or hyper vigilance could, in fact, be the symptoms of adoption stress and/or PTSD (Post Traumatic Stress Disorder).

Chronically stressful situations may lead to deficits in learning (www.futureofchildren.org). PTSD is unique in that it is an initial emotional response that can, if stress is sustained for a long enough period, cause temporary or permanent neurological damage to the sufferer (Perry). So, PTSD is the bridge between the emotional and neurological issues of the typical post-institutionalized child. Our Survey reports a large number of neurological and emotional problems. It thus becomes clear that it is impossible to ignore the consequences of this key piece. There is much excellent material available that can help parents and teachers better understand the underlying causes of stress and ensuing neurological changes stemming from life in an institution. Adopting or teaching a child who has experienced such stress and not realizing how

The Eastern European Adoption Coalition

When reports began coming out of Romania in the late 1980's about the grim conditions of children in orphanages, willing parents from around the world rushed to that country and began adopting children. In the early 1990's, Russia and countries from the former Soviet Republics opened their borders to adopting parents. Some of these parents sought support through electronic mailing lists and Internet websites. The A-PARENT-RUSS mailing list and its associated website were established in 1995 to help provide this support. In order to expand this support to parents adopting children from other Eastern European countries and to post-adoptive parents, the Eastern European Adoption Coalition (EEAC) was formed in 1998. EEAC currently operates 20 mailing lists and its website at;
www.eeadopt.org.

Over the years that children from orphanages have been joining families, EEAC's mission has been to educate adoptive parents concerned about the effects of post-institutionalized life. Its approach has always been that a well-prepared adoptive parent will be a more satisfied and capable parent. The ultimate goal of all its work has been the welfare of both the children and parents who have created these new families.

Further support and advice can be found on Harriet McCarthy's website:
www.postadoptinfo.org

much of an impact it will have does a huge disservice to all concerned. Dr. Bruce Perry at www.ChildTraumaAcademy.com and Dr. Boris Gindis at www.BGCenter.com have on-line training programs available for parents and teachers.

Institutionally Caused AD/HD Symptoms.   Dr. Jerri Jenista writes "Adopted children's problems seemed to be related mostly to language difficulty and attention deficit and hyperactivity." This is corroborated by an extremely thorough and in-depth study by Kreppner, O'Connor and Rutter,of the English and Romanian Adoptees Study Team who have identified a strong correlation between inattention/overactivity and former life in an orphanage. Current research by this same group is addressing the question of "whether the inattentiveness and overactivity observed in the present sample is different in type from that which is normally defined as AD/HD in clinical practice." Our Survey suggests that the underlying cause of what appears to be AD/HD in these children may actually be specific neurological damage which manifests itself as inattention and overactivity but is unique in composition to each child. If that is proven to be true, it would partially explain why many of these children react so adversely to traditional pharmaceutical, behavioral, and therapeutic approaches to AD/HD. We may be seeing inattention and hyperactivity when, in fact, these behaviors are the results of the sustained stress of life in an institution. It's clear from our reported data that this AD/HD-like presentation exists in a very large number of those we surveyed.

Where Do We Go From Here?

The current thinking among many adoption professionals and adopting parents is that we should prepare for the worst and hope for the best when we adopt post-institutionalized children. A far more realistic approach might be to expect and thoroughly prepare for the worst so that we are ready for the realities of parenting these children, many of whom will need therapy and special services throughout their school years. The 'best' may be nothing like you expected. Realistic expectations correlate with overall satisfaction.

How likely is it that the child you have adopted or are going to adopt will need considerable help getting an appropriate education?
Enough post-institutional children and their families are struggling with academics to necessitate the preparation and planning it takes to be an effective therapeutic parent and an educational advocate for your child. Evaluations for developmental delays, sensory and processing disorders, language delays, and disabilities are just as important as general pediatric appointments, re-immunizations, and dental interventions. Parents bringing children home who are young enough to qualify for Early Intervention should be applying to this program whether or not they believe their child has an immediate need. Agencies should insist this be a requirement, right along with the post-placement reports and visits from social workers.

Are adoption agencies and social workers adequately preparing their families for what may lie ahead during school years?
At the present time, good pre-adoption education is falling far short of need. It's not that agencies aren't trying to cover all relevant pre and post-adoption topics, but they need to

re-evaluate the programs to insure that truly relevant issues are being presented. Post-adoption preparation and support is sorely lacking. In light of the fact that children have died tragically in families overwhelmed with post-adoption stress, the creation of dependable, comprehensive, and accessible support departments should be the number one priority for every single agency placing children from orphanages. Continuing education programs need to be developed and encouraged.

Do school systems understand the cognitive and emotional dynamics of children who have previously been living in institutions?

Every person who becomes involved with a post-institutionalized child needs to be cognizant of the significant possibility that child will need assistive services in school. A thorough understanding of the psychological and emotional changes that happen to institutionalized children is necessary to do that. Parents need to learn their rights and how to effectively advocate for their child's appropriate education. Teachers and school administrations must become more aware of the complexity of teaching these children. The only way any of this will ever be accomplished is by us as responsible parents pushing for change.

~ Harriet McCarthy is a free-lance writer whose primary interest is the challenging issues of post-institutionalized children. Over the past ten years she has been involved with support groups for parents of Eastern European adopted children and children with learning differences. She has managed the Eastern European Adoption Coalition's PEP-List (Parent Education and Preparedness) since its inception in 1998 and is a current EEAC Board Member. In 2003, she received the Congressional Angels in Adoption award.

Home Schooling
A Positive Alternative for Post-institutionalized Kids
By Dawn Mercer

Home Schooling and Us.
We were already home schooling when we adopted our daughter. We fell into it with our first child. We had friends who didn't send their kids to school so we knew about the option and had seen it work. Our son was also an extremely active little boy who we could see having difficulty in a traditional schooling environment. We gave home education a trial of six months and have continued home educating ever since. We follow a pretty relaxed approach, basic maths, reading and Chinese and take advantage of other opportunities that arise. We tape TV programs for the kids, they participate in sporting activities, 'after school' classes like Drama, drawing lessons with Nanna, Chinese tutoring etc–lots of reading and visits to the library fill our days. There never seems to be enough time to do everything that we want and I often wonder how on earth I would ever get anything done if the kids were at school.

Advantages for our Family.
Our son was seven and a half when we adopted our daughter, aged 3 years 4 months. That he didn't go to school made it easy for him to come with us to China to adopt his sister. We spent three weeks travelling around before we adopted our daughter and the travel was a learning experience for all of us! After we returned home our priority was our daughter, she needed lots of intensive attachment parenting and intensive care and we let everything else drop in order to give this to her. We figured that for our son five weeks in China was the equivalent of 6 months to a year in school in terms of the amount of learning that happened and so we weren't stressed about doing anything formal in terms of learning. That he was around a lot was a great thing for the two kids. They really got to know one another well and spent a lot of time playing. Our daughter learnt a huge amount from her brother including language, how to play with Lego and so on- but probably the most important thing she learnt was how children interact with their parents. There was lots of watching going on!

If our daughter had started school, she would have done so a bit over a year ago. I guess that school presents extra challenges for many adopted children, at least those who have a history of neglect or abuse or changes in primary caregiver beyond infancy. I know that this would have been the case for our daughter and I'm really glad that that was something that we didn't have to stress about.

Home Schooling and the Post-Institutionalized Child.
There are a number of ways in which I think that school would have been difficult for or detrimental to our daughter. Our daughter doesn't cope with competition very well. If she feels deficient in any way she'll fall apart. For a long time our daughter also stressed out if she was expected to do anything in the presence of other children (performance anxiety). At home neither of these things are an issue, we can just go at our own pace and there is no need for her to perform at a particular level. I also feel that she still benefits from lots of contact with me and our current level of contact would not be possible if she were at

school. In addition, not being at school removes to a large degree the peer pressure to act a certain way. I think that this is significant because having been home just three and half years a lot of our daughter's needs are closer in some areas to what an average three year old needs than to what you would expect from an almost seven year old.

Our daughter is always looking around for the 'right' way to do things–a survival mechanism, I think, but when her needs conflict with the expected norm this can be problematic. Such conflicts are easier to manage outside of school.

It has taken our daughter a long time to overcome the trauma of placement and to developmentally catch up. Until recently, she really did not have the head room for learning things like math or reading. This would have been a real problem if she had started school and been expected to learn at the same pace as other kids. However, since she was not at school this was not an issue and she's just started learning how to read. She will be able to grow as a confident learner at her own pace and with no stigma attached to learning at a different rate to other children.

Finally, because we can essentially do what we want as far as our children's education goes we have the freedom to choose to spend time on things that are important to us, like learning Chinese which has become a family activity rather than something that just the kids do.

I anticipate that neither of the kids will ever go to school. I really value the ability we have as home educators to just go with the flow and move at the rate and in the way that best fits our children. I'll end with a summary of what I believe are the pros and cons of home schooling for adopted children:

How do children learn when they are Home Schooled?

There are as many different ways of pursuing home education as there are families who home school. I've found that it can be difficult for those outside of the home school community to understand how it all works (kind of like adoption really). Just about everyone comes from a background of having been in school and so we don't have the personal experience of alternatives to draw upon.

Home educators can do everything from 'school at home', (a highly structured approach with lots of similarities to traditional schooling) to natural learning/unschooling (learning through experience), to classical approach (following the trivium), to 'Charlotte Mason' (learning via living books) to unit studies (all subjects via study of different topics) etc etc. Many families use a combination of approaches and usually the way a family home educates changes over time (often from more structured to less).

Many families use real-life as the 'school room'. Counting, drawing, reading and writing use real situations–working out the cost of food in the supermarket, entering artistic competitions, writing letters. Play scaffolds learning–bath-time teaches science, with volume (jugs and water) and states (once bubbles disperse they can't be recreated). Libraries and museums are important, the garden a nature paradise, with the children logging what they find. Home schooling families often combine to hire experts to teach the children music, dance, art etc. A child's current 'interest' can also be used to underpin all aspects of their learning parents get adept at using, for example, princesses and pirates to educate across the board!

Home Schooling Resources

Home-School Legal Defense Association – State by State advice on laws, and legislation, curricula, issues, and support organizations
www.hslda.org/laws/default.asp

Dumbing Us Down: The Hidden Curriculum of Compulsory Schooling
by John Taylor Gatto

Teach Your Own: The John Holt Book of Homeschooling
by John Holt

Home Learning Year by Year: How to Design a Homeschool Curriculum from Preschool Through High School
by Rebecca Rupp

The Well-Trained Mind: A Guide to Classical Education at Home
by Jessie Wise, Susan Wise Bauer

The Teenage Liberation Handbook: How to Quit School and Get a Real Life and Education
by Grace Llewellyn

Deschooling Society
By Ivan Illich

Homeschooling Our Children, Unschooling Ourselves
By Alison McKee

The Potential Advantages:

• Opportunity for parents to spend lots of time with their child.
• Opportunity to focus on learning things that are of most value to a particular child/family.
• Opportunity to value different aspects of learning.
• Opportunity to tailor learning to the child's needs.
• Reduction in pressure (or the ability to have greater control over pressure) to be performing at age level in all sorts of areas.
• If in a non-racially diverse area it may be easier to facilitate racially diverse relationships/role models.

The Potential Disadvantages:

• If in an area with racially diverse schools it may be easier to facilitate racially diverse friendships/role models therein.
• The primary caregiver can get very tired!
• It can be difficult to arrange work around schooling.
• In some instances special services that are available in schools may not be available to home educators.

Home schooling can be a very compelling way to educate our post-institutionalised children, giving them much needed time to bond with us. Parents need however to remain advocates for their children in acquiring the specialist services that some of our adopted children need. These services are often more easily accessed within the formal school setting, and parents should check out local education departments for policy on providing home educated children with such services.

~Dawn Mercer, Bio and Adoptive Mom

School

W.I.S.E. Up
Tools to Empower Your Children
By Ellen Singer, LCSW-C

Where Did You Find Him? How Much Did She Cost?

It is the rare adoptive parent who has not encountered questions or been subject to comments about adoption. In same race adoptions, it will be by people who know your family was formed by adoption; in trans-racial adoption, it may come from complete strangers. Well-meaning people may ask to be friendly, out of curiosity, or to express their own opinions. They often are not aware that they are inappropriate. Questions and comments like,

"Oh, is your husband Asian?"

"Do you know anything about her real parents?"

"Are they really brothers?"

"Oh, those children are sooo lucky!"

"She's so adorable, how could anyone give her away!"

New parents especially, often describe a range of emotions, feeling 'caught off guard', angry, violated, scared, sad, and helpless, to name a few. They may feel compelled to respond and share aspects of their story that later they regret, may display anger that is uncharacteristic and unsettling, or just generally feel miserable. When this happens in front of children old enough to be aware of what is happening, parents may feel especially concerned about the impact of the questions on them, as well as what they are demonstrating to their children with their reactions.

Most parents quickly learn that in order to minimize and cope more effectively with the distress these experiences can bring, they must prepare themselves for the questions, and develop responses that they can comfortably use. Adopted children and teens are likely to encounter these very same experiences (with their peers, friends, classmates, and neighbors) when they are alone, and not under the 'protection' of parents. It is imperative that they too get help and guidance. It is clear that many adults and children often do not have accurate information about adoption, and do not realize the impact of their insensitive questions on adoptive families

School-aged children in particular are typically frightened by the thought of adoption. The idea that one can 'lose' parents is very scary, and is often the subject of many childhood stories and fairy tales. The 'mother' replacement is usually wicked (Cinderella, for example). Children also receive the same misinformation from television, movies and the media that their parents do, and are subject to popular adoption myths:

Do birth mothers sell their babies on the Internet?

Are some adopted children kidnapped from their birth parents?

If you're not biologically related, you don't really have the same bond.

Driven by fears and understandable curiosity, with little understanding of what adoption means, non-adopted children may relate to the adoptee as they might to a child with a physical disability, by asking questions and making comments to accentuate how they are different (to distance themselves from the adoptee in order to comfort themselves that this could never happen to them). Knowing that they are delving into private territory, non-adopted children are likely to ask these questions when other adults are not around.

Are You From Asia? Are Your Real Parents Still There?

These questions are just samples of the of the ones hundreds of children seen at The Center for Adoption Support and Education, Inc. (C.A.S.E.) report getting from their peers. Add to that list questions like,

"Why were you adopted?"

"Can I see a picture of your first mother?"

"Why don't you look like your mother/father?"

and comments meant to tease like, *"Chinese Eyes!"*

These questions, coming from the 'outside', often mirror the exact questions that adopted children are asking themselves 'inside' as they struggle to make sense of what being adopted means about them and to them. These experiences create an added burden of emotional vulnerability.

Empowering Our Children

In response to this predicament, The W.I.S.E. Up! Program was developed to empower children to respond to questions and comments made about adoption. It is a powerful tool used at C.A.S.E and world-wide, and taught to children in groups; in individual and family therapy; at camps for adopted children; programs run by adoptive parent support groups; and parent workshops. *The W.I.S.E. Up! Powerbook*, written by Marilyn Schoettle, an educator and former Director of Publications and Education at C.A.S.E, was created so that parents could teach this empowering tool to their children. A complete facilitator's guide for teaching the program to parents is also available.

What Is W.I.S.E. Up!

Before children can think about responding to questions and comments about adoption, the W.I.S.E. Up! Program first helps children realize that they are smarter than their peers–or WISER about adoption because of their experience of growing up in an adoptive family. They can take on the role of 'expert'. This understanding helps introduce and prepare adopted children for the distinct likelihood that they will get asked questions and helps explain the reasons why.   Second, children learn to think about who is asking the question/making the comment and evaluate the motivation behind the question. Is the question coming from a trusted friend, from the class bully, from a teacher? Is the person just curious or trying to tease? Third, children learn to identify how they feel about:

1) The person asking the question/making the comment.
2) When the question is being asked–are they alone with their friend, or in front of other classmates; what kind of mood are they in–how are they feeling at that particular moment.
3) How they feel about the question/comment. Children are usually shown a list of possible feelings including–sad, angry, surprised, shy, happy, etc. Obviously there may not be much time for long reflection in this process, but it may be just long enough to help children 'slow down' and take charge, in preparation for the next empowering step which is to actively choose how to respond..

Power To Control The Situation

In the final and fourth step, children learn that they have four possible options for responding – each represented by the four letters of W.I.S.E., a tool designed for quick memorization:

> **W = WALK AWAY**, or ignore what you hear.
> **I = IT'S PRIVATE** I do not have to share information with anyone, and I can say that appropriately, even to adults.
> **S = SHARE SOMETHING** about my adoption story, but I can think carefully about what I want to let others know.
> **E = EDUCATE OTHERS** about adoption in general, for example, I can talk about how adoption works today, successful adoptees, inaccurate information in the media, etc. I know a lot about it.

With practice, children can choose between W, I, S, or E without hesitation. In the process of embracing the W.I.S.E. Up! Program into their lives, they sometimes find themselves able to 'take the sting out' by laughing at the question. They also learn to anticipate additional questions that may come when they respond with S or E. The W.I.S.E. Up! tool can turn a challenging moment into an experience of confidence and success.

Parents and therapists who use this program with children also find that it is often a door opener that can lead to other important discussions/conversations about adoption.

~ By Ellen Singer, LCSW-C, Program Specialist, Education and Publications,
The Center for Adoption Support and Education, Inc.
For more information, visit C.A.S.E. at www.adoptionsupport.org

Adoption Goes to Kindergarten
How Stuffed Bears and Rabbits Expand a Child's View
By Shanti Fry

The parents in my daughter Victoria's kindergarten class were invited to visit and talk about what they do for a living. My husband and I are both bankers. He got banking and I got adoption. Victoria knows of my work as president of the New England chapter of Families with Children from China. She and I decided that I should talk about it to her class. Which also meant talking about adoption.

I first thought of the adoption talk as a version of Chinese New Year. The kids in Victoria's class love Chinese New Year. They love the painted glass lantern I light with a candle and the not-culturally-correct fortune cookies, as well as the red envelopes (with real money!) and a rousing reading of the Mulan legend. We had established our place alongside Hanukkah and Kwanzaa.

When it was too late to back out, I considered the potential for inflicting life-long trauma on my daughter and the other adopted children. One adoptive parent had expressed 'deep concern' about my adoption talk to the teacher. I began to measure the distance between the culture of FCC families and that of the other adoptive families in Victoria's class—at least one of whom hadn't revealed their child's adoption to the teacher last year.

"Victoria," I asked my daughter in that upbeat but carefully neutral Mommy tone adoption experts advise, "What would you like me to say about adoption?" she said she wanted all the kids in her class to get FCC tee-shirts because the parent who talked about his job managing the local Hyatt hotel had distributed Hyatt tee-shirts. "Would you like to talk about being adopted?" I persisted. "You do it, Mommy. You are the boss of FCC. You talk good about adoption." Victoria replied.

I talk good about adoption to infertility patients, waiting parents, and adoptive parents. In other words, adults. Not kids. Not kids who are a little shaky on the specifics of how anyone joins a family (read: the birds and the bees). Not kids whose parents are quiet on the subject of adoption. It struck me that I didn't even know how Victoria had internalized our talks about adoption. A few days passed. "Do you think the kids in your class understand adoption?" I asked Victoria. "No" she said, "P.J. doesn't know about it." "How would you explain it?" I asked. "A baby grows in one mummy's tummy and gets growed up by another mummy," said Victoria. Bingo. You can waltz around it but that is the hard truth of adoption. A baby grows in one mummy's tummy and gets growed by another mummy. Once I accepted that I had to start with that stark fact, the rest of the talk fell into place.

Victoria and I arrived in the classroom with two boxes full of props. The one lesson I could carry over from Chinese New Year is that kids like props. Victoria sat beside me.

What is Adoption?
I posed the question, "What is adoption?" for the children and then answered it with Victoria's definition. The kids wanted to tell me about adopted kids they knew. No other adopted children identified himself or herself as adopted. The only other adoptive mother I know lingered in the back of the class to listen. There were a few other parents. Were

some of them adoptive parents?

I took out five stuffed bears. On one side of the rug I placed three perfectly matched 'Pooh' bears: a daddy bear, a mommy bear in a dress, and a little tiny baby bear. I called them the birth family. "Everyone in the whole world has a birth family, no matter what," I explained. "Every single child has a birth mother and a birth father from the moment that child is born." On the other side I sat two mismatched bears. These bears were the adoptive daddy and the adoptive mommy. These bears looked older and more worn, not the visually satisfying matched set of the birth bears.

"Sometimes a birth family can't keep a baby." I decided to give no explanation unless the kids asked. Many times we don't know why birth parents made this decision. Even with a reason, the decision retains some mystery. "This is very sad for the whole birth family." I paused and put the baby in the middle of the rug, away from the birth parents. "Some people want a baby but can't grow one. This is also sad for people. People love babies and children and want to have them in their family."

The class was completely quiet. All eyes were riveted on the baby bear alone in the middle of the rug. No one was smiling. "Babies and children need parents to grow up. They need parents to love them and teach them. Babies and children who don't have families are sad. How should we help the baby bear?" The kid waved their hands and half rose from the floor. "Give the baby bear to the parents who don't have a baby!!!" said the children in a cascade of voices. "This is adoption," I said, placing the baby bear with the mismatched bears. The class heaved a collective sigh of relief.

"Real adoption requires more work," I said as I continued taking out a stuffed female rabbit with a fetching straw hat and a stuffed male rabbit. "This lady rabbit is the orphanage rabbit who looks after the baby bear, while the gentleman rabbit looks for new parents for the baby. "What do you think the gentleman rabbit asks people before he lets them adopt a baby?" I asked. This question was beyond the 5-year-olds because their parents are just their parents. They don't ask what qualifies a person to be a parent.

"The gentleman rabbit asks many questions: Will the new parents love the baby bear? Are they nice to other children? Do they have enough room for a child? Where will the child go to school? Do they have enough food for a child? The gentleman rabbit has to tell the lady rabbit that the parents will be good parents before the lady rabbit will let the child leave the orphanage."

"What happens when the new family comes together?" Everyone looked alert when I posed this question. "It's scary," I said, "because everyone is a stranger the first time they meet. Very little babies are usually fine but older babies and children have to get used to new parents, a new language, and new food. When everyone is used to each other, the fun of being a family begins."

"Lots of good people work together to find a new family for a child," I said touching each of the animals. "A chain of goodness stretched half way around the world to bring Victoria and Julia home to us."

We moved to the next topic which, for my daughter's benefit, might as well be called how to make every kid think being adopted in China is an unbelievable treat that comes with more holidays, more presents, and more trips.

"In our house we celebrate two countries," I said unfurling large American and Chinese flags. The Chinese flag was the surprise of my prop boxes. One teacher snapped a photo. The kids liked the vibrant red color. We touched on Chinese New Year and other festivals, Chinese dance class, and Chinese language class. The crowning prop, however, was the album of Victoria's recent trip to China with a photo of her atop a live camel at the Great Wall. The album also contained photos of Victoria visiting her orphanage. As we talked about seeing other children waiting for adoptive families in the orphanage (just like the baby bear), the children reached for the album.

Expanding a Child's View

Although the children I spoke to were 5 and 6 years old, I wanted to go beyond defining adoption as another flavor of family. "Sometimes children are in need. They might need a new family or they might need something else. In our family we work to send money back to Chinese orphanages through the Red Envelope campaign. These are items we sell to help the children in the orphanages. We buy the orphanages washers and dryers. We help the children get foster mothers to care for them before their permanent families arrive." I showed the class a picture of Victoria's foster mother with Victoria as a baby. The kids scrambled to look at the photos.

"Sometimes we see problems in life, but we can work hard to solve those problems." I touched the baby bear and the new parents. "We can find happiness by solving our problems. Every year we celebrate our children's adoption anniversaries with candles," I said. I whipped out two large candles and a small candle. I placed one large candle before the birth bears and the other before the adoptive bears. I lit the birth bears' candle. Victoria lit the small candle from the birth bears' candle and then lit the adoptive bears' candle.

"The flame represents the love that a child receives from the birth family. It's part of her being and is carried to the adoptive family. People who do adoptions have big hearts, because there are so many people to love: the birth mother and father, the adoptive mother and father, and the children, and lots of other people in both families."

This was the conclusion of the talk. Victoria and I passed out FCC tee-shirts to each child and teacher. One of the teachers then sat beside Victoria and me and helped field the children's questions. Later that evening, I asked Victoria what she though about the talk. "Good," she said and skipped off, seeming somehow lighter. "The tee-shirts were good, too."

~ Shanti Fry is the president of Families with Children-New England and FCC-NE's Foundation for Chinese Orphanages, which cosponsors the FCC Orphanage Appeal. She has two daughters from Hubei Province

This article first appeared in Families with Children from China-New England's newsletter, China Connection, and is reprinted with the permission of FCC-NE.

~It Worked for Me!~
Confronting Questions with Classroom Education

My daughter is Haitian and I am not. It was blatantly obvious that we are not biologically connected and E. took some hard questions from her Kindergarten classmates last year. E. knows her story. She is nearly 7 years old, home almost 3 years, so
she remembers her life in Haiti. It took a therapy session for her to reveal that the
kids in her class were saying things like, "That's not your real mom. Where is your
real mom?" and other comments that kids usually make when they are too young to
be sensitive. I contacted her teacher immediately and asked if I could come in for
about 25 minutes to answer questions and share a book called, *How I Was Adopted*
by Joanna Cole. I sent the book in and the teacher looked at it. We both agreed that
the two pages devoted to how babies grow in uteruses and stuff would not be
shared, but the rest of the book is awesome.

I read the book, showed them where Haiti is on the map, and gently answered as
many questions as they had, teaching them terms like Birthmother and Birth family,
and Forever mom and Forever family. E. was thrilled to be able to share part of her
story. She sat next to me, and talked about being hungry and she spoke of her mis-
treatment at the hands of a worker. She talked about being scared and wanting a
family to love her. I was so proud of her. Attachment therapy has made this all
possible!

One question that a little boy had, "Why didn't her Birthmom love her?", was hard
for E. to hear, but we have had these tough talks and she knows her Birthmom did
everything she could to keep her alive; E. was left in a hospital because she was very
sick (nearly dead) from starvation. We have presented this to E. as an act of desperate
love on the part of her birthmother and it works for her.

The biggest thing was the 'real' mom stuff. I asked what a real mom was, and then I
asked one rather vocal little boy (yes, the one who seemed to antagonize E. the
most) if he lived with his 'real' mom. When he said yes, I asked him what his real
mom does. He listed several things. I asked E. if I did this, if I did that, and as it
turned out, I did everything his 'real' mom did, so guess what? I'm her real mom,
too!

Our classroom presentation really made the rest of her year easier.
                    ~ By Jackie Rancourt, smother to4 children–2 bio sons (18 and 12)
                              and 2 daughters adopted from Haiti

School Daze: Hang on for the Ride!
THE B.E.L.T. Model for Talking about Family Formation in the Classroom
By Deb Capone

Issues surrounding family formation (including adoption), need to be addressed systemically and with the same vigor that other 'isms' receive. When we look at adoption through the broader prism of family formation and recognize that ancillary issues like inclusion and diversity are also part of the mix, we sometimes feel that we are living our lives on a roller coaster. Then we realize that all parenting, regardless of how your family was formed, is a roller coaster ride. And that as advocates for our children it is our job and responsibility to help our educators address family formation in a way that works for everyone, and especially for the children.

Our goal as parents and as advocates for our children is to make it easy for everyone to be successful in addressing adoption and family formation. We need to find ways to keep an incredibly complex subject straightforward, fun and inclusive. To do this, the As Simple As That Foundation has developed a simple model to help. We have found through talks and presentations with hundreds of parents and teachers that the model works! The model is built around an acronym: B.E.L.T. As you prepare to work with schools and teachers keep these 'belt notches' in mind as your build your strategy and presentations. Then fasten your seat BELT and hang on for the ride!

The B.E.L.T. Model for talking about family formation in schools:

Bias: we all have them and they come in all shapes and sizes. They are positive and negative as well as conscious and unconscious and they shape how we all see the world. Make sure that you evaluate and 'own' your biases and help your teachers do the same. Plan your meetings and presentation with them in mind. Resolve not to pass your biases to your children and expect teachers to do the same.

Environment: Help your teachers build environments that support all kinds of families, family formation, races, cultures, and choices. Make sure that your children's classrooms are stocked with books you think are great and that really resonate with the children. A well-thought out approach to a multi-cultural environment will speak louder and longer than any presentation you do in school. And remember what is missing is sometimes more revealing than what is included. Try to focus on inclusion.

Language: Before you can insist on positive adoption language you have to alert people that there is such a thing as positive adoption language. You might want to take it a step further and incorporate 'people-first' language, i.e., people who are blind, not blind people, and sitting like a pretzel and not an Indian. Remember that you must also 'walk the walk and talk the talk' at home.

Teach the Teachers: Teachers truly want all children in their classrooms to be successful and don't knowingly give assignments that put some children at a disadvantage. Give your teacher the resources he/she needs to make assignment broad enough that all students can succeed. And remember, if your teacher doesn't know about your child's needs he/she cannot shape assignments appropriately. As you build your conversations and presentations using the BELT model, you should also consider the following 'do's':

Do focus on inclusion: First, you will get better response from the teachers if they can do things that include more students, and second, you are less likely to make any individual child-especially your own-feel singled out. Make your presentation on adoption within the broader topic of family formation.

Do the work for them: Donate books to the classroom, offer to come in and read; prepare a 15-30 minute talk and present it yourself, offer to help 'decorate' the classroom with images and tools that reflect the diversity in the classroom, school, community and the world.

Do believe that teachers want every student to succeed: if you prepare material with that in mind, you will be more successful.

Do recognize that teachers are not trained in family formation: they are truly grateful when you can help and support their efforts in the classroom.

Do provide an appropriate amount of material: you can you can let the teacher know that you have a plethora of resources if they need more information, and leave it at that. Respect their time; most teachers are overwhelmed with classroom curriculum and have broader goals in mind.

Do provide suggestions for alternative and inclusive spins for problematic assignments like the family tree: your teachers simply may not know why certain assignments might be potentially angst-producing, or not know how to tweak them to reflect adoptive families.

Do check your own biases at the door: and understand that everyone has conscious and unconscious biases (both positive and negative).

Do consider your child's needs in the mix: your child may have strong feelings about being the center of attention. Be sensitive to your child's needs when preparing your presentations and talks in schools.

Do call in the experts when necessary: Not only are there plenty of written resources that are available, there are also many people in the community that are prepared to help you get the message across. You can find 'human' resources in the ranks of adoption social workers and adoption support groups.

Do have fun and enjoy the process: Roller coasters can be scary, but they are fun, too. Enjoy the ride! It is a great lesson for your children!

And don't forget to fasten your seat belt!

~By Deb Capone, Founder of As Simple As That Foundation and adoptive mom

When School Projects Deal with Adoption
"If You Know Where You (are going to) Fall,
You Would Spread Some Straw" ~ Russian Proverb
By Nancy Ng for FAIR

As the Boy Scouts have long advised, it is better to 'Be Prepared'. The task of every parent sending her child off to school is to be prepared for challenge without predicting failure. The parent who 'knows' that his little girl will be miserable when he drops her off at kindergarten's door is likely to have a clingy, unhappy daughter. Conversely, the mom who confidently tucks a smiley face note in her son's snack bag and matter-of-factly reminds him that she'll be waiting on the blacktop when the dismissal bell rings, will probably experience a more cheerful child.

Most parents have left their moms and/or dads to go to school and many, remembering the common annoyances of elementary school, are well prepared to help their kids weather phonics, bullies, and long division. But unless she herself was adopted, the ordinary parent might not recognize the additional challenges of the adopted child at school.

Like the wise Russians, adoptive parents may want to 'spread a bit of straw' around the following potential pitfalls:

Baby Pictures
From preschool through high school graduation, children may be asked to bring in a photo of themselves as babies. Many adopted children as well as many others may not be able to fulfill this assignment. Wise parents can encourage teachers to broaden the assignment when the purpose is understood.

Preschool- Kindergarten
Bring in a baby picture
Illustrate growth, change
Ask children to bring in a picture of themselves when they were younger and smaller. One child might bring one from his first birthday party, another from birth, one six months ago. Compare and contrast.

Kindergarten- Third Grade
VIP Day or Week
Get-to-know-you
This is your day (or week). You and the adults at home can work together on something that will tell us more about you. Children have brought their favorite books, some a soccer uniform and trophy, some a family picture, some a pet...

Any Age
Can you guess who this is?
Reasoning ability
Bring in a picture of yourself or someone we all know-- but make sure the picture won't be easily recognized. Describe that person using three clues; add one at a time until someone guesses correctly.

High school graduates
Baby photo slide show
Just for fun
All are welcome to submit photos from memory lane.

Family Trees

Perhaps the most dreaded of school assignments for those families touched by adoption is the ubiquitous Family Tree. Students may encounter versions of the Family Tree assignment many times during their academic careers, from pre-school through high school graduation. The very idea can raise issues of belonging, of relatedness, of difference, of divided loyalty, of confusion, and embarrassment–not only for the student; but for her birth and adopted siblings, for the children of adopted persons, for students in foster families and for all the adults who are part of these students' lives

Parents can help teachers design an assignment that can be done by all the students, if the purpose of the assignment is clearly understood. Generally preschool and kindergarten family trees are meant to emphasize caring relationships. It is not important that children illustrate genetic relationship but rather honor those who care for the child.

In **elementary school** the Tree might be used to help children understand their individual story; to introduce the concept of history; or, as a foundation block to begin the study of societal structure. Many variations are available to adoptive parents and teachers. It is important to present alternative assignments not as deviations from the norm but rather as valid variations on a theme.

Older elementary students may encounter a Family Tree assignment at a time when it is extremely important to them to 'fit in'. Wise parents need to tailor their response to the particular needs of their child and be willing to accept the child's choice to include or exclude birth family, to assume a culture not their own or to engage in a bit of fiction, as just that: the child's choice. As always it is far easier to discuss possible assignments with a child proactively and ahead of the actual assignment than to respond to a surprise project.

Middle and high school students may find a Family Tree assigned specifically for the purpose of the study of genetics. The assignment is educational whether or not the family studied is related to the student. It is not unusual, though, for the nature of the study itself to bring up issues and questions for the adopted student. Parents can welcome the opportunity to normalize the feelings of their teenager, to acknowledge grief and to open up a discussion which might otherwise be more difficult.

At any age, students are helped when parents and teachers evaluate the assignment with the following criteria:
- What is the educational objective of the assignment?
- From a developmental perspective, what does the student understand about the concept of family.
- Are there particular cultural implications for this assignment in this class, this community or this family?
- Is the assignment broad enough to allow all children to participate?

Student of the Week, I Am Special Day

Frequently teachers plan getting-to-know-you activities at the beginning of the school year or attempt to build self-esteem by affording every student with an opportunity to bring in and display mementoes, photos or family traditions in front of the whole class. An adopted child may feel embarrassed by the differences these opportunities point out,

School Presentation Guidelines

So, you have decided to take the plunge and do an adoption-related presentation in your child's classroom. Where do you begin? Why do you want to do it now? What does your child want? There are as many styles of classroom presentations as there are adoptive parent-child combos, but some guidelines are helpful.

- Gear the presentation to the ages of the children and your child understands of his story at this time. For example, preschoolers love music, food, motion, and being the center of attention. Most eighth graders love music, food and motion but would rather die then be the focus of parental attention in the classroom. So, most preschoolers would love a classroom celebration which included music and food from their birth
culture and an acting-out of their journey home to their families. Young teenagers want to fit in with their peers and often do not welcome parent presentations.

- Involve your child and respect his wishes. Kids, adopted or not, come in a variety of styles; some need to be gently encouraged and some need help to reign in their enthusiasm. It is wise to remember that the classroom is the child's turf and her adoption story is her personal story.

Some resources for parent and/or educator:

An Educator's Guide to Adoption
Institute for Adoption Information, Inc.
www.adoptioninformationinstitute.org
A 22-page booklet for parents to give to their child's classroom teacher to create a partnership on how to handle adoption in the classroom.

Adoption and the Schools
By Lansing Wood and Nancy Ng, FAIR available directly from EMK Press
www.emkpress.com

Children of Intercountry Adoptions in Schools: A Primer for Parents and Professionals
By Ruth Lynn Meese

S.A.F.E at School – A Manual for Teachers and Counselors
By the Center for Adoption Support and Education

S.A.F.E. at School presents five proactive strategies to help teachers and counselors create a positive adoption environment in school: Acceptance, Accuracy, Assignments, Assistance, and Advocacy. S.A.F.E. is a complete–but simple–tool for addressing the complex topic of adoption in any school.

especially if s/he was adopted as an older child. If the teacher encourages diversity and originality rather than competition, all students can fell comfortable being 'special'.

Autobiographies
Some adopted children love to tell the story of their lives; for some it is an impossible task. For many the assignment presents two negative possibilities: not telling the truth or revealing more than classmates need to know. Understanding the purpose of the assignment and encouraging the teacher to broaden the assignment to include biographies, a story about one particular incident in one's life or a favorite experience at school allows students to make respectful choices. As always, choice provides safety.

Confronting Genetics and Sex
Middle school science class may be the first time an adopted student confronts the reality of their genetic connection to birth parents. When a student is asked to trace a genetic marker such as red hair or brown eyes in his/her family s/he is presented with concrete implications of difference. Family life projects may include the care of a 'baby' in the guise of a sack of flour, a doll or an egg. Such assignments are certain to raise issues for a child whose birth parents couldn't care for him. Health and family life classes present the opportunity to increase awareness of adoption built families. It is almost always a mistake for parents of middle-schoolers to use their own adoption stories in the classroom, but generic information particularly if it normalizes the adoption experience can be helpful.

Parents who bring adoption education to any grade in school should heed this advice from experienced parents. See the resources on page 295 for some wonderful publications to help you get started.

Remember: most adopted students do fine in school; most encounter at least one assignment made more difficult because of their adoption. Kids end up reacting in sync with their parents; if moms and dads exude confidence that their child can handle the situation, children absorb that surety.

Act as you instruct your children: do your homework; plan ahead; cooperate rather than confront whenever possible; stand up for justice; have fun.

~Nancy Ng has nine children, eight of whom are adopted. She is a board member of FAIR (Families Adopting in Response), and editor of FAIR's magazine, and editor (with Lansing Wood) of the acclaimed book Adoption and the Schools. Nancy has a particular interest in special needs and multiculturalism. Nancy has a master's degree in marriage and family therapy and specializes in working with adoptive and foster families. She has served on the Governor's Adoption Policy Advisory Council in California and on the advisory board of Adoptive Families of America. She is a master trainer for Kinship Center's Adoption Clinical Training and is still learning from her children.

Repeating Kindergarten/First Grade or Moving Up:
What is Right for My Adopted Child?

So much of the answer to this question lies with a child's personality and emotional maturity. The Center for Adoption Support and Education (C.A.S.E) (www.adoptionsupport.org) lists several adoption-related developmental milestones that first-graders may experience:

- A six year old may realize that 'to be adopted one must be given away'.
- Their 'early positive feelings about adoption may turn to uncertainty'.
- Children may feel a 'sense of loss; grieving for birth parents'.

These big, confusing emotions may be present at a time that young children are learning to grapple with all-day school separation from a parent, and the introduction of serious academics. What can your child handle? How does she react to emotional stress? How does that impact what is being absorbed in the classroom?

Some important issues to consider:

- What is your school's policy on retaining a student? Would the school work with you once a joint decision was made, either way?
- If you decide to hold her back would she get differentiation in subjects she is particularly strong in? Would she be bored, or excited to conquer the material?
- If she advances to second grade with her peers, would she get extra help in the classroom or in private pull-out sessions in the subjects she is weak in?
- Does your daughter qualify in any area for a specialized 504 plan that requires the school to accommodate her specific learning needs? See page 258 for more information.
- Would your child feel a huge blow to her confidence and self-respect? Could your daughter transfer to another public or private school in your district that might be less demanding if she goes on to second grade, or less embarrassing for her if she feels badly about remaining in first?
- Have you considered home-schooling for a year?

Find out if your school is flexible. Figure out all of your possibilities and determine what would be acceptable to school administration. If they are not flexible and are not willing to work with you creatively for your daughter's success (academically and personally), then you might need to find her another learning environment.

Remember to consider your daughter's emotional level, and factor in adoption. Learning to cope with the lifelong issues of adoption is a positive skill, but an overload of academic and social situations can make a normal adoption transition more difficult. Make a list of pros, cons and options, and figure out the individual formula that works best for the 'whole' child.

~ By Jean MacLeod

Gifted Children, Adoption, and School

Giftedness is hereditary, and in an adopted child, it may unfold as a surprise. Typically, gifted children are very intense at a young age, often displaying traits of empathy, perfectionism, and advanced abstract reasoning. There are different levels on the giftedness spectrum: gifted, highly gifted, exceptionally gifted and profoundly gifted. Some children excel in one or two areas and some, who excel in both right and left brain activities, are considered 'globally gifted'. Giftedness is measured by an Intelligence Quotient (IQ) evaluation, where typical gifted IQ scores range from 130 to 180+. An assessment of traits that are common to gifted children is another, equally valid tool for parents and educators to utilize, particularly in very young children. It's important to understand that giftedness can co-exist with learning disabilities, which can be doubly frustrating for a child and for their classroom teacher. A gifted child is likely to experience asynchronous emotional, social and physical development, meaning a six year old gifted child could intellectually be twelve, and socially, at age four. Imagine how some of this plays out with the unique life experience of internationally adopted children:

- A gifted child of two or three understands and acutely feels what has happened to him through the process of being adopted, but has no context for what he has gone through. Without being able to verbalize his feelings he internalizes them, and may deduce his parents are to blame for choices that were out of his hands.
- A gifted child may have intense feelings but no acceptable outlet for them, which can produce tantrums, avoidance or sadness.
- An unusually young abstract thinker can 'logically' jump to the wrong conclusion when her thinking is older than her experience. One preschooler tearfully admitted that she thought her adoptive mother had stolen her from her birthmother... a fairly typical thought among adopted children, but not so typically spoken at age three.
- A gifted child can push themselves to compensate for post-institutional problems.

Gifted children tend to get the 'big picture' of a situation instantly, and can be taught to use coping skills at a young age. However, parents can expect to deal early with the extra layer of adoption with gifted, young children. Teaching these children coping skills is often accomplished through storms of emotion, or even through the hyper-sensitivity, hyper-vigilance, and anxieties of post-institutional behaviors. It helps to have a child IQ-tested so you can understand and define where the big feelings and frustrating outbursts are coming from. It is reassuring to know that giftedness can exacerbate almost all behaviors in a young child, and that the mystifying asynchronicity a parent witnesses is normal for many gifted girls and boys. Understanding helps a parent better deal with the challenges of giftedness, and fuels a mom or dad to become their child's advocate.

Some gifted children have difficulty in fitting into a 'one size fits all' school classroom or curriculum. Parents can help achieve a good fit for their son or daughter by being learning about the educational needs of gifted children, and the parallel emotional issues of adoption. It will be up to the parents to advocate for the best placement for their child, with the school administration:

Know your options, and do your homework. What programs are available in your school system and what is the district's philosophy on educating gifted children?

Understand exactly what your child requires, and what you are requesting. If your gifted child has special needs, learn about 504 Plans and Individualized Educational Plans (IEPs) before you call a meeting. Know your State and Federal mandates! (see www.wrightslaw.com)

Schedule a conference. Meet with the Principal, the Teacher, and the School Psychologist to respectfully discuss the best options for your child. Stress partnership; have a plan in mind, and map out how the school can best fill your child's educational needs.

Come prepared. Present the Principal and School Psychologist with a portfolio containing your child's IQ test scores, testing psychologist comments and teacher remarks. Some parents are wary of IQ tests for their children, but it can provide helpful, 'official' evidence that you are not just an over-involved mom or dad.

Be persistent. One Principal told a mother who was advocating for her child, "All children are gifted". "All children have special gifts" the mom replied. "But not all children have IQs of 165 and I need to know how the school is going to accommodate my child's classroom learning." Even in an accommodating school it is imperative to be proactive, to really map out a strategy, and to help implement the strategy in a positive manner.

Get involved. Plan on volunteering regularly in your child's classroom. It is an excellent vantage point for discerning success, failure, social difficulties and emotional maturity. Your child has a lot of issues on her or his plate: giftedness/asynchronous development, adoption, and possibly a trans-racial or trans-cultural adoptive family. An involved parent can help their child find a comfortable niche or outlet at home and at school.

Develop a Team. Most children benefit from a team approach from home and school. Develop good working relationships with administrators, staff and teachers, and be supportive of the school in general; you will stand a better chance of getting what you want for your child if you are a visible and helpful presence.

Gifted children desperately need attuned, common-sense parenting. They want a mom or dad who can help them fly, and who can help ground them by modeling organized, regulated behavior. Parents need to normalize the highs and lows of giftedness for their child, and teach their son or daughter the coping skills that will help bridge the child's intellect, emotions, academics and social life.
                                    ~ By Jean MacLeod

Recommended

Helping Gifted Children Soar: A Practical Guide for Parents and Teachers by Carol Ann Strip, Ph.D with Gretchen Hirsch

The Gifted Child's Survival Guide for Ages 10 & Under by Judy Galbraith, M.A

Empowering Gifted Minds: Educational Advocacy that Works By Barbara J. Gilman, M.S

Visual-Spatial Learners

Upside-Down Brilliance: The Visual-Spatial Learner By Dr. Linda Kreger Silverman

Raising Topsy-Turvy Kids: Successfully Parenting Your Visual-Spatial Child By Alexandra Shires Golon

Websites:

www.hoagiesgifted.org

www.gifted development.com

Bullying
A Real Problem/Some Real Solutions
By Sherryll Kraizer, PhD

Bullying is an integral part of our culture. It happens every day in classrooms, in bathrooms and hallways, on playgrounds and in the neighborhoods of all communities. It is insidious and it is hurtful. Children who are bullied, physically, emotionally or socially, are deprived of their right to go to school and to live in communities where they feel safe.

Being bullied is linked to depression and low self-esteem. Many adopted children suffer with these also – linked to loss, feelings of 'not being good enough' to remain with birth-family, and also feelings of being different to their (often white) adoptive parents. Some adopted children are vulnerable with regard to social skills, other with regard to language capacity. The baggage that being adopted brings these children means that they are open to becoming bullied or bullies. Some adopted children present as easy prey to classroom bullies, while others bully as a means of bolstering faltering esteem.

What can adoptive parents do to help things in the classroom change? Most adults easily remember a specific bullying incident from their past. If they were the victim, they remember the panic, the sick feeling, wondering why no one was helping. If they were the bully, they remember the feeling of power and perhaps the shame for what they did to others. Some were bystanders. They remember the anxiety of not wanting to be the next target and often guilt for failure to intervene, even though they didn't know how.

Is Bullying Really That Harmful?
Bullying is the deliberate and repeated infliction of harm on another person. It takes many forms. It may involve one child bullying another, a group of children against a single child or groups against other groups. Bullying includes many behaviors. Common forms of physical, verbal, emotional and social bullying are shown below:

Physical	Verbal	Emotional	Social Bullying
Hitting	Name-calling	Exclusion	Peer pressure
Pushing	Teasing	Rumors	Exclusion
Kicking	Belittling	Acting superior	Making fun of
Shoving	Making fun	Being mean	Taunting / Baiting
Pinching	Bad language	Not caring	Set up to get in trouble
Violence	Verbal Abuse	No conscience	Threats
Abusive	Mimicking	Thoughtlessness	Ganging up on someone
Destructive	Shouting	Gossip	Name-calling
Spitting	Taunting	Threatening	Pranks
Tripping	Cursing	Belittling	Internet harassment

Whether the bullying is direct or indirect, perpetrated by an individual or a group, the key component of bullying is that the physical or psychological intimidation occurs repeatedly over time and is designed to hurt. Young people who are bullied are more likely to be depressed, to feel isolated, anxious, to have low self-esteem and to think about suicide. Bullying, as most children know, starts early and it is devastating. And as we have seen, it impacts all the harder on adopted children with their intrinsic vulnerability as regards self-esteem, and damages these children all the more.

What Is the Role of Adults?

All forms of bullying are opportunities to teach children how to get along, how to be considerate of all people, and how to be part of a community or group. But, children do not learn to solve conflicts and get along with others naturally. They have to learn specific skills that will prevent and thwart problems with bullying. As soon as children are old enough to interact with others, they can learn not to be bullies and not to be targets. This includes giving them the words to express their feelings, skills to monitor and change their behavior, and conflict resolution strategies.

When preschoolers begin to call people names or use unkind words, we should intervene immediately and consistently. In kindergarten, children learn the power of exclusion. We begin to hear things like, "She's not my friend and she can't come to my party." Respond with, "You don't have to be friends with her today, but it's not all right to make her feel bad by telling her she can't come to your party."

In the early elementary grades, cliques and little groups develop which can be quite exclusionary and cruel. Children need to hear clearly from adults, "It's not all right to treat other people this way. How do you think she feels being told she can't play with you?" Kids don't have to play with everyone or even like everyone, but they can't be cruel by excluding others. Children who are not bullies or victims have a powerful role to play in shaping the behavior of other children. We need to teach these children to speak up on behalf of other children being bullied. "Don't treat her that way, it's not nice."

What Is Role-Play?

Role-play is the tool that turns theories about prevention into reality. It is the game parents and teachers can use to coach children to better life skills. It is the way to find out what children think about the social problems they encounter and how they actually handle them. It is the primary skill-builder for prevention of bullying. It's also a lot of fun!

Role-play is really just practice for life. It's a way of preparing for what we can anticipate. Everyone does it. If you are going to your child's school to discuss a significant problem with a teacher, you probably rehearse what you are going to say, or mentally practice how to approach the issue, thinking through how to respond if the teacher says this, or that. It is perhaps the most powerful way to prepare to be effective.

Learning to speak-up is also a skill learned by doing. When a child is able to say "Don't do that to me, I don't like it." in a tone of voice that is clear and assertive, while standing up tall and looking directly at the person, you will know that role-playing has worked.

Role Play
Some Good Ways To Respond To A Bully

It is helpful to have a range of statements, behaviors or actions in mind as children are role-playing. The following chart will help you get started.

Statements	Behaviors
"That wasn't nice."	Walk away
"Don't do that."	Join another group
"I'm going to tell if you do that again."	Laugh and leave
"That really hurts my feelings."	Ignore them
"That's not a very nice thing to say."	Act like you don't care
"Give that back or I'll tell the teacher."	Avoid the bully
Make a joke–"Whatever" "No kidding"	Get away and tell
"Leave me alone"	Ask a friend to help

Children should also develop action plans to get help. This might include:
• Go and tell a teacher.
• Tell a parent or another adult.
• If they are really afraid, run to someone who can help.

Practice, Practice, Practice
Role-play takes these concepts and makes them skills. Be sure to have fun putting an end to bullying with role-plays. Children love to role-play and will rapidly use it as a way to address other concerns they have. This is invaluable for parents and teachers. The "What if..." questions or scenarios kids suggest reflect their fears, concerns, anxieties and curiosities Children hear stories about things that have happened to other children, or they witness something in school or on the playground. They naturally think about what they would do. They want to role-play so they know how to handle a similar situation. By eliciting children's ideas through role-play, we discover how they think, how they solve problems, their concept of how the world and their social groups work, and what they know and don't know about solving interpersonal conflicts. Always look for the skills children are bringing to these problem-solving What if... scenarios and acknowledge them. These are the building blocks for all future skills.

Role-play scenarios are easy to create and modify according to the situation or the skills and needs of an individual child or group. Always keep the experience positive, empowering and fun! Remember that interpersonal skills are learned a little bit at a time, so each step a child takes in the direction of being a clear, powerful and assertive communicator is important.

How Do I Get Started?

Initiating role-play is as simple as asking a "What if..." question or responding to a child's "What if..." question. For example, you might begin with, "I heard that there was a problem in the lunchroom with one of the boys taking other kid's desserts. What would you do if that happened to you?" When the child begins to tell you, suggest, "Show me what you would do, I'll be the kid trying to take your dessert." Play it out. See what resources the child already has.

If the child isn't particularly effective, suggest you switch roles. The child is now the bully. You should model standing up straight, looking the bully in the eye and clearly saying. "Do not touch my lunch." Then change roles and let the child try it again. If he gets part way there, provide coaching. Whenever you role-play, remember, it is a process. You are learning what the child's skills are and helping to develop new ones. Avoid judging or making an issue over any part of the role-play or the value will be lost. Role-play is never a confrontation. It is an opportunity to share ideas, initiate discussion and learn new strategies.

The three key elements of role-play are:
1. **Speaking** – this includes deciding what you want to say and then saying it in an assertive manner, paying attention to tone of voice, volume, pitch, clarity, etc.
2. **Body language** – this includes posture, facial expressions, the distance between the people involved, use of hands, etc.
3. **Eye contact** – communication that is delivered face to face, eye to eye is more powerful.

Consistently combining all three of these elements takes time and practice. Children most often learn the skills one at a time and then integrate them. Practice and successive approximations is the key. Role-play teaches children how to communicate effectively and consistently so they can utilize the skills automatically.

Family Ethos

Perhaps your child isn't being bullied or isn't a bully, but children are very aware of it occurring. Ask any children from kindergarten through high school who is bullying whom. A teacher or parent may not know, but the children always know and they don't want to be next. They are also highly conflicted because they don't want to be marked as a 'tattle tale.' OK – let them become **advocates**. Children like to speak up for others!

Advocates are those children who are neither bullies nor targets and they have the most powerful role to play in shaping the behavior of other children. They tend to have better social and conflict management skills. They are more willing to assert themselves without being aggressive or confronting. They suggest compromises and alternate solutions. They tend to be more aware of people's feelings and are the children who can be most helpful in resolving disputes and assisting other children to get help. Very often adopted children who have proactive parents will have already been discussing the key elements of bullying (difference, weakness) with their parents, because adoptive parents are aware. Maybe they

What If a Child Wants To Disclose Bullying?

Children use "What if…" scenarios as a way to tell their parents and teachers things that have happened. It seems less like tattling to them and makes incidents easier to talk about. For example, "Mom, what would you say if some of my friends were making the little kids miss the bus and blaming it on someone else?" To follow up, you would want to explain that telling about a problem is not tattling and that you would like to help without making the situation worse. You might role-play your child talking to someone at the school, with or without you. Or decide together that this is a situation you should handle with the school directly. Always remember to thank your child for speaking up and for being an advocate for another child.

will have discussed the effects of difference and feelings of inability, loss and vulnerability.

Schools need a policy and an educational plan regarding bullying that targets the entire student body. It should include:

- A clear statement regarding bullying: that it is unacceptable.
- A plan for student and parent education about the policy.
- Adequate and active supervision, especially at times when students are moving about freely such as recess, class breaks, lunchtime and after school is dismissed.
- A policy of immediate and early intervention (always too early rather than too late).
- Training that makes every child an advocate for every other child.

We should scrutinize our schools for diversity and empathy for difference. And, we need to become advocates against bullying. If each of us is willing to speak up and to learn the skills to intervene effectively against bullying, this can no longer be a culture of meanness and violence.

~Sherryll Kraizer, PhD is the founder and director of the Coalition for Children

Some Additional resources:

Bullying At School: What We Know and What We Can Do, D. Olweus

Take A Stand Prevention of Bullying and Interpersonal Violence Program **www.safechild.org/bullies.htm**

The Safe Child Program, **www.safechild.org/program.htm**

Women's Educational Media, uses film to train parents, staff, faculty, administrators and students in schools. **www.womedia.org/abouttraining.htm**

www.tolerance.org

Adoption and Sports:
Playing for Self-Esteem
By Ron Margolin

Our first daughter, Olivia, was physically precocious. Adopted in 1992, she walked before she was ten months old. By the time she was two she could kick a soccer ball and hit a baseball. Her coordination and body control was amazing. Our second daughter, Lili, was adopted in 1997 at twenty-one months of age. She was a special needs child because of rickets, a deficiency of vitamin D that causes bone deformities. Her legs were bowed and her chest deformed. She had the neuromuscular complications of rickets resulting in severe weakness. She was just starting to walk. She could barely get herself from lying to sitting, and needed assistance getting from sitting to standing. Once home, Lili did improve rapidly, but remained far behind other kids her age in physical development. Our hope was that she would some day progress enough to keep up with her playmates.

When Olivia was seven and Lili four, our neighbor's daughter convinced Olivia to go to gymnastics with her; Lili, like any little sister, wanted to go also, so they started in beginner's classes. A few weeks later the instructors said they wanted to move Lili into Olivia's class because her class was 'too baby' for her. That summer they did two weeks of camp at the gym. On Thursday of the second week when I went to pick them up, Lili was nowhere to be found. She finally appeared 10 minutes later. I asked where she had been. She said some of the instructors asked her to 'do some stuff.' Same thing the next day, but this time I could see Lili out on the floor surrounded by a bunch of coaches and counselors. Finally, Lili's camp counselor, whom I recognized as one of the gym's competitive team members, came out and said that the team coach wanted to talk to me about Lili. The coach, a fortyish Chinese woman, said she thought Lili could be a great gymnast, and wanted her to start competitive team training. "She has everything–coordination, speed, flexibility, balance, fearlessness. And she loves it. She has everything except strength. She's very weak. But we can give her that. We can make her strong." She said training started at two hours twice a week. We thought that a lot for a child barely five years old.

We thought it over for a week or so, Lili begging the whole time to be allowed to do it, and Olivia complaining the whole time that it wasn't fair. We finally decided to let Lili try

Perhaps the greatest benefit of being a high level competitive athlete is the contribution athletics makes to the development of their self-identity, their body image, and their self-confidence. This is especially true for an adopted child, who faces unique obstacles in the development of a strong and positive self-identity. Whatever problems they have with their cultural and racial identity, with understanding their place in the family, and their role in society, the child involved in athletics can always derive self-confidence from their physical strength, the special skills they possess, and the respect of their teammates.

~ Ron Margolin,
adoptive Dad

it, and called the coach. Two and a half years later Lili won the state championship in the vault in her division.

Now ten years old, Lili continues to be a top gymnast. She trains sixteen hours a week. In the five years we've been involved in competitive gymnastics we've learned a great deal about Lili, about competitive gymnasts, about the contribution high level sports can make to a child's, particularly an adopted child's, development, about the pitfalls of competitive sports, about being parents to a competitive athlete, and even about Olivia.

We've learned that in addition to the qualities her coach listed, Lili is also relentless, a perfectionist, and highly competitive. In her first year of training Lili was so tiny that she crashed into the vault at least five hundred times before finally clearing it. But each time she got up, smiled, and ran back to try it again. All of the competitive gymnasts are very competitive and perfectionists by nature. As parents, we have to make sure they (and the coaches and the other parents) don't get too competitive or too hard on themselves. These kids have a very real need to compete hard, but they also have to learn to remember it's not the end of the world if they don't perform at their best every time.

Perhaps the greatest benefit of being a high level competitive athlete is the contribution athletics makes to the development of their self-identity, their body image, and their self-confidence. This is especially true for an adopted child, who faces unique obstacles in the development of a strong and positive self-identity. Whatever problems they have with their cultural and racial identity, with understanding their place in the family, and their role in society, the child involved in athletics can always derive self-confidence from their physical strength, the special skills they possess, and the respect of their teammates. One of the things we have always marveled at is the friendship and respect the older team members show toward the younger ones.

The psychologists tell us that self-confidence in one area tends to spill over into other areas. Competitive gymnasts and other dedicated or high-level athletes tend to do very well in school. That's partly because of their confidence generated by their physical abilities, but also because of:

- their self-discipline
- their ability to follow instruction precisely
- their ability to focus on a task
- and their willingness to work hard

Because of the time demands of gymnastics they need to stay well organized. Homework needs to be done immediately after school. Projects cannot be left to the last minute. *Importantly, kids heavily involved in competitive sports don't have the time, and have too much self-respect, to get in trouble.*

All kids eventually quit gymnastics. There are no thirty-year-old competitive gymnasts. Some quit early, some compete through college. What they all get to keep from gymnastics is a life long self-image as being an athlete, of an ability to do other sports well, and physical strength. Even for the child who is not a special athlete, competitive athletics can have benefits. Olivia is a perfect example. While well coordinated and precise in her techniques, she lacks some of the natural abilities of a very high quality gymnast. She's much better suited to sports like swimming and golf. But competitions and training bring a lot of fun, the opportunity also to win medals and gain pride in prowess. Olivia won a medal at her level of state championships. We were very proud of her.

What do parents need to remember if a child shows interest in a competitive sport?

First and foremost, it has to remain fun. As parents it's our responsibility to see if they're having fun. If a kid is no longer enjoying herself, it's time for a break or to quit. All the kids have periods of burn out, especially at the end of the competition season. Usually they bounce back. Almost all of them need a break every once in a while.

A gym or sports facility has to be chosen with care. The coaches must be able to balance the demands on the kids necessary for them to compete successfully, with positive reinforcement. In a meet in New York City this year, Lili fell off the beam four times, a complete disaster. But her coach hugged her and teased her about doing the worst beam in the gym's history. Two hours later she was happily running around a restaurant with her teammates. She finished 2nd and 1st on beam in her next two competitions.

The coaches should never, ever discuss weight. They should just emphasize healthy eating. I can't think of a better way to set a young girl up for an eating disorder than to put that much emphasis on their weight. Good competitive gymnasts come in all sizes and shapes.

It is crucial for us as parents and for our child to have realistic expectations. Too many parents envision their child winning Olympic medals. The reality is far from that. Mainly, as parents we have to remember that these are still little kids. I'm always reminded of it when the team goes out to lunch or dinner together after a meet. At the meet they've been intense, competitive, and highly skilled athletes who are truly amazing to watch. Then we go to a restaurant and they're sitting together, with all their medals still hanging around their necks, drawing pictures with crayons and doing the games on the children's placemats, laughing, and being just regular nine and ten year old girls.

~ Ron Margolin and his wife, Lesley Sneddon, are parents of two daughters adopted from China and he is the moderator of the internet e-mail Yahoo discussion group RaisingChinaChildren.

Identify the root of the fears. Why is your child afraid to participate? Is she afraid to fail? Is she crumbling under the weight of early-life rejection? Is her being 'not good enough' an adoption issue? Helping a child understand what might be holding her back from participating in a sport she's interested in, and helping her 'fight' her ghosts, is empowering!

~Jean MacLeod

Team Sports can be win/win. Some children who crave control and need to win simply thrive in team sports. The losing is less personal and the winning means working with others. Adopted kids with a need to succeed can derive support from working as a team, and (yes!) moving to captain the team. The drive then becomes the welfare of the team, and the personal becomes integrated in making team spirit real.

~Sheena Macrae

Friendship Resources

Helping the Child Who Doesn't Fit in By Stephen Nowicki and Marshall P. Duke

Good Friends Are Hard to Find : Help Your Child Find, Make, and Keep Friends By Fred Frankel, PhD

Nobody Likes Me, Everybody Hates Me: The Top 25 Friendship Problems and How to Solve Them By Michele Borba

The Unwritten Rules of Friendship: Simple Strategies to Help Your Child Make Friends By Natalie Madorsky Elman and Eileen Kennedy-Moore

Teaching Your Child the Language of Social Success By Marshall P. Duke, Elisabeth A. Martin, Stephen Nowicki Jr.

Raise Your Child's Social IQ By Cathi Cohen

The Art of the Successful Playdate

I found that age five was the absolutely most brutal time for social skills with little girls. They are just starting to learn the power of 'liking' and 'not liking' and are starting to use it with great ruthlessness. I think parents need to be alert to these dynamics to ensure that one child does not get scapegoated, or become a nasty little power broker. Socializing is something that needs to be taught. Children don't naturally get along; it takes practice and learning, and just a structured school or daycare situation alone won't give them all the needed skills.

What worked in our situation was to arrange 'play-dates' and to have some rather structured time with some nice hooks to ensure that the children don't have to spend too much time actually relating to each other. So maybe a Saturday afternoon with a lunch trip to favorite restaurant, some free play, then an outing of some sort, and home by supper. This way a positive connection gets established and next play-date the children have some basis of previous fun to start from. Gradually more free play and less adult intervention, and by the time they are six, things go smoothly. Mostly.

The word spreads, and other kids want to come for some fun also, so your child has a higher likelihood of receiving positive overtures from peers and is more open and able to form relationships–bribery and manipulation maybe, but it really helps. Also when conflict arises, as it will, you can figure out what's going on and can help your child learn to navigate problems. Sharing is hard –so teach your child that this is necessary when she has friends over. Help your child plan some play-date activities which don't involve sharing!

~By Lynn Sherwood

Articles on the building blocks of friendship:
Young Children's Social Development: A Checklist
by Diane McClellan & Lilian G. Katz
www.nldontheweb.org/Mcclellan_Katz.htm

Learning the Language of Relationships By Ann Siegel
**www.ldaamerica.org/aboutld/teachers/
social_emotional/language.asp**

Race

The Color Connection
Transracial Adoptive Families
By A.R. Sakaeda

Making the Connection

It's often said that one of the best things about the Internet is that it allows us to be color blind. Since we don't see the faces of those with whom we communicate, it allows us to make race a non-issue. It allows us to forge connections without ever knowing or caring about color.

But when race does become an issue, the illusion and the connection are shattered. Like in real life, divisions are often drawn between whites and people of color (those who identify as not being white). Noting the disconnection that occurred in an e-mail discussion group, a friend wrote the following: *They keep saying that they don't know how to make friends with people of color—that just bugs the hell out of me. That's exactly where the problem is. They are so darn scared of people who look/talk different. On the other hand, we have to deal with [white people] on a daily basis (willingly or unwillingly).* **For adoptive parents, the ability to connect is crucial.**

When we form our families through intercountry/interrace adoption, we are choosing an intimate relationship with a child whose life may unfold much differently from our own. Most of us did not grow up apart from our birth families. Many of us may never have had significant peer relationships with people of other races. For white families who adopt children of color, race takes on a new, more critical importance.   How do we foster relationships with those who have previously walked where our children will walk? How do we maintain connections with our children? How do we learn to understand race and racism in a way that will facilitate these connections?

Understanding Race

Understanding race in a way that will benefit our children means understanding how racial identity develops throughout a lifetime, for both our children and ourselves. It means understanding how to support our children's identity development and how to further our own growth and development. **Understanding racism in a way that furthers connection means being able to work past fear, anger, and denial.** It requires that we understand our own privilege, acknowledge injustice and become active anti-racists. Additionally, it means examining the ways in which racism is perpetuated in our words and actions, both overtly and covertly.

Racism, and the divisions caused by race, harm us all by preventing us from truly knowing ourselves and others. As an entrenched system of privilege for some groups to the detriment of others, racism supports the false ideology that some people are superior to others. Racism prevents us from seeing a truer reality. Additionally, it is contradictory to ideals of fairness and justice. Racism strips us of the opportunity for personal growth and the ability to experience a full and rich life. We also deny ourselves the ability to make real and lasting connections with others. Being able to forge and maintain these connections is vital. We need to connect with other parents, role models, mentors and friends. Most of all, we need to be able to connect with our children.

The ability to connect is critical to both our own and our children's well-being. Jean Baker Miller, a Clinical Professor of Psychiatry at Boston University School of Medicine, notes *"… people develop by interaction with other people. No one develops in isolation … if women or men are not acting in ways that foster others' development, they are inevitably doing the reverse."*

The process of furthering development is especially important when we consider the developing racial and ethnic identity of our children. The ways in which racism harms us all—through creation of a false reality, contradictions to our sense of justice, denial of our humanity and loss of connections with others—also affect our children on a very personal level.

Racial Identity. Racial and ethnic identity development for children of color typically progresses through a number of stages. Initially, there may be no desire to learn about this part of the self. Later, the child may seek out information and begin to actively explore.

What I Wanted to Hear:
Being Different in an All White Family

The one thing I wanted to hear as an adopted child in an all white family during a troubled time of defining who I was and where I belonged, was:

"You are different. You come from a different country, rich with heritage and the spirits of your ancestors. You carry that within your soul, and in your appearance. You were an orphan. It is tragic to lose your mother, father and the brothers, sisters you may have. You carry a sorrow of war and separation like those in your country of birth. You need time to grieve.

You were adopted by us. The world is a wide and varied place. You now live with us and we love each other, love having no boundaries. Others may never learn this, or understand it. It is a gift to treasure if one is lucky enough to know this. A gift to all of us.

Because we love, the hardest road is over. You have our support to explore your heritage and share in ours. It is also yours. You have our support to one day search for your biological family. We are also your family. We don't expect you to be like us. We want you to be yourself, but you are never by yourself. There are many people adopted just like you and we will help you meet them."

By Indigo Williams (Thuy Thi Diep Huynh) Group Organizer: Adopted Vietnamese Australians and Adopted Vietnamese International

Questions of Color

Parents need to ask about their own feelings...

- How do I feel when I am the minority in a setting?

- What would it be like to be in an environment in which I am always the minority?

- What is my race? How do I feel about my own race?

- What did I learn about people of other races as I was growing up? Do I accept those beliefs now?

- How do I feel about adults of other races? Adults of color? How do I feel about adults who share my children's race or ethnicity?

- What types of remarks do I make about people of color? How do my children interpret these remarks?

- How do I feel about my children joining a community of which I am not a member by virtue of race or ethnicity?

- How do I feel about my children dating other people of color?

- Do I see my children as belonging to a community of color? Can I envision my child as an adult of color?

- If I am white, how will I feel about my children viewing me as white?

- Is it difficult for me to make friends with people of other races?

- Do I have peer relationships with adults of color? Do I have friends with whom I can speak candidly about race?

To understand their transracially adopted children, parents need to ask themselves...

- What do my children see when they survey their environment?

- What are my children's everyday experiences like? What do I imagine it would be like to be the minority in a setting?

- Are my children reflected in the books our family reads and in the movies we watch?

- Are people of color reflected in the history that is taught to my children?

- Do my children see reflections of themselves in their school, in their place of worship and in their neighborhood?

- How are people of my children's race or ethnicity portrayed in the popular media? What are some of the common stereotypes? How do they affect my children?

- Who are the role models for my children as they develop their identity?

- Who do my children see in positions of authority?

- Who is invited into our home? What does this say about who we value?

- How are heritage and culture connected to their people? Can children explore identity in the absence of their community?

- Do I incorporate my children's heritage into my own?

Parents need to ask about racism...

- Do I have a vested interest in ending racism?

- Do I believe that the responsibility for ending racism belongs to people of color?

- Is racism a problem for me if I am white?

- What is privilege? What are the implications of privilege on my children?

- When I fail to speak out against racism, what does that mean? What message does that convey to my children?

- Is tolerating divergent opinions the same as tolerating racism?

- Am I able to listen when others accuse me of racism? Do I view such accusations as an opportunity for growth, or do I deny or defend?

- How do my words convey how I feel about racism?

- Do I believe in a just world? Are my words backed by action?

- What is the role of intentionality in racism? If people are unaware that they are being racist, is the effect changed?

- Can good people be racist?

- Do I believe that the problem of racism is exaggerated?

- Have I spoken honestly with friends of color about racism?

- What have I learned about racism through books and other materials? What do I need to know about racism that will help my children?

By A.R. Sakaeda

Ideally, racial and ethnic identity is incorporated in a way that enriches and enhances self-esteem. Since we cannot predict when our children may begin this exploration, we need to make sure that this information is readily available and accessible. It is vitally important for children to see themselves positively reflected in their environment.

Racial identity development is not static, and can progress throughout a person's lifetime. It is critical that parents additionally seek to understand and explore their own race and racial identity simultaneously. This is because our own racial identity and the way we think about race and racism is reflected in and absorbed by our children.

For parents of color, understanding racial identity means exploring internalized racism as well as racism manifested towards other groups of color. Internalized racism refers to the way in which we may have accepted and learned to believe negative messages about ourselves and our worth. For white parents, understanding race and racial identity involves exploring the meaning of whiteness and privilege and learning to understand alternative viewpoints. For all of us, developing a healthy racial identity for ourselves and our children means we need to pay close attention to the way race and racism is enacted in our speech and actions. Our children are taught both overtly and covertly about race. Adoptive parents sometimes say, "My child is just a regular kid," without recognizing that children and adults of color are also just 'regular people.'

A child may show no interest in his or her heritage or racial identity, but that does not mean this information is unneeded. It is difficult for children to choose to explore their heritage if opportunities have not been readily available to them. Additionally, the absence of materials reflecting our children's heritage and the absence of people who look like them sends a clear message that our children's heritage and community are not important to us.If we assume our children have no interest in heritage, this may lead them to prematurely foreclose their identity. In so doing, they deny a critical part of themselves in the interest of pleasing their parents. Later, children or adults may find they wish to explore their heritage and may choose to sever ties with those who deny its importance. These are rifts that may never be healed.

Empathy, Not Advice. If we are white parents, we must be especially careful that we do not cause disconnections with our friends of color or our children through our inability to extend empathy, or accept the validity of their experiences. Listening empathically allows the speaker to frame an incident without attempts on our part to define the experience for them. Suggesting how they should feel or react, focusing on the good intentions or good character of the perpetrator, and/or attempting to relate it to our own experience are all sometimes felt as disconnections. (This is also true in relationships with others who have widely varying life experiences. Empathic listening can similarly be applied to adoption-related issues.)

Building Connections. Identity exploration must be encouraged in our children, and we must give them explicit permission to do so. We can provide them with books, videos and other materials that relate to their ethnic and racial identity as well as exploring these materials ourselves. We can give them space to make same-ethnicity and same-race friends and we can connect them with communities that share their race and ethnicity. It is especially important to interact with role models of color to counteract the pervasive stereotypes that exist in our culture.

Our children must see themselves mirrored in the faces of their peers, their neighbors, their teachers and their school environment. It is tremendously isolating for children of color to be in environments in which they do not see reflections of themselves. Parents who have been in the minority in a setting can use this information to try to understand what it is like for our children to experience this constantly. Because identity formation is derived largely through relationships with others, our children need to have regular, consistent interaction with others who share their race or heritage.

Support of Heritage. It is important to note that we must also incorporate our children's racial and ethnic heritage within our family heritage. It is equally important for us to establish peer relationships with people who share our children's race and/or ethnicity, to read widely and to learn about and experience our children's cultural heritage.

Often parents will discount the importance of heritage, noting that they don't know much about their own heritage. They joke about being 'mutts' and disclaim the idea that heritage is of any importance. Heritage perhaps seems less important when access to that heritage has been readily available; such is not always the case for our children.

Sociologist Mary C. Waters notes that part of ethnic identity development involves selective identification, which occurs "when parents decide what they will tell their children about who they are and who their ancestors were." Adoptive families similarly make choices about what to tell their children about heritage and ancestry. Heritage may be of special importance when our children have no biological relatives from whom information can be gleaned and when they have been removed from their culture.

A salient difference also exists between white ethnicities and ethnicities of persons of color. For white ethnics, there are few social costs in choosing either to embrace or to ignore ethnicity. Children of color cannot choose to ignore their ethnicity as it is inextricably tied to race.

Making and maintaining authentic connections are key to ethnic identity development. Identity development is relational; how people react and interact with you serves to form your image of yourself, including your ethnic and racial identity. For people of color, self-identity is negatively affected in reaction to both overt and covert racism.

For children of color in particular, the ways in which parents react and respond to racism is critical for development. Our children need to learn that we will not tolerate racism, that we are active in opposing racism and that we value and validate their perspective.

As parents, we will have to take the lead in racial discourse and speak openly about race and racism. We additionally need to learn how to listen to our children's experience of racism without denying, defending, or discounting. Incorporating culture and heritage is not enough, however. As our children develop their racial and ethnic identity, it is imperative that we actively work to counter racism in our environment and in ourselves. Words without action are meaningless.

Conveying a Consistent, Positive Message. Children very quickly sense when a disparity exists between what they are told and what they perceive. One commonly-espoused belief is that color or race does not matter. We may try to teach our children to be color blind, but in the words of activist Dr. Cornel West, *"race matters"*. Children learn at an early age that these distinctions are real and meaningful. Sociologists Debra Van Ausdale and Joe Feagin, who examined how pre-school children learn about race and racism, note the following:

This failure to acknowledge the importance of racial groups in children's lives arises from the twin adult convictions that children are naïve and that color blindness is not only desirable but achievable. To reach this goal, many adults verbally discourage children from recognizing that skin color is a critical social marker. This professed color blindness denies the racially and ethnically divided world that kids observe and function in on a daily basis. The primacy of race and color cannot be denied. Insistence that race doesn't matter will ring false for our children. Instead, what they learn is that it is not polite to mention race, and race becomes a taboo subject. For our children of color, this may create a disconnect between our words and what they observe and experience. Moreover, they learn that an intrinsic part of themselves—their color—makes others, including their parents, uneasy, defensive, and angry.

Lessons About Race and Racism

Lessons about race and racism are often inherently contradictory. We teach our children that justice is a worthy ideal; simultaneously we are either not attentive to injustice or we accept it uncritically as a part of our lives. We may remain silent when others are mistreated because we do not feel that it is our concern. And if we are white, we have the luxury of choosing not to address racism because we benefit from a system in which people are treated differently because of race. Sometimes these advantages are small, like when a store clerk passes over the next person in line in order to wait upon us. Sometimes the stakes are enormous and seem so overwhelming that we shrug them off as 'well, that's life'.

Accepting racism as a normal, expected fact of life gives our children the message that we are merely paying lip service to ideals of justice and fairness. Worse yet, the message conveyed to children of color is unmistakable: You are a second-class citizen. No words can make up for the damage to our children's self-esteem when we convey through our non-action that they are not important, that they do not possess rights, that they do not deserve equal treatment. When we do not act to right injustice, we risk damaging our relationship with our children, our own self-growth and our children's developing identity. The message we send needs to be clear, consistent and just. Additionally, we must back our words with action.

Often the lessons we teach about race are wholly unconscious on our part. Professor Charles Lawrence notes as follows: "*Most of the lessons are tacit rather than explicit. Children learn not so much through an intellectual understanding of what their parents tell them about race as through an emotional identification with who their parents are and what they see and feel their parents do. Small children will adopt their parents' beliefs because they experience them as their own ... we are not likely to be aware that the lessons have even taken place. If we are unaware that we have been taught to be afraid of blacks or to think of them as lazy or stupid, then we may not be conscious of our internalization of those feelings and beliefs.*" Children's exposure to racist ideology is especially harmful because it can lead to internalized racism and shame. In other words, when people of color are exposed to stereotyping, prejudice and racism, they may begin to believe those negative messages about their abilities and intrinsic worth.

We must assist our children in developing a protective, healthy identity that incorporates their racial and ethnic heritage. But purchasing toys, books and dolls that reflect our children's heritage, while important, lacks the key component of connection: **We need to provide opportunities for our children to connect with children who share their heritage, to be surrounded by racial and ethnic diversity and to connect with adults who can serve as role models.**

Additionally, we need to be anti-racist role models ourselves. We need to actively examine how we think about race and racism, how we communicate these thoughts to our children and how we explicitly and implicitly teach about race. Our beliefs must be communicated in a way that is consistent both with the way we live our lives and the way in which our children experience the world.

An adoptive parent who is also an intercountry adoptee wrote: "*I have certain animosity towards my own adoptive father because he's white. He held some pretty strong racial views without realizing how it affected me. I remember he was talking about 'colored' people and used racial slurs, etc. I used to scream inside my head, 'Dad, I'm a person of color!'*"

We cannot teach our children that they are equals in our eyes if we express a viewpoint that 'those people' are not our equals. But achieving consistency in the principles we endorse and our everyday speech and action requires critical thought and careful attention. Moreover, it requires education on matters of race and racism. While learning through experience is valuable, there is no substitute for reading widely. Learning to understand the alternative viewpoint is critical to development of both our racial identity and our moral sense. Reading the accounts of others allows us to begin to understand that our worldview is largely shaped by our environment. If we have always lived within a homogenous community, we may find it difficult to relate with those who do not share our experiences.

Psychologist Beverly Daniel Tatum, who writes widely on issues of race and racial identity, noted the disconnection that is experienced when a listener is unable to identify with an account of racism: *"… in many situations people who try to comfort often end up invalidating the person's feelings by saying things like, 'Oh, come on, it wasn't that bad.' What happens is that you withdraw from the conversation. The feeling is 'Well, you don't get it, so I'll find somebody who does.'"*

Discounting racism by denying its effect on others is a common defense mechanism used to avoid race-related anxiety. Often, talking about racism makes us so uncomfortable that we inadvertently break connections with others in a desire to lessen our own anxiety.

Validating Our Children's Experience

To maintain connection with our children, we need to listen to them, to empathize with them and to validate their experiences. Specifically, we must be mindful not to offer excuses for others or minimize or discount the experience. Psychologist Shelly P. Harrell notes that the damage of racism *"lies not only in the specific incident, but also in the resistance of others to believing and validating the reality or significance of one's personal experience."*

It is important to encourage our children to talk about even their most painful experiences without attempting to offer alternative explanations or denying their reality. We have to be able to sit with their pain and tolerate it ourselves—for if we can't, how can we expect the same of our children? Adult adoptees surveyed by the Evan B. Donaldson

How Would You Answer?
Reactions to Racist Remarks in the Family

Decide how you would react in each of the six situations. What would you say? How would you act? What would your nonverbal communication include (rolling your eyes, leaving the room, etc.)? Write down ways you would handle each situation:

1) Grandfather Wilson tells a racist joke that causes laughter from your family, but at the same time insults you and your child during a holiday gathering.

2) Aunt Mary is noticeably uncomfortable being alone in the same room as your adopted African American son. She clutches her purse rather than leaving it by her coat.

3) Your brother's children tease your child about her hair and complexion during family gatherings. When you mention your concern to your brother, he brushes it off as child's play.

4) One Sunday brunch spurs a discussion of genetics: everyone in the Johnson family has a long, stern nose. Your Vietnamese adopted daughter is ignored.

5) Your parents announce that they will divide their inheritance among the grandchildren: $2,000 for natural children; $1,000 for adopted children.

6) Your African American son is told by his Caucasian cousins that he should go out for sports because all Blacks are athletic.

~ By Jeanette Wiedemeier Bower, MPA,
excerpted from "Transracial Parenting Project Self-Awareness Tool" (NACAC, 2/1998).

Adoption Institute reported they did not want their parents to try to fix things. They wanted them to listen.

The cost of not validating our children's reality is high. Jean Baker Miller notes that the threat of isolation raises so much anxiety that most people will try to avoid it at all costs. This means that a child may try to make and maintain connections with parents in any way possible, even if it means denying a significant part of him- or herself. *"In order to twist herself into a person acceptable in un-accepting relationships, she will have to move away from and redefine a large part of her experience—those parts of experience that she has determined are not allowed."*

Children feel a strong need to fit in. Additionally, they also feel a very strong need to be loved by and approved of by their parents. Because they cannot afford to lose a parent's love, children will internalize racism rather than speak up. The power dynamic inherent in the parent-child relationship means that we must be especially careful about the messages we convey to our children as they develop their racial and ethnic identities. If we validate our children's experiences but discount the experiences of other people of color in our everyday conversation, our children will recognize the disparity.

Part of the critical exploration for parents is the consideration that our children may develop a racial and ethnic identity we do not share. This may be especially difficult for parents who form their families through adoption, as often we try so hard to claim our children and mark them as our own. Once again, thinking critically about race and racism is crucial to enhancing both our own and our children's development and our connections with others. This involves being able to see a viewpoint that is different from our own.

When we made our commitment to our children, part of that commitment included the need to grow and become the parents our children need. In so doing, we embrace our own personal growth, contribute to the positive development of our children's identity and build stronger, more authentic connections.

~ A.R. Sakaeda is a parent and a writer who concentrates on issues of race and social justice

www.pactadopt.org
for those wanting to understand the racial component in transracial adoption

www.birchlane.davis.ca.us/library/10quick.htm
How to analyze books for racism and sexism

www.wcwonline.org
White Privilege: Unpacking the Invisible Knapsack by Peggy Macintosh
a must read for transracial adoptive families

Sites for educators and school resources:

www.tolerance.org

www.teachingtolerance.org

www.misf.org/educatorstoolkit/mce/curriculum.htm
including an excellent explanation of the differences between contributions and additive approaches to multicultural education and the transformative approach.

Preparing Our Children for Racism
How do we do this without making them expect it?
By Frances Kai-Hwa Wang

I always knew that this day would come. I have been preparing my children for it since they were born. I tried to put it off as long as possible. I read countless books and talked to many people, searching for a better solution than what I did when I was their age (which was nothing). I secretly gave my children the tools with which to fight it, but without actually telling them what the battle was all about. I did not want to taint their innocence or to create paranoia, but I knew that they had to be ready when that day came. Still, I was unprepared for how sad I would feel when my daughter, Hao Hao, told me about her first brush with a racist slur in kindergarten. I say 'brush' because the comment made by one of her classmates was not really directed at her. It was not meant to be insulting or malicious. It was intended simply as an observation or description. Uttered in innocence, it hurt her nevertheless.

At lunch one day, my daughter used her hands to make a funny face, about which her classmate observed, "Those are Japanese eyes." My heart sank at my daughter's report, but I tried to control my expression as memories of my own classmates' chanting came flooding back. My daughter said to the girl, "No it's not." "Yes it is." "No it's not." A student teacher happened to overhear the conversation and stepped in right away to say, "My eyes are a little bit slanted, but I'm not Japanese."

I asked my daughter how she felt and she said, "Bad," although she said she felt better after the student teacher stuck up for her. When I asked why she felt bad, she said, "Because Andy is Japanese!" Andy is her best friend (He is actually Chinese, but he speaks Japanese). Then she said, "I saw a Japanese person once and his eyes weren't like that." She points to the Mulan plate in front of her and explains to me what Mulan's eyes, my eyes, her sisters' eyes, and her eyes look like. "Nobody has eyes like that."

She is indignant and angry, but she does not understand why. She does not know the rest of that dreaded rhyme, that it slurs Chinese eyes, too. She does not know that some people confuse Chinese and Japanese and other Asian people. She does not know that there are those who do not like Asian people, or who think that we do not belong here. Still, she feels it in the pit of her stomach.

Racism takes many forms at different ages, and it is different for boys and girls. There are many possible strategies depending on the personality of the child and the circum-

Outside Difference, Inside Sameness

A great exercise for children from pre-K to second grade is one Deb Buckingham and I developed to go with a book I wrote: *I Don't Have Your Eyes.* We talk age appropriately about how people judge others on what they look like. We look at the things that make us different on the outside (skin, hair, eyes, height) and the things that make us the same on the inside (feelings and talents). We take out sheets of construction paper in black, red, white, and yellow and we all place our arms on them to see where we match. Then we use paint chips to find a more accurate skin color and discover that we are all some shade of brown. The kids then cut a circle out of the paint chip and use it for the head to a small person they create that looks just like them. You can download all the materials from **www.emkpress.com/school.html**

Carrie Kitze

stances. It is a politically charged topic so nobody wants to talk about it or believe it still exists. It is not fair, but to keep our children resilient and safe, we must prepare for it.

How do we prepare a child for racism **without making her expect it?** How do we recognize and combat racism, especially if we have not had experience dealing with it directly? How do we keep our children safe in a sometimes hostile and xenophobic world without causing even more damage? Here are some of the lessons that I have learned from other parents, educators, child development experts, and my own experience: learn as much as you can ahead of time through literature and history, start early to build self-esteem and a strong sense of ethnic pride, practice coping methods ahead of time, teach your child to always tell an adult, and show your child how to take action.

1. Laying the Groundwork: Literature, History, Politics, News. Many parents who adopt internationally feel inadequate to prepare their child for racism because they have not had personal experience with racism. They feel that they cannot understand what racism is like. Others are not even aware that racism could be a potential problem. Many international adult adoptees tell of parents who are so obviously uncomfortable when the subject comes up that the adopted child decides that it would be better to shield her parents and handle it alone. It does not have to be this way.

If you have not had personal experience with racism, you can draw from parallel experiences with difference, standing out, being excluded, insults, and teasing. Think about all the times you were 'the only one'—the only woman with a bunch of men watching a football game, the only man at a baby or bridal shower, the only left handed person in a world of right handed scissors, the only vegetarian at Thanksgiving dinner, the only sane person at your spouse's last family reunion. Think about the times you or other people made unfounded and mistaken assumptions—like assuming that the only woman at a business meeting was the secretary, or assuming that the woman health care provider was the nurse and the man assisting her was the doctor, or mistaking the African American CEO for the janitor.

Try to remember how you felt when you were teased for being the only kid wearing glasses, the fat kid, the skinny kid, the only kid who did not celebrate Christmas. Recall the hurt you felt when you were the only one not invited to little Suzie's birthday party, or when you were sure that you were the only one in the world without a date on Saturday night. If you have girls, you will also have to think about sexism, as they go hand in hand. Parents should get informed by reading Asian American, African American, Hispanic American, Native American literature and history to learn about the experiences of people of color in America.

Your child's history in this country did not start the day she arrived, and her experiences with racism are not unique—literature helps us better understand the ripples and texture of how it feels, and history helps us understand how it all fits together in time.

Parents should also keep up to date by reading the ethnic media, online or in print, and utilizing resources like tolerance.org. Follow the trends and celebrate the cool people in your child's ethnic/racial community. Keep track of what the community's leaders and activists are working for and why. Try to understand and support boycotts and other calls to actions. Join in the fight against stereotypes and hate crimes and glass ceilings. Get political. Tapping into this rich network of activism and scholarship and creative arts gives

Books on Parenting & Race

Inside Transracial Adoption
by Gail Steinberg and Beth Hall

40 Ways to Raise a Nonracist Child
by Barbara Mathias and Mary Ann French

Everyday Acts against Racism: Raising Children in a Multiracial World
by Maureen T. Reedy

Racism Explained to My Daughter
by Tahar Ben Jelloun

Loving Across the Color Line, A White Adoptive Mother Learns about Race
by Sharon E. Rush

Dim Sum, Bagels, and Grits
by Myra Alperson

Nuestros Ninos, Bringing Up Latino Children in a Bicultural World
by Gloria C. Rodriguez

The Black Parenting Book
by Linda Villarosa

Stickin' To, Watchin' Over, and Gettin' With, an African American's Guide to Discipline
by Howard C. Stevenson, Gwendolyn Davis, Saburah Abdul-Kabir

Hate Hurts: How Children Learn and Unlearn Prejudice
by Caryl Stern-LaRosa and Ellen Hofheimer Bettmann

Teaching Tolerance: Raising Open-Minded, Empathetic Children
by Sara Bullard

Anti-Bias Curriculum, Tools for Empowering Young Children
By Louise Derman-Sparks and the A.B.C. Task Force

Beyond Good Intentions
Cheri Register

Does Anybody Else Look Like Me? A Parent's Guide to Raising MultiRacial Children
by Donna Jackson Nakazawa

Why Are All the Black Kids Sitting Together in the Cafeteria? And Other Conversations about Race
By Beverly Daniel Tatum, PhD

White Privilege: Essential Readings on the Other Side of Racism By Paula S. Rothenberg

In Their Own Voices Transracial Adoptees Tell Their Stories by Rita J. Simon and Rhonda M. Roorda

Uprooting Racism: How White People Can Work for Racial Justice by Paul Kivel

For a great list of recommended books, visit PACT An Adoption Alliance
www.pactadopt.org/favoritebooks/

For Kids
Dealing With Racism
by Jen Green

The Skin I'm In: A First Look at Racism
by Pat Thomas and Lesley Harker

For an age appropriate list of children's books on race, diversity and fitting in:
www.understandingprejudice.org/ readroom/kidsbib.htm

a person a larger collection of experiences from which to draw—voices which are not generally heard in the mainstream.

2. Start Early: Build Strong Self-Esteem and Ethnic Pride. Start early. Just as you would not want to wait until after your child has been molested by the neighborhood pedophile to teach her that her private parts are private, you should not wait until after her first encounter with racism to teach her to be proud of her heritage. Racist comments can come as early as preschool, although preschoolers generally do not understand the connotations of what they are saying. They are beginning to notice differences among them, and are perhaps repeating things they have heard at home. Sometimes children not used to people who look different will try to scrub the brown doll 'clean,' or refuse to play with the 'dirty' dark-skinned child, or fear the child who speaks accented English. Children of color, unused to racial diversity, might do this too--an invitation for unfortunate comments. Starting early, using different age appropriate techniques also gives you, the parent, a few years' head start to figure it out.

Expose your child to all different types of people, use books, dolls, television, real people. Help your child make friends with other international adoptees, other children of her ethnic/racial group, and other children of color. Teach your child to look past stereotypes and to examine differences for herself. Correct your child when you hear her making stereotypical statements like, "Boys do not have eyelashes," or "This brown doll is dirty." It is important to educate your child's peers and expand their experience too.

Developing strong self-esteem and ethnic pride are critical for preparing your child to resist racism. You do not want your child to internalize the racist attitudes she encounters. You want her to be so sure of herself that it is obvious to her that racism is the other person's problem, not hers. Be proactive in teaching your child about race, ethnicity, and culture (if not about racism directly) to ensure a positive message. Just as you do not want your child to learn about sex from strangers, you do not want her to learn about race, ethnicity, and culture from bullies on the school bus or well-meaning but ignorant old ladies. Read adult Korean adoptee Dottie Enrico's essay, *"How I Learned I Wasn't Caucasian."*

Child development experts say that one of the best defenses against child molesters is simply teaching a child the correct names for their private parts because then she has the words to tell someone else exactly what happened. A similar case can be made for anti-racism education. You do not need all the gory details about racism, but you can still give generalized rules and ideas about tolerance like "Do not exclude people," "No put-downs," "Treat people with respect." That way, when your child does encounter racism, she can identify it and deal with it as a case of someone else behaving poorly, rather than a case of her not being able to 'take a joke.'

3. Practice. Always be on the lookout for 'teachable moments' in situations that parallel an experience of racial stereotyping or bullying but are not so loaded. These help your child practice how to deal with unfairness and teasing, preferably with her occasionally on the offending side, too, so that she is not always the victim.

For us, a moment presented itself one day during Chinese summer camp when all the girls ganged up on the one boy and made fun of him on the monkey bars. All the children were Chinese American and all the offenders were girls, so the lesson was not directly about racism or sexism, but a more general lesson about not harassing people who are different from you: "It's not his fault he's a boy. He was just born that way. It's ok to be a boy. Daddy's a boy, and you like him."

Give your child the words to use so when that moment comes she will know what to say, and so she can answer quickly without fumbling for words. Let her practice on siblings and with less-loaded incidents. For example, when one sibling tortures another, let her practice using her words, "Please stop," "No, that's not true," or "I feel hurt/angry/sad when you say…"

4. Tell an Adult. Teach your child to always tell a teacher, a trusted adult, and most importantly, you, her parents if someone slights her or makes a racist comment. Do not just dismiss racial harassment as 'kids will be kids'; bullying is never ok, and these days, bullying is becoming more and more dangerous, even deadly. Even if you feel uncomfortable talking about race and racism (just as sex education talks make many feel uncomfortable) you have to get over it and let your child know that she can always talk to you about this.

When she comes to you, do not panic or overreact. Take a deep breath and ask open-ended questions to find out what really happened. *Listen.* Let her talk about how she feels. Let her express her anger and hurt. Let her know that you are listening. Let her know that she is not alone, that it has nothing to do with her personally, and that she is not the first person to whom this has ever happened. Tell her stories and read her books about how other people have faced and dealt with similar situations. Give her tools and ideas with which to cope. Help her strategize what else she could have said or done. Let her know that it has less to do with her than with the bully's own insecurities and shortcomings. Assure her that home will always be a safe haven where she is loved unconditionally. Kiss and hug her.

5. Take Action. If a racist incident has occurred, then you need to take action. If you say nothing, your silence gives your

Hot Spots:
Racism in the Family
Families who have adopted internationally are often surprised (or not) to discover racism within their own families…

When dealing with racist family members, it is important for both spouses to present a unified front. The first rule is that each spouse has to deal with his or her own family members (If the husband's uncle is a problem, the husband has to be the one to talk to him). Do not allow racism of any sort (not just the kind directed at your child's own particular ethnic or racial group) in your own home, jokes included. Limit contact with the worst offenders.

However, it is trickier when you are going to someone else's house. If you are going to a big family reunion and you never know what Uncle Joe might say, prepare a strategy and a plan of escape ahead of time. When racism is subtle and the kids are very young, you might not want to draw attention to it if you think the kids did not pick up on it. However, if they are old enough to understand, then it is important to debrief the kids and talk about it on the way home. Explain how you love old Uncle Joe because he is family, but you do not agree with his opinions. Saying nothing just indicates your agreement with him and teaches your child that it is ok to disparage others on the basis of race, ethnicity, gender, difference.

Also be prepared for backhanded compliments and stereotypical flattery ("Such a cute China doll, I bet she's really good at math." "Why are you teaching her Chinese? She's American now.") Educate your family as gently as you can, and have research to back you up.

~Frances Kai-Hwa Wang

assent and allows racist incidents to be perpetuated. Your child needs to see you stand up for her so that she can learn to stand up for herself and it must be done.

Some people think that children should 'work it out themselves,' however children often do not have the tools to do so. It is important to work together with your child's teachers and school to bring multiculturalism and tolerance into the curriculum. Getting your child involved in the process is especially empowering. If the teacher is the problem, or if the teacher does not acknowledge that there is a racial problem, then you need to work up the chain of command and talk to the principal and the School Board. If you are worried that you might be making a big fuss over nothing, ask other parents of color what they think (especially those who have grown up in America). Get them to rally with you. Make waves. Call in outside experts. Worst-case scenario, move, or get your child out of that classroom and into a more multicultural and tolerant environment. Make sure that that classroom is not her whole world, that she has a community outside of school.

Chinese Eyes and Other Slurs–a Child Empowered

My daughter's first brush with racism was relatively benign. Everything that should have happened did happen. It happened at her hip and liberal multicultural school which is 30% Asian. The slur was not really directed at her and was not intended with malice. She had the words and the self-confidence to say, "No, it's not like that." A vigilant teacher overheard the exchange and intervened immediately. My daughter told me about it within two days. I talked to her teacher about it the next day. I knew the other child and her family—they are not racists—and talked with them about it. My daughter remained happy at school, popular and social, and she bounced back with no problems. She continued to sign her name in Chinese and to sing her Chinese poems to the class at circle time.

However, she did spend several weeks drawing odd kimono-clad Japanese ladies with the big elaborate hairdos, chopsticks in their hair, and little squinty, slanty line eyes, as if to try to understand what people could possibly see in the stereotype, to deconstruct it, and then to take control of it so that it did not have control of her. She would not talk about it at the time, but simply had to work it out for herself. A year later, when she had her second brush with racism in first grade, "Hao Hao, don't you know how to speak English yet?" she did not even miss a beat in transforming the mild insult into an empowered declaration, "Yes, I speak English, and Chinese, and Spanish, too—the three most spoken languages in the world."

~ Frances Kai-Hwa Wang, is IMDiversity.com's Asian American Village Contributing Editor. An earlier version of this article was first published by IMDiversity.com

Hot Spots: *Unconscious Racism*

Many of us are loathe to acknowledge even the possibility of our own unconscious racism, but as Dr. Phil says, "You can't change what you don't acknowledge." This is not an easy process, but examining our own beliefs and paying attention to the words we find coming out of our mouths can often reveal surprising attitudes that we have picked up and held onto unreflectively. Once we start to think about them, then we can free ourselves of the subtle and not so subtle brainwashing of our youth. We need to challenge ourselves to think outside the box and to look at things from other perspectives, so that we can learn from people of all races and cultures.   *~Frances Kai-Hwa Wang*

Language: Social Groups and Adoption

Defining Who We Are
By Riam Sangdoung Kidd

How do people define a word? Does one simply look it up in the dictionary? Does a 'term' have different meanings with social contexts? If Chinese American person heard a 'term', does it carry the same meaning to a recent Chinese immigrant? It is important to explore the issues of how 'language' can have different meanings within defined group of people. The words we choose and how we use language can convey what we value and how we 'think'. We can't deny that words don't elicit emotions, but we can learn and understand how words can mean different things to different people.

Social Groups Have the Right to Define Themselves As an Asian American woman, I didn't have to refer to a dictionary when someone called me a 'China doll'. As with racial slurs and terms such as chink, jap, mail-order bride, I learned these terms from different social interactions. When I met other Asian American women, it was validating to 'hear' from other Asian American women or women of Asian ancestry who felt the same way I did. I needed that validation for a number of reasons. It doesn't surprise me when someone 'outside' the group exclaims these terms 'I' hear aren't meant to be rude. They're thinking of terms defined by their own social interactions and not understanding that they aren't part of that group.

Social groups have the right to define their own terms. Since I identify as part of an Asian American woman, I have the right to define myself and those rights are transferred to other Asian American women. People who are outside this social group do not have the right. When a dominant group

~IN MY WORDS~
Talking About Race

We tell our children about the dangers of strangers (unprotected sex, date rape, drugs, alcohol, and getting into the car with drunk drivers). We need to tell our children about racism. We are helping to keep them safe, whether it is physically or psychologically, when we help prepare them to deal with the real world. Racism will happen whether or not we talk about it, and our children will find out about racism much earlier than we suspect. My child was eight, in second grade, and had been here less than three months when she put her little brown arm against mine and said, "White good, brown no good". Our children need to be prepared for racism when it happens so it doesn't take them by surprise. They need to have a number of choices for how they can respond and to know it is okay to talk to us about it.

Kids draw their own conclusions about overt racism, subtle racism, and skin color. We need to help them draw conclusions that are consistent with their own self esteem and not ones that have them deciding that somehow they are lesser than others because of how others perceive them (kids commonly deal with problems by blaming themselves). To help them means that we need to initiate conversations before they experience racism for the first time. We need to prepare them and arm them to face a world that isn't always going to play fair or be nice; where kindergarten rules aren't always in effect.

~Carolyn Birmingham is mom to a child adopted at nearly 8 years old, has worked in adoption, with adjudicated youth, and in personal growth outdoor programs.

redefines or imposes a definition, the lesser dominant group is silenced into accepting the terminology. This act in itself diminishes empowerment. When you are outside an ethnic, social, or 'X' group(s), then reflect upon instances where a person from that particular group objected to the 'term' you used. How did you feel? Did you attempt to redefine the term for them? If your child identified with that particular social group confronted you with 'your chosen' word, how did you react to the situation?

Adoption and Language How does language involve adoption? Families formed by adoption, especially in transracial families, will eventually confront what is appropriate in their adoption social group with those outside the group. Terminology and positive adoption language has become an adoptive family's ongoing education to outsiders to the world of adoption. Think about how you reacted to loaded words such as 'real' parents/siblings, 'natural', and/or 'very own child'.

Stereotypes and Language When using a term to represent a group (i.e., defining an ethnic group), this practice can perpetuate stereotypes. Referring to the term 'China doll', to me, it brings up an image of the passive, sensual Asian woman stereotype that is portrayed in numerous films and real life social interactions. Even when a term is meant to be complimentary, it still labels a person to a set of preconceived ideals. Another example is the term 'Model Minority'. When using this to describe an Asian American or anyone of Asian ancestry, it assumes this person is good at math, successful, and other attributes that may or may not be true.

When you first met a person from a specific ethnic group, did you have preconceived ideas about that person? What did you expect and what unexpected social interactions did you experience?

Riam Sangdoung Kidd is Thai adoptee who adopted her daughter from China

Rude Stares: *How to Confront Them*

Rude stares are something that adoptive families with kids and parents of differing races may encounter. I am mom (by birth and adoption) to black children, but I am white. How do I deal with stares like this, and how do I deal with it on behalf of my children? I used to try to be polite and teach my kids to do this also. Yes, some stares are friendly and simply inquisitive. based on the place and situation. But I am tired of other types of stares: the nosey stare, the disapproving stare, the 'your family is inferior' stare, the laughing stare where apparently some rude comment about my family has just been made to a co-starer. It is obvious that people feel my family is less deserving of respect and privacy–and so is less legitimate –than others. I am a single older parent of transracially adopted young children. I provide a variety of reasons for disapproval to those who like to judge. As a single transracial parent of a bio daughter for over 25 years, I have lived the majority of my adult life with this form of judgement. I no longer tolerate it as I used to, nor do I encourage my kids to do so. Often one of us will just pointedly turn and confront the person staring with a stare of our own. Not a threatening stare and not when it could lead to our own endangerment. I consider returning the stare to be a way of taking a silent stand that says: This is my family. Your rude stare is violating our privacy and space. It works as a reminder that staring is rude and the person will glance away with an embarrassed expression. This is a boundary for me and for my family.

Virginia Farr, biomom to a biracial 25 year-old, transracial adoptive mom to two

So What is Asian American Culture to Me?

By Byron Han, adoptive dad

It is being able to eat dim sum, sushi, kimchee, pizza, hamburgers, tacos, hotdogs, chicken feet, turkey, bagels with lox, PB&J, spam musubi, bok choy, deep fried twinkies –without having to give it a second thought .

It is listening to 'Mouse Loves Rice' in Mandarin, laughing to Margaret Cho, and listening to the Asian American rapper Jin, whilst still enjoying my Star Wars, Madonna, and Jerry Seinfeld.

It is celebrating Moon Festival, Chinese New Year, Christmas, Thanksgiving, St. Patricks Day, Valentine's Day and a myriad of other secular and formerly non-secular holidays without having to give it a second thought.

It is to be with people who have shared the experience of 'The Look' when you are the only Asian looking person for a hundred miles, to have been asked the questions "where are you from–Ohio–no I mean where are you **really** from?" and "how did you learn to speak English so well"–and to be able to make jokes about this with people who just 'get it'

It is to be proud of the great accomplishments of America and of our ancestral countries. And to be willing to criticize and work to better what is wrong here in our home country and in our ancestral countries.

It is to be with other people whose parents also worry about how Americanized we are, yet whose parents' friends marvel at how Chinese we still are.

Most of all, Asian American culture is being caught (forever) between two worlds–America and Asia. I don't raise my children to be little Chinese boys and girls, dressing them up in traditional outfits, doing the ritualistic kowtowing 3 times in the morning (though I've tried), memorizing Confucian proverbs out the ying-yang (pun intended), and force-feeding them Chinese culture until they gag on it. What I do is:

- Impress on my children that everyone is different and differences are to be celebrated and respected.
- Discuss what parts are good in Asian and American cultures and to be adopted (belief in hard work, education, and personal responsibility and freedom), and what parts are bad and to be avoided (materialism, provincial thinking).
- Teach my children to be respectful of their parents, other adults, and other children and always say please and thank you (something that should transcend all cultures).
- Teach my children not to be boastful (Asian) yet at the same time be able to stand up for themselves (American).
- Cook a bewildering variety of initially strange and yet delicious and ultimately embraced dishes (pigs feet, duck tongue, fried rice mountain with ice cream volcano...turducken is the next on my list).
- Make them go to Chinese school on Saturday afternoons (I know, I know, violating the force-feeding clause mentioned above).

Can you Erase Hurt?

Ask children to draw a picture, then crumple it into a ball. Tell them this is what it's like to hurt somebody's feelings. Then ask them to flatten the paper back to its original state. Explain that no matter how hard you try to undo the damage, the initial hurt can't be smoothed out completely.

Daisy Girl Scout Activity

Confronting Racism
United States Customs
By Usha Rengachary Smerdon

Although she was not cognizant of it, my adopted daughter experienced racism for the first time as a nine month old upon arriving at the Los Angeles airport in October 2004. We and another Indian family consisting of a Sikh son and his elderly parents were leaving the INS processing area. Confused, the other family took a wrong turn and began exiting immigration the wrong way. U.S. Customs agents started shouting at them and one mocked them by bobbing his head in a gesture similar to the typical Indian manner indicating agreement. I was distraught for the other family and dismayed that my infant daughter was confronted with racism almost immediately upon touching down on U.S. soil. Gee, how would this incident figure into her lifebook?

I thought about this incident at the airport for days and weeks afterwards. My heart ached for the immigrant family who were 'welcomed' to the U.S. in this manner. My heart also ached for my baby daughter, currently unaware, but not forever. Incidents like these are bound to happen to me and around me, to my daughters and around them, over and over. My friend Sunny Jo remarks in her essay, "*The Korean Drop*", that the drops of racism will fall over time. Will the weight of these drops wear my children down, or will they be strengthened and rise above them?

Subtle Racism is a Slippery Animal

In thinking of racism, I know from my own experiences as a minority in the United States, that subtle racism is much more prevalent in my daily life than acts of overt racism. Subtle racism is a slippery animal. It can leave the target second guessing oneself as to whether racism is truly at play. I believe that the yardstick is whether a white person would have been treated the same. For example, as I am alternately ignored by salespeople or followed around in stores, I can't help but wonder if this is happening because of the color of my skin. The answer is rarely clear. That is why for all parties, subtle racism is easy to dismiss and easy to deny.

Would you characterize the Customs incident I recount above as overt racism, subtle racism or perhaps you feel that no racism was involved at all? I felt it was an act of overt racism that was propagated towards the Sikh family, and I also felt indirectly attacked as a member of the same ethnic group. What can I do as a mother to help ensure that my daughters not only survive negative experiences, but that they also emerge from them as strong individuals?

Acknowledge that Racism Exists Acknowledgement does not mean that we are looking under every stone, actively seeking out racism. Acknowledgment simply means that we believe our kids when they tell us racism exists. When it happens to our children, we are saddened by it, but are no surprised that it has occurred. Recognize that not only will our children face one or two incidents of racism in a lifetime, but that they will face various shapes and forms of it repeatedly. Most importantly, acknowledgment means that we are not dismissive of our children's experiences or how they might feel. More than once, I have been more hurt by the reaction that I am 'overreacting,' 'too sensitive,' or need to 'lighten up', than I am by the actual racist incident itself.

Speak Critically with Our Kids about Racism   As parents, we may be concerned that initiating a conversation about racism may be equivalent to falsely 'planting the seed of racism' in our children's tender brains. But I do think we need to help our children see racism, by pointing it out in popular culture (e.g., African Americans frequently cast as criminals, Asians often portrayed as nerdy, etc.)

Be sure to ask enough questions about an unpleasant incident they describe at school or elsewhere, to help them work out if it was a racist incident. I think the most important tools we can give our children is the ability to think critically. They need to be able to recognize that they are responsible for their own success and to know that people in power will sometimes try to get in the way of their success

Confront the Beast   The racism our children face demand action on our part. Confrontation is the next step after acknowledgment and talk. The type of action to be taken obviously will depend on the circumstances. Do not discount the need for physical safety. At the LAX airport, I felt intimidated by the actions of the U.S. Customs agent. I felt vulnerable because I did not want to somehow jeopardize my daughter's entry into the country by confronting the agents at that moment. However, once we were home, I wrote a letter to U.S. Customs that included the following statement: *"I am shocked that this family's first incident of racism occurred before they even left the airport, by federal US government employees no less. I would never conduct myself in such a hateful manner. Being a woman of color and because we were processing my daughter's entry into the country, I was too intimidated to confront these men in person. That is why I am writing this letter to you. I question what kind of future my daughter will have in this country when government personnel treat fellow human beings this way, and I am disgusted at the behavior I witnessed."*

Confrontation need not always be reactionary. Confrontation can also be preventive, recognizing however that even preventive measures will not be 100% effective. For example, surrounding our children with a diverse set of friends is a terrific way to arm them against racist incidents to come.

Having a peer group with whom to take solace and provide support was paramount to me, particularly in my teen years.   When confronted by racism, I could seek solace in my friends, even if I didn't feel like going to my parents. My friends met me and my problems with acknowledgment, comfort, and humor.

~ Usha Rengachary Smerdon is the mother to two children adopted from India

Invisible Adoption
My Child is Just Like Me
By Karen Holt

My daughter looks like me. My daughter was adopted in Russia. Because she looks like me, we can go to the grocery store, mall and zoo without being noticed, which is a blessing. However I am not sure that it is a blessing to have her hear constantly that "she looks just like me". People say that "she looks like me" as if to validate the adoption. Since we look alike, we must belong together. Doesn't she belong with her birth family too? Does saying she looks like me invalidate her connection to her birth family? She may look similar to me, but she looks like them, not me. People who introduce my daughter to new church members often add, "You know she is a special child, she was adopted in Russia." To the people who really count, it is not a very 'invisible' adoption after all.

Does being an invisibly adopted child/young adult/adult lessen a child's need to know about their birth culture? Can same race international adoptive families ignore the language and cultural issues that visible/transracial adoptive families work hard to incorporate into their families? I don't think so. I think the culture and heritage is a key piece of a person's identity. An adopted person has two sets of culture and heritage to assimilate.

Knowing Roots

Generations of same race domestic adoptive families before us have learned that the need to know about their past is critically important to many adopted people. That is one reason we have so many open or semi open domestic adoptions today. It is why adult adopted people are still fighting to open their birth records in many places in the USA and around the world.

Peter F. Dodds, the author of *Outer Search, Inner Journey: An Orphan and Adoptee's Quest* was adopted in 1957 at age three from a German orphanage by an American couple. He features this quote prominently on his website: *There is no greater sorrow on Earth, than the loss of one's native land.—Euripides, Medea*

His experience as an invisibly adopted person left him feeling different. Although he and his adoptive parents were the same race, he did not feel that he looked like his parents at all. *"I looked nothing like my adoptive parents. Francis Dodds was 5'8", stockily built with blond, wavy hair and sky blue eyes. Tattoos covered the biceps of his muscular arms and he had a pug nose. My mother was small–5' 2", plain looking with a long nose, medium build, brown hair and hazel eyes. I would grow to be 6'1", had angular facial features and a Roman nose beneath dark blue eyes and straight dark hair. Our physical differences glowed like a neon flashing sign; we weren't the same blood."*

Peter felt like an outsider in both Germany and the United States, and said, *"Peter Friedrich, wer bin ich? Peter Frederick, who am I? German or American? The answer was neither and both. I had German blood but an American mentality."* His adoptive family apparently did not celebrate his birth culture and told him they didn't trust Germans due to the World Wars.

Most white children who are adopted internationally by same race families are going to be from 'former enemy countries' of the US, Canada, England, and other industrialized countries. It is the nature of international adoption that the children from second and third world countries are adopted by families in first world countries.

Adoptive parents of children from 'former enemy countries' need to be especially careful that they are supportive of the child's birth culture. There will be plenty of negative inferences about these countries on the playground and in everyday life. The Cold War and fear of communism is not that far behind us. The placing countries of Eastern Europe and the former Soviet Union are often portrayed as dirty, backward, and corrupt, rather than interesting and exotic as many other child placing nations are portrayed. Families need to be proactive in understanding the history of their child's birth country to provide a stable base on which their child can build an identity.

> *Peter Friedrich, wer bin ich? Peter Frederick, who am I? German or American? The answer was neither and both. I had German blood but an American mentality.*
> *~Peter F. Dodds*

Adoption into a Similar Culture Does Involve Loss

Even internationally adopted people who were invisibly adopted by similar-culture families experience loss. Maggie Biddle, born in Ireland in 1951 and adopted at age one by a Roman Catholic Irish-American family in New England, was quoted in the LA Times:

"You were cut off from your name, from your history and from your country," she said. *"You were sent into exile. You are supposed to be grateful for what was done for you. But that shouldn't negate the fact that you want to meet your mother."* Maggie now lives in Dublin, Ireland.

Parents of invisibly adopted international children need to work harder at making connections with similar families because they are invisible. I often babysit for children adopted from Asia and Central America. When I run into other similar looking families while caring for these children, there is an instant rapport, a smile, a nod. It is much harder to connect with families where the children are adopted invisibly. One invisible-adoptive family struck up a conversation with my friend because her children were visibly adopted. The family had a child from Russia, but although I was at the same event, we would have never met: it wasn't obvious to me or to them that our children had similar backgrounds.

Invisibly adopted children can and do hide their adoptive status from the world at times. It is important that we as parents don't hide it from ourselves.

Will my child be offended at the constant reminders that she looks like me? Will she feel those comments belittle her genetic heritage and discount the value of her birth family?

Children who are invisibly adopted are not exempt from the need to understand their birth culture. They are not exempt from the losses of birth family, language, and heritage. Children who are adopted by same race families do have the advantage of learning directly how people of their race function in their adoptive community. But that isn't enough. I work hard to incorporate my daughter's family and heritage into our life; I think the experiences of the Peter Dodds and the Maggie Biddles show that birth culture, language, heritage, and family are not to be forgotten.

~ Karen Holt is an adoptive mom to a child from Russia and she maintains a comprehensive list of adoption resources **www.karensadoptionlinks.com**

~The Scarlet Letter Experiment~
A Parent Exercise in Exploring Visible Difference

In Nathaniel Hawthorne's The Scarlet Letter, Hester Prynne is forced to wear a Scarlet A on her chest because she was caught committing adultery during Puritan times. Imagine wearing an A on your blouse—or to update it, a D for Divorced, G for Gay, or PS for Premarital Sex.

You may not think there is anything wrong with being divorced or gay or having premarital sex any more, but some people still do. Because of the D or G or PS on your chest, they know who you are, but you do not know who they are. Suppose you have to wear a big D on your chest for 'Divorced.' When you go to a club and ten people ask you to dance, is it because you really look so beautiful today, or because they think divorced people are desperate? When you try to rent a house and do not get it, is it really because it was rented to someone else or is the landlord afraid of the wild drunken orgies he knows divorcees have? If your child's friends cannot come play at your house, is it really because she has to practice violin or is it because her friends' parents are afraid you will have lots of strange men hanging around? When you meet someone new, do they expect you to teach them everything there is to know about the experience of being divorced?

It does not take long before you start double guessing people's motives or you simply get tired of the same dumb question over and over again. These examples are minor compared to getting beaten up or killed by illiterate skinheads who cannot tell a D from a G from a PS, but they still chafe like a burr under the saddle-pad of supposed equality.

Then compare your experiences to that of The Scarlet Letter's adulterous Reverend Arthur Dimmesdale, who also wears a scarlet letter on his chest, but hidden, under his clothes. He is able to hide it until he chooses when and to whom to reveal it.

If thought experiments are not your thing, then try the real thing: Put yourself in situations where you are 'the only one' and pay attention to what it feels like. Resist the urge to hide behind your child or an explanation. If you are Caucasian, go to an African American nightclub or an African-American church. If you are in your thirties or forties, go to a college frat party and try to blend in. If you are a man, go to a woman's beauty salon or lingerie department (and only look at items in your size). If you are straight, go to a gay bar. If you are a woman, go watch a football game or go to a strip club with a bunch of men. If you speak only English, go to an ethnic neighborhood or organization where everybody speaks another language. Go to a black tie event wearing torn jeans, or go to a child's birthday party wearing diamonds and a fabulous evening gown. Dye your hair blond and wear a slinky red dress. Sometimes something as simple as saying no to a glass of wine or a piece of chocolate cake is enough to arouse strange looks and suspicions.

Try it and deal with feeling uncomfortable and vulnerable. Then imagine that it is something you cannot escape, like the color of your skin. This is what our children potentially have to deal with every day.

~ Frances Kai-Hwa Wang
IMDiversity.com Asian American Village Contributing Editor

Older Child Adoption

Lessons I Learned
From a 4 year-old...
By Cindy Champnella

When the child came to me, I was whole and she was broken. Or so I thought. If I had only known then that in the process of her becoming whole, of her reconciling her past with her new life, that the veneer of my life, my assumptions, the things I had formerly believed to be true, would be stripped away...

I can now say, five years later, she has become whole or maybe as whole as she will ever be. Her teachers tell me with a mixture of pride and wonder that she blends invisibly in any group of children that she is in and that no outside observer would ever sense where she had been or what she had been through. I credit her with this. If sheer force of will can be used to put back together the pieces of a shattered life, she had this in spades. If you can make yourself love and trust and believe again, when absolutely nothing in your previous life gives you any reason to think that your heart will not be once more trampled, she succeeded in doing so. If you can embrace a foreigner, one whose very countenance makes you recoil, and claim her as your mother by willing yourself to do so, she did. I am humbled by her strength; thank goodness one of us possessed it.

Adopting Jaclyn was a decision I made solely with my heart; if I had stopped to think about the adoption, even for a moment, I would never have done it. I never read anything about older child adoption until I got on the plane to go to China. And, truthfully, if I had read any of it I would never have gotten on that plane in the first place.

My first year with Jaclyn was an amazing roller coaster ride of ups and downs. The dizzying downward slides made me, at times, question my saneness. But always, the joy that Jaclyn brought into my life helped balance the angst. But I desperately needed support. I struggled. I was discouraged and confused and amazed and bewildered—often at the same time. I lost perspective as I broached the challenge of becoming a mother to this unfamiliar four-year-old that had claimed my heart.

I wish there was a way that I could now tie those lessons up with a bow and offer them in some formulaic manner to those with the fortitude, heart, and spirit required to venture into the unknowns involved in older child adoption. But for this experience, there are no easy answers. I guess the single most reassuring piece of advice I can give is simply to admit that I am living proof that you can have no idea what you are doing, manage to do just about everything wrong and still have things somehow turn out OK. So here's a chance to learn from my mistakes, to do as I say not as I did, and to hopefully glean something helpful along the way. For me the light at the end of the tunnel was the eventual love and trust of a remarkable child who has changed my life in more ways than I can count. It ended up fine. But it didn't start out that way....

Expect Rejection.

To say that Jaclyn was disappointed when she met us would be the understatement of the century. In fact, on the return visit to the orphanage a few days post adoption she marched up to the orphanage director with this disparaging pronouncement: "My parents are foreigners!" This was clearly not the deal she had signed up for. Jaclyn, very conscious of issues of race from the start, wanted desperately to be adopted by a Chinese family. Any Chinese family. In fact, on our last day in China she begged plaintively with our driver to adopt her–any reprieve from going off with the foreigners was welcome. Much later, when she had both the language and the courage to express herself, she told me that the reason she did not like me in the beginning: "Your nose and eyes are a little bit yucky!"

But fear can also play a part in rejection and, as a result, you must be continually vigilant. If I live to be a hundred, I'll never forget the heart-pounding panic that ensured when I realized that while we were distracted looking at some tourist attraction, Jaclyn had stealthily gotten away in a crowded park and hidden from us. It didn't bode well for my mothering abilities to have already lost the child I had parented for all of three days.

Advice I'd offer to handle this:
Preparation Helps. Make sure you send a photo book in advance so the child can be prepared for your yucky face. Remember, however that the child is often not shown the book until right before the adoption.

Get Out. Don't sit in the hotel room and look at each other. Not only did her anxiety increase as she came face to face with me, but mine increased as well and she could sense my fear. Most children have a natural curiosity about what is in the outside world so getting outside to see the sights tends to district the child.

Hang On. While you are out and about keep your eyes on your child and their hand in yours so that they don't get away from you. Jaclyn could not remember much about life outside the institution so some of her natural curiosity and lack of socialization also caused potential safety concerns–twice she tried to run into five lanes of heavy traffic.

The Food Factor. An important first step in establishing trust and minimizing fear is food. Jaclyn told me later that her biggest fear in coming with us was that she would not get any food. Almost immediately I offered her snacks, which she hid in a stash, but her spirits rose considerably at every meal.

Expect to Have Second Thoughts.

Rejection can be a two-way street and the shame that comes from the realization that you are secretly hoping for some way out of the commitment to the child you have longed fo forever can lead to all kinds of self-recrimination. Love doesn't happen overnight on either side of the equation. I had formed a vivid impression of my future daughter based on a few photos and some second-hand information from a family who had met her. Imagine my shock when the sweet, quiet, shy child that had been described to me turned out to be a tiger. The fact that she was completely and totally unfamiliar to me somehow surprised me. An older child has already formed a distinct personality and you need to discover that; you cannot predetermine it. And it takes a long time to see who they really are as you peel back the layers of what they have been through.

Strategies here include:

Fake It Until You Feel It. In a performance that should have garnered an academy award, I feigned love and caring for a child that I sometimes didn't even like. And, to be truthful, I believe the faking went both ways—once Jaclyn realized there was no way out she, too, determined to try to love the yucky-faced mom she was saddled with. But a scary accident that resulted in my first tears cried with her and for her and the surprising knowledge that came with them—that I truly loved this child and she was now my own—somehow was sweeter because of the time it took to get there.

Don't Be Too Hard on Yourself. You're not a bad mom if you don't fall in love right away—you're an honest mom. Love can't be willed and doesn't have any 'shoulds'; love has its own time and path.

Love is Not Enough.

If I only had a nickel for every well-meaning person who congratulated me on my bravery and assured me that with enough love everything would be OK. Here's a reality check— for some of these kids, many who have suffered unspeakable trauma, there isn't enough love in this world to make it OK. They need more, much more. Some need structure. Some need reassurance. Some need support. Most need all three. And many need professional help and guidance.

Remember this:

Real Problems Need to be Dealt With in Real Ways. Read everything you can get your hands on. Use internet adoption groups to get advice and support. Seek out therapists or social workers who specialize in adoption issues. And don't get scared.

Adjustment is Not a Linear Path.

I somehow thought that every day would be better and certainly that every week should be. Wrong. Often there is a 'honeymoon period' and then a crash. In my case, the honeymoon never happened. We went from problems to getting-used-to-problems to life-now-seems-normal-with-these-problems to disaster. In fact, the most trying period of time came about 8 months post-adoption. A friend congratulated me at that milestone indicating that it was now evidence that Jaclyn trusted me enough to show her most challenging self—it was the ultimate test to see if I would stick around when times got tough. But it was hard to celebrate this, much less to endure it. Spending every minute of every day with a cranky, difficult, bossy, I'm-going-to-challenge-everything kid nearly did me in.

In hindsight, I offer this:

Remember, This Too Shall Pass. When you're in it and things are going badly it feels like it's going to last forever. You are not going to be able to 'fix' all that has happened before in a few months. Or years. Or maybe ever. And 'fixing' isn't the goal. It's about acceptance and overcoming and learning and growing. Keep a long term perspective— you're on a journey of discovery together.

Maintain Control and Structure. Do not change any rules or routines just because it appears that they will never be adhered to. Consistency is critical.

Keep Calm. Your anxiety, fear, and anger ratchets up the child's anxiety, fear and anger. Count to a hundred. Count to a million. Take a walk. Scream into a pillow. Cry in the shower.

Keep Loving Them. At their worst, and most out-of-control, is when they desperately need to know that they are loved and accepted and that you are never, ever going to give up on them.

Socialization Takes Time.

In an incredible act of sheer lunacy I scheduled a trip to Disney World, the land of sensory overload, three months post-adoption. Then I was somehow surprised when I found Jaclyn head first in a fountain congratulating herself on her good luck in finding so many coins that others had left behind Later in the day her older sister tattled that Jaclyn was chewing gum. My husband and I exchanged puzzled glances as neither of us had given her any. Then finally the light bulb went off—she was happily chomping on gum that she had scraped off the bathroom floor! I reprimanded her severely and was sure that this matter was taken care of...until the next day when her sister reported once again that Jaclyn had gum. Of course she was clueless as to how to behave and what was expected of her! Only much later was she able to explain to me how confusing this had been for her. When they told her at school that food on the floor was dirty and had germs she puzzled over it and then concluded: *"In China there no such thing as germs! You find food on the floor, it your lucky day!"*

Some thoughts on this:

Review Expectations. In any and every new situation, you need to tell the child what behavior is expected. Be specific on what is OK and what will not be tolerated. Expand the list as you go along because it is nearly impossible to think of all the 'don't dos'.

Watch Their Reactions. Unlike other children her age who had been socialized in the US, Jaclyn was terrified of many things that she had never been exposed to; she simply didn't understand what would happen next. When she was ready to get on the bus to go to school she asked: "Mama, will I ever come back from kindergarten?"

Explain, Explain, Explain. For a period of time I thought of my life as a continual game of 'Jeopardy' as I tried to answer all the questions of one very short contestant. They need to understand; show them how things work. Just like you need to explain to a toddler the fridge door must be kept shut, many older adoptees need to be told these things too.

Be On Guard for Sensory Overload. TV, cars, movies, the circus—all of them may be new experiences. Advance preparation on what to expect is helpful but also ease them into new stimuli.

A New Value System Takes Time to Develop.

Many older adoptees not only have institutional behaviors, but may also exhibit behaviors that were at one time integral to their survival. For Jaclyn, stealing was one of those. The teacher called to report that she had been caught going through her classmates' coat pockets. She shoplifted from the store on the field trip. She tip-toed out of bed to sneak things from her sister's room. She hid candy in her underpants. She later told me she had often stolen food to give to one of the younger children in the institution who had food taken from him by older kids. For her, stealing was an adaptive behavior not a 'wrong' one. My job was to help her understand a whole new moral code based on 'right' and 'wrong' instead of survival.

Sisters Don't Happen Overnight.

Along with my other delusions, I had a fantasy of a new playmate for my other kids. After the first few days my older daughter had only one question: "Why is she so mean?" Jaclyn brought with her wariness of older children. In the orphanage she had often seen the older kids bully and take advantage of the younger ones. Survival of the fittest was her norm and, as a result, she often was aggressive. She had a menacing stance with upraised fists that appeared, always behind my back, at the least provocation and sometimes without any provocation at all. She also saw other children as competitors for scant adult attention. But I believe that there was another issue here, too. She had left behind in the orphanage two children that had become family to her. About one of them she stated simply: "I gave him all my love." She had now lost them both, in addition to her birth family who she also recalled. Given this, how willing was she to love again?

So how can you facilitate the sibling bond?

Prepare Your Children. They need to understand the 'whys' behind the new sibling's often puzzling behavior.

Encourage Empathy and Support. Make this a family issue—you're all in it together. Ask for their help.

Empathize With Their Frustration. They're kids after all, not saints. They don't have the perspective of adults. And it is annoying to have a new sibling steal your stuff and become the mom-hog.

You Now Have a New Job: Educator.

One of your primary duties will be helping those who interact with the child, especially teachers, understand the 'whys' of your child's behavior. I had a livid teacher call me to relate that the children had all been in line to go to the bathroom. A child cut in line in front of Jaclyn and she exploded. The teacher intervened and instructed Jaclyn to 'let it go'. Assuming compliance, she was furious when Jaclyn neatly checked the other child into the sink as soon as they got out of the teacher's eyesight. Understanding that Jaclyn's former life experience involved living in an orphanage with 380 children that lined up daily for virtually everything and that being in the back of that line often meant no lunch if they ran out of food, or wearing the left-over shoes that were two sizes too small, helped the teacher understand that 'place in line' was not a trivial matter for this child.

Strategies that might help here include:

Seek First to Understand. Unfortunately, most older adoptees are not as disclosing about their past lives as Jaclyn was. So read all you can on institutional behavior and think about cause and effect responses. For example, I could hear Jaclyn on the playground when I was two football fields away. But she had also clamored for adult attention with hundreds of others so her piercing voice was simply a way to be heard. Once you 'get it', it somehow becomes easier to tolerate.

Help the Child Understand. Use positive reinforcement to encourage them to abandon old behaviors. But remember, too, that this is also a process and feeling safe is a prerequisite to letting go of what worked in the past.

Help Others Understand. Speak candidly with those who will be an on-going part of your child's life. Then, ask for them to be your partner in encouraging new behaviors.

Feelings Are Paramount.

You can't have the rug pulled out from under you and not feel anger and confusion and grief. Jaclyn told me once: "I don't know how to make the mad go away." She came to me with not only a list of grievances, but also with deep anger about being wronged. And judgments about those who had wronged her, including her birth mother. In the beginning, I recoiled from those outbursts and tried to make her understand a different perspective. I thought I could somehow talk her out of her anger. The truth was I felt uncomfortable with the depth of her rage. What I didn't get was that it was hers, not mine, and only she could find the key to releasing it. Forgiveness, if it ever comes, is only hers to bestow.

What would have worked better:

Allow the child to feel it, own it and express it. Her teacher often used the expression that many use with angry toddlers: "Use your words, not your fists." If anyone can tell me what the words are that would be big enough to express her feelings, I'd love to hear them. In hindsight I'd let her use her words, her voice, and her, fists, too, if she needed to. Get a punching bag. Show them how to punch a pillow. Give them a safe place to scream if they want to. And don't try to use logic and facts to counteract feelings.

Understand that sadness and grief can happen anytime with no seeming connection to current events. To know Jaclyn was also to know sorrow. When the demons of her past grabbed hold of her she sobbed, nearly catatonic, while I attempted to comfort her. Her grief had such depth that I don't believe any of my attempts to calm her make the slightest difference. At first I was puzzled by the lack of triggers—what in the world had caused this crash? Then I finally realized that the triggers were unknown to me, like fleeting ghosts that only she could see.

Make it safe for them to tell their story. Pieces of the past seemed to come out at the most inopportune moments—when I was exhausted and hoping to crawl into bed, when we had to rush to the airport, when we were at the doctor's office. And then Jaclyn would watch carefully for my reaction before going on. If I seemed upset or sad or too interested or probed too deeply with my questions, the conversation stopped. A neutral expression and reaction were critical to her continuing to speak of the recollection. And this was anything but easy to pull off when the story being recounted would make me want to recoil or sob or pound something with my fists. I sometimes felt that if I gave into the sadness that I felt about where she had been and what she had been through that my tears would fill the room. But getting it out was healing for her and she needed for me to be able to handle it.

Realize that you may never get the missing pieces. Most older adoptees talk very little about the past. For some the memories are too deep, for some they are too wounding. And if they don't want to talk, or can't find the words or don't know why they feel the way that they do, that has to be OK, too.

Control Equals Safety.

When the world turns upside down with no say on your part, the need for control becomes the invisible elephant in every interaction. Jaclyn would eat noodles only with the little white fork. She would drink only from the red glass. Each item on her plate could not touch another. Her pony-tail could only be in the sparkled rubber band. Jaclyn was crushed that no one wanted to play with her because her version of playing involved barked orders like "You will be this!" or "You will do that!" But I often wondered if your whole life has spun out of control, when you had been uprooted from home, friends and family and all that is familiar twice before you were five years old, how big your need for control should be? When she felt safe, the need for control diminished. Notice that I didn't say it went away.

What does help:

   Provide Structure. Jaclyn was used to the structure of an orphanage routine where children walked in lock-step to a rigid schedule. When given time for 'free play' at kindergarten she immediately organized a small posse to invade the little kitchen and showed the kids neat ways to throw the plastic dishes like Frisbees. She simply did not know how to handle 'free choices'. In fact, the routine at school was much easier for her than figuring out how to live in a family. Structure and the certainty that came from knowing what would come next helped provide her with security and some continuity in a world that had turned upside down.

   Understand that a Strong Will is also an Adaptive Behavior. Many older adoptees survived, when others did not, because of their fortitude. So I think of it this way—if I survive Jaclyn's childhood, to say nothing of her adolescence, I'm pretty confident she will be a woman to be reckoned with.

   Choices. Whenever possible give them choices. This allows them control within boundaries that you have defined.

   Choose Your Battles. A battle of the wills better be over something huge.

Food is Fundamental.

Although many adoptees have a variety of food issues, an older adoptee may have a longer history of deprivation. For Jaclyn, food was the most tangible sign of security. She had to have food with her all the time, everywhere she went and in every situation. I found stashes of potato chips behind my couch and under her bed. She took food with her in her backpack even on trips to the corner store. If we were going anywhere, she had to know what food would be there. And even if we were going somewhere to eat, she still brought food along just in case. She not only had to have food with her always, but had to be in control of any situation that involved food. When I served dinner, she had to monitor what went on her plate. If a doggie bag came home from a restaurant, she needed to grab it, examine it, know what it was and who had eaten it and, most importantly, why she was not there when it was consumed. And if I refused to tell her what I had eaten, she'd smell my breath.

What manages this:
Never let Food be an Issue. It was obvious, even to me, that this was a biggie. And I eventually learned to open my horizons on issues like what was an acceptable breakfast. Jaclyn simply didn't like American breakfast foods, and still doesn't. So we learned to compromise; I abandoned cereal and eggs and she abandoned popsicles and mandarin oranges. We settled on peanuts, dill pickles and spinach with lots of garlic.

> *"When I lived in China I wished for only one thing— a mama. If you wish for too many things your heart aches."*
> Jaclyn Champnella

Let them have Access to Food Without Permission. Control on something this primal to security doesn't work. I showed her shelves of low-fat, low-sugar snacks that she could help herself to whenever she wanted.

There is no timeline. Five years later, food is still fundamental. But I am happy to report that there are no longer potato chips under my couch.

Race Matters.

And if you don't think race matters, you're going to learn otherwise. I never really thought race would be an issue because it wasn't for me. My first clue was Jaclyn's birthday party. I had given her invitations for all the girls in her class. I noticed on the day of the party that she had invited only other children of color. Then I made time to notice her interactions at school and discovered that she segregated herself at lunch and often stood in tight circles with other children of color while keeping her back to the Caucasian children. One day Jaclyn came home and told me that she needed an eye examination because something was wrong with her eyes. "Eyes supposed to go like this," she said while pulling hers open. Later came the story about why she didn't like a boy in her class: "He always call me 'Jaclyn, you Chinese girl,'" she said sadly.

And how does a parent without any first-hand experience regarding issues of race tackle this?
Ask Adult People of Color to Help You. Talking to Jaclyn's Asian tutor helped me understand that separating along racial lines was sometimes OK. "You don't understand," the tutor said to me. "Sometimes you just want to be with your own people. Then you can relax and you don't have to explain why you're not good at math since all Asian people are."
Be Inclusive. We have dear friends that are Chinese in addition to friends of other ethnic backgrounds. Jaclyn loved having a chance to spend time with others who shared her heritage.

Mingle with Other Families that Look like Yours. It goes without saying that the groups such as Families with Children from China provide wonderful opportunities for socializing with families that share your child's heritage.

Make Them Proud. I told Jaclyn to proudly affirm that she was Chinese. After all, she was from a spectacular country with a proud and noble history. I also told her that I believed that some of the most beautiful and smartest girls in the world came from China. I wasn't sure if it was the right response until I saw her eyes fill with tears and heard her heart-felt words of thanks.

Be There.

You have to just be there constantly and consistently for as long as it takes. And everything else in your life needs to take a back seat. I got a call one day from a friend with a very serious problem. I went to the basement to talk to her because I could not hear her over the ruckus in my living room. After a few minutes Jaclyn noticed that I was missing. I found her in the front yard, on her knees, hands outstretched to the heavens screaming; "MAMA! MAMA!" Her terror was palpable. When my husband had to work late she would call down from her bed: "Daddy? Daddy?" every time she heard a sound. This went on once until 3:00 am.

Six weeks after I adopted Jaclyn she told me for the first time that she had two mamas. One she called her 'go-away China mama' and I was dubbed 'this-a mama'. And then she shared her most basic fear: "I scared this-a mama go away."

How do you respond to this?

Develop a Mantra. For me it was "Mama goes. Mama always comes back." I said this every day, every time I went anywhere. I hoped that if she heard it enough, she would one day believe it.

Actions Speak Louder than Words. Over time, just being there counts.

Every Child's Story is Different.

The tough thing about preparing is that there simply isn't anyway to know what's ahead. Your child may have none of the issues described here, but others that we didn't experience. Different histories present different issues. And similar events can trigger different responses. The value in preparation and in reading is that you at least know where to get help, that others have managed similar issues and that you are not alone. But you have to manage the fear factor, too. During the waiting phase, I found myself for a time addicted to an internet adoption group. But the more I read, the more I panicked. I suddenly began to envision a child with Reactive Attachment Disorder, parasites, Post-Traumatic Stress Disorder, sleeping issues and an identity crisis all happening simultaneously. Not a pretty picture. For some expecting the worst makes the rest seem manageable. For me it was easier to just stick my head in the sand.

And so, after reading all of this, are you left wondering "is it all just too hard?" What I would say is this: my experience in life has been that things that prove to be the most satisfying are often the most difficult. I think of Jaclyn as both the greatest sorrow and the greatest joy in my life. But when I close my eyes and think of my proudest moment, it certainly must be the day that I graduated from "this-a mama" to "always-come-back

Mama." Jaclyn explained to me why her younger sister was whimpering when I dropped her off at Sunday school. "She doesn't understand that you always-come-back, Mama," Jaclyn said. "She doesn't know mama always comes back." And then, in her impish way she added, "And I be always-come-back, Jaclyn!"

When I think of my greatest triumph, it was surely the day that I noticed that the suitcase Jaclyn had kept at her bedside for almost two years, neatly packed with her favorite treasures in case she once again had to leave, was now gone. But nothing compared to the day she told me, with great anguish, about what it felt like to live in an orphanage and stand and watch "the mamas" arrive over and over to adopt babies while the older kids languished. When I asked her if she felt sad she explained by saying; "I happy for the babies to get mamas. But I not sad for myself. I didn't want those other mamas." Then she gave me her brilliant smile and added; "I was waiting for you!"

A few months ago we had a dear friend who was going through a tough patch. The combined stress of work problems, family problems and financial problems had culminated in some frightening chest pains. Jaclyn, an inveterate eavesdropper, heard us discussing this troubling situation and had her own insight: "I know what's wrong with Uncle Al," she said solemnly. "He's wishing for too many things." And then she added quietly, "When I lived in China I wished for only one thing—a mama. If you wish for too many things your heart aches." And so, if you're reading this and your heart aches because you want to parent one of these remarkable older kids, I guarantee you there is a not-so-small person somewhere on this earth who shares that ache.

But can you do it? If you understand parenting as a marathon, not a sprint, if you aren't too proud to ask for help, if you're open to the unexpected, if you have a strong support system, if you're prepared to commit for better or for worse, in sickness and in health, this may be for you. But it's also for you if you want to hear the word "WOW!" shouted in exuberance over the ordinary things in your life, if you want to see the world through the lens of wonder, if you want to try to hang onto the hand of a child who runs joyfully into new life, if you want to hear a heart-felt "thank-you" over something you formerly took for granted, if you want to fall in love in a way that you never saw coming or see a smile that rivals the beauty of even the most magnificent sunset.

Just remember to hang onto your hat…it's a wild ride!

~ Cindy Champnella is the author of "The Waiting Child: How the Faith and Love of One Orphan Saved the Life of Another". All proceeds from her book are designated for the charity, Half the Sky Foundation. This foundation, which was founded entirely by parents of Chinese adopted children, is intended to benefit children who live in Chinese orphanages. Champnella is mother to six children including two adoptees from China. She has worked as an adoption social worker and is currently pursuing her PhD in psychology with a specialty in adoption issues.

Grief and Loss
In Older Child Adoptive Families
By Susan M. Ward

Feelings from the Past

My daughter, Hannah, was six when I adopted her from a Russian orphanage. As I prepared to travel to Russia, reading everything I could about what to do and how to act at the orphanage, I saw a list of questions to ask of the orphanage staff about your child's background and early years. That didn't seem particularly important to me; her past was her past. Her 'real' life would begin with me. ***How wrong, naive, and uneducated I was!***

Within 48 hours of being home, Hannah was talking about her birth brothers! How could that be? I knew she had birth brothers, but I'd been told she had not interacted with them in quite some time, and had no memory of them. Why was she talking about them...?

During the first couple months home, Hannah shared stories with me about the orphanage, and about her birth mom. My Russian was limited so I couldn't understand all of it, but I did realize that she was sharing lots of emotional experiences from her past.

Four months after Hannah came home, I took her to a therapist to for help with her outbursts, aggression, and noncompliance. During the sessions, the therapist talked about 'the hole' in Hannah's heart due to the gaps in information I had about her past, and about being adopted. She also mentioned Hannah's possible grief about being separated from her birth brothers. I started to understand. I began to read. I found out about grief and loss in adopted children, especially in older children.

Later on, when Hannah and I started seeing an attachment therapist to help with Hannah's just-diagnosed Reactive Attachment Disorder (RAD), this therapist too, talked about grief issues, especially grief and loss in children. I continued reading.

I began connecting the grief and loss to post traumatic stress disorder, and the post traumatic stress disorder to attachment and bonding challenges. I finally understood why I should have asked those questions at the orphanage about Hannah's past. Her past was part of her present. And, grief and loss were woven into all parts of her life.

Exploring Grief and Loss in Adoption

My new understanding led me first to explore grief in children, then grief in adopted children, then to the topic of grief and loss throughout the lives of adoptive families. My newfound interest provided me with an opportunity to help educate other adoptive parents. It also showed me how seldom the topic is of grief and loss is discussed, whether in the context of children and their healing, or families and their parenting challenges

Part of the reason that the information is limited is that the topic of grief in children is fairly new; it wasn't too far back when it was assumed that children simply did not grieve. There is now an awareness that children do grieve, and that they grieve differently from adults. Most resources available, however, are for children dealing with death–death of a grandparent, sibling, or parent. Our children are more commonly suffering from loss–the loss of their everyday life, of who they are, of all that is familiar to them. And, when it comes to parental grief and loss in adoption, there's a hesitancy to cast a pall of somberness over the excitement of creating a new family.

Few joyful occurrences in life come without some measure of difficulty, challenge, or even grief. In the joy and excitement of adoption, don't be surprised or overwhelmed to find elements of grief and loss intruding upon your life, and your child's life. Read about it, understand it, and use the information to grow the strongest family you can.

Adoptive Parents: Grieving the Dream

As parents, adoption agencies, and social workers, we view adoption as happy and joyful. A child without a family now has one. A family yearning to share its love can now open its heart. Most adoption books, web sites, agencies, and social workers use words and phrases like, "fulfilling, joy, happiness, tears of happiness, meant to be together."

Adoption, however, often involves the hurtful, pain-filled, gnawing emotion of grief. The grief can be for us, for our children, or it can be our children's grief.

At the beginning stages of adoption, grief may be part of pre-adoptive couples as they face issues of infertility. It can be part of a single parent's issues of loss in not finding a spouse. It can also be an emotion of birth parents who want to parent their child, but realize they don't have the resources and choose to place their child with adoptive parents.

As parents go from adoption planning to placement, expectations for the child they plan to adopt may include words like "smart, sweet, athletic, curious." But adopted children, like biological children, come with no guarantees. After a child is home for a while, parents may realize their child has a physical, emotional, behavioral, psychological, or learning disorder. All of these can mean abandonment of your dream child. As you grieve and grow, you must learn to let go of what you hoped your child would be, and to embrace what your child is.

As adoptive families adjust to their new lives, there can be substantial changes in relationships: relationships between spouses, siblings, extended family, and friends. These changes may be temporary, or sometimes, they may be permanent, requiring a period of grieving for relationships that may be changing significantly, or even ending.

One mom of an older adoptive child shares, *"The grief that has most touched our family is the loss of the life we had pre-adoption. Everything changed, more than we were prepared for, even though we had prepared. We grieved (and sometimes still do) the loss of independence, freedom, a relatively calm and happy home, lost friendships (or the time to maintain these friendships). We miss being able to have a conversation without being interrupted! We grieve when special occasions are overshadowed by child's loss of control and manipulation.*

"Having said this, we are adjusting and we have grown and changed in positive ways. We are very slowly coming to love our son, to believe in him, to want to assist him to be the best he can be even if it costs us. He has totally changed our lives but some of those ways are very positive. It is now hard to imagine our lives without him."

> *In the joy and excitement of adoption, don't be surprised or overwhelmed to find elements of grief and loss intruding upon your life, and your child's life. Read about it, understand it, and use the information to grow the strongest family you can.*

Tools to Tackle Grief

I'm a big fan of solution focus strategies. Here's my 'short list' of very concrete ways to help our children be very resourceful in dealing with their own feelings, including those of grief and loss.

Validation

In my worldview, Validating is an important resource. To validate another's experience means to accept that for them it is real. We can offer empathy to our children for their grief.

Affirmation

Affirmations are positive statements that reinforce feelings about grief
"I'm sure if that were me, I'd feel (insert feeling here)."

Ritual

Rituals are really lacking in today's world. Children derive feelings of security and safety from them. Developing family rituals and traditions are great ways to build family strength and increase parent/child bonds.

Measuring Success–Journaling

As children learn to process, a Journal can be an effective means of helping them not only recognize their feelings and successes, but allow them to look back over time and see how much progress they've made.

~Deborah Anderson, birthmother, bio mother and adoptive mother to many

Grieving Children: How Can Parents Help?

In considering our children's new life with us, intellectually, we understand that our children may not have that same sense of joy that we do about being adopted, especially during the first weeks and months. Practically, though, do we allow and even create enough opportunities for adopted children to grieve their losses and their past?

In *Helping Children Grieve and Grow*, Donna O'Toole and Jerre Cory write, "Especially for children, a loss may be based on safety, comfort, and familiarity, rather than on what adults speak of as love or affection." Additionally, O'Toole and Cory write, "When children feel overwhelmed by intense feelings they may naturally make their world safe by distancing themselves physically or emotionally, by pretending or by denying the reality of the loss."

Nine-year-old Hannah, adopted at age six, said, *"The hardest part of grieving is learning to say good-by. We have to say good-by to things that are in our hearts but sometimes these things in our heart gave us bad habits...habits that we can't let go of easily."* As adoptive parents, we must not overlook our children's grief because it is not easily seen or noticed. We need to listen, watch, discuss, and comfort, even when the grief is not easy to identify. Our children have left familiar surroundings... people they know... school... food... language... routines. Attending to their grief is a critical element to integrating them into our family.

Dr. Victor Groza, an Associate Professor and the Interim Associate Dean for Research and Training at Case Western Reserve University in Ohio, and author of *A Peacock or a Crow? Stories, Interviews and Commentaries on Romanian*

Adoptions, suggests that prospective adoptive parents should read about the abandonment, separation, grief, loss and mourning of adoptees, that is evident throughout the life cycle.

When helping your child, newly home or home for years, here are some tips for helping them to acknowledge, accept, and grow from their grief:

- Talk about your own and other people's losses and grief.
- Read books to your child about loss and grief and show how others have lived through their losses.
- Suggest that your child keep a journal where she or he writes or draws about feelings.
- Find ways for your child to commemorate their past: light candles, create a special section in their life book, frame a particular drawing pertaining to their memories.
- Help your child to find positive ways to express their feelings: physical activities, praying, crying.
- Help your child learn to cry. Many of our children have been taught not to cry. Help them understand how healing crying is. Let them see you cry.
- Share a therapeutic story with your child, a story about grief that can be adapted to fit a variety of scenarios relating to grief and loss in children. (See page 238 for an example)

For many children impacted by issues of grief and loss, parent interventions like discussion, activities, and stories, will eventually ameliorate the issues of grief and loss. But, some children may need additional help from a therapist or grief-counselor.

Many of us are taught that grief, sadness, and loss are negative emotions, to be hidden away. In fact, grief is a process that brings us to reconciliation. Our pain doesn't disappear. The issue we're facing isn't gone. But, through discussion, tears, and sometimes prayer, we can grow, change, and become stronger.

The book *Healing and Growing Through Grief* presents grief as a journey towards growth. As the loss is remembered and integrated into the present there is once again energy to invest into the present and the future. This is more than survival. Personal strengths, insights and compassion have been gained. A future can once again be imagined and new relationships and opportunities can be explored and experienced. Grief, in some way, will touch all adoptive families. Accept it, learn from it, and grow from it.

~ Susan Ward is the founder of Heritage Communications , a writer/lecturer, an adoptive mother, and also runs Older Child Adoption, a site with many resources for adoptive parents. Her website is www.olderchildadoption.com.

Adopting an Older Sibling Group
Joys, Challenges, and Issues
By Cathy & Chas Long

My husband and I have six biological children. We love parenting, and had talked of adopting older children someday, as the older children generally get overlooked when people are considering adopting a child...

We turned to international adoption and adopted a sibling group of four from Russia, which consisted of one boy and three girls. We also adopted a girl from another orphanage at the same time, and three years later we adopted another daughter. Some of what we have written about are the behaviors these children had to learn in order to survive.

Our children were ten years old, eleven years old, thirteen years old, almost fourteen years old and almost fifteen years old when we adopted them. Today, we have two fourteen year old daughters, a fifteen year old daughter, a seventeen year old daughter, an eighteen year old son and a nineteen year old daughter. Not all of their behaviors were due to their early upbringing or orphanage life; some of it was normal, run-of-the-mill teenage angst. My children are like most teenagers. They worry about their skin, their weight, being physically fit, their grades, and being pretty. They are interested in members of the opposite sex, and a wide variety of music. They throw fits and slam doors. They criticize each other and nit-pick each other unmercifully. In essence, they are just normal teenagers that happen to talk with a lovely accent and an interesting turn of phrase. They are our children, stinky feet, pimples, dimples, and all.

Our 3 Greatest Challenges
Combating Their Fear and Lack of Trust. Our children still have horrible nightmares about their 'papa' in Russia and will wake up afraid that he will come back to steal them. They are ever watchful. When they first came to America, the girls would all stand behind their brother and peek around him, to look at us or at a stranger. They were uncomfortable when someone just dropped by without calling. We always told them when we knew we would be having company, who the company was going to be, the purpose for their visit, and how long they would stay. They did not like us leaving the house without them. The children wanted to go with us, and when we got to our destination, they immediately wanted to know when we were going home. It took a long time, but they did learn the routine of our lives. Their fears become less evident the longer they are with us, because they feel more secure about their environment and our commitment.

When we got upset with them, they reacted as if we hated them and would be mad at them forever. They had to be reassured a lot, and we still give our sons and daughters hugs and tell them we love them. The children were never allowed to hug anyone in the orphanage.

Teaching Effective Listening and Communicating Skills. The children are easily distracted so we have to keep them focused on a conversation. They just were not used to adults actually talking to them. We sit around our dining table and talk after most meals. Some of the children will stay and ask questions, while some will leave the table in favor of finishing homework, or watching a favorite program on TV. Usually, when one of the children says, "I have a question", the other children will stay to hear the question and listen to the answer. Sometimes we have some very long, in-depth conversations about bodily functions, two-faced people, or why there are different cultures and different traditions in the family.

Communication is vitally important to everyone's growth, development, and understanding. They have needed to learn to talk to other people. The children were never taught manners and had to learn acceptable social behaviors. We have one daughter that simply does not apologize. If she accidentally runs into one of them, her attitude is, "Well they shouldn't have been in my way". If I ask her to say "thank you" when someone does something nice for her, she will tell me, "I didn't ask them to do that nice thing, so why do I have to thank them?" Those conversations are long.

Irrational Love/Hate for Old Relationships. The children have mixed feelings about their biological parents. On one level, the children love their birthmother, and on another level they feel sorry for her. Another child will talk about how much he or she hates her. The best thing we can do is to listen to them talk. We encourage them to try to see their mother as an individual, not just as their mother, so they can understand the problems she was dealing with. The children's parents drank heavily and would leave the children along for long periods of time. When their parents were home and drinking, they would fight with knives and hurt each other and the children. We have tried to help our children see that this was perhaps the only way their birthparents could cope with life. Their parents had almost no education, and could not read or write. We talk about how important a good education is, as it brings understanding and knowledge on a personal, as well as academic, level. Our son, Matt, still says he hates his mom because she did not love them enough to do the right thing. When asked "what was the right thing she was supposed to do", all he could answer was, "She was supposed to love us and care for her family like a good mom; not be a drunk—or worse".

Their mother passed away a year and a half ago and it was tragic. All four of our children grieved, but in different ways. Emily, the oldest, cried a lot, and talked about all of the wonderful and loving things she remembered about her mom. Matt just said, "She lived like a drunk and she died like a drunk!" Harsh words for sure, but he has always blamed his mother for his being sent to an orphanage; oddly, he never blames his father. Chloe cried and rocked. She talked about wishing that her mother could have loved her, and then said, "Now I guess I will never know."

Our children have two older sisters. The oldest is six years older than Emily, and was not very nice or loving. The children have another sister who is a year and a half older than Emily, who lived in the same orphanage. They were very close to her. We learned about this older girl just before we came to Russia to adopt the children. We were told that we could not adopt her as she was over sixteen years old and that she resided in a hospital for very ill patients with tuberculosis. We didn't learn until months later that we were lied to. Emily misses Ula the most; she writes to her sister and talks with her on the phone. She wants Ula to come and live in the United States, but Ula is afraid to leave Russia.

The 3 Biggest Issues for Our Children

Learning Expected Social Behaviors. The children had to fend for themselves when they were not much more than toddlers. They had to scrounge through their neighbors' trash for their food, or raid a local garden. In the orphanage, life was also survival by their wits.

They had to eat their food very fast or the older, stronger kids would take their food away from them. They learned to hoard their food in case one of the caregivers became angry at them and deprived them of their meals. They had to be sneaky and secretive in order to survive; the children have the ability to look you in the eye and lie through their teeth. We had to teach the children social skills slowly. Once one skill was mastered, we moved on to the next.

We had to teach the children table manners first. We started by passing bowls of food around the table. The curious thing was that although the children would readily pass the food, they never took so much as a spoon full for themselves. We realized that the children we taught not to touch the food, but wait to be served. Also, they were unsure how much food they should serve themselves, never having done that before. The children were home two years before they would take what they needed! They are all very bright and quickly learned the correct way to use their utensils and their napkins. It took a while for them to learn that it really was alright to drink their beverage during the meal instead of waiting until the meal was over.

Next we taught them to use polite words for what they wanted or needed. Words like "please pass the potatoes", followed by "thank you". They learned so fast. We had to work on being respectful and not talking loudly over everyone else. Also, if someone asked them a question that they either did not understand, or just refused to answer, they would avoid eye contact and act as though the other person had not spoken at all. If they felt they were being criticized, they would many times stare straight ahead and freeze their movements. It took a lot of talking, but the wall slowly came down. We learned that they froze up in the orphanage

Lying.

Growing up in an orphanage with hundreds of other children, our children had to be very resourceful in getting what felt they needed in order to survive. They all came home with the ability to lie in the most convincing way! They lied, because to tell the truth was to be vulnerable, causing them to get beaten by the caregivers in Russia. Learning to tell us the truth was a gradual process, as they had to learn to trust us and trust that we were not going to hurt them in any way.

Hoarding.

Hoarding may be a life-long issue for the children. Most of the time, they did not have enough to eat in the orphanage and were hungry. I always kept fresh fruit on the table when they came home, along with nuts, granola bars, crackers, and peanut butter. Plus, we raised a large garden and they could pick, clean, and eat food whenever they wanted it. After they had been here a few months we learned that they also used to sneak and eat the cat food. They found it to be quite tasty and could not figure out why I didn't pour them some in bowls like I did for the cat. Because of being hungry for so long, they would take extra food and stash it somewhere in their room; mostly under their pillows or under the covers at the foot of their bed.

The hoarding did not stop with food. When I bought school supplies, they

Common Issues of Older Child Adoption

hoarded mechanical pencils, erasers, folders with cute pictures on them, and markers. I still keep the school supplies in a cabinet where they have free access to it all. The only rule is to tell me what they took, so if we run low I can purchase more. They keep their clothes...all of them. We have just in the last year been able to get them to let us have their out-grown clothes to replace with new items. They tell me they are saving the clothes to give to their children some day.

Discipline.

We found early on that when you discipline the children, you don't spank them. They were beaten at their orphanage by mean caregivers. You also don't take away something they value because they were used to having things taken or stolen from them at the orphanage. Taking the girls makeup or CD Players away, then telling them they have to earn the right to get their things back, is a lot different than just removing their favorite possessions.

When our children get in trouble they have to do extra chores. In the beginning we would tell them what chore they had to complete as punishment. The chore may be pulling weeds in six rows of beans in the garden or scrubbing the front porch with a small bucket of hot soapy water and using an old tooth brush. Or they were given the task to take a pitch fork and turn the compost pile out by the garden. None of these are pleasant chores, but the children get the added bonus of spending time with one of us while they work. They get attention from mom or dad, and at the same time are being taught the value of tempering their actions.

We made up a list of acceptable behaviors and posted them in my work room, as they spend a lot of time talking to me, individually and as a group, while I'm working. My work room is not a public room in our house so they don't get embarrassed by visitors being able to see our list. We also made another list of all of the chores they could do for unacceptable behaviors. They get to pick a chore on the list, which gives them a certain amount of control over the situation.

Mothering By Older Sib.

Emily felt that since she was the oldest then she had to mother her younger siblings and keep them in line. She was so afraid that if she didn't make them behave, that they would all be sent back to the orphanage. We had to sit her down and tell her that this was her time to be a teenager, not 'the mother' or even the 'caregiver'. Over time she let go of the role of authority figure. We had to have many conversations with her about letting herself enjoy life now, before she has the responsibility of her own family.

~ By Cathy & Chas Long

Older Child Adoption Resources

The Waiting Child:
How the Faith and Love of One Orphan
Saved the Life of Another
By Cindy Champnella

Our Own: Adopting and Parenting the
Older Child by Trish Maskew

Parenting the Hurt Child
by Gregory Keck, PhD and Regina M.
Kupecky, LSW

Toddler Adoption: The Weaver's Craft
By Mary Hopkins-Best

Attaching in Adoption: Practical Tools
for Today's Parents
by Deborah Gray

Real Parents, Real Children
by Holly van Gulden and
Lisa Bartels-Rabb

Help for the Hopeless Child: A Guide for
Families (Second Edition)
by Ronald S. Federici, PhD

Susan Ward's Older Child Adoption
website:
www.olderchiladoption.com

because the caregivers so often beat them or demeaned them, that the only way to survive was to close in on themselves.

We had to teach the children that running across the couch, loveseat, and recliners, was potentially dangerous! I finally figured out that was how they secured their spot for television viewing for the evening. They had to learn to go into the living room and gently sit down in their preferred seat. When we went out in public I had to teach them how to cross the street. They were not used to so much traffic and simply would not look in either direction. We spent time every day for the first four months at our local library. We would only stay for about ten minutes before the children felt insecure and wanted to go home. This did not change until the children had been home for almost a year. By then we were up to staying thirty minutes. We used the same routine with grocery shopping, where they also had to learn not to pick up or try to unwrap any item. Again, they learned quickly.

Living in One Culture After Growing Up in Another Culture. Their Russian holidays were different from ours, as were their traditions. Our children don't remember much celebrating before they went into the orphanage. They came to know about the holidays and some of their traditions through different caregivers, but never celebrated their holidays in the orphanage. Christmas was not observed, but they did get a piece of candy on New Years day. They knew about Mother's day, but it was not observed. Many celebrations were all toasted with vodka, much drinking and singing or dancing.

The children had never celebrated their birthdays or even knew of anyone who celebrated the day of their birth. They had never seen fireworks before, and were utterly fascinated with the Fourth of July.

Halloween was really confusing for them, but the children had a lot of fun dressing up in homemade costumes and going trick or treating. Thanksgiving was overwhelming because of the amount of food that was put on the table. Their first Christmas with us, was also the first Christmas they had ever celebrated and they got to learn about why this was such a special time for us. They loved to sing the old carols. In Russia they did color Easter eggs, but only used red onion to dye the eggs. They were gleeful participants in their first Easter egg hunt!

Understanding the Concept of Family. The children did not understand what family meant, except that they were brother and sisters. 'Mom and dad' were adults that would go away for weeks at a time and leave them with no food, water, or heat in the winter. When the parents did eventually come home they would get drunk and fight with knives. Our children have been with us over four years now and every once in a while they will say something like, "we have been here four years and you have not beaten us yet." Or, "we are waiting for you to get drunk and leave us." Slowly they have learned that this is who we are: we work to pay the bills and take care of our children. We are active in their educations, their sports, and their interests. We spend long hours talking to them and answering their zillions of questions. We love them and give hugs goodnight. Our son Matthew is a senior in high school this year. When we went to College Night, he would not look at any college that was more than an hour away. He said, "That is too far from my home".

Our 3 Greatest Joys

Witnessing Their Love of Being Educated. The children have learned so much and it seems that the more they know, the more they want to know. Their teachers are so surprised at how respectful they are to their educators. The children will sat and watch the history channel with dad and ask a lot of questions, then watch the science fiction channel and want to know about fictional characters. We've read to them from the very start and they always listened in earnest. They are so curious about their whole world!

Listening to their never-ending questions and answering their questions has been a gift. It's like looking at the world again, but this time through different eyes. As we explained and answered their many questions, the children would ask more or different questions. We learned a lot about ourselves as we explained our thoughts, beliefs, and how the world worked. Our older children were charmed by their new siblings and greatly fascinated by their perspective.

Simply enjoying each unique individual and watching them grow. We have been given a unique opportunity to get to know these incredibly resilient children. They were all physically delayed due to poor nutrition, and emotionally undeveloped. We have watched immature kids grow into intelligent, self-possessed young adults. It has been a joy to witness their personalities bloom and their individuality come forth. Their journey has proved what a strong, intelligent group of young people we have added to our family.

~ Cathy and Chas Long are bio parents to six children, and adoptive parents to six children from Russia, 4 of whom are bio sibs and the fifth was in the same orphanage.

Older Child Adoption
Transitioning from Primary School
By Julia Rollings

Middle School and High School Bring Big Changes

The transition to upper levels of school are tough on any youngster, but for adopted children it can be very difficult. No longer is there one teacher who is (hopefully) familiar with the child's history and knows them personally.

The child has to cope with a lot of change: new school, new students, a whole range of unknown teachers, changing classrooms for each class rather than having a classroom and desk of their own, and a whole load of novel demands such as managing a timetable and study program. Add to this the personal challenges occurring at this time in their lives, as they hit puberty and have to cope with a rapidly changing and unfamiliar body, and complicated new social expectations. Moving to middle or high school can be exciting but it is tough on adolescents.

High school is especially tough on parents. It can come as a real surprise how quickly a child seems to grow up after starting high school. Suddenly their child's social life seems centered around friends rather than family, and peers become a huge influence. It is hard not to feel that you've lost some of your influence as you see the first glimmer of adulthood behind your adolescent's eyes.

My first experience of cutting the apron strings came with seeing my youngsters off on their first day of primary school, but the move to high school felt more like a gentle farewell to childhood. Goodbye hugs were given at home to avoid any embarrassment in front of friends, and there was no question of following them to the classroom to see how they'd cope!

Some of my adopted children have needed a formal support structure, but others haven't and would have resented the intrusion. It is up to parents to foresee which child might drown without help, and for those children it is important to put support in before they start to flounder. My son Sadan's transition to high school involved some planned steps. Sadan was aged around five on adoption, and mute from the day he was abandoned until a few weeks after joining our family (something we were unaware of until his older brother, Madhu, aged around 10, had sufficient English to explain why his brother didn't speak). Sadan's trauma was deeply internalized and hard to access. Abandonment had, I believe, permanently wounded his psyche. His schooling required us to meet a whole different set of challenges to those of his brother–and Madhu's were grave, given many missed years of education,

We took Sadan to all the open days and nights at his new high school so he could learn the layout of the buildings and start recognizing a few of the teachers. His primary school also arranged for him to visit the school for a day and to take along one friend from primary school with him. We spoke about his new high school whenever we drove past it, and involved him in selecting his school clothes. Finally, with Sadan's permission, I made an appointment to meet his principal, school counselor, year coordinator, and a teacher before the school year began. I explained in detail Sadan's early deprivation, his insecurities, his ability to mask a lack of understanding, and his vulnerabilities. His success, or lack of success, at school could depend on the crowd he fell in with, as we believed he would be easily led astray. The high school identified a boy, Simon, who was willing to act as a mentor for Sadan in the first week, and this helped Sadan considerably. On the first day of school Sadan asked me to come in with him but once inside the school he spotted Simon and was happy to go off with him to the school assembly.

Suggestions That Might Help the Middle/High School Transition: Minimize Challenges. One of Sadan's biggest fears was traveling to and from school on a bus. It took a few weeks of negotiations with the local bus company for us to succeed in having a minor route change that allowed Sadan to catch one bus from near our home to his school rather than have to change buses at the terminal. This made a huge difference in his confidence. There was no worry about what to do if his bus didn't arrive, as he was either still at school or still near home, so help was at hand.

Make it Clear that This is not the Only Option. We chose the school we thought would suit Sadan, but we made it very clear to him that he could change if it didn't work out. We told him he needed to give it a fair go, but if after some time he was still unhappy we would look with him for another school.

Think laterally about your child's talents: a few of us might adopt a budding Charles Dickens or Greg Louganis (both adoptees) but don't count on it. More likely we will

Delaying School Entry
for an older adopted child

Advice now given to Australian families adopting older children from overseas is to delay school entry in order to give the child time to settle into the family. I can now recognize my son Madhu's (aged ten on adoption) eagerness to attend school as being rooted in his early deprivation. He'd asked his Indian father if he could go to school but was told "School is for rich children. Poor children work." This explained in part his desire to go to school, just as his years of being barefooted explained his particular affinity for shoes.

I also now recognize that starting school a few weeks after joining our family allowed Madhu to maintain an emotional and physical distance from us. It relieved him of much of the daily challenge of negotiating emotional relationships. This didn't cause us long-term difficulties, but if Madhu had been a different child it may well have negatively impacted his attachment. It was a time when he was grieving and going through monumental adjustments, I realize now that several more months at home would not have damaged his education. I kept my other older adopted children home for an extended time. This has meant they are generally a year or more older than their classmates it has not caused anyone any difficulties.

I believed an extra year under their belts might help counter the imbalance created by their difficult experiences, lack of English, and lack of familiarity with Australian culture. They needed a little extra time to understand some of the basic building blocks most children acquire early in life.

~ By Julia Rollings

parent children who struggle in the classroom and whose early deprivation leaves them with lifelong challenges. School is the center of a child's world, the place they negotiate friendships and sort out social groupings. School can offer opportunities to the athletic, artistic, dramatic, or empathetic child, and this may be the area where you can build your child's self-esteem when the academic side of school doesn't come easy. Whether the academic side of schooling is a challenge or not, all children will have a few areas where they shine. Sadan still couldn't read in fourth grade, but he was king of the monkey-bars at lunchtime. His palms were always calloused but his self-esteem grew. He would come home from school and tell me what new feat he'd learned on the playground that day. We enrolled him in gymnastics classes for older boys.

Choose the Right Clothes and Accessories. With a large family on one income I buy things that are bargains rather than trendy brands or styles. This works fine with the younger children, but with older children it matters what they are wearing. I still don't spend a lot of money but I made sure Sadan came with me and had a choice of style when I bought his things for high school. It would do him no favors if his hair cut, sneakers or school bag was a source of teasing at school.

Academic Success is not Critical. Some of our children will be permanently impaired by their early deprivation, so for some older children the aim should be functional literacy and numeracy, and decent social skills. Make sure your child doesn't feel that their worth is dependent on their ability to get top marks. I've demonstrated this to all my children by reading their school reports with them and always reading the 'teacher's comments' section first. I've told them I'd much rather read that they are trying their best and are considerate of other people than see how many As and Bs they received. Their effort matters more than the results.

Postscript. Sadan moved to his new high school at the start of our school year in January 2004 and he has just completed his first year. He is in a small special education class for some lessons and joins a larger class for less academically challenging lessons such as P.E. and cooking. The structure and spirit of his small school means that the adolescents receiving special education support are not teased, and his friendships extend throughout the school. On the final evening of school before our Christmas break we received a letter inviting us to the presentation evening. Sadan was one of only three students in his class, and the only student receiving special education support, to be given an annual award: an engraved trophy for 'Academic Excellence'. He loves high school.

~ Julia Rollings has been involved in adoption support and education for the past 19 years, both through her local adoptive family support group and alongside the state government adoption unit which processes all application for intercountry adoption. She is the mother to eight children, both bio and adopted.

Challenges

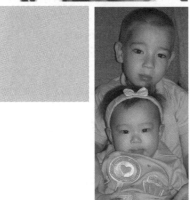

Unexpected Special Needs
The Loss of a Dream and Learning what is Truly Important
By Nancy Hemenway

From Infertility to Adoption.
We went through 7 years of infertility and lost four angels to miscarriage before we had our one and only live birth. My conception and pregnancy were both nightmares. There was nothing easy we did to either get or stay pregnant and giving birth was not much different. These experiences were filled with fear, dread and dealing with multiple roadblocks. There were a number of midnight trips to the emergency room before my one scary live birth story. But, at the end of this ordeal, was a healthy, happy baby. We were overjoyed and set-tled quickly into everyday parenting of our first miracle child.

It is no surprise then, that it took us four years to even begin to discuss how we would add a second child to our family. We decided we wouldn't pursue fertility treatment but instead adopt to grow our family. We used a local agency, added our names to a number of listservs, and jumped feet first into the throes of the 'paper chase'. As in birth, our adoption was eagerly anticipated with great exuberance and expectations of a future filled with happy parenting complete with a built in big sister. Add we did on May 23, 2001 in the lobby of the third floor of the China Hotel, a stunning little Cantonese beauty! Another long road traveled but this time through adoption. Our expectations the second time were the same—a healthy baby. This time, however, the twists and turns were not in the conception or adoption, but in the parenting of our new little miracle.

Adoption is a Leap of Faith
So often I heard other eager waiting parents refer to their adoption as a 'leap of faith'. But then life is a leap of faith too. No one is guaranteed tomorrow or a perfect child—not through birth or adoption. Although feeling thoroughly pre-pared through research, education and support groups, our life changed in a number of ways the day little Xiao Rong entered our family.

It was a heart-pounding, exciting and exhilarating experience full of anticipation when the orphanage personnel handed over this little tiny twig of a baby. This minuscule little girl was 14 months and a 'whopping' 13 pounds (the size of a four-month old). In the months to come, we would discover our sweet little girl had a number of developmental delays, chronic anxiety, post traumatic stress disorder (PTSD) and a variety of letters and acronyms all boiling down to one damaged little girl who had suffered. She desperately needed a great deal of professional care as well as a savvy family to navigate a labyrinth of procedures, treatment and a magnitude of healing. I remember flying home from China and wondering how this child was going to change our family dynamic. Our life would be out of the ordinary and not what we had planned. Having had more than a decade of experience teaching handicapped children, and being an older parent, I knew life would be 'special' and I worried about being 'up to' the tasks ahead.

Accepting the Loss of a Dream

Before we made this trip to China, my husband and I agreed the child selected by the CCAA (central adoption authority for intercountry adoptions in PR China) and entrusted to us would be the child we were destined to parent. This was our leap of faith. I think to deny the feelings of loss, loss of that dream, of a whole child, a 'normal' little sister to our birth child Zoë, would be to deny what everyone hopes for when they have a family. But I felt to accept this circumstance as a loss of a dream was somehow rejecting our child. I came to learn that accepting this loss was the biggest hurdle to clear and doing so enabled me to move on and to truly appreciate the miracle this baby was in our hearts and lives.

At first I felt very alone. It was another loss in a string of multiple losses, more challenges and added stress. I think a key component to successfully working through this is the strong bond between my husband and me. Our marriage withstood the loss of four babies and because of the willingness to communicate on new levels and to work as a team, we continue to carefully navigate the maze in order to meet our daughter's special needs, taking them one day at a time.

My Child is My Hero

Sometimes I feel myself tensing up, thinking about what the future holds. I worry about what I might have to cope with tomorrow. But then I look to my daughter. She is my hero, my miracle. What adult do you know who could have survived abandonment at birth, month after month of neglect in severe physical pain, all with no coping skills, no language with which to answer back, no support group, no therapist to talk to, no friends, and no family to nurture her. She was stripped of her dignity, her future, and her culture; kidnapped by strangers (that's us, as adoptive parents) but she never gave up. I see her tenacity and her strength. It gives me strength. I am so honored to be her mother. God must really believe I have the integrity, skill and love to have put this little life in my hands. Yes, it is a responsibility and sometimes feels like a weight on our shoulder; but it's also an awesome gift and a miracle.

Trauma, Anxiety and PTSD Resources

Freeing Your Child from Anxiety: Powerful, Practical Solutions to Overcome Your Child's Fears, Worries, and Phobias
by Tamar E. Chansky

Worried No More - Second Edition: Help and Hope for Anxious Children
by Aureen Pinto Wagner, Ph.D

Parenting the Hurt Child: Helping Adoptive Families Heal and Grow
by Gregory Keck and Regina M. Kupecky

Websites of Interest

ChildTrauma Academy (Bruce D. Perry, MD. PhD)
www.childtrauma.org

National Center for Post Traumatic Stress Disorder
www.ncptsd.gov.va

The Child Trauma Institute
www.childtrauma.com

How Our Family has Grown

It's been 5 years and thousands of miles since I first experienced those feelings of grief on the plane ride home to the US. Instead of loss, I am just beginning to realize how really fortunate we are. When adopting internationally, you'll often hear how wonderful it is that you 'rescued' an orphan. But the truth is, our little Cantonese beauty rescued all of us. To live life without our youngest family member is unthinkable. We've been so fortunate and not once, but twice blessed with beautiful daughters; one who grew under my heart and the other who grew in it. Zoe born after a 7 year struggle with infertility and pregnancy loss, and Rebekah Ruth Xiao Rong adopted May 23, 2001 in mainland China. What more could any parent ask for?

My Balance.

I have discovered some helpful tools to take care of myself, your other children and your marriage.
- Find a network of other families who have similar circumstances
- Learn how to relax (still working on this one)
- Learn to take one day at a time
- Exercise, walk that extra bit
- Keep a journal
- Take a mental vacation, imagine your on a beach, riding my horse, biking
- Therapeutic riding isn't just for kids–it's for mom too;
- Take the time to listen to music
- Deep breathing exercises
- Find or develop a hobby (sew, build a doll house etc.)
- Take at least two days a month to have a date with your husband where talking about the children is 'off-limits'
- Go have your hair cut, perm it or have it colored, or have a massage or pedicure
- Take time with your other children, be sure they feel your special touch
- Eat healthy foods and drink lots of water (but don't forget that occasional chocolate!)

~ Nancy Hemenway, Executive Director of INCIID, the largest infertility information and support organization in the US. **www.inciid.org**
She is a mother by birth and adoption.

Positive Outcome:
How Can You Combat the Effects of an Orphanage
By Mary Beth Williams, PhD, LCSW, CTS

The Situation in Orphanages

As an adoptive parent, or as a professional working with post-institutionalized internationally adopted children, it is important to be thinking about the impact of the world in which that child lived prior to being adopted. The child may have lived with a foster care family rather than in an orphanage. In others, the child will have known only one or several institutions. In those institutions, the child may have been unable to meet her needs for food, attention, touch, and comfort when in pain. Over time, she may have learned not to look for those needs to be met and may have come to distrust the adults in his or her world. Also, the child may have experienced neglect, poor nutrition, lack of stimulation, and potential for attachment, inconsistent caregivers, and various forms of traumatic experiences including physical abuse, sexual abuse, and witnessing of violence toward others (including other children). Parents need to understand a child's orphanage life in order to understand what makes their child think and behave the way she does. It is very hard to help a child join a family without being fully aware of her history. In general, what might a child's life have been in an orphanage? Even the best institutions have the following:

- uneducated or minimally trained caregivers
- rotating caregivers on shifts
- abrupt transfers to different orphanages or sections of an orphanage
- loss of peers as those children are adopted or transferred
- limited language interaction with adults
- regimented daily activities: eating, sleeping, toileting all at the same time
- lack of spontaneous activities
- absence of personal possessions
- limited activities to develop motor skills–no use of markers, pencils, equipment
- exposure to toxins, including lead

Children in many orphanages are frequently nutritionally deprived and often have low muscle tone. Playground equipment may be non-existent or, if present, may be in disrepair. Children may be over-responsive when put in high-stimulus situations. Speech acquisition, because of minimal exposure and subsequent minimal usage of words, may be extremely delayed and it may take a long time to develop appropriate articulation and grammar. At an orphanage, children do what everyone else does, eat when everyone else eats, go to school when they are told, and even use the restroom on a schedule.

What this means is that orphanage children are never encouraged to make (good) decisions and no one talks to them about choice making–key essentials to personal success and active coping. At first sight, the child may appear to be overly mature and 'too good' or 'well trained', ready at age four, for example, to learn how to work with and care for younger children. They may know how to dress themselves, go to the bathroom totally independently, sweep floors with a large broom, and sit quietly without any argument for long periods of time. Older siblings in a sibling group may also be 'parentified', having been taught to take care of younger brothers and sisters.

In reality, their often traumatic experiences within the institution have taught and conditioned these children to be hypervigilant (on constant high-alert) and to take on expected roles without recognition of their own individual desires or needs. Their emotions and 'feelings' are never considered in decision-making or in complying with institutional life. Asking these children how they feel leads to a blank or questioning expression, rather than to words such as 'happy, sad, scared' that a normal three-year old understands, uses, and applies to herself. Internationally adopted children, whether from an institutional or deprivational environment, quite possibly have not had the positive human contact necessary for social and emotional communication post-adoption.

Helpful Factors in Adoption Transition

There are pre-institutional and institutional factors that help children adjust to their adopted families (Hopkins-Best, 1997). These factors are helpful for a parent to reflect on, as the transition at the time of adoption may impact a child's adjustment into the family:

- Children who have had few moves during their pre-adoptive years fare better, unless they have been seriously abused and/or neglected in any placement. Those who have had a secure attachment to a caregiver are more likely to attach to new parents.
- Giving the child an opportunity to see her caregiver/foster parent figure before leaving the institution or giving her the chance to go back to see her caregiver to say good-bye, allows the child to transition with the blessings (and often tears of joy) of that care-taker.
- Toddlers who have had a chance to transition to the adoptive family with preparation, gradual visitation, and even overnights, do better than those who suddenly are placed with a family–never to return to the orphanage again, not able to say good-bye to friends and caretakers.
- Some children are just inherently more resilient than others. Resilience is a relational trait. An adoptive parent can consciously help instill a healthy resilience within an adopted child.

Your Role as a Parent

A major task of parenting is first to give a child emotional and physical safety, above all else, and to help a child develop the abilities to meet all of the needs with self, others, and the world. (Rosenbloom & Williams, 1999) All parents want a healthy child, whether that child joins a family through birth or adoption. It's probable that they want a child to

- be able to attach and be intimate
- become autonomous and independent over time
- feel safe and secure with them
- trust them
- develop self esteem
- develop a conscience

You need to remember that the child may have experienced neglect, poor nutrition, lack of stimulation or potential for attachment, inconsistent caregivers, and various forms of traumatic experiences including physical abuse, sexual abuse, and witnessing of violence toward others (including other children). *It is important to begin to think about what will happen in this child's life as she grows into maturity, and how her early environment has impacted her.*

Attachment between a parent and a post-institutionalized child begins with the parent. It is up to the adult to begin the process by creating an empathic, safe, caring, loving environment for a new child. It is up to the adoptive parent to model communication, affection, coping, and emotional modulation. It is up to him or her to remain in control if and when the child does not. It is also up to the parent to take good care of him- or herself in order to take good care of the family. Parents provide the love and nurturing and also provide the rules and structure. Treating new children with respect and maintaining a sense of hope will affirm and reaffirm that they have found a forever family. Suggestions for modeling and instilling hope include the following:

New parents sometimes confuse a Trauma Bond (instantaneous and based on terror) with an Attachment Bond when they adopt a child who clings to them immediately.

- addressing the child in positive language
- setting a sense of order and structure
- setting realistic limits and rules
- providing physical nurturing and attention
- providing emotional nurturing
- having consistency in bedtime, mealtime and other routines
- using eye contact with the child
- praising the child's behavior ("you did a good job")
- keeping calm when the child is having a meltdown
- recognizing and stating that a behavior is bad, the child is not
- being the lead on giving affection and encouraging reciprocity from the child
- stopping manipulation of parents (if there are two)by being on the 'same page'
- holding the child accountable to learn and to abide by the rules
- practicing healthy self care by having a life outside the home
- teaching the child to problem solve as soon as language allows; prior to that, keeping language short and simple
- giving the child choices right from the beginning
- developing non-punitive strategies for bad situations

The Negative After-Effects

What does a deprived or neglected institutional background mean for a newly adopted child and his family? The issues below affect many adoptees to many different degrees. Parent awareness and/or professional assistance can help turn-around, or at least modulate, the negative after-effects of institutional living. Not every issue will disappear entirely, but a parent's initial high expectations may shift to an enormous appreciation for the courageous work a post-institutional child is willing to do, in order to become 'family'.

Medical Records. Parents may not get an accurate medical history or may have no medical history or family background; the medical records may be sporadic and spotty. When parents bring a child home, it is important to get a thorough medical examination, including age-appropriate screenings and an assessment of the child's growth and development. In addition, it is important that the child have an assessment of her nutritional status. Contact and meet with a pediatrician familiar with the height and weight charts for the child's birth country (or supply them yourself), to set norms for your child.

Emotional Development. Many children have slow emotional development because they have never been allowed to express emotions (some call this 'The Silence of the Kids'). Many have never learned how to modulate emotions. They may have problems with affect dysregulation (emotional reaction) and be diagnosed as hyperactive or attention deficit disordered. They may have problems putting feelings into words and act out with poor impulse control instead. They may not have the words to describe internal physical or emotional states. They have never even been asked how they feel, let alone know what a sad, mad, or glad feeling is.

Attachment Difficulty. Those children may have an attachment problem and have difficulty with affection and emotional intimacy. On the extreme end of the attachment spectrum, children have Reactive Attachment Disorder, which is a complete inability to connect in a reciprocal fashion. Many post-institutional children have difficulties giving and receiving love (because of their own absence of positive touch and loving,) and do not trust others, primarily due to lack of physical and emotional contact with a primary care-giver. Attachment is reciprocal, is based on love, and takes time to develop. New parents sometimes confuse a Trauma Bond (which is instantaneous and based on terror) with an Attachment Bond when they adopt a child who appears to attach immediately.

Loss and Grief. Many children have a true of loss at leaving the orphanage and feel grief when they are separated from that world, no matter how awful it was. Even children adopted as babies and toddlers can internalize sad events of their young lives and exhibit ambiguous loss.

Age. A child adopted at over eighteen months of age, in particular, may have notice-able developmental delays. There is always the possibility that the child has a history of abuse, stored as pre-verbal memories and unable to be recounted. They may even be dissociated or repressed memories.

Sensory Issues. Some children may have problems regulating and filtering sensory input. These children may have problems regulating behavior control, temper control, and adapting to changes.

- The hypersensitive child can be fearful, cautious, negative, and/or defiant. The under-reactive child may be withdrawn, hard to engage, or self-absorbed.
- The motor-disorganized, impulsive child may have an extremely high level of activity and a lack of caution. She may appear to be 'driven' and unable to settle down or organize behavior. She may over or under-react to loud, high, or low-pitched noises, bright lights, touch, foods with certain textures, coordination, touch, pain, odors, temperature, motor planning, attention, and focusing, among others
- Some children may be inconsolable when hurt or frightened, unreceptive of attention or touch
- Some may have little or no conception of personal space and property, constantly tripping over their feet, or falling down easily
- Some may have no skills for conversation or friendship

Post Traumatic Stress Disorder (PTSD). Some internationally adopted children may have symptoms of Post-Traumatic Stress Disorder. PTSD is defined in part in the DSM-IV as: *Being exposed to a traumatic event where a person experiences, witnesses, or is confronted by event(s) involving actual or threatened death or serious injury, and a response that involves* *intense fear, helplessness, or horror.* Abandonment, institutionalization, loss of a primary caregiver, abuse, neglect and the swift and traumatic life changes in a child's world through the act of international adoption, can contribute to a child developing PTSD. PTSD must be addressed and treated for the child to realize his full emotional and cognitive potential. Not addressed and treated, a child's PTSD can impact the parent-child relationship, the child's self-perception, and other areas of the child's life. The symptoms of PTSD can interfere with or affect a child's attachment to her parents by limiting safety and trust development.

A few of the symptoms of PTSD in young children:
- Hyper-vigilance, anxiety and exaggerated startle response–some children will be constantly on guard, looking for any danger that might befall them, and fearful of exploring the environment around them.
- Problems concentrating and focusing, and ADHD type behaviors due to increased levels of cortisol [a hormone secreted by the adrenal glands in response to any kind of physical or psychological stress].
- Less ability to give emotionally in a reciprocal fashion .
- Irritability or outbursts of anger.
- Difficulty with falling or staying asleep; including nightmares, night terrors or non-specific distressing dreams.
- Trauma-related fears that may not appear to be related directly to the original trauma (e.g. animals, darkness, and other triggers).
- Increased somatic (body) aches, and problems with stomachaches and headaches.

"Love is not enough" for some of these children who are 'at risk'. They may have a multi-system developmental disorder that includes PTSD, attachment, and sensory difficulties. They cannot just be loved into normality and may need intervention programs. In time, these children do develop warm relationships, *"logical thinking and problem solving, and interactive communication"* (Doolittle, 1995) if they have access to the right types of therapy and highly involved parents. *"All adoptions of orphanage children should be considered by both prospective parents and adoption officials to be special- needs adoptions"* that require *"extra commitments of parents' time, energy, acquisition of expertise, and willingness to work"* with professionals, agencies, and others who have adopted." (Ames 1997)

The Positive Outcome
In spite of the possible abuse, deprivation, neglect, and lack of stimulation in the lives of many children who are available for international adoption, most children from orphanages and from the foster care system can and do adjust well to their new lives. Motivated, aware parents are a wonderful source of information, security, support, and love for a new child. *"Parents are the one most important educational tool for a child who is being adopted internationally or nationally."* (Kincaid, 1997).

What this means is that, in spite of all the possible negative outcomes that might occur due to institutionalization, there are also positive outcomes to placement and adoption that are within a parent's power to influence. A child's ability to recover from trauma is heavily based in innate or learned emotional resilience "an ability to recover from or adjust easily to misfortune or change"

What Does PTSD Look Like in Children?
Researchers and clinicians are beginning to recognize that PTSD may not present itself in children the same way it does in adults.

Criteria for PTSD now include age-specific features for some symptoms.

Very young children may present with few PTSD symptoms. This may be because eight of the PTSD symptoms require a verbal description of one's feelings and experiences. Instead, young children may report more generalized fears such as stranger or separation anxiety, avoidance of situations that may or may not be related to the trauma, sleep disturbances, and a preoccupation with words or symbols that may or may not be related to the trauma. These children may also display posttraumatic play in which they repeat themes of the trauma. In addition, children may lose an acquired developmental skill (such as toilet training) as a result of experiencing a traumatic event.

Elementary school-aged children may not experience visual flashbacks or amnesia for aspects of the trauma. However, they do experience 'time skew' and 'omen formation,' which are not typically seen in adults. Time skew refers to a child mis-sequencing trauma related events when recalling the memory. Omen formation is a belief that there were warning signs that predicted the trauma. As a result, children often believe that if they are alert enough, they will recognize warning signs and avoid future traumas. School-aged children also reportedly exhibit posttraumatic play or reenactment of the trauma in play, drawings, or verbalization. Posttraumatic play is different from reenactment in that posttraumatic play is a literal representation of the trauma, involves compulsively repeating some aspect of the trauma, and does not tend to relieve anxiety.

Other Signs of Trauma in Children
Besides PTSD, children and adolescents who have experienced traumatic events often exhibit other types of problems... fear, anxiety, depression, anger and hostility, aggression, sexually inappropriate behavior, self-destructive behavior, feelings of isolation and stigma, poor self-esteem, difficulty in trusting others, and substance abuse. Children who have experienced traumas also often have relationship problems with peers and family members, problems with acting out, and problems with school performance.

Along with associated symptoms, there are a number of psychiatric disorders that are commonly found in children and adolescents who have been traumatized. One commonly co-occurring disorder is major depression. Other disorders include substance abuse; other anxiety disorders such as separation anxiety, panic disorder, and generalized anxiety disorder; and externalizing disorders such as attention-deficit/hyperactivity disorder, oppositional defiant disorder, and conduct disorder.

~ From PTSD in Children and Adolescents, A National Center for PTSD Fact Sheet
By Jessica Hamblen, PhD

Creating the 'Whole Child'–Teaching Resiliency.   Parents can help a child successfully combat the effects of his or her pre-adoptive life by using a team approach. Seeking prompt professional help for the specific medical or psychological issues a child exhibits is extremely important, however, parents can also help to create a 'whole child' at home. A resilient child with coping skills is equipped to overcome many of the effects of trauma, PTSD and institutionalization. Resiliency is an invisible protective shield; the good news is, it is a trait of internal strength that can be taught by parents, and intrinsically developed.

What are Four Traits of a Resilient Child?   A resilient child is *socially competent* and exhibits empathy, flexibility, and caring. These children understand interpersonal give-and-take and have a sense of humor and a cooperative nature. A resilient child has *problem-solving skills* and can seek help, plan and look for alternative solutions. They use abstract thinking, can look ahead to the future and are able to delay gratification. *Autonomy* (ability to act and think independently) and self-esteem empower a resilient child with the ability to bounce back with confidence and faith in personal ability to prevail. Resilient children have a *sense of purpose and future*. They are hopeful, and own a positive view of reality. Their lives have meaning and a spiritual context, and they have a celebratory nature.

Teaching Resiliency. Awareness of the traits that emotionally strengthen a child allows the parent to design daily living activities to teach and reinforce the tasks and skills that build resiliency. To help a child learn problem-solving skills and autonomy, and to develop social competence and a sense of purpose and future, a parent can deliberately include the following into family life:

- Assign the child small tasks; break larger tasks down into manageable segments.
- Establish simple rules that the child can understand easily; do not make them abstract or complex.
- Identify any interests/skills the child has and use them for positive reinforcement. Help the child become open to new experiences.
- Notice when the child responds by laughter or makes a joke, then compliment his abilities and responses; agreeableness is a desirable trait in a child. Try to encourage it.
- Give the child choices among two or three items, situations, or activities that are 'no loss' choices (all choices are positive). Then commend the child for choosing, whatever his choice.
- When the child has appropriate language skills, ask the child to identify and name the possible choices, and then choose one.
- Use play to reinforce problem-solving skills
- Affirm the child's perception of reality
- Introduce new activities consistently, again in small doses
- Help the child find an outside interest or hobby and pursue it
- Celebrate the child and his or her life in any way possible!

Children who gain coping skills and mastery over their environment are building resiliency. It is a trait that empowers a child to deal with childhood trauma, and is key to the healing, therapeutic process. It may take a team of parent, child and professional(s), including a multi-disciplinary approach to bring a post-institutionalized child a positive outcome. Trauma, attachment, sensory, and speech and language work benefit by being addressed simultaneously as part of one whole: the child. The parent is integral to a child's positive outcome, and can support the work of professionals by reinforcing the healing process at home.

Helping Children Heal. Parents can make the home, and the parent-child relationship, an emotionally safe place for recovery and re-growth. They can provide comfort and reassurance for their child, set clear boundaries and maintain routines. In addition, a parent can:

- Respect the child's fears (avoid giving the fears too much credit)
- Avoid new and challenging tasks; use consistency and repetition
- Monitor and limit exposure to fearful situations
- Increase child's physical outlets
- Give child opportunities to talk about feelings (in limits); listen to and accept the strong feelings of the child
- Expect regression to a degree
- Listen for distortions and misunderstandings, and take the opportunity to offer facts
- Keep anniversary reactions in mind (a child can be affected by abandonment or adoption dates, birthdays, etc)
- Help children focus on images of strength and survival

A parent who can teach active action-based coping skills, foster resilience, and maintain a healing environment at home can heavily stack the child toward a healthy new beginning. Combatting the effects of an international orphanage takes patience and hard work and may also need specialized professional intervention. Strong parental love, commitment, and determination help children who have the ability to attach and love develop positive relationships.

~ Mary Beth Williams, PhD, LCSW, CTS specializes in the treatment of trauma-based disorders, including those related to disorganized attachment. Dr. Williams was a school social worker for many years and is familiar with special education related issues, as well. She is the author of many trauma-based workbooks and texts, including Life After Trauma (1999) with D. Rosenbloom and The PTSD Workbook (2002) with S. Poijula. She is the parent of seven children. Four of her children were adopted, two of them domestically, and two from Kazakhstan. She has a forthcoming book on Trauma in Adoption from Rutledge Press.

Unknown Triggers to Trauma
Collapsing Under the Weight of the Past

When a child has been traumatized, if the cause isn't addressed and the child is not helped to separate the past from the present, events in the present can re-trigger the past. Many adopted children have suffered the shock of intercountry adoption, compounding loss of birthfamily. We have vulnerable children. Loss, loss of familiarity, loss of daily rhythms, loss of esteem compounded by the possible indignity of institutional life, and our children bring much that can be used–subconsciously–to hook the past into the present, and to lasso the present by the past.

For many adoptive parents, it's hard to know what the triggers might be, but the child's reaction to them makes it plain that they are indeed triggers. An event most kids would take in their stride escalates to momentous anguish in seconds in some adopted kids – and commonly the child blames themselves for being bad/useless. The triggers tend to be events where the child is expected to achieve something – and fails to accomplish it. For example, some children are triggered by difficult homework, some by handling new and awkward social situations, some simply by necessary transitions, such as from school time to holidays. What is common to these situations is that the feelings raised in the child from the present event simply collapse back into the engulfing tragedy the child has experienced in the past. They cannot cope. That 'tragedy' may in itself be an amalgam of successive traumas: loss of birthfamily, carers, foster family, familiar settings, foods, smells, language, cultural rhythms- and transition to institutional care, environmental damage, and yes, intercountry transracial family (however loving).

The CD, *Warming the Stone Child: Myths and Stories About Abandonment and the Unmothered Child* by Clarissa Pinkola Estes explains the concept of 'collapsing'. Under pressure, traumatized children will flashback to those original deep, dark feelings of fear and abandonment. They will become overwhelmed with a flood of emotion instead of shaking off a momentary dejection and moving on. They will **collapse under the weight of past baggage and bring it to the present, as trauma triggers that automatically call up the big guns, instead of the appropriate 'in the present' guns.**

What do we adoptive parents do? We need to 'learn' our children, get to know when and where they may be triggered, and to be prepared to help them both in the present and to sort the trigger of the past. Learning to place the triggers in perspective and to understand where they come from is powerful in the management of the feelings that surface for both us and our children.

Sensory Integration
And the Internationally Adopted Child
By Barbara Elleman, MHS, OTR/L, BCP

Have you ever wondered why the fast, spinning rides that you repeatedly enjoyed as a child, now make your head spin and your stomach turn? As we mature, our brain's ability to organize and interpret information from our senses (touch, taste, smell, movement, sight, sound and body awareness) improves. This is a process called sensory integration. For most children, sensory integration occurs automatically. These children naturally seek out the sensory information they need to grow and mature. Some children do not. Some children experience Sensory Processing Disorder (SPD).

Children, who have been adopted internationally, particularly from an orphanage, may be at risk for Sensory Processing Disorder. This may be due to early environmental circumstances, prenatal or medical factors that predispose a child to altered sensory input during the first year of life.

large amount of sensory integration occurs during the first year of life. The integration of simple sensory information becomes the basis for more complex tasks as a child develops. For example, an infant integrates information from vision, touch, and body awareness to locate and reach for a brightly colored toy held above her. Sensory information comes to the brain as input from sights, sounds, taste, smell, touch, movement, and body position.

The touch **(tactile)** system is highly responsive during the first years of life. It allows us to determine if we are being touched and to locate that touch (such as when a fly lands on our leg). The tactile system also provides us with the ability to react when the touch input is harmful (such as a hot or sharp surface). When a touch sensation is provided, our brain registers the sensation and determines a reaction (such as withdrawing a hand from hot water or swatting away a fly).

The movement **(vestibular)** system is also highly responsive during the first years of life. It informs our brain about the direction and position we are holding/moving in space and provides the foundation for coordination, balance, eye movements and posture.

Sensory processing disorders (SPD) is the current term used to describe the diaspora of outcomes that may happen when the brain can't make sense of what the senses tell it. It is synonymous with dysfunction of sensory integration (DSI) and sensory integration disorder (SID) - which are terms found in some literature. The current trend is to use "sensory processing disorders" to refer to the condition or problem and to use "sensory integration" when referring to the theory (based on the original work of A. Jean Ayres) on which treatment and interventions are based.

Barbara Elleman, MHS, OTR/L, BCP

Proprioception is the term used for the sense of body position. It provides information about the position of our body in space. It allows us to perform tasks such as turning on a light switch in the middle of the night.

SPD occurs when sensory integration does not develop as efficiently as it should. It may result in problems with learning, behavior, or development.

Older children with SPD usually exhibit more than one of the following symptoms:
• Over or under-reactive to touch, movement, sights, sounds, food textures, tastes

- Easily distracted
- Unusually high or low activity level
- Clumsiness or difficulty with coordination
- Difficulty making transitions or accepting change
- Inability to unwind or calm self
- Poor self concept
- Difficulty with academic achievement
- Social and or emotional problems
- Speech, language, or motor delays

Younger children with SPD usually exhibit more than one of the following symptoms:
- Poor muscle tone
- Slow to achieve developmental milestones
- Unusually fussy, difficult to console
- Failure to explore the environment
- Difficulty tolerating changes in position
- Resistance to being held or cuddled
- Difficulty with sleep
- Difficulty with sucking

Not all children who have been internationally adopted will have Dysfunction of Sensory Integration. Often, symptoms may be present right after adoption, during the transition to a new culture and new environment. Dysfunction of Sensory Integration usually presents as a pattern of symptoms that persist beyond the initial period following adoption.

Immediately following adoption, parents can begin to provide activities to promote a sensory rich environment. Parents should incorporate a variety of sensory experiences into their child's everyday routine, introducing new activities slowly. They should provide an opportunity and encourage participation, but not force the child to perform.

Suggestions for Activities.
Caution should be used regarding the child's age and ability when choosing activities
Touch Activities
- Finding small toys in sand or a container filled with macaroni or beads
- Rubbing with lotions, powders or towels
- Finger-painting, playing in pudding

The Lively, Loud, Kid Book List
Sensory-reads for noisy, wiggly little readers

The Wheels on the Bus
Paul O. Zelinsky

There Was an Old Lady Who Swallowed a Fly
Simms Taback

My Aunt Came Back
Pat Cummings

Silly Sally
Audrey Wood

Napping House
Audrey Wood

Brown Bear, Brown Bear
Bill Martin, Jr.

Some Dogs Do
Jez Alborough

No, David!
David Shannon

Doggies
Sandra Boynton

Animal Kisses
Barney Saltzberg

Chugga Chugga Choo Choo
Kevin Lewis

Head to Toe
Eric Carle

Ten Little Monkeys: Jumping on the Bed
Annie Kubler

Resources

The Out-of-Sync Child: Recognizing and Coping with Sensory Integration Dysfunction by Carol Stock Kranowitz

The Out-of-Sync Child has Fun by Carol Stock Kranowitz

Raising a Sensory Smart Child: The Definitive Handbook for Helping Your Child with Sensory Integration Issues by Lindsey Biel and Nancy Peske

The Sensory-Sensitive Child: Practical Solutions for Out-of-Bounds Behavior by Karen A. Smith and Karen R. Gouze

Raising Your Spirited Child: A Guide for Parents Whose Child Is More Intense, Sensitive, Perceptive, Persistent, Energetic by Mary Sheedy Kurcinka

The Fussy Baby: How to Bring Out the Best in Your High-Need Child by William Sears, MD, Martha Sears RN

- Dress up activities
- Building forts with blankets, towels, or sheets

Movement Activities
- Playgrounds or backyard equipment–swing sets, slides, tire swings
- Gym programs
- Riding toys
- Sit 'n spin or spinning activities and games
- Gentle bouncing on an old mattress, cushions, lap, or when held securely on a ball.

Proprioceptive (Body Awareness) Activities
- Crawling and climbing
- Wheelbarrow walking, jumping, hop-scotch
- Tug of war or obstacle courses
- Pushing or pulling weighted objects such as a wagon, laundry baskets, filled buckets
- Position games such as Twister or Simon Says

Visual Activities
- Punching bags, balls, balloons, and bubbles
- Target games such as tee ball, tennis, or soccer
- Puzzles, tracing, dot to dot, mazes
- Scissor activities
- Mobiles

Sound Activities
- Whistles, bells, and horns
- Listening to stories, tapes, and songs
- Repeating sequence of sounds
- Naming sounds for animals
- Rhythmic games and activities

If you suspect your child may have SPD, an evaluation may be beneficial. Occupational therapists with training in sensory integration can provide evaluations and develop individualized treatment programs to help children who struggle with the world around them.

~ By Barbara Elleman, MHS, OTR/L, BCP

A Sensory Story for Kids!
The Goodenoughs Get in Sync: A Story for Kids by Carol Stock Kranowitz
This book helps a child with sensory issues understand what they are feeling.

Sensory Learning
Figuring out the Puzzle Pieces that Work
By Catherine Mossup

How my nine year old daughter thinks has been an enigma to me. The best way to describe it is to imagine the *Good-Housekeeping Cookbook*. On every page there is a picture of the finished product, pictures of all the major steps, and a step by step guide of how to assemble the recipe.

This is my daughter. She has an audio-cognitive processing disorder, a very small short-term 'working memory', a huge long-term memory, and what I describe as poor access pathways. Her problem was recognized by her inability to solve some of the most basic problems, and a complete inability to read words. If a sentence was 'the red apple fell from the apple tree', she would not recognize the second 'apple' or the second 'the' (working memory problem). In her brain, she had never seen these words before. The reason why she can play piano with astounding skill is part of her cookbook approach. She:

1) sees the symbol (see)
2) hits the key (touch)
3) sound is instant (hear)

This also works for her in the other order, hear-touch-see. Harmonious music patterns also repeat, as do the patterns on a Chess board (she started playing in kindergarten and was on the competitive chess team starting in first grade).

In Chess, there are clear rules, structures and patterns (like in a cookbook!). Her kindergarten teacher taught the students to play using one role at a time: pawns only, then add the bishop; then add the rook, etc. The board is static (it doesn't move or change shape, which would over-stimulate); you can see everything on the board (nothing is outside the parameters); the chess pieces all have a spot and a role; you control the moves; the pieces move in patterns (stored in long-term memory); and it fits the see-touch-hear profile.

To teach my daughter how to read, I finally found a fantastic tutor who works with special needs children. She gave me a 'sand plate' to use. The recipe:

• get a bag of colored sand from the art supply store

• spread the sand on a large cookie sheet

• daughter says the word 'apple'; at the same time as saying the letter and sound (A ah, P peh), she uses her fingertip to form the letter in the sand, then says the whole word to finish

So to create pathways from long-term to working memory she needs multi-sensory input (not overstimulation!). She can not conceptually extend herself to feel the end of a pencil or feel the end of a paint brush, and the idea of gentle, firm, soft is difficult to grasp! Writing letters in the sand is sensation on the finger tip, she has total control of the fingertip, and she inputs the visual, the touch, and the sound. My daughter is now improving her writing significantly. Her printing is messy, which is all part of the same disorder. It doesn't occur to her to use the lines, keep the paper from moving, or keep the paper crinkle-free. But it is coming!

To get her to understand the difference between a good feeling and a bad feeling (she would hit other kids, and since she can not conceptually extend herself in space, she had no clue that her hit was like a ten-ton truck. She would hit or bite just to generate a feeling) I started many years ago with massage and she just loves it. She will rarely hug, but every night she gets a massage, and always wants a massage. We have made a bit of a ritual out of it–she can choose the massage oil and body parts. As I massage her, I speak to her about how good it feels, how it feels relaxing, and how my gentle touch is how she knows how much I love her.

I also do some really odd-ball things: I wake her up in the middle of the night to go out and look at the moon; after a spring rain, I take her outside to smell the spring air or have her look at a beautiful flower: see it, feel it, smell it; see it in the garden, see it with the other flowers, what do you see? I do the same thing with food. What does it smell like, look like, feel like, taste like? When something bad happens, I ask her how it feels in her body; where does she get a feeling, what does she want to do (hit, scream, cry)?

I was overjoyed when she told me she would be very disappointed if she didn't make the swim team. That is a concept: anticipating a feeling, knowing how to label the feeling, and sharing her concern with me. A breakthrough!

~Catherine Mossop lives in Canada and is the adoptive mother to two children—a daughter from China and a son from VietNam. She owns and runs Sage Mentors Inc. which designs and manages mentoring programs to accelerate high potential talent in organizations around the world.

A Parent's Letter to a Second Grade Teacher
explaining the classroom needs of her child with SID

I write regarding some therapeutic needs that my daughter G has regarding the Sensory Integration Dysfunction (SID) that she exhibits at times. There are days when it is not apparent and other days when you will discover a different child. She was in private Occupational Therapy once a week during the first grade school year. I am assuming that you already know about these things from her first grade teacher, 'Mrs. D', but in case not...

In her first grade class we discovered some useful things. My daughter feels a bit shy in the new setting about introducing them:

Weights. G has some ankle weights that she wears during sit down times (i.e. writing). They should be worn for about twenty minutes, a couple of times a day. My daughter learned to monitor this herself.

She has a lap weight (another fitness weight, rectangular in shape, weighing about three pounds) that she might need during circle or floor time. Again she monitors her own need with it. Mrs. D. gave her a carpet square to sit on so she could stay in her own personal space, which she has trouble with at times.

Gum. Mrs. D. did allow G to chew gum in the classroom. This regulates her for better focus. She tries to do it discreetly. It may help her impulsivity, talking out of turn, etc. D taught her to put her finger to her lips to remind herself to not talk. Can you allow gum chewing? She would use gum only if she feels she needs it.

Direction. Another useful therapy for G, if you find her moving around a lot or acting giddy or silly, is to give her the job of 'helping' you by carting some heavy things around the classroom (like crates of books). G needs weight to bring her 'down to earth'. We refer to this state as her 'engine being on high'. She knows what that means.

Start Up. G may have auditory and visual processing problems at times. If there is a lot of visual stuff on the walls for her to process she sometimes 'shuts down' and can't move on with activity. It's the same with lots of oral instructions. If she is dawdling it's often a sign of avoiding sensory overload, and she may need help in getting started on her work.

We had a great summer (constant 'sensory diet' of sand, water, and physical activity), but of course, G has not been in the classroom setting all summer. She is due for a re-evaluation of her SID. At her karate classes, the instructors have seen tremendous growth in her physical coordination, particularly balance and left/right body coordination, as she is doing things she could not do just a few months ago. She learned to ride her bike without training wheels, and for her that was a huge accomplishment. I am looking forward to seeing you on the 16th, and sooner if need me! I would definitely like to volunteer in the class and help you in any way I can. Feel free to email me if you have any questions!

~Cynthia B. Baker, adoptive mom

Parenting Children with FASD
Things I wish I had Known When we Started...
By Andrea Horman

I've always been a believer in the maxim 'forewarned is forearmed' but nothing prepared my husband and I for the life changes that came with adopting two older special needs children with Fetal Alcohol Syndrome Disorder (FASD).   There must be some divine reason that of the more than one billion orphaned children in the world, we were paired up with Sam and Heather. We would never go back, or think of what could have been with a different child because they are ours, that much is clear.

Our two children, adopted from Kazakhstan a few years ago, have turned out to have FASD with attendant diagnoses: institutional autism, sensory integration disorder, hearing and vision problems, post-traumatic stress disorder, auditory processing problems, severe speech and language delays, overall developmental delays, attachment issues, even dental and bone structure problems. We have seen over twenty medical practitioners since they have been here in an attempt to determine what we ought to work on and when; whether their behaviors were from attachment and emotional problems, or something medical, or could be helped at all. Some of the visits were a waste of time, and many were useful. One of the reasons so many professionals were consulted is that when you get to this level of insult to the brain, everyone is a specialist.

I would describe myself as a therapeutic parent. It was clear after Sam and Heather came to live with us that there were multiple issues that we didn't understand. There were behaviors we couldn't put a diagnosis on, or sometimes there were more than one possible diagnosis and each required a different parenting or therapeutic response. **Our premise for being therapeutic parents to our children is:** Very few professionals in the U.S. know about FASD. Far fewer have seen a patient who also have the other diagnoses. Having figured out over the first eighteen months that we didn't have an expert in our midst who could cover these diverse issues, we had to become the experts. In order to do that, we needed to know as much as possible. What we learned:

Time is of the Essence.
The accepted time frame for the brain to more easily lay down neural pathways is up until the ages of about ten to twelve years old. There is evidence, according to Dr. Harry Chugani, Chief Pediatric Neurologist at Detroit Children's Hospital, that it can be stretched through ages thirteen or fourteen. One thing is certain: early intervention is of the greatest benefit to the child. Our approach has been:

1) Address medical needs first

2) Begin Occupational Therapy and Speech and Language Therapy as soon as possible

3) Address emotional and psychological issues when they were able to use language

Sam and Heather came to our home for in the summer of 2003 through the Kidsave Summer Miracles orphan camp program. Summer Miracles makes it possible for children living in orphanages in Columbia, Russia, and Kazakhstan to spend a few weeks experiencing life with an American family. Many children end up being adopted as a result of their visit, and we hoped that would be our outcome too. They are accompanied by a caregiver from the orphanage that stayed in our home. We got a photo and an almost blank medical record in advance. I wondered about what looked like a flat filtrum on Heather's face, so we took her photo to a physician who was supposed to be knowledgeable in international adoption. She said she couldn't tell anything from just a picture, and neither could anyone else. We inquired about getting more information but were told it would be nearly impossible, so we let it pass.

That first meeting was quite something. Sam came bounding forward with a grin from big ear to big ear and stuck out his hand for a shake. He was ready for America. Heather was being carried by the caregiver and was wailing and took a swat at me when I tried to say 'Hi'. Our summer visit was busy but we'd been warned about over stimulating them so we kept it low key.

Sitting around the deck with plates of watermelon and bottles of bubbles kept us all laughing into the summer evenings. Later we learned that their total life experience was severely limited, mostly to two rooms in the orphanage with a little daily playtime on a cement playground with no toys. They chattered away constantly to each other in Russian, which I could understand a few words of for daily basics, but mostly we tried to anticipate their needs so they didn't have to ask for things.

They had the utmost respect for their caregiver and would line up if she lifted an eyebrow at them, although I only heard her scold them once. Later I found out that one punishment for infractions of the rules was to lose your meal and watch other kids eat it while you stood for hours. They were and are so eager to please it is both sad and heartwarming. I'd like it if they stood up for themselves a little more. Any indication of issues to come was easily explained away with excuses: they're just little kids alone in a new place, tiredness, lack of life experience, and Heather's chronic sniffles.

The kids came home with us permanently in late March, 2004 after a long trip to Kazakhstan. Sam was seven years old and Heather was six.

The First Six Months.

As the first weeks went by it was obvious they weren't making any attempt to learn English. They didn't seem to see any need to talk to us so we could understand. I had entertained ideas of home schooling but it soon was obvious to me that their needs were so disparate that trying to teach one while the other one hung on me was not going to work. We put Sam in the local first grade so he'd be forced to make an attempt to learn English. The school assured me he would pick up functional English in just matter of weeks. They had him in an ESL group for two hours a week. He loved it because they assigned two students each day to be his buddies so he had built-in friends. I only found out the final week of school that the teacher had discontinued the buddy system a few weeks after he got there and he'd been going it alone the rest of the time. With his poor language skills he would mostly nod and smile. It is Sam's modus operandi to tell the world that he is ok, even if he's not.

Heather and I spent the days at home that spring doing nothing in particular. I was a new mom and she couldn't remember having had one. She was very resistant to being held, making eye contact, or doing anything together. FASD kids often have various sensory issues and she was severely sensory disordered. What makes it difficult is that children with attachment disorders can behave very similarly. Also, children with institutional

> *The 'Wait and See' advice we got from a number of professional sources is absolutely wrong for children that have neurological damage.*

autism or autistic tendencies can exhibit the same issues

We went to the pediatrician monthly for Heather's constant upper respiratory infections, and she finally ended up with surgery for an adenoidectomy, sinus cauterization and tubes in her ears. The Ears, Nose, Throat doctor said the thick fluid behind her ears was so great that she probably could scarcely hear at all. As time went on we found out that she does indeed have permanent hearing loss in both ears.

I kept Heather at home that spring as it was obvious that she was having a much more difficult time transitioning to her new home and continued to have sore throats and sinus infections one after the other that made her tired. She had such poor balance that she sometimes would have to bend over and put her hands on the floor to keep from falling down. She would turn a corner too hard and run right into the wall on the other side. One thing that will sound foolish now is that being a new mother of six and seven year old children, I didn't really know any other mothers on the level of discussing their children's issues. I was involved in my career for over twenty years and the daily head colds of little children just wasn't on my radar screen. I didn't have a check-list of things to look for or things to do. I didn't know a single thing about normal or abnormal child development. Being resourceful, I looked up a lot of things on the internet and read a lot of books.

I knew they needed basic physicals and vision and hearing screens from participating on the PEP-L internet list (a knowledgeable network of adoptive families at www.eeadopt.org). I also knew they might need Occupational Therapy and Speech and Language evaluations based on the amount of time they had spent in the orphanage. We began with a series of three pediatricians, and I became increasingly frustrated with doctors who knew next to nothing about older children coming into the United States from such a disadvantaged situation.

The first pediatrician tried to tell me to take it easy and give them time, and disregarded the protocols set out by the American Academy of Pediatrics for internationally adopted children. She dismissed the idea of repeating infectious disease tests and doing parasite screens as 'not necessary', and seemed a bit defensive about the former Soviet Union's health care system. As part of our initial visit she was supposed to evaluate their language capability. We had chosen her because she spoke Russian and was described as an International Adoption Physician. She asked them a few questions, which they answered yes or no or nodded their heads to. She was satisfied they were on target with language. I showed her a white thing that was stuck far into Sam's ear which she thought was ear wax. Later I insisted we try to get it out and we discovered an entire cotton ball that had been in the ear canal for months, since before we adopted him. It had dried blood stuck on the back of it. Sam's comment going out the door, was "Mom, I hears better!"

The second physician was a well respected Chief Developmental Pediatrician who had an urban practice. Her comment was that the children looked happy and smiling while I seemed very hyper about them, and maybe I was the problem. "Give them two to three years", she said. "They'll be fine". Finally we found a thoughtful pediatrician. Although many of our problems are completely unique to his practice, he has given us so much of his time that we are sure he has earned the keys to heaven early.

During the first six months Heather was also evaluated for two crossed eyes, and had surgery to correct them. Both eyes immediately flopped out and we patched for four months. She was diagnosed with Monocular Vision, meaning the neural pathway in the brain that should take input from both eyes and show it to your brain as one continuous field of vision, was not present. She used one eye or the other, but not both together. It was a toss-up as to whether her brain could still form this pathway at her age, but we hoped with all the stimulation she was receiving that maybe she had a chance. We suspected she might be seeing double, but even with a Russian speaker, she didn't understand what we were asking her and kept saying "My eyes don't hurt". A year later, she was finally able to say, "Mom, I see two of you" and we were back to monthly ophthalmologic visits again. At that time there was exciting evidence that she might be developing the neural pathway that would allow her eyes to work together to present a fuller field of vision. The small miracles do happen.

They both had audiology exams, with Sam being normal and Heather having permanent hearing loss. The audiologist recommended that Heather's classroom be outfitted with an FM system and that she wear a headset so that she could hear words spoken directly into her ear. (The public school dragged their feet for seven months and finally told me they were implementing a trial in the spring of her school year. They used it a few times and dropped it. I was too tired to go fight with them). In addition, living with the two children every day, and talking to other parents, led us to believe that they were not transitioning as quickly as the

Definition of Fetal Alcohol Spectrum Disorders (FASD)

Prenatal exposure to alcohol is one of the leading preventable causes of birth defects, mental retardation, and neurodevelopmental disorders–American Academy of Pediatrics

Experts now know that the effects of prenatal alcohol exposure extend beyond FAS. 'Fetal alcohol spectrum disorders' (FASD) is an umbrella term describing the range of effects that can occur in an individual whose mother drank alcohol during pregnancy. These effects may include physical, mental, behavioral, and/or learning disabilities with possible lifelong implications. FASD is not a diagnostic term used by clinicians. It refers to conditions such as:
* Fetal alcohol syndrome (FAS), including partial FAS (pFAS)
* Fetal alcohol effects (FAE)
* Alcohol-related neurodevelopmental disorder (ARND).
* Alcohol-related birth defects (ARBD)

From the Office of the United States Surgeon General:
* No amount of alcohol consumption can be considered safe during pregnancy.
* Alcohol can damage a fetus at any stage of pregnancy. Damage can occur in the earliest weeks of pregnancy, even before a woman knows that she is pregnant.
* The cognitive deficits and behavioral problems resulting from prenatal alcohol exposure are lifelong.
* Alcohol-related birth defects are completely preventable.

From SAMHSA, Fetal Alcohol Spectrum Disorders Center for Excellence. U.S Department of Health and Human Services, Center for Substance Abuse Prevention and the U.S. Office of the Surgeon General -0- 02/21/2005 /

Thinking About Adopting?
Facts About Parenting a Child with Fetal Alcohol Spectrum Disorder

What every adoptive parent needs to understand about children who have been affected by Prenatal Exposure to Alcohol (PEA):

1) There is no way of knowing for sure if a child without obvious symptoms has been adversely affected by PEA, as symptoms may appear later, at or around adolescence. If the child is later found to have Fetal Alcohol Spectrum Disorder (FASD), there is a 90% chance the child will need long-term support throughout adulthood.

2) There is a very wide spectrum of effects ranging from full Fetal Alcohol Syndrome (FAS) to the so-called 'milder' Fetal Alcohol Effect (FAE). The children with the milder effects are actually at greater risk of having serious problems later on in life. Since the symptoms are not visible, the expectations of others are unreasonably high (normal) and set the child up for failure and frustration that can lead to depression or aggression.

3) There is also a very wide spectrum of behavioral disorders among the kids who are exposed and/or affected. More than half the children with FASD have ADHD, some have ADHHHHHHD, and some are not hyperactive at all. More than half of the adults with FASD suffer from clinical depression, some of them become suicidal, and some of them cope and adapt very well to the stress of living with FASD.

4) There is another segment of kids with FASD: children who also have mental health issues. Some of the children have diagnoses that are directly related to the FASD, such as the ADHD and depression mentioned above. Other children who have FASD may also have a serious mental illness such as Bipolar Disorder or Reactive Attachment Disorder (RAD). While most people with FASD have some mental health issues, most do not have problems to this degree. Most of our kids are very sweet, friendly (overly so), sociable (without social graces) and would not hurt a bug.

There does seem to be a higher rate of mental illness among FASD than in the general population, due to the fact that women with hereditary mental illness are at high risk of self-medicating with alcohol. The children with FASD who show signs of anger toward their mother or show violent behavior with pets or siblings, are most likely among the small percentage who have a serious mental illness. These children need an entirely different set of intervention strategies and medication than those we suggest for kids with classic FASD.

5) Expect the worst, hope for the best, pray for guidance, seek support of others, and plan on spending a lot of time and energy looking for solutions to problems as they pop up along the way. If the child does not have a serious mental illness, the chances are becoming greater that he or she will be able to live away from home as an adult. A good support system needs to be established over the years, and the child must be able to accept the reality of the FASD and the limitations and restrictions that will be necessary to maintain success.

~ By Teresa Kellerman

other adoptees. Talking to Heather, it is almost like you can see the words washing over her. Sometimes she can repeat back what she hears, but often there is no comprehension or response given. She is currently scheduled for a Central Auditory Processing evaluation. The audiologist typically does not test kids have overlapping diagnoses where its difficult to ascertain what the problem is, but I convinced her that in this case, the additional information might be useful for designing remediation. Sam tries very hard to understand, but usually he will not volunteer that he doesn't comprehend.

In the first summer, four months after they arrived, I determined that we had seen enough issues and made an appointment with the Chief Neurologist at a regional Medical Center. After a three hour intake, he said "I don't know what to do with Heather. Without being able to assess her in the Russian language, it's very hard to determine her status. My recommendation would be to find someone who can do that."

We moved on to the doctor we should have started with, Dr. Ron Federici, neuro-psychologist in Alexandria, Virginia. Dr. Federici's practice specializes in older adopted children from the Eastern European countries, and he has possibly seen more of these patients than anyone else in the world. He was able to test in both Russian and English, so we traveled to his office five months after we came home from Kazakhstan. At this point the findings were not so un-expected for Heather; Fetal Alcohol Spectrum Disorder, Post-Traumatic Stress Disorder, Institutional Autism, Sensory Integration Disorder, and severe speech and language delay.

At the age of six and a half, she possessed a vocabulary of about eighty words. Her aggregate developmental equivalent age was a little more than two years old and her IQ tested below average, although we were warned that IQ tests at this stage are unfair and could change as she gained life experience. The findings on Sam were shocking to us however. We were suckered in the same way the first pediatrician was. Sam tested as FASD, PTSD, Sensory Integration Disorder, Severe Speech and Language Delay. At eight years old, he possessed a vocabulary of one hundred and forty words.   He had an Aggregate Developmental Age Equivalent of about three and a half years old. He tested as having a low IQ, although we were warned again that this was inconclusive. He should not have been an English as a Second Language (ESL) student.

We came home from Virginia and I got busy calling the school district to request information on how to get Individualized Education Programs (IEP) for Sam and Heather. One of the outcomes of many conversations was a warning from other parents that the school district might try to dismiss an out-of-state physician's findings for the IEP. To head that off, we went to a geneticist, a gruff old guy who knew his stuff inside and out. The neuropsychologist had recommended we do this anyway. He did many tests to rule out any genetic or chromosomal abnormality, and in the end gave a confirming diagnosis of FASD to both kids based on physical features of the face, hands, head, and body. In addition, we repeated the speech and language portion with a Pediatric Speech and Language Pathologist, arriving at virtually word for word the conclusions of Dr. Federici.

Some of the evidence that they had not developed normally was:

1) **Physical:** Microcephaly, dental and jaw malformations, small hands and short fingers, thin upper lips, ear placement, epicanthal folds, vision problems, digestive problems, hearing problems, poor balance and coordination, poor musculature, immune system

Resources

Fetal Alcohol Syndrome; A Guide for Families and Communities by Ann Streissguth

The Best I Can Be - Living with Fetal Alcohol Syndrome or Effects by Liz Kulp

Recognizing and Managing Children With Fetal Alcohol Syndrome/ Fetal Alcohol Effects: A Guidebook by Brenda McCreight

Fantastic Antone Grows Up and *Fantastic Antone Succeeds! Experiences in Educating Children with Fetal Alcohol Syndrome* By Judith Kleinfeld and Siobhan Wescott

Fetal Alcohol Syndrome, Fetal Alcohol Effects: Strategies for Professionals by Diane Malbin

The Broken Cord By Michael Dorris

Visual Strategies for Improving Communication, Volume I: Practical Supports for School and Home By Linda A. Hodgdon, MEd, CCC-SLP

deficiencies, malnourished. The stunting of their size could be explained by a number of factors such as malnutrition and emotional and sensory deprivation, which certainly might collude with FASD to worsen the problem.

2) **Neurological:** Memory and retrieval problems, such as great difficulty with repeating words, remembering words, or short word sequences. Speech, language, and auditory processing problems, inability to follow patterns of movement, and problems with visual tracking and discrimination. Sam and Heather didn't seem to be interested in learning new things at any great speed. All that warm talk about 'they'll just soak it up like sponges' was not what we were seeing.

3) **Behavioral:** Autistic-type activities like rocking, self mutilation, self stimulation (biting their own arms, picking skin or scabs), only parallel play with us or other children, lack of direct interaction with people, not recognizing or taking social cues.

It's a good thing I have a medical background, because of all the evaluations we had only three physicians recognized FASD. I have acted as the central coordinating person for all of their medical care because I haven't found a physician in our area that seems to know much about FASD. My children were diagnosed by a neurophysiologist, a geneticist, and a pediatric ophthalmologist who took one look at my daughter's hands and told me she was FASD. Having the hard diagnosis will be important to the children's future support and services through the education system and probably in adulthood. My husband and I are older than the average parent and these are our first children, so at least we have life experience to bring to the tasks and joys of raising Sam and Heather.

We had another surprise when our daughter went into precocious puberty a few months after arriving in the United States. See article on page 400. Little is known about why children do this; it is postulated that the endocrine systems of children with FASD have been damaged by pre-natal alcohol exposure and simply do not respond correctly to stimuli. Others think that the hormones contained in our dairy and beef stimulate hormone production in children. Still others think that there may be an enzyme missing in the liver to metabolize and eliminate estrogen, thus allowing it to accumulate in the body.

Our daughter's immune system is very weak. Even a

normal scratch becomes inflamed and sometimes infected. Not only did our daughter have eye surgery to correct esotropia, ear surgery and adenoidectomy, but she also developed a softball sized abscess at the site of an injection of a drug to suppress estrogen production. She ended up in surgery again, and experienced four months of wound care, including skin grafts. It was a Catch-22 situation. Heather is so delayed; she needed a chance to have some little bit of childhood and an opportunity to catch up, but unfortunately her body would not tolerate the traditional medical approach to suppress precocious puberty. We are looking into alternative therapies now.

Parenting Tools

Attachment-Parenting. It was important to keep Sam and Heather home after arrival, and I can't emphasize this enough. The adoption trip and jetlag alone took its toll. The attachment and bonding, and the development of routines, were crucial. Individually they had huge emotional needs and they competed with each other for attention. There was no substitute for bonding with their new parents so my husband and I took turns with each child almost daily to make sure they each got attention from both of us. I have come to believe that the attachment and bonding piece of both FASD and adoption parenting is one of the most important lifetime gifts you can give a child.   Their neurological deficits make life just plain more difficult wherever they fall on the FASD spectrum, and they are prone to misunderstand (and to be misunderstood) in even the tiniest nuances of everyday life and human communication. It's kind of like having undiagnosed vision or hearing loss; you miss a lot of what's going on and you appear to others as if you aren't paying attention, or that there is something wrong with you. So I believe it all starts with bonding with parents. It takes a tremendous amount of energy to parent this day in and day out, but I believe it's the key to later life success.

Meet Individual Needs. I think it was okay for Sam to have the half-day experience in the public school. There were few expectations and everyone was nice to him. He met and played around other kids. It would have been fine to have kept Sam home and found a tutor, or a way to get him into planned activities to encourage language development. Heather, on the other hand, needed to stay home. It was very important to Heather to be with a mother so she could find out what a mother was. Building this trust continues to be an ongoing task with both of them.

Use Language–Age Equivalent. You have to determine the child's developmental age and then parent at that level. Treating Sam and Heather like their chronological age was a losing strategy, especially at the beginning when language was a huge barrier. It just caused frustration for everybody. Now when we coach them to think about what they could be doing, at least we can comment that kids their age do or don't do certain things, and they understand what we are saying. FASD kids are often developmentally delayed and having appropriate behaviors for the age level may not ever occur. After some of our testing was completed, we began to parent them at their language equivalent age rather than their chronological age. This helped us to remember to set our expectations at the right level. The television and music they listened to was much younger than their ages. This made it impossible for them to play with kids their own age, so we just stopped letting them play with neighborhood kids except when we could direct the action. When their language ability, social skills and self regulation became more age appropriate, we could begin to have other kids over to our house.

Family Time. Sam and Heather were forced to get along and play with each other and with their parents. We fly glider planes together, do family sledding, fishing, visits to all kinds of places, picnics at the river, play pirate, and hide and go seek. We spend a lot of time with favorite aunts and uncles and the grandparents. They have learned to be creative, to find ways to occupy themselves, to play independently and together. Heather never used to dress her dolls, but now she dresses dolls and animals, and plays house with them. Sam's initial play consisted exclusively of lining cars up and looking at them. Now he takes them places, while talking and making up stories. We are pleased to see that Sam can manage having certain friends over now, or going to play at friends houses. He is interacting well and the kids invite him back. Heather hasn't quite identified a playmate yet and continues to engage in parallel play and some inappropriate behavior. But she's making progress every day and her brother's role modeling helps a lot.

Evaluations. I tend to be an analytical person, and although some people have felt that we over-evaluated the kids, I don't agree. We needed to know as much as possible to even begin to figure out what to do. And we didn't get any help from anyone. The wait and see advice we got from a number of sources was absolutely wrong for our children. In concert with the occupational therapist, speech and language pathologists, neuropsychologist, pediatric endocrinologist, and their pediatrician, we have developed a game plan of what to work on and in what order. If I had waited for the public education system, or their first pediatrician to tell me anything, my children's chance at an independent future would be totally lost.

Support Network. We gave the public school district a try and worked through the IEP process for Sam and Heather. We were disappointed with their responsiveness, and unwillingness to learn about FASD and execute a plan. They did not comprehend the language deficits and what that would mean to future comprehension. We took our son out of public first grade a few months into his first formal year of school, and put him in a school for kids with learning disabilities with very small class sizes. He went from crying every night and showing all of his autistic and anxiety-related behaviors to flourishing and making friends, and is now almost at grade level after not knowing even 1, 2, 3 in Russian. Our daughter went to the public Kindergarten and received many special services, but it was only after I took her to a private Occupational Therapist, Audiologist and Speech and Language Pathologist, that she began to learn. We have removed her from the public school system to go to the same school as her brother. We don't know what their total capabilities are, but we are giving it all we've got to make sure that they are getting help in each area.

Emotional Age. In the midst of my searching and networking I found an ongoing research project at a University. We volunteered to be a beta test family for a research project on parenting for the bonding and attachment of internationally adopted children. We had two social workers come to our house for floor-time play therapy every week for six months. Then we used the week's technique and practiced it with the kids every day for thirty minutes. The other children in the project were many years younger than our children, but because of the developmental age of our kids, they fit right into the study parameters.

More than anything, this taught us that we had to get down on the kids level and play with them as if they were infants or toddlers. A year later, we have probably advanced by an equivalent of three years. Sam and Heather moved through developmental stages as if they had started at 'birth'. If we had not spent so much time in evaluations we would never have given a thought to regressing to such a young age to interact with the kids, which especially helped them with language. The floor time play worked very well. Due to FASD and other co-morbid factors, the kids were 'stuck' at earlier developmental stages. It was allowing them to work through the stages (and teaching them along the way) that helped them to lay down neural pathways. They began to acquire an accumulated knowledge base to experience life and develop the tools for learning.

Nutrition. Nutrition is a subject that seems to have gone by the wayside in modern America. Despite our national interest in looking good, too few people bother to adhere to the Food Pyramid. Even the schools are full of sugar snacks. Every single day in Kindergarten, a parent brought a white sugar snack to the class. I knew that intestinal digestion and uptake of amino acids and nutrients was the beginning of feeling good, and of adding weight and muscle mass. I knew that their brains needed the right calories to support all the stimulation we were giving them. We had to improve the children's' nutritional status and eliminate over-riding factors that affected their ability to concentrate, learn and retain information, in order to work on the FASD-related neurological deficits.

I give them extra of all the water soluble vitamins, especially those diminished by stress. In addition, I use protein shakes and sometimes PediaSure or Ensure for extra calories and vitamins. I have no empirical evidence to support the following observation but I believe the extra weight they have gained and the extra vitamins they take contribute to stronger, happier, and more capable children. They seem to shake off the sensory issues more easily, and are better able to talk. My experience with physicians tells me that most do not think of proper nutrition as a starting point for reducing a disease state. Not one of them suggested additional nutrient studies or even a multi-vitamin. My children remain on the tenth and fortieth percentile lines on the Center for Disease Control (CDC) Weight Charts.

Occupational Therapy. Occupational therapy has been very important for us. Our OT has been a genius in designing daily work for the kids to do. Heather and Sam would get upset at the slightest thing, so she had us doing crossover brain organizing work from BrainGym, PACE, and NeuroNet four times a day in a proactive attempt to keep them calm and organized, rather than disciplining them afterward. Today, we do a ten minute routine every day, plus we are doing a Tomatis-style Listening Program, meant to stimulate the brain and promote crossover activity. At her recommendation, we also have a music therapist once a week. We do so many things it's hard to discriminate and decide which activity is making the difference; I think the combination of various exercises and music stimulation is having a positive effect on both their language and their development toward chronological maturity.

Skill-Based Activity. The kids swam on the swim team, and Sam shows real promise. The coach, who has worked with state and national champion swimmers, has asked if we plan to try to keep him in swimming. It would be a great lifetime sport. Your children must find something they are good at and enjoy working on to improve. They need something that makes them feel competent, self confident, and that earns them recognition. Their little lives are so difficult already. School is tough for them; it must be difficult to struggle so hard for what they can see comes easily to others. Whether its sports, art, singing, drama, or reading, help them learn the self discipline that keeps them involved with something they enjoy.

Positive Learning. We found a small Catholic school for kids with learning issues and enrolled Sam last year. This year we put Heather in as well and it is a joy to see them succeed. The class sizes are small, the place is quiet and gentle. They wear uniforms so there is no confusion at home or competition at school over clothes. Sam hugged me this year after the first day of school and said "Mom you love me, you took me out of my old school and brought me to XX. I love it!" For him, stress and anxiety are always present; he really appreciates the quietness and smallness of the place. In addition, because of the time required to drive them to school, our family has to follow a fairly strict routine, and this has turned out to be good for them.

Advice to Parents

The most important thing I've done for myself and my husband is to Read Read Read about FASD so I can help educate doctors and teachers, and know something about the behavior that I see at home. There are more knowledgeable parents than professionals out there and the combined wisdom is so helpful. Learn about your state and federal support services, and investigate your options. In my state we have a state funded program that helps us out with some of the extras like Occupational Therapy and Therapeutic Riding. Check with your State Education Department or search your State website for its Drug and Alcohol Department. Call them and ask what they can do for your children–even if it's just educating you. The biggest thing I've learned from my parenting experience is that early intervention is the most important thing you can do for your children. You get the picture. Better to start now.

~Andrea Horman and her husband Mark adopted two older children from Kazakhstan. Andrea had no previous training in child development or pediatric medical and mental health issues, however her education in genetics and business coupled with longtime work experience in the healthcare industry was good preparation for the research required to determine how to evaluate and assist their children.

Resources for Parenting Children with FASD

Education, evaluation and support
Dr. Harry Chugani, Chief Pediatric Neurologist, Detroit Children's Hospital. See 2004 National Conference presentation available through FRUA at www.frua.org

Dr. Boris Gindis www.bgcenter.com

Dr. Ron Federici www.drfederici.com Site offers research and treatments and support

Dr. Jane Aronson at www.orphandoctor.com

American Academy of Pediatrics www.aap.org

FASlink www.FASlink.org

PEP-L list-serve www.eeadopt.org

Amen Clinics www.brainplace.com Trauma therapy–investigations by SPECT Scan

Ohio Coalition for the Education of Children with Disabilities–offers sister state information which helps parents from other states find help www.ocecd.org

Mother's With Attitude www.motherswithattitude.com/about.html, with Hot Links devoted to offering further reading, contacts, support and treatments for FASD

Teresa Kellerman, Director of the FAS Community Resource Center's website www.fasstar.com. Extensive links to treatment centers, research, reading and support (See Kellerman article, pages 380 and 388)

Wrightslaw www.wrightslaw.com Advocacy and resources for children with special educational needs

Therapies
Brain Gym www.braingym.org. Theory and exercises designed to help re-organize and re-order the brain through cross-lateral movement Andrea's Occupational Therapist suggests this site as a portal to Brain Gym® www.learning-solutions.co.uk/brain_gym.php PACE is a group of exercises within Brain Gym that help with organizing the brain

The Neuro Net therapy program, devised by audiologist Nancy Rowe, helps "improve vestibular control of body management (attention) and integrate vestibular-motor, auditory-motor and visual-motor skills" www.neuronetonline.com/bg.php?contentFile=bg5_content

Tomatis Listening Therapy www.tomatis.com Theory and exercises designed to help those with listening/learning disorders

S.C.R.E.A.M.S. Then S.M.I.L.E.S.
How to Parent a Child with FASD and Look after Yourself
By Teresa Kellerman

I'll never forget the day that I first realized the success I had achieved as a mother of a young adult with Fetal Alcohol Syndrome Disorder (FASD). I had been somewhat depressed over the hopelessness of the idea that FAS is permanent brain damage, for which there is no cure. My son John, diagnosed with FASD, had just turned 18, that magical age when a person legally becomes an adult. But I knew that he really was and always would be a boy in a man's body, never able to function independently in the true sense of the word. He would always need supervision and support services. I felt discouraged that nothing I could do for him would reverse the physiological damage of FASD. Until my 'awakening' to a reality. I attended a conference where Dr. Ann Streissguth revealed the results of her long-term studies on secondary disabilities associated with FASD disorders. Streissguth noted the primary disabilities associated with FASD–the delayed growth, the facial characteristics, the physiological anomalies, and the dysfunction of the central nervous system. I recognized that John had just about every primary disability that was mentioned. Then Streissguth talked about the secondary disabilities that the individuals in her study developed: mental health issues such as clinical depression that in 23% of adults led to suicide attempts, dropping out or getting kicked out of school, getting in trouble with the law, sexual assault, abuse of alcohol and other drugs. The secondary disabilities that can result from of having FAS disorders are more devastating than the primary disabilities, but all were preventable!

It was at that moment that I realized that John had reached the legal adult age of 18 without having incurred any of the secondary disabilities! Streissguth reported that the protective factors include early diagnosis, stable home environment, and appropriate support services. John came to me with the first, and I provided the others. The strategies I had been using while John was growing up were not just haphazard ideas applied blindly, they were carefully thought out strategies based on what I had learned from Streissguth and other FASD experts. There are seven basic components that I apply, and they happen to form the acronym SCREAMS.

- **S**tructure: a regular routine with simple rules and concrete, one-step instructions
- **C**ues: verbal, visual, or symbolic reminders can counter the memory deficits
- **R**ole models: family, friends, TV shows, movies that show healthy behavior/life styles
- **E**nvironment: minimized chaos, low sensory stimulation, modified to meet individual needs
- **A**ttitude: understanding that behavior problems are primarily due to brain dysfunction
- **M**edications: most often the right combination of meds can increase control over behavior
- **S**upervision: 24/7 monitoring may be needed for life due to poor judgment, impulse control

Structure. Most people who know about FASD disorders are aware of the need for structure, but sometimes this is confused with control. While providing structure as a foundation, we need to offer choices they can handle, remain flexible, and remember KISS –Keep It Simple, Sweetie!

Cues. Giving cues can be tricky, as we tend to only give verbal reminders. I call it cueing; John calls it nagging. Kids with FASD respond well to visual cues, to symbols and signs, to music and rhythm.

Role models. Children with FASD learn behavior primarily by mimicking the behavior of others. This makes healthy role models extremely important. I am reminded of this saying: "Children learn by example; unfortunately they can't tell a good example from a bad one." We need to provide positive examples for dealing with frustration and anger, for appropriate social interactions, and for life styles that are healthy.

Environment. Behavior modification is not on my list,what works better for our kids is to change the environment. Avoid noisy, crowded places; reduce the chaos; and prepare in advance some coping strategies for unavoidable situations that might be too stimulating. One overlooked factor in environment is diet–avoid all artificial additives (preservatives, coloring agents, aspartame, etc.), which may increase behavior issues.

Attitude. Understanding the nature of FASD as a neurological disability helps to minimize unrealistic expectations. The greatest obstacle our kids must overcome is chronic frustration from unreasonable expectations of others. The parents whose children experience the most success are the parents who have achieved an 'attitude of acceptance', and who understand that their child may not fulfill their dream of 'normalcy.' Again, unrealistic expectations for full independence might set the teen up to fail. The teens and young adults who enjoy the most success are those who have accepted the limitations of their disability and the need for protective restrictions.

Medications. The right meds or combination of meds can normalize the balance of brain chemicals. Meds can somewhat restore function and give the individual more control over behavior, increase memory and learning, and enable the individual to behave more appropriately in social interactions.

Supervision. Close monitoring is difficult to impose, especially as the child reaches the teen years and wants the same independence as they think their peers are given. I have overcome criticisms of being overprotective and of not letting go. But my son is healthy and happy and productive, and I am proud of the success he has achieved. His quality of life is better than that of most non-disabled people. The only screams in our family are screams of excitement and joy.

And our S.M.I.L.E.S???

Once you have learned about the SCREAMS intervention strategies and have applied them, over time you have probably seen some success. But even though life may be more manageable for your child, you may find that your life is still in chaos, with more stress than you can handle. Applying the SCREAMS strategies is a daily battle, and maintaining success requires an unusual amount of effort and energy, sometimes more than should be expected of a normal person. So SMILES are the intervention strategies that I have applied to my own life to help me cope with FASD parenting. Try them:

- **S**tress Management: minimizing the chaos
- **M**edications: balancing the brain chemicals
- **I**nspiration: finding the strength to go on
- **L**etting Go: planning for future 'independence'
- **E**xternal Brain: providing the safety net
- **S**upport: taking turns leaning on each other

Stress Management. Some methods that are helpful for stress management include eating properly, adequate sleep, daily exercise, avoiding alcohol, music, prayer, and a friend who is a good listener. For those who live where chaos reigns, try logging on to www.FlyLady.Net. This web site taught me that not only is structure and routine good for my son with FASD, but it helps reduce my own stress as well. And try massage therapy, even if simply a 1-minute self-administered one.

Medications. Studies show that chronic stress depletes the levels of serotonin produced by the brain. Just as with FASD disorders, we need to recognize the physiological basis for our own distress. Helping to maintain a balance in the brain is the responsible, healthy thing to do, if that is what is necessary, and if meds are recommended by your doctor, then use them.

Inspiration. Just when I feel I am at my lowest point emotionally, I will get a message from a parent who helps me see my life and my child in a different perspective. It is easier for me to accept advice and suggestions from someone else who has walked this walk, and support from parents is usually more helpful than what I have received from professionals.

Letting Go. As parents, we have the natural instinct to raise our children to become independent. Helping our child with FAS transition from living at home to living in the real world can work, but only if it is done in a way that minimizes the risk of the secondary conditions like getting arrested, becoming addicted to alcohol or other drugs, or beginning another generation of alcohol affected babies. We can only let go when there are adequate supports in place to help our children to succeed. And then we are only letting go to allow some other persons to hold on or to be there if they fall.

External Brain. Our children have brain damage (whether you like the term or not, that's what it is). There is no artificial brain that can be dispensed to my child. Therefore he needs to 'borrow' my brain in order to control his impulses or make important decisions. If my brain is not available, he needs the brain of his brother or his job coach. When children who are disabled turn 18, we don't take away the wheelchairs or the hearing aids and tell them they are expected to be independent without those devices. They need them the rest of their lives. Our children will need that 'external brain' for the rest of their lives too.

Support. We need support from our spouses, our family members, our friends. Those who find support close to home are lucky. We need support from the social services system, from church, from the community. But often the support we get is not the support we need. We wish someone would say, "What can I do to make things easier for you?"

Teresa Kellerman is the Director of the FAS Community Resource Center in Tucson, Arizona, President of Fasstar Enterprises, and cofounder of FASWORLD. www.fasstar.com

Alcoholism and Addiction:
the Birthfamily Factor

When you adopt a young child it's so hard to look beyond tomorrow and begin preparing for the future. That's exactly what parents need to do, but adoptive parents also need to look into 'yesterday', at a child's pre-adoptive history.

When children are adopted, parents try to learn about attachment, speech and language issues, obtaining early intervention, immunizations, and blood-work. An area that is easy to ignore, but should be considered, is the influence on a child of having a birth family with addiction issues, including alcoholism.

Children coming from Eastern Europe are most likely at higher risk for this concern. A quick review of the news indicates that Russia and the CIS (Commonwealth of Independent States) have a huge problem with alcohol and drugs, but it's important to realize that the problem exists around the world. Families who are adopting from Eastern Europe are initially worried about Fetal Alcohol Syndrome Disorder and the effects of alcohol abuse on their children. But there are other addiction issues related to our children's history that could eventually impact even a healthy child:

- We know very little about our children's birthfamilies, and must assume the possibility that addiction could be part of their history. We need to consider what children who were adopted at an older age might have experienced before they were placed. Did they see parents unconscious from drinking? Were they given alcohol? Were they hungry because all of the money was regularly spent on alcohol?

- Alcohol affects the brain of child differently than the brain of an adult. In addition, there are physiological events that happen to the brains of people with addiction potential that is different than what happens to people without that factor. This risk is similar to that physical fact that some people have a higher risk for heart disease or diabetes than others do. Alcoholism is a disease, and much research is occurring related to the hereditary aspects of addiction. The findings are mixed, but tend to support a genetic component.

- A child who was adopted is at greater risk for problems related to identity and self-esteem. Poor self-esteem can lead a child into undesirable peer groups, troubled behavior, and drug and alcohol usage.

- There are problems in many countries with drugs and alcohol, and easy availability to both for children with an unknown addictive component. It is important for adoptive parents to arm themselves with knowledge as early as possible about alcohol and addiction. The unknown details of an internationally adopted child's family history make substance abuse a possible challenge for any of our adoptive families.

> *~ By Mary Ellyn Lambert, President of Families for Russian and*
> *Ukrainian Adoption-Michigan, bio and adoptive mom.*

Abuse and the Adoption Connection
The Extra Layer May Make Our Children Easy Targets
By Sheena Macrae

Shame: at the Core of Abuse and at the Core of Adoption

Being rejected is shameful, and being abused is sometimes kept a shameful secret. Shame is pervasive. Adopted children need help to understand that abandonment and loss of birth-family are impositions on them; abandonment and loss are not caused by the child's actions. Children who don't get beyond this first pervasive sense of shame often carry it to other situations in their lives.

Adopted children, rejected by birthparents, often feel intrinsically 'bad'. This sense of guilt and shame leaves the door wide open to a child feeling so worthless that abuse is something they somehow deserve. Being abused simply confirms the sense of shame. Further, an adopted child already affected by trauma and loss may simply be overwhelmed by an abusive situation. Such children may think that abuse is too shameful to report; they may believe that in some way 'they asked for it'.

How Abuse can Reinforce Shame in our Adopted Children

No young child deals easily with abuse, but the words that sexual molesters use to 'persuade' might deliberately manipulate our adopted kids' fragile sense of worth. Many potential abusers are fatally aware of just the 'right' words with which to intimidate a child. For our adopted children, with issues centering on those detailed by Kaplan and Silverstein, abuse targets where they are vulnerable. Read the words of actual sexual offenders and consider their effect on a child dealing with the core issues of Loss, Rejection, Guilt and Shame, Grief, Identity, Intimacy and Mastery/Control. Imagine how these statements might silence an adoptee-victim:

- It is all your fault.
- Everyone will think you're nasty and dirty.
- You will be taken away from your family.
- Your parents won't love you anymore.
- Who will take care of you if I go to jail?
- You will be put in a foster home.
- Everybody will know what a bad girl/boy you are.
- *I will hurt you, your dog, your family (anything of value to the child)*.
- You would be responsible for destroying our family.

(Excerpted from Sexual Offender Behavior, Street Level Consulting. Used with permission)
It is our job to help our children know how to deal with abuse and have the words to speak of it. We need tools for ourselves and for our children, too.

Abuse and Adoptive Parents

There is much evidence available from experts that we parent as we ourselves were parented. We need to seek help for any dark corners and abusive secrets in our own lives before we go onto parent adopted children successfully. If we ourselves don't have secure boundaries or feel that we are in charge of our past, how can protect a child or teach them self-protective behaviors?

Adopted children are vulnerable to parents who are unable to cope, especially if the parents have latent problems with handling stress. Adoptive children, especially in the first days and months when they are terrified, may try and test a new adoptive family to their limits. We need to be prepared and to know where to find help for both ourselves and for the adopted child.

A child who has survived traumatic pre-adoption care and carries the scars of attachment disorder, may know all the buttons to press to destabilize a new parent with a less than 100% sense of boundary and self. A parent pushed beyond the limits may over-react physically or verbally, with devastating effect on the trusting bond that we all hope to develop with our children. Horribly, in some cases, a parent's reaction goes beyond any acceptable limits and ends in a termination or parental rights, or in a child's death.

> Adoption experts Debra Silverstein and Sharon Kaplan Roszia in their article, *Seven Core Issues in Adoption* consider Guilt and Shame a critical issue of adoption. The other core issues they highlight are Loss, Rejection, Grief, Identity, Intimacy and Mastery/Control

Abuse and the Post Institutional Child

As adoptive parents, we parent our children with the extra layer of adoption parenting, and they come to us with the extra layer of an often unknown history.

Abuse in the Orphanage. We need to remember that some of our kids may well have experienced abuse while being cared for in orphanages. Institutions may attract workers with capacity to harm as well as care, and the abuse may be physical, sexual, emotional, or deprivational. There's also evidence that older orphanage inmates abuse younger children. Abusing younger kids that can't hit back gives older children a sense of power; ultimately the younger kids repeat the pattern of abuse as they grow, and become perpetrators themselves. The pattern can be hard to erase and some kids come home knowing only how to relate to others by abuse. These children may go on to become bullies and may abuse their parents. On the other hand, a child who has been abused in the orphanage may have such low-esteem that she may be a perfect target for an abuser, or a bully, once adopted and home.

Attachment Issues and Abuse. Attachment issues in our adopted kids may also impact on how they might deal with abuse in an abusive, post-adoption situation. Children with attachment disorders who have never been given the chance to develop a secure notion of boundaries between 'self' and others, cannot be expected to defend against an abusive invasion of personal space. It becomes all the more critical therefore, that we as adoptive parents instill a sense of secure personal boundaries in our children,

Resources

When the Body Is the Target: Self-Harm, Pain, and Traumatic Attachments,
by Dr. Sharon Farber, has linked the addictive nature of both Eating Disorders and Self-Injury to each other

A Very Touching Book...for Little People and Big People
By Jan Hindman

My Body Is Private
by Linda Walvoord Girard

Parenting the Hurt Child: Helping Adoptive Families Heal and Grow (Hardcover)
by Gregory Keck, and Regina M. Kupecky

Center for Behavioral Intervention
Cory Jewell Jensen & Steve Jensen
4345 SW 109th Ave
Beaverton, OR 97005
A full set of tools for understanding abuse and protecting our children from it can be found in their work
Understanding and Protecting Your Children from Child Molesters and Predators

while engaging them in trusting us. *"... Adopted children may be abusive due to a variety of circumstances in their backgrounds. They may have grown up in violent and abusive birth-families, foster homes, or orphanages. They may be affected by reactive attachment disorder, bipolar, or other disorders that can include violent behaviors. They may be filled with so much grief and anguish that they it seems to them that their only release is through violence."* Susan Ward

Race as a Factor in Abuse. Race and ethnicity may impact on abuse by giving predators 'permission' to prey on children who have been sexualized by popular racial stereotypes. Most documented perhaps is the racist Asian stereotype of the exotic China Doll, the submissive comfort woman, the GI brothel girl. Our adopted Asian children are often seen by the general public as part of this broad-brush stereotype. Our daughters are called 'dolls' and 'cuties'. To a predator, they are simply toys to be used

Is 'Being Adopted' a Factor in Abuse? Lynelle Beveridge has written in her book *The Colour of Difference* that transracial adoptees are more vulnerable to abuse in their adoptive families simply because they are 'different'. She also writes that if adoptees are abused then *'they suffer the effects worse because they have a 'double whammy' situation to deal with, i.e., they have adoption issues and abuse issues. Both are traumatic and would cause anyone to suffer mental health issues unless given appropriate support and professional intervention'.*

Further, our adopted children may be sitting ducks in a sexually abusive family setting, because the 'incest taboo' is off. Our children are not genetically related to other family members, which may make it easier for a relative-predator to justify molestation.

Helping our children stay safe requires proactive thought and action by us, as responsible parents. Helping our children who have been hurt requires an understanding of the core issues of adoption, and therapeutic intervention with experts experienced with the issues of abuse.

~ By Sheena Macrae

Self Harm and the Adopted Child

Children who have been abused or grossly neglected are at high risk for self injury. It affects those who suffered childhood trauma and who later face the resulting emotional pain without resiliency or internal resources. Children who have not been helped to deal with issues from their past may be more prone to physical manifestations of a need to feel in control, or for a release from deep emotional pain.

Tweenies (children 8-12) are moving toward early teenhood, where the eating disorders of anorexia nervosa and bulimia, and self-harming behaviors such as 'cutting', become more prevalent. Dr. Sharon Farber, author of When the Body Is the Target: Self-Harm, Pain, and Traumatic Attachments, has linked the addictive nature of both Eating Disorders and Self-Injury to each other:

'Both of them seemed to be an individual's attempt to solve emotional problems, to make himself or herself feel better. They really served as a form of self-medication. Just as drug addicts and alcoholics use drugs or alcohol in order to medicate themselves, in order to calm themselves down or to rev themselves up, they use self-mutilation to make themselves feel better.'

Adoption doesn't cause eating disorders or self-injury, but unresolved trauma from an adoptee's past can contribute to their occurrence. A child's underlying trauma issue must be treated for the self-injurious behaviors to stop. Cutting among some children is treated as a peer group fad, but for other tweenies and teens, cutting is a sign of their high anxiety over attempts to control extreme emotional distress.

"For many people it's a form of their body's speaking for them… the body says for the person what they cannot allow themselves to say or know in words. It's about speaking about emotional pain…" (Farber)

What can adoptive parents do to prevent their tweenies from expressing emotional trauma through self-harm? It helps to be proactive, rather than reactive, by strengthening a child's internal resources:

- We can teach our children to identify and appropriately express their feelings
- We can teach our children to communicate and share their thoughts and daily experiences
- We can help them build resiliency (see Positive Outcome, page 366)

Another factor contributing to cutting, or other self-mutilating behavior that can become 'addictive' (tattooing or body piercing, for instance), are the sensory issues that many post-institutional children exhibit. Sensory issues may, or may not, be coupled with psychological issues. A sensory-deprived child who picks at scabs or scratches her skin, may be simply looking for the alien physical sensation of feeling, and an Occupational Therapist can offer evaluation and guidance.

Children Who Abuse
Being Prepared is Your Best Offense
By Kelly Killian

The sad reality is that many children come into adoption from a history of abuse or neglect. For some children, violence is a way of life, and a way of mind. This violence can, and often does, carry over to the new adoptive home. How this violent past manifests itself varies from child to child. There may be temper tantrums, destruction of property, abuse of animals or other children, and in some cases, parental abuse. It can also manifest in false allegations of abuse against the parent. These children are angry and their parents are the safest place to vent this anger. If they feel you are getting too close, they will do everything possible to push you away, physically and emotionally. It is hard to accept that the child you lovingly took into your home can be abusive toward you, or make allegations that can destroy your life, but there are things you can do to protect yourself.

Preparing to parent a possibly violent child. Prior to placement, obtain as much history on the child as possible. Some important questions to ask are:
- Has the child witnessed domestic violence?
- Has the child been a victim of abuse, and if so, in what form?
- Has the child ever made allegations of abuse against anyone?
- Is the child violent toward animals, other children, or adults?
- Does the child have a history of property destruction?
- Does the child have a history of self-injury?

Once your new child is placed in your home, prepare for the worst. Preparing yourself for the worst, and never having it happen, is far better than being caught off guard.

What to do if your child abuses you. Children with a background of exposure to violence often seek to gain power by pitting one adult against another. One of the ways they do this is by claiming they have been abused by a parent or caregiver. They may tell a teacher their parents are not feeding them, that a parent is beating them or that they are being locked in their room. All of this is done with the most sincerity, and is completely believable to the person hearing it.

Do research and find a lawyer who specializes in family law. If possible, meet with the attorney and discuss your child's history, and what steps you can take to protect yourself, or what to do in the event of an investigation. Should you ever come up against allegations, knowing who to call will help to ease some of the panic and fear. The more documentation you can bring into a meeting, the better off you will be.
- Document any damage to your home with photographs. If your camera has a date and time stamp, use it. Otherwise, make sure you write this information on each photo. Also include a narrative of the events preceding the damage, as well as steps taken to deter it and any consequences given afterward.
- If at all possible, video tape or audio tape your child's outbursts and destruction. Again, use the date and time stamp if possible and write up a narrative afterward. Some children will stop the behavior once the video camera is on.

- If your child is in school, meet with the teachers, principal, and counselors and explain the situation in your family. You may feel this is violating your child's privacy, but it will enable the teacher to work with the unique situations that may arise.

- If your child is in day care, have the day care document any and all events. Many day cares give out a daily behavioral sheet. If yours does not, ask them to do so and document what happens throughout the day.

- Make sure your pediatrician is educated in adoption issues, especially those involving abuse.

- Take photos of any injuries you sustain from your child. If you have someone who is able to come and be a witness, use that person. If your child self-injures, take photos of any injury you find and note the circumstances surrounding the injuries.

- Keep a diary of all events. You may begin to see patterns emerging. Many children have difficulties with anniversary dates and holidays. It may help you to defer events in the future, and warn those who deal with your child, when you are approaching a difficult time. It can also serve as your source of protection later on.

- If there are witnesses to any events, ask them to write a narrative as well.

- If you find yourself in an investigation, do not allow yourself to be interviewed without a witness present. A witness can be your attorney, a friend, neighbor, family member, or anyone that you trust. If you can not have a witness present, write a summary of the interview afterward, and mail it to the investigating person and his/her supervisor. Start with, "this is what I heard you say" and summarize the meeting. Keep a copy for your records and give a copy to your attorney as well.

There is little awareness among professionals and the general public about children abusing parents. That may be due to several issues:
- It's hard to grasp the idea of a blond-haired, blue-eyed, eight-year old girl, inflicting body and facial wounds to her mother.
- There's been such strong (and needed) effort to educate people about parental child abuse, that the reverse situation seems unthinkable.
- Many professionals are untrained and unaware of the potential violence that young children can bring upon their parents due to their mental, emotional, and behavioral issue.

Susan Ward,
olderchildadoption.com

When you are in the middle of an investigation, emotions run high. Having the documentation will prevent you from forgetting details, and will serve to show the history of events in your home. It will also aid in getting the help you need for your child. Trying to prove that you did not abuse a child who abuses, manipulates, or triangulates relationships, is very difficult to accomplish.

~ Kelly Killian is an adoptive and foster parent of children with various emotional and physical special needs. As a volunteer advocate, Kelly has worked with, and counseled, many families who have been through abuse investigations. She works for the Attachment Disorder Network www.radzebra.org.

Visible Difference
Parenting a Child with a Minor, Physical Special Need.

Adopting an Older Child with a Special Need. Having adopted one daughter, we decided that we would adopt again. Our eldest was adopted as an older child and we decided to adopt from the same age group again. At the same time, we also decided that we would request a child with a minor special need. We received a referral for a very lively little four year old with a 'club foot' (talipes equinovarus) affecting her left leg. Referral information included photos specifically of the leg concerned. We discussed the condition with our family doctor and got a referral to an orthopedic surgeon to make appointments for when we got home. Based on our previous experience with attachment difficulties, we planned to give our new daughter some time to adjust before undertaking any invasive medical procedures, but appointments also need to be made months ahead.

Home, First Investigations, then Surgery. When we got home, I really don't think that we thought much about her foot much until our appointment with the surgeon. She did have a limp and a few people would mention it, but the vast majority did not even notice. From his examination, the surgeon suggested that her foot had previously been 'cast' while in China (a standard non-surgical approach to straighten the foot). The surgeon recommended surgery to lengthen the Achilles tendon, to be followed by casting the foot again. Surgery was a day procedure and proved very successful. We painted her cast (and let her paint it too) to make it more interesting for her and to give her a feeling that she contributed to her foot getting better.

The Reactions of Others. It's amazing how people start taking an interest once a physical special need is more obvious. We received sympathy and offers of help, including from a physiotherapist who made up a splint for night-time use once the cast was off and also advised on exercise. In our case, dealing with a physical special need has been relatively easy because it is visible and more readily understandable to friends, family, and acquaintances. In comparison, educating those around us to attachment issues was significantly more difficult. Of course, the visibility of a special need can also mean that you (and your child) are never allowed to forget.

Difficulties Beyond the Special Need. Our daughter had a difficult transition and to not thinking about her foot until the surgeon's appointment. Our daughter was quite traumatized by the suddenness of the change and in a word, 'angry'. She would rage for forty to fifty minutes, with all the considerable vigor and volume that a four-year-old can muster. She would do this three plus times in a night. She continued to do this for a good five months before the frequency even started to diminish. By nine months it was down to a few times a week. After only five months with us, she was able to express a wish to visit China. This took a few months to organize, but at ten months post adoption we had a return trip to China to properly say goodbye to her old life. This resulted in an almost complete cessation of the rages. The visit that she requested had clearly met some psychological need. For our family, we have learned that dealing with a physical special need has been minimal in comparison to the other issues from institutionalization.

~Vivienne and Paul Webb, adoptive parents of two daughters.
Viv is a legal librarian and Paul is a railroad engineer. They live and work in Australia.

The Lifelong Impact of Birth Defects
How My Cleft Palate has Shaped My Life

I'm 36 and I was born with a cleft palate. Any child with a birth defect has to go through operations and visits to hospitals. Mine spanned the period shortly after I was born until my early twenties. Repair work meant I had to attend both a dental hospital and a plastic surgery clinic. These involved tedious trips to stuffy buildings with bright lights and harsh chemical smells. I remember having to wait for what seemed like hours before someone in a white coat would peer down my throat, photograph me, or stick some implement into my mouth or nose, often in the presence of medical students. I am certain that these trips, although brief, did have an impact on who I am today. The other constant memory of these appointments was of having my mother with me, which was always great comfort although it must have been difficult for her.

The first time I was exposed to other children was when I went to school. I made a friend on the first day; I was accepted as part of the group and it was very rare for anyone to make any comment about my appearance. If they did, it was more out of curiosity than malice. As a pre-teen and teenager, however, I faced challenges relating to the image-consciousness that surrounds children approaching 'adulthood' and I was subjected to bullying. I feared being viewed as different, and I became self-conscious about my image and how other people related to me. Being naturally introverted, I found it difficult to interact with people out of my immediate circle of friends and would avoid situations that exposed me to new groups. This was ostensibly because I was 'different'. I would be lying if I said that this period of my life was happy.

There is no doubt that having a birth defect presented me with difficulties that I would not have wished for had I been given a choice. My experiences have given me understanding, sympathy, and empathy for others who are experiencing difficulties in their life–and I think they have made me a better person. Dealing with my birth defect has helped me learn that many of the limitations that surround us we impose on ourselves. In adulthood, appearance matters less to us and those around us. I have set myself goals I would not have dreamed of setting a few years ago. I have no idea what I would be like if I had been born without my cleft palate–but I am pleased with who I am.

~ Andrew McArthur

From His Mom

The first of Andrew's surgeries closed his lip (3 months old) and improved his appearance; the second closed his palate (15 months old) and enabled him to eat normally; and the last, at 18, improved his general appearance. He had a plate to hold replacement teeth and to support his weakened palate. This required constant inspection and upgrading as he grew. The Speech Therapist worked wonders on his speech. Prior to attending school he played with his friends and they accepted him– the deformity being hardly noticeable. When he went to school he suffered some teasing, which I only found out about when he was in his late teens. What could we as parents have done differently? Possibly we were over-protective and did not appraise him of his 'different' appearance and prepare him for the jibes and challenges ahead? Perhaps we should have been more involved with him in out side activities and expanded his circle of friends and generally tried to boost his moral.

Ruth McArth

Books on Puberty for Boys

What's Going On Down There? Answers to Questions Boys Find Hard to Ask By Karen Gravelle (ages 10-14)

It's Perfectly Normal: Changing Bodies, Growing Up, Sex, and Sexual Health By Robie H. Harris (ages 10-14)

Books on Puberty for Girls

The Care & Keeping of YOU, the Body Book for Girls By Valorie Lee Schaefer

The Feelings Book, the Care & Keeping of Your Emotions By Lynda Madison
Both titles from the American Girl Library
www.americangirl.com

The Period Book: Everything You Don't Want to Ask, But Need to Know by Karen Gravelle, (ages nine and up)

It's Perfectly Normal: Changing Bodies, Growing Up, Sex, and Sexual Health by Robie H. Harris (ages nine and up)

Precocious Puberty
Why Internationally Adopted Children are Affected
By Laurie Miller, MD

Parents who prepare to adopt internationally are faced with learning about a host of infectious diseases and medical problems that they probably never imagined they would need to know about. Most parents become experts in understanding 'PCR tests' for Hepatitis C, the difference between 'surface antigen' and 'surface antibody' tests for Hepatitis B, and how vaccination with BCG may affect the results of skin tests for tuberculosis. However, for many parents, the topic of precocious puberty is especially daunting.

What is precocious puberty? Precocious puberty means early puberty. Puberty is the complex series of hormonal events that control the development of secondary sexual characteristics and rapid growth of adolescents. Secondary sexual characteristics include pubic and axillary (under-arm) hair. In addition, the testes and penis of boys enlarge, their voices change, they develop axillary sweatiness, facial and chest hair, and acne may appear. For girls, the most obvious signs are breast development and the beginning of menses; they also develop axillary sweatiness and may have acne. Both boys and girls experience a growth spurt as a part of the changes of puberty.

In about one in every 5,000 to 10,000 children, these changes start earlier than expected. This is known as precocious puberty. Rarely, precocious puberty results from serious medical conditions, including tumors (brain, testes or ovaries, adrenal glands), genetic disorders, or various hormonal problems. However, in most cases, the precocious puberty is 'idiopathic'–meaning there is no obvious underlying cause. Idiopathic precocious puberty is also known as 'Central Precocious Puberty', or CPP. Far more girls than boys are diagnosed with CPP.

When is puberty considered early?
Pediatric endocrinologists disagree, to some extent, about the definition of precocious puberty; that is, the age at which pubertal changes should be considered abnormally early. There is some evidence that the age of onset of puberty differs among children of different races and ethnic origins; however the exact differences have not yet been completely

defined. This becomes very important when internationally adopted children are considered. Although there is a great deal of research on the normal and abnormal timing of puberty in various ethnic groups of children in the U.S., less information is available on the normal onset of puberty in children in other countries. Moreover, research indicates that body mass index, malnutrition, chronic infections, or some illnesses alter the timing of puberty. Most girls menstruate for the first time when they weigh approximately 100 pounds. A 2002 study of 1623 girls in the U.S. found differences in the age of appearance of signs of puberty in different ethnic/racial groups. For example, nearly 50% of African-American girls aged 9 years had breast development, compared with about 24% of Mexican-American girls and 16% of white girls (Wu et al., Pediatrics, 2003,110:752-757). Variations in this study are shown in the following table.

	Age (years) at appearance		
	Breast development	Pubic hair	1st menstrual period
African-American	9.5	9.5	12.1
Mexican-American	10.3	10.3	12.2
White American	10.3	10.5	12.7

Onset of puberty also relates to social class and ethnic subgroups. In Madras, India, age at first menstrual period varied from 12.8 years for urban, privileged girls to 14.2 years for rural, less privileged girls (Proos et al., Acta Paediatr Scand, 1991, 80:852-58). In comparison, Indian girls adopted in Sweden had their first menstrual periods at age 11.6 years. However, some researchers argue that American and other Western doctors over diagnose precocious puberty because they are not familiar with the normal expectations for pubertal timing in other countries.

What are the concerns related to precocious puberty? Children with early puberty grow quickly, and soon become taller than most of their peers. When puberty ends, however, hormones signal the bones to cease growth. Thus, many end up significantly shorter than their peers, as they stop growing sooner. In addition, children appear more mature than their peers, which can lead to teasing. People may assume that the child is more capable and mature than he or she really is. Hormonal changes make some children moody and irritable; these changes can be harder for young, immature children to handle. Girls who menstruate early need to be able manage their hygiene during their periods.

What is the connection of precocious puberty to international adoption?
In 1981, researchers from Sweden noticed a cluster of 7 adopted girls from India and Bangladesh with early puberty (Adolfsson et al., Pediatr Res, 1981,15:82). Additional reports from Sweden, France, Italy, and Belgium suggest that a surprising number of internationally adopted children develop precocious puberty: as many as 45% of girls in one study. Both boys and girls adopted from other countries have developed early puberty; children from South Asia seem most likely to be affected. To date, no reports from

American investigators have been published about children adopted from other countries with precocious puberty.

Why would internationally adopted children develop precocious puberty more frequently than the general population?
There are several possible explanations for the apparent increase in precocious puberty among children adopted from other countries. Some of these theories are based on research in animals, where adjustments in food supply (feast/famine) can alter the timing of puberty. Researchers believe that the improved diet children receive after adoption (from low protein, low energy diet to a more balanced, enriched diet) may trigger earlier onset of puberty. The better quality diet induces the body to produce the hormones that signal puberty. Other speculations include possible contributions of psychological factors, rapid growth, and changes in body mass to the development of early puberty.

Can precocious puberty be treated? Should internationally adopted children with precocious puberty be treated? Any child with precocious puberty should be examined by a pediatric endocrinologist to determine if there are related conditions or other problems causing the early puberty. CPP is treatable with hormones that block the signals causing the pubertal changes. When the medication is withdrawn, puberty then progresses. Internationally adopted children should be evaluated like any other child who has these symptoms, and a decision to treat made on an individual basis.

What about premature breast development (thelarche) alone? Some children, especially girls, prematurely develop breasts but no other signs of puberty. This condition is differentiated from precocious puberty as no other signs of hormonal activation are present. Usually this condition resolves with time, suggesting that it is a response to hormones or hormone-like substances from outside of the body (in food or medicines, for example).

As a parent of an internationally adopted child, should I worry about precocious puberty? Although clusters of children with precocious puberty have been reported, this condition remains rare among international adoptees. Over-zealous diagnosis may have falsely inflated some of the statistics related to the frequency of this condition. However, any parent who observes the development of signs of puberty in their young child (8.5 years) should schedule an examination with a pediatric endocrinologist.

~ By Laurie Miller, MD, author of The Handbook of International Adoption Medicine: A Guide for Physicians, Parents, and Providers, Oxford University Press

Dealing With Doctors and Hospitalization
Opportunities to Build Trust

Hospitals, doctors, dentists, and their procedures can be frightening for any child, but for post-institutionalized children there are additional reasons for anxiety. Caregivers in institutions often wear 'white coats' and our children may have experienced terrifying breaks from daily institutional normality when undergoing tests for medical reports when sick, or in order to be cleared for adoption. Our children may both fear the environment for the painful things that occurred in medical testing, and may also fear that hospitals are a part of the past that has come back to haunt them.

> **For the New Adoptee:**
> Explore delaying non-essential medical or dental procedures that require hospitalization. Allow the child time to adjust to life in their new family, and for strengthening the parent-child relationship prior to another stressful event.

Children may:
- React to the stress of hospitals by shutting down, disassociating, talking incessantly, becoming hyperactive or uncooperative.
- Become disregulated by a trip to a medical professional. Even a short visit can disrupt the child for several weeks. They may need a parent's help in processing their reaction.

Parents/Professionals may find it helpful to:
- Arrange for the child's history to be discussed with health care professionals via telephone in order to stay out of the child's radar.
- Minimize the waiting before an appointment (parents may wait outside the hospital building and be called by mobile phone when their child is to be seen).
- Permit post-institutionalized children who are hospitalized to have their parents with them at all times, even at night, regardless of their age.
- Understand that the child is difficult or uncooperative because of fear and anxiety, perhaps based on past institutional experience.
- Be aware that parents can often understand their child's reaction to the hospital environment better than the doctors and staff; parents should be prepared to advocate.

Parents can:
- Use a child's hospitalization and need to be cared for as a tool in furthering the bond with the child. Use child's increased dependence on you while ill as an opportunity to create trust and build attachment.
- Tell the truth to a child; never tell them "it's not going to hurt" or try to minimize either their fears or what they are experiencing physically.
- Address a child's feelings while staying calm and positive.
- Practice and role play what happens at the dentist or at the doctor in advance of an appointment. Explain why shots or drawing blood is necessary. Put together a Dr.'s bag of instruments and pretend pills and 'role play'. Saying AHHHH with a tongue

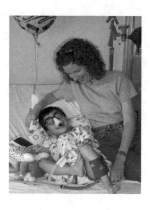

depressor in the mouth is hard for an orally defensive child, but it won't be as traumatic at the Dr.'s if it's been practiced (and rewarded) at home.

- Reward with hugs and even some candy when the child emerges from the doctor, dentist or hospital. Make the special treat contingent on getting through the experience, not on getting through it without tears or trauma.

When a Parent is Ill or Hospitalized

An adopted child may be terrified that he or she will lose a parent who is ill or who must be hospitalized. Loss issues may manifest in anxiety or anger, which both can mask the child's underlying fear. A child may appear to be coping, but may experience nightmares or breakdowns over small provocations at home or at school. Children may not 'allow' an ill parent to be sick, and escalate their own needs in order to hold the sick parent's attention.

The hospitalization of mom or dad should be treated by the parent as a short 'break' of attachment, and mending the break should begin when the parent is able.

- Phone contact and visits to the hospital should be regular and encouraged.
- Child needs to know he or she will be well-cared for regardless of how long the parent is gone from the home. Tell your child about the caregiver plan-of-action that you have in place, even if it's not necessary to use it.
- Establish a regular routine for child at home when possible.
- Openly acknowledge child's mad/scared feelings; understand child may feel out of control.
- Explain to your child's caregiver, and to your extended family, what your child is experiencing and how they can be supportive.

Text based on work by Sheena Macrae, Jean MacLeod, and on
The Post Institutionalized Child by Karleen Gribble.

Support

Women Who Notice:
Speaking Up and Reaching Out

My second daughter, adopted as a baby, was a challenge to parent. She came to me with an awareness of her loss, memories of a woman she loved, a sensitive nature, and an intense personality. My first three years with this beautiful and intelligent child drained me emotionally and physically. I learned what I had to do in order to help her with her adoption issues, and re-wiring my life, I did what was needed. I don't remember the details...but I remember the anxiety and resignation, and being tired! We made progress together, but teaching a baby to love you is a lonely business.

My daughter grew to feel safe and secure in tiny little steps. I rejoiced in the smallest of things: her first unsolicited kiss at fifteen months old almost stopped my heart! I spent most of my day, every day (and a lot of my nights) meeting her needs and teaching her to trust. It's hard to comprehend the immense amount of energy that can go into adoption-parenting, unless you're familiar with the bittersweet experience of bringing a child back from the edge.

I had a lot to learn about support systems, both for my child and for myself, and if I had to do it again I would be as proactive in finding assistance for myself as I was about finding resources for my daughter. I would help my family and friends understand the work I was doing with my child, and I would ask for their emotional support. I would let them know exactly what I was dealing with, and how important it was for them to put their arms around me and my baby, literally and figuratively. Adopting a child opened a whole new world for me, but I think I was too blurry-eyed to realize that my friends and family weren't sure of how to offer to help, or even what I was trying to accomplish.

I needed a coach, a mentor, a friend who understood–I wanted the village that was supposed to help me raise my child! I didn't get the whole village, but I did find women who reached out to me, who extended sisterhood and who told me I was doing something valuable by mothering. They noticed. I held on to their words of honesty and support, and was enormously touched whenever another mom mentioned how well my little girl was doing. Simple words had a powerful impact:

"You are a great mom," my own mother said to me one day, after watching me slog through months of attachment-parenting.

"You are a strong woman," an adoption therapist told me, which gave me the mantra to get through my week.

"We are so thrilled for her!" a group of moms told me with excitement when my one year old was finally able to sit happily on the play parachute at the toddler class. It was a big day when she decided to go for a gentle circle ride with the other babies, instead of clinging to me in fear. The moms' sincere celebration of my baby's big step forward surprised me; that they had noticed what my daughter was working to overcome, and had shared their appreciation of her accomplishment, meant the world to me.

More than time alone or bubble baths or even chocolate, the words and company of other mothers re-energized me to be the kind of parent I wanted to be. Moms who understood what I was trying to achieve, who acknowledged and validated my time with my daughter, were my cheerleaders–giving me the words to go forward and the words that re-filled my inner reserve. I was, and continue to be, extraordinarily grateful for the women in my life who spoke up and reached out to me, who helped keep my attitude healthy and happy, and Who Noticed when I needed it most.

There is invisible strength in Motherhood, and we need to watch out for one another. Giving a struggling mom a compliment, noticing the incremental progress of her child, or offering your encouragement (or shoulder to cry on) are not-so-random acts of kindness that fuel the thankless job of parenting. Showing up with a flat of flowers and planting them, dropping off a video and a bag of chips and dip, or simply sending an admiring email, are motherly gestures we can do for other women that help void the feelings of isolation that parenting challenging children can engender.

We can do this for each other. We can extend a hand. We can connect. We can all notice, and tend to a mom in need of the essential, human magic of other mothers.

~ Jean MacLeod

The Power of Connecting

Whether it's online or off, the most powerful thing we can do for ourselves is to connect to other parents with shared experiences. Being able to talk in person or online to a mom or dad who has shared or is sharing similar parenting experiences can really make a difference. Ask your adoption social worker for local on the ground support groups, or join one online. Yahoogroups (found at yahoo.com) have a wide variety of groups to meet many specific family needs. Our favorite? Adoptionparenting.

Find it at groups.yahoo.com/ group/adoption parenting/

It's a topic driven group that changes topics every two weeks. There's lots of thoughtful discussion, and it is the group that made this book possible....

The Learning Curve
Learning That We Aren't Alone

In international adoption, most of us adopt a child who is close to being a year old, or older. They bring their own secure or insecure attachment history with them. Some of these kids have to be taught what a mom or dad is and does, and what it means to be part of a family.

New parents expect to fall in love with their newly-adopted child, but post-institutional kids have learned to survive without that kind of intimacy. In the dance of attunement, bio-parents get back those tiny, intimate rewards from their children for their parenting efforts: hugs, kisses, preferential treatment, self-regulating behaviors, that adoring gaze that babies reserve for their moms and dads–it all keeps the parent dancing!

It is grueling, heartbreaking work to parent a child who has ambivalent or avoidant behaviors, and who resists conforming to our own concepts of affection or behavior. No one likes to feel a failure at life's most important 'job', but with a parent's desires and a child's history on opposite tracks, the disconnect will sadly feel very much like a failed or partial relationship.

Being abruptly thrown together with a grieving-neglected-sick-abused-deprived toddler without the societal 'it takes a village' kind of support that pregnancy and childbirth engender, is frightening, fatiguing and lonely. Our internalized working model of attachment, motherhood, and self-esteem has been hard-wired into us by our early primary caretakers. If a parent has internalized disorganized or insecure attachment from his/her own mom, the parent's emotional skill-set of attachment will be shaky under stress and duress. This makes parenting the way an adopted child needs to be parented, very difficult.

It is depressing to be caught in this kind of vicious circle. Birth children bring a readiness to trust and love to 'the dance', and so, are easier to parent on the most primary level. Even when the 'mom' and mothering a parent has internalized is a strong, healthy model, the demands of an unconnected adoptee, combined with the total lack of preparation that most of us get for adoption-parenting, can bring a parent to her/his knees. Where many of our adopted kids have adoption issues that are completely normal for their circumstances, I also think that cold-parenting the adoptee is a completely understandable catalyst for Post Adoption Depression.

Sometimes it is meds and therapy that get us through. Sometimes the simple, surprising realization that adoption-parenting is different, and that we are not alone on our learning curve, will encourage us to find the resources that help our kids and strengthen ourselves and our families. In parenting, our tools lie mostly within ourselves. It doesn't mean we can't replace a tool with a better model–it is our awareness of the mom we had and the moms (and dads) we are now, that give us the power to make that change.

~ by Jean MacLeod

Making Connections with Support Groups
By Bert Ballard and Sarah Ballard

International adoptees occupy a very unique place in the world. Often they find themselves 'between' cultures, not fully understanding or feeling accepted into their birth culture and not fully welcome or comfortable in their adopted culture. We believe that this 'space' between cultures does not have to be viewed as a negative or a hindrance. Certainly occupying this space comes with its own challenges unique to the international adoptee but it provides an opportunity for growth and connection unique to these adoptees as well.

One way to deal with both the challenges and the opportunities related to being a member of this community is to build connections through a support group for international adoptees or a support group for their families. For the most part, children can begin attending a support group around the age of five. It may seem young, but laying down the foundation for connections can never begin too soon. Five is an age when kids can begin to articulate what they feel and think. And there is no age too old to begin! We know of an adoptee who began attending support groups when he was 45. You can remain a part of a support group as long as it continues to benefit you and your child. As for families, there is no set time either. We encourage you to see attending a support group as a way to strengthen the family. Do not wait until anything is 'wrong,' but consider attending a support group to improve on what is working, to improve communication between everyone, and to learn how to better relate to one another. No matter where we are in life, we can always work on these areas!

The final piece of advice, and probably the most important, is do not push! Adoptees are diverse individuals. Each person has his or her own set of challenges, and there is no way to predict when, or if, a certain question will arise. Some adoptees will benefit from a support group. Others might not. Some may need it. Others may not. Allow your child to process at his or her own pace. This may happen at a young age. It may happen a long time after they have moved out. Offer your kids the opportunity of a support group. Encourage them to attend. Don't force them to go if they do not want to, and don't force them to go back if they had a negative experience. Allow your adoptee to become who he or she is; sometimes this will include a support group, other times it may not. Support groups are offered as one of many resources available to the adoptee and the adopted family.

Some Reasons Why
Understanding. Adoptees understand each other in ways no one else can. To have others who can relate is invaluable to helping adoptees struggle through experiencing racism and difference, feeling lonely, desiring to fit in, coming to terms with how one looks, returning to birth country, searching for birth parents, relating to individuals from birth culture, dating, and reconciling loss of birth culture.

Find a Local Support Group

To locate a support group in your area, contact the following websites. (Please note that the following are primarily resources for North America):

Database of parent support groups by state or Canadian province: **www.nacac.org/pas_database.html** (search by state and transracial/transcultural adoption)

Online support groups or list serves: **www.adoptioninformation.com/ directory/ supportgroups1.htm**

Locate a support group by state and type: **www.adoptivefamilies.com/ support_group.php**

List of on and off-line support groups: **www.adoptionsupportgroups.com**

The value and history of adoptive parent support groups as well as further resources for locating groups: **naic.acf.hhs.gov/pubs/f_value.cfm**

If you do not find any support groups in your area you can contact the National American Council of Adoptable Children **www.nacac.org** for additional resources and suggestions for starting one of your own.

Parents as Facilitators. We want to answer all of their questions and protect them from harm. However, for many challenges other adoptees serve as a better resource, and a resource that parents cannot offer. Encouraging your child to participate in a support group demonstrates your love for them. It is healthy for your child to find connection, not a badge of failure or inability!

Awareness. A support group introduces adoptees to others who are asking similar questions and going through similar challenges. A support group can help adoptees become aware of issues of which they were previously unaware. This knowledge can aid in adjustment and the forming of healthy relationships, and a chance to prepare for questions that otherwise might have caught them off guard.

Peer Support. Adoptees, like all people, are complex. Each person journeys on his or her own, and each will have different and unique questions. A support group offers adoptees the chance to learn about themselves and others, and the chance to receive and give support in a way that no one outside of the group can.

Safety. Support groups are typically based on two values: freedom of expression and confidentiality. Together, these create a safe environment for the adoptee. In this space, the adoptee is free to be angry at birth parents, be stressed by adopted parents, grieve the loss of birth culture and birth parents, and be depressed about their situation without the fear of hurting others' feelings. They are also free to feel lucky about their life, adopt their adopted culture as their main culture, and express a longing to be something other than who or what they are. In short, a support group offers safety that no other interactions in their lives can offer.

Just Being There. Knowing there are others who understand is important; even if the adoptee never interacts with or builds a relationship with another adoptee, the knowledge that other people are going through the same issues, challenges, and questions can be enough.

Rarely Used. It might sound opportunistic, but support groups are rarely used. They exist, but people often view support groups as signs of failure. This is simply not true! Accessing a support group is a sign of a healthy individual!

Support Groups for the Whole Family. This aspect is even less considered than accessing a support group for an individual, but support groups are a great place for adopted families to talk. Today's support groups are no longer staid, boring discussions. Today, they offer opportunities to role-play, dramatize, play games, draw pictures, and a host of other 'innovative' techniques that foster healing and promote positive interaction..

Belonging. As mentioned at the beginning of this list, international adoptees can feel as though they are between two cultures. In the support group, this becomes the norm and not the exception. It becomes a place to talk about identity and how one feels. It becomes the place to share and give and receive support. It is feeling part of a community

A New Sense of Belonging

It is very complicated being a multi-racial, multi-ways-of-looking family. However, adopting my children has really increased my own sense of belonging in the world; it has enormously enriched my life. I now belong in the world of mothers, of adoptive families, of mixed race families, of international adopters, of families with children from China, of families with children with attachment problems, and so the list goes on. I even feel I belong in a sort of peripheral Chinese community. All these things have greatly enhanced and enriched my life experience, and have given me many interesting contacts and friends. I suspect and hope that all of this increases my children's sense of belonging with us, and in our homeland.

~ By Charlotte Holtam ,
adoptive mum

Normalizing. As one becomes involved and connected with a support group, the 'in between' culture becomes its own culture. Realizing that other adoptees think, feel, interact, and reflect in similar ways becomes a bridge between the 'in-between' space and the greater world. The adoptee is able to 'normalize' what it means to be an international adoptee by connecting to others who share his or her outlook, struggles, and feelings.

By Bert Ballard, Vietnamese adoptee who did not connect with other Vietnamese adoptees until he was 25 years old, but wishes he had connected with them when he was younger. He is Vice President of the Vietnamese Adoptee Network and a board member with Colorado Heritage Camps, a culture camp for international adoptees and their families. Sarah Ballard holds a masters degree in counseling and is a practicing psychotherapist and runs support groups for adoptees and adopted families.

Single Parenting
The Joys and Challenges of Parenting with One Pair of Hands
By Leanne King

Who are Single Parents?

The vast majority of single adoptive parents are women who choose to adopt so that they may experience the joys and challenges of raising a child. They are usually older mothers (30 to 55) who are well established in their careers and who want to share their lives with a child. Most have never married, while some are no longer married (because of divorce or death). International adoption is particularly attractive to single parents because in many countries single applicants receive the same treatment as partnered parents, and singles may apply to adopt a healthy infant.

However, some countries are tightening restrictions–a singles quota is in effect for adoptions from PR China, for example. As China tightened their single parent program, agencies were left scrambling to find single-friendly countries to meet the growing demand of singles wanting to adopt. Many singles have turned to waiting child programs where they are able to adopt children designated as having minor special needs or because of their (older) age are deemed difficult to place.

Domestic adoptions to single parents are also on the rise as child placement agencies recognize the valuable resources found in the single parent family. It has been suggested that placement in a single parent family may be preferable for some children as the parent is completely able to focus on the child's needs. Children adopted out of our foster care systems and from institutional settings often have special needs (physical, emotional and mental) and if the single parent has the appropriate resources, then it may a win-win situation for both parent and child.

Balancing the Care. Single parents are often extraordinarily organized individuals. Balancing caring for ones children and working often requires the precision of a tight rope walker. Most single parents work fulltime to make ends meet. Many look for employment that offers flexibility in hours worked and time off. Being able to work from home when your child is sick is a true bonus. Although some of these technicalities may also be felt by partnered parents, it is so much more critical to plan ahead when there is only one parent to juggle changing childcare needs. Schools and daycares are often chosen with job location and needs in mind. Many singles also find once they are home with their child and have returned to work after parental leave that they must look for alternative employment that better suits the needs of their family. Others come to the realization that dreams of early retirement are unlikely to materialize when one faces the prospect of putting their child through university at the same time. Some employers are supportive and understanding of the single parent, while others feel that singles chose this path and do not allow flexibility of any sort in the workplace. Most single parents feel it is imperative to establish a strong support network for times when day to day life is challenged by the many variables of parenting young children.

In my home, making and maintaining lists of things that need to be done and keeping an accurate daily planner has greatly helped our day-to-day life. If we look at the planner each night before bed, I am able to pick out appropriate clothing for the day, pack skates, etc., so that we are prepared in advance. Not only does this make for better time management but it lowers my stress level greatly! I plan meals two weeks in advance and shop accordingly. Birthday party gifts are bought on sale and kept in a bin in the closet – my daughter shops out of the bin when she needs a gift.

Single Parents and School-aged Kids. Most singles also agree that once their children reach school age and are involved in extracurricular activities, the balancing of the schedule becomes even more challenging. Arranging after school care, transportation to swimming, soccer and whatever can use up valuable energy and resources. Single parents with two or more children sometimes have to miss soccer games to attend ballet recitals and so forth. It is a constant balancing act and it is very important for the single parent family to establish supports within their child's circle. I know making friends with the parents of my daughter's friends has provided us with invaluable support in getting through scheduling challenges and I am always grateful. It is also wonderful when I can reciprocate the favors although I do fear that I am more often on the receiving end.

Finances. Finances are a challenging issue and even though many of us were financially successful and secure when we adopted, we find ourselves stretched to the limit with childcare and household expenses. The cost of adoption alone can set back a single income home. But in two parent families when kids are school age and parents return to the work force full-time, it is quite reasonable for many families to simultaneously save for university and retirement. Many single parents have no hope of retiring before age 65 or older or being able to pay for their children's education. I am not in position to contribute anything extra to my retirement savings and I will not be able to pay for my daughters' education entirely. The current task of organizing our small home for a second adopted child has been overwhelming at times. We will eventually need to move or build an addition

Adding a child is an incredible financial worry and is often the main factor in this decision for singles. I knew when I adopted my daughter that I could not afford two in fulltime daycare on my salary and so was not able to consider a second adoption until my daughter was in school fulltime. Single parents also need excellent life insurance, disability insurance, and health insurance. The cushion for when things may go wrong needs to be very wide and diverse as there is not another adult or income to fall back on.

Circles of Support. The growing popularity of single parent adoption has brought large groups of single parents

The Singles Toolbox

What needs to be in there? For any sort of single parent? Do the same tools last a lifetime? My kids are small and what works changes about every month.

I need a daily routine, it's a sort of lived in planner…

The Exiting the House to Start the Day Strategy: The Routine Tool

Daycare Strategy: The other Carer Tool

Work Strategy: The Money/Adult World Tool

Back-up Strategy: The Network Tool

Corporate Strategy (the body as a Temple!): Respect for Self Tool

The Evening Strategy: Focused Time Tool

The Sleep Strategy: Together Tool

The Weekend/Spare Time Strategy: Battery Charger Tool
    ~Becky Miklos, single mom to two

together, connected through online support groups, agency groups, and cultural groups. We share both the joys and challenges of raising our children solo. As our children grow, we learn more and more from each other and face the unique challenges of single parenting with an adoptive family perspective. It is participation in these groups that has given me so much knowledge and wisdom, that I am confident of my ability to raise my children in an insightful way.

So, circles of support are paramount to the success of the single parent family yet our safety nets can be fragile. Online support groups are often active with discussions of how to cope with some of the complicated situations single parents can find themselves in. Single parents do not enjoy the luxury of running out to the store for a carton of milk, birthday present, or medicine for a sick child. This problem is magnified when our children are sick. Establishing a relationship with neighbors and community is crucial to the single parent. I can call my neighbors to either pick up something from the store for us or stay with my child while I run out. Some singles are blessed with family close by and grandparents, aunts etc. may fill this role. Some singles have even returned to their home cities to have this type of support.

Many singles connect to other single parent families and provide wonderful support to each other. Connecting with other single parent families has been a true positive for my daughter – it allows her to feel like her family is not 'unusual' which in her grade one class, she is starting to feel. Having a single parent family to socialize with has true benefits to both parents and child. Many singles trade childcare, and help each other out when possible. Clothes and toys are handed down and information shared between parents. I have learned a great deal from my single friends who are parenting older children and I consider them a very valuable resource.

Single Parenting can be Lonely. Not only does facing the hardships of single parenting leave you with a sense of loneliness or isolation, but so does celebrating the joys of parenting. There is no one to chat with at the end of the day about what cute/funny/smart or incredibly annoying thing your child did that day, about how beautiful you think she is, what kind of person you think she will grow up to be, about any of these things that create the joys and sorrows of parenting. This is what I miss most about doing it alone–not being able to share all these things that are really only of interest to a child's parents. Single parents will often tell you that you need to know when to ask for help and as difficult as this can be for some of us, it allows our neighbors, families and friends to see where our challenges lie. I think in order for the single parent family to be running as a well oiled, functional machine, we must open our minds to receiving help. As many of us single parents are strong and independent women, it can be humbling to accept help. But in my opinion, it is necessary.

As a single adoptive parent I have found that many of the issues we face (being a biracial, no daddy, adoptive family), we face very much on our own. Discussing them with friends and family often results in my feeling hurt and invalidated. The early years were particularly challenging as I faced my daughter's attachment and trauma issues completely alone. I was accused of making a 'mountain out of a molehill' and the absence of knowledgeable professionals (of the issues of post-institutionalized children) in our area, had me questioning my sanity some days. I believe single parents are at high risk for post-adoption depression because of this isolation.

Dealing with Loss, Dealing with Identity, and Looking after Yourself.
As with all adoptive families, we deal with the difficult task of helping our children to feel good about themselves and their adoptive family despite the very basis of adoption being one of loss. Loss of birth family, loss of country of origin and loss of culture all can weigh heavily on the adopted child's mind. Building positive racial identity is another challenge for the adoptive parent as many of our children are of racial minorities while their parents have enjoyed the benefits of white privilege.

The daddy issue (or mommy issue for the single dads) can be difficult for a child to understand. Toddlers and preschoolers become acutely aware of not having a dad and some are subsequently drawn to men. I remain vigilant of my daughter's safety and work hard to educate her to look after herself and know what is appropriate and what isn't. I worry about sexual abuse because my daughter is so eager to have the attention of the males in her life. Providing a male role model is not easy and most of us hope that frequent exposure to men will suffice. Some families are fortunate to find someone to take on a 'big brother' role which is ideal but many of us find that potential big brothers are either too busy with their own kids or not that interested in spending time with another child. Many kids fantasize what a daddy would bring to their families–cooking dinner, rough and tumble games, and mowing lawns are my daughter's expectations of a dad!

The myriad of issues our children will work through is hard and sometimes overwhelming for the single parent. It is with amazing dedication and skill that many singles balance the needs of their children with their own. Singles recognize the importance of looking after themselves in order to be the best parents they can be. Eating well, exercising, getting enough sleep, taking time for things you love that do not necessarily involve your children are all important in keeping parental energy positive. Although all of us make daily sacrifices for our children, we do them no favors by not looking after ourselves. Helping the child of a single adoptive parent with the many complex issues she will face requires a strong and dedicated parent. Is the single parent prepared for this task or does she grow as the needs of her children change? I suspect there is only so much preparation that can happen in advance.

The Joy of Single Parenting. It is flying solo and growing as a mother and woman as your children lead you down different paths. My expectations of single parenting have changed so much! I am able to sit down and play with my child and ignore the messy house and dirty dishes in the sink. I am recreated by motherhood and for that I am eternally grateful. The joy my daughter (and hopefully soon to be daughters) brings to my life is worth every second of worry, work, and time I expend. I love being the one she hugs and asks "Guess how much I love you?", I love listening to her talk lovingly to her stuffed animals, I adore watching her skate around the ice rink astonishing me with her skill, and I have found true peace in this world when I gaze at her sleeping face. She has breathed new life into me and her laughter is the song my heart sings. It is in these times that I am not even aware of the challenges of parenting solo.

Most single parents will tell you that parenting alone is not for everyone. Most are very clear of their limits and make the best decisions for their families based on this awareness. We are a group who wants our families to be recognized as the viable, strong family units that we are. We do not want to be pitied but we want our unique challenges to be recognized. We don't understand when partnered parents claim single status for a week or month while their partner is away. It is not the same as parenting solo! Nor is the divorced parent who sends her kids off to dads on the weekend and receives child support. These are significant resources for these families! We want our kids to be included and we want to be included in the social lives of our two parent family friends. We want our friends and families to accept and support us as we help our children navigate issues of race, adoption and not having a father. We want our male friends and relatives to build relationships with our children. We want our neighbors, friends, and families to offer concrete help, not the ambiguous "well, if you ever need anything...." Most of all we want people to respect us and our choice to be a single adoptive parent.

We are truly blessed to have so many choices in building our families and we are forever grateful for the countries who allow us to be the families that we are today. It is the joy that has captured so many of us in this wonderful journey of solo parenting and for that we thank our children.

Leann King, RN (ICU), BScN, single parent to Ella and currently awaiting referral for an infant from China. She is co-moderator of the attach-china yahoo group for parents with an adopted child suffering from attachment or trauma issues.

One Pair of Hands and Switching Hats

I've learned that solo/single parenting is very much about endurance and survival. Adoption parenting adds another layer because many children absolutely need the parent to remain in control even while they themselves absolutely need to keep testing. The cycling can be vicious. And add other stresses: exhaustion, financial, work, commuting, daycare, illness.

I've learned to keep a hatbox, and I am hoping to learn how to do switches of headgear fast enough to match my children's growing needs. Do any of you with 'One Pair of Hands' out there recognize how hard it is to get one off and the other one on with just that one pair of hands? Being a single parent (of whatever sort) means working out just those logistics. Here are my hats: Nurturer, Provider, Disciplinarian, Maid, Playmate, Handyman, Financial Planner/Investor, Nurse, Therapist.

Too often I feel conflicted as I have trouble wearing more than one hat at a time. By far the biggest, heaviest, most stifling (and dizzily intoxicating) hat is that of Nurturer. When I'm with my children, I'd better have it on, or my children sense my being disconnected and re-begin to feel unsafe. Defiance, testing, misbehavior follows as they grasp for my attention. Disorder: and the house gets messier and messier. Can one be a Nurturer all of the time? How does one ever get anything done? It is exhausting to live with the clutter and piles and disheveled toys, puzzles, books. Getting on the Disciplinarian hat over the Nurturer hat is a conundrum struggle. But is this unique to solo parenting? I think what I struggle with the most as a partner-less parent is the exhaustion from enduring the march of days, children, work, errands, and never feeling as though any progress is being made.

But, I've made a promise I'll give myself a break. I've promised myself I'll get everything cleaned up and organized when they go off to college...

~Becky Miklos, single mom to two

A Dad's Role

In order to find our role, I think it is vital in a two parent, Mom-Dad household that we adoptive Dads understand the dynamics involved in family development. We have to understand the need for bonding between Mom and child, even if this means our role is initially as a parenting 'assistant'. Most of the adoptive Dads that I have talked to seem to imply that it is their wife's job to keep up with all the emotional 'stuff': attachment issues, sense of loss, and sense of belonging. When I recommend resources or books, they almost always say, *"Great, I'll make sure my wife knows about that."*

I think it's just as important that we Dads know what's going on if we are to discover the important parenting role we play, and be comfortable in that role.

What can Dads do to educate themselves about adoption, and adoption parenting? Simply by modeling on what women do! Meet with other parents, talk, and exchange views. Also:

Get involved. More dads are taking time to attend adoption events.

Get info. Join online e-lists, but be prepared to be in the minority. I rarely see men responding to topics, and frequently only see a female perspective. However, that helps me to better understand where my wife is coming from. I need to keep in mind that the connections my wife and daughter are establishing are primary and not be jealous when my daughter bumps her head and runs to Mom for comfort. I'm seeing the ben-efits of taking a temporary backseat. My daughter sleeps well by herself, makes prolonged eye contact with us both, seeks comfort from us both now, and will give a kiss or a hug even when she doesn't want something.

Work as a Team. I think the role of adoptive Dads will be strengthened if, during the homestudy or parenting classes (mandatory for adoptive parents in some states), time is taken to educate both prospective parents about the issues they may face and strategies for handling them.

Get Balance. This quote about the husband-wife relationship says it best from Sheena Macrae: *"If a mother's need to mother engulfs a father's right to commitment to his children (however the children enter family) then at least for adoptive parents it is right to look pre-adoption at what your relationship is. If it falters because you have no balance with each other, stop there. Your children-to-be, already in imbalance because of loss of birthfamily, will flounder on your imbalance.*

If you are there now, seek help. Get balance. Kids always see where parents fail. We adoptive parents cannot fail our kids (and that means making available fathers and mothers, moms and dads) without disastrous result."

~ By Craig Morgan

Older Parent Toolkit

Helpful Things I Have Finally Learned
By Carrie Kitze

The Patience Tool. As a younger person, I had no patience. My husband and I fall into the same category and were always looking for places to acquire some. I discovered it came with age and experience. And I thought perhaps I could get some on Ebay. I am certain I am much more patient with my kids than I would have been had I become a parent in my mid to late twenties.

The Modeling Tool. I have come to realize that I can learn a lot from others just by observing and listening. Since I have had a few extra years to do that, it has been helpful as a parent. I watch teachers, caregivers, other moms, friends. It's a great resource and it is just before your eyes. And it actually works for kids too! (Unfortunately they model both the good behavior and the bad...)

The Understanding Tool. I have also discovered that everyone does things a bit differently and has their own unique life experiences that impact them and

Motherhood and Menopause

Being an 'older parent' at my kindergartner's public school PTA meeting was a shock. I could have been some of the parents' mom! I have also had another shock. I passed though menopause. Yippee. Over the past year I finally passed that doorway to a new world. In some ways it is a wonderful milestone, and I feel like I should celebrate. Only I haven't got the energy. See, I have two adorable little girls from China. When I was doing paperwork for #2, I remember joking about how I would be going through menopause with a two year-old in the house. I had no idea.

I love both my girls and my baby is wonderful. But busy and stubborn and ornery and loving and fast. Very fast. There was the Vaseline incident. Two child-proof cap incidents. Hair trimming adventures with big sister's scissors.

There are more incidents, of course. But I can't remember them. I read on the WebMD website that the symptoms of menopause (pre-, during and post) may include memory problems. Probably a blessing. Plus...fatigue, lower metabolic rate (I gained 20 pounds last year!), irritability, emotional swings, depression, did I mention fatigue? And the best of all, the hot flashes. Just try to maintain your cool during a two year old's tantrum over which way you tucked in her blankie–all the while steaming.

Sometimes, it seems like there is good reason why Mother Nature designed us to be moms of toddlers before we went through menopause. I came to parenting late. And I laugh every day at the antics of my baby girl. Then cry. Then yell. Then laugh again.

~ *By Marina VanRenssen,*
mom to two daughters, five and two

make them who they are. There are no right or wrong answers but I can listen and learn from them and then apply things to my life experience and make the best decisions for myself and my family because I really do know them best. And for someone else, it will probably be different. I can also support others that do things in a different manner than I have chosen to do.

The I Don't Give a Rat's A$# Tool. This is probably the most freeing tool I have discovered. I really don't care what people think. About me, about how I am parenting my kids. I have learned to smile and nod or make some kind of random small talk and move on. I have come to the realization that I know my kids and myself best and thanks for the advice, but see 'the Understanding Tool'.

The Boundaries Tool. This is a great tool because it helps you to dump the things that are just causing you pain and frustration. I have strategies for dealing with family visits and dealing with relatives. I choose outside activities not by what everyone else is doing, but by what gives me satisfaction, or good friends, or some benefit for my children (either short or long-term). I do things which don't make me resentful but give me joy. As I have started looking for joy in the things I spend my limited time with, I have found myself more content...which just makes life better.

The Humor Tool. I couldn't get through life without this. The ability to laugh at yourself and with others is one of life's greatest gifts. I am also fortunate to have one of the funniest kids living under my roof. I can't wait to see where she ends up, but she keeps me laughing, even when I want to wring her neck!

The Support Tool. This has been really important to me and keeps me sane. My support is not family but instead my circle of friends. I have become selective with friends and I have a wonderful group of supportive, caring moms who I share a cup of coffee, a walk, or an email. They listen, I listen and we have a wonderful give and take. Some of my friends I can sit across the table from and others are around the world. How do you build a network? It doesn't happen overnight. It is a process that requires tending and maintenance, like any good relationship. It's never too late to start...

The Wisdom of Knowing Me. Understanding myself has been key to me in being a good older parent. I am not sure I would have been ready or capable of embarking on the work I have had to do to become the parent I want to be for my children. That has been my best gift to myself and has really made me a more centered and happier person, which just makes all of the above easier. My tribal wisdom has been hard won and I have been able to help others with some of the things I have learned realizing that those I share my thoughts with will take what is helpful to them and discard the rest...

Sandwich Parenting
An elderly parent, a middle-aged mom and an eight year old daughter negotiate connection
By Lynn Sherwood

Well, we've got another holiday weekend coming up, and we'll be going to visit grandma. After finishing work on Friday, I'll be packing up the car with clothing for myself and my daughter, dog gear, dog, roller blades, helmet, wrist guards, Game Boy, books, the security pillow, portable DVD player, DVDs, hair dryer, my hypoallergenic pillow, allergy medication, headache medication, fully charged cell phone, a plant, baked goods for the festivities, snacks for the trip, a digital camera, and chargers and batteries for the cell phone, Game Boy, DVD player, and camera.

After popping a load of wash into the dryer so we'll have clean clothes for school when we get back, I'll put out the garbage, fill the pet dishes, make sure the cat sitter has emergency numbers, water the plants, and bring in the lawn furniture. Then we'll hop in the car and drive five hours down the busiest highway in Canada to grandma's house. When we get there I'll unload everything and walk the dog before settling in to listen to grandma tell me that she expected us earlier, and don't I have anything to put that child in except jeans.

At the age I am now, 58, my mother was already well settled into this routine holiday weekend pilgrimage across the province. The fact that I am no longer young, am working, raising a child by myself, and bone tired almost all the time, does not enter her consciousness. Going 'home' proves to her, and to her neighbors, that I am a 'good daughter'. Saturday morning, after rising really early to walk the dog again, I'll spend several hours listening to grandma review each detail of her daily life since I last visited six weeks ago. My daughter has wisely learned to disappear during these sessions, hence the DVD player.

Grandma comments acerbically on the quality and quantity of food my daughter eats, and is likely to tell her that she is a big girl and not a baby if she sits on my lap at any point during the meal. My daughter tends not to eat a lot at grandma's house. Grandma finds my daughter 'too demanding' if she at any point interrupts grandma's three day monologue. Grandma tells her that if she lets hair fall in her eyes she will go blind. Grandma doesn't believe in praising a child for achievement too much, because then if the child fails at something the next go round, she will be disappointed. Likewise playing games and giving too much attention leads to the dreaded spoiling.

My mother never worked after her marriage, raising her family according to traditional notions of parenting. Blessed with excellent health, affluent, and mentally alert, she still lives independently, driving her own car and volunteering at the local hospital a couple of days a week. Widowed for 25 years, after caring for my dad through the tragedy of Alzheimer's disease, she has been able to do just as she pleases for quite some time now. She is quite lonely, but refuses regular invitations to visit because she feel more comfortable in her own home. Grandma lives with the persistent fantasy of a nineteenth century extended family gathered around a harvest table partaking of her great food and gentle wisdom.   The fact that this fantasy never really was reality, that her nineteenth century family existed at a time of backbreaking manual labor, stultifying boredom, starchy food, and sudden death from any number of causes, has drifted far from her awareness. Upon her oldest daughter, me, has devolved the task of preserving a semblance of that fantasy family.

I figure the fantasy stems from my parent's generation growing up at a bad time. Their parents fought the First World War, and raised my parents during the Depression when old rural ways of life were being transformed into the modern urban world. The Depression was terminated only by the Second World War, which marked my parent's abrupt entry to adulthood. Today we would call this a traumatic childhood environment. Those tough enough to survive into their eighties are all a bit crazy – fiercely protecting their alternate reality against all evidence to the contrary.

Grandma likes to spend a lot of time talking about this. This past summer we reviewed her life history while driving down to the Family Reunion, a two hour drive back the direction I came from the day before. Then we visited the pioneer cemetery where her parents were buried, and the following day met with her financial advisor to review her situation. My daughter handled all this with apparent serenity but on return home became obsessed with the fear that I would die. She slept in my bed for the following six weeks. My daughter came to me prepared to love her grandma, and she does, unquestioningly, despite the fact that birthday gifts arrive a week or so late, and grandma frequently appears to be more affectionate with Fred the dog.

How To Cope?

First, I try to keep the front of my mind an uncompromising and realistic view of the situation at hand. Talking to grandma about the way she behaves with my daughter, for example, is a non-starter. Grandma is becoming disinhibited, a common feature of old age. She says whatever she thinks, wherever she happens to be. Grandma's feelings would be severely hurt by any admonishment on my part. Family warfare would be triggered, as my siblings discovered with their children. The most positive outcome in this case would be an injured and suffering silence, punctuated with sarcastic comments about overprotecting children, or how grandma always says the wrong thing. Worst outcome, grandma gets on the phone to the rest of the family and tells them I'm having trouble with my adopted daughter, as she predicted, and my daughter receives the permanent label of 'problem child'.

The Sandwich Generation: A Cluttered Nest from website developed by the University of Nebraska at Lincoln. It offers financial advice and discusses emotional support for members of the sandwich generation. *Highly recommended:* ianrpubs.unl.edu/family/g1117.htm

Hot Flashes, Warm Bottles: First Time Mothers Over Forty by Nancy London which describes the older parent dilemma; it has a chapter on adoption.

OlderAdoptiveParents @yahoogroups.com a group designed for older parents to discuss their difficulties and successes in parenting adopted children.

www.caregiving.com online forum about caring for elderly parents

I acknowledge that my own needs are not going to be met. Allergy medication, for example is necessary because grandma does not believe that I am actually made ill by her ancient, dusty, feather pillows. She still doesn't know what kind of work I do, and isn't interested in finding out. Similarly, a lot of support from my mother around the daily issues and problems of child rearing is not going to happen.

Talking about day-to-day life, telling cute stories works well, as does describing problems that have been solved. Despite the heavy use of Tylenol I require on outings together, this activity seems to help to keep the best balance between grandma's inappropriate interventions, need for something to occupy her time, and my daughter's need to spend time with her. I try to include other people in our excursions. This necessitates a degree of creative imagination since my siblings' children are now young adults. Fortunately my second cousin's grandchildren are the same age as my daughter. Acknowledging that my nephew with ADD would wreak havoc in grandma's retirement style home, we had a great time taking them all miniature golfing last summer. Grandma even commented, "I guess I've forgotten what young children are like," as she listened to them giggling in the back seat of the car. And my daughter loves to talk about 'all my cousins'.

I try to pace my own coping ability, and to not get caught up in a futile attempt to meet all my mother's needs. I try to get rested up for the pilgrimage during the week before the holiday. And I don't make the pilgrimage in the winter. The roads are dangerous, the weather unpredictable, and grandma can come to my home for Christmas by train. Despite initial resistance grandma has come to accept this new 'tradition' and last year stayed for a week, enjoying herself making Christmas dinner while I hosted friends and neighbors, and my daughter ran about the house with her friends.

Also, I try to anticipate that my daughter will react to these trips to some degree, and accept that there will be a few subsequent, difficult days. We keep activities for the week following the pilgrimage fairly low key, for myself as well as for my daughter.

Finally, I try to remember that my daughter will, for better or worse, have these memories to carry forward into the rest of her future. Therefore, I need to live with wisdom in the forest , not the trees, and take a long-range view of this situation. My daughter needs to remember her mother handling grandma's neediness and inappropriate statements with grace and serenity. She needs to see me treating my parent with respect, and fostering her dignity as she prepares for the dark road we cannot journey together on. She needs to remember a loving and secure childhood so that she, in turn, can journey forward into a future that my own forbearers could not even imagine.

~ Lynn Sherwood is Canadian, and has a BA degree in sociology, a child care workers certificate, (CCW), a Masters degree in social work (MSW) and is a registered social worker (RSW). Lynn and her daughter and share their home with two cats, a Yorkshire terrier, nine goldfish and, lately, uncounted numbers of invisible (but high maintenance) sea monkeys. She is passionate about social justice and breaking down barriers between people. Adopting her daughter was the best decision of her life, and that raising her is a profoundly satisfying experience.

Ten Survival Tips for Sandwichers

1) Develop a game plan. Sit down and have a pragmatic conversation with yourself. Ask yourself these questions. What kind of relationship with my family was I expecting/hoping for when I decided to adopt? What is the reality of the situation as it now stands? What can I realistically do in these circumstances? What is the long-term outcome for my child? How do I feel about it all?

2) Decide the level of involvement, balancing the needs of your parents, your child, and yourself, to which you can realistically commit, and let your family know.

3) Plan time for yourself prior to an anticipated 'sandwich session'. Do something you enjoy; take care of yourself.

4) Don't expect your family to change because, through adoption, you have. Family attitudes and expectations may or may not change, but predicting/expecting change can lead to hurt feelings all around.

5) Keep your priorities straight in your own mind, remember that everyone else will have their own differing ideas of what you can or should do.

6) Talk to your family and find out how they want potential care-giving situations handled. Develop a list of people you may need to be in touch with while supporting ageing family members including the financial advisor, the doctor, and most importantly, the neighbor or friend who is most frequently in contact with your family member.

7) Don't spend lot of time trying to 'educate' older family members about adoption issues, attachment theory, or the latest toilet training techniques. Do share memories of your childhood, and of your parent's childhood, together with your parents and your child.

8) Plan so that time together will be as pleasant as possible. Ageing parents can become impatient and overwhelmed with active children who are just doing what children do. Don't expect them to provide childcare; don't put them in the position of disciplining your child.

9) Keep visits short and sweet, as opposed to long and tedious. Plan a manageable, structured activity that promotes pleasant interaction, whether this is baking the Christmas cookies together or going on an excursion. Remember that your child will treasure the strangest things – my daughter loves grandma's 'white broccoli (i.e. cauliflower) with melted cheese on it' – and that these will be her important and lifetime memories.

10) Repeat to yourself, "you can't please all of the people all of the time" three times while getting dressed each morning!

~ Lynn Sherwood

Poised on the Edge of Middle Age...
What are the factors we need to consider as older parents?

I consider myself an adoptive parent poised at the brink of middle age. I am 58. My wife is younger at 41. We have four adopted daughters, ages seven, five, three, and two. I don't know if there will be a fifth. When our eldest graduates high school I'll be thinking in terms of being three score years and ten. I will never retire and so have had to re-engineer my work life into a field where there is no pressure to retire at some predetermined age.

What are the factors we need to consider in parenting at an older age? I suspect we all recognize that actuarial tables and probability about health and death apply only to large number populations. When we talk about one adoptive family, about one child or four, the tables and the equations of probability become just what they are; academic exercises. Even when we talk about the universe of all international adoptive parents, the sample size is too small to apply actuarial tables. More to the point, it is so very difficult to convert matters of the heart to numerical values in terms of years, likelihood of illness, and longevity prognostications based on genetic history.

As one of those older parents, I don't have any answers, but I can share my own experience. I am not adopted. I was born into a two-parent family. When I was twelve my father died suddenly. In her grief, my mother succumbed to alcoholism almost immediately, although she lived physically for another forty years. I had my Dad's love and nurturing for just twelve years. Yes, I would have loved to have experienced all the father-son transitions and growth in relationship over the lost years from twelve to adulthood. I would have loved and valued his physical presence as I encountered all the challenges, joys, and sorrows of growing up. I would most have loved for my daughters to have known this extraordinary father-grandfather.

But, in the world of 'what ifs' I would not trade a moment of those twelve years for the absolute certainty of a different father guaranteed to live to be ninety. He was my Dad. Had he lived longer maybe I would be a different, better person. But he shaped me in those twelve short years. I miss him every day, just as every day I value his presence in my memories and in the core of who I am.

There are practicalities that cannot be ignored. We do what we can to prepare for the possibilities. In the interim, my daughters will experience more love each and every day, more nurturing care, more support, more over-filling of their buckets of self-esteem, more affirmation of their worth as persons, more loving challenge to be and grow and learn than ever they would have in an orphanage.

~Mike O'Neill, middle-aged adoptive dad

Same-Sex Parenting
Challenges and Tools
By Susan Harrington

Family by Choice

In the LGBT (lesbian, gay, bisexual and transgender) community, the concept of 'family by choice, not by blood,' has a long history unrelated to adoption. In most parts of the world, gay families exist with few, if any, legal acknowledgements: they are sustained by loving networks which may or may not involve biological connections or state sanction. Increasingly, gay and lesbian families include children, many of them adopted. There are challenges facing same-sex adoptive families, but lesbian and gay parents can use the nature of their families and their own awareness, as an asset in adoption parenting.

Around the world, there are growing numbers of children being raised in families with two parents of the same gender. In the 2000 United States census, same-sex families were recorded in every state in the USA. About a third of lesbian households and about a fifth of gay male households had children under eighteen living at home (and more than half the households had two or more children). The most recent census in England and Wales recorded almost seventy thousand same-sex couples, while Scotland reported nearly seven thousand. Same-sex households with children were found in all but one Canadian province and territory. We are, indeed, everywhere.

Let me describe the view from my study window. As I look out the driveway, I see my partner waving as she hustles our toddler daughter (adopted internationally as an infant) into the car for a late afternoon trip to a children's museum. I see the houses of our neighbors: straight and gay people living in a delightful mix of multi-racial, multi-generational, adopted and bio families. Our lawns extend our living rooms as our children play with each other while their moms chat before dinner. All of the children witness the different ways families work, and have a network of adults who see them almost every day, who take an interest in their lives, and who are helping them grow. Without any coordination, our block has come to represent the rainbow diversity in American families. This small stretch of a near-downtown neighborhood is among the most valuable social resources any of us can offer our children, and it's all the more wonderful for being totally unplanned. Each family moved to the block independently, not knowing the diversity in the neighborhood. But now that we're here, we all plan to stay.

Strengths. Our block is a resource because it illustrates to all the children that there are many ways to make a family. That is important, particularly for the non-traditionally-structured families (those with transracially adopted children and/or with lesbian parents). But the strength of our block goes far beyond its ability to exemplify diversity. Simply living in a same-sex family amid such diversity builds strengths that support the hard work of adoption parenting. Negotiating life in an LBGT family (even without children) lays the groundwork for good adoption parenting later on. On the whole, same-sex families learn how to negotiate the gaps between the law and real life. Most same-sex families aren't recognized by the government (although a number of countries are allowing same-sex couples to legally formalize their relationships). We don't depend on legal definitions to endorse our families. Rather, we define family by living it. A family is the people we come home to every day, the people we have chosen to share our lives.

Our families have biological components, but they have plenty of non-biological components too, and this makes a shift into adoption parenting arguably more natural than it might for heterosexuals. Another factor that can ease the move into adoption parenting is the widespread acceptance of adoption as a usual means of bringing children into a family. Many lesbians choose donor insemination, but adoption and pregnancy are considered more equal than they may be in the straight world. And for gay men having children together, adoption is common. In the LGBT community, adoption is not considered an unusual or second choice.

'Coming out' as a gay, lesbian, bisexual or transgender person isn't always easy. One's 'original' or 'biological' families may withdraw love and support (either temporarily or more permanently); the months and years following coming out can help a family renegotiate relationships, which may also be tested when partners are brought into the family. But these issues get magnified further when children enter the picture:

Redefining Family. Successful LBGT families learn to define family as what supports healthy relationships: the slogan 'Love Makes a Family' was the title of a 1992 documentary by Bonnie Tinker about LGBT Quaker families, and it's a slogan that has long spoken to LGBT people whose loves and families are often invisible to the larger straight culture. We know that it's not the legal recognition from the government that makes us a family

Complex Structures. We usually have some practice in explaining our relationship choices ("No, Aunt Mary, she's not my friend, she's my partner") and in tracing the multiple strands in an extended family/friendship network. The complexity of family for gay and lesbian people can be a good basis for understanding the complexities of adoptive family structures. Birth families and adoptive families co-exist in our children's lives (even when birth family information is scanty at best), and the emotional resiliency captured in gay family networks can help develop flexible attitudes toward the richness of relationships around adoption.

Family Layers. Creating and redefining a family means creating communication strategies and relationships. My partner and I have created an extended family that brings all kinds of people into our lives. Our relationships with neighbors form one part of our notion of family. We cherish the day-in, day-out support that comes from our contacts. At times we may be having a heartfelt chat on a stoop, comparing notes about what to say (or not) about adoption or our families to teachers at the start of the school year. While our children play, we share recommendations for children's books, ask parents of the older children on the block how kids on the bus have reacted to friends with two moms, or wonder how to answer emerging questions about birth parents. At other times we may simply wave as we pass on the street. Our neighbors constitute one layer of family, a layer formed through the kid connections that bring the adults together, and through geography.

We add another dimension with our adult friends (and increasingly their children as well). Here in a city, miles away from our bio families, we have created our own holiday traditions. We celebrate most holidays with a particular group of friends; they are another layer in our extended family. This layer is mostly constituted of straight couples with children, and each year we gather for Thanksgiving, Passover, Hanukkah and Christmas. What's this got to do with adoption parenting? By celebrating life cycles within this extended family we show our daughter (and all the children) how we muddle through this complicated world. We laugh together, grieve together, and draw strength from shared tradition. We show that all kinds of families can love, together. Whether there are two parents in the home or one, working parents or stay at home parents, we all share the work and pleasure of watching our children mature.

So where's our bio family in all this? They're important, too. We may fly home to celebrate holidays with our bio families who live at a distance, and every other summer we vacation with my parents and my sister and her family. Cousins and grandparents play a real role in our daughter's life, connecting through visits several times a year, phone calls, and mail.

We nurture these relationships and show that distance is no barrier to love, and that the celebration of roots is important. We model love and respect for the families we come from and the families we build. These are precisely the qualities we hope our daughter will use when she is an adult. As she grows, she will integrate her understandings of her biological family, our family, and the family she will create for herself one day.

With these interlocking networks we create rituals and regular gatherings at which all the children can see families with different sets of parents, and where all the children see adults who care about each other and them. Some of the families have two moms; some of the parents are divorced and remarried, others divorced and single; some of the families are single-parent households, others have a mom and a dad. But what they mostly have in common is love. Let me be clear: I'm not saying that love is all a family needs to make an adoption successful. But a commitment to love is the foundation a family needs in order to do the work of building attachment and life-long relationships. This understanding of family as intentional and chosen is one of the central lessons we want to teach our child.

Learning to Manage and Live with Compromise and Conflict Compromise and conflict are parts of any family, but LGBT families have often had particular occasion to make peace with compromises. Coming out invariably causes ripples in existing family relationships. Some parents, siblings, cousins, or other family members may never accept an LGBT relative, and may cut off all contact. This hurts, and if it happens, we need to address it by getting the help we need to be functional adults. In other cases, we may move through some messy moments (lasting for months, years or decades!) as relatives work through discomfort, religious objections, or disappointment about a child turning out not as expected. In other cases, we may come out to a wholly supportive parent who is happy to share our lives. We make our own choices about how to respond to our family's responses to our sexuality, and in the course of so doing, we may learn to live with compromise.

The Lesbian Parenting Book: A Guide to Creating Families and Raising Children, 2nd edition by D. Merilee Clunis, PhD and G. Dorsey Green. PhD

Love Makes a Family: Portraits of Lesbian, Gay, Bisexual, and Transgender Parents and Their Families photos by Gigi Kaeser

How It Feels to Have a Gay or Lesbian Parent: A Book by Kids for Kids of All Ages by Judith E. Snow, MA

Out of the Ordinary: Essays on Growing Up with Gay, Lesbian, and Transgender Parents edited by Noelle Howey and Ellen Samuels

My own parents would probably say they wished I weren't a lesbian. They had hoped I would marry a man and settle into the life they dreamed for me. We went through some difficult years, although their love for me always led them to keep contact open, even when our relationship was strained. Their overall generosity has led them to treat me and my partner exactly evenly with my sister and her husband: when they travel, they bring back a t-shirt for each of us; at holidays, we each get the same number of gifts. I've come to see their generosity as a sign of their love, even if they still have trouble actually saying lesbian. I learned to live with my own disappointments about their response, and to appreciate the relationship they were able to offer.

With a child in the mix, things change somewhat. All the jockeying and negotiating about one's own status in the family, is good preparation for hard conversations about gay parenting or adoption. I found it easier to speak frankly to some relatives about the language they use about our adoptive family because of the work I had done negotiating family relationships after I came out. Years of practice answering questions about my primary relationship came in handy when I started to get intrusive questions about adoption. In addition to facing the same questions any adoptive parents may face about their relationships to their children, same-sex parents face homophobic slurs and questions about the very legitimacy of their family.

Challenges of Same-sex Adoptive Parenting

Most of the same-sex parents I know spend much more time struggling with the challenges of parenting in general than same-sex parenting in particular. It's not easy for any of us to learn to set limits, promote attachment, enforce boundaries, and establish family discipline. As the mother of a toddler, I've not yet had much personal experience with questions from my child about why or how our family is different than anyone else's. Yet one issue that does weigh heavy on my heart is the knowledge that I will one day have to explain homophobia to my child. Aside from the personal cruelty which any child may occasionally encounter, our children will also hear homophobic views articulated in 'balanced' news coverage of gay issues like the struggle for marriage rights.

It is hard to know when and how to introduce the darker sides of human nature to our children without making them scared, yet also hard to risk not giving children the tools they need to protect themselves from intolerance. Parents of minority children also face these same issues: how do you explain racism? It is a burden we share, and I hope that we can help each other through the challenges. We have much to learn by pooling resources about all kinds of hard parenting issues.

Like single parents, gay and lesbian parents face questions about how we deal with the 'missing' gender role in the family ("Doesn't every child need a mother/father?"). For most of the same-sex families we know, the 'missing' role really isn't an issue. Even though we've chosen to parent and partner with someone of the same gender, we value the opposite sex. My partner and I see our daughter growing up with many men in her life. We focus our energies on thinking about our roles. It's our job to keep our daughter safe, to help her develop, to help her become civilized, to support her education, and to show her myriad possibilities for what she can grow into.

It's our job to help her learn a language and strategies for coping with the fact of her family: with her own background in Europe, with the fact of her adoption and with the

Tools in the Same-Sex Family Home that Support Adoption Parenting

The negotiating of relationships with each other, our biological families, and the world around us offers several emotional strengths which support adoption parenting. These include:

- The ability to define family as people living and loving together: the place we come home to that makes us safe, that protects us, that challenges us. Our experiences consciously defining family for ourselves may prepare us to define and create family for our children.

- The ability to focus on attachment. We have needed to cultivate trust in our own family structures, to create secure attachments as adults even when the dominant culture didn't always support that. We need to do the same with our children.

- The ability to stand up to public scrutiny gracefully. We all have to decide which battles to pick, which stares to return, which rude comments to reply to or ignore, which stories to rehearse in private so we can decide how to respond in public. It's easier to make those choices about our daughter's adoption stories for having spent time making choices about our sexuality and when, why, and how to discuss it.

- The ability to balance public and private. The fact that we're LGBT people is fundamental to our identity and culture. It's an important aspect of identity and as such it's something we share. But it needn't always be the first thing we share and we get practice deciding whom to come out to, when and why. Similarly, aspects of our children's adoption stories and pre-adoption stories are fundamental to their identity and culture, yet not necessarily something shared always and with everyone.

- The ability to think about multiple identities. Most LGBT people move in and out of different cultures and identities. We are members of religious organizations, families, and professions. We have children. We are mentors. We travel. We play sports or have hobbies. Like anyone else, different aspects of identities are more important at different points in time. As we think about adoption parenting, we know that adoption may sometimes be the central issue for us as parents and for our daughter, but at other points, it may not. That she has two mothers raising her may at some points be a hard issue; at others it will be a joy. Our own experiences moving within and between cultures will help us help her do the same, and help us parent without expecting that we know all the issues up front.

~Susan Harrington

fact that she has two moms. It's our job to help her understand the complexities of gender roles in the world, as well as the complexities of race, class, and religion. In the course of her regular life she meets men and women, girls and boys, people with varied religions, occupations, and interests, and people with varied racial and cultural backgrounds. We can work to accomplish our jobs by making connections with all kinds of families. The collective wisdom that accumulates from sharing stories about the questions children ask about their birth families and their adoptive families benefits us all.

Our child will learn how to navigate the world, we believe, by living in the environment we provide. One in which she will gain the emotional resources to handle all the questions she'll ever have about her birth family, her adopted family and the larger culture framing those questions. Living with parents who believe that love makes the work of a family possible can only help her as she grows up.

*~ Susan Harrington is a university professor and adoptive mother.
She and her partner of twelve years co-parent their daughter.
Her academic interests center in writing assessment, and she has been
surprised to discover how much her interests in teaching and learning writing
intersect with her parenting experience. She has offered a local workshop
in lifebook writing and has an emerging interest in the role of writing in the
development of parenting skills and identity*

Ten Books for Young Children Featuring Gay and Lesbian Families

Heather has Two Mommies
by Leslea Newman

The Family Book by Todd Parr

Who's in a Family? By Robert Skutch,
and Laura Nienhaus

*One Dad, Two Dads, Brown Dad, Blue
Dad* by Johnny Valentine

*How My Family Came to Be: Daddy,
Papa and Me* by Andrew R. Aldrich

123: A Family Counting Book
by Bobbie Combs

Felicia's Favorite Story
by Leslea Newman

Mama Eat Ant, Yuck!
by Barbara Lynn Edmonds

All Families are Different
by Sol Gordon

Molly's Family by Nancy Garden

Therapy

Directions Not Included
Seeking therapy for an adopted child
By Jean MacLeod

Parenting is a tough job. Adoption Parenting is a tough job that comes without directions. Baby books, child-care books, and parenting and discipline Books are all based off the societal, biological 'norm'. Without any kind of a map, how can you discern which of your child's problematical behaviors are derived from age-related flare-ups and which are evolved from the life-long issues of adoption?

Without some help, you probably can't. Adoptive parents are not prepared by the adoption process or by the model of child-rearing they themselves were raised with, to understand the extra layer of emotions that adopted children live with. Moms and Dads have not been taught to recognize the masked anger, sadness, shame or fear that is a part of some adopted and foster children's psyche, and they have not been trained to help their children deal with the emotions that spring from the pain and loss of their children's early lives. Adoption Parenting is different; children who were adopted domestically and internationally, at birth or as an older adoptee, will process core issues and experience life transitions on a different timetable and with a different twist than their biologically parented peers.

The cause of troubling behavior in a child is a tough call to make when a parent is left in this kind of uncharted Adoption Parenting twilight zone. It is easy when a child is young to rationalize his or her objectionable behaviors as being part of the terrible twos, threes or even fours. It becomes more difficult to accept as the child gets older, and it becomes terribly frustrating for an adoptive parent trying unsuccessfully to use traditional disciplinary methods on a rebellious pre-teen or adolescent. It's important for a parent to realize that a child's behavior is only a symptom. The real underlying problem may be an adoption-related issue…the difficulty is deciding if your child's issues are disturbing enough to himself or to others, to seek professional assistance. Children who harm others, animals or themselves, or act destructively, need immediate help. For other children, who move in and out of intense emotions or behaviors, it's harder to discern if therapy is required.

All children may exhibit some of these issues while growing up, but parents usually recognize a red-flag behavior by its intensity and persistence. Worrisome moods and behaviors can fall at either end of the 'healthy' spectrum; everything is a matter of degree, but if your parent instinct has 'concerns', you are wise to listen to it and to seek help.

Finding a therapist skilled in the specific issues of adoption and attachment can be a challenge. Your homestudy or placement agency may have the names of highly regarded local contacts. The Association for Treatment and Training in the Attachment of Children (ATTACh) is a national organization that lists member therapists and clinics on their website: www.attach.org. ATTACh has instituted a detailed membership registration, which is now required for qualified therapists who wish to be eligible for referral. Other highly informative websites that provide names of parent-recommended adoption and attachment therapists can also be found by doing an online search.

Attachment therapists recognize that a child's minor or major adoption issues can interfere with a secure, intimate attachment with his or her parents, and can negatively impact the family as a whole. Attachment is about relationships, and a reputable adoption/attachment therapist will treat not just the child, but include the immediate family. Traditional talk therapy and behavior modification may not be as effective in correcting adoption-based problems as some of the methods used by attachment therapists. Theraplay, nurturing Holding Time, Re-parenting, EMDR and Narrative Therapy are popular techniques, and a competent therapist should empower the parents with the knowledge and skills to reinforce the emotional work at home.

When parents are finally at the point of seeking outside help for their child, they are usually stressed, worried and confused. Many parents have had no previous experience with psychotherapy and are not sure what to expect during the process. An initial parent-only consultation with a potential therapist to discuss his or her philosophy and methodology is important to finding the best 'fit' for your family. If you have adopted internationally, it is essential that the therapist you choose is aware of the realities of institutionalization and its effect on a child, developmentally and emotionally. Is the therapist knowledgeable and experienced with:

Attachment Theory and Treatment?
Post Traumatic Stress Disorder (PTSD)?
Fetal Alcohol Syndrome (FASD)?
Institutional physical or sexual abuse?

Does he or she understand that post-institutional or internationally adopted children may also display sensory, neurological, or speech and language issues that need to be addressed by a 'team' of specialists, concurrently with attachment therapy, for best results?

Domestic adoptions bring their own set of complexities. Is the therapist experienced with the intricacy of open adoption, birthparent search or the data compilation and personal review of a child's pre-adoption history? Many children adopted domestically, particularly from the foster care system, have vivid and often painful memories of living with their birth families.

An informed therapist will understand that your child's present behaviors are in part a consequence of his or her past, and will not blame the child's resulting conduct on your 'inadequate' parenting.

Parents should not be afraid to ask what a therapist charges per session and how they accept payment. How long is each session and is there some flexibility built into the session time (can you go overtime five or ten minutes for an appropriate closure)? Is the therapist available for consultation in between sessions by phone or email, and does she or he charge extra for these services? How can the therapist be reached in a crisis?

Parents should also ask what therapies will be used in the office and what your role as parent will be. Unlike most traditional therapy, you should expect to be participating fully and interacting with your child in each session; for an adopted child, attachment and security with you is the primary point, with the ultimate goal of the child internalizing that strength and self-regulating their own behavior.

Every therapist works a little differently; styles vary with the different kinds of therapists, the work they do, and the needs of their clients. A child may really benefit from multiple approaches, including the services of other professionals from neuro-psychology, sensory integration, and speech and language. Your therapist may continue to strategize as your child progresses through the stages of healing, building on treatment with variations. Successful adoption or attachment therapy takes a creative and united team of therapist and parents to support the child while trauma is resolved.

The timeframe for treatment is also varied, ranging from a few consciousness-raising sessions to a much lengthier process for more severe problems. As therapy advances a therapist will constantly reassess the client's progress and treatment plan, and therapy can be either shorter or longer than originally anticipated.

Support for parents is an important component of successful adoption or attachment therapy. If a Mom or Dad is too overwhelmed, depressed or emotionally burned out to participate in the child's treatment, then therapy will fail. A therapist should ideally provide the parent with educational resources, a parent support group and if necessary, a referral to a personal therapist and anti-depressive medications. Recognizing that the parent continues the work done in the office at home, seven days a week, is vital on the part of an empathic therapist.

Adoptive parents need to realize that their child's troubled behaviors can be a normal result of what their child experienced before joining their present family. As parents, you look for ways to protect your children and to soften the kind of life-blows that some of our children have received, and that no child deserves. Therapy can be challenging work for any family, and it won't allow you to soften or protect. It will open feelings and conversations over the truthful realities of your children's beginnings and will give you the insight and the capability, the map and the directions, to bring your family very close together.

~by Jean MacLeod
Originally published in Adoption TODAY

Questions adoptive parents can ask themselves to help evaluate the need for a therapist consultation:

- Is your child's behavior interfering with her own, normal enjoyment of life, school and family?

- Is your child's outward compliance or quiet opposition really a control, anger or fear issue? Is she passively angry at you for leaving her at school or at daycare; are there hidden or underlying abandonment issues?

- Is your child acting out (angry, disruptive) or acting in (depressed, withdrawn)?

- Is your child's anger frequently inappropriate?
  Is it directed at mom?

- Is your child's supreme 'self-control' or
  manipulative behavior really a desperate need to control you, and everything else in her life?

- Do you find yourself parenting 'around' your child's issues and hot-buttons? Do her tantrums (and the timing of when she decides to have one) control family life and activities?

- Does your child whine constantly?

- Does your child have anxieties and fears that she can't control? Do her fears change over time, but never really go away? Do they rule where she'll go, what she plays or whom she'll see?

- Does your child have difficulty with her identity? Are there cross-cultural or trans-racial concerns to factor in?

- Does your child's behavior affect her relationship with you, your spouse or her siblings?

All children may exhibit some of these issues while growing up, but parents usually recognize a red-flag behavior by its intensity and persistence. Worrisome moods and behaviors can fall at either end of the 'healthy' spectrum; everything is a matter of degree, but if your parent instinct has concerns, you are wise to listen to it and to seek help.

~Jean MacLeod

Tips on Selecting an Adoption Therapist
Knowing the Types of Help is the First Step
By the National Adoption Informaion Clearinghouse

Adoption is an event that has a life-long effect on everyone involved. Adoption brings unique rewards as well as challenges to families, and sometimes families will need or want professional help as concerns or problems arise. Timely intervention by a professional skilled in adoption issues often can prevent issues common to adoption from becoming more serious problems that might be more difficult to resolve.

The type (e.g., individual, family, group) and duration of therapy will vary depending on many variables, including the kinds of problems being addressed. Some families build a relationship with a therapist over years, 'checking in' for help as needed. Other families might find they need a therapist's help only once or twice. Sometimes a difficulty a child is experiencing is very obviously connected to adoption, but sometimes the connection is not readily apparent. On the other hand, issues that seem to be related to adoption, after investigation, turn out not to be related to adoption at all. Clinicians with adoption knowledge and experience are best suited to help families identify connections between problems and adoption and to plan effective treatment strategies.

Finding the right therapist can seem like a daunting task, especially when parents may be feeling overwhelmed or burdened by the difficulties for which they are seeking help. Parents should take the time to shop around for a mental health provider who has the experience and expertise required to effectively address their family's needs. At minimum, a therapist must:

1. Be knowledgeable about adoption and the psychological impact of adoption on children and families
2. Be experienced in working with adopted children and their families.
3. Know the types of help available.

Check on Insurance

The search for a therapist can be complicated by restrictions imposed by insurance companies or health management organizations (HMOs); however, it may still be possible to choose from a list of approved therapists. Check with your insurance company to find out:
• The extent of your coverage for mental health treatment
• Specialty areas of approved providers
• Company policies regarding referrals to, and payment for, treatment provided by therapists outside the plan.

You may be able to justify using a therapist outside of the network for specialized services if the insurance company does not have providers with the required expertise. Although you might meet some resistance, persevere to secure the needed services-you are your child's strongest advocate.Some therapists accept Medicaid reimbursement. The challenge is to locate a therapist who accepts reimbursement and who has experience in foster care and adoption. Your local public foster care agency may be able to give you referrals to therapists they use for children's treatment.

Know the Types of Help Available:

Many different professionals provide mental health services but not all may be available in your area. It helps to know the training and credentials that various professionals attain.

Pediatrician or Family Practice Physician.   Medical doctor (MD) who specializes in childhood or adolescent care and who typically treats routine medical conditions; a primary care physician who refers a child for additional lab studies or diagnostic procedures and who coordinates referrals to other specialists.

Psychiatrist.   Medical doctor (MD) who specializes in the evaluation of major mental or emotional disorders which may require medication. Psychiatrists complete medical school and follow with post-graduate training in psychiatric disorders and perhaps subspecialties in child and adolescent psychiatry. Psychiatry's primary focus is on medication consultation and management, and only a few psychiatrists have formal training in psychotherapy, counseling, or interventions that address child and adolescent behavioral or emotional disorders. Rather, most work with or refer to specialists in child and family evaluation and therapy.

Clinical Psychologist.   A clinical psychologist has completed a doctoral degree (PhD or PsyD) in psychology and usually has completed advanced courses in general development, psychological testing and evaluation, as well as psychotherapy techniques and counseling. Many clinical psychologists develop a subspecialty in child and adolescent development, psychological testing, and family therapy.

Clinical Neuropsychologist.   Clinical neuropsychologists hold a PhD They complete undergraduate and graduate training in biological and medical theories pertaining to human behavior and doctoral studies in clinical neuropsychology, followed by post-graduate specialty training in the assessment and treatment of neurodevelopmental disorders, neurological and medical conditions, traumatic brain injury, learning and memory disorders and the differential diagnosis of organic versus psychiatric or psychological disorders.

Clinical Social Worker.   A clinical social worker (LCSW or MSW) has completed a master's degree in social work with emphasis on family structure and children's interactional strengths and weaknesses. Social workers typically focus on social, educational and family adjustment issues, but usually do not have professional training in psychological testing. Many complete advanced training and licensure in order to be qualified under state licensure requirements to offer counseling to individuals and families.

Marriage and Family Therapist.   Marriage and family therapists (MSW) have a master's degree in counseling techniques that mainly focus on family relationships and couples. Family therapists focus on communication building and on family structure and boundaries within the family.

Licensed Professional Counselor. A licensed professional counselor often has graduate training in a specialty such as education, psychology, pastoral counseling, or marriage and family therapy. Licensed professional counselors focus on brief problem-solving therapies with a focus on reorganizing the family, building communication skills, and strengthening family relationships.

Pastoral Counselor. A pastoral counselor has a minimum of a master's degree (many have completed doctoral training) and focuses on supportive interventions for individuals or families, using spirituality as an additional source of support for those in treatment.

Ask for Referrals

Locating a therapist does not have to be difficult. You may want to contact community adoption support networks, use the Internet, and/or ask your placement agency. Many adoption agencies have either consulting mental health therapists trained in adoption on staff or referral resources in the community. Public agencies may have a list of therapists who have effectively worked with children in foster care and adoption. In addition, there are independent social service organizations throughout the United States that provide post-adoption services, which may include parent support groups, individual and family counseling, children's support groups, educational seminars, consultations and advocacy.

Check with the following resources for therapist recommendations:
- Agency social workers involved in the original placement
- State or local mental health associations - most offer referral services and list specialty areas for therapists
- Public and private adoption agencies
- Local adoptive parent support groups
- Specialized agencies providing post-adoption services.

Using those recommendations, call therapists for a phone or face-to-face interview. Many therapists will offer a 15- or 20-minute initial consultation free of charge. In contacting a community mental health center, parents should ask for names of the center's family and child specialists and then leave messages for those clinicians requesting a short phone interview.

Phone Interview Questions

Parents should start by giving the clinician a brief description of the concern or problem for which they are requesting help.
Listed below are some questions to discuss.
1. What is the therapist's experience with
- Adoption, in general?
- Infertility?
- Special needs adoption?
- Open adoption?

Evaluating Help

It is very difficult to be a therapeutic parent without professional input; your own upbringing, your expectations, your fears and anxieties and your lack of preparation for parenting a traumatized child can interfere with your connection to a child needing help. If your family is encountering problems, it is important to seek support from a therapist trained in attachment theory and experienced with international adoption, and you should evaluate your family's treatment protocol by reading the ATTACh Professional Practice Manual found on the ATTACh website: www.attach.org Therapy to address a child's adoption or attachment issues should never be coercive or abusive. Some methodologies should only be used with the careful guidance of a trained professional, and only within the safe guidelines proscribed by the international ATTACh coalition.

- Transracial adoption?
- Identity issues in the context of adoption?
- Search and reunion?
- Adoptive families?
- Adopted children?
- Children who have histories of loss, abuse and/or neglect?
- Children who may have learning or developmental disabilities?

2. How long has the therapist been in practice, and what degrees, license or certification does he or she have?
3. What continuing clinical training does he or she have on adoption issues?
4. Does the therapist include parents in the therapeutic process?
5. Does the clinician prefer to work with the entire family or only with the child(ren)?
6. Will the therapist give parents regular reports on a child's progress?
7. Can the therapist estimate a time frame for the course of therapy?
8. What is the therapist's theoretical orientation regarding treatment? Many therapists treat from one or more of the following approaches:
   - behavioral therapy, which focuses on treating overt behaviors
   - cognitive therapy, which focuses clinical intervention on thinking processes, motivation, and reasons for certain behaviors
   - family systems therapy, which views family members as a unit and focuses on their interpersonal and communications patterns
   - psychoanalysis, which is based on psychosexual development theories, personality structure and psychotherapy techniques pioneered by Sigmund Freud.

Other Practical Considerations

Most therapists or clinical practices have policies regarding late or missed appointments, notice required for rescheduling appointments, and filing for insurance reimbursement. Parents should ask for this information.

- What is the therapist's arrangement for coverage when he or she is not available, especially in the event of an emergency?
- Are daytime, evening, or weekend appointments available? What about after-school appointments?
- Does the therapist offer discounted or sliding scale fees if he or she is not an approved provider for your health coverage?
- Does the therapist accept adoption subsidy medical payments or Medicaid reimbursement payments?
- Does the therapist have experience working collaboratively with school personnel including attending any appropriate school meetings.

Working with a Therapist

Parents may request an evaluation meeting with the therapist 6-8 weeks after treatment begins. This evaluation meeting will help all parties 'take a pulse' on progress of the treatment and to discuss the following areas:

- Satisfaction with the 'chemistry' between the therapist and family members. (It is important for parents to understand that a trusting relationship between clinician and

"The world breaks everyone and afterwards many are strong at the broken places"
~ *Ernest Hemingway*

The wounds of broken trust can be healed; healing can happen. However, as parents it is also important for us to understand the analogy of the scar that forms over an old wound. When the wound is fresh and open and infected, the pain is intense anytime we touch on it, even when we 'bump it' accidentally.

Every time we work to evacuate the pain of broken trust, by talking and working it through as best we can, we churn up the pain. But as we progress in the healing, a scar begins to form over the site. Finally, just as with a scar covering a wound, when we touch our 'broken places' there is no remaining pain… but we always remember the origin of the wound. The sign of the healing is not that we forget. It is that when we touch on it, the pain no longer brings us to our knees.

I believe that as parents (and/or therapists) one of our roles is to empower our children with the tools to survive the healing process, to be able to touch on the scar and deal with the memory, to discover the ways in which we truly become stronger in broken places. We are not called upon to help our children find ways around the pain. We are called upon to love them and support them and help them find a way through it to the other side without ever losing sight of the wonder of creation embodied in each one of them.

~ *Mike O'Neill*
adoptive Dad

the child may take several weeks or longer to establish. This is particularly true of children who have had histories of significant loss and separations.)
- Mutually agreed-upon goals for treatment approaches and desired outcomes.
- Progress on problems that first prompted the request for treatment. Parents should realize that some behaviors need extensive intervention before progress can be identified.
- A tentative diagnosis.
- The therapist's evaluation of the chances that therapy can improve the situation(s) which prompted treatment.
- Follow through by the family with the therapist's recommendations. Practiced any 'homework' assignments? (Parents should know that most of the 'work' in therapy occurs between, not during, sessions and that it is a reciprocal process.)

The family's involvement and support of the therapy is often critical to a positive outcome for the child. Families must commit to keeping regularly scheduled appointments, and parents should not use therapy as a tool for discipline. Family members must communicate regularly with the therapist and ensure that the therapist has regular feedback about conditions at home. The success of therapy depends heavily on open, honest and trusting communication. Recognizing the need for outside support and early intervention when problems arise will help adopted children and their families navigate the challenges adoption presents as they grow and develop.

By National Adoption Information Clearinghouse (DHHS)
www.naic.acf.hhs.gov/pubs/r_tips.cfm

A Mother's Touch
Treating Attachment Issues through Occupational Therapy
By Doris A. Landry, MS

Children who are able to enjoy relationships were provided constant contact when in need as babies (and at many other times, simply because they were so cute and cuddly). Their mothers filled their hungry bellies while talking, smiling, and interacting with them. Their mothers rocked, lifted, and moved them, and provided stimulating environments in multiple ways, particularly through touch. Their mothers presented warm and loving faces to them, with a strong interest in eye contact. Their mothers connected with the babies' inner world, almost downloading their own inner experiences. Such moments not only create and shape the relationship but these *"dyadic, reciprocal interactions that arise within a (parent/child) relationship are central to young children's neuro-psychological development"* says Daniel A. Hughes, PhD. Such mother-child interactions are not only rich emotional experiences, but also rich sensorimotor (senses and movement) experiences for developing babies.

Adoptive parents of children institutionalized from birth may find that their children resist comforting and show little interest in exploration. Some parents are concerned that their children do not seem to know when they are hungry or full. Other parents are saddened that their new child will not look at them and do not seem to know how to seek comfort or even safety. There are worries that their child does not 'track' or heed a call of fear from a screaming mother who is seeing her child running toward a busy street! And, there are concerns over 'affect regulation' making an adoptive parent feel that the words 'temper tantrum' do not aptly describe the intensity of the explosiveness and impulsivity their child displays. One of the most disturbing things for adoptive parents to witness is self-injurious behaviors, such as intense rocking or head banging. These are all poignant signs of not having been mothered.

Clinical research conducted by Neil W. Boris, MD and Charles H. Zeanah, MD and colleagues, has provided professionals with a set of emotional-behavioral symptoms for children who suffer from not having been mothered. Their findings indicate a spectrum of attachment disturbances, with the severe Reactive Attachment Disorder being but one type. They suggest a diagnostic scheme that includes children suffering from a 'Disorder of Nonattachment' because the etiology and symptomology differ between bad care versus no care. It is important to differentiate children who have not been mothered from those who have known uncaring, cruel or terrorizing mothers, because their plights differ. The children identified as 'not having been mothered' are the children who have never experienced 'her'. They have no memories of 'her' embedded deep within, and this is the basis of the sensorimotor issues that compound the emotional issues facing un-mothered children and their adoptive parents.

Institutionalized babies adopted within the first year of their lives seem, for the most part, to have a resiliency that allows them to thrive in a family setting. However, children who are adopted later seem to be in need of relationship treatment at a higher rate due to behavioral problems stemming from their inability to enjoy the sensations of their adoptive mother and/or father. Many of these families seek 'attachment oriented psychotherapy' and engage in a treatment model called Dyadic Developmental Psychotherapy (DDP)

Resources

The American Psychological Association (APA)
www.apa.org

The American Psychiatric Association
www.psych.org

The American Association of Marriage and Family Therapy
www.aamft.org

The National Association of Social Workers
www.naswdc.org

The Association for Treatment and Training in the Attachment of Children (ATTACh)
www.attach.org

developed by Daniel A. Hughes, PhD.

This treatment model, which can be found within the pages of Hughes' book, *Building the Bonds of Attachment,* is designed to help a child feel emotionally safe so their energy can be spent enjoyably engaging others, especially their primary attachment figure. It is also designed to create the experiences of 'affect attunement', the emotional sharing that occurs between a child and his/her parent, which may not have been experienced prior to adoption. This treatment model focuses on the relationship, giving us a model for occupational therapy–the sensorimotor-mothering piece that is sorely needed in many cases.

The deprived infant/child, the one not held, fed, cuddled and 'claimed', (the children identified by Drs. Boris and Zeanah as having a Disorder of Non-Attachment) needs to be given the opportunity to experience missed sensations. This is most often accomplished through occupational therapy, but in the past, the missing component has usually been the parent. Most naturally, the un-mothered child will have practical physical issues to be addressed, but treatment also needs to be experienced within the context of a meaningful relationship.

If the child does not have a relationship with his/her parent, there is the likelihood that there will not be one with the occupational therapist. In addition, having a parent in the occupational therapy treatment room, versus watching a therapist with the child through a one-way mirror (or sitting in a waiting room), can take advantage of the developing parent and child relationship that psychotherapeutic treatments, such as DDP, are working to create.

Further, it is suggested that the treatment be performed through the parent. This means the occupational therapist must work with the parent to teach them to do the interventions. *"When a child is in attachment-oriented therapy, the occupational treatment plan will always include the parent in the treatment room,"* says Sandra Glovak, owner of Sensory Systems Clinic in St Clair Shores, Michigan. Having occupational therapy mirror attachment-oriented psychotherapy creates more opportunities for the child's sensory issues to heal, and more opportunities for the developing parent-child relationship to flourish.

~ By Doris A. Landry, MS

Dealing with Young Children, Adoption and Anger

"Those of us who weren't adopted cannot fully grasp the meaning of being given away. As I work with adoptive parents on listening to their child, this issue becomes paramount. From the adult perspective, the adopted child was taken out of an unsafe environment and this should be seen as good. From the child's point of view, however, something very valuable was taken away: their home, their identity, their family. Children are quite adept at communicating their feelings. Strange as it is, adults consistently miss the messages. For the adopted child, anger is his way of communicating feelings of loss, grief, fear, and terror. Unfortunately, these messages get misinterpreted and the child subsequently gets labeled as defiant."

~ Christopher Alexander, PhD, *The Inner World of the Adopted Child*

As adoptive parents, we need to stop and think what we are reacting to when our children act-out or misbehave. Adoption doesn't excuse bad behavior, but it should influence how we choose to deal with it. Sometimes, demonstrating our understanding, or pro-actively going for the 'core issue', can nip a tantrum in the bud.

Identify feelings. Teach your children to use the 'Four Feelings' (mad, sad, happy and scared) to identify and express what they are feeling inside. This takes practice, and it helps for a parent to model usage, too.

Go to the core issue. What is really producing the anger? "For the adopted child, anger is his way of communicating feelings of loss, grief, fear, and terror." Not everything goes back to adoption, but it is a big relief even for a very young child, to be able to sort out the root of their feelings and behaviors with the help of a parent.

Adoption discipline. For little kids, a **time-in** is generally more helpful for emotional issues than a time-out. Hold the child in your lap (face in or face out) for a period of time until they have calmed down, stopped raging, or are ready to talk and listen. A time-in is done in a quiet place (no toys or TV), in a non-punitive manner. The goal is to help a child understand expectations and their own motivations, and to help them process and internalize their feelings. The parent's quiet, calm, hands-on presence helps a child with behavioral self-regulation. A time-in takes the "abandonment-isolation" aspect out of time-outs for adopted children. Adoptees with control issues don't care for time-in, but it is an appropriate, gentle, disciplinary action. See **Discipline** chapter pages 145-164.

~*Jean MacLeod*

Helpful Resource for Parents Dealing with a Child's Anger:
A Volcano in My Tummy: Helping Children to Handle Anger:
A Resource Book for Parents, Caregivers and Teachers
by Elaine Whitehouse, Warwick Pudney

How is PTSD Treated in Children and Adolescents?

Although some children show a natural remission in PTSD symptoms over a period of a few months, a significant number of children continue to exhibit symptoms for years if untreated. Few treatment studies have examined which treatments are most effective for children and adolescents. A review of the adult treatment studies of PTSD shows that **Cognitive-Behavioral Therapy (CBT)** is the most effective approach. CBT for children generally includes the child directly discussing the traumatic event (exposure), anxiety management techniques such as relaxation and assertiveness training, and correction of inaccurate or distorted trauma related thoughts. Although there is some controversy regarding exposing children to the events that scare them, exposure-based treatments seem to be most relevant when memories or reminders of the trauma distress the child. Children can be exposed gradually and taught relaxation so that they can learn to relax while recalling their experiences. Through this procedure, they learn that they do not have to be afraid of their memories. CBT also involves challenging children's false beliefs such as, 'the world is totally unsafe.' The majority of studies have found that it is safe and effective to use CBT for children with PTSD.

CBT is often accompanied by **psycho-education** and **parental involvement**. Psycho-education is education about PTSD symptoms and their effects. It is as important for parents and caregivers to understand the effects of PTSD as it is for children. Research shows that the better parents cope with the trauma, and the more they support their children, the better their children will function. Therefore, it is important for parents to seek treatment for themselves in order to develop the necessary coping skills that will help their children.

Several other types of therapy have been suggested for PTSD in children and adolescents. **Play therapy** can be used to treat young children with PTSD who are not able to deal with the trauma more directly. The therapist uses games, drawings, and other techniques to help the children process their traumatic memories. **Psychological first aid** has been prescribed for children exposed to community violence and can be used in schools and traditional settings. Psychological first aid involves clarifying trauma related facts, normalizing the children's PTSD reactions, encouraging the expression of feelings, teaching problem solving skills, and referring the most symptomatic children for additional treatment. **Twelve Step** approaches have been prescribed for adolescents with substance abuse problems and PTSD. Another therapy, **Eye Movement Desensitization and Reprocessing** (EMDR), combines cognitive therapy with directed eye movements. While EMDR has been shown to be effective in treating both children and adults with PTSD, studies indicate that it is the cognitive intervention rather than the eye movements that accounts for the change. Medications have also been prescribed for some children with PTSD. However, due to the lack of research in this area, it is too early to evaluate the effectiveness of medication therapy.

Finally, **specialized interventions** may be necessary for children exhibiting particularly problematic behaviors or PTSD symptoms. For example, a specialized intervention might be required for inappropriate sexual behavior or extreme behavioral problems.

From PTSD in Children and Adolescents, A National Center for PTSD Fact Sheet
By Jessica Hamblen, PhD

The Perfect Child
When Fear and Anxiety Drive Goodness

My older daughter was the easiest and most compliant child I could have imagined (a true joy to be around) from the time she was adopted. But she buckled under incredible stress after starting school. For her everything came to a head in 2nd Grade. She quite literally had a 'nervous breakdown' and left school for a few weeks while we found a therapist and picked ourselves up off the floor (totally mystified by what was happening with her). Her breaking point didn't provoke rage, but rather depression. We learned that she had basically run out of steam in working so hard to promote the image of the 'perfect' child all those years. She truly wanted to be a good girl, never wanted to be in trouble or thought badly of by anyone. I did not realize this was the lesson she learned in those early years in her institution—good babies live, bad babies and toddlers are abused, neglected and in other terrible ways mistreated. During her pre-school years, we controlled her environment so nicely (loving family, set boundaries) that she was able to manage being so good most of the time. But once she got to school, it was no longer easy....and the effort it took was overwhelming her.

When she started 2nd grade, there was another little girl in her class who had some behavior issues. The other girl, as kids often do, figured out very quickly that it wasn't hard to 'push Elena's buttons' and so manufactured ways of making Elena think she was going to get "in trouble'. Elena slowly began deteriorating as the year progressed. She forgot how to tie her shoes, she cried in class if she couldn't finish a paper, she couldn't remember the words the teacher had just said during spelling tests...and so on. Initially we didn't understand what was going on, and neither did her teacher!! Finally it all came to a head with one dramatic incident– and it was the straw that broke the camel's back!

Once we began working with a wonderful (gentle, loving) therapist, I was happy to finally understand what was going on inside her, but at the same time felt so bad that I had missed some symptoms she had displayed early on. Her basic issue was fear/anxiety....she was living in constant hyper-vigilance all of the time, from the moment I got her, but I didn't realize it. I just thought she was a 'good' child, and I was doing a good job of parenting her. Honestly, I don't believe any different parenting style would have changed a thing. She was going to 'be good' for whomever adopted her; she internally wanted to be good, motivated by overwhelming life-or-death fear for what the repercussions could be for being 'bad'.

Today she is sixteen and still a 'good girl' at heart. She hates to get in trouble, but has learned it's not the end of the world. She has so many things going for her that help her compensate for the ways in which she is different than other people. As she has matured she has learned to cope with her assumptions and perceptions of things that are often born out of her internal fears, rather than based in reality. I have learned so much from parenting her, and know in my heart that she is a miracle girl just to have survived what she lived through in Romania, and come out on the other side as a strong, competent, and successful individual today.

~ By Jill Lampman

You Can't Treat One Without the Other!
Children with Attachment and Sensory Processing Disorders
By Susan Olding

Flips and Dips, Rights and Wrongs.   Here's an image from my memory scrapbook. My daughter, adopted from China at ten months, is somewhere between the ages of two-and-a-half and three. I'm standing in a doorway, saying goodbye to an adult guest, and she is climbing on me, grasping my hands, digging strong feet into my thighs and stomach and then flipping herself over, as if I were a piece of park equipment. I pick her up and hold her, thinking she needs the closeness–but after a moment, she squirms to get down–and when she goes down, she goes with a hard jump onto the floor. She begins to spin, round and round, circling my legs and the guest's, a bit the way a cat will. She grabs my hands again, hoping for another flip, and when I gently tell her no, she just returns for more. Meanwhile, she talks almost non-stop, trying to get us to pay attention to her, yet when we do pay attention to her, she only wants to show off more of her 'gymnastics' moves. I sit her on the steps beside us for a short time in; she accepts this willingly enough but then, when I tell her she's free to get up, she leaps into my arms unannounced.

What my daughter is doing is difficult for me to label 'bad' or 'wrong,' yet something doesn't feel right about it. She is mostly, at this stage, sunny, bright and on the face of things, co-operative. She does nothing purposely to hurt me. Yet by the end of the day I feel like a towel wrung out in the wash. My body is covered with bruises. So she's active, so she's physical–what's wrong with that? I just need to learn to ignore her when she is vying for my attention that way. Or maybe I should speak sharply to her, as my husband does. It works for him. Well, I do speak sharply to her sometimes–and then I feel both guilty and inadequate. What's going on? There's got to be a better way.

Attachment Issues?   I had known from the start to look out for attachment issues, and using the advice I gleaned from Mary Hopkins-Best's *Toddler Adoption: The Weaver's Craft*, and Caroline Archer's *First Steps in Parenting the Child Who Hurts*, I had been parenting for attachment from the beginning. Yet my daughter did seem attached. She looked to me for guidance, clearly preferred me to anyone else, was affectionate, made great eye contact, and had always loved me to hold her. Yet something wasn't quite right – and most of what didn't feel right I associated in some way to movement and touch. She loved me to hold her, but had never liked me to hold her in the cradle position. Even though she loved books and looked forward to story time, we often got into awkward and emotionally confusing power struggles because she could not or would not sit still enough to listen. In groups, especially groups of children, she became hyperactive and sometimes even indiscriminately affectionate. And more and more I noticed that she seemed to need movement, especially hard and crashing movement, or spinning

Sensory processing disorders (SPD) is the current term used to describe the diaspora of outcomes that may happen when the brain can't make sense of what the senses tell it. It is synonymous with dysfunction of sensory integration (DSI) and sensory integration disorder (SID) - which are terms found in some literature. The current trend is to use "sensory processing disorders" to refer to the condition or problem and to use "sensory integration" when referring to the theory (based on the original work of A.Jean Ayres) on which treatment and interventions are based.

Barbara Elleman, MHS, OTR/L, BCP

and hanging upside down, more than many other kids her age.

Sensory Processing Disorder (SPD)? I started doing research and took her for numerous evaluations. No one then diagnosed the attachment strain that I believed and still believe is a factor in her behavior. But I did find a wonderful occupational therapist (OT) who confirmed what I had come to suspect from reading Carol Stock Kranowitz's The Out-of-Sync Child: my daughter had a disorder of sensory integration processing (SPD). We began working together with the OT when my daughter was just over three years old, and in the next year we saw considerable improvement in the ways she sought to use movement and touch for self-regulation. Once I understood some of the physiological drives that were motivating her more annoying and confusing behaviors, I could empathize and redirect her more effectively some of the time. Not only that, but these therapy sessions themselves became like a form of Theraplay - www.theraplay.org. I was present and involved in activities such as throwing and catching (making eye contact), playing with water and shaving cream (touch), pushing my daughter on a swing and catching her, making a 'people sandwich.' We brought many of these games home with us, prolonging the fun and increasing opportunities for healing.

The Relationship between Attachment and SPD. The more we worked on my daughter's sensory issues and the more reading I did, the more I began to wonder about the relationship between SPD and 'attachment strain'. I still don't claim to understand this relationship completely. But common sense suggests that children who have failed to complete and repeat the bonding cycle in their first two years of life or who have suffered neglect or abuse will be at increased risk for developing sensory processing disorders,

Umbrella Therapy
Make Strides by Treating All Apects

There's a growing awareness that just as children are individuals first, and more than any sum of their needs, so the therapies and therapists we choose for them may need to be multi-faceted.

For example, a child with attachment issues gets that way because a nurturing bond with mother or significant care giver was broken. That's on the emotional axis. Just so that child who has not been held and rocked in the loving arms of that same care giver, or helped take first steps holding onto those loved hands - doesn't feel safe, and may not have appropriate use of sensory affect. That's the sensory axis, and, with the emotional is a component of trust. And just so, the child who hasn't had a safe harbor (mother or care giver) from which to explore the world (feeling safe and emotionally secure) lags in using sense and security to go on to make sense of the world by herself. That's the axis of learning, and without those same safe welcoming arms to run back to, the child can't learn.

More and more, parents and therapists alike have come to realize that all aspects of a child's development need to be treated if one area has been impacted by hurt. Without this, treating a hurt child is like trying to keep the broken lid of a jack-in-the-box closed. Impossible: stuff it in, and it pops out again. Parents and therapists often report remarkable strides forward when all aspects of what might under pin an issue are treated.

~Sheena Macrae

just as they will be at increased risk for developing 'attachment strain' – they are children who have difficulty bonding.

They haven't experienced through their senses (yes all five of them) the mother-child bond that underpins attachment, and that is the crucial connection. Throughout the attachment cycle the mother (or primary caregiver) acts to regulate the child. Eventually, over many repetitions of the cycle, the child internalizes the mother's messages; the child thus learns to modulate her responses by to fit the situation. This capacity for modulation grows, in part because throughout the cycle, the mother is providing the infant with physiological experiences (rocking, swinging, sucking, touch. eye contact) that are foundational for all future development. Security is learned through the senses. A child who has been institutionalized or otherwise neglected has been short-changed of these fundamental experiences. As a result, she is neurologically and physiologically disadvantaged. No wonder she has difficulty processing sensory messages from the environment in as efficient a manner as her more 'typical' peers.

In a developing child, sensory experience helps to shape neural connections and to prime the areas of the brain having to do with emotional regulation. If those connections are absent or minimal, the child may struggle to feel genuine trust or love. Instead, she relies on more primitive, primed pre-birth, areas of the brain and shows an exaggerated fight or flight response to stress. In short the child is 'stuck' at a sensory stage younger than her age.

It's not surprising, then, to find that while it is possible for a child to be diagnosed with sensory processing disorder alone, or with attachment issues, many children coming from backgrounds of neglect suffer from both attachment disorders and sensory integration dysfunction. In practice, it can sometimes be difficult to distinguish attachment issues from SPD, since the symptoms can overlap. For example, children with sensory processing disorder may avoid eye contact, just as some children with attachment issues do. Children with sensory processing issues can be extremely controlling–just like children with attachment strain. Children with sensory processing disorders often show extreme and inappropriate reactions–just like children with attachment issues or issues related to early trauma. Add to this inborn temperament, and it's no wonder it can be confusing to determine precisely what is going on for our Post Institutional (PI) children. But maybe distinguishing the disorders is beside the point. Perhaps we should take it for granted that many of our children could be labeled with both SPD and attachment issues. How do these interact?

Unpacking the Connections. One way of explaining what was going on would be to say that as a 'sensory seeking' child my daughter's flips and leaps were simply her attempts at 'self-therapy.' Interestingly, children with SPD often do choose the kinds of movements that their bodies need more of, to regulate. This is one instance where kids 'know what's good for them' and it may simply be a question of re-directing them to meet these needs in socially appropriate ways, or in the case of sensory-avoidant children, to tolerate touch and movement or to find polite ways to excuse themselves. The child who practices her flips at the park will have a much easier time than the child who practices those flips on her parent; the child who says to her school-mate, "Please don't stand quite so close to me," will have an easier time of it than the child who shrieks at the slightest touch from another. A 'sensory diet' for the home, and programs such as BrainGym® and the How Does My Engine Run? are useful adjuncts to occupational therapy here.

But my daughter, while a sensory seeker, does not always show the kinds of behaviors she was showing at that moment. She is capable of sitting still, of focusing on a task, and of polite behavior. My theory is that my daughter's sensory issues become most noticeable and most acute at precisely those moments when she is feeling the greatest strain in her attachment, and that she exhibits her sensory seeking behaviors in response to her inner state of stress. In the example I've given, Mum was talking to someone else – always a cause of jealousy in three-year-olds – especially three-year-olds who are anxiously attached. Not only that, but a transition was in process; our beloved guest was about to leave, and loss of all kinds threatens my daughter enormously. Why? Because of her early losses and trauma. Why the back-forth, push-pull behaviors, the wanting up and wanting down? A partial answer is that this kind of movement was meeting her sensory needs. But critically, another answer (I know it now, but didn't know it then) is that she is anxiously attached with ambivalent presentation, and with the absence of sophisticated language skills, her body was the only tool she had to express that conflict. Interestingly, now that her language is more developed, she never uses me as a piece of climbing equipment! Instead, she speaks her ambivalence.

The key is the construct resulting from how the interacting disorders merge, and how that in turn interacts with a child's temperament. I think that children with disorders of in both sensory and emotional regulation will present on and across the axes of these two disorders. A different child, one with a more avoidant attachment style, might tend toward more sensory-avoidant behaviors when her attachment anxiety was provoked–resistance to eye contact and touch. Perhaps this child would have gone to hide behind the couch when it came time for the guest to say goodbye. Later, as an older child, this child might refuse to express her feelings or deny having any feelings; she might show more interest in a toy than in the people around her. These differences may in turn correspond to basic temperamental differences. Research examining the relationship of temperament to attachment style is underway, and clearly, we need more information before we can reach any firm conclusions, especially as regards our PI children, who remain an exceptional population.

I know that my daughter's SPD is 'real' because she continues to seek unusual sensory input even in situations where her attachment strain is not especially activated; time and occupational therapy have helped her learn to meet her sensory needs in more adaptive ways, but days when she does not get opportunities to jump, run, spin, climb and leap are days when her moods are more difficult to regulate. On days when her emotional reactivity is high, I can often help her by proposing calming sensory activities. Even so, her emotional needs remain greater than those of most children her age, and while improved language skills and a deepening attachment to me have helped her learn to express and meet those needs more effectively, I know the attachment strain is 'real' as well. SPD and attachment issues are not an either/or proposition for my daughter, but rather 'both/and'.

The ideal treatment for many of our children will include more than just occupational therapy or trauma therapy or attachment therapy, but will best instead build a team of people who can work together to understand the complex interrelationship of our children's challenges. Such a team would meet my daughter's needs more completely. For now, we try to offer a sensory diet at home while we work on high-structure/high-nurture parenting and with an adoption/attachment therapist. Our daughter is making progress in school and socially and while she is volatile and often controlling she is also loving and affectionate.

–Susan Olding, step mother and adoptive mom

The Attachment Project Turns on a Stream of Services
Could Your Agency Learn How to Make a Team Like This?

The Attachment Project (TAP) is a new pilot service provided by Surrey (UK) Adoption and Fostering services to promote stable permanent and adoptive placements and to prevent crisis breakdown for such placements. It's additional to ongoing services for attachment problems in permanent placements. TAP is based on attachment theory, assessments and interventions and takes as its starting point the need for a holistic assessment of a child's attachment history and needs prior/close to placement. Additionally, TAP works on the premise that the attachment between care givers and children placed, and the relationship between care givers (when there's a partnership) is central to understanding the dynamic that occurs in newly formed families. Understanding individual attachment styles helps to establish whether care givers have barriers to seeking help, the ways in which they may interact with the child and the extent to which they can provide a secure base for the child. Providing extra support for both care givers and children post placement can be critical to placements stabilizing and remaining permanent. TAP has two components:

1. Consultation Panel–a team of professionals from different child-care agencies (psychologists, education experts, adoption & permanence workers) who meet monthly to use their combined skills to make recommendations about how to take forward placements that are having difficulty. Panel also offers advice on the therapeutic and permanent placement needs of attachment disordered children. This enables expert advice on psychological issues (including psychiatric and psychotherapeutic) and educational issues to be combined with experienced social work input.

2. Direct Work–once a family has been considered at Consultation Panel, they may be referred to work with social workers who can provide direct work with the family including additional assessments and therapeutic interventions. This includes life-story work and Theraplay. Work with consultant and educational psychologists and consultant psychiatrists can be undertaken alongside the social work intervention, or as a discrete piece of work, according to the needs of the child and family. Key areas include:
- Supervision of social workers involved.
- Advice from experts. TAP consults with Family Futures consortium (www.familyfutures.co.uk) for training in attachment-centered techniques for working with children and families.
- Research base. TAP has consultation with a research unit at Royal Holloway College, University of London who advise on advanced assessment techniques for care givers/aid in support, resilience assessment and matching of child to care giver. They also evaluate TAP and its impact on children and families and stability of placements.
- Workers and families involved in TAP feel their experiences are valued, which promotes positive outcomes.

~Wendy Hirst, Surrey Children's Service and Toni Bifulco, PhD, Royal Holloway College

Journey

The Search for Identity in Adoption:
Understanding the meaning of one's life
By Hollee A. McGinnis, MS

Where did I come from?

Like many adopted people I never had a simple answer to the question, "Where did I come from?" For most people who are raised by their biological parents, this question can be answered by simply gazing at their parent's face. There in the turn of a nose and the curve of the eye is one reminded of where they came from, undeniably, bound by blood, a part of a human continuum passed from mother to daughter, from father to son. There in the touch of a hand, in the family smile, one is secure in knowing they belong, are part of a legacy that started long before their birth and will continue long after.

I, on the other hand, seemingly dropped out of the sky on a Boeing 747, walking, talking, and potty trained. The life I know began at the age of three when I stepped off the plane from South Korea and into the waiting arms of my American family. As a child it did not matter that I did not share my father's Irish ancestry, or my mother's blond hair. Unfettered by blood ties, the ties that bound me to my family were love ties and I never questioned my belonging.

Unfortunately, despite how much I felt I was a part of my adoptive family, my parents' love could not shield me from the inquisitive questions or the puzzled faces that did not understand how a White couple could have an Asian daughter; or protect me from people who assumed I was not American because I did not have blond hair and blue eyes. Knowing that I came from Korea could not answer the curiosity of who gave me my artistic talents, my eyes, or shape of my face. And even though my parents could expose me to Korean food and history, they could not teach me how to be Korean.

The search for identity in adoption is similar to any quest to understand the meaning of one's life. After all, the question "Who am I?" has been pondered by philosophers, scientists, and theologians for millennia. For everyone, the development of identity is a complex, ongoing, life-long process that is unique to each individual. It involves the incorporation of one's self-definition with an understanding of the past, present and future, multiple relationships and contexts over time. For adopted people and their families by birth and adoption, this natural process is complicated by experiences of loss, lack of access to one's past, and societal assumptions of adoption, race and culture. I weave vignettes of my own search for identity in adoption to provide a window into one adopted person's experience, and to give guidance for adoptive parents as they raise their children.

Acknowledge when you do not know-that means talking about difference. As a child, I understood that I was different than my parents, but I was not aware of its implications. When I was growing up, Korea described my physical appearance, and was a mystical fairytale land where I was born. Korea meant a special dinner at a Korean restaurant, a culture day where I learned a Korean song, the television show M*A*S*H, a reminder that I was different. I always felt a strong connection and pride in being Korean, but as I reached my late adolescence, I also began to feel like an imposter. I looked Korean but did not feel Korean. I did not know what Korea looked like, smelled like, or tasted like. I could not speak the language. Whatever memories I had once had, I had lost. I only knew American culture.

As I entered college, the culmination of incidental moments (strangers complimenting my English, being asked where I came from, being spoken to in every Asian language) had me keenly conscious of the fact that I was judged differently than my White parents because I had an Asian face. Pride and awareness of my birth culture could not protect me from the horrifying realization of the stereotypes and prejudice toward my race. It angered me that people would make assumptions about who I was based on things I could not change: my gender, my race, my adoption status. In college, I sought to understand the racial implications of my face, and reconcile my self-identity, based on my experience within my adoptive family, and the identity imposed by the racial stereotypes of my society.

Having cultural pride and awareness does not replace the need to talk about racism. This exploration of difference can be particularly stressful for transracially adopted people because it can result in feeling disenfranchised from, or choosing to reject, the values and beliefs that had comprised their adoptive family's culture (i.e. the White dominate cul-

Acknowledge when you do not know (that means talking about difference).

Having cultural pride and awareness does not replace the need to talk about racism.

Be comfortable in your own skin and your children will be comfortable in theirs.

Understand your own adoption losses, gains and "ghosts".

Be confident in your relationship with your child; nothing can take away your years of nurture.

Give space for your child to create their own identities and integrate their dual identities.

Change the world: challenge the bigotry and prejudice that exist in society.

ture). Because of their race, adoptees are excluded from this culture despite being raised in it; and it can be potentially explosive within a family if discrimination and racism had never been addressed. Today, adoption practitioners and adoptive parents are more aware and active in helping adopted children maintain connections with their biological roots, whether by maintaining relationships with birth mothers through open adoption, or exposing internationally and transracially adopted children to their birth culture through heritage camps, trips to their country of origin, or culture day celebrations.

Be comfortable in your own skin and your child will be comfortable in theirs. While these efforts are important for fostering connections and pride, providing cultural awareness is not talking about racism; and having contact with a birth parent is not talking about having been 'given away'. Families need to determine how to cope with discrimination in a healthy and adaptive manner. Denial of difference or over-emphasis of difference may be problematic for transracial adoptive families. It is important to find the right balance, which may be achieved by first admitting, without resignation, fear, guilt or anger, those experiences you have and those you simply will never have; this is at the heart of recognizing difference. I will never know what it is like to be a 5'11" Caucasian male, or have the privileges that come with it. Likewise, my adoptive father will never know what it is to be an Asian woman and the interactions I have because of it.

The point is not to assert our differences, and so justify misunderstandings and inaction, but rather to use the acknowledgment of difference in order to become better listeners. When we listen, we demonstrate honesty and empathy, and validate our children's experiences and feelings: I do not know what it feels like to be teased for being Asian; it is normal that you should feel hurt; it hurts me because it hurts you, and I think it is wrong. We then make it possible to work in collaboration with our children and have them feel supported to learn how to navigate a race-conscious society.

Understand your own adoption losses, gains and 'ghosts'. One of the cornerstones of adoption is the belief that a human life is best nurtured within a family and not an institution; however, the possibility of gaining a new family through adoption can only exist in the wake of the loss of another family. The experience of loss, gain, and the search to reconcile these experiences is shared by all members of the adoption triad: adoptive parents, birth parents and adopted people. The adoption memoirist Betty Jean Lifton, herself an adopted person, has described these losses in adoption as "ghosts". For adoptive parents, the ghost can be the biological child they did not have; for birth parents, the ghost can be the child they did not get to raise; and for adopted people, the ghost can be the family they did not grow up in and the person they might have become in a different family and culture. On the flip side of the losses of adoption are the gains. For adoptive parents, the gains of adoption can include the opportunity to become parents; for birth parents, the prospect of not having the burden of raising a child; and for adopted people the opportunity to be raised in loving families.

When these 'ghosts' are not understood, acknowledged or avoided, they can 'haunt' the relationships between members of the adoption triad. Often adoptive parents may seek to mitigate the perceived losses of their adopted children, without first recognizing how their own adoption losses may be motivating their behaviors. An over-zealous attempt to search for birth relatives on behalf of an adopted child may be motivated by an adoptive parent's unconscious feeling that they are competing with the birth parent for the love of their adopted child. Certainly all adopted people think about the people who gave them birth, but not all are interested in searching or finding biological relatives. Even for those adoptees that do find biological family, not all decide to continue ongoing relationships with them. In fact, one of the barriers for many adoptees in conducting a search for birth parents is the loyalty many feel toward their adoptive parents, and the desire not to hurt their adoptive parent's feelings. This, however, may prevent an adopted person from exploring a fundamental adoption loss, that of birth kin, and the healing that may come with it.

The experience of loss in adoption is different from other kinds of losses, such as the death of a relative, because they are the losses of 'what-might-have-been' and as such can never be fully known. For adopted people in particular, initially the losses in adoption can feel more like missing pieces. After all, the only 'real' parents adopted children know are the ones that are there tucking them into bed, helping them with homework, making them do chores. It was not until I returned to Korea for the first time at the age of 24, that I fully comprehended the losses in adoption. My life up until then had been filled with the gains: the gains of a loving family, a good education, and life-long friends. But when I returned to South Korea I became keenly aware that there were two levels to culture: a learned culture and a lived culture. One I could reclaim, the other was lost to me forever.

Be confident in your relationship with your child; nothing can take away your years of nurture. I think of learned culture as the symbols of a culture that anyone can learn and share. It is the language, the customs, the dress, the food, the ceremonies and holidays. Lived culture is a culture of being, shaped by our experiences of being a woman or a man, being adopted or not adopted, being an American or a South Korean. It is the culture we gain from the skin we live in, and the environment that surrounds us. I realized that no matter how long I studied the Korean language, learned the customs, and even lived in Korea for the rest of my life, I would not be able to regain the lived culture of the native Koreans I met who had grown up there. I would never be Korean in the same way they were because my being had already been shaped by my experiences of being a Korean woman, adopted by a non-Asian family, and raised in the suburbs of New York City.

It was in confronting, mourning, and accepting these adoption losses that I came to fully understand and appreciate my adoption gains. Nothing could take away the years of nurture my adoptive parents gave me. In the same way, nothing could take away the genetic endowment my birth parents had bestowed upon me. Adoptive parents must have confidence in their relationships with their children and understand that nothing–even meeting birth parents–can take that away.

All members of the adoption triad must come to reconcile the paradoxes of adoption: that one can be loved and be given away; that we are a product of nature and nurture; and that to have gains is to have losses. The point is for adoptive parents to work on being comfortable in their own skins, to know their own meanings of these adoption paradoxes and so have capacity to support their children when they begin to explore the dualities inherent in adoption.

A Dance of Identities: Declaring Who I am

When I graduated from college I realized the conflict I felt about my identity arose in part because I felt I only had two choices: Korean or American. When I tried to learn everything about Korean and Asian cultures, I felt I was just fulfilling the racial stereotypes of my society. I had also been raised as a McGinnis. I felt caught between two worlds, walking on a fence between two identities until I realized I could embrace both. In coming to accept the paradoxes and contradictions in my identity, rather than accommodating the identities imposed upon me, I realized the question "Who am I?" can only be answered by our declaration: "Who I am." Who I am is a transcultural, multicultural, interracial, hybrid, bridging worlds, being. I am Hollee McGinnis, also-known-as Lee Hwa Yeong. I have an Asian face, an Irish last name, a blond haired mother. And that is who I am.

Give space for your child to create their own identities and integrate their dual identities. As I began to appreciate the richness of my life because of my dual identities, rather than frustration because I did not 'fit in', I sought to connect to the thousands of other internationally and transracially adopted people I knew who shared my experiences. I felt that as a community we could truly create a physical space in which we could explore, and come to embrace and celebrate our dual heritages given to us by birth and adoption. The organization of adult intercountry adoptees was formed in 1996 and was named Also-Known-As in recognition of the identities we create that may not be apparent on the surface. Since its inception the organization has developed post-adoption services informed by the experiences of adult adoptees with the goal of serving the younger generation of intercountry adoptees and their families.

Who we are is a complex web of ancestry, traditions, language, looks, experiences, and choices. While some aspects of identity involve a degree of choice such as occupation, religion, or political values, others do not. Like race, gender and sexual orientation, being adopted is an imposed identity. The adopted person has no choice in being relinquished or being adopted. For some adopted people this lack of choice and control in their own adoption can be a source of anger, especially when fantasizing about the 'what-might-have-been' in their lives. However, if identities are ultimately formed by our declaration, then adopted people do have a choice: they get to choose the meaning of being adopted.

We sometimes think that Life is a book, written, bound, and handed to us. But in fact our lives are more like loose-leaf binders to which we add pages, erase and modify. While the facts of our lives we can not change, the meaning we make of those facts is essentially a narrative we create to organize the past and present. As the authors we control the meaning-making of our lives. As a child, adoptive parents provide the initial meaning of being adopted. The goal for parents, however, is to support and empower their children to make their own meaning as they enter adolescence and young adulthood. To have choices is to also be responsible for those choices, which might feel frightening to an adolescent. But when we feel we can choose, we also feel empowered to be the director of our lives. In supporting adopted children in creating their own meaning of being adopted (which may involve a search for birth relatives) or being a person of color (which may involve interacting with different communities), we instill in them a feeling that they can be the masters of their lives.

Change the world: challenge the bigotry and prejudice that exist in society. Ultimately our declaration of who we are should not only be about our past, but about our future. Who I am is not just about who I know myself to be, but who I want to also be known as. Parents must be responsible for helping their children navigate the culture and societies in which they live, but they are also responsible for giving their children hopes and dreams for the future. Hopefully your adopted child will grow up in the most important culture: a culture of love. From this foundation they will be able to explore in a safe way their past, present, and future, always knowing there is a safe place to retreat when the going gets tough. But that is not enough. Part of the complications of adoption, and especially adoptions that cross race, nationality, and culture, is because it does not fit within the 'status quo'. We have the choice of trying to make our families 'fit', and reinforcing the merits of the status quo, or we can change those perceptions to accommodate our non-traditional families. My choice is to change the status quo.

Part of the meaning-making of adoption is thinking about what one can do with the life one has been given. I see my experience of being adopted transracially as a unique opportunity to talk about racism and shatter racial stereotypes. Intercountry adoption inspires me to imagine a world in which strangers are embraced as daughters or sons, as sisters or brothers. After all, I was a foreign child in a foreign land until my parents opened their hearts to love me as their daughter. But I also know that adopting across race, nationality and culture is complex and requires courage, honesty, commitment and love. To make a real difference in our children's lives, we must be willing to make a difference in the environment in which they grow up. The greatest gift we could give our children, besides love, is a world that values them for who they are and who they will be–irregardless of race, nationality, culture, or circumstance.

~ By Hollee A. McGinnis, MS,
Adoptee, Policy and Operations Director at the Evan B. Donaldson Adoption Institute.

Building Bridges:
Connections in International Adoption
By Indigo Williams Willing

Two Sides of the Bridge

Family histories and the stories that we build around them are never as neat as diagrams of family trees are prone to suggest. There will always be main characters, such as a 'mother', 'father', 'daughter' and 'son' and so on to help us to begin to sketch out a map of 'who' we are in relation to significant others. But, the individuals who actually take up these roles following the birth of a child are not necessarily cast through blood or bound by any culture or country.

We should not give into the temptation of thinking that a mum, dad and two kids, who all bear the same ancestry and history is the ultimate norm. Not to do so is hugely important for trans-nationally adoptive families. We must not forget that we live in an era where there are families made up of step-mums, dads and kids, single parent households, same-sex ones as well as IVF, foster, adoptive and birth families. Families can also be multi-racial and transnational, with members sometimes spread across many borders. Adoption cuts across these possibilities.

It is important to recognize that any and all of these combinations involve social relationships, cultural identifications and emotional bonds that will make them 'real' families. No family, whatever its composition, is more authentic than any other and we need to remind others of this if ever they question our place in the world. And so it is for adopted people and their families

With this in mind, how can we help people who are adopted from overseas develop a healthy sense of identity and belonging? How do we celebrate the fact that adopted people and their families have multiple heritages? One of the ways is to work through some of the more subtle processes that underpin them. It's like trying to check that the foundations on two sides of a 'bridge' are robust enough so that the center point will be as strongly supported, even, and balanced as possible. For the adopted person, whose sense of identity we can think of as this center point, we might view the strength of one side of the bridge being reliant on what knowledge they have of their first family and first country. The other side of the bridge might be thought of as being reliant on how strong their sense of 'place and belonging' is in their adoptive family and adopted country. I call the sides of the bridge 'Over Here' and 'Over There', with the adoptee as the coping stone, holding up the edifice.

'Over There'

Adopted people can learn to cope with their separation from their first family and country through the narratives, the stories, that they are offered about how they got from 'over there" to 'over here'. I would argue that the most important tools or support we can give adopted children today to assist them to look to their past, and to accept what are separated from, is by letting them know it is OK for them to grieve, while simultaneously allowing them to develop empathy and affection for what they left behind.

Even recently, many adoptees have had their grieving process cut short via being distracted by societal pressure to only feel 'grateful' from being adopted. The narratives sent out through these adoptees' families and the media, sent a strong message to adoptees that they were 'rescued' from people and places that were irredeemably negative. It was essentially suggested, and the adoptees believed, that that their whole history 'over there' was deeply inferior to their post-adoption lives 'over here'.

I am an adopted person myself, adopted from Vietnam and I have made an academic study of the one-dimensional portrayal of my birthcountry as suggested to many others adopted from Vietnam. Our country was described as 'a war zone' where Communists were thought to kill babies, and first mothers (birthmothers) were 'prostitutes' and / or incapable women who abandoned their children. It is certainly a grim picture of one's past. What is missing in the narratives adopted Vietnamese were offered about their past, is how Viet Nam also has a history of culture, beauty and humanity, including an intense literary tradition. The offered narratives ignored the bravery, compassion, intelligence and spirituality of the Vietnamese citizens, and failed to mention the dreams, aspirations, disappointments and grief of Vietnamese birthmothers.

I believe that one–dimensional and derogatory narratives about their first family and first country affect adoptees as a double trauma, or at the very least, gives them an uneasy feeling about their pre-adoption past:

- They not only have to make sense of their separation from a past with only second-hand knowledge to fill in the gaps
- They are then further challenged to do so through deeply denigrating and speculative representations of what they left behind

This is not a pathway to grief, recovery and acceptance; this is a process that is ripe for producing blame on the first parents, as well as shame of their ancestry as a whole. It leaves adoptees with a shaky sense of permanence for that first side of the bridge…

What we can do is find ways for young adopted children to learn about their separation and adoption in a way that is unpolluted with negative 'gossip' about 'over there'. We owe it to the children of the world who are adopted not to talk about the people and places they left 'over there' in a way that is less kind and less informed than the ways we talk of about people and places 'over here'.

There are also other 'tools' we might utilize to assist adopted people to feel less distanced and overwhelmed by what they left behind in the past. Adoptive parents can provide concrete information about their child's journey to them, particularly through supplying things such as passports, official migration papers and orphanage mementos. Information to the past, no matter how little, can become very important to how an adopted child makes sense of their past. For example, in interviews I conducted with adopted Vietnamese such 'artifacts' were described by them as 'important' and 'vital' as well as a 'link' or 'key' to discovering the past, rather than completely illustrating that past.

Adoptive parents, please hold on to whatever mementos of your child's past that you can, collect everything and keep it safe so your child can have access to them when they are old enough. The more elusive part of an adopted child's past is their first family. How do we help 'new generations' of adoptive families to develop better, more sophisticated ways to prepare for the possibility that their adopted child may want to find and develop a relationship with their first family? The main questions that they need to ask themselves are:

- What information do I already have?
- What support do I have to help me decide how to gather and hand-over this information to my child?
- What issues may emerge and what areas of expertise do I lack?
- Who do I need to make connections with to make this process as easy and undaunting as possible?

It is important to remember that a collective approach can help you through almost any challenge. If you can write down a strategy, and then share it with others, almost anything is possible.

'Over Here'

How do adopted people develop a sense of place in their 'new' family and country (the other side of the 'bridge')? It is reasonably common for adoptive family members to all be deeply bonded and it is clear that most adopted Vietnamese enjoy 'real' and deeply loving parent and child relationships with each other. Adoptive family members also generally all call the same nation 'home', although the adopted child may also call an overseas nation 'home' as well. So, on the surface, this side of the bridge looks pretty strong.

The problem is that others outside the family and in general society will often bring our familial attachments and other forms of belonging into question. This is because there are often visible differences between trans-nationally adoptive parents and adopted people that can lead to others asking all kinds of racial, cultural or national identity questions. Given that intercountry adoption more commonly is from underdeveloped countries to First World countries, this sends a resounding message to many adoptees that 'west is best'– which undercuts heritage and pride.

Adopted persons will face challenges in trying to define their sense of place and identity in the context of their adoptive families and adopted societies. Initially there may be none when the children are still young, but we need to consider the long term. The majority of the adopted Vietnamese I interviewed said that in their early years they initially felt the 'same' as their adoptive parents. The main problem was that although the adopted Vietnamese recalled feeling the 'same' as their parents in childhood, they were actually referring to feeling like they shared a 'white' identity, which was seen by them as being the 'norm' and in opposition of being 'non-white'. The adoptees' recollections of their childhood upbringing include statements that they were raised as a 'normal Australian lad', 'all American', 'raised as normal', and 'white...just like my family'. Challenges then began to emerge when the adopted Vietnamese entered school and were seen by their peers as being 'Asian' or 'different' to whites. In these cases, the adopted Vietnamese then found that they were forcibly dislocated and excluded from the only identity they knew and felt comfortable with.

   An adopted Vietnamese-Australian provides us with some insight into how her own sense of identity at home was contradicted by how others saw her at school, stating, "I felt I was white, but because I don't look like my parents or the majority of students at school I was treated like I was Asian." One of the problems for this adoptee was that being seen as Asian also meant that she was made to feel inferior because of racist views she received, "Directly and indirectly, by students, teachers and people walking past who believed they had the right to have a go and judge me".

   Adopted Vietnamese were left feeling excluded from the side of the 'bridge' that connected them to their adopted family and home, due to their physical appearances setting them apart. They were also left unable to draw support from the other side of the 'bridge' from people who shared their Vietnamese ancestry, as they had little positive affirmations or knowledge available about this part of their personal history and identity. You cannot build a coping stone in mid-air. Left in the center with shaky foundations on either side, we can consider that standing 'tall and proud' for these trans-national adoptees was not always easy.

Bridge Building
How do we help adoptees develop a sense of pride in their post-adoption settings?
Parenting. There is definitely a large amount of literature that takes a more psychological approach to explore how the formation of identity and self-esteem in children who are adopted from overseas can be improved by new parental approaches
Travel. We now live in a global era where, arguably, we are able to become much more international or cosmopolitan. Affordable birth country travel for those of middle-class dispositions in the West definitely has made a difference.
Internet. There is also the Internet and many other technologies that can bring people from around the world much closer together.
With these transformations, there is talk that the boundaries between nations and cultural communities are becoming more blurred and that old stereotypes and prejudices towards difference are lapsing and being replaced with an enthusiasm and acceptance of diversity. If this is true, what are the implications for the new generation of adoptive families?
   Mary Watkins is an adoptive parent and researcher; she proposes that adoptive parents are now better able to take up an "ethical and societal responsibility to open up personal and public space in which otherness and difference can be articulate". In the new 'space'

which she now sees as possible, adoptive parents can then bring forward the diversity within their families as a shared process rather than one just carried by the adoptee. One of the ways she does this is through her discussions on her relationship and travels with her adopted daughter from China, which she finds has the profound effect of building a joint sense in both of them of being connected to a range of people and places across borders. What she is finding is that China (and Chinese-ness) is no longer just this mysterious place 'over there'; it can be a living and dynamic part of her and her child's own lives 'over here'.

This opening up of a multicultural and empathetic space between 'over there' and 'over here' is not always easy. New identities and senses of belonging are not all fun and games, they are commitments that require us to do a lot of groundwork and to hold a lot of conviction while remaining open to new dialogues and experiences.

The hazards for adoptive parents to being subject to overly simplistic praise or harsh critical remarks by outside observers are also highlighted in researcher Toby Volkman's study of Chinese adoptive parents. In particular, as an adoptive mother from China herself, she skillfully highlights a new kind of sensitivity in her own community that stems from others' claims that adoptive parents from China only have a superficial commitment to diversity. Volkman states "While it is easy to parody the compulsion to consume–to spend lavishly on Asian dolls or search the Web for panda pajamas–or to scorn the superficiality of a celebratory multiculturalism, many parents strive for some deeper transformations of their own identities and lives."

Adoptive Parents: Outside the Center?

In instances of tension and conflict we are able to see how adoptive parents are also 'outside the center, the norm' and have to find ways to re-negotiate a position from which to find support for their multicultural family.   While doing this, they may come across a range of judgements and opinions that can be a little jarring. The main benefits of Volkman's philosophy, (*Cultures of Transnational Adoption* (Paperback) by Toby Alice, ed. Volkman) are that adoptive parents can see that their own identities come with nuances, and histories. At the same time, their actions towards developing a new understanding of the world around them also means that their identities are as just as open to transformations as their child's.

Past attitudes towards trans-national adoption generally came with the expectation that it was the child would come to blend in with their new families and homes. We might also consider the reverse is just as possible for adoptive parents. We might turn the question around and ask: in what ways can trans-national adoption have a significant impact upon the identity of adoptive parents?

If adoptive parents are more multicultural, worldly and internationally empathetic, then it is likely that adopted children will feel less pressured to only identify with one (white or non-white) identity, less influenced by racism and more comfortable with all facets of their personal history and sense of self.

How do adoptive parents make this journey to meeting their adopted children and create a space in their own lives and homes so that diversity is not only appreciated, but it becomes their own new 'norm'? Activities might include:

- learning the language
- joining overseas cultural community networks
- regularly visiting the country
- practicing cultural traditions in the home
- moving family activities to more multicultural neighborhoods with diverse peoples, foods, languages and cultures

Adoptive parents might also begin to read up on the ancient and modern history of the country they adopted from, seek out books and films produced about it and other materials that can help familiarize them with their adopted child's past. If adoptive parents do these things regularly enough, they can then offer a diverse range of networks and knowledge to their adopted child in a more even, natural, unforced way.

Traffic Over the Bridge

There are no 'hard or fast' rules or strictly set out diagrams to answer our questions or to get that bridge built. Every family still has a unique quality to them and what may work for some families, may not work for others. What we can do is share our ideas, experiences and proposals on these issues with each other within environments that encourage constructive advice and ongoing support.

Adult adoptees are working together with adoptive parents and adoption professionals to provide a more detailed history of what adoptees struggled with in the past, and what they believe can remove or ease them. Through such endeavors, recent adoptive families are now able to access a range of opinions and experiences that might help younger (and future) inter-country adoptees to develop and maintain a more secure sense of pride in their identity, cultural ancestry, and sense of place in their new homes.

Many confusing and unsettling feelings and experiences that older adoptees are now reporting, such as encounters with racism, cultural loss and estrangement from people who share their cultural background, all suggest that there was/is a need in their lives for more firm and regular affirmations of racial pride and cross cultural exposure.

Adoptive parents today can also give their adopted children the option of knowing other inter-country adoptees on a reasonably regular basis through putting them in contact with the various emerging groups that have worked hard to initiate such opportunities. It is hoped that as adoptive families be, and become, more multicultural this process can pre-empt the confused stage that many older inter-country adoptees reported going through when they reached ages where questions of their racial and cultural identity became more pronounced. In addition, by spending time with a wider and more diverse range of people, we can all break down the unnecessary barriers between us.

~ Indigo Williams Willing, BA, MA,
Adoptee, founder of Adopted Vietnamese International (AVI)

Preventative Medicine

The most important thing a child returning to any birth country can come home with is liking their country of birth and feeling good about their experience

I frequently refer to the practice of traveling with children to their birth country to learn about their culture and heritage as 'preventative medicine'. The entire experience creates a 'toolbox' for your child. Travel itself is an educational experience for children and a valuable means for creating dialog and learning about culture and adoption. Exploring your child's birth country while they are elementary school age sends them a signal that their birth country is important to your family. The early travel experience allows the child to have information to share with their peers at school about where they are from. This is different than reading books, seeing movies, and being an observer of life that is far away from their daily reality. They need to be a participant in their culture and see it, touch it, smell it. Then, as they encounter questions about themselves from peers, or perhaps even teased, they will have a host of things to say about being from that country based on their own personal experiences.

The most important thing a child returning to any birth country can bring home with them is liking their country of birth and feeling good about their experience there. It creates a powerful toolbox that a child can build upon later in life. It does not mean that everything in the toolbox will be perfect, positive images, or experiences, but they will be real and they will be 'theirs' and not something they've learned second-hand from someone else.

If you can model for the child intercultural understanding and create opportunities for your child to experience different cultures then they will accept differences and learn to adapt to them. They may even decide they don't like something but it will be based on their experience and an understanding, versus through your filters.

Internationally adopted children need a positive connection to their birth culture and people for their life-long self-worth. The positive, hands-on experience of homeland travel can help a child stock her personal toolbox, and provide a lasting foundation for further journeys.

~ By Dr. Jane Liedtke,
Founder and Director of Our Chinese Daughters Foundation

Homeland Visits
Preparation is essential for a positive trip
By Carrie Kitze and Jean MacLeod

What to Pack

A sense of humor

A sense of adventure

An ability to be flexible

An open mind and heart

One small piece of luggage, packed lightly

A Piece of the Puzzle? Going back home is a rite of passage, and something that most of us take for granted.   For an adoptee, going 'home' has an extra meaning, and a Homeland visit can include the powerful extra dimensions of self-understanding, discovery, and closure. It doesn't matter if a return trip is done domestically, or if the place of birth is somewhere halfway around the world. What families are finding is that 'going back' is helping their children with a foundation for identity.

When is the Right Time? Homeland visits can help play a pivotal role in identity formation. When you are trying to decide what is right for your own child, you might want to consider that the middle school years can be difficult for a child who is suddenly defining himself by his peer group. Dr Jane Liedtke, of Our Chinese Daughters Foundation, recommends a first trip between the ages of 6-10; it is easier for a child to internalize a positive view of their birth country when the trip is seen as an awesome adventure. Many parents who have taken trips with their children before they reach adolescence report that their children are more open to cultural differences, and are less judgmental of the harsh socio-economic realities of some sending countries.

Keep in mind, that for each child the answer of when to go back will vary, and that maturity and personality are big factors. Some parents have made the journey earlier in their children's lives, due to either circumstances or requests of the child, others later. Personal finances may also play a role if international travel is involved. What if a Homeland visit is not financially feasible for your family? Look ahead at future travel possibilities, and use the present to learn about your child's heritage. Make local connections with people from your international community, and perhaps learn the language. Consciously celebrate the importance of your family's ties with the country that will always be part of your child.

It's a Process! Taking a visit to a birth country should begin as a family process a year before the trip is actually taken. Age-appropriate books and videos should be read and discussed together, both about the country and about adoption. A child's reactions (physical/verbal) to these topics are going to give you some insight to a child's readiness. Does your son or daughter have a great desire to travel back to the land of their birth? Do they have fears associated with a proposed trip? Does your child clearly understand what will happen on the trip, who they will meet, and that they will be returning home with you? Communication about a trip's potential scenarios can be used to address both an adoptee's emotional readiness, and their trip expectations.

Culture or Adoption? What is the purpose of the trip? Is it an exposure to a culture and a place? A getting-to-know-you type of trip? If so, enjoy soaking in the sights. Many people have chosen to create positive memories of your child's homeland on a first trip,

Homeland Trips:
Part of the process

Understanding birth culture is important. Homeland Trips are important if conducted when and if the child is ready. They can fill in the pieces, or help 'put the puzzle pieces together.' The next step is to be able to put that in context and realize/accept that birth culture is but one facet of many parts of adoptee identity.

Christopher Brownlee, Adult adoptee, founder of the Vietnamese Adoption Network

and return later to do the harder work surrounding adoption-issues.

If your child is ready, seeing the place where they started life can be a wonderfully affirming choice. Visiting orphanages and meeting with birth siblings and birth parents requires more serious thought and up front planning. A child should have a thorough grasp on his or her birth and adoption story, and be able to express their feelings about the tougher adoption elements of loss and anger. Creating a Lifebook together before a Homeland trip is a concrete form of communication, and an important 'tool of talk' for parent and child.

When pursuing a child's personal history on a Homeland visit, parents need to be ready for the unexpected to occur. Have a plan in place for dealing with negative, positive or surprising information about your child's early life, and be prepared to be supportive. How will you deal with finding out information that is different from what you have previously told your son or daughter? What is your responsibility toward a newly discovered birth parent, or your child's biological siblings? As a parent, you are the emotional model for your child and can assist him or her in integrating new facts or ideas. Knowing when to pull back from situations in which your child feels uncomfortable will help your child feel safe and in control. Set up a plan in advance, a signal for "I need to get out of here", and observe your child's cues. They will know how far their comfort zone extends. This is a very personal journey that your child will need to guide.

As a Family or With a Group? Families we have talked to report that both types of travel have worked very well. Are you able to follow a routine and a schedule set by someone else? Do you need the comfort of a group and the companionship of others going through the same thing? For many kids, having travel-mates with their same history and past is a powerful added benefit. It gives them a secure place to diffuse feelings and share emotions.

For others, the privacy of an independent trip might allow a more personal examination of feelings, in a more flexible environment. Group tours are not an option in some countries, but an experienced guide/translator is a necessity. Either way, make sure to hire an interpreter for important meetings, if the language is not one you speak. Plan and get permissions in advance, so you can go to the places and see the sites you want to see.

How do We Prepare for the Journey? Preparation is essential for a positive trip. Talk with your child about the emotional implications of returning to their starting place in life and deal with normal adoption issues well in advance. Don't overlook discussing the physical requirements of international Homeland travel, and the culture shock that most adults and children will experience to some degree. Jet-lag, summer heat, strange food and unaccustomed physical exercise will affect some travelers far more than others. Prepare your family for the customs and behavioral expectations of another country, and for the dynamics of group travel. Model flexibility, and help your kids go with the flow!

Is it for Me or for Them? Homeland trips are all about the child. But it is surprising how many of our own parent-issues will crop up and take center stage if we let them. Spend some time preparing yourself as a parent with what your expectations are for the trip (cultural? educational? emotional?), then separate them from the ones your child has. Listen to your child and do what it takes to meet their needs.

> For a series of free articles on homeland trips, visit the parent resources section at www.emkpress.com

What Happens if it Doesn't Work... Always have a Plan B. If things are not working out as planned, or the emotional toll is unexpectedly hard on your child, then you need to be prepared to scale back on your daily schedule. Find alternative activities, and help your child re-gain a comfortable balance, without blame or repercussions. Understand that positive AND negative experiences are both part of the ongoing process of learning about your child's country and culture of origin. A trip doesn't have to be perfect to be effective or memorable. Your attuned support to your child can make a Homeland trip a valuable step in the life-long experience of adoption.

Carrie Kitze is publisher, author, and adoptive mom.
Jean MacLeod is Director of OCDF Institute, a Homeland tour leader,
adoptive mom, and author. Originally published in Adoptive Families Magazine

Impact of a Birthfamily Reunion
What to consider before planning a birthfamily reunion for
your elementary or middle-school aged child

- *Decide if the trip is for the child, and plan for that, not for your own needs*

- *Preparation: what will the child need to know about to make the trip successful. Think about journaling before the trip, so that the child has some basic understanding of what that she'll see. Look at this from a child's viewpoint. Children don't 'see, hear, think' lifestyle in the same way as adults. They may be oblivious of dire poverty, yet hone in on smells and sounds*

- *Decide before hand on long-term goals about continuing contact and support for the birthfamily. Explore how you feel about extending financial assistance before you go, and give yourself permission*

to change your mind if you learn something that influences your original decision

- *Prepare for your child to have an emotional need to reconnect after the visit. Put your own needs aside and work to support your child.*

- *Decide what to do about coping with new information that may be hard to hear*

- *Consider how a birthfamily meeting will impact other children in your family, especially those whose circumstances don't allow them the same opportunity.*

Jill Lampman, adoptive mom

Sari. Hanbok and Cheongsam

I've seen several documentaries over the years in which second-generation immigrant teens and young adults discuss the difficulties of feeling "too American" when they're with their parents, and "too ethnic" when they're with their school friends. They talk about the two halves of themselves, as represented by the split wardrobes in their closets.

- Cheryl Leppert, writer, adoptive mom to daughters from India

I Am Who I Am

By Christopher Brownlee

As an adoptee, I spent a long time struggling to fit in. I was American, but not really American. I was Asian, but not really Asian. Or so they said. I was getting told what I was not more than what I was. What a horrible way to try to formulate my identity; to scavenge for scraps of my personality based on what I couldn't be, rather than what I could be. Not a healthy way to grow up.

So I adapted. I learned a lot about American culture and took what I liked and discarded the rest of the dross. I learned a lot about 'Asian culture' and took what I liked, and discarded the rest. I became very adept at 'walking between two worlds'. Adoptees all experience a strong sense of duality, of coming from two cultures, but belonging to neither. I believe that wrestling with this duality is a crucial turning point in most adoptees' lives.

Anyway, I got really adept at being American when it served me, and I was able to utilize my 'Asian-ness' when it suited me. So, slowly, I became comfortable living in both worlds. I knew enough trappings and nuances of my birth culture to get by to an extent, and I knew enough about mainstream (White) culture to get by to an extent. I was comfortable enough in myself to shake off the 'Whitewashed' and 'Twinkie' (yellow on the outside and white on the inside). Unfortunately for me, the better at it I got, the faker I felt. I didn't like putting on a face, or a show, and it really bothered me that I was in a way 'faking the funk'. I wasn't being truthful to others, and more importantly, I wasn't being truthful to myself. I got sick and tired of feeling like I had to justify or validate myself to every questioning White and to every questioning Asian who had the audacity to question my legitimacy in society.

The fundamental issue I had with all of this, after a while, is that I found myself falling victim to the Model Minority myth, which sadly many first and second generation Asians buy-off on. By trying to assimilate into the norm of what was generally and superficially accepted as 'Asian' (even within my own Vietnamese-American community), I was accepting uninformed mainstream views of what it meant to 'be Asian', and I was basing my identity development against that view.

The bottom line was that my white adoptive parents taught me better than that, and I refused to accept becoming a stereotype in my own quest for self/acceptance.

Who am I: am I American, or am I Asian-American? Can an adoptee really assimilate into either culture and still be true to one's own adoptee identity? I don't think so. The more I looked at it, the more I realized that it's not ME that needs changing. I thought "There's nothing wrong with me, so why am I turning into a neurotic wreck trying to mold myself into the image of what others perceive I should be?" Which is the ultimate irony, because 'American' has no singular definition, and neither does 'Asian-American'.

It's a false dichotomy. We build categories and definitions around every culture, every ethnic group, every socio-economic substructure and culture, and God help you if you don't fit into one of them. This is what adoptees deal with every day. Based on the color of my skin, I am lumped into a box with every one else that 'looks like me', and a ton of cultural expectations are automatically heaped upon me from within and without. Based on the color of my skin, I am shoved out of other boxes which I have a claim to as an American. It kills me that I have been (and other transracial adoptees still are) twisting around in the wind still trying to fit into boxes that others have created for them.

I believe that it's not adoptees that need to change; it's the definitions that others are trying to force us into that need to change. Transracially adopted people, by the very nature of who we are, have the inherent ability to challenge the stereotypes that others heap on us and to really effect some social change through broadening the boundaries of diversity. Simply because we don't fit into everyone else's boxes.

I am who I am.

Adopted children and adults are in an incredibly powerful position to educate and to effect change in society. Adoptive parents need to know that adopted children, by virtue of their heritage and collective history, have the power to change the perception of what it means to be Asian/(insert your child's ethnicity here), to change the perspective of what it means to be adopted, to be a family, to be American (or insert your nationality here).

I think that that a transracially adopted child's 'culture', and that of the adoptive parents/family 'culture' is what you make of it. Adoptees and adoptive parents have the power (and to put it strongly in my opinion, the responsibility) to influence typical societal norms, both mainstream, and within the communities of your country.

Me? What do I do to promote a deeper understanding of transracial adoption? I keep my name. No, not my Vietnamese name, Tran Quoc Tuan (I've already 'reclaimed' it within myself and that's what is ultimately important to me), but my adoptive name. If I went back to my Vietnamese name I feel that I would be letting a lot of people off the hook. The name fits the face, the stereotypes live on, and half the battle is lost because people will remain comfortable in their unspoken conclusions. Conversely, by keeping Christopher Carroll Brownlee, nobody can ignore the Eastern face and the Western name.

There is more. How I was named by my adoptive parents followed their family tradition. Hence my middle name of Carroll, which is my father's first name. My father's middle name is my grandfather's first name. My younger brother (who is also adopted) received my grandfather's middle name as his middle name. That is the tradition that I was raised in, and even though it does not allow for my Vietnamese name, is still a valid and important part of my history as a member of the Brownlee family, of which I am proud to be a part. I feel that for me to change my name back to what it was before, would in a way devalue the importance I put on my adoptive family experience; I was named what I am now for reasons that were considered; my name was not an attempt to eradicate my Vietnamese identity and 'assimilate' me into mainstream America.

My adoptive name for me is the summation of my experiences, and because I have a Western name, it hints at a deeper story and experience. I believe all adoptees from our generation at some point in their life have dealt with the "you don't look like a Johnson," or the "where are you really from" comments, which stem from us being outside of the typical categories that mainstream society tries to put us in. Our Western names and our Eastern faces are an obvious collision of the status quo, and this collision was a defining point in how I chose to identify myself as Vietnamese, as Asian, as an American, as me.

~ *Christopher Brownlee*
adult adoptee,
co-founder, Vietnamese Adoptee Network

Choosing a Mask
Making family our priority

Children choose the mask (group) that allows them to either hide or stand out, and to fill a void they have within their lives. The mask the child chooses, at least in our community, does not fall along racial boundaries, or even economic, as we are on the same socio-economic playing field with an incredibly broad racial diversity. Rather, it seems to me that the kids fall into various groups according to the voids the children feel they have in their lives. I say "feel" because teens really act primarily on feelings, and often cannot look inward or rationalize their choices. These feelings sometimes do not reflect the realities in their lives, but more often than not they do point to that void.

My daughter and I talked a lot about kids that do not require "masks" and about the type of kids she knew who were totally comfortable in their own skin, and what qualities made them so. Each one of the children that she felt were comfortable with themselves were children with enormous amounts of parental involvement ; not suffocation, just real interest and caring.

Our society has so relegated parental responsibility to peers and schools that there are many lost children out there floundering for some leadership. In our family - the kids always come first and all our decisions are always made as to what is in their best interest. Hopefully in the end, they will be well-adjusted adults, which I believe should be the goal of all parents.

~ *By Jennifer Dawson*
adoptee , advocate and adoptive mom

Jumbotha
the Family 'Stew'

My girls understand that family means being there for one another, in good times or bad. And we have found a way to meld our Italian/Scots-Irish heritage and our Chinese family into one big Jumbotha stew.

This past summer, I took my girls back to China. We spent a week in their birth city, visiting the orphanage and their foster family, and then went to Beijing and Guangzhou. It was a very special trip, wrought with all kinds of emotions, some expected and some unexpected. It was also filled with 'duties'. I was fulfilling responsibilities as the leader of our parents group. I also had my responsibility as the mother of two wonderful girls, and as the 'head' of our family in China. We have a deep connection with my daughter's foster family in China, and that foster family views me as the matriarch; YiMah and ShouShou are very much a part of our lives. I have paid for their son to go to school. They mourned and burned the traditional paper money when my Father passed away. Although we are separated by an ocean and a language, we are a family who loves and worries about each other.

When we returned from China this summer, we traveled to Pennsylvania for our orphanage group reunion. One of the keynote speakers was a young woman, adopted as a baby from Thailand by a Caucasian, single woman of Jewish faith. The girl spoke of how she envied our children, for when she was growing up, there were no Families with Children from Thailand support groups, there were no orphanage groups, or reunions, or travelmates. Our children, she said, had a benefit of having each other in a way that previous international adoptees did not.

But she also told us that while we might try to bring as much 'China' into our homes as we could, that we had to stop beating ourselves up for not being Chinese. She said we needed to do what we could to introduce our children to Chinese culture, and give them an appreciation of their heritage, but that it was equally important to give them a rich understanding of who we were and how we appreciated where our own heritage comes from. We need to teach our children about our family traditions and celebrations. We need to give our children a history that is rich in our family myths and recipes, stories and memories. Our children are not simply children of China, but children of America. Yes, visit the Great Wall, but also the Grand Canyon. If we give our children the world, literally, they will have a perspective beyond our current hopes and dreams. These connections, our family stew, warms my heart.

~Bonnie Ward is an adoptive mom to two daughters from Changde, China

Return to the Unknown

By Analee Matthews

I am sitting in seat 56C on flight TG992, on my way to Vietnam. The country where I was born. A country I know nothing about. I can't believe I'm finally returning for the first time since I left at ten months of age, and will experience the culture, see the country and visit the orphanage where I first began. I feel like I could sleep for a decade. Understandably, of course, considering it's taken me almost thirty years to board this plane. Here I sit, finally feeling that I can allow my eyelids to relax. It sounds odd, I know, but for some thirty years I've felt the need to keep my eyes propped wide open. After all, I couldn't have anyone assuming I'm Asian, could I? That would never sit comfortably with me. Well, until now that is...

Looking around at the Asian flight attendants, I finally begin to gain a sense of pride in having similar features. Well, maybe not 'pride' at this point in time, perhaps it's more accurate to say 'less shame'. I've always harbored a sense of embarrassment about looking Asian. Being raised in a rural town, I grew up with a sense of isolation and a constant niggling of loneliness. I didn't have any other Asian faces around me. I never had anyone around who I looked like or that I could relate to, and I never had the opportunity to develop a sense of pride in looking the way I do. When we moved to Melbourne, in time for me to attend secondary school, I was fortunate enough to attend a private school where there were many Asian faces. Although none of them were adopted and I wasn't actually introduced to any Asian cultures, it did make me feel less isolated having similar-looking people around me. Still, it wasn't enough motivation for me to lay claim to my birth origins and I still lived in denial that I was actually Asian. If anyone ever asked where I was from my standard response would always be "I was born in Vietnam, but I'm adopted". I felt compelled to add "but I'm adopted", because to me, that translated into "So, I'm not really Vietnamese".

But here I am. The sense of ownership I am developing for my birth country is like nothing I've ever experienced. I really do feel like I can be Asian and not have to explain my adoption or make excuses for not knowing anything about the country or the culture... after all, that's exactly why I'm here: to learn, and hopefully come home with a real sense of pride, and a thorough

Photos by
Anh Đào Kolbe
on her first trip back to
Vietnam in 30 years.

understanding about the place where I was born.

I used to think that my own repulsion of Asians stemmed from primary school days, where the other children teased me for being the only Asian-looking child on the playground. I used to think that it was their taunting that caused me to feel that being Asian was bad; that being Asian meant being a lesser person. And maybe in part it was, but I think it's more likely that my fear of embracing an Asian birth culture was what really caused my racist feelings. It is not uncommon for inter-country adoptees to experience a conflict between their extrinsic and intrinsic sense of self. For me, I grew up in a beachside town, feeling like a blonde haired, white surfie chick. As it's human nature for people to judge and treat others based on how they look, you can imagine how frustrating and confusing it can be when you look one way but feel a completely different way. Being adopted from one culture into another is like having registration plates on your car that are from another state...borrowed plates you can't give back. Being adopted from a different country is similar to living with someone else's registration plates.

I want to cry. I'm sitting on this plane and I feel like at any moment I could burst into tears. I have no idea what to expect when I get off the plane but I do know one thing: I feel sad. It's a sadness that stems from a sense of not knowing; a loss of identity. How can I visit this country and not look at these people and wonder--are you my biological family? I can't help but look at the Vietnamese people on this plane and ponder-- are you my brother? My sister? My uncle? My cousin? Are you my mother? And if you are my mother, why did you give me up? Why did you leave me all those years ago when I needed you most? I was just a baby. Have you missed me? Thought about me? Have you ever wanted me back?

I hope that this journey will provide me with a sense of peace from knowing and learning about the place I was born and the culture I have missed out on growing up with. The goals I have for this trip are:

- To gain an understanding and appreciation of my birth country and culture.
- To be proud of my origins.
- To visit the orphanage where I spent the first ten months of my life.
- To want to return again.

And here we go. The plane hits the runway and my tears fall like rain. I am in my birth country. This is the actual country that I was born in. For some reason all I want to do is cry. I can't understand why I am so overwhelmed at being here, but I am. And I am really here. I can barely believe it.

Tuesday
Here I am, in Hanoi, lying underneath a silk sheet listening to the noises of Vietnam. It's only 6:50am so I'm surprised when the phone rings. It's Tom, my friend who has been organizing his side of this trip for the past twelve months. He volunteered to be my pillar of strength over here. Being adopted himself, he is all too aware of the necessity of unconditional support

during what is bound to be an emotional journey. I am happy to hear from him. He is due to arrive here in Hanoi in just four days and I can't wait. I don't want to be alone in this country. It feels strange. Foreign. Almost scary.

Before he can speak, I answer the phone with "I can't wait for you to get here!"

There is silence at the other end of the line, and then he speaks. He tells me there has been a hiccup to our plans. The 'hiccup' turns out to be that his wife thinks the trip is selfish. They were apparently up all night talking about it and the bottom line is that he is no longer coming over. The rest of Tuesday is spent crying. I phone my travel agent and shuffle things around so that I can leave Vietnam early. I don't want to be here on my own. I don't even want to be here at all now. How could he do this? How could he abandon me like that? On this trip, of all occasions, how could he abandon me?

People who are adopted tend to carry around an ingrained fear of abandonment, which stems from being abandoned at birth. There's something in my psyche, and in the subconscious of many other adoptees, that says, 'I must have been a bad person for my mum to not want me/discard me/abandon me/leave me'. Now obviously there are no such things as 'bad' babies, but many adoptees feel that because their parent(s) abandoned them at birth, they must be unworthy of truly being cared for. And often, we carry that into our adult lives.

Wednesday

Well, today came with more inspiration in the shape of one Marco from Holland. He is traveling on his own too, and he reminded me that I'm supposed to be soaking it all up, seeing the sights and getting out and amongst it. Sadly though, all I'm doing is spending my currency in internet cafes, and racking up the biggest phone bill in the history of telecommunications by phoning home in a poor attempt to avoid feeling like I'm alone. I'm also in SMS contact with Ed–we have a special rapport and I hope it will grow into a long-lasting relationship when I get home. Then it dawns on me–Ed is my support, simply because he wants to listen and support my sadness without presuming to know it. I now see that this journey has to be about attitude. Take the right attitude and it changes experiences. Yet it's hard to journey on....

I didn't want to feel alone during this trip. And that's all I feel. Not only abandoned by Tom, but so lonely. And that is precisely why I didn't want to undertake this trip on my own. To face what I'm here to face is challenging enough without the added dimension of feeling isolated and ostracized. My strongest emotion right now, is to go home. Not once so far have I had that feeling of 'I am so glad to be here'. Not once. And that's worrying me. It's a battle to not grab a flight and just head home.

I feel like all the positive things I used to pride myself at being, have gone. I feel so stripped of my courage, my inner strength, and my intuition. I feel completely bare and foreign to my own self. I don't know this person who lies here bawling uncontrollably. How did this person emerge? Where did she come from? Will she ever leave and let the old Analee shine through? Maybe part of this excruciating anxiety is the realization that if I don't fit in here, where I was born, then I really don't fit in anywhere. This pain is so intense and I can't even figure out why or where it's come from, let alone how to combat it. Obviously the universe thinks I need this push to better myself and get the most from this journey, and I will trust in that higher power. I just hope it gets easier. This is so incredibly painful that I can't even describe it accurately. It really does feel like the loneliest thing I've ever done. I know I have to not fight these emotions in order to deal with them and for that reason alone, being here with no one else is probably the best thing.

Saturday

I finally got it! That 'I'm so glad to be here' feeling! I am so happy! As I watched the countryside roll past last night on the train journey from Hanoi to Ho Chi Minh City (36 hours!), I began to fall in love with it's beauty. Today I feel excited and calm all at the same time. I feel safe here and relaxed. The train was definitely a great decision. The scenery is so picturesque; I absolutely love it, and am so proud to have come from this countryside.

Friday

Happy Birthday (my 30th) to me!
Today I am returning to the orphanage where I spent the first ten months of my life. From the research I conducted prior to leaving Australia, I know that the orphanage still exists and that the nun who signed my adoption paperwork is still alive. I just don't know exactly where it is or where she is. But I have the name of the orphanage and a district where it should be.

So 9.30am strikes and 'uncle' has arrived, ready to act as my chauffeur and interpreter. He's the uncle of the lady who manages my hotel. I hopped aboard uncle's motorbike; it took a few times to start and visions of

Returning: The Journey of the Soul

Returning to the country of birth is a journey, at once real, spiritual and emotional

To return is both a journey from home to the homeland and a rite of passage in the life of the family. It's a pilgrimage, to thank the people and the country for your mutual child. It is emotional balm and healing for a child who grapples with loss. And it's a travel trip, to drink in the culture of your child's birth.

Being there with your child and the smells and the food and the sheer immense difference of it is 'the journey real'. Walking with your child in the streets where perhaps their birthparents walked, looking round a corner for a fleeting glimpse of face that looks like your child is headily emotive and deeply spiritual. Watching your child grasp hold of history and roots is real and emotional, and stitches the family together. This latter links your child's first community of care.... with you.

Every language has words for all these journeys. This in itself is headily powerful in its welcome. The people will understand why we return:
a pilgrimage, the journey of the soul.

~ By Sheena Macrae

being stranded in the middle of nowhere ran through my head. Third time lucky and we were off. Into the traffic we merged, abiding by Vietnam's stringent road rules:

- The largest vehicle has the right of way.
- There is no requirement to stay on any one side of the road.
- You may load any number of people, livestock, or products onto your bike.

So we merge into the organized chaos and off we go. I am filled with excitement, anxiety and anticipation. Here I am, placing my entire experience in the hands of a man who drives a scooter very well, but whose name I don't even know and who speaks very limited English. I decided it best if I leave the navigation up to uncle. We traveled terrain of all sorts. Bumping up and down over bitumen, sealed, unsealed, rain puddles–we ventured over and through it all. *And then we arrived.*

The giant sign on the security gates that read 'Tam Binh' confirmed that we were in the right place. Those were the words contained on my adoption paperwork. With a sense of deja vu I handed over my paperwork to this security guard. He looked solemnly at me and said 'You wait here.' I'd taken 30 years to get here, what was a few more minutes? I wasn't going anywhere. After what seemed like a decade he came back to us. He unlocked the gate and invited us in. Oh my God–this was it. We were going in!

One of the young employees, Minh (I found out he had been in the orphanage with me), made a phone call. He called Sister Tan, the nun whose name was plastered all over my adoption paperwork. She had been the one to confirm and process my adoption. She was the director of the Sweetwater Orphanage (name changed after 1975) and the closest thing to a biological mother that I'd ever had! My heart was pounding. I was really going to meet this woman. I felt excited and nervous. Why was it taking so long?

Minh came back to us and said he would take us to Sister Tan. We were then informed that this meant another ride with uncle. Sister Tan was at another nearby location. So I hopped behind uncle again and Minh led us out the gates and down the dusty road. We pulled up to a similar security gate with the same 'Tam Binh' writing on it as the one we'd just left behind. This must be Sister Tan's home. Uncle gestured to me to dismount and said the only two words of English that I didn't have to ask him to repeat. He said, 'your mummy'. He was telling me that I was about to meet the first woman that I ever knew as my mother.

We walked into a typical Vietnamese building. Open plan, old décor and a lot of con-crete. A religious sister, whose name was Hai, greeted me with a giant beaming grin. She grabbed my arm, said 'hello' and asked me my name. I said 'Analee' and she shouted 'It is Analee' to a moving shape in the background. That moving shape was none other than Sister Tan. At 81 years old, Sister Tan still lives and breathes childcare. She was so fragile looking but had a definite resilience about her. She, too, greeted me with a giant smile and warm hug. As the Sisters looked through my paperwork, Sister Hai let out a scream of delight. 'It's your birthday!' she exclaimed. I answered 'yes' and beamed at her with appreciation for noticing that, based on my fictitious birth certificate, I was 30 years old today.

Sister Hai confirmed that my orphanage still existed and she placed a phone call seeking permission for us to visit. Could this day get any better? After a short while, the phone rang. Permission had been granted. A car came by to collect the Sisters and me. It took us some ten minutes to travel what seemed only a few meters around the block, until we pulled up at another set of security gates. This was the very place where I began my life.

The buildings are dull and concrete dominates the landscape. Everyone knows the Sisters and they are met with smiles and constant head nodding. I have the sense of being in the presence of royalty. I guess in childcare circles, I am. We walk up a driveway. Sister Tan uses me for support, holding my arm at all times.

After a few short steps we were all stopped by a vibrant, energetic young girl whose smile was infectious. As she climbed a few stairs to greet us, I found myself doing a double take in her direction. My heart sank; she was a victim of the atrocious Agent Orange herbicide. Her name was Tham and she looked like she was only ten years old. Tham was a resident at the orphanage, having been abandoned at birth like me. Unlike me however, Tham's biological father was one of the Vietnamese soldiers exposed to the Agent Orange herbicide spray during wartime. The effects of the chemical spray have been seen more than ten years after the event. Not only do the veterans themselves suffer physical consequences, such as blindness, but their children and even their grandchildren have been known to be affected. And Tham was affected; but as the day progressed I saw how much she put into her life here.

Sister Hai led me around the grounds of my orphanage. It was old and sterile. But then the sound of crying babies grew louder and louder. Panic rose within me as realization hit. Oh God, this was where they kept the babies. I wasn't prepared for what I saw. We slipped our shoes off at the entrance to the building and walked through the doors. I couldn't believe the sight. A room full, wall to wall, with stainless steel baby cots. And inside every cot was at least one baby less than twelve months old. This is what had happened to me. This is where I had been. This was my existence once before. I, too, had been the same as all these poor, helpless, abandoned babies. Only I was luckier than this lot. I promptly burst into tears.

My tears fall at a rapid rate. I can't stop them. What am I I doing here? I wasn't quite expecting to feel so overwhelmed with empathy and sadness for these children. I draw deep breaths and compose myself and really look around.

There were ladies everywhere. Ladies to care for these babies and give them love and affection. Sister Tan and Sister Hai had wandered off to pick up and cuddle any distressed or crying infants. The other ladies in the room were doing the same and before long, the sound of crying had stopped. All that was left was the joyful tone of a giggling child. We left that ward and walked over to another.

> *I feel completely spaced out. Vacuous. Numb.*
>
> *I thought I would next see older children but I am wrong.*
>
> *How many orphaned babies can there be?*

I feel completely spaced out. Vacuous. Numb. I thought I would next see older children but I am wrong. How many orphaned babies can there be?

There were more of the same–more babies–and my heart felt heavier. I wondered if these children were destined for families or whether they would simply spend the rest of their lives in this place. I was later advised it was most likely to be the latter. We moved across to another ward. More babies. Only these babies, I was told, all suffered from some type of hepatitis. The first infant I saw was dressed in a tiny yellow singlet. He stared blankly at me. I smiled and began to cry again. Staring back at me was an almost exact replica of my own baby picture. His blank gaze slowly turned into a tearful cry. A heartfelt wail escaped from him and my heart snapped in two. I knelt down to comfort him by placing my warm hand firmly on his little back and I squeezed him gently. His crying stopped, and with it came my own realization that these babies need love and physical affection to survive. That's what these ladies knew and therefore provided. The children may grow up in this facility, but at least they would grow up with love around them. It was a small, but significant consolation.

I know right then and there that I want to give some of my time and love to the orphans in Australia when I got back. It is my destiny to help support these abandoned children as I was once helped.

When we arrived back to the security gates, Uncle was there, ready and waiting for me. I gave Sister Hai a hug and thanked her for her time and love. She called me her daughter for the hundredth time that day; She insisted I come back and spend a whole day with her and Sister Tan.

I agree and tell her my next visit will be with my parents.

My visit had been perfect. This milestone birthday was unequivocally one of the greatest in the history of birthdays. And this trip was one of the most amazing, most rewarding and most memorable journeys I could ever hope to experience. My goals were all achieved; I did learn about and truly experience my birth country and culture; I will definitely leave with a sense of pride at being Vietnamese; and I absolutely have a yearning to return with my folks and the man whom I hope will become increasingly special to me.

And as a bonus, I am returning home with a sense of inner peace that I have never felt before; nor did I expect to ever feel. Despite the trauma and the emotional roller coaster, I know that everything happened as it was meant to happen. I now understand that this journey really was something I had to do on my own.

Analee Matthews, BA, DIp, was adopted from Vietnam to an Australian family at the age of 10 months. She has no factual information about her biological family or early beginnings. Analee volunteers much of her spare time to present at forums and workshops held across Australia, where she presents information to those involved in intercountry adoption, including prospective parents, social workers, and fellow adoptees. She is a contributor to Australia's first book exploring intercountry adoption, The Colour of Difference, and is the NSW representative and Editor for the Intercountry Adoptee Support Network (www.icasn.org).

My Mother's Daughter
The Definition of Kinship
By Mary Hart

I was adopted in 1955. It was a different world altogether. Birthmother, adoptee, adoption triad–none of this was part of the vocabulary of my growing up. Although adoption was not often a topic of discussion in our family, I was aware of my adoption from a very early age. Indeed I have no memory of any time when I did not know that our family was formed by adoption.

While I was aware that we were different, I had no sense of being 'second best' or 'less than' a biological family. This simply never entered my mind. I confess to having no interest whatsoever in searching for my birthmother or knowing of her. The sole exception to this was my occasional awareness as a child that out there somewhere was a person with a claim to me, a thought I found frightening.

The family I was raised in defined kinship in broader terms than were considered the norm of the 1950s and 1960s. In addition to relatives in the conventional sense, my mother and father drew those bonded by spirit and deep friendship close to us. This formed the circle of kinship in which I grew. As an adult adoptee, there is a comforting analogy between this family of kinship and the family formed by adoption. My family bonds were formed not of blood but of kin, and not with titles but in the way my mother and father lived their lives.

I discovered fairly early on in life that once the 'adoption' piece of my life was out of the bag people moved quite quickly to intrusive questioning. "Have you looked for your real mother?" "Aren't you curious?" or my personal favorite: "Now that your adoptive mother is dead, will you look for your real mother?" (After my mother's death in 1997, I took to answering the first of these questions with, "I have buried my mother". I found that this ended this line of questioning quite nicely).

I have also learned to be careful about sharing my views on my own adoption, and my feelings about birthparents, even within the adoption community. On more than one occasion it has been suggested to me that my feelings about my adoption and my family are build on a structure formed of denial. That if I was open to my 'true' feelings I would find that I was denying my connection to and need for a connection with my birthmother. In conversation with another adult adoptee I expressed my view that my birthmother's decision to place me for adoption was an act of great love. The response was a very curt, "You didn't really buy that line, did you?"

I can't tell you how much I hated these questions and the commentary on denial that have come my way. The level of intrusion is appalling to me. Mostly I hate the assumptions underlying all these questions–adoptees are all the same, they all have the same feeling about search and reunion and where the adoption part of their lives fits with all the rest.

We live our lives within a dominant culture that is often in conflict with us as families. Which is why I so relish the "I have buried my mother" comment. I throw down the gauntlet. Waiting for it to be picked up. The dominant culture is so very very sure that they have the patent on this thing called family. And are quite taken aback, affronted when someone has the unmitigated gall to thumb nose.

All children need to know who is theirs. To whom do we belong and who belongs to us? I belonged to my mother and she was mine. I was claimed and claimed her in return. We moved beyond biology to family. It is said that the biological link allows one to look at child, parent, grandparent and back through time and through this understand the link of family and history. I, not born to my mother, was so much like her that we were forever hearing comments like, "You are your mother's daughter". And I am. I see my mother in our oldest daughter. The link is not biology–it is a link of family.

Becoming a transracial adoptive family redefines us. Ours is a melding of old lives (whatever they were) and new.   Regardless of what prior expectations we may have had, we now find we must reach out.   Look and keep looking until we find the people and ways that can fit the new present and future that belongs to this new family.

Adoption support groups draw the community of adoptive families together. We grow familiarity and sometimes friendships, exchange resources, ideas. We meet up at events, celebrate festivals, all of which are cause for celebration. But I think we need more. Our families need to stretch the boundaries by which we define family. I am convinced that in so doing we go some way in providing our children with scaffolding to take them over the top of the collisions they will inevitably have with the dominant culture.

Certainly I had none of this in mind in the summer of 2001 as I sat cradling my daughter in my arms. But I did pick up the telephone and invite five families to lunch.   Five years later I cannot help but think that those were among the most important telephone calls I would make.

In the absence of my parents and with few relatives on my husbands side we have created a different family. Grandparents that are grandparents in every sense but blood. These wonderful people are neighbors who entered our lives by serendipity and stand clearly and firmly in the Grandparent place. They are ours and we are theirs. Bui, who came into our lives and announced she was the honorary Vietnamese grandmother and was to be listened to and heeded on all matters. She is ours and we are hers.

We have met families because our children were born in the same country. Some of these relationships grow to hold particular significance - not 'just' the children - but the adults also. Not just friends. Family.   Several of our children have known each other from babyhood. They have grown together and know the comfort that comes of this closeness. Our circle widens from time to time and there is no closing time for admission.

The joy in all of this comes because it is both remarkable and so ordinary. The melding of our lives is not something we 'do' for our children–it is who we are now. For me a sight most clearly bespeaking this is the two Grandmothers at my kitchen sink fighting over who will do the dishes. Grandmother Bui says, "Listen old woman, I am going to do the dishes". Grandmother Mary Anne says, "Move over old woman, I was here first". Large irreverent personalities come together over my kitchen sink. Children from all parts of our lives whirl and run and laugh loudly through the house as food is dished up, eaten and cleaned up. So the grandmothers can fight over who has the sink honors.There is no better place to be.

With our two daughters, I travelled to Boston in April 2005 to attend the VAN conference. The experience was extraordinary for me. Of all I saw and heard, what most stays with me is the sight of the adult adoptees gathered together in the hallway between sessions, cross legged on the floor, talking, laughing. In the air, I felt a sense of pure comfort.

I see that our children share a palpable bond. This past winter seven families holidayed together. We were a group of families some with transracially adopted children and others not formed by adoption. And we were more than a group of families. Friends and kin. Beach time and family time. Parents do what parents do–swim and watch children swim and talk and drink rum. The children ran like a tribe. They have long histories together and our family lives are woven together like a tapestry. The important part for me is that this is not special, not some adjunct to our main life, it is our lives. Of course we are together–how else could it be?   Entering our midst on this holiday, one child, almost six, said to her mother "These are my people!" Which is exactly right.

We are all different. My views on adoption have changed much over the years and mellowed considerably. This is a life journey. My journey has led me to define family in an increasingly broad and inclusive way. By moving past the construct imposed by biology, I found a place in which family is defined by kinship and my life has been immeasurably enriched. My heart is larger than it has ever been. There is plenty of room to leave my own daughter a broad map on which to begin to trace her own journey. My daughter's journey will be different from mine for many reasons. She is very much her own person in personality and temperament. Daily, in taking on the world, she will trace her path through constructs of family and race. To define in her terms, her own words and her own time what it means to be a child of our family, a Canadian child and a child of Viet Nam. Look out world.

I have come to the point where my heart is full–my place in family unshakable, despite early fears that my birthmother would claim me back. The gift of my family was belonging. I was claimed through acts of love and in turn claimed my family as my own. I have claimed both my children. I believe I see in my daughter's eyes her claiming of me. She is my child. Her journey has just begun. She will grow and make choices of her own. She will search or not. There will be many others who lay claim to her dear heart. There is room.

~ Mary Hart, her mother's daughter- and her daughters' mother,
through birth and adoption

Dear Mum

I wish you...

- hadn't changed my name–it was the only tangible thing my birthmother could give me.

- hadn't said I was special and chosen because it just made me feel even more different.

- hadn't smiled smugly when people said I looked like you–your private joke made me remember I wasn't really yours.

- hadn't overfed me gallons of milk to comfort me. I cried not because I was hungry but because I missed my mother. I still do, but the comfort-eating you taught me goes on. So now I'm fat as well as having adoption related issues.

- had realized that the small 10 day old baby you took home to make you happy was one day going to turn into a real life person who would want to know all about her roots.

- hadn't scared me off my search with all the 'facts' you had. Turns out they weren't facts but your paranoid suspicions.

- had told me what you knew, how close I really was to my genetic family. Instead you explained that you wouldn't tell me lies but I would have to ask the right questions. Why make me play such a frustratingly cruel game–where did your loyalties lie?

- had the insight to realize that when you said you would support me in looking for my birthmother you actually meant that you would do everything to protect yourself.

- hadn't told me I would do so much harm by contacting my birthmother and that I'd hurt so many people, disrupt their lives. I was a secret, no one knew. So I buried my needs and yearnings for her until it was too late–she was gone. And guess what–they all knew about me, I wasn't a shameful secret.

- understood that the hurt you encouraged me to avoid for everyone else's sake was the hurt you feared you would feel. Your hurt was imaginary, borne out of your insecurities and fears and you avoided it–well done! My hurt is real. I wish you could feel, just for a day, the hurt I have to live with now, knowing it's too late, that I can't meet her, or talk to her or say the things I need to say and hear the things she needed to say. I'll always be your daughter and I love you but I was hers first and we needed to be reunited and have a chance at healing each other.

~Elizabeth, adult adoptee whose birthmother
committed suicide before they could reunite.

The One Thing I Wish
Adult adoptees tell us what they wish we would give our kids.

❝One piece of advice is hard! I'd suggest adoptive parents should give their kids permission to feel sorrow and sadness surrounding their beginnings, and help them develop a real connection to their birth country and culture and pride in the culture to which they were born into.❞

Analee Matthews, adoptee,
Vietnamese by birth and re-finding,
Australian by belonging

❝No matter what the adoptee says, make your home a place where their voice is heard. Listen more than talk, they're the adoptee. ❞

Riam
Adoptee, ddoptive mother

❝If I had just one thing to say, it would be that we live, talk, work, sing, and dance with the certain knowledge that we are family. That this knowledge (not belief) is so ingrained that the rest of that wrongheaded crazy world can just go on thinking whatever they want about the biology trump card—we know it ain't true. My family-centered mother gave me this gift. Adoption was how our family came to be. For that we cheer. But nowhere in my upbringing did I ever have to feel that this fact defined my existence. I still get mad, sometimes very angry, at the efforts made to define us throughout our lives by the fact of adoption. This view is born purely of ignorance—and I continue to take that gift of my mother's and use it both as shield and sword. ❞

Mary,
Adoptee, adoptive mother

❝I believe that with adopted children is it is not the outside features which are the ones most significant. It is the 'stuff' inside. What sets us apart–the mixed genetic pool of countless generations of personality, thoughts, moods, sense of humour, intelligence, and potential of diversity that makes all humans different–is what makes us so alike. Genetics just isn't over one generation. The success of adoption is not that the child does not look like you but rather within the 'culture' of your 'family' you can find enough in common when the 'baby stuff' is over that you can laugh with them, talk with them, delight with them and realize their journey in their adoption will be different, just as your own journey was different to your own parents. ❞

Jane, adoptee

❝The best thing for adoptive parents on how to raise adoptive kids can be summed in this: Love and communicate with your child. Your child is unique. No studies, no experts, and no older adoptees know your child as well as what you and your child come to learn together. Each child is unique, and each family is unique. Don't pressure them into being something they're not; listen to them when they don't want to be something you think they should be. Let them be uniquely who they are–after all, that is why you adopted them in the first place! And above all, there is not perfection, just what is perfect. Enjoy the journey, share your love, and always cherish the relationship you have! ❞

Bert Ballard, born Vu Tien DoII.
Vietnamese Adoptee. An Lac Orphanage,
Saigon, Vietnam, April 1975

"It is no coincidence that you are the parent of this child! You, more than anyone–therapists, teachers, friends–have been given an intuition to know his/her heart. Go forward with confidence, even when the waters are rough, which they eventually will be for the majority of parents, adoptive or biological. Even though it may not seem like it during the rough times, keep your eyes on the day when your child will someday thank you for not abandoning him/her when she was unlovable."

Sherrie Eldridge, adoptee, adoptive grandmother Author of "Twenty Things Adopted Kids Wish Their Adoptive Parents Knew" and "Twenty Life-Transforming Choices Adoptees Need to Make"

"Don't expect your child to have the same approach to life and social (political, religious, other) values that you have, even though you have brought them up. We are all individuals, whether adopted or not, and the greatest gift you can give your child is independence and support in becoming the person they are going to be, whether that is the person you want them to be or not."

Adoptee

"Adoption is not for the fainthearted. The feelings take your breath away when you least expect it. And they never go away—just get recycled. So my one piece of advice? Don't forget to laugh. A good sense of humor is essential for this journey."

Beth O'Malley 'older' adoptive Mom, adoptee, professional in the field

"Having told your child that they are adopted, don't then discourage them from asking questions at any stage later in life."

Penny Jack, adoptee

"Just love your adopted child and treat them as you would had they been born to you, remembering to tell them they were adopted when they are very young and confirming this and your love regularly. Mistakes are not unhealthy, all parents make them, as do all humans. My adopted parents did all of the above, including the mistakes, and I love them to bits."

Richard Perkins, adoptee

"Don't react in the way mine did, when I used the word 'adoption' in a sentence, after decades of family taboo. I was trying to signal, in the gentlest way and without hurting your feelings, that I needed to know more about myself. I wish that you had not reacted by shouting and screaming abuse at me. That you had not chosen this moment to tell me that my father was dying of cancer. That I was ungrateful and disloyal, and had not so much as repaid the price of my first pair of shoes. That you had not been able to enjoy a single moment of having me; not even my graduation or wedding. That you would knock on every door, until you found my mother, and expose her as a slut. That you would disinherit me. That I had no feelings; only your feelings mattered. That you had rather I had died in the gutter, than you had to face this moment."

Elizabeth, adoptee

"Remember that your blessings and joy is built on someone else's tragedy, including that of your child. Only by acknowledging the losses and grief involved can you help your child heal the pain and make her feel that you respect all of her, including her past before she became your child. The focus in adoption is not and should never be that of you, your grief, your issues, or your path to the child, but instead your child's path to you. Until you have fully understood and accepted this, you simply are not ready to adopt! "

Sunny Jo
Adult adoptee

"Love is essential, but it is not enough on its own. You need to be fully aware and committed to adopting a culture and a country when you adopt your child from overseas. Offer the culture to them repeatedly so they can retain ties with where they come from and develop a healthy sense of esteem and pride in who they are and where they have come from. This may come in the form of dance classes, celebrating national cultural days, language classes, etc. Understand that at times your child may reject your opportunities to remain connected with their birth culture/country but you should continue to offer them. "

Adult adoptee

"I'm an adult adoptee, I'm 38 years old now but only found out last year that I was adopted at 19 months old. I wasn't told, I found out by accident. As soon as I found out, I wanted to trace my birth mother and any more family that I may have.

I was very lucky to find out and then search when I did. Only 6 months after first making contact, my youngest sister called to say mom was poorly and I should go to see her. Sadly she died shortly after I arrived. I only met her twice. Don't do what my adoptive parents did, and not tell your child about being adopted. My adoptive parents didn't tell me because they were afraid to lose me. I sometimes wonder if I should be angry with them. But they made a decision, and I have to live with the consequences. They haven't lost me, and were never going to. They should have told me, as I have always had my doubts, and surely I should have had the option to search for my birth family when it suited me. And when I was properly prepared. "

Simon Stearne, adoptee

"The one thing I would like adoptive parents to understand is that we are a family. Not an adoptive family, not a multi-racial family, just a family. We are not your 'adopted' children but rather, just simply your children. Love us with unconditional love and the rest all just sorts itself out over time. We need to justify our relationships to no-one. We just are. "

Jennifer Dawson
Adoptee, adoptive mother

I wish you would listen. And really hear.

Resources
Additional resources can be found at www.emkpress.com

Getting Started

Lifelong Issues in Adoption By Deborah N. Silverstein, LCSW, and Sharon Kaplan Roszia,MS

Orphans and Warriors: The Journey of the Adopted Heart By Dee Paddock, MA, MTS,NCC

The Resilient Self: How Survivors of Troubled Families Rise Above Adversity By Stevan J Wolin MD and Sybil Wolin PhD

Real Parents. Real Children By Holly van Gulden and Lisa M. Bartels-Rabb

Sleep

On Becoming Babywise By Gary Ezzo and Robert Bucknam

Solve Your Child's Sleep Problems By Richard Ferber

Attaching in Adoption Practical Tools for Today's Parents By Deborah Gray

The post-institutionalized child. Benevolent Society, February 2004. March 12, 2005. Karleen Gribble www.bensoc.asn.au/ parc_search/transracial_article_educate.html

Sleeping through the Night: How Infants, Toddlers, and their Parents Can Get a Good Night's Sleep.Jodi Mindell

The No-Cry Sleep Solution: Gentle Ways to Help Your Baby Sleep through the Night By Elizabeth Pantley

The Baby Book By Martha and William Sears

The Baby Sleep Book By Martha and William Sears, Robert Sears, James Sears

Claiming

Change Your Brain, Change Your Life. By Daniel Amen

First Steps in Parenting the Child Who Hurts. By Caroline Archer

Parenting with Love and Logic: Teaching Children Responsibility. By Foster Cline and Jim Fay

Transforming the Difficult Child: The Nurtured Heart Approach. By Howard Glasser and Jennifer Easley

Attaching in Adoption: Practical Tools for Today's Parents By Deborah Gray

The Child with Special Needs: Encouraging Intellectual and Emotional Growth. By Stanley I. Greenspan,Serena Wieder,Robin Simons

Building Healthy Minds: The Six Experiences that Create Intelligence and Emotional Growth in Babies and Young Children. By Stanley Greenspan

Toddler Adoption: The Weaver's Craft. By Mary Hopkins Best

Building the Bonds of Attachment. By Daniel Hughes, PhD

Language

1. General Information on Facilitating Speech and Language Development

Beyond Baby Talk: from Sounds to Sentences, a Parent's Complete Guide to Language Development By K Apel and J Masterson (Ordering information available at www.asha.org/public/beyond_baby_talk.htm)

www.asha.org/public/speech/development/ Parent-Stim-Activities.htm (Specific age-appropriate suggestions for encouraging language development in general–not specific to internationally adopted children)

www.hanen.org (parent training programs for family-focused early language intervention programs)

www.babysigns.com (books and videos on how to teach and use baby signs with your child before they are able to talk)

2. Websites for Speech and Language Development in Internationally Adopted Children

Language Development in Internationally Adopted Children Sharon Glennen

pages.towson.edu/sglennen/index.htm

Speech-Language Development in Children Adopted from China Karen Pollock

www.rehabmed.ualberta.ca/spa/phonology/ Chinadopt.html

3.How to find a Speech-Language Pathologist or Audiologist (searchable databases)

American Speech-Language Hearing Association
www.asha.org/proserv/

American Academy of Audiology
www.audiology.org/consumer/find/

Canadian Association of Speech-Language Pathologists and Audiologists
www.caslpa.ca/english/profession/find.asp

(UK) Association of Speech and Language Therapists in Independent Practice
www.helpwithtalking.com/search.asp

Speech Pathology Australia
www.speechpathologyaustralia.org.au/Content.aspx?p=115

4. Mitigating Language Losses

Speech and Language Disorders
www.nlm.nih.gov/medlineplus/speechandcommunicationdisorders.html

Information on developmental delay, developmental milestones and how to read these with regard to individual children and different needs see **www.zerotothree.org, www.howkidsdevelop.com** and **www.aap.org**.

Our Children in School: A new Challenge for Teachers and Parents By Boris Gindis
www.bgcenter.com/interview.htm

English Language Learning in Internationally Adopted Children: Communicative language and cognitive language By Boris Gindis
www.bgcenter.com/interview2.htm

5. Communication Gains

Attunement Daniel Hughes, PhD
www.danielahughes.homestead.com

Daniel J. Siegel, MD
www.parentinginsideout.com

Professional Interview–Daniel Siegel, MD, at Mental Help Net **mentalhelp.net/poc/view_doc.php/type/doc/id/818**

Attunement: Reading the Rhythms of a Child by Bruce Perry, MD, PhD
www.teacher.scholastic.com/professional/bruceperry/attunement.htm

Emotional Intelligence. By Daniel Goleman

Building Healthy Minds: The Six Experiences that Create Intelligence and Emotional Growth in Babies and Young Children.
By Stanley Greenspan

The Out of Sync Child & The Out of Sync Child has Fun. By Carol Stock Kranowicz
Lots of ideas for work on the senses and movement. The suggested activities are great and not expensive to set up.

University of Minnesota International Adoption Project–longitudinal study of language delay in children adopted from China–social skills a predictor of language success
education.umn.edu/icd/iap/Results4.25.htm

Brain Gym ®
www.braingym.org
Exercises for the brain carried out through positioning and movement

Food
Adoption Comeunity
www.comeunity.com/adoption/index.html

Baggage
1. Adult Attachment

Mothering Without a Map. By Catherine Black

Parenting from the Inside Out: How Deeper Self-Understanding Can Help You Raise Children Who Thrive. By Dan Siegel and Mary Hartzell

The Whole Parent: How to Become a Terrific Parent Even if You Didn't Have One.
By Debra Wesselmann

Books for Helping Parents With Their Issues
Homecoming: Reclaiming and Championing Your Inner Child. By John Bradshaw

2. Resilience
A quick and interesting resiliency test can be found at **www.resiliencycenter.com/resiliencyquiz.shtml** After you get a sense of how resilient you are you may want to pursue different resources for beefing up your resiliency.

These books provide a great starting point for enhancing an adult's resiliency:

The Resilient Self: How Survivors of Troubled Families Rise Above Adversity By Steven J. Wolin, MD and Sybil Wolin, PhD

The Resilience Factor: 7 Essential Skills for Overcoming Life's Inevitable Obstacles. By K. Reivich, & A. Shatte

Facilitating Developmental Attachment: The Road to Emotional Recovery and Behavioral Change in Foster and Adopted Children.

By D. Hughes, PhD

Becoming Attached: First Relationships and How They Shape Our Capacity to Love. By Robert Karen

Attaching to Your Newly Adopted Infant or Toddler. By Lynne Lyon, MSW
www.attach-china.org.

Discipline

Lifelong Issues in Adoption By Deborah Silverstein and Sharon Kaplan Roszia
www.adopting.org/silveroze/html/ lifelong_issues_in_adoption.html

Building the Bonds of Attachment. By Daniel Hughes, PhD

1-2-3 Magic: Effective Discipline for Children 2-12. By Thomas W Phelan., PhD

How to Talk So Kids Will Listen & Listen So Kids Will Talk. By Adele Faber and Elaine Mazlish

Parenting With Love and Logic: Teaching Children Responsibility. By Foster Cline, MD and Jim Fay

Loss and Grief

Finding the Missing Pieces: Helping Adopted Children Cope with Grief and Loss available through Adoption Learning Partners
www.adoptionlearningpartners.org
Adoption Learning Partners offers education and training to the adoption community via the Internet through a series of e-learning courses of a variety of adoption topics.

Promoting Successful Adoptions: Practice with Troubled Families. By Susan Livingston Smith and Jeanne A. Howard

A Child's Journey Through Placement By Vera I. Fahlberg

Helping Children Cope with Separation and Loss By Claudia Jarrett Jewett

Real Parents, Real Children: Parenting the Adopted Child. By Holly Van Gulden and Lisa M. Bartels-Rabb

Homeworks #1: At-Home Training Resources for Foster Parents and Adoptive Parents By Wendy Whiting Blome, Maureen Leighton, and Eileen Mayers-Pasztor

Being Adopted: The Lifelong Search for Self By David M. Brodzinsky, Marshall D. Schechter, Robin Marantz Henig

Toddler Adoption: The Weaver's Craft By Mary Hopkins-Best

Our Own: Adopting and Parenting the Older Child By Trish Maskew

Twenty Things Adopted Kids Wish Their Adoptive Parents Knew By Sherrie Eldridge

Adopting the Older Child By Claudia L. Jewett

Transitions

Disruption

Families who are in crisis and contemplating disruption should seek professional advice. Calling your agency is important. Support can also be obtained from support groups locally and on the internet. Nancy Spoolstra's Attachment Disorder Network (ADN) has associated listservs with experienced members who can support you: **www.radzebra.org**.

This site **www.karensadoptionlinks.com/ disrupt.html** speaks to the need to seek advice from agency and social worker; has general process listserv advice, and useful links to Residential treatment Centers (which could shelter a child post-disruption if no further family is found (parents liable for cost) or provide respite and staying the disruption.

Siblings

Siblings Without Rivalry By Elaine Mazlish

Narratives

EMK Press Parent Guides and selected titles on Lifebooks and resources for families working on their children's stories **www.emkpress.com**

Learning

1. Adopted Children in Schools

Adoption and the Schools: Resources for Parents and Teachers. By Lansing Wood and Nancy Ng

Center for Cognitive-Developmental Assessment & Remediation **www.bgcenter.com**

Identifying Learning Problems in Adopted Children Annie Stuart
www.schwablearning.org/ articles.asp?r=689&g=1

2. Special Education Resources

www.wrightslaw.com
Website with comprehensive explanations of special education laws, including information on the reauthorization of IDEA 2004 and the impact of the various changes under this law.

www.nichcy.org/pubs/genresc/gr3.htm
Website of the National Dissemination Center for Children with Disabilities. Contains lists of state contacts in special education, early intervention and local parent support and advocacy groups. Available through this site is each state's Parent Training Institute (PTI), a great resource for learning more about the state's regulations and how to advocate for children with disabilities.

www.partnersinpolicymaking.com
Partners in Policymaking is a competency-based leadership training program for adults with disabilities and parents of children with disabilities. It's purpose is to teach best practices and the competencies of influencing public officials.

3. Attachment and Trauma Information

www.teacher.scholastic.com/professional/ bruceperry/index.htm
Dr. Bruce Perry is an international expert in childhood trauma. This website contains several articles about dealing with traumatized children in the classroom and has great information for both parents and teachers. For more information see also www.childtrauma.org. This site contains on-line course offerings to learn even more about childhood trauma, PTSD and interventions.

www.radzebra.org
The Attachment Disorder Network website contains comprehensive information on attachment disorder and related issues/diagnoses as well as treatments.

School

Adoption and the Schools: Resources for Parents and Teachers. By Lansing Wood and Nancy Ng

Dickens, Boys, Town or Purgatory: Are Institutions A Place To Call Home? Victor Groza, Daniela Ileana, Ivor Irwin, **www.comeunity.com/adoption/ institutionalism.html**

Adopting an Institutionalized Child: What Are the Risks? By Dana Johnston MD **www.adoption-research.org/risks.html**

Can Inattention/Overactivity be an Institutional Deprivation Syndrome? By Jana M Kreppner, Thomas G. O'Connor, Michael Rutter, and the English and Romanian Adoptees Study Team

Adoption Stress By Mark Lerner, 2005 **www.adoptiondoctors.com/articles/Article/ Adoption-Stress-and-International-Adoption/39**

Race

Color of Difference By Sarah Armstrong and Lynelle Beveridge

Outer Search, Inner Journey By Peter F. Dodds

So You Think You're an Anti-Racist? 6 Critical Paradigm Shifts for Well-Intentioned White Folks. By Paul Gorski
www.edchange.org/multicultural/resources/ paradigmshifts_race.html

Inside Transracial Adoption By Gail Steinberg and Beth Hall. See also **www.pactadopt.org**

Loving Across the Color Line: A White Adoptive Mother Learns about Race. By Sharon Rush

Why Are All the Black Kids Sitting Together in the Cafeteria? And Other Conversations About Race. By Beverley Tatum

It's the Little Things—Everyday Interactions that Anger, Annoy, and Divide the Races By Lena Williams, 2000.

I'm Chocolate, You're Vanilla—Raising Healthy Black and Biracial Children in a Race-Conscious World—A Guide for Parents and Teachers By Marguerite A. Wright

Online Resources

Evan B. Donaldson Adoption Institute. The Gathering of the First Generation of Adult Korean Adoptees: Adoptees' Perceptions of International Adoption, June 2000. **www.adoptioninstitute.org/proed/ korfindings.html**

IMDiversity.com and the Multicultural Villages (Asian American Village, African American Village, Hispanic American Village, Native American Village) **www.imdiversity.com**

How I Learned I Wasn't Caucasian, By Dottie Enrico, **www.fwcc.org** and **www.nysccc.org/ T-Rarts/HowILearned.html**

Scholastic Magazine on Diversity, **www.teacher.scholastic.com/ professional/teachdive/**

Writing for Change, Parenting for Tolerance at Tolerance.org, and *10 Ways to Nurture Tolerance*, Teaching Tolerance Magazine, **www.tolerance.org/teach/index.jsp**

A Question of Color, Teaching Tolerance, Parenting Magazine **http://www.parenting.com/**

Bully Proofing Your Child, and *Effective Anti-Bullying Programs in Schools*, By Robert Needlman, MD, FAAP, **www.DrSpock.com**.

Older Child Adoption

www.olderchildadoption.com

Resources and links for parents contemplating or having completed an adoption of an older child.

Challenges

Institutionalism

The post-institutionalized child. Benevolent Society, February 2004. March 12, 2005. Karleen Gribble **www.bensoc.asn.au/parc_search/ transracial_article_educate.html**

Adopting for good: A guide for people considering adoption By J. Kincaid

Medical and developmental sequelae of early childhood institutionalization in international adoptees from Romania and the Russian Federation By Dana Johnston

Children of intercountry adoptions in school: A primer for parents and professionals. By R. L. Meese

Life after trauma: A workbook for healing. By D. Rosenbloom & M.B. Williams

What do you do with a child like this: Inside the lives of troubled children. By L. Tobin

Parenting Children with FASD-.Education, Evaluation and Support

Dr. Harry Chugani, Chief Pediatric Neurologist, Detroit Children's Hospital. See 2004 National Conference presentation available through FRUA at **www.frua.org**

Dr. Boris Gindis **www.bgcenter.com**

Dr Ron Federici at **www.drfederici.com** Site offers research and treatments and support

Dr Jane Aronson **www.orphandoctor.com**

American Academy of Pediatrics **www.aap.org**

FASlink **www.FASlink.org**

PEP-L list-serve **www.eeadopt.org**

Amen Clinics **www.brainplace.com** Trauma therapy – investigations by SPECT Scan

Ohio Coalition for the Education of Children with Disabilities – offers sister state information which helps parents from other states find help **www.ocecd.org**

Adoptive mother Terri Mauro's website **www.motherswithattitude.com/about.html** with Hot Links devoted to offering further reading, contacts, support and treatments for FASD

Teresa Kellerman, Director of the FAS Community Resource Center, Tucson, Arizona's website **www.fasstar.com**. Extensive links to treatment centers, research, reading and support

Wrightslaw **www.wrightslaw.com** Advocacy and resources for children with special educational needs

Abuse

Center for Behavioral Intervention
(503) 644-2772/Cory Jewell Jensen & Steve Jensen, 4345 SW 109th Ave, Beaverton, OR 97005

Darkness to Light –site setting out what can be done to prevent sexual abuse and molestation:
www.darkness2light.org/KnowAbout/statistics_2.asp
www.darkness2light.org/7steps/download_7steps.asp

How abusers operate
www.streetlevelconsulting.ca/rareTreasures/sexoffender1.htm

Parenting the Hurt Child: Helping Adoptive Families Heal and Grow by Gregory Keck, Regina M. Kupecky

Support

LGBT Resources

The Queer Parent's Primer: A Lesbian and Gay Families' Guide to Navigating Through a Straight World. By Stephanie Brill

The Lesbian Parenting Book: A Guide to Creating Families and Raising Children By Merillee D. Clunis, and G. Dorsey Green

Out of the Ordinary: Essays on Growing Up With Gay, Lesbian, and Transgender Parents. By Noelle Howey, and Ellen Samuels

For Lesbian Parents: Your Guide to Helping Your Family Grow Up Happy, Healthy, and Proud. By Suzanne Johnson, and Elizabeth O'Connor

The Lesbian and Gay Parenting Handbook: Creating and Raising Our Families. By April Martin

Therapy

If you feel that you need to seek an attachment therapist, information can be obtained from www.attach.org and www.attach-china.org as to how to obtain a registered therapist.

Dyadic Developmental Psychotherapy
www.center4familydevelop.com/therapy.htm
www.danielahughes.homestead.com/Model.html

Brain Gym
www.braingym.org. Theory and exercises designed to help re-organize and re-order the brain through cross-lateral movement

A portal to Brain Gym
www.learningsolutions.co.uk/brain_gym.php
PACE- processing and cognitive enhancement - is a group of exercises within Brain Gym that help with organizing the brain

EMDR
www.emdr.com
www.emdria.org

Narrative Therapy   **www.narrativeapproaches.com**
www.dulwichcentre.com.au
www.familyattachment.com

Neurofeedback
www.eegspectrum.com

The Neuro Net therapy program, devised by audiologist Nancy Rowe, helps "improve vestibular control of body management (attention) and integrate vestibular-motor, auditory-motor and visual-motor skills"

www.neuronetonline.com/bg.php?content File=bg5_content

Theraplay **www.theraplay.org**

Tomatis Listening Therapy **www.tomatis.com** Theory and exercises designed to help those with listening/learning disorders

Useful tools:
www.childanxiety.net
www.mindworksforchildren.com
www.familyattachment.com
www.emkpress.com
www.alertprogram.com
www.speechmark.net

Journey

Evan B. Donaldson Adoption Institute
www.adoptioninstitute.org

Index

About the Publisher:

EMK Press:
Resources and books for families formed by adoption

16 Mt. Bethel Road
Warren, NJ 07059
732-469-7544
732-469-7861 fax

Titles currently in print:

I Don't Have Your Eyes

We See the Moon

At Home in This World, A China Adoption Story

*Adoption Parenting: Creating a Toolbox,
Building Connections*

We publish books for the adoption market and work
to fill voids in that market. We also provide a wealth
of resources and web links on our site that are
available for free download, as well as a monthly
newsletter on topics of interest to adoptive families.

www.emkpress.com

(every link discussed in this book is listed there and
will be the most up to date. Please advise us if a link
is broken or not working.)

If you have a manuscript to submit to us, please
follow the submission guidelines found here
www.emkpress.com/contact.html.